Bibliography on American Prints of the Seventeenth through the Nineteenth Centuries

Bibliography on American Prints of the Seventeenth through the Nineteenth Centuries

Edited and Compiled by

Georgia Brady Barnhill

Andrew W. Mellon Curator of Graphic Arts
American Antiquarian Society

Oak Knoll Press

The American Historical Print Collectors Society

2006

First Edition, 2006, Published by
Oak Knoll Press
310 Delaware Street
New Castle, Delaware, 19720 USA
Web: http://www.oakknoll.com
and
The American Historical Print Collectors Society
P. O. Box 201
Fairfield, Connecticut 06824
Web: http://www.ahpcs.org

ISBN: 1-58456-193-9

Title: Bibliography on American Prints of the Seventeenth through the Nineteenth Centuries
Editor/Compiler: Georgia Brady Barnhill
Designer: Angela Werner
Typographer: Angela Werner, Michael Höhne Design
Publishing Director: J. Lewis von Hoelle

Library of Congress Cataloging-in-Publication Data
available from Oak Knoll Press upon request

The following prints appear on the dust jacket
and are reproduced courtesy of the American Antiquarian Society:

Paul Revere. *A View of the Obelisk erected under Liberty Tree in Boston.* Boston, 1766.
John Hill. *Menage Horse.* New York, ca. 1835.
Currier & Ives. *General Francis Marion of South Carolina.* New York, 1876.
Winslow Homer. *The Coffee Call.* Boston: Louis Prang, 1863.
Robert Cooke. *Singletarry Pond.* Boston: Thomas Moore, 1835-41.
A Select Committee of Enquiry at Hard Work. New York: Henry R. Robinson, 1839.
William Sidney Mount. *Power of Music.* New York: Goupil, Vibert & Co., 1848.
Father and Child. New York: Nathaniel Currier, 1849.
R. H. Hubbard. *Lake George.* Philadelphia: Edward Sintzenich, 1865.
David Claypoole Johnston. *Mr. E. Forrest as Metamora.* Boston: John and William Pendleton, ca. 1830.
The Gingerbread Man. New York: George Endicott, ca. 1840.
John Hill. *Matteawan Manufacturing Village, Near Fishkill Landing. N.York.* New York: O'Neely, 1832.
Lucian Gray. *Geo. W. Phillips, Builder.* New York: C. L. Crapper & Bro., ca. 1875.
Thomas Nast. *The Tammany Tiger Loose. "What Are You Going to Do About It?"* in *Harper's Weekly,* November 11, 1871.

This work was printed and bound in the USA on
archival, acid-free paper meeting the requirements of the
American Standard for Permanence of Paper for Printing Library Materials.

TABLE OF CONTENTS

This volume is dedicated to
David F. Tatham,
Friend and Scholar,
To recognize his many contributions
To the study of
American Prints and Illustrations

ACKNOWLEDGEMENTS

This bibliography came to be as a result of a discussion during a board meeting of the American Historical Print Collectors Society over a decade ago. The board felt that a bibliography on American prints of the eighteenth and nineteenth centuries would be a useful tool for collectors, dealers, curators, and scholars. I mentioned that I had compiled such a work that was published as a section in *Arts in America,* a four-volume compilation under the editorship of Bernard Karpel issued by the Archives of American Art and the Smithsonian Institution in 1979. That seemed to be a good beginning. The Archives of American Art and the Smithsonian Institution Press were kind enough to give permission to reprint the information from *Arts in America* in this new format. In the early 1980s, the Garland Publishing Company invited me to participate in another bibliographic initiative, but the project collapsed. In the meantime, I continued to keep track of current literature as it came across my desk at the American Antiquarian Society because that seemed to be a worthwhile effort.

The board of the American Historical Print Collectors Society provided substantial assistance in the compilation of this bibliography. They purchased a bibliographical software package for me, Pro-Cite, and paid Caroline Wood Stoffel, a cataloguer at the American Antiquarian Society, to put the entries in the bibliography published in 1979 into the database as well as several hundred that I had compiled in the 1980s. She also did a great deal of editing. Even after that work was completed, Caroline continued to assist me since I am challenged by anything that is very technical. I want to express my very great appreciation to Caroline Wood Stoffel for all of her work on this project and her continuing friendship.

Jane Neale, my former assistant at the American Antiquarian Society and a long-time volunteer in the graphic arts department, was kind enough to read through the bibliography, finding many misspelled words as well as inconsistencies and errors. Reading bibliographies can be a cure for insomnia, so I thank Jane for taking so much of her time to read through the draft. Lauren Hewes, the principal bibliographer for the Print Council of America and an assistant in the graphic arts department at the American Antiquarian Society, also read through the bibliography and found several lapses.

Several friends have sent me citations to articles that I might have missed; others sent me copies of essays and books. David Tatham has been very generous with his knowledge over the years as has Philip Weimerskirch, Michael McCue, Wendy Wick Reaves, and the late Thomas Beckman. Several years ago, Jonathan Flaccus cautioned me about how few references I had to the poster movement of the 1890s leading me to exclude such material from the bibliography altogether. To these friends and many others I offer my thanks.

The bibliography has languished far too long. Wendy Shadwell, a board member and former president of the AHPCS and curator of prints emerita at the New-York Historical Society, brought the bibliography to fruition by challenging the board of the AHPCS and its members to match a very generous gift that she made towards the publication of this volume. It was her generosity and that of others including Phyllis Brown, William Cook, Jody Gill, Harry Katz, Lois Newman, Donald O'Brien, The Philadelphia Print Shop, Jane Pomeroy, Sue Rainey, and Charlotte Rubinstein that made me bring this project to closure. The International Fine Print Dealers Association also made a generous grant to the AHPCS to support this publication. I greatly appreciate all of this support and tangible encouragement. The community of collectors, dealers, scholars, and curators who will make use of this information will appreciate the generosity of all of these supporters of this bibliography. I also want to thank Oak Knoll Books for their willingness to assist the AHPCS in the publication and distribution of the bibliography.

This is the perfect moment to express my gratitude to the American Antiquarian Society for its unparalleled collection of periodicals and books on American history and culture. Without such a strong collection literally at one's fingertips, compiling a bibliography such as this one would be far more difficult than it has been. Founded in 1812, its collections continue to grow with the generous support of members, friends, and grants from foundations and government agencies, including the National Endowment for the Humanities. I want to acknowledge my indebtedness to Marcus A. McCorison, president emeritus, who has always been supportive of my scholarly activities, and to Ellen S. Dunlap, president, and John B. Hench, vice president for collections and programs, for continuing that tradition. The current librarian, Nancy H. Burkett, continues the program of acquisitions that enriches the great collection.

I have dedicated this bibliography to David Tatham for several reasons. First is his friendship that began in 1969 when I became curator of maps and prints at the American Antiquarian Society. My predecessor, Louise S. Marshall, told me that one of the people I would come to know in my new position would be this young scholar at Syracuse University. Over these many years, he has been supportive of my own research and has been an active member at the American Antiquarian Society on various committees and on the governing board. I also want to recognize the fact that David, now professor emeritus at Syracuse University, is the only academic art historian who has devoted so much of his time, energy, and good will to the study of American prints. He has organized his share of conferences and has used his presence at Syracuse University to encourage the University's Press to publish several of the conference reports. All of these reasons, but most importantly his friendship and his belief in the importance of American prints to art history, lead to the dedication of this volume.

Most of the work that I have done on this compilation has been done at home where I have a study that looks out over beautiful Brooks Pond. I spend hours upon hours at my desk and my husband, Jim, never complains. I greatly appreciate his quiet support of my many professional activities and his pride in my accomplishments.

Georgia B. Barnhill
Oakham, Massachusetts
April 2006

PREFACE

For twenty-five years scholars, collectors, and students interested in American historical prints and printmakers have had the advantage of a very useful research tool, Georgia B. Bumgardner's "Graphic Arts: Seventeenth – Nineteenth Century" that appeared in *Arts in America. A Bibliography* (Washington: Smithsonian Institution Press, 1979) edited by Bernard Karpel.

Fortunately, Mrs. Barnhill continued to add to her published bibliography as new material appeared in print. In 1992, the AHPCS board encouraged her to combine the Smithsonian publication with additional entries published in the intervening years. Those describing articles that appeared in *Imprint* (the journal of the American Historical Print Collectors Society), Volumes 1-25, were published in the Autumn 2000 issue of that journal and are on the AHPCS website. However, the remaining entries, consisting of hundreds of titles that had been published since 1975, were still unavailable to the general public.

Now Mrs. Barnhill's complete bibliography is available to all who have an interest in and love of American historical prints. As president of the American Historical Print Collectors Society, I am delighted that our Society has had the opportunity along with Oak Knoll Press to publish this magnificent, scholarly work.

Donald C. O'Brien
President
American Historical Print Collectors Society

INTRODUCTION

This bibliography is based on and supplements "Graphic Arts: Seventeenth – Nineteenth Century" that I compiled for *Arts in America,* a four-volume reference work edited by Bernard Karpel under the auspices of the Archives of American Art, a bureau of the Smithsonian Institution in Washington, D.C. That work covers literature published through the middle of the 1970s and contains 1175 entries, arranged topically. I have arranged this bibliography in a similar fashion although several topics have been omitted since they are of less interest to members of the American Historical Print Collectors Society.[1] Limits needed to be set to make this bibliography feasible to compile, print and distribute. This bibliography covers books and articles published through the year 1999.

Asserting that any bibliography such as this one is complete reflects an optimism that is untenable. There are undoubtedly wonderful articles and books that are not in these pages. I apologize for such omissions, but the literature on American prints is expanding so that it becomes impossible for any one individual to be responsible for it. For those interested in exploring the full range of articles on any given topic, the best advice is to read the footnotes of the most substantial study that one can find. That will inevitably lead to additional useful literature. I have tried to note publications with particularly important bibliographies for the same reason.

A great proportion in the expansion of the literature on American prints is due to two factors. The first is the initiation of a series of scholarly conferences in 1970 that eventually came to be called the North American Print Conference. Jonathan Fairbanks and Sinclair Hitchings cajoled a variety of museums, historical societies, and libraries to organize the early conferences; to date twenty-six conferences have been held; the most recent one occurred in 2000 at Syracuse University. Seventeen conference publications were published prior to the year 2000, each with eight or more scholarly essays.[2] The other factor was the founding of the American Historical Print Collectors Society in 1975.[3] The Society's journal, *Imprint,* has published over 150 essays on American prints. The AHPCS website contains a list of all the articles along with brief synopses. Journals such as *Antiques* and *The Winterthur Portfolio* continue to publish articles on American prints from time to time.

Another important phenomenon in this field is that scholars in the academy are beginning to write about American prints and to use them as primary documents in their scholarly efforts. This is a rather recent development and one that curators welcome because such scholars bring a contextual knowledge to the interpretation of prints that can show them in a different light. Tracking this literature, however, can be difficult. Electronic bibliographic resources, such as *America: History and Life,* enabled me to track down some studies that appeared in academic journals in the 1980s and 1990s, as opposed to periodicals on art, in which one would expect to find such essays. I recommend this electronic resource to those who want to find recent essays in this field. The Internet also offers great resources for research purposes.

Some might question why a printed bibliography is a useful adjunct to electronic and internet resources. It is only through the gathering of information within a given field that new and significant research can be undertaken. Fortunately, Oak Knoll Press understands the role of printed bibliographies. I hope that the users of this publication will use this volume to not only find out what has been published on a given topic, but where needs and opportunities exist for future research. The future of studies on American prints and printmakers is rich with possibilities. There are, for example, few complete catalogs of printmaker's works or for genres. Nancy Finlay and her colleagues at the Connecticut Historical Society are engaged in compiling a complete list of the lithographs printed by the Kellogg firm. The completed project will enable scholars to look at the products of a firm that rivaled Currier & Ives in the breadth of their output and distribution. Similar projects will help define the importance of American popular prints in the nineteenth century. One of the earliest catalogs of an engraver's work was compiled by Clarence Brigham on the engravings of Paul Revere. Yet, even Revere's work can use a reappraisal because the historical context is more complex than Brigham presented. John Reps's publications on city views are superlative and he has enabled us to understand the full range of that genre. Wouldn't studies on other genres be equally useful?

One of the new academic disciplines is the history of the book. The American Antiquarian Society is one of the leading institutions that enable scholars to assess the creation of literature, its distribution, and reception. There are many aspects of this approach to American publishing that can be applied to studies of prints and their creators. Who were the creators and the publishers? What were the relationships among artists and engravers and lithographers and publishers? What did the public think of prints and illustrations and what were their reactions? These are questions that can be addressed by future scholars, collectors, and curators.

Arrangement of the Bibliography

ARTISTS AND PUBLISHERS

Arranged alphabetically by surname, the first section of the bibliography is devoted to studies on individual graphic artists and print publishers. It is in this section that books and articles on artists such as Winslow Homer and publishers such as Nathaniel Currier and Currier & Ives will be found. As anyone knowledgeable about American prints will discover, there are many important graphic artists and publishers about whom little or nothing seems to have been written. However, other sections of the bibliography should be checked because articles on several etchers, for example, will be found in that section.

BIBLIOGRAPHIES

This bibliography is in fact based in part on other bibliographies that are listed in this section. Noting these important bibliographies is one way to pay homage to the efforts of others in this field. Some of the early works are interesting as historical artifacts because they demonstrate the growth of the scholarly literature in this field and they offer contemporary assessments of printmakers. I have tried to be consistent in incorporating appropriate works in the present bibliography.

BOOK AND PERIODICAL ILLUSTRATION

Before there was sufficient patronage for the publication of large numbers of separately published prints, publishers and printers in colonial America incorporated illustrations in their books and pamphlets. The practice continued throughout the nineteenth century. Since I have long been interested in the history of book illustration, this is a large section, although additional works on individual illustrators such as Hammatt Billings, F. O. C. Darley, Winslow Homer, and other practitioners are found in the opening section on artists. With the creation of the relatively new academic discipline of the history of the book, scholarly interest in book illustration is increasing as scholars seek to find documentation on the relationships between illustrators and authors and publishers and on the reception of images in books. Sections on Political Prints and Social History in Prints also have important articles and books on periodical illustration.

CITY VIEWS

City and town views are among the earliest prints relating to America. The section on city views is a substantial one for two reasons. First, city views are certainly a popular genre of prints among collectors and curators. Views document space and its use in specific ways; panoramic views can be regarded as simply beautiful. They can be used to show towns and cities in a most attractive way and can also demonstrate change over time for major cities for which there are multiple views, such as Boston, New York, Philadelphia, and other great cities. In addition, for over thirty years, John Reps, now professor emeritus at Cornell University, has gathered many bibliographical references for his extensive publications on this genre, many of which have been incorporated in this bibliography. He has also reproduced a large number of views through his commercial firm, Historic Urban Plans. Any scholar interested in following Professor Reps's footsteps should consult the bibliography in his *Views and View Makers of Urban America.* Also included in this section are works on architectural prints.

COLLECTING AND COLLECTORS

What resources are available to the new collector? The section on collecting provides some basic references as well as a few books on the care of prints. This latter subject is too vast for the present bibliography and those interested in the care of works of art on paper should consult the publications of some of the major conservation facilities as well as those of the American Institute for Conservation of Historic and Artistic Works in Washington, D.C. Also of interest is information about collectors of American prints such as Harry T. Peters and J. William Middendorf.

COLLECTIONS

The American Historical Print Collectors Society has provided a valuable service by publishing articles in *Imprint* on institutional print collections throughout the country. Curators in these collections are usually only too happy to hear from collectors and scholars with questions. There are also major catalogs of print collections in this section, such as those compiled by Karen Beall at the Library of Congress and E. McSherry Fowble on the collection of British and American prints at the Winterthur Museum. These are models for other institutions. This section is arranged by the name of the collection.

DICTIONARIES OF PRINTMAKERS

This section contains a variety of reference works under the loose rubric of dictionaries. Included are biographical dictionaries of engravers and their works, lists of engravers and others gleaned from city directories, and compilations of advertisements from newspapers. It is astonishing that such reference works were compiled in the generations before computer databases simplified such undertakings. This kind of painstaking accumulation of factual information is now facilitated by access over the Internet to the full text of newspapers.

ENGRAVINGS

This section is quite small in comparison to those on etching, lithography, and wood engraving. It contains general works on engraving and its various applications to genres such as trade cards, bookplates, the production of currency, and the training of engravers. Although I have excluded most of the literature on ephemera, there were several articles that seemed important to include because of the information presented on engravers who also made separately published prints and book illustrations. Likewise, the important book on American bookplates by Charles Dexter Allen includes substantial information on colonial engravers and those of the New Republic.

ETCHINGS AND OTHER PROCESSES

The last quarter of the nineteenth century witnessed a resurgence of interest in artistic etching, as opposed to the use of this process with engraving in the production of reproductive prints. Sylvester Koehler was one the proponents of what has become known as "The Etching Revival." There is a substantial amount of literature on etching, both old and new. Some of the older literature is interesting because the writers were able to communicate directly with artists and describe their working methods. More recently scholars such as Elton W. Hall, Rona Schneider, Thomas Bruhn, and Lauren Hewes have appreciated these uncommon works. The catalogs of several excellent exhibitions on The Etching Revival are found in this section.

EXHIBITION CATALOGS

This section of exhibition catalogs can be used to trace the interest in American prints. The earliest exhibitions were enormous in size, but the publications usually have only the scantest information on each print. Far more useful are modern catalogs that provide analytical discussions of each print. Quite a few important exhibitions were created for meetings of the North American Print Conferences; unfortunately few of them are completely documented. Major commercial galleries, such as Hirschl & Adler and Kennedy Galleries in New York, publish exhibition catalogs as well. The user of this bibliography will find exhibition catalogs on specific topics, such as landscape prints or portrait prints in those sections.

HISTORICAL PRINTS

There is a body of prints that depict significant events in America's past. Oddly, relatively little has been written about prints that depict historical events, with the exception of those by Currier & Ives, as well as naval and military prints. An exhibition being prepared by the Huntington Library and the American Antiquarian Society is addressing this body of material. Clearly this topic presents great opportunities for future scholars.

LANDSCAPE PRINTS

Landscape prints are among my favorites and for this reason I created a new category for this genre. This is a topic about which much more could be written, although it must be admitted that the works of William Henry Bartlett, John Hill and Thomas Moran, among others, are well described and documented by articles listed in the section on artists. Additional articles on landscape imagery are found in the section on Regional Studies.

LITHOGRAPHY

Developed in the late eighteenth century, lithography arrived in the United States early in the nineteenth century and became a useful process for the creation of a wide array of artistic prints and commercial ephemera. Because of the popularity of the prints by Currier & Ives, many collectors wrote about lithography early in the twentieth century. Interest in the process continues because of the widespread availability of lithographs in the nineteenth century. The relative cheapness of lithographs in comparison to folio engravings made them available to the working and middle classes and of interest to those studying popular culture of the nineteenth century. The broad strokes of the histories of many firms are well established, but more research can be done on the publication and distribution of lithographs in general.

MARINE PRINTS

Perennial favorites of collectors, these prints appeal to individuals and institutions because of their emotional and visual appeal. American artists, engravers, and lithographers excelled in this genre from the late eighteenth century on. Foremost among collectors of this genre was Irving Olds, whose collection is at The New-York Historical Society. Much of what has been written about these prints relates to their artistic qualities, not on issues related to the authenticity of the views. Nor have scholars tried to assess the emotional impact of these prints on their contemporary purchasers. The conference sponsored by the New Bedford Whaling Museum in 1977 focused its attention on maritime prints. There is also a substantial literature on American ships that are illustrated with prints, but without any attention paid to the prints themselves. Such works fall beyond the scope of this bibliography.

MILITARY PRINTS

Military prints are almost as popular as naval prints. There are important recent works on prints depicting the War of 1812, the Mexican War, and the Civil War. Even so, there is much to be explored in terms of assessing the impact of heroic military prints on the American public. Among other issues about military prints that have been raised is their authenticity.

POLITICAL PRINTS

Since they are laden with historical significance, political prints have always been of great interest to scholars, collectors and to institutions. There is, therefore, an excellent mix of studies in this section. Frank Weitenkampf's checklist of separately published political prints published in 1953 has yet to be superseded. Fortunately many well-illustrated exhibition catalogs appeared during the celebration of the Bicentennial in 1976 that made political prints available to scholars and others. Bernard Reilly's excellent catalog of political prints at the Library of Congress contains a wealth of explanatory material. The bibliography of Roger Fisher's *Them Damned Pictures* is excellent and Gary Bunker continues to do research on political prints found in periodicals. Works on specific artists who did political cartoons, such as Edward Williams Clay and Thomas Nast, are found in the section on artists.

PORTRAIT PRINTS

Printed portraits of American political, social, religious, and military leaders have been collected and researched extensively. Likewise, there has been great interest in the nineteenth-century portfolios of Native Americans. Obviously, George Washington is the subject of several important studies. The National Portrait Gallery in Washington, D.C., part of the Smithsonian Institution, is dedicated to collecting and preserving the images of Americans; its print collection has been growing steadily in the past quarter century.

PRINTS

Although I tried to find appropriate categories for each article and book, this section contains a variety of publications on the American Art Union, descriptions of several of the North American Print Conference volumes, broad chronologically or topically arranged overviews of American printmaking, and miscellaneous items that seemed to fit nowhere else. Frank Weitenkampf's *American Graphic Art* remains an indispensable reference work.

REGIONAL STUDIES

Incorporated in this section are works on specific geographical regions of the United States, the West Indies, and Canada. In part, this section is driven by the subjects addressed in several of the North American Print Conferences that often have had a regional emphasis such as New England, Boston, Philadelphia, Texas, and the Adirondacks. Of course, prints relating to the Gold Rush and California have been perennial favorites of collectors and scholars of western Americana. The great interest in local history fuels some of these studies. There is, of course, some overlap between this section and city views.

RELIGIOUS PRINTS

There has been an increase in the interest in religious imagery in the past twenty-five years; this interest will undoubtedly increase in the years ahead given the interest of art and social historians in the intersection of religion and popular and material culture. Elizabeth Gilmore Holt was one of the first to write about this genre of imagery; others have followed in her footsteps. Several important studies on the imagery of the Shakers have been published recently; they are included even though these works are drawings, not prints.

SERIALS

The section listing the titles of important art serials and periodicals of the nineteenth and twentieth centuries should aid the scholar in identifying publications important to the study of American prints. Sound View Press published Mary Morris Schmidt's *Index to Nineteenth-Century American Art Periodicals* in 1999. This valuable resource facilitates access to a wealth of information covering far more than American prints.

SHEET MUSIC ILLUSTRATION

One important application of lithography was to print music less expensively than the earlier process of engraving at a time when the piano became available to the public. In Europe, music publishers commissioned artists to provide illustrations for the covers; the practice became widespread in the United States in the late 1820s. Pictorial lithographed sheet music covers contain a wealth of important imagery, running the gamut from portraits of singers and dancers to political and military leaders, from scenes of courtship and romance to political satire. Several articles in this section suggest some themes that have been explored; others await the scholar. In the past, use of sheet music as a source for imagery was hampered by a lack of access by subject. This problem has been alleviated by the inclusion of several important collections of sheet music in the American Memory Project of the Library of Congress and by the digitization of the Lester Levy Collection at Johns Hopkins University. Both collections are available on the Internet.

SOCIAL HISTORY IN PRINTS

Several scholars have started to use prints to explore various aspects of society—romance, gender, labor, urban life, holidays, and sports among other topics. Ewell Newman's 1981 article in *Imprint* on images of women in lithographs published by Currier & Ives suggests an approach that can be replicated using prints of other eras or in other media. Studies on the Mormon religion have been placed in this section because often criticism of this religious movement carried such important social overtones. Surprisingly, little has been written about the pictorial components of and responses to reform movements of the nineteenth century.

WOOD ENGRAVING

The dominant reproductive process by far is relief engraving on wood. This section contains general studies on the subject as well as detailed articles on wood engraving of the last quarter of the nineteenth century when there was an enormous change in style and technique, discussions of which erupted in many serials. Edward Gokey summarizes this literature in his essay published in 1990. Rollo Silver's 1974 article reminds us that in the second half of the nineteenth century, illustrations were printed by electrotyped plates made from wood engravings, not from the blocks themselves. Again, studies on specialists in wood engraving such as Alexander Anderson and William Linton are found in the section on artists and publishers.

• • • • •

Again, I offer my apologies to those whose books and articles have been omitted from this compilation. I hope, however, that this volume will prove useful to scholars, curators, collectors, and dealers; and I once again offer my thanks to the American Historical Print Collectors Society for its assistance and to Caroline Wood Stoffel.

Notes

[1] Sections that have been omitted include the following: Bookplates, Currency, Maps, Broadsides and Posters, Trade Cards and Ephemera.

[2] The conference volumes are listed as are the separate essays in this volume. A published list, accurate through 1997 may be found in *Adirondack Prints and Printmakers,* Caroline Mastin Welsh, ed. (Syracuse: Syracuse University Press and Adirondack Museum, 1998).

[3] Ruth Alden Graham's history of the AHPCS is in volume 25, no. 2 of *Imprint* (Autumn 2000).

Bibliography on American Prints of the 17th through the 19th Centuries

Artists and Publishers

1. Barnhill, Georgia B., Diana Korzenik, and Caroline Sloat. *The Cultivation of Artists in Nineteenth-Century America.* Worcester, Mass.: American Antiquarian Society, 1997. 225 pp., index.

The volume contains essays based on lectures presented at a conference held at the American Antiquarian Society in 1993. The titles of the essays and their authors are as follows: "Training in the Workshop of Abner Reed" by Donald C. O'Brien, "The Lithographic Workshop, 1825–50" by David Tatham, "American Drawing Books and Their Impact on Fitz Hugh Lane" by Elliot Bostwick Davis, "The Plan Book Drawings of the New Orleans Notarial Archives: Legal Background and Artistic Development" by Sally K. Reeves, "Set to Music: The Engravers, Artists, and Lithographers of New Orleans Sheet Music" by Florence M. Jumonville, "Art, Industry, and Education in Prang's Chromolithograph Factory" by Michael Clapper, "Quiet Pleasures" by Sinclair Hitchings, "The Imp of the Reverse" by Bruce Chandler, "The Graver, the Brush, and the Ruling Machine: The Training of Late-Nineteenth-Century Wood Engravers," by Ann Prentice Wagner, "John Sloan's Newspaper Career: An Alternative to Art School" by Elizabeth H. Hawkes, "Educating American Designers for Industry, 1853–1903" by Nancy Austin, and "Art Museum Schools: The Rise and Decline of a New Institution in Nineteenth-Century America" by Joyce Woelfle Lehmann. Those relating to the history of prints are indexed in their appropriate sections of this bibliography.

2. Dunlap, William. *A History of the Rise and Progress of the Arts of Design in the United States.* Boston: C.E. Goodspeed & Co., 1918. 3 vols.

Frank W. Bayley and Charles E. Goodspeed are the editors of Dunlap's *History*, first published in 1834. The third volume of this edition of Dunlap's *History* includes a list of painters, sculptors, architects, and engravers, with brief notes about each, that is supplementary to those names mentioned by Dunlap. This work contains much information gleaned from correspondence and personal knowledge making it a valuable resource.

3. Little, Nina Fletcher. "The Cartoons of James Akin Upon Liverpool Ware." *Old-Time New England* 28 (January 1938): 103–108.

This article discusses an unusual application of caricature—a cartoon by James Akin (ca. 1773–1846) on a Liverpool pitcher. The cartoon concerns the "long embargo" which preceded the War of 1812. Little also discusses the cartoon, *Infuriated Despondency*, which was printed upon pitchers and bowls in England, and then shipped back to Newburyport, Mass.

4. Quimby, Maureen O'Brien. "The Political Art of James Akin." *Winterthur Portfolio* 7 (1972): 59–112.

Akin was a proficient etcher and lithographer. Quimby concentrates on his political and satirical prints, for which excellent historical background is provided. A lengthy checklist of Akin's works, including book illustrations, bookplates, trade cards, caricatures, cartoons, portraits, and miscellaneous prints is appended. This well documented and illustrated study is based on the author's 1969 master's thesis for the University of Delaware, *James Akin, Engraver and Social Critic.*

5. Sanborn, Franklin B. "Thomas Leavitt and His Artist Friend James Akin." *Granite Monthly* 25 (October 1898): 224–234.

A native of South Carolina, Akin established himself about 1808 as an artist and engraver in Newburyport, Mass. In 1811 he went to Philadelphia, where he spent the rest of his days. The article concentrates on his stay in Newburyport, where he did the portraits of Thomas Leavitt and his wife. Sanborn suggests that his satirical prints were made for personal amusement.

6. "American Pioneer Wood Engraver." *American Historical Record* 2 (May 1873): 201–205.

This article discusses several of Alexander Anderson's engravings. It notes that Anderson executed one hundred and fifty wood engravings after his ninetieth birthday. The engravings have been printed from the original blocks by Charles L. Moreau in an edition of fifty copies, with an introduction by Evert A. Duyckinck.

7. Burr, Frederic M. *Life and Works of Alexander Anderson, M.D., The First American Wood Engraver.* New York: Burr Bros., 1893. 210 pp.

The biographical details vary little from those presented in the memoir by Lossing in 1872. However, this volume reprints Anderson's diary for the years 1795 to 1798 and the autobiography he wrote in 1848.

8. Dingman, John F. *Alexander Anderson, 1775–1870, and the back-ground of wood-engraving in America.* San Marcos, Ca.: The author, 1984. 45 pp., biblio.

Dingman touches briefly Anderson's life, the wood engravings of Thomas Bewick, the state of wood engraving in Anderson's lifetime, publishers of children's books and magazines, and his creative work. This is a handsome, limited edition publication.

9. Duyckinck, Evert Augustus. *A Brief Catalogue of the Books Illustrated with Engravings by Dr. Alexander Anderson, with a Biographical Sketch of the Artist.* New York: Thompson & Moreau, 1885. 35 pp.

The biographical sketch is based upon Benson Lossing's published in 1872. The catalog is arranged by the title of the volume in which Anderson's illustrations appeared. Although far from complete, it provides an indication of the range of Anderson's work.

10.———. *A Collection of One Hundred and Fifty Engravings by Alexander Anderson Executed on Wood After His Ninetieth Year.* New York: C.L. Moreau, 1873. 8 pp.

This article discusses the difference between Anderson's wood engravings commissioned by booksellers and publishers and the works he produced during the last years of his life when he engraved solely for his own pleasure.

11. Gardner, Albert Ten Eyck. "Doctor Alexander Anderson, the Pirate's Friend." *Metropolitan Museum of Art Bulletin* (July 1951): 218–224.

The main subject of this article is a portrait of Anderson by John Wesley Jarvis. The author also makes an assessment of Anderson's standing among his peers and provides biographical information. He notes that Jarvis made some of the drawings which Anderson engraved on wood.

12. Knubel, Helen M. "Alexander Anderson: A Self Portrait." *Colophon, New Graphic Series* 1, no. 1 (1939): 33–36.

In 1846 Anderson had a daguerreotype taken by John Plumbe at the urging of Benson J. Lossing. Anderson made a wood engraving of the daguerreotype, which was published in the *London Art Journal* for September 1858 together with the first printed resume of Anderson's life, written by Lossing.

13.———. "Alexander Anderson and Early American Book Illustration." *Princeton University Library Chronicle* 1 (April 1940): 8–18.

Knubel interprets Anderson's career by discussing his contacts with other artists and publishers. She provides a thorough checklist of his engravings and an assessment of his work as a whole. This article quickly passes over the well-known biographical facts of his life and concentrates on his adaptation of Bewick's technique, his pupils, the New York publishing business, his illustrations for the American Tract Society publications, and his involvement in the "visual method of education" for children.

14. Lossing, Benson John. *Memorial of Alexander Anderson, the First Engraver on Wood in America.* New York: Printed for the subscribers, 1872. 103 pp.

Preceded by a brief history of wood engraving, the memoir provides a biographical sketch of Anderson, the son of a printer in New York. Always fascinated by pictures, Anderson began engraving at the age of 12 and continued doing so even during his medical studies. Many of Anderson's earliest engravings are mentioned. Lossing has relied on Anderson's diary for much of his information on the artist's life and work and discusses some of his pupils and contemporaries. Lossing makes general observations on the business of book publishing. Appended to the memoir is Anderson's autobiography written in 1848.

15.———. "Alexander Anderson." *London Art Journal* 10 (September 1858): 271–272.

This is the earliest known biographical sketch of Anderson. The titles of several books that Anderson illustrated with engravings are cited.

16.———. "Alexander Anderson, M.D." *Harper's Weekly* 14 (5 February 1870): 84–86.

This biographical sketch, published just after Anderson's death, indicates that some appreciation of his work existed during his lifetime.

17. Pomeroy, Jane R. "Alexander Anderson's Life and Engravings, with a Checklist of Publications Drawn from His Diary." *Proceedings of the American Antiquarian Society* 100, no. 1 (April 1990): 137–232.

Pomeroy bases her article on a close reading of Anderson's diary covering the years 1790 to 1799. From it she has drawn a complete picture of Anderson in this formative period and an annotated checklist of almost one hundred publications that incorporate his copperplate engravings and relief cuts. Much of what Pomeroy has learned about Anderson extends to other practitioners of his trade. Pomeroy spent many years studying Anderson's work and her definitive catalog of his work was published in 2005.

18. Smith, Malcolm S. *Alexander Anderson and American Wood Engraving.* M. A. Thesis, University of Delaware, 1973. 110 pp., biblio.

Smith focuses on Anderson's background and development as an engraver on metal and wood. One chapter sets Anderson's work in the context of changes in education in the nineteenth century. Smith also stresses the American nature of Anderson's oeuvre, even when he uses English engravings as his sources. An appendix lists 693 books with illustrations engraved by Anderson in four research libraries.

19. Sugden, Thomas D. *A Few Timely Remarks on A. Anderson and His 300 or More Blocks That He Engraved After Mr. T. Bewick's Quadrupeds, Etc.* Bridgewater, Conn.: 1918. 4 leave.

The author at one time possessed two hundred wood blocks engraved by Anderson. He discusses the disposal of the collection through auction and gift. The four illustrations are printed from original blocks.

20. Thompson, Lawrence. *Alexander Anderson: His Tribute to the Wood Engraving of Thomas Bewick.*

Princeton, N.J.: Princeton University Press, 1940. 12 pp.

Thompson praises Anderson for copying Bewick's style of wood engraving, and mentions some of Bewick's illustrations copied by Anderson. The fourteen plates are reproduced from original wood blocks owned by Helen M. Knubel.

21. Haugen, Eva L. and Ingrid Semmingsen. "Peter Anderson of Bergen and Lowell. Artist and Ambassador of Culture." *Americana Norvegica* 4 (1973): 1–29.

Anderson emigrated from Bergen, Norway, to Boston in 1830. This biographical sketch is based on his autobiography housed in the manuscript collection of the University Library in Oslo among the papers of Wilhelm Boeck. Anderson started to work in the textile mills in Ware, Massachusetts, later moving to Lowell where he became treasurer of the Baldwin Manufacturing Company. He was talented as an artist and, at the time of the 1837 financial crisis, supported himself by making panoramic views of Ware, Worcester, and Washington. The author traces the rest of Anderson's life until his death in 1874.

22. Boston Art Club. *Report of the Proceedings at the Memorial Meeting in Honor of the Late Mr. Joseph Andrews (Engraver)*. Boston: 1873. 21 pp.

This memorial volume contains two essays on Andrews (ca. 1805–1873). The first, by Sylvester R. Koehler, "Biographical Memoir of the Late Mr. Joseph Andrews, Engraver," is based on interviews that Koehler had with Andrews. His childhood, apprenticeship, studies in Europe, and subsequent career are described in detail. The second essay, "Remarks on the Life and Character of Joseph Andrews," is by the Reverend R. C. Waterston, who concentrates on Andrews' character rather than on his engraving.

23. Fielding, Mantle. "Joseph Andrews." *Pennsylvania Magazine of History and Biography* 31 (January and April 1907): 107–113; 207–231.

Joseph Andrews served his apprenticeship with Abel Bowen in Boston and learned copperplate engraving with William Hoogland. He established a publishing and engraving business with his brother in Lancaster, Massachusetts, in 1827. Fielding discusses specific prints of Andrews that are in the author's collection. The list includes separately published prints as well as book illustrations.

24. Schrock, Nancy Carlson. "Joseph Andrews, Engraver: A Swedenborgian Justification." *Winterthur Portfolio* 12 (1977): 165–182.

Andrews (1806–1873) was a major portrait engraver in Boston. Apprenticed to Abel Bowen, he learned line engraving from William Hoogland. Schrock provides excellent descriptions of his further training in England and his major prints and relates his art to his religious affiliation with the sect founded upon the revelations of Emanuel Swedenborg.

25. Wheeler, Leeds Armstrong. *Armstrong & Company. Artistic Lithographers*. Boston: Boston Public Library, 1982. 67 pp.

The lithography company of Charles Armstrong (1836–1906) flourished in Boston in the final quarter of the nineteenth century. Armstrong's grandson, Leeds Armstrong Wheeler (1897–1969), assembled the materials for a complete history of the firm (manuscript at the Boston Public Library), from which this publication is derived. The chronology begins with Armstrong's birth in England and mentions the most significant publications of the firm, including such fine portfolios as *Upland Game Birds and Water Fowl of the United States* and *The Celebrated Dogs of America* both by A. Pope and *American Yachts* illustrated by Frederick S. Cozzens. A chapter from the manuscript, "The Lithographic Artists at Armstrong's," provides an excellent sense of the ambience at the firm.

26. Garrison, Lloyd. "The Work of a Great Cartoonist." *Cosmopolitan* 29 (September 1900): 550–60.

Francis Gilbert Attwood (1850–1900) was educated at Harvard, where he was one of the five founders of the Harvard *Lampoon*. He pursued a career as an illustrator of books and periodicals, including *The Cosmopolitan* and *Life*. He was also renowned as a political cartoonist. The article is well researched and informative.

27. Museum of Fine Arts, Boston. *An Exhibition of the Drawings of Francis Gilbert Attwood*. Boston: Alfred Mudge & Son, 1901. 8 pp.

This exhibition catalog lists about two hundred drawings, most of which were political or social in nature. Many of his drawings were published in *Life*, although his work appeared in other magazines and books.

28. Blaugrund, Annette. "John James Audubon: Producer, Promoter, and Publisher." *Imprint* 21, no. 1 (1996): 11–19.

Blaugrund provides an excellent introduction to Audubon's (1785–1851) life and the importance of the *Birds of America*, focusing on his attempts to sell subscriptions to his work. The article concludes with his death and his widow's sale of the original watercolors to the New-York Historical Society.

29. Blaugrund, Annette and Reba Fishman Snyder. "Audubon, Artist and Entrepreneur." *Antiques* 144, no. 5 (November 1993): 672–681.

This article focuses on the exhibition of ninety of the watercolors owned by the New-York Historical Society prepared by Audubon for his *Birds of America*. The authors discuss the project from its inception and include information on his exhibitions of the watercolors as part of his marketing strategy.

30. Braun, Robert. "Identifying Audubon Bird Prints: Originals, States, Editions, Restrikes, and Facsimiles and Reproductions." *Imprint* 21, no. 2 (1996): 12–22.

Braun, an amateur ornithologist and print collector, provides a useful guide to differentiating among the various editions of Audubon prints, as well as later reproductions. The essay features enlargements of details of prints that are helpful in distinguishing different editions and states.

31. Dwight, Edward H. "Audubon in Kentucky." *Antiques* 105 (April 1974): 850–54.

Audubon spent the better part of the years between 1807 and 1821 in Kentucky. He spent as much time as possible studying and drawing birds, but also ran a general store in Louisville for a few years with Ferdinand Rozier. Dwight discusses his other business ventures, most of which failed.

32.———. "Unpublished Audubon Originals." *Antiques* 87 (April 1965): 454–55.

Dwight describes and illustrates five previously unpublished works by Audubon, including three birds and two portraits executed between 1821 and 1824. Pertinent information about this period of Audubon's life is supplied.

33. Field, Richard S. "Audubon's Lithograph of the Clapper Rail." *Art Quarterly* 29, no. 2 (1966): 146–53.

During the summer of 1832, Audubon visited the lithography workshop of Cephas G. Childs where a print of the Clapper Rail was executed after one of Audubon's drawings. Field documents the print and relates it to the corresponding engraving in *The Birds of North America*. He doubts that Audubon himself did the lithograph, but attributes it to Albert Newsam in this well-documented study. This is Audubon's only lithograph, and it is known by just three impressions.

34. Fries, Waldemar H. *The Double Elephant Folio: The Story of Audubon's Birds of America*. Chicago: American Library Association, 1973. 501 pp., biblio., index.

Fries spent nearly fifteen years compiling his detailed history of the publication of *The Birds of America*, which includes a census of the extant copies of the work. The narrative begins with Audubon's search for an engraver in 1823 and ends with the completion of the project in 1837. Information is given on the original subscribers, the octavo edition, the Bien chromolithographed edition, reproductions, locations of the original copperplates, chronology of the engravings, variants in watermarks and legends, and lists of owners. This monumental work is superbly documented and researched.

35. Low, Susanne M. *An Index and Guide to Audubon's Birds of America*. New York: The American Museum of Natural History and Abbeville Press, 1988. 255 pp., biblio., index.

Low has produced an exhaustive compendium to Audubon's *Birds of America* prefaced with a brief introduction to Audubon and the publication of his work. Succinct biographies are given of the naturalists whose names appear on the plates, each of which is reproduced in a small black and white photograph with text descriptive of each species and the plate. There are indices by common name, title of plate, and by name of the original watercolor.

36.———. *Analysis of the Bien Edition of Audubon's Birds of America*. New York: American Museum of Natural History, 1994. 109 pp., photocopy of manuscript.

This publication discusses the chromolithographic facsimile production by Julius Bien in 1858 to 1860. Audubon's son, John Woodhouse Audubon initiated the project with the assistance of the publisher of the Royal Octavo edition, Roe Lockwood. Between the death of the younger Audubon in 1862 and the Civil War which hampered publishing in general, the project ceased after the publication of 105 plates. Low provides information about the process used to create the plates and describes each one.

37.———. *Catalogue of the New* Birds of America *Section of the Audubon Archives*. New York: American Museum of Natural History, 1993. 19 pp.

This publication is a census of the copies of the *Birds of America*, including complete and incomplete sets that have vanished or been destroyed by natural disasters and war.

38.———. *All Species of Birds Painted and/or Described by John James Audubon*. New York: American Museum of Natural History, 1995. unpag.; photocopy of manuscript.

This list includes all the birds painted by Audubon for the various editions of the *Birds of America*.

39.———. *Two Audubon Essays*. New York: American Museum of Natural History, 1995. 40 pp.

This slender publication includes two essays by Low. "The History of Audubon's Paintings from which the copperplates for *Birds of America* were etched" provides a chronological arrangement for Audobon's paintings. In "The History of the Royal Octavo Edition of *Birds of America*" Low describes the process for the creation of the small reproductions of the original plates and compares the two publications.

40. McColgin, Helen. "The Audubon Prints." *Antiques* 8 (December 1925): 361–63.

Audubon's training as an artist under Jacques Louis David, the formulation and execution of his work, and the printing and coloring of the plates are all touched upon in this informative article.

41. Murphy, Robert C. "John James Audubon (1785–1851): An Evaluation of the Man and His Work." *The New-York Historical Society Quarterly* 40 (October 1956): 315–50.

Murphy reviews Audubon's merits as a person and attributes his failures to financial depressions, the War of 1812, and an often uncompromising quest after his goals. Written from an ornithologist's point of view, Murphy emphasizes Audubon's dedication in studying and recording American birds at a time when there was little printed on the subject, and traces the history of his publication. The reception of the public and scholarly audience to his *Birds of America* is noted, and the author emphasizes the importance of the bird biographies themselves, an often neglected aspect of publications on Audubon.

42. Shelley, Donald A. "Audubon's Technique: As Shown in His Drawings of Birds." *Antiques* 49 (June 1946): 354–57.

Among the collections of The New-York Historical Society are the original water colors and drawings for the Audubon's *Birds of America*. Shelley has studied the drawings closely and analyzes the change in Audubon's style, from the early drawings to the more mature works, in terms of technique and composition. This excellent study contributes to the understanding and appreciation of Audubon's monumental work.

43. Tyler, Ron. *Audubon's Great National Work. The Royal Octavo Edition of The Birds of America.* Austin: University of Texas Press, 1993. 213 pp., biblio., index.

Tyler writes about the octavo edition of Audubon's *The Birds of America* published in nine editions from 1840 to 1889. The first two chapters concern Audubon's life and the publication of the first edition. The publication of the octavo edition was by subscription and Tyler has sought out information about the trips Audubon made to gain subscribers as well as biographical information on those who did agree to purchase the book. Other chapters discuss later editions and Audubon's place in the history of American art. This scholarly volume is eminently readable and handsomely produced. The bibliography is excellent.

44. Welch, Margaret. "'Gentlemen of fortune and liberality': The Original Subscribers to the Audubon Folios." *Imprint* 16, no. 1 (1991): 11–19.

Derived from her doctoral dissertation, *John James Audubon and His American Audience: Art, Science, and Nature, 1830–1860*, Welch discusses the patronage that Audubon sought and received. She concludes that it was the enthusiasm of these patrons and collectors that ensured the production of such lavish publications.

45. Wiehl, Lee. "Four Lithographs of John Woodhouse Audubon's Gold Rush Journey." *Imprint* 5, no. 1 (1980): 15–19.

During 1849 Audubon traveled to the California gold fields, making numerous sketches during his trip. Four lithographs were published by Nagel and Weingartner in 1851. Wiehl describes the circumstances of their creation and publication, noting that although an ambitious publication was evisioned, only one part of *Notes of an Expedition through Mexico and California* was issued. Wiehl compares the drawings and the prints.

46. Goodman, Ted, and Angela Giral. "Samuel Putnam Avery, Patron of the Arts." *Art Documentation* 16, no. 2 (September 1997): 6–8.

Samuel Putnam Avery (1822–1904) was, in his early life and through the 1850s, an engraver on wood. In the years before the Civil War, Avery began to work as an art dealer, advising patrons such as William T. Walters of Baltimore, and Colonel J. Striker Jenkins. By the middle of the 1860s he was working as an auctioneer. This essay really focuses on the Avery Architectural and Fine Arts Library at Columbia University, founded by Avery and his wife as a memorial to their son who died in 1890. This is, however, a useful biographical sketch of Avery.

47. Sieben-Morgen, Ruth. *Samuel Putnam Avery (1822–1904), Engraver on Wood: A Bio-Bibliographical Study.* New York: Columbia University, 1940. Mimeographed, 157 pp.

Samuel P. Avery was best known as an art connoisseur and philanthropist. He is less well known as an engraver on wood, an activity that occupied his time for the twenty-five years before the Civil War. The author traces his career and corrects errors in the scant biographies of Avery. The appendices are helpful and include information about him in the New York City directories from 1821 (under his father's name) to 1871, descriptions of his scrapbooks and albums, a bibliography, and a checklist of his engravings chronologically arranged from 1841 to 1866. This is an excellent study. Revised edition (1942).

48. Koehler, Sylvester R. "Mr. Bacher's Venetian Etchings." *American Art Review* 1, no. 2 (1881): 231–32.

In 1880, Otto Henry Bacher (1856–1909) moved from Germany to Venice. Koehler makes a stylistic comparison of the work done in Germany with that of Italy, then compares Bacher's work to the etchings of Duveneck, his teacher. Using the plate of Venice as a point of departure, Koehler discusses impressionism and the problems of representing nature faithfully.

49.———. "Otto H. Bacher." *American Art Review* 1, no. 1 (1881): 51–52.

A native of Cleveland, Ohio, Bacher was studying in Europe with Duveneck's "boys" when this article was written. His first etching dates from 1876, but it was not until 1879 that he began to apply himself seriously to the art. A list of twenty-four of his plates is given, all of which depict European subjects. Koehler feels that Bacher's choice of realistic subjects is preferable to the romantic subjects of earlier artists.

50. Nash, Chauncey C. "John Warner Barber and His Books." *Walpole Society Note Book* (1934): 30–60.

John Warner Barber (1798–1885) grew up in Windsor, Connecticut, where he expressed an early interest in drawing. After serving his apprenticeship with Abner Reed in East Windsor, he moved to New Haven where he began his own engraving business. Nash draws much of his information from Barber's diary, which he kept from 1813 to 1884, and mentions a number of his engravings and books. In addition to engraving book illustrations, Barber traveled extensively and wrote a number of books on history and geography, many of which he also illustrated. Nash compiled a list of eighteen books written by Barber and seventeen books containing his illustrations.

51. O'Brien, Donald C. "John Warner Barber: A Connecticut Engraver." *Imprint* 4, no. 1 (1979): 20–22.

O'Brien provides an excellent review of the life and work of John Warner Barber, an author and illustrator of historical works who resided in New Haven for most of his life. Sources for this essay include Barber's diaries located in the collections of the New Haven Colony Historical Society.

52. Jacobs, Phoebe Lloyd. "John James Barralet and the Apotheosis of George Washington." *Winterthur Portfolio* 12 (1977): 115–138.

Barralet (ca. 1747–1815), an Irishman of French descent, became an important American illustrator and artist beginning with his arrival in Philadelphia in 1795. Jacobs closely examines his allegorical commemoration of Washington's death setting it in the context of Barralet's other prints and those of other engravers. Barralet drew upon Cesare Ripa's *Iconologia* and other European sources for much of his imagery.

53. Hine, Robert V. *Bartlett's West. Drawing the Mexican Boundary*. New Haven: Yale University Press, 1968. 155 pp., biblio., index.

Hine has provided an exceptionally full account of the life of John Russell Bartlett (1805–1886), concentrating on his drawings and watercolors executed during the three years that he spent surveying the Mexican border between 1850 and 1853. Also present during this survey were Seth Eastman and Henry C. Pratt. Bartlett's sketches were used to illustrate his *Personal Narrative of Explorations and Incidents in Texas, New Mexico, California, Sonora, and Chihuahua* published in New York in 1854. The watercolors and sketches and personal papers of Bartlett are deposited in the John Carter Brown Library.

54. Arnot Art Gallery. *William H. Bartlett and His Imitators*. Elmira, N.Y.: Arnot Art Gallery, 1966. 36 pp.

A survey of the engraved work of Bartlett (1809–1854), this exhibition catalog demonstrates that Bartlett's work had a wide ranging influence on other artists. Many art teachers used his engravings as models for their pupils. The work of Bartlett and his imitators provides an insight into artistic taste in America between 1840 and 1870.

55. Cowdrey, Mary Bartlett. "William Henry Bartlett and the American Scene." *New York History* 22 (October 1941): 388–400.

Cowdrey addresses herself to the interesting problem of the many mid-nineteenth-century paintings attributed to Bartlett. She discusses the drawings he made to be copied as engravings for travel books, noting that he probably had no time for oil painting in the last fifteen years of his life. She concludes that many of the landscapes attributed to him are copied from the engravings or are more recent frauds. Also there is no contemporary documentation that he painted in oil. Cowdrey points out that only American landscapes are attributed to Bartlett although he made thousands of drawings in Europe and the Near East. To assist in straightening out the confusion, she includes a list of the engravings in Bartlett's *American Scenery* (London and New York, 1840).

56. Diebold, William. "Bartlett's Hudson River Prints." *Imprint* 3, no. 1 (1978): 8–11,15, 19.

Diebold discusses the collaboration between Nathaniel P. Willis and William Henry Bartlett that resulted in the very popular *American Scenery*. Diebold sets Bartlett's views in the context of other Hudson River views by William Guy Wall and Jacques Gerard Milbert, trying to explain the choice of views and the differences between views by the different artists of identical locations. Diebold also discusses the reproductions of the engravings by other engravers and in different media.

57. Dintruff, Emma Jane. "The American Scene A Century Ago." *Antiques* 38 (December 1940): 279–81.

In 1840 the London publisher George Virtue simultaneously issued English, French, and German editions of *American Scenery*. This popular publication, written by Nathaniel Parker Willis, contained one hundred engravings after drawings by William Henry Bartlett. Dintruff discusses the historical accuracy of the book and its engravings, also mentioning views on Staffordshire china and other prints that were copied from

Bartlett's work. The Imprint Society, of Barre, Massachusetts, reprinted portions of *American Scenery* in 1971.

58. Earl, Mary-Ellen. "William H. Bartlett and His Imitators." *Antiques* 92 (November 1967): 722–25.

The author focuses on Bartlett's background, artistic training, and the production of his volume *American Scenery*, from which several engravings and original sketches are reproduced. The author of this article substantiates Bartlett Cowdrey's views on the oil paintings attributed to Bartlett, and points out the influence of his engravings on amateur artists, noting that even Currier & Ives copied some of them in their lithographs. The engravings also served as sources for glass and Staffordshire pottery.

59. Major-Marothy, Eva. "The Wild and the Tamed: Bartlett's Canada Versus Views by his Canadian Contemporaries." *Imprint* 20, no. 1 (1995): 22–28.

The author compares the views of Canada by William Henry Bartlett for Nathaniel Parker Willis's *Canadian Scenery Illustrated* with works by Canadian artists. In order to appeal to a European audience, Bartlett emphasized the wild nature of the country. In contrast, views made for home consumption focused on progress and development. Prints after views by James Pattison Cockburn (1779–1847), William Eagar (ca. 1796–1839), Robert Auchmaty Sproule (1799–1845), Thomas Young (d. 1860), and John Gillespie (fl. 1841–59) are compared to Bartlett's views.

60. Worman, Eugene C., Jr. *The University of Guelph Collection of Original Drawings by W. H. Bartlett.* Guelph: University of Guelph, 1997. 112 pp., biblio.

Located in the library of the University of Guelph is a portfolio of drawings by Bartlett, including those for *Footsteps of Our Lord* (1851), *Pictures from Sicily* (1853), *The Pilgrim Fathers; or, The Founders of New England* (1853), and *Jerusalem Revisited* (1855). Worman describes Bartlett's career, particularly his last years covered by these publications. The catalogue is arranged by book title and Worman provides excellent information on each drawing and publication. All of the drawings are reproduced, but the quality unfortunately is compromised by the use of digital technology.

61. Worman, Eugene C., Jr. "*American Scenery* and the Dating of Its Bartlett Prints." *Imprint* 12, no. 2 (1987): 22–27.

Worman has traced the publication history of this very popular travel book by examining copies in original wrappers as issued in parts as well as many bound copies. His study will assist curators and collectors in dating impressions of prints removed from volumes. Worman also notes that no copies were issued by George Virtue, the English publisher, with handcoloring.

62. Worman, Eugene C., Jr. "A Geographical Catalog of Bartlett Prints in *American Scenery*." *Imprint* 19, no. 2 (1994): 2–16.

Worman, the authority on Bartlett, provides excellent background on the publication of *American Scenery*. Also of interest are titles of volumes bearing contemporary reproductions of the engravings such as American periodicals, histories, biographies, and guidebooks. In a compact format, the geographical catalog presents valuable information including the number of each plate, whether or not German and French subtitles are present, dimensions, earliest imprint date, location of the engraving in the published work, and the location of any original drawings.

63.———. "W. H. Bartlett and American Magazine Illustration." *AB Bookman's Weekly* (23 March 1992): 1114–1134, passim.

Worman correctly proposes the importance of the engravings of Bartlett's drawings of American scenery by documenting their immediate reuse in periodicals published in the United States.

64.———. "W. H. Bartlett and American Book Illustration." *AB Bookman's Weekly* (20 April 1992): 1568–90, passim.

Worman has found reproductions of many of Bartlett's American and foreign landscapes in American gift books, guide books, histories, biographies, religious texts, view books, and literary works suggesting the widespread popularity of the publications containing reproductions of Bartlett's views.

65. Wainwright, Nicholas B. "Education of an Artist: The Diary of Joseph Boggs Beale, 1856–1862." *Pennsylvania Magazine of History and Biography* 97 (October 1973): 485–510.

In the introduction to the diary, Wainwright relates information on Beale's (1841–1926) family, education, and later professional career as an artist and illustrator. The section of the diary that Beale wrote from the age of 15 until he became an art instructor at Central High School in Philadelphia at the age of 21 is reprinted. The diary is concerned with a variety of topics, and provides insights into Beale's artistic development. The diary, which continues to 1865, and other papers belonging to Beale are located at the Historical Society of Pennsylvania.

66. David, Beverly R. "The Unexpurgated A Connecticut Yankee: Mark Twain and his illustrator Daniel Chester Beard." *Prospects* (1975): 98–118.

The author discusses the humorous illustrations by D.C. Beard (1850–1941).

67. Beckman, Thomas. "The Beck and Pauli Lithographing Company." *Imprint* 9, no. 1 (1984): 1–6

Located in Milwaukee, the Beck and Pauli Company was best known for the printing of panoramic city views. Beckman provides a carefully researched history of the two partners, both German immigrants, Clemens J. Pauli (1835–1896) and Adam Beck (1847–1922). They were in partnership for only nine years (1878–1887), but their output remains historically significant.

68. Koehler, Sylvester R. "Albert F. Bellows." *American Art Review* 1, no. 2 (1880): 293.

In this brief note on Bellows's (1829–1883) etchings, Koehler notes that his work is a potent argument in favor of etching as painter's art. A list of his best plates is given.

69. Deak, Gloria-Gilda. *William James Bennett: Master of the Aquatint View.* New York: New York Public Library, 1988. 92 pp., biblio.

William James Bennett (ca. 1784–1844) was a master of the aquatint process as well as a skillful topographical artist. This exhibition catalog celebrates Bennett's skills. Dale Roylance provides an essay on aquatint engraving in England and America. Gloria Deak's essay discusses Bennett's early years in England and his American career that began in 1826. His prints are glorious and are well served by this publication. Deak's well researched essay is followed by a chronology of Bennett's life. The exhibition included fifty-two prints, each of which is well described and many of which are illustrated, some in color.

70. Virginia State Library and Archives. *Album of Virginia: Picturesque Views of the Old Dominion.* Richmond: Virginia State Library, 1994. 10 pp.

This checklist for an exhibition mounted in 1994 describes Edward Beyer's *Album of Virginia* printed in Berlin in 1858 for distribution in the United States and Europe. Brief mention is made of other artists who depicted Virginia scenery.

71. Wright, R. Lewis. "Edward Beyer and the *Album of Virginia.*" *Virginia Calvacade* 22, no. 4 (March 1973): 36–44.

Wright presents biographical information on Edward Beyer (1820–1865) and on the publication history of his *Album of Virginia* issued in 1858 with lithographs printed in Germany from sketches made in 1854 to 1856. Beyer returned to Germany with his sketches and never returned. The portfolio contains forty plates and is highly regarded by collectors. The article contains a couple of photographs that contrast Beyer's views with the present reality.

72. Craven, Wayne. "Albion Harris Bicknell, 1837–1915." *Antiques* 106 (September 1974): 443–49.

This reassessment of the artist contains some references to Bicknell's etchings, six of which are illustrated.

73. Marzio, Peter C. "Mr. Audubon and Mr. Bien: An early Phase in the History of American Chromolithography." *Prospects* (1975): 138–154.

Marzio begins his discussion with the meaning and effect of chromolithography on late nineteenth-century American life. Julius Bien's chromolithographs for the American edition of Audubon's *Birds of America* (1859–1860) is one of the high points of the process. This aborted publishing project is described (only 105 plates appeared) in detail.

74. Morgan, Ann Lee. "The American Audubons: Julius Bien's Lithographed Edition." *Print Quarterly* 4, no. 4 (December 1997):

Morgan's excellent article discusses the publication of the lithographed set of Audubon's birds in 1859–60 by Julius Bien. The reasons for the project, the process, and reasons for the abandonment are all provided. The essay is well illustrated with details to show the differences between the etched and lithographed versions.

75. Wright, Helena E. "Bierstadt and the Business of Printmaking." in *Albert Bierstadt: Art & Enterprise,* 267–288 in Nancy K. Anderson, and Linda S. Ferber. New York: Hudson Hills Press and The Brooklyn Museum, 1990.

Bierstadt capitalized on all of the reproductive arts during his lifetime—chromolithography, photography, photomechanical processes, and engraving. Wright's brief essay focuses on the ways in which these processes were used by him and publishers to reproduce his drawings and paintings. A carefully prepared checklist of the reproductions made during his lifetime includes engravings in periodicals and other books as well as separately published prints. The commentary is extensive and very useful.

76. O'Gorman, James F. *Accomplished in All Departments of Art: Hammatt Billings of Boston, 1818–1874.* Amherst: University of Massachusetts Press, 1998. 291 pp., index.

O'Gorman's thoroughly researched monograph describes all facets of Billings's career: illustrator of books and periodicals, designer of monuments and other public art, architect, and decorative artist. Among the several appendices are lists of books illustrated by Billings and books owned by the artist. The commentary on Billings as an illustrator is the summation of many years of collecting and research on O'Gorman's part.

77.———. "The Poet and the Illustrator: Longfellow, Billings, and the Disproportion Between their Designs and Their Deeds in the 1840's" in *Aspects of American Printmaking, 1800–1950,* 31–51. ed. James F. O'Gorman. Syracuse, N.Y.: Syracuse University Press, 1988.

Hammatt Billings was the foremost book illustrator of Boston in the mid-nineteenth century. O'Gorman focuses on American illustrators for Longfellow's poetry including one title page by an anonymous designer issued by Carey and Hart and a cycle by Daniel Huntington whose figures were rather too Italian for Longfellow's taste. Billings was chosen by the poet to illustrate *Evangeline* in 1847, but the illustrations never were produced except for one drawing. The reason is unknown, but English illustrators Jan E. Busham, Birket Foster, and John Gilbert illustrated *Evangeline* and subsequent works. This chapter in the history of American literary illustration suggests that significant English competition existed.

78.———. "War, Slavery, and Intemperance in the Book Illustrations of Hammatt Billings." *Imprint* 10, no. 1 (1985): 2–11.

O'Gorman provides biographical information about Billings and focuses on the themes of the Mexican War, slavery, and intemperance which dominated Billings' oeuvre. Among books illustrated by Billings was Harriet Beecher Stowe's *Uncle Tom's Cabin* of 1852. O'Gorman closes his essay by summarizing the other genres which Billings illustrated.

79.———. "Hammatt Billings (1818–74) Book Illustrator of Boston." *Private Library* 7, no. 3 (1994): 102–113.

Obviously overshadowed by the author's monograph on Billings (1998), this article provides the basic facts of Billings's life and provides an excellent summary of his work as an illustrator. O'Gorman also talks of his own experiences as a collector.

80. Bender, J. H. "Catalogue of Engravings and Lithographs After George Caleb Bingham." *Print Collector's Quarterly* 27 (February 1940): 106–108.

Bender lists eleven prints after Bingham's paintings. The information provided for each print includes background for the painting copied. In some cases publication data for the print are lacking.

81. Brown, Phillis Y. "George Caleb Bingham." *Imprint* 2, no. 1 (1977): 7–9.

Several paintings by Bingham (1811–1879) were reproduced as prints. Brown points out that Bingham credited the reproductions published by the American Art Union with enhancing his reputation. A list of those prints as well as several published by Goupil & Co., and three others are appended to the article.

82. Casper, Scott. "Politics, Art, and the Contradictions of a Market Culture, George Caleb Bingham's *Stump Speaking*." *American Art* 5, no. 3 (1991): 26–47.

Casper thoughtfully analyzes and sets Bingham's paintings within his active political life, focusing on *Stump Speaking*, orginally known as *The County Canvass*. In addition, Casper briefly considers the publication of prints after Bingham's paintings, *The County Election* and *Stump Speaking*, by Goupil & Company. John Sartain engraved *The County Election* over a two or three year period in the early 1850s; the latter was engraved by Louis-Adolphe Gautier. Casper quotes letters by Bingham showing how involved he was in the publication process and how concerned he was with the commercial success of them.

83. Hall, Virginius C. "George Caleb Bingham, the Missouri Artist." *Print Collector's Quarterly* 27 (February 1940): 8–25.

Hall briefly discusses Bingham's background, training, and a few of his paintings. Engravings and lithographs after his paintings are the subject of this study. Goupil & Co. of New York and Paris and the American Art Union were two organizations that reproduced his paintings as prints.

84. McDermott, John Francis. "Jolly Flatboatmen: Bingham and His Imitators." *Antiques* 73 (March 1958): 266–67.

The "Jolly Flatboatmen" by George Caleb Bingham was purchased by the American Art Union in 1846, and was the subject of one of its large engravings. McDermott recounts the history of the painting and then describes the many woodcuts, lithographs, and engravings copied after the painting.

85. Tucker, Joseph L. "A Collector's View of the Prints of George Caleb Bingham." *Imprint* 14, no. 2 (1989): 2–10.

Tucker has identified seventeen nineteenth-century reproductions of the paintings of Bingham, eight of which concern him in this essay: the four prints in the Election Series, the two river prints, and the two history prints. He believes that Bingham considered the prints the end product of his painting and demonstrates how involved Bingham was in their production.

86. Boorse, Henry A. "The Third Street House in Philadelphia by William Birch: The Inside Story." *Imprint* 14, no. 2 (1989): 11–17.

One of the views in Birch's *City of Philadelphia* depicts William Bingham's house, then the finest residence in the city. Boorse recites the history of the house and its owner for whom Birch (1755–1834) worked as a drawing instructor to Bingham's daughters. After the building passed out of the family, it served as a hotel and was destroyed by fire in 1847. Boorse's knowledge of this landmark provides important background for an appreciation of Birch's *City of Philadelphia*.

87. Snyder, Martin P. "Birch's Philadelphia Views: New Discoveries." *Pennsylvania Magazine of History and Biography* 88 (November 1964): 164–3.

Since publishing his first article in 1949 on Birch's Philadelphia views, Snyder has found new material to prove that four, not three, editions of the Philadelphia views were published. The newly found edition was issued in 1809. The contents of that edition are carefully described and compared to earlier editions. Also discussed is a broadside advertisement which reveals several details about the first edition. Snyder found a map of Philadelphia printed in 1794 which was the source for the map included in the first three editions.

88.———. "William Birch: His 'Country Seats of the United States'." *Pennsylvania Magazine of History and Biography* 81 (July 1957): 225–54.

Birch was the first artist to depict the rural way of life in the early years of the nation's history. From studying Birch's unpublished autobiography at the Historical Society of Pennsylvania, Snyder has been able to explain Birch's motivation and background for this ambitious and novel undertaking. The series of twenty plates, published in 1808 and 1809, are discussed in detail.

89.———. "William Birch: His Philadelphia Views." *Pennsylvania Magazine of History and Biography* 73 (July 1949): 271–315.

The publication of *The City of Philadelphia* containing twenty-seven engraved views by William Birch and his son, Thomas, was a monumental task. Snyder discusses Birch's artistic background, the genesis of the project, the production of drawings and plates, and other details relating to the publication of the volume. A second edition appeared in 1804, and this article contains a comparison of the first two editions, with information about the third edition of 1827–1828. Later restrikes from some of the plates were also made. In the appendix of his article, Snyder collates the various editions and lists other views of Philadelphia by William Birch.

90. Hunt, David C. "Karl Bodmer and the American Frontier." *Imprint* 10, no. no. 1 (1985): 11–19.

The Joslyn Art Museum in Omaha, Nebraska, has among its collections four hundred watercolors and sketches by Karl Bodmer (1809–1893) that document the scientific expedition of Prince Maximilian of Wied from 1832 to 1834. Hunt clarifies some of the misconceptions about Bodmer and writes about the journey and the circumstances surrounding the publication of the narrative and its accompanying atlas volume of eighty plates. Hunt discusses various states of the prints and restrikes from the plates, together with comments about the coloring of the prints. A full description of the Bodmer collection is contained in *Karl Bodmer's America* published by the University of Nebaska Press in 1984.

91. Hunt, David C. and Bockhoff, Esther. *Tribes of the Buffalo. A Swiss Artist on the American Frontier.* Cleveland: The Cleveland Museum of Natural History, 1994. 64 pp.

This exhibition catalog describes the collection formed by John Painter of Cincinnati. Painter not only owns a magnificent set of the aquatints after Karl Bodmer's drawings, but also many objects reflecting life among the tribes of the Great Plains. Hunt's essay provides biographical sketches of the artist and his patron, Maximilian, Prince of Wied, and describes their travels in America. Bockhoff's essay focuses on the objects in the exhibition and their meaning to the Plains natives. There is a checklist of the artifacts and prints in the exhibition. The catalog is thoroughly illustrated in color.

92. Mann, Maybelle. "Karl Bodmer: From Frontier American to the Barbizon Woods." *American Art & Antiques* 5, no. 2 (March 1982): 52–61.

The artist Karl Bodmer accompanied Maximilian, Prince of Wied-Neuwied, on his expedition through the American West. The author describes the trip and sorts out some of the editions of the published account of the trip. On his return to Europe, Bodmer joined the circle of artists in Paris known as the Barbizon school. He died in poverty at Paris in 1893.

93. Tomko, George P. "The Western Prints of Karl Bodmer" in *Prints of the American West,* 46–55. Ron Tyler ed. Fort Worth: Amon Carter Museum, 1983.

Tomko discusses Bodmer's art training, the poses of the Indians he depicted, and overall compositions. Bodmer's landscapes are important documents of the terrain as well as works of artistic merit.

94. Whitmore, William H. *Abel Bowen, Engraver.* Boston: Rockwell & Churchill, 1884. 32 pp.

Prepared for the Bostonian Society, this is a biographical sketch of Abel Bowen (1790–1854), an engraver on copper and wood. Many of the publications that he illustrated are cited, and the article is illustrated with restrikes from copperplates and wood blocks engraved by Bowen and owned by the Bostonian Society.

95. Tatham, David. "The Photolithographs of L.H. Bradford" in *Aspects of American Printmaking, 1800–1950,* 105–140. ed. James F. O'Gorman. Syracuse, N.Y.: Syracuse University Press, 1988.

Lodowick Harrington Bradford (1820–1885) was active as a lithographer in Boston for some years. He experimented with photolithography from 1857 through the 1860s. Tatham describes the process as well as shop practices of the 1840s and 1850s before the practice of lithography in Boston became intensely competitive. James Ambrose Cutting was a photographer who joined with Bradford to create the first photolithographs. Tatham provides a definitive checklist of Bradford's photolithographs based on the collections of the American Antiquarian Society and the Smithsonian Institution.

96. Koch, Robert. "Will Bradley." *Art in America* 50 (1962): 78–83.

Bradley (1868–1962), one of the foremost exponents of Art Nouveau, spent the years between 1893 and 1898 as a draftsman. Koch discusses his work before 1900 and cites a number of books and magazines bearing his designs.

97. Koehler, Sylvester R. "Alfred Brennan." *American Art Review* 1, no. 2 (1880): 330.

Brennan (1853–1921) was one of the young etchers whose illustrations frequently appeared in magazines. In spite of certain inadequacies in Brennan's style, Koehler uses examples of his work to support his conviction that inventiveness and expressiveness in an etching are more important than academic preciseness. One of Brennan's original plates serves as the illustration.

98. Snyder, Martin P. "William L. Breton, Nineteenth-Century Philadelphia Artist." *Pennsylvania Magazine of History and Biography* 85 (April 1961): 178–209.

William Breton (ca. 1785–1855), in his fifties when he came to Philadelphia from England, started sketching the city immediately upon his arrival. In 1828, the Philadelphia historian John F. Watson, who had been accumulating material for his *Annals of Philadelphia*, met Breton and hired him to prepare sketches for publication in the *Annals*. Through this contact, Breton secured other commissions. Snyder discusses Breton's sketches and watercolors (many of which are located in the Historical Society of Pennsylvania), and the publication of them as wood engravings and lithographs. It is in the latter medium that most of Breton's work from the 1830s has survived.

99. Craven, Wayne. "Hugh Bridport, Philadelphia Miniaturist, Engraver, and Lithographer." *Antiques* 89 (April 1966): 548–52.

Little documentation about the life of Hugh Bridport (1794–ca. 1868) exists, but Craven has successfully unearthed some contemporary records of his life. The author was able to locate some miniatures and several prints by Bridport at the Historical Society of Pennsylvania.

100. Erickson, Bruce T. "Eliphalet M. Brown, Jr. An Early Expedition Photographer." *The Daguerreian Annual* 1 (1990): 145–156.

Brown (1816–1886) worked as a lithographer in New York from 1839 onward. In 1852, he was part of the military expedition sent to Japan by the federal government under Perry's command. His daguerreotypes were the sources for many of the illustrations that appeared in published reports. Erickson provides an excellent commentary on Brown's career as a daguerreotypist, adding to what has been previously known about this lithographic draftsman.

101. Koehler, Sylvester R. "George Loring Brown." *American Art Review* 2, no. 2 (1881): 192.

All but one of the etchings by Brown were executed in Italy in 1853 and 1854. They were published in New York under the title, *Etchings of the Campagna, Rome*. Koehler compares these early etchings to those produced during the etching revival, and notes that the earlier works are more like engravings in technique because they lack the spontaneity he feels a true etching should possess. Koehler attributes the difference in style to the age in which they were done, not to any lack of talent in the artist.

102. Courtney, Rosemary. "M.E.D. Brown (1810–1896): American Lithographer and Painter." *American Art Journal* XII, no. 4 (1980): 66–77.

Rosemary Courtney has uncovered a great deal of biographical information about Brown, including his full name: Mannevillette Elihu Dearing Brown. She follows his professional career from the Pendleton shop in Boston (1827–1831), to Philadelphia where Nathaniel Currier worked for him a year. Courtney discusses several of his works in lithography. In 1834 he left Philadelphia for a brief sojourn in Boston, settling in Utica, New York, in 1849 where he remained until his death in 1896. He also painted portraits and a few landscapes.

103. Bates, Albert C. *An Early Connecticut Engraver and His Work*. Hartford: Case, Lockwood & Brainard Co., 1906. 48 pp.

There are few engravings actually signed by Richard Brunton (d. 1832), but Bates has attributed over thirty engravings to Brunton on the basis of style. Among the most interesting are two family registers, a portrait of Washington, and a view of Newgate Prison in which Brunton was imprisioned for counterfeiting. The rest of his work consists of bookplates. Bates was unable to find much biographical data on Brunton, beyond tracing his path as he moved around New England.

104. Warren, William Lamson. "Richard Brunton, Itinerant Craftsman." *Art in America* 39 and 41 (April 1951 and Spring 1953): 81–94; 69–78.

Warren updated the book on Brunton by Albert C. Bates, and included new biographical data. The article adds several new family registers and a few other prints to Brunton's production.

105. Deak, Gloria. *Discovering America's Southeast: A Sixteenth Century View Based on the Mannerist Engravings of Theodore de Bry*. Birmingham,

Alabama: Birmingham Public Library, 1992. 205 pp., biblio.

An essay on discovering the new world is followed by one on the work of Theodore de Bry (1528–1598), a mannerist engraver born in Belgium but who worked in Strasbourg. Deak sets de Bry in his historical and artistic context and provides important information on the engravings that he did after the work of the English artist John White who did a series of sketches in Virginia. These, of course, led to other engravings after Jacques Le Moyne de Morgues. Deak describes the various publications of de Bry, explores his impact on his contemporaries, and their importance today. Almost fifty plates are reproduced, each with extensive annotation.

106. Hugo, E. Harold, and Thompson R. Harlow. *Abel Buell, a Jack of All Trades, and Genius Extraordinary: His Life and Trials.* Meriden, Conn.: Columbiad Club, 1955. 7 pp.

Buell (1742–1822) seemed to have a propensity for getting into legal and financial difficulties, and the authors touch upon them briefly. Two of his engravings are reproduced: the chart of Saybrook Harbor and the writing sheet, both done about 1774. Several newspaper advertisements issued by him and his wife are reprinted in full. They reveal the scope of his talents and inventiveness.

107. Newman, Ewell L. "Abel Buell: Errant Genius." *Imprint* 1, no. 1 (February 1976): [7–8].

Newman's brief biography of Buell mentions his training as an apprentice to a goldsmith in East Guilford, Connecticut. As a young man, Buell forged some currency, for which he was briefly imprisoned. Upon his release he established a type foundry in New Haven. In 1770 he engraved a map of Saybrook Harbor, the first significant engraving in the Connecticut Colony. His most ambitious work was a map of the United States published in 1784 in New Haven. He apparently was a mechanic with many interests for he later invented agricultural implements, was a part owner of some sloops, and also worked as a coach and sign painter.

108. Wroth, Lawrence C. *Abel Buell of Connecticut: Silversmith, Type Founder & Engraver.* Middletown, Conn.: Wesleyan University Press, 1958. 102pp., index.

First published by the Acorn Club in 1926 in a limited edition, this volume was enlarged and revised for publication in 1958. Wroth begins with a well-written biographical sketch and devotes separate chapters to Buell's activities as jeweler, silversmith, typefounder, and engraver. The author discusses each of Buell's engravings, including a chart of Saybrook Harbor (1774), a form for Yale's diploma, a writing sheet, "The Sequel of Arts and Sciences," a large map of the United States, and armorial cuts. Wroth's documentation and style are superb.

109. Tatham, David. "John Henry Bufford, American Lithographer." *Proceedings of the American Antiquarian Society* 86, no. 1 (April 1976): 47–73.

Tatham asserts that Bufford (1810–1870) was a significant figure in the history of American lithography because of his own skill as an artist on stone, his role as a publisher and printer of prints, and as an employer, teacher of sorts, and colleague of a notable number of artists, including Winslow Homer. This essay begins with an appraisal of Bufford's career. Tatham also provides an excellent biographical sketch based on information provided to him by Bufford's descendants. His activities in New York are well documented by surviving prints as are his activities in Boston beginning in 1840. Among the artists associated with his firm in Boston were John P. Newell (c.1831–1898), Joseph E. Baker (1834–1914), and Homer. Tatham contrasts Bufford's business with that of Nathaniel Currier and concludes the essay by discussing five prints in detail that Bufford had drawn.

110. Holman, Richard B. "William Burgis." in *Boston Prints and Printmakers 1670–1775,* 57–82. Boston: Colonial Society of Massachusetts, 1973.

William Burgis was involved in printmaking in colonial America as a designer, publisher, and engraver for about a dozen years. Holman discusses the small group of his known plates, including one map and nine views. Each print is reproduced and discussed in detail. Holman has located all known copies of each print. A checklist follows the article containing short descriptions of each work. A short bibliography supplements the notes in the text.

111. Burt, Alice. *Catalogue of Line Engravings, Etchings, and Original Drawings by Charles Burt, Dec'd.* Brooklyn, N.Y.: 1893. 50 pp.

Born in Edinburgh, Scotland, Burt (1823–1892) came to the United States after completing his apprenticeship in engraving. He concentrated on bank notes and postage stamp engraving and was for many years the principal engraver for the Bureau of Engraving and Printing. In the catalog, 310 small portraits are described, as well as 144 prints of varied subjects (unidentified subjects, large portraits, genre scenes, allegorical figures, etc.). Forty drawings are also included. Dimensions, dates, and publishers are included in the catalog descriptions. The collection is at The New York Public Library; 125 copies of the catalog were printed.

112. Thomas, Thomas H. "Charles Burt: Bank Note Engraver." *Print Connoisseur* 4 (April 1924): 114–29.

This article begins by explaining the necessity for high accomplishment and large editions in bank note engraving, noting that there is no public recognition and little financial reward. Charles Burt kept a collection of prints from his own plates and his daughter published a catalog of this work, with a biographical note, after his death in 1892. He engraved vignettes of many types: fancy heads and figures, a few landscapes, allegorical subjects, etc. He also engraved a number of portraits in a larger format. The author analyzes Burt's style with care and finds it to be of high quality.

113. Williams, Jennifer. "Color From Stone." *Michigan History* 70, no. 1 (January 1986): 18–22.

This article, well-illustrated, discusses chromolithographs produced by the firm founded by Thomas Calvert (1828–1900) in 1861. An Englishman, Calvert built up his company so that it was employing twenty workers within five years. The firm continued until 1970 when it was absorbed into the Canadian firm of Lawson and Jones. An exhibition of works issued by the firm was held in Michigan in 1986 under the sponsorship of the Detroit Institute of Arts.

114. Breeskin, Adelyn D. *Mary Cassatt: Graphic Art.* Washington, D.C.: Smithsonian Institution Press, 1981. 25 pp. and plates.

Breeskin's introduction provides the outlines of Mary Cassatt's (1844–1926) life in Europe, the creation of her prints in France, the impact of Japanese prints on her art, and her use of color. There is a useful technical discussion of dry point, etching, aquatint, and color prints. A chronology of her life precedes the catalogue of the exhibition of forty-nine prints.

115.———. *Mary Cassatt. A Catalogue Raisonne of the Graphic Work.* Washington, D.C.: Smithsonian Institution Press, 1979.

The introduction focuses on Cassatt's life and her art. This catalogue reproduces 220 prints and other items related to them. The entries include information on various states of these prints. A chronology of the artist's life, a technical discussion, and a list of early exhibitions completes this work.

116.———. "The Graphic Works of Mary Cassatt." *Prints* 7 (December 1936): 63–71.

The author presents a short biography of Mary Cassatt and then concentrates on a discussion of her drypoints, which constitute about one hundred of the approximately two hundred prints she made. She categorizes her prints by date: early 1879 to 1880--pure etching, soft ground, and aquatint; 1887 to 1891—drypoints and color prints; after 1900--drypoints, many of which are in color. Breeskin considers the color prints unique in the history of color printmaking and among the finest work produced by the artist. She also feels that the scarcity of Cassatt's graphic work in the United States was partly responsible for the general lack of appreciation of her work during the late nineteenth century.

117. Mathews, Nancy Mowll, and Barbara Shapiro. *Mary Cassatt: The Color Prints.* New York: Harry N. Abrams, 1989. 207 pp., index, biblio.

The two authors each explore Cassatt's graphic production. Mathews's, "The Color Prnts in the Context of Mary Cassatt's Art, " observes that her attitudes were often influenced by the American or Anglo-American art world of which she was a part. She explores the artist's studies and her introduction to Impressionism and provides an overview of her graphic production. Shapiro's essay, "Mary Cassatt's Color Prints and Contemporary French Printmaking" sets her in a European context. The catalogue entries describe as many states of the twenty-three color prints as could be located. The bibliography should be consulted by any collector or scholar seeking more information.

118. Museum of Graphic Art. *The Graphic Art of Mary Cassatt.* Washington, D.C. and New York: Smithsonian Institution Press and Museum of Graphic Art, 1967. 111 pp.

The introduction by Adelyn D. Breeskin, the foremost authority on Mary Cassatt, emphasizes the artist's work in the graphic processes in relation to her other works and to the work of her contemporaries in Europe. Most of her prints were not printed for sale and are, therefore, very scarce. The catalog includes about eighty Cassatt prints, almost all of which are reproduced. A chronology of her life and a list of exhibitions featuring her prints are helpful features of this book. The selected bibliography is excellent.

119. Weitenkampf, Frank. "The Dry Points of Mary Cassatt." *Print Collector's Quarterly* 6 (December 1916): 397–409.

Weitenkampf appreciates the uncompromising directness of Cassatt's drypoints, noting that it is her manner of presentation and her technique, rather than the subject matter, that impresses the student of etching. Weitenkampf also admires Cassatt's ability to produce multiple variations on a theme without lapsing into a sentimental or anecdotal manner. Technically, her freedom of handling never degenerates into looseness.

120. Comstock, Helen. "An Eighteenth Century Audubon." *Antiques* 37 (June 1940): 282–84.

Mark Catesby was an English naturalist fascinated by the flora and fauna of America. He illustrated *The Natural History of Carolina, Florida, and the Bahama Islands* (London, 1731–1743), for which he made the original drawings and engraved all but three of the plates. Containing 220 plates, this volume preceded Audubon's work by a century. Comstock discusses Catesby's life, research, and artistic style. Catesby's *Natural History* was reprinted in 1974 by the Beehive Press in Savannah with introduction by George Frick and notes by Joseph Ewan.

121. Frick, George Frederick, and Raymond Phineas Stearns. *Mark Catesby: The Colonial Audubon.* Urbana: University of Illinois Press, 1961. 137 pp., biblio., index.

This biography covers many aspects of Catesby's life: his background as a naturalist, his apprenticeship as a naturalist during his first trip to America, his twenty years of work, which culminated in the publication of *The Natural History*, and other scientific projects of his. A checklist of Catesby's published works is included.

122. Graham, Ruth Alden, and Frances M. Sheppard. "Mark Catesby." *Imprint* 1, no. 2 (1976): 5.

This brief article describes how the English naturalist Mark Catesby produced the two-volume *Natural History of Carolina, Florda and the Bahama Islands* from 1731 to 1743, after two sojourns in America. To keep costs as low as possible he etched the plates himself, after his watercolors, and then hand-colored the prints.

123. Trechsel, Gail Andrews. "Mark Catesby (1682–1749): Revelations of the New World." *Imprint* 8, no. 2 (1982): 12–18.

The first major description of America's natural history was Mark Catesby's *Natural History of Carolina, Florida and the Bahama Islands* published from 1731–43. Trechsel's article provides solid biographical information on Catesby, his trips to the colonies, his training as an engraver, and his contributions to popular natural history study. His *Natural History* was extremely labor intensive, but he was able to publish one book and two essays before his death.

124. Troccoli, Joan Carpenter. "First Artist of the West. Paintings and Watercolors by George Catlin." *American Art Review* 5, no. 5 (1993): 150–157.

Catlin (1796–1872) devoted most of his life to the West and he was a skillful observer and translator of what he saw. Early in his life, he was a lawyer, but by 1821 he was in Philadelphia painting and exhibiting miniatures. He left the East in 1830 and settled in St. Louis. A remarkable body of his work, in watercolor and oil, survives at the Gilcrease Museum in Tulsa and at the Smithsonian. Many of his works were reproduced as prints and book illustrations.

125. Truettner, William H. "For European Audiences: Catlin's North American Indian Portfolio" in *Prints of the American West*, 25–45. ed. Ron Tyler. Fort Worth: Amon Carter Museum, 1983.

For six years from 1830 to 1836, George Catlin travelled thousands of miles from the Mississippi River to the Rocky Mountains gathering the nucleus of his Indian Gallery, some 470 paintings and Indian manufactures that he displayed in New York, Washington, and other cities in the United States and then in England from 1840 to 1844. The *Portfolio* was published in London in 1844. Sixteen of the twenty-five plates were hunting scenes or related subjects, sure to please a European audience. Truettner discusses the choice of subject matter and the reworking of Catlin's paintings by the London lithography firm and their artist Mr. McGaney. Also of interest to Truettner are the additions to the Indian gallery made by Catlin during his residence in Europe. Catlin ended his years bankrupt in England and he fled to Brazil.

126. Champney, Benjamin. *Sixty Years' Memories of Art and Artists*. Woburn, Mass.: 1900. 178 pp.

Benjamin Champney (1817–1907) began his formal artistic training in the Moore lithographic shop in Boston. His reminiscences of that period are of interest to those studying early American lithography. Most of his memoirs concern artists and painting, and they are a fascinating and often amusing chronicle of his times.

127. Tatham, David. "The Lithographs of Benjamin Champney." *Old Time New England* 67, no. 1–2 (1976): 1–6.

Tatham provides a useful biographical sketch of Champney which focuses on his years as a lithographer. Following the biographpy is a check list which lists twenty lithographs by Champney and includes background information on the prints.

128. Hosmer, Herbert H., Jr. "John G. Chandler." *Antiques* 52 (July 1947): 46–47.

Chandler (1815–1879), engaged in wood engraving and lithography in Boston from about 1840 to 1860, worked primarily on children's books. The article is based on materials which have descended through Chandler's family: wood blocks, proofs for labels and trade cards, his engraving tools, and other odds and ends.

129. "Collection of Paintings, Drawings, Engravings, Etc. by John Gadsby Chapman and Conrad Wise Chapman in the Virginia State Library." *Bulletin of the Virginia State Library* 12, no. 3 and 4 (July and October 1919): 77–104.

The preface to the checklist contains biographical information on the two artists. John Gadsby Chapman (1808–1889) produced a number of etchings in Italy in the 1850s and 1860s. The impressions of these prints described in the checklist are overpainted with oil colors. Paintings by J. G. Chapman and his son, Conrad, are also described.

130. Diers, Herman H. "The Strange Case of Alonzo Chappel." *Hobbies* 49 (October 1944): 18–20.

Alonzo Chappel (1828–1887) was a prolific painter of historical scenes. His paintings, reproduced as engravings, adorned many books, particularly those published by Johnson, Fry & Co. A biographical sketch is followed by descriptions of a number of his paintings, whose locations in public collections are given.

131. Meschutt, David, and Barbara J. Mitnick. *The Portraits and History Paintings of Alonzo Chappel.*

Chadds Ford, Pa.: Brandywine River Museum, 1992. 82 pp., biblio.

Alonzo Chappel was one of the foremost historical illustrators of nineteenth-century America. This exhibition catalog contains a biographical sketch and an essay by David Meschutt on Chappel's portraits reproduced in Evert A. Duyckink's *National Portrait Gallery of Eminent Americans* (1862) and *Portrait Gallery of Eminent Men and Women of Europe and America* (1872–3). Meschutt discusses sources for Chappel's portraits (none were done from life) and suggests their value as historical documents and as works of art. Barbara J. Mitnick's essay on Chappel's history paintings discusses the "taste for reading history" among his contemporaries and the publications which Chappel illustrated. The catalog describes eighty-nine works, mainly paintings. The book as a whole is extremely informative and well researched.

132. Fowble, E. McSherry. "William Charles *Family Electioneering or Candidate Bob in his Glory.*" *Imprint* 3, no. 1 (1978): 16–18, 20.

Although recorded by Stauffer, no impression of this important, early political print by Charles (1776–1820) was known until the Winterthur Museum acquired this impression. Fowble explains the historical background to this satire issued at the time of a New York City mayoral election in 1806.

133. Lanmon, Lorraine Dwelling. "William Charles and His War of 1812 Caricatures" in *Philadelphia Printmaking. American Prints Before 1860*, 90–109. ed. Robert F. Looney. West Chester, Penn.: Tinicum Press, 1976.

Charles, born in Edinburgh, was active in London in 1803 and 1804, in Edinburgh from 1804 to 1805, and in New York from 1806 to 1808. In Philadelphia from 1808 until his death, he worked extensively for the publisher Mathew Carey. Lanmon discusses Charles' remarkable series of caricatures, numbering some seventeen, published during the War of 1812. She analyzes his iconography and his sources which included works by Thomas Rowlandson, James Gilray, George Woodward, and Isaac Cruickshank. Fourteen of Charles' cartoons are illustrated.

134. Lanmon, Lorraine Welling. "American Caricature in the English Tradition: the Personal and Political Satires of William Charles." *Winterthur Portfolio* 11 (1976): 1–51.

Charles (1776–1820) was born in Scotland and worked in New York and Philadelphia from 1806 to his death. Lanmon focuses on Charles' satires and their relationships to English prints of the same era, and sets the prints in their historical context. Following the article is an excellent catalog of Charles' satirical prints, most of which are illustrated.

135. Koehler, Sylvester R. "William M. Chase." *Art Review* 2, no. 2 (1881): 143.

At the time this brief notice was written, Chase (1849–1916) had etched three plates, one of which is printed with the article. No biography is given because Chase's paintings were the subject of a two-part essay in the same volume of the *Review*. Koehler mentions Chase's early experiments with monotypes, some of which were exhibited in *Black and White*, an exhibition at the Salmagundi Sketch Club in 1881.

136.———. *Catalogue of the Engraved and Lithographed Work of John Cheney and Seth Wells Cheney*. Boston: Lee & Shepard, 1891. 161 pp.

The introduction adequately characterizes the work of both men. The catalog itself is chronologically arranged beginning with John Cheney's prints, which are carefully described. Descriptions of the engravings of Seth Cheney follow, and finally a volume the two engraved together is described. There are various indexes at the end as well as reprints of several letters.

137. Museum of Fine Arts, Boston. *Exhibition of the Works of John Cheney and Seth Wells Cheney*. Boston: 1893. 33 pp.

John and Seth Wells Cheney both began as line engravers but Seth turned to crayon portraiture, an art which flourished before the days of photography. The exhibition profited from the assistance of members of the Cheney family, who loaned prints and drawings. The 338 entries provide a good checklist of works by the two brothers, but little information is provided on each item.

138. Cheney, Ednah D. *Memoir of John Cheney, Engraver*. Boston: Lee & Shepard, 1889. 53 pp.

Much of this *Memoir* is based on family papers and documents, many of them preserved from the early 1820s when John Cheney was in New York. All phases in his career are discussed and entire letters are reprinted, which reveal information not only about Cheney, but about his contemporaries in the art world. Unlike other memoirs which tend towards sentimentality, this one contains much valuable information.

139. James, Claudia Esko. "John Cheney (1801–1885): 'First-rate Engraver'." *Imprint* 11, no. 2 (1986): 14–19.

Reproductive engraving was an important and respected trade in the nineteenth century and Cheney was among the best. James provides important biographical information on this graphic artist, who worked for John Pendleton in Boston in the late 1820s as a lithographic draftsman. His engraving skills were highly prized by the publishers of gift books and Cheney's engravings appeared in the best of them throughout the 1820s and into the 1850s. After the death of his brother

Seth, also an engraver, in 1856, he retired, although he continued to draw from plaster casts and European engravings.

140. Owen, Hans C. "John Cheney, Connecticut Engraver." *Antiques* 25 (May 1934): 17–75.

A biographical sketch, correcting some earlier mistaken impressions about John Cheney, precedes a general description and appreciation of his engravings. Owen compiled a valuable checklist of 103 engravings found in gift books whose specific titles and publication dates are given.

141. Cheney, Ednah D. *Memoir of Seth W. Cheney, Artist*. Boston: Lee & Shepard, 1881. 144 pp.

This biographical memoir, based largely on family correspondence, documents the state of arts and the business of engraving and lithography in Boston and elsewhere. In addition to his artistic endeavors, Seth Cheney (1810–1856) entered the family silk culture business for a period of time, a venture carefully described here. This memoir is at once both personal and factual.

142. Koehler, Sylvester R. "F. S. Church." *American Art Review* 2, no. 1 (1881): 143–44.

Koehler cautiously admires Church's (1842–1923) phantasmagoric imagery and regrets Church's dissatisfaction with his etchings, which resulted in the destruction of nearly all his plates. As a consequence his etched works, one of which is reproduced, were rare and "almost unique" even when the article was written.

143. Davison, Nancy R. "E.W. Clay and the American Political Caricature Business" in *Prints and Printmakers of New York State, 1825–1940*, 91–110. ed. David Tatham. Syracuse: Syracuse University Press, 1985.

Derived from Davison's doctoral dissertation on Clay (1799–1857), this essay focuses on the political cartoons that he produced from 1834 through 1840. The earlier prints were published by Henry R. Robinson of New York. Davison describes Clay's print production, the importance of New York as a center for print publishing, the rise of political parties, and Robinson. Davison describes a number of prints in detail. From 1838 to 1840 Clay worked in conjunction with John Child, another lithographer who worked in New York from 1836 to 1844. Clay and Robinson produced additional political prints during the 1844 presidential election. This essay provides an excellent glimpse of Clay's output during a fruitful period.

144. Davison, Nancy Reynolds. *E. W. Clay: American Political Caricaturist of the Jacksonian Era*. Ann Arbor, Mich.: University Microfilms, 1980. 408 pp., biblio.

Davison's doctoral dissertation on Clay contains chapters on the artist's family and background, his early life and work in Philadelphia, his move to New York and his work there, the Panic of 1837 and the 1840 presidential campaign, and his later work that became more diffuse. The text provides copious information on the political and social context for his prints, many of which are reproduced in a small but useful format. A catalog of the 212 prints located by Davison in public collections follows.

145. "William B. Closson." *Scribner's Magazine* 17 (April 1895): 459–60.

Closson (1848–1926), who was praised by Hamerton in an essay on the art of the American wood engraver, began his career in Boston, where he developed an acquaintance with the artist George Fuller. This sketch, like many others concerned with wood engraving of the period, dwells on the technical difficulties of the craft. Closson's paintings are mentioned as well.

146. Koehler, S. R. "J. Foxcroft Cole." *American Art Review* 1 (1880): 191.

Cole (1837–1892), a native of Maine, studied in France, where he came under the influence of Charles Emile Jacque. A well-known painter of landscapes, he had etched only one plate by 1880, done at the time Cadart arrived from France to introduce this new process to New York.

147. Hudson River Museum. *To Walk With Nature: The Drawings of Thomas Cole*. Yonkers, N.Y.: Hudson River Museum, 1981. 64 pp., biblio.

In the introductory essay, Howard S. Merritt writes of Cole's (1801–1848) love of drawing and his early ambition to be an artist. Merritt discusses his early drawings and his keeping a list of potential subjects for paintings drawn from his extensive reading. The relationship of his sketches to his painting is also considered as is his working methodology. The catalogue is divided into the studies, imaginative sketches, landscape studies from nature, and the lithographs he did in 1825–29 and 1847. The entries are informative and relate the sketches to paintings whenever possible.

148. Cole, Alphaeus P., and Margaret Ward Cole. *Timothy Cole, Wood-Engraver*. New York: Pioneer Associates, 1935. 172 pp., index.

Written by Cole's (1852–1931) relatives, and published in a limited edition, this is a biography of the artist. The book also contains the artist's own recollection of his childhood. A brief biography also appeared in the *Print Collector's Quarterly* 1 (July 1911): 334–46.

149. Print Club of Philadelphia. *Timothy Cole Memorial Exhibition*. Philadelphia: 1931. 71 pp.

The brief foreword by Robert Underwood Johnson outlines the importance of Timothy Cole to the wood engraving movement, and provides some information on his life. The catalog is divided into engravings, drawings, wood blocks, books, manuscripts, photographs of Cole, and miscellaneous items. Engravings are listed by date, beginning in 1874. Titles of the volumes that contain his book and magazine illustrations are noted. Over 400 engravings are listed in this well-organized catalog.

150. Ristow, Walter W. "Eliza Colles America's First Female Map Engraver." *Map Collector* 10 (March 1980):

Benson Lossing in 1884 attributed some of the plates of Christopher Colles' *Survey of the Roads* to Colles' daughter. She also engraved maps in the *Geographical Ledger and Systemized Atlas* (New York: John Buel, 1794). Ristow provides biographical background on Eliza and her family, noting also her death in 1799 at the age of twenty-three.

151. Koehler, Sylvester R. "Samuel Colman." *American Art Review* 1, no. 2 (1880): 387–88.

A member of the New York Etching Club, Colman (1832–1920) made several etchings based on nature both here and abroad. No dominant influence from other artists is apparent in his individualist style. Nine of his plates are listed.

152. Middleton, Margaret Simons. "Thomas Coram, Engraver and Painter." *Antiques* 29 (June 1936): 242–44.

Born in England, Coram (1756–1811) went to Charleston, S.C., to join other members of his family who had settled there. He began engraving in the late 1770s and quotations from contemporary newspapers show that he engraved many things other than copperplates for prints. After 1802 he executed several paintings; a few of these are described and illustrated. This brief study is worthwhile, and suggests that much remains to be said about this versatile artist.

153. *Currier & Ives. The New Best 50*. Fairfield, Conn.: American Historical Print Collectors Society, 1991. 80 pp., biblio.

The AHPCS sponsored a competition to select a new "best 50" of lithographs by Currier & Ives. This volume and an accompanying exhibition in Milwaukee in 1990 presented the selection to the public together with excellent comments about each one. Marshall Berkoff's introduction discusses the selection process. Christopher Lane compared the old list with the new one and made some interesting observations about the changing taste for specific types of subject matter. Tables comparing the old lists with the new and numbers of votes are interesting.

154. Abbatt, William. *A Selection of Lithographs Published by Currier & Ives, New York 1825–1866; Comprising Forty-Seven Examples*. Tarrytown, N.Y.: William Abbatt, 1929. Unpag.

These forty-seven reproductions of Currier & Ives prints were selected by William Abbatt, a dealer. There is a one-page prefatory statement, but no text. The edition was limited to 200 copies.

155. Bland, Jane Cooper. *Currier & Ives: A Manual for Collectors*. Garden City, N.Y.: Doubleday, Doran & Co., 1931. 349 pp.

This volume contains an alphabetical list, by title, of prints by Stodard & Currier, Charles Currier, Nathaniel Currier, and Currier & Ives. The corresponding numbers in Harry T. Peters's volume, if recorded there, are noted. Recent auction price and a record of sale also form a part of each entry. The compiler has added some 1,600 titles to Peter's first volume on Currier & Ives. At the end of the book is a checklist by subject.

156. Bonfante-Warren, Alexandra. *Currier & Ives: Portraits of a Nation*. New York: MetroBooks, 1998. 128 pp., biblio., index.

Bonfante-Warren provides a brief history of printing, a synopsis of the history of the firm established by Nathaniel Currier, and a survey of the history of the nation from the 1830s to the Civil War as seen through the prints. The final chapter focuses on prints of the 1860s and 1870s when domesticity reigned. The text is a good summary of the history of the firm and their prints. The illustrations are all in color from the distinguished collection of the Museum of the City of New York.

157. Brust, James. "A Photograph by Currier & Ives." *Imprint* 16, no. 2 (1991): 2–3.

Brust has discovered a photograph of the Supreme Court of the United States taken by Napoleon Sarony and published by Currier & Ives in 1890. It suggests that, perhaps following Sarony's lead, the firm was interested in branching out into photography.

158. Brust, James and Wendy Shadwell. "Unconventional Currier & Ives." *Imprint* 24, no. 1 (1999): 2–26.

In the spring of 1998, Brust and Shadwell assembled an exhibition of uncommon objects relating to Currier & Ives at the New-York Historical Society. This article discusses these items and others, including cases for daguerreotypes, wood engravings of lithographs, unusual lithographs for the firm, job work, trade cards published by the firm based on earlier larger prints, and photographs of their prints. Also noted are works by other artists who copied prints by the firm. This is a fascinating excursion into little-known images.

159. Carini, Anselmo. *The Esmark Collection of Currier & Ives*. Chicago: Esmark Collection, 1975. Unpag.

This exhibition catalog contains a brief history of the collection formed by Roy M. King for Esmark, a history of the lithographic firm, comments on the pictorial record left by Currier & Ives and on some of the artists who made the prints. The collection numbered almost 700 items in 1975, 123 of which were circulated in exhibitions. This collection is now owned by ConAgra in Omaha, Nebraska.

160. Conningham, F. A., and M. B. Conningham. *An Alphabetical List of 5,735 Titles of N. Currier and Currier & Ives Prints*. New York: Privately Printed, 1930. 301 pp.

This volume gives dates of publication, sizes and recent (1930) auction prices for the known prints issued by Nathaniel Currier and Currier & Ives. In 1931 the authors issued a supplement, which added additional titles and auction prices. A listing of 6,879 prints is in *Currier & Ives Prints: An Illustrated Check List* (New York: Crown Publishers, 1949). Most of the supplementary prints were found in Harry T. Peters's voluminous work on Currier & Ives. Colin Simkin compiled a revised edition (New York: Crown Publishers, 1970), which adds only seventeen prints to the 1949 publication. Approximate prices for prints in good condition are given, providing a reflection of current market conditions.

161. Crouse, Russel. *Mr. Currier and Mr. Ives: A Note on Their Lives and Times*. New York: Doubleday, Doran & Co., 1930. 138 pp.

After making preliminary comments on Currier & Ives, the author writes about subjects portrayed in the lithographs, including women's rights, temperance, the Chicago fire, whaling, trotting and horse racing, the Gold Rush, Amelia Bloomer, firemen, courting and marriage, boxing, steamships, the world of finance, P.T. Barnum and Tom Thumb, winter in New York, railroads, and baseball. There is no commentary on the plates illustrating the chapters. The text is enjoyable in style but is not scholarly.

162. Fowble, E. McSherry. "Currier & Ives and the American Parlor." *Imprint* 15, no. 2 (1990): 14–19.

In an interesting look at material culture through the medium of lithography, Fowble examines how Currier & Ives prints both influenced taste and reflected taste of the nineteenth century. The parlor depicted in Currier & Ives' 1868 lithograph, *The Season of Rest* (Plate 4 in *The Four Seasons of Life* series), is compared with arrangements suggested in manuals for young housekeepers such as Frances Byerly Parker's *Domestic Duties* (New York, 1828), Catherine Beecher's and Harriet B. Stowe's *The American Woman's Home* (1869), and Almon C. Varney's *Our Homes and Their Adornments* (1882). Fowble concludes that the prints do reflect the dictates of these manuals but also show that housewives and artists were not enslaved by them.

163. Gale Research Company. *Currier & Ives. A Catalogue Raisonne*. Detroit: Gale Research Company, 1984. 2 vols., biblio., index.

Although no compilation of this sort can ever be definitive, this two volume reference work is the most complete listing of the prints published by Nathaniel Currier and Currier & Ives issued to date. The introduction by Bernard F. Reilly, Jr., discusses various aspects of nineteenth-century lithography including the importance of job work, the public's appetite for decorative prints met by Nathaniel Currier, the artists who worked for the firms, news reporting, their political prints, strongly racist prints, and reasons for the demise of the firm. He concludes with a summary of twentieth-century interest in these prints among various collectors and institutions. The list is arranged alphabetically by title. Each entry records the title, any identifying numbers on the plates, dimensions, publisher, date, and notes about the prints. The bibliography is exhaustive and should be consulted by any serious student of the firm's production. The concordance is useful as are the subject, artist, chronological, and illustration indices.

164. Gifford, James P. "The Celebrated World of Currier & Ives." *The New-York Historical Society Quarterly* 59 (October 1975): 348–65.

In this article Gifford concentrates on one category of Currier & Ives lithographs: scenes of fires and firemen. He includes background information on volunteer fire companies. Gifford speculates on reasons why Currier & Ives did not depict policemen in their lithographs in the then popular romantic fashion, concluding that various political and social factors were responsible.

165. Goyle, G. A. R. "An Addition to Currier Incunabula." *Antiques* 20 (September 1931): 100–1.

Currier & Ives occasionally reprinted old copperplates, adding their own imprint. The subject of this study is an engraving of George and Martha Washington framed by an elaborate border. It was copyrighted in Massachusetts in 1838 by G.F. Storm and T. Pollock, two engravers. It was published by Nathaniel Currier sometime later, or perhaps in collaboration with Storm and Pollock in 1838.

166. Hall, Virginius C. "The American Dream." *Print Collector's Quarterly* 26 (February 1939): 8–29.

Writing in the dreary days of the Depression, Hall advises those who have lost their faith in their country to search for the American Dream in the lithographs of Currier & Ives. After generalizing about Currier & Ives's business and the appeal of their lithographs, he discusses several prints in detail. It is an enthusiastic article full of praise and nostalgia for a bygone era.

167. Hall, W. S. *The Red Indian. Currier & Ives Prints, No. 2*. London and New York: Studio and William Edwin Rudge, 1931. 8 pp.

The introduction discusses Indians in American literature and history. Hall lists forty Currier & Ives prints of Indians and reproduces eight of them here.

168.———. *The Spirit of America: Currier & Ives Prints*. London and New York: Studio and William Edwin Rudge, 1931. 6 pp.

The introduction adds nothing new to the story of Currier & Ives. The eight plates cover a variety of subjects.

169. Heartman, Charles F. "Random but Sane Remarks About the Lithographs Issued by Nathaniel Currier and James Merritt Ives." *American Collector* 1 (March 1926): 226–31.

Heartman, a renowned collector of his time, comments on the quality of Currier & Ives lithographs. He remarks on the poor drawing style of most of their lithographers, noting that a few of the prints are quite good while others are garish. Heartman discusses the varied subject matter and judges the relative qualities of the different prints. He concludes by lamenting the lack of attention paid to other nineteenth-century lithographers.

170. Heritage Plantation. *Currier & Ives: Nineteenth-Century Printmakers to the American People*. Sandwich, Mass.: 1973. 64 pp.

This exhibition catalog contains the foreword written by Harry T. Peters for *Currier & Ives, Printmakers to the American People*, a brief introduction to the exhibition by Ladd MacMillan, whose collection was on display, a discussion of American lithography and Currier & Ives by Ewell Newman, a listing of the best fifty large and small folios, a note on modern reproductions of Currier & Ives lithographs by Katherine and John Ebert, and a discussion of popular prints by William Lipke. Eighty prints, with adequate captions, are illustrated, many in color. An additional list of prints on display but not illustrated follows the reproductions.

171. Holmer, Richard P. "California Currier & Ives: From Amusement to Admiration." *Imprint* 20, no. 1 (1995): 13–21.

Forty-two prints published by Nathaniel Currier and Currier & Ives depict California subjects. Holmer discusses these prints as well as the market for them. A list of the prints, arranged chronologically, follows the text.

172.———. "Currier & Ives Do California." *The Californians* 12, no. 6 (December 1995): 8–11, 51.

Holmer explains that Currier & Ives published prints of California because it was good for their business. Holmer has identified 42 that relate to the state, noting that 13 were issued between 1849 and 1851 by Nathaniel Currier and the others were published after 1865. He explains the differences between the two groups, includes a list of the prints, and explains the most interesting of them.

173. Holzer, Harold. "Currier & Ives: America Imagined." *Art & Antiques* 5, no. 6 (November 1982): 60–65.

Holzer provides historical background of the firm, categorizes the prints the firm published, and explains marketing techniques. The role of the lithographs as reflections of nineteenth century culture is also explored. A few of the major collectors who began the vogue for Currier & Ives prints are also mentioned.

174. Landauer, Bella C. "Some Trade Cards With Particular Emphasis on the Currier & Ives Contributions." *The New-York Historical Society Quarterly* 17 (October 1933): 5–8.

This study explores the change which occured in advertising when lithography, as opposed to line engraving, became the most economical medium for printing trade cards. Landauer mentions several lithographic firms, concentrating on the trade cards issued in the last quarter of the nineteenth century by Currier & Ives. The article is well illustrated, and provides a good introduction to the late nineteenth-century advertising art that was the specialty of several large firms.

175. LeBeau, Bryan. "'Colored Engravings for the People.' The World According to Currier & Ives." *American Studies* 35, no. 1 (1994): 131–141.

The article describes the collection of 650 Currier & Ives prints owned by ConAgra in Omaha, Nebraska. LeBeau describes the process, provides brief biographies of Currier & Ives, and then focuses on the arrangement the lithographs in the corporate headquarters by subject. He concludes by describing the fall and rise of these evocative images in terms of public appreciation of them. The collection was formed by Ron M. King of New York in the 1950's and was previously owned by Esmark and Beatrice corporations. The Smithsonian Institution Press published LeBeau's monograph on Currier & Ives, *Currier & Ives: America Imagined* in 2001.

176. Lubbers, Klaus. "Popular Models of National Identity in Currier & Ives's Chromolithographs." *Amerika studien / American Studies* 40, no. 2 (1995): 163–183.

Among the topics discussed by Lubbers is the overall nature of the prints produced by Currier & Ives and their "plagiarism of high art," drawing parallels with the American Art Union. Lubbers has astutely found, for example, an excerpt of Bingham's popular *Jolly Flatboatmen* in Fanny Palmer's *The Mississippi in Time of Peace*. Lubber's important contribution to the Currier & Ives literature is his discussion of the firm's output that reflects national identity, looking at representations of the locomotive in detail.

177. Mayer, Grace M. "A Century of Currier & Ives." *Antiques* 71 (May 1957): 451–54.

This article accompanied the exhibition celebrating the donation by his family of Harry T. Peters's collection of Currier & Ives prints to the Museum of the City of New York. Mayer discusses the collection briefly and then turns to Currier & Ives. She has found much information about the firm in a catalog they issued in 1860, a copy of which is in the Museum's collection. The catalog notes that amateurs were encouraged to handcolor black and white impressions of lithographs.

178. Miller, Steven. "A 1986 Currier & Ives Lament." *Imprint* 18, no. 1 (1993): 15.

This brief note by the former senior curator at the Museum of the City of New York suggests strategies for research on the output of the firm, such as looking at sources for the prints, reviewing Harry T. Peters's research records, writing about political prints, and using the methodologies of the historian and art historian. In an editorial footnote, Rona Schneider says that there has been progress on the Currier & Ives research front since Miller wrote in 1986.

179. Newman, Harry Shaw. "The Continued Popularity of Currier & Ives Prints." *American Collector* 8 (October 1939): 6–7, 14.

Newman states that Currier & Ives intended their prints to be of high quality, low cost, and suitable for framing, in order that they would appeal to a large public. He seeks to explain their continued popularity among collectors in the twentieth century, citing their wide range and choice of subject matter, the long and successful publishing career of the firm, and the quality of the prints. It is interesting to hear from a dealer on this subject.

180. O'Rourke, Kevin. *Currier and Ives: The Irish and America*. New York: Harry N. Abrams, Inc., 1995. 144 pp., biblio., index.

The text to this handsomely produced book begins with a brief history of Currier & Ives. O'Rourke has analysed the output of the firm and found that just over two hundred of their prints relate in one way or another to the Irish in America or Ireland. The subject matter of nearly one hundred is described in detail; seventy-seven of those are reproduced in color. Of particular interest to collectors is a history of O'Rourke's collection, a list of dealers, and a list of the 204 Irish-American prints and locations in public collections and his own.

181. The Old Print Shop. *Best Fifty Currier & Ives Lithographs*. New York: Old Print Shop, 1933. 2 vols.

These two unpaginated folios of fifty plates each are included here because they form the canon of any serious collection of Currier & Ives prints. The series was based on an exhibition held at the Old Print Shop. Among jury members selecting the fifty best in each series were Harry T. Peters and Frank Weitenkampf. There is a short preface and summary descriptions of the plates.

182. Peters, Fred J. *Clipper Ship Prints, Including Other Merchant Sailing Ships by N. Currier and Currier & Ives*. New York: Antique Bulletin Publishing Co., 1930. 109 pp., index.

Peters discusses the growth of the merchant marine and the concomitant popularity of marine prints. He further mentions the artists and collectors of these prints, and his own interest in the subject. Each print is illustrated, its size and state noted, and the history of each ship recorded.

183.———. *Railroad, Indian, and Pioneer Prints by N. Currier and Currier & Ives, Being a Pictorial Check List and Collection*. New York: Antique Bulletin Publishing Co., 1930. 109 pp., index.

This volume contains separate sections on railroads, Indians and pioneers, and the West. A page or two in the general introduction is devoted to each subject, providing general background and a few specific details on the prints and their artists. All the prints are illustrated and the size of each is noted.

184.———. *Sporting Prints by N. Currier and Currier & Ives, Being a Pictorial Check List and Collection*. New York: Antique Bulletin Publishing Co., 1930. 205 pp., index.

The sporting prints are divided into separate sections according to subject: fishing, game birds, bird shooting, camping, hunting, etc. Each chapter is preceded by a short introduction which gives details for a few specific prints, including the history of the sport or activity, the locale depicted, the artist, and the names of the people who appear in it if known. Relatively few prints are described so completely, but each print is illustrated and its size noted.

185. Peters, Harry T. *Currier & Ives: Printmakers to the American People*. New York: Doubleday, Doran & Co., 1929. 2 vols., biblio.

The first volume of this mammoth reference book contains a detailed history and description of the Currier & Ives firm, information on the best-known artists associated with the firm (Tait, Maurer, Worth, Palmer, Durrie, etc.) and their specialties, and notes on different subject categories. A chapter is devoted to collectors and is followed by reproductions of 142 prints. The checklist in the first volume numbers over 4,300 lithographs arranged by subject. The second volume adds new information on the firm and gives a more detailed analysis of the subject matter of the prints. An additional 177 lithographs are reproduced, and there is a revised checklist with 1,600 new titles added, alphabetically arranged by title. It is obvious that most publications on Currier & Ives owe a great deal to this work. Peters' collection is at the Museum of the City of New York.

186.———. *Currier & Ives: Printmakers to the American People*. Garden City, N.Y.: Doubleday, Doran & Co., 1942. 41 pp.

Discussed in the introduction are the techniques of lithography, Nathaniel Currier's career, his association with James Merritt Ives, their business methods of publication and distribution, the artists they employed, and the different subjects they portrayed in their prints. The plates present a representative selection of the firm's production.

187. Rawls, Walton. *The Great Book of Currier & Ives' America*. New York: Abbeville Press, 1979. 487 pp., index., biblio.

This enormous volume provides extensive and well-researched background information on the subject matter and context of the production of the Currier & Ives firm. An introduction to the firm and its general history is followed by chapters describing various genres of prints—history, city views, childhood, the West, prints of the home, politics, images of hunting and fishing, landscape depictions, trotters and thoroughbred horses, and genre prints. Most of the reproductions are in color and a generous selection of prints are reproduced.

188. Reisenberg, Felix. *Early Steamships. Currier & Ives Prints, No. 4*. London and New York: Studio, 1933. 10 pp.

The introduciton provides background on steamships, then discusses the eight reproductions included in the pamphlet. A checklist of 204 Currier & Ives steamship prints follows, arranged by the name of the vessel.

189. Rudisill, John and Barbara. "Some Previously Uncataloged Currier & Ives Prints." *Imprint* 22, no. 1 (1997): 16–24.

The authors summarize the available catalogs of Currier & Ives prints and list 115 unrecorded items. They are eager to receive information on additional prints.

190. Simkin, Colin. *Currier & Ives' America: A Panorama of the Mid-Nineteenth Century Scene*. New York: Crown Publishers, 1952. 13 pp.

The author writes briefly about the invention of lithography, its beginnings in the United States, and the business conducted by Nathaniel Currier and James Merritt Ives. Simkin emphasizes their popularity during the 1850s and 1860s, and attibutes the decline of lithography to the invention of photography.

191. Tatham, David. "Poetry, the Stage, and Currier & Ives." *American Art Journal* 24, no. 1/2 (1992): 94–102.

Of the more than 7,000 lithographs published by N. Currier and Currier & Ives, fewer than 100 pertain to literature and authors. For this article, Tatham has focused on about two dozen prints illustrating Lord Byron's *Mezeppa* (1846), Longfellow's *Song of Hiawatha* (1858) and Tennyson's *Enoch Arden* (1869). Tatham discusses the circumstances of the publication of these prints, pictorial sources, and the public performances of these narrative poems on stage. Tatham speculates that these subjects were chosen because they were dramatized for a popular audience.

192. Thomas, Phillip Drennon. "The West of Currier & Ives." *American West* 19, no. 1 (January 1982): 18–25.

Thomas suggests that lithographs of western frontier life, although highly romanticized, fired the public's imagination. James Merritt Ives is credited with taking Louis Maurer and A. F. Tait to the Astor Library to examine the works of Catlin and Bodmer to add to their knowledge. Thomas focuses on the work of Maurer, Tait, and Palmer, noting how they used their pictorial sources and worked collaboratively.

193. Truesdell, Winfred Porter. "The Lithographs of Currier & Ives." *Print Connoisseur* 7 (July 1927): 162–91.

Truesdell approaches Currier & Ives prints as sources of historical information. He briefly surveys the spread of lithography from Germany to France and England, then its growth in the United States to the 1840s. By that time Nathaniel Currier had become active in New York. After a short discussion of Currier, Truesdell turns to the various series published by Currier & Ives before mentioning individual prints. He finds the series of particular importance because they recorded life in the nineteenth century with great fidelity.

194. United States Naval Academy Museum. *Currier & Ives Navy. Lithographs from the Beverley R. Robinson Collection*. Annapolis: Naval Academy Museum, 1983. 97 pp., biblio.

The Beverley R. Robinson Collection at the Naval Academy Museum contains nearly 5,000 prints. This selection of seventy-six prints, all by Currier & Ives, is accompanied by explanatory text, focusing on subject matter. The introduction by Paula L. Lieberman includes photographs of the publishers, Frances Flora Palmer, Louis Maurer, and Napoleon Sarony, among the most important and prolific artists working for the firm. The introduction discusses the output of the firm, lithographic technology, marketing, and the artists who worked for the firm.

195. Weaver, Warren A. *Lithographs of N. Currier and Currier & Ives*. New York: Holport Publishing Co., 1925. 147 pp.

The book contains a short historical introduction to Currier & Ives's prints, followed by an alphabetical listing of lithographs with recent (1925) sales prices.

196. Weitenkampf, Frank. "Currier & Ives, 'Picture Makers' to Uncle Sam." *Antiques* 7 (January 1925): 10–14.

This introduction to the lithographs of Currier & Ives seems to be the first in a long series of books and articles. Weitenkampf presents some sparse biographical information, then discusses the many subjects depicted in the prints. Although fully aware of the work of many other lithographers, he praises Currier & Ives in particular for their prolific and consistent production which reflected the "activities, interests, and ideals of the American people."

197. Yochelson, Bonnie. *The Wood, Struthers & Winthrop Collection of Currier & Ives*. New York: Wood, Struthers & Winthrop, 1996. 56 pp.

The introduction by Bonnie Yochelson discusses the core of the Wood, Struthers & Winthrop Collection—depictions of American homesteads, reflective of twentieth-century yearnings for a simpler era. She discusses Currier & Ives' history briefly and mentions a number of themes portrayed by that firm. Twenty lithographs are reproduced in color with informative captions. A checklist of the complete collection completes the volume.

198. Zaldin, Donald. "Currier & Ives Lithographs: Nineteenth Century ad hoc American 'Democratic Vistas'." *Ephemera Journal* 5 (1992): 6–11.

The author relates Currier & Ives's prints to the struggle for a distinct, national character, and their expression of manifest destiny. This is an interesting and thought-provoking look at these most popular of American prints.

199. Brust, James. "A Nathaniel Currier Family Photo Album." *Imprint* 20, no. 1 (1995): 3–6.

Brust's article provides genealogical information on and photographs of Nathaniel Currier and family members. Although his name is familiar to all print collectors and scholars, little is known about the man and Brust remedies this situation.

200.———. "Prints of Questionable Taste That Nathaniel Currier Would Not Sign: An Update." *Imprint* 23, no. 2 (1998): 25–6.

This brief article provides further information on two of the four prints described by Brust in *Imprint* in 1995. He has located an impression of *The Celebrated Terrier Dog Major* with an imprint. However, he no longer believes that *The Seven Stages of Matrimony* is by Currier, since an impression has surfaced with a plate number that does not correspond to Currier's numbering system.

201.———. "Prints of Questionable Taste That Nathaniel Currier Would Not Sign." *Imprint* 20, no. 1 (1995): 7–11.

Several prints issued during the nineteenth century bear the signs of having been published by Nathaniel Currier, but lack an imprint. Brust illustrates and describes *The Wedding Night, When! Shall We Three Meet Again?*, *The Celebrated Terrier Dog Major Performing His Wonderful Feat of Killing 100 Rats in 8 m. -58 sec.*, and *The Seven Stages of Matrimony*. Brust's attributions are carefully considered.

202. Raisig, L. Miles. "Currier's 'Express Train' and Legal Tender." *Antiques* 66 (September 1954): 210–11.

Although the "Express Train" by Nathaniel Currier is not dated, it was probably issued in the mid-1840s. It served as a source for vignettes on at least twenty American bank notes, issued between 1855 and 1865. Raisig lists the bills based on this print, then comments on two examples.

203. *...Illustrated by Darley*. Wilmington, Del.: Delaware Art Museum, 1978. 21 pp.

The introduction provides an excellent sketch of the life and work of Felix Octavius Carr Darley (1822–1888), one of the foremost illustrators of the nineteenth century. This sketch is well researched. It is followed by a selection of published designs and drawings from a number of collections. This is a valuable record of Darley's output. There is also a chronology of his life.

204. "Darley's Outline Illustrations of *Margaret*." *Crayon* 3 (December 1856): 370.

The author distinguishes between creative and illustrative art, praising Darley for his illustration of ideas, a Ruskinian ideal. He goes on to call these illustrations of *Margaret*, "the most effective drawing we have ever seen by Darley.".

205. Barnhill, Georgia B. "F. O. C. Darley's Illlustrations for Southern Humor" in *Graphic Arts & the South. Proceedings of the 1990 North American Print Conference*, 30–61. ed. Judy L. Larson. Fayetteville: University of Arkansas Press, 1993.

Between the years 1844 and 1849, the Philadelphia publisher, Carey & Hart, commissioned F. O. C. Darley to illustrate ten works of humorous literature set in the southeastern states. This essay focuses on this portion of Darley's prolific career using original drawings, letters, and account books as documentation.

206. Bolton, Theodore. "The Book Illustrations of Felix Octavius Carr Darley." *Proceedings of the American Antiquarian Society* 61 (April 1951): 136–82.

Bolton provides a brief but adequate biographical sketch of Darley, and discusses his earliest drawings in some detail. The greatest contribution of this work is its listing of books illustrated by Darley, and of references made to Darley. The informative entries are chronologically arranged.

207. Ewers, John C. "Not Quite Redmen: The Plains Indian Illustrations of Felix O.C. Darley." *American Art Journal* 3 (1971): 88–98.

Darley was fascinated by Indians from an early age, yet there is no indication that he ever traveled west of the Allegheny Mountains during his forty year career. Consequently, his illustrations of Indians, drawn in his studio, contain many errors.

208. Finlay, Nancy. *Inventing the American Past: The Art of F.O.C. Darley*. New York: New York Public Library, 1999. 52 p., biblio.

Finlay describes Darley's career as a book illustrator, focusing on his works that interpreted the nation's history such as his illustrations for Cooper's historical fiction, Irving's biographies, and his separately published historical prints. The Civil War prompted further historical images. The collection of Darley's books and drawings at the New York Public Library is an important one. The checklist of the exhibition includes 126 books, sketches, and prints.

209. Hoover, John Neal. "Felix Darley (1822–88): A nineteenth-century vision of America and the world." *Private Library* 7, no. 3 (1994): 114–129.

Hoover has created a special collection of Darley's works at the St. Louis Mercantile Library. In this essay he summarizes Darley's immense output focusing on his outline sketches for *Scenes in Indian Life*, *Rip Van Winkle*, *Sleepy Hollow*, and *Margaret*. Another theme of interest to Hoover are the works by Darley that present aspects of American history.

210. King, Ethel. *Darley: The Most Popular Illustrator of His Time*. Brooklyn, N.Y.: Theo Gaus' Sons, 1964. 156 pp., index.

Poorly written in an anecdotal style, this study's main merit is its citation of numerous books illustrated by Darley. King includes an overwhelming amount of incidental and generally useless material, yet occasionally presents information which sheds light on Darley's talents, contemporaries, and cultural milieu. The bibliography is basically concerned with books on the nineteenth century, rather than on prints or artists.

211. Reed, Sue W. "F. O. C. Darley's Outline Illustrations" in *The American Illustrated Book in the Nineteenth Century*, 113–135. Gerald W. R. Ward. Winterthur: The Henry Francis du Pont Winterthur Museum, 1987.

Reed describes and analyzes four series of illustrations produced by Darley between 1847 and 1856 and printed as lithographs. The analysis of the production of an illustrated edition of Sylvester Judd's reform novel, *Margaret*, is important because the project occupied Darley's attention for almost a decade. Over sixty drawings and a number of unpublished proofs provide the basis for Reed's analysis. She concludes that the outline style enabled Darley to idealize the story's earthy characters successfully. The article concludes with a table listing the illustrations and the original drawings extant for each one.

212. Stoddard, Richard Henry. "Felix O.C. Darley." *National Magazine* 9 (September 1856): 193–97.

Stoddard begins with an eloquent discourse on book illustration in which he judges Darley to be superior to any other illustrator. Stoddard mentions many of Darley's illustrations in a stylistic review of his work.

213. Weitenkampf, Frank. "F.O.C. Darley, American Illustrator." *Art Quarterly* 10 (1947): 100–113.

Darley's period of activity lasted about forty years, beginning in 1843. Weitenkampf discusses his development as an illustrator for book and magazine publishers, his wide range of subject matter, and his versatility as an artist. In his discussion of the artist's style, Weitenkampf compares Darley's drawings to the finished wood engravings, and reveals characteristics of his work which remained constant for much of his career.

214. Stapp, William F. "The Life and Work of Francis D'Avignon" in *American Portrait Prints*, 194–231. ed. Wendy Wick Reaves. Washington: National Portrait Gallery, 1984.

Born in France in 1813, D'Avignon was brought up in Russia, and returned to France to study painting in Paris. He settled in Hamburg, but lost everything in the 1842 fire, at which time he emigrated to New York. Stapp discusses his American portrait prints, the best known of which were published in Mathew Brady's *The Gallery of Illustrious Americans* in 1850. He produced additional prints after daguerreotypes by Philip Haas and others. In 1858 D'Avignon moved to Medford, Massachusetts, and he produced several prints for Charles Brainard for a projected series that collapsed like the earlier *Gallery*. After a brief period of service in the Union Army in the Civil War, this skilled lithographer faded from public view. His date of death has not been uncovered. Following the essay is a definitive checklist of over 200 lithographs by D'Avignon, reprints of two biographical sketches, and a chronology of the artist's life.

215. Broome, John. "The Counterfeiting Adventure of Henry Dawkins." *American Notes and Queries* 8 (March 1950): 179–84.

A counterfeiting episode in Dawkins's life is examined in detail, with much documentation provided.

216. Cole, Wilford P. "Henry Dawkins and the Quaker Comet." *Winterthur Portfolio* 4 (1968): 35–46.

One of Dawkins's prints depicted Benjamin Lay, an eccentric Quaker, based on a painting by William Williams. Copies made after Dawkins's engravings are also described. This article presumably formed part of the author's master's thesis for the University of Delaware, *Henry Dawkins, Engraver* (1966).

217. Decatur, Stephen. "The Conflicting History of Henry Dawkins, Engraver." *American Collector* 7 (January 1939): 6–7.

The author provides a brief sketch of Dawkins's life including his plea to be sentenced to death while in jail on a charge of counterfeiting. A number of separate prints are discussed and illustrated. The author owns some interesting plates engraved by Dawkins.

218. Hearn, Michael Patrick. "An American Illustrator and His Posters." *American Book Collector* 3, no. 3 (May/June 1982; July/ August, 18–24): 11–18.

William Wallace Denslow (1856–1915) collected the artistic posters of the 1890's and wrote about them in *The Bill Poster*. He also designed posters in Chicago after he served years as a newspaper artist. Earlier, Denslow had worked for the lithographic firm of Thomas Sinclair & Son in Philadelphia. Hearn sets Denslow's contributions in this field within the context of the poster movement. The second part discusses Denslow's designs for book wrappers and posters. Near the end of 1890's Denslow began illustrating books, the most famous of which is the *Wonderful Wizard of Oz* (1900).

219. Allen, Francis W. "Notes on the Bookplates of Amos Doolittle." *Old-Time New England* 39 (October 1948): 38–44.

Following the biographical sketch of Doolittle (1754–1832) is a list of nineteen bookplates either signed by the artist or attributed to him. Two of the attributions are controversial and Allen presents both points of view.

220. Andrews, William Loring. "Early American Copperplate Engraving." *Book Buyer* 15 (January 1898): 652–58.

Andrews discusses Amos Doolittle's engravings of Lexington and Concord and John Norman's "The Death of Warren" and "The Death of Montgomery" in terms of their historical importance, which he feels is as slight as is their artistic merit.

221. Beardsley, William A. "An Old New Haven Engraver and His Work: Amos Doolittle." *New Haven Colony Historical Papers* 8 (1914): 132–50.

Beginning with an eloquent defense of collecting "quaint prints" and "musty volumes" for their historical significance, Beardsley describes Doolittle's life, and then discusses his major engravings in detail. Various book illustrations and bookplates are mentioned more summarily. In a reprint of the article, there is an appendix listing the engravings of Doolittle known to Beardsley, but the checklist could be expanded.

222. Metcalf, Frank J. "Amos Doolittle, Engraver and Printer." *American Collector* 4 (May 1927): 53–56.

This biographical sketch provides background on the engravings of Lexington and Concord, and cites several books containing engravings by Doolittle. Also listed are a few maps by the artist, Bible illustrations, and *A Display of the United States of America* with Washington's portrait.

223. Ormsbee, Thomas Hamilton. "Amos Doolittle Originated Chain of States Design." *American Collector* 11 (August 1942): 5, 15.

A Display of the United States of America, engraved by Amos Doolittle in 1790, provided the motif for a set of Canton china presented to Martha Washington and for some later Staffordshire china. Two states of the engraving are well described and an impression of the second state is reproduced.

224. Porter, Edward G. *Four Drawings of the Engagement at Lexington and Concord, April 19, 1775*. Boston: 1883. 5 pp.

This pamphlet, reprinted from *Antique Views of Ye Towne of Boston*, contains a text describing the subject of Doolittle's four engravings.

225. Quimby, Ian M. G. "The Doolittle Engravings of the Battle of Lexington and Concord." *Winterthur Portfolio* 4 (1968): 83–108.

Much of this well-illustrated article is devoted to background discussion of the events depicted in Doolittle's prints such as the British expedition, prior incidents, and subsequent battles. Doolittle's engravings are well described as are later prints based on them.

226. Sawitzky, William. "Ralph Earl's Historical Painting, "A View of the Town of Concord"." *Antiques* (September 1935): 98–100.

Since the publication of John Barber's *History and Antiquities of New Haven* in 1831, which quotes Doolittle on the subject of his engravings of the battles of Lexington and Concord, it has been generally concluded that Doolittle copied four paintings by Ralph Earl. Earl's paintings, however, have never been discovered, and there was no trace of them in the nineteenth century. Sawitzky here analyzes Earl's "A View of Concord," which is apparently one of the four paintings, and compares it to the Doolittle engraving. Sawitzky supposes that Earl's name did not appear on the engravings because he did not want to be associated with such amateurish efforts.

227. Sherman, Frederic Fairchild. "Amos Doolittle's Engravings of Lexington and Concord." *Art in America* 24 (January 1936): 43–44.

In an article in *Antiques* (Sept. 1935), William Sawitzky attributes the originals of the Doolittle engravings to Ralph Earl on the grounds that Doolittle was not capable of producing designs equal to the quality of Earl's work. Sherman disagrees with Sawitzky's premise since he feels that Doolittle was capable of painting such a picture. Moreover, the artist's custom was to engrave from his own originals. Sherman also doubts the attribution of the original to Earl since his landscapes are rather different in style.

228. Whitehill, Walter Muir. *Amos Doolittle's Engravings of Lexington and Concord.* Chicago: R.R. Donnelley & Sons, Co., 1974. Unpag.

Whitehill provides detailed historical background on this important set of prints. It is accompanied by full-size color reproductions made from the set owned by the Chicago Historical Society. Notes on other reproductions are also included.

229. Owen, Hans C. "America's Youngest Engraver." *Antiques* 26 (September 1934): 104–105.

The author owned three manuscripts written in 1804 by a young girl, Rebecca Hillhouse. Two of them are embellished with engravings by Horace Doolittle (b. 1792), then aged twelve. It had been thought, before these signed engravings came to light, that Amos Doolittle had a son, A.B. Doolittle, who started engraving at an early age. Owen feels that A.B. Doolittle was of another family and was not Amos Doolittle's son. The texts of the manuscripts are reprinted and some biographical information is provided for various members of the Doolittle family.

230. Looney, Robert F. "Thomas Doughty, Printmaker" in *Philadelphia Printmaking. American Prints Before 1860*, 130–148. ed. Robert F. Looney. West Chester, Penn.: Tinicum Press, 1976.

Although Thomas Doughty (1793–1856) is recognized as a painter of landscapes, his work as a printmaker is not well known. Looney focuses on Doughty's contributions to *The Cabinet of Natural History and American Rural Sports* published in Philadelphia in 1830–1 and on several separately published prints. Looney provides the outlines of Doughty's life and discusses several engravings for gift books that reproduced Doughty's early landscapes and views. *The Cabinet* was published by Doughty and his brother John until John Doughty published it on his own beginning in 1833. Looney documents Thomas's role in producing the illustrations for this magazine.

231. Looney, Robert. "Thomas Doughty, Printmaker." *Imprint* 4, no. 2 (1979): 2–10.

As the title suggests, this essay is a reprint of the author's essay in *Philadelphia Printmaking* (1976).

232. Craven, Wayne. "Asher B. Durand's Career as an Engraver." *American Art Journal* 3 (March 1971): 39–57.

The author attempts to rehabilitate appreciation of Durand's (1796–1886) graphic work, which has been overshadowed by his reputation as a painter. The first twenty-five years of Durand's career were devoted to engraving, but by 1836 he had surrendered the craft for painting.

233. Durand, John. *The Life and Times of A.B. Durand.* New York: Charles Scribner's Sons, 1894. 232 pp., index.

This handsomely produced and well-illustrated biography covers Asher B. Durand's entire life. The first few chapters are particularly pertinent to the study of his prints, concentrating on his experiences with Peter Maverick, his engraving of Trumbull's "Declaration of Independence," and his other works and activities before 1836, at which time he turned to painting. This book also provides information on Durand's contemporaries and artistic milieu.

234. The Grolier Club. *Catalogue of the Engraved Work of Asher B. Durand.* New York: 1895. 103 pp.

In the introduction, Charles H. Hart provides a biographical sketch of the artist, an enthusiastic appreciation of his engravings, and a discussion of his most important prints. Hart feels that Durand's engravings are superior to his paintings. The catalog lists 237 prints, an impression from each plate that Durand engraved; and often several states of the plate were included. The exhibition was based on the artist's own collection of reserved proofs.

235. Hendricks, Gordon. "Durand, Maverick and the Declaration." *American Art Journal* 3 (1971): 58–71.

A carefully researched and reasoned discussion of Asher B. Durand's engraving, *The Declaration of Independence*, after the painting by John Trumbull now at the Yale University Art Gallery. Documentation for the study includes contemporary newspaper articles and advertisements as well as manuscripts.

236. Huntington, Daniel. *Asher B. Durand, a Memorial Address.* New York: Century Association, 1887. 48 pp.

Durand was one of the founders of the Century Association, and the one illustration in this book is a portrait of him etched by James Smillie after a painting by Huntington, president of the association. The biographical sketch is excellent and there is a discussion of Durand's engravings and later paintings.

237. Montclair Art Museum. *A.B. Durand, 1796–1886.* Montclair, N.J.: 1971. 111 pp., biblio.

Before becoming a painter, Asher B. Durand was an apprentice to Peter Maverick as a line engraver. His production was mainly bank notes, book illustrations, and portraits. By

1835, he had ceased engraving and turned to painting. David B. Lawall's introduction is excellent and is followed by a chronology of the artist's life. There are about twenty-five engravings in the catalog, and excellent background information is provided for each.

238. Hudson River Museum. *Asher B. Durand: An Engraver's and a Farmer's Art*. Yonkers, N.Y.: The Hudson River Museum, 1983. 96 pp., biblio.

This exhibition catalogue contains a thoughtful essay by James Thomas Flexner on Durand's training and work as an engraver, the importance of engravers to the reputation of painters, his engravings of female nudes, and his turning to painting at the age of 40. Two essays by Barbara Gallati discuss Durand's engravings and his drawings. There are 129 entries in the catalog, many of which contain lengthy captions providing a great deal of information about the works.

239. Donnell, Edna. "Portraits of Eminent Americans After Drawings by Du Simitière." *Antiques* 24 (July 1933): 17–21.

In 1779, Pierre Du Simitière (1736–1784) made a series of fourteen profile drawings of American statesmen, which he sent to France to be engraved. The French edition, published in late 1781 or 1782, was pirated by two English publishers in 1783. The English engravings served as sources for portraits of the statesmen that appeared on English pottery and textiles. Of great value in this excellent article is a checklist of the French and English editions. Excerpts of letters by Du Simitière are also included that provide excellent documentation of the artist's problems with the publication of the portraits. All the engravings of the French edition are reproduced.

240. Huth, Hans. "Pierre Eugène Du Simitière and the Beginnings of the American Historical Museum." *Pennsylvania Magazine of History and Biography* 69 (October 1945): 315–25.

Among the artist's projects in Philadelphia between 1764 and 1784 was the establishement of a history museum to collect materials pertinent to America and the Revolution. This is a good description of the collection, which contained broadsides, newspaper clippings arranged by subject, maps, plans, and views. Du Simitière's proposal to Congress to write a history of the Revolution is examined. The collection was unfortunately dispersed at the artist's death, much of it going to Peale, and thence to Barnum. Fire destroyed the major part of it in 1845. Huth speaks briefly of Du Simitière's series of portraits and his designs for seals, illustrations, and maps. This is thorough and well documented.

241. Potts, William J. "Du Simitière, Artist, Antiquary, and Naturalist: Projector of the First American Museums, With Some Extracts From His Notebook." *Pennsylvania Magazine of History and Biography* 13 (October 1889): 341–75.

This study opens with a lengthy sketch of the artist's activities, written by several authors. Included is a letter from Du Simitière to Governor Clinton in 1779. The published notebook entries contain references to drawings and paintings by Du Simitière, receipts of antiquities for his museum, and records of loans of books and other items.

242. Sifton, Paul G. "Pierre Eugène Du Simitière: Illustrator of Nascent America." *Antiques* 78 (December 1960): 576–78.

Drawing upon the artist's Memorandum Book deposited in the Library of Congress, the author has been able to identify six entries for illustrations that appeared in the *Pennsylvania Magazine* in 1774 and 1775. The illustrations include a title page vignette, three mechanical diagrams, and an allegorical engraving presaging American independence.

243. Cary, Elisabeth L. "Frank Duveneck's Etchings." *Art in America* 13 (August 1925): 274–76.

Based on a small group of Duveneck's (1848–1919) etchings at the New York Public Library, the article concentrates on his views of Venice. Cary discusses the characteristics of the artist's style.

244. Cincinnati Art Museum. *Exhibition of the Work of Frank Duveneck*. Cincinnati: 1936. 82 pp., biblio.

This exhibition focuses on Duveneck's paintings, although some thirty etchings and monotypes were included. The introduction by Walter H. Siple provides information on the artist. A full list of the artist's paintings is appended to the catalog. The bibliography is excellent.

245. Poole, Emily. "The Etchings of Frank Duveneck." *Print Collector's Quarterly* 25 (October and December 1938): 312–31; 446–63.

Duveneck etched about thirty plates between 1880 and 1885. For the most part, they are architectural views, chiefly of Venice. In 1915 the artist presented an almost complete collection of the etchings to the Cincinnati Art Museum. This article discusses Duveneck's painting career briefly but concentrates upon his etchings, which are catalogued by date in the second part of the article.

246. Parry, Elwood C., and Maria Chamberlain-Hellman. "Thomas Eakins as an Illustrator, 1878–1881." *American Art Journal* 5 (May 1973): 20–45.

Between 1878 and 1881 Eakins (1884–1916) supplied eight illustrations to popular magazines. The authors discuss changes in Eakins' style, and relate the illustrations to paintings of the same period. There is some comment on the relationship between Pennell and Eakins.

247. Boehme, Sarah E. "An Officer and an Illustrator on the Indian Frontier" in *Seth Eastman. A Portfolio of North American Indians*, 1–35. Sarah E. Boehme, Christian F. Feest, and Patricia C. Johnston. Afton, Minn.: Afton Historical Press, 1995.

Characterized as an accurate reporter of Native American life, Eastman (1808–1875) spent many years among his subjects. Educated at West Point, he received some artistic training from 1824 to 1829 and then taught drawing there from 1833 to 1840. Boehme thoroughly describes Eastman's years at West Point and relates his work there to his later career, setting it in the context of other artists. Many of his illustrations appeared in Henry Schoolcraft's *Historical and Statistical Information Respecting the History, Condition and Prospects of the Indian Tribes of the United States* (1852–7). Many of his works found a subsequent use in his wife's publications.

248. Rugg, Harold Goddard. "Isaac Eddy, Printer-Engraver." in *Bibliographic Essays: A Tribute to Wilberforce Eames*, 313–29. Cambridge: Harvard University Press, 1925.

As an engraver, Eddy (1777–1847) is best known for the naive engravings on copper which he made for the first edition of the *Vermont Bible*. The author summarizes what little is known of Eddy's career, and examines all of his known engravings. A list of Eddy publications and authenticated engravings is included.

249. *James Eddy: Biographical Sketch, Memorial Service, Selected Thoughts*. Providence: J.A. & R.A. Reid, 1889. 66 pp.

At an early age James Eddy (1806–1888) became an engraver in Boston, later working in New York. He did not remain an engraver for many years, but turned to the importation and sale of foreign paintings. The biographical sketch reveals little about his artistic training or work; rather, it is a eulogy.

250. The Newark Museum. *Oliver Tarbell Eddy, 1799–1868: A Catalogue of His Works*. Newark: 1950. 68 pp.

Oliver Tarbell Eddy began his artistic career engraving for his father, Isaac Eddy. Most of the exhibition was devoted to Oliver Tarbell Eddy's paintings, as discussed in the introduction to this catalog after a biographical sketch. The catalog is by Edith Bishop.

251. Fielding, Mantle. *Catalogue of the Engraved Work of David Edwin*. Philadelphia: 1905. 62 pp., index.

The introduction provides an excellent biographical sketch of Edwin's (1776–1841) life and even includes anecdotes about him from the writings of his contemporaries. Fielding discusses the technique of stipple engraving, Edwin's style, and his friendships with other artists, including Gilbert Stuart. The 263 entries include the full inscriptions taken from the prints. Many of the engravings are book illustrations; unfortunately, the titles of the volumes from which they came are not included. The introduction was also printed in *The Pennsylvania Magazine of History and Biography* 29 (Jan. 1905): 79–88. The catalog is based on lists completed by Hildeburn and Fielding in the same periodical in volumes 18 (1894), 28 (1904), and 29 (1905).

252. Hanson, David A. "Baron Frederick Wilhelm von Egloffstein: Inventor of the First Commercial Halftone Process in America." *Printing History* 15, no. 1 (1993): 12–24.

The Prussian Baron von Egloffstein (ca. 1824–1898) served as a topographical engineer in Fremont's final expedition across the Rocky Mountains. During the 1860s he produced several maps using an experimental halftone method which he patented in 1865. In 1867 he established a company to produce halftones, the Heliographic Engraving and Printing Company, which survived until 1870. The firm produced separate prints and book illustrations, but failed because the process was not economical.

253. Shadwell, Wendy. "'1 Year at the Business'—George B. Ellis of Philadelphia." *Imprint* 16, no. 2 (1991): 26–28.

This brief article discusses an engraving signed by George B. Ellis, *The Peaceable Kingdom of the Branch* done in 1819 while Ellis was an apprentice to Francis Kearny. The illustration later appeared in a Bible published by Carey & Lea in 1823.

254.———. "St. Lawrence County, 1838 As Seen Through the Eyes of Salathiel Ellis" in *Prints and Printmakers of New York State, 1825–1940*, 67–89. ed. David F. Tatham. Syracuse: Syracuse University Press, 1986.

The impetus for this essay is a group of eight lithographs depicting scenes in St. Lawrence County. Four were produced by the Speckler firm in Hamburg, Germany; the others were by Eugene Ciceri of Paris. All but one are in the collection of the New-York Historical Society. They were commissioned by the Parrish family, successful merchants in Scotland, who owned substantial amounts of land in New York State. Shadwell discusses the family, subjects of the prints, and the artist, Salathiel Ellis (1803–1879), who later worked as a sculptor. An appendix to the article lists the eight prints and locations in publications.

255. Bumgardner, Georgia B. "George and William Endicott, Commercial Lithography in New York, 1831–1851" in Prints and Printmakers of New York State, 1825–1940, 43–65. ed. David Tatham. Syracuse: Syracuse University Press, 1986.

Documented by Charles Hart's manuscript history of the Endicott firm, *Lithography, Its Theory and Practice* (located at the New York Public Library), this essay provides information on the business of the Endicott firm, which produced sheet music, book illustrations, portrait prints, city views, and topical prints. Among the artists who worked sporadically for this commercial firm were John H. Bufford, William Ball, Edward Williams Clay, Eliphalet H. Brown, and Eugene Sintzenich. Names closely associated with the firm's output included George T. Sanford, John Penniman, Francis D'Avignon, and Charles Parsons. Representative prints by these and others are discussed in this essay.

256. Koehler, Sylvester R. "J.M. Falconer." *American Art Review* 1, no. 1 (1880): 190–91.

A Scot by birth, Falconer (1820–1903) resided in Brooklyn. He was a member of the American Water Color Society (a catalog of its thirteenth exhibition enumerates seventeen of his watercolors and etchings). Influenced by Cadart, he made some early attempts at etchings. In 1878 he resumed the practice, producing about thirty plates, many of which are scenes of picturesque ruins. A sample list of his etchings, created from 1878 to 1880, is appended to this article by Koehler, which is illustrated by an original etching.

257. Newman, Ewell L. "The Graphic Art of Henry F. Farny." *Imprint* 8, no. 1 (1983): 13–25.

Held in high esteem by Theodore Roosevelt and Joseph Pennell, Farny (1847–1916) specialized in depictions of the West. He was a frequent contributor to *Harper's Weekly*, *Century Magazine*, *Frank Leslie's Illustrated Newspaper* and others. He also illustrated for book publishers, posters, etc. Born in France in 1847, Farny's family fled France in 1853 settling in western Pennsylvania. They moved to Cincinnati in 1859. He began working in a lithographic firm by 1865 and soon moved to New York where he worked briefly for Harpers'. His enthusiasm for the West developed slowly but was well in place in 1884. His interpretations of the American Indians and the West were realistic. In the 1890's he turned away from book and periodical illustration to painting.

258. Koehler, Sylvester R. "Henry Farrer." *American Art Review* 1, no. 1 (1880): 55–56.

Farrer (1843–1903), born in England, was a proponent of the American pre-Raphaelite school early in his career. His first attempts at etching were made about 1868, but he did not devote his full time to the craft until the foundation of the New York Etching Club in 1877. His early plates illustrate "Old New York." A list of his best plates, produced from 1877 to 1879, is given. A further comment on Farrer's work and a later etching can be found in the *American Art Review* 1 (Pt. 2, 1880): 525.

259.———. "New Etching by Henry Farrer." *American Art Review* 2, no. 1 (1881): 184.

This follow-up to an earlier article on Farrer in the *Review*, this notice focuses on the New York City plates done in 1879 and 1880, praising their delicacy and subtlely.

260. Marks, Matthew S. "Henry Farrer's Early Etchings of New York." *Imprint* 7, no. 1 (1982): 2–6.

Farrer (1843–1903), one of the first American etchers, produced an important series of New York views between 1870 and 1877. Marks discusses the importance of these prints and corrects several misconceptions about these rare views of a city undergoing rapid transformation. The New-York Historical Society has twelve of the fifteen prints.

261. Parker, Alice Lee, and Milton Kaplan. *Charles Fenderich, Lithographer of Amreican Statesmen: A Catalogue of His Work*. Washington, D.C.: Library of Congress, 1959. 79 pp., index.

This catalog describes 261 items (including some drawings) which are arranged according to the places where Fenderich worked: Switzerland, France, Philadelphia, Washington, and California. The Library of Congress owns a small collection of drawings and watercolors, as well as most of the published lithographs. In the introduction, Fenderich's early training and career in Germany and France are discussed. In 1831 he fled with his family from Switzerland to the United States. His career in Philadelphia and Washington is outlined. When daguerreotypes became popular in the 1840s, his own portrait production decreased, so he left for California in 1849. Little is known of his work there, although he was listed in the city directories until 1887 as an artist.

262. Koehler, Sylvester R. "Stephen J. Ferris." *American Art Review* 1, no. 1 (1880): 104

An admirer of Fortuny, whose paintings he often reproduced in etching, Ferris (1835–1915) was only known in Philadelphia as a painter. His early attention to reproductive etching gave him a wide reputation as an etcher, however, and a number of his plates were published in New York City and Philadelphia. A sample list of his reproductive work is given and the above article is illustrated by an original etching.

263. Byrne, Janet S. "An America Pioneer Amateur." *Princeton University Library Chronicle* 6 (June 1945): 153–70.

Jonathan Fisher (1768–1847), a Congregational minister in Blue Hill, Me., is the subject of this excellent article. As a child, Fisher experimented with drawing on slate and scratching on wood with a pin, then later painted and made wood engravings. Byrne concentrates here on his painting of Nassau Hall at Princeton (copied from Henry Dawkins's engraving of 1764), but also discusses his wood engravings. He engraved on boxwood as early as 1793, at the same time as Alexander Anderson. Entries from Fisher's diary that provide details about the wood engravings are reprinted. He compiled and illustrated *Scripture Animals; or, the Natural History of the Living Creatures Named in the Bible,* published in 1834. The sources for this children's book, both literary and pictorial, are discussed in detail, as are several of his other productions.

264. Lieberman, Frank. "J. F., The Woodcuts of Rev. Jonathan Fisher." *Print* 9 (March 1955): 22–33.

In 1953 Frank Teagle discovered 121 woodcuts by Fisher used in *Scripture Animals*, some of which were reprinted from the blocks to illustrate this article. Lieberman quotes extensively from Janet Byrne's article and lists six works illustrated by Fisher. The chief value of this article is the quality of the reproductions of the woodcuts.

265. Rossiter, Henry P. "Drawings and Wood-Engravings by the Rev. Jonathan Fisher, 1768–1847." *Bulletin of the Museum of Fine Arts, Boston* 47 (June 1949): 31–33.

In March and April of 1949, the Department of Prints and Drawings of the Museum of Fine Arts, Boston, had an exhibition on Fisher, largely borrowed from Gaylord C. Hall and other private collectors. This article outlines Fisher's life and activities and briefly describes the drawings and prints on display.

266. Winchester, Alice. *Versatile Yankee: The Art of Jonathan Fisher, 1768–1847*. Princeton: Pyne Press, 1973. Unpag., bibio.

This beautifully produced volume concentrates on Fisher's water colors and oils, but the introduction includes material on his wood engravings and drawings. An excellent bibliography and a list of books illustrated with Fisher's engravings is given. For her earlier study on Fisher, see "Rediscovery: Parson Jonathan Fisher," *Art in America* 58 (Nov.-Dec. 1970): 92–99.

267. Bickford-Swarthout, Doris. *Mary Hallock Foote: Pioneer Woman Illustator*. Deansboro, N.Y.: Berry Hill Press, 1996. 119 p., biblio.

Probably the most prolific of American women illustrators, Foote (1847–1938) led a difficult, but memorable, life in the west. Bickford-Swartout provides a biographical sketch of the artist and author and reproduces over 150 of her illustrations.

268. Foote, Mary Hallock. *A Victorian Gentlewoman in the Far West*. San Marino, Cal.: Huntington Library, 1992. 419 pp., biblio., index.

Mary Hallock Foote was an illustrator and writer of some note. These reminiscences, edited by Rodman W. Paul, provide a great deal of information about the life and work of a professional woman who had a great many obstacles to overcome to pursue her craft. Her work was published in the *Century Illustrated Monthly Magazine* and *Scribner's Monthly*. Among other works, she illustrated *The Scarlet Letter*. Her life is also the subject of Wallace Stegner's novel, *The Angle of Repose*. The bibliographical note includes many articles on her as well as information on primary sources, including extant drawings.

269. Dawson, William Forrest. *A Civil War Artist at the Front*. New York: Oxford University Press, 1957. Unp., 40 plates and text.

Dawson's foreword provides background information on the youthful Edwin Forbes's (1839–1895) Civil War experiences as a sketch artist for *Frank Leslie's Illustrated Newspaper*. In 1876 Forbes published a series of forty etchings which this book reproduces together with useful explanatory text by Dawson. The Library of Congress has an extensive collection of drawings by Forbes, who also worked as an illustrator. This book was reprinted by Dover Publications in New York in 1994.

270. Forbes, Edwin. *Thirty Years After. An Artist's Memoir of the Civil War*. Baton Rouge and London: Louisana State University Press, 1993. 319 pp.

William J. Cooper's introduction to the illustrated memoir of the Civil War artist Edwin Forbes discusses the artist's work for *Frank Leslie's Illustrated Newspaper*, and sets Forbes' work in the context of the reporting of Civil War news in general. Forbes' experiences during the war were central to him for the rest of his life. After the War he prepared drawings from his sketches, and then made forty etchings that were published as *Life Studies of the Great Army* in 1876. In 1890 he produced *Thirty Years After: An Artist's Story of the Great War*. He died in Brooklyn on May 6, 1895.

271. Holzer, Harold. "The Bohemian Brigade's Best." *MHQ: The Quarterly Journal of Military History* 11, no. 1 (1998): 54–61.

Military artist Edwin Forbes recorded the lives of common soldiers in his Civil War works, many of which he reproduced as etchings in *Life Studies of the Great Army*. In addition he created important sketches of the Battle of Gettysburg that he turned into paintings. Holzer reviews Forbes's training, Civil War experiences, and his paintings, sketches, and etchings. J. P. Morgan acquired Forbes's archive from his widow in 1901 and later presented it to the Library of Congress.

272. Deane, Charles. "Notes on Hubbard's Map of New England." *Proceedings of the Massachusetts Historical Society, 2nd Series* 4 (November 1887): 3–21.

Deane describes the two editions of John Foster's (1648–1681) map of New England, published in 1677 as an illustration to William Hubbard's *A Narrative of the Troubles with the Indians in New England*, and compares the place names and other legends for errors in spelling. He suggests that both editions were printed in Boston, the "Wine Hills" map first. The second issue of the volume contained many textual corrections, and Deane feels the map would have been corrected at the same time. Since he had seen copies of the London edition with the "White Hills" map inserted, he concludes that the

Boston printer sent extra copies of the map to the London publisher for use in the volume.

273. Green, Samuel A. *John Foster, the Earliest American Engraver and the First Boston Printer*. Boston: Massachusetts Historical Society, 1909. 149 pp., biblio., index.

Separate chapters in this volume discuss Foster as an engraver and printer, elegies written about him, and his other intellectual attainments as an almanac compiler. An excellently prepared bibliography of Foster's imprints, and a short title list of engravings ends the book. There are several errors in the volume, which more recent scholarship has corrected, but it remains a valuable bibliographical tool, particularly for its list of imprints. Green was the first to link Foster with the portrait of Richard Mather, so his work is of importance to later scholars.

274.———. "John Foster, the Earliest Engraver in New England." *Proceedings of the Massachusetts Historical Society* 19 (January 1905): 51–60.

This sketch of Foster was inspired by the exhibition of American engravings at the Museum of Fine Arts, Boston. The earliest print on display was Foster's portrait of Richard Mather. Green discusses that print, the "Indians' ABC" (no copy extant), the seal of the colony, the map of New England, and a map or view of Boston made by Foster (also no longer extant). Foster's will and the inventory of his estate are reprinted.

275. Griffin, Gillett. "John Foster's Woodcut of Richard Mather." *Printing and Graphic Arts* 7 (February 1959): 1–19.

John Foster's woodcut of Richard Mather was the first print made in the English colonies in 1670. This article includes facsimiles of the five of the known copies, printed side by side to facilitate study. Griffin carefully compares the five and attempts to explain the split in the block which separates the head and shoulder from the body in some of the copies. Appendixes contain information on the oil portrait of Mather at the American Antiquarian Society, the provenances of the five copies of the woodcut, and the signs of the zodiac which appear on the robe in four of the five prints.

276. Hamilton, Sinclair. "John Foster and the "White Hills" Map." *Princeton University Library Chronicle* 14 (1953): 177–82.

A brief biography and short descriptions of Foster's other wood engravings precede the author's analysis of the map of New England engraved by Foster in 1677. One of the questions Hamilton raises is whether or not Foster was the draftsman as well as the engraver, but the documentation is inconclusive on this point.

277.———. "Portrait of a Puritan, John Foster's Woodcut of Richard Mather." *Princeton University Library Chronicle* 18 (1957): 43–48.

This article was written to celebrate the donation of an impression of the Foster woodcut of Richard Mather to the Princeton Library. Hamilton describes the provenance of the print and the five known impresssions, also providing biographical information on John Foster and Richard Mather.

278. Holman, Richard B. "John Foster's Woodcut Map of New England." *Printing and Graphic Arts* 8 (September 1960): 53–93.

The definitive article on Foster's map of New England, this discusses the two variant forms printed in William Hubbard's *A Narrative of the Troubles with the Indians in New England* (Boston, 1677). Hamilton concludes that both forms were cut by Foster in Boston, and that the "Wine Hills" version was cut first and sent to London to be published with the London edition of the book. However, letters on the subject by William Jackson and Roderick Stinehour in *Printing and Graphic Arts* 8 (No. 4), refute Holman's conclusions and suggest that the "White Hills" version was cut first, and that Foster did not cut the London edition. A variant state, Stinehour notes, is in the Massachusetts Historical Society.

279.———. "Some Remarks on 'Mr. Richard Mather'." *Printing and Graphic Arts* 7 (June 1959): 57–33.

In response to Gillett Griffin's article in *Printing and Graphic Arts* 7 (No. 1), Holman submits that the blocks were not properly cared for, thereby producing the variations in the prints. He suggests that the zodiac signs were mistakenly pushed into the soft pine of the body to identify them, with no thought given to the fact that the experiment was being done on a woodcut. Furthermore, Holman believes the Harvard copy was printed on a press, while the other four were rubbed proofs. Lastly, he speculates that Foster engraved Mather's head but an apprentice completed the body.

280. Nichols, Charles Lemuel. "Justus Fox: A German Printer of the Eighteenth Century." *Proceedings of the American Antiquarian Society* 25 (April 1915): 55–69.

In the early nineteenth century, William McCulloch compiled many editions and corrections to Isaiah Thomas's *History of Printing in America*, first published in 1810. Many of the notes were not included in the 1874 edition, and Nichols draws upon these for his narrative of Justus Fox (1736–1805). Hired as an apprentice by Christopher Sauer in 1750, Fox learned the various phases of the business, including the cutting of wood blocks for illustrations. Nichols enumerates some of the cuts attributable to Fox which appeared in Sauer's publications (mostly almanacs), then discusses almanac illustration in general before the Revolution and makes a few comments about book illustraion.

281. Severns, Martha R. "Charles Fraser of Charleston." *Antiques* 123, no. 3 (March 1983): 606–611.

A childhood acquaintance of Thomas Sully, Charles Fraser's (1782–1860) first instructor was Thomas Coram (1756–1811), an engraver of currency, bookplates, and seals as well as a painter. Trained as a lawyer, Fraser practiced for eleven years before devoting himself to painting miniature portraits on ivory. He was also commissioned to do a series of landscapes published in the *Analytical Magazine*. Stevens discusses his training and style and mentions a number of his portraits. During his travels in the north, he occasionally made oil paintings, and he based others on print sources. This article is derived from *Charles Fraser of Charleston: Essays on the Man, His Art, and His Times* compiled by Severens and Charles L. Wyrick and published by the Carolina Art Association in 1983.

282. Brainerd, Ira Hutchinson. *Edwin Davis French, a Memorial: His Life, His Art*. New York: Privately printed, 1908. 95 pp.

French (1851–1906) did not begin engraving bookplates until 1893. The introduction provides a lengthy sketch of the man and his work. The catalog of bookplates designed or engraved by French includes almost 300 entries ranging in date from 1893 to 1903. A second list includes about thirty miscellaneous designs and engravings used on certificates, letterheads, or as book illustrations. There is an index to the book plates and one for the miscellaneous group.

283. "Frank French." *Scribner's Magazine* 17 (June 1895): 689–91.

This short article emphasizes French's (1850–1933) New England heritage and his independence as an artist, even though his name is usually associated with the New School of wood engraving.

284. Smith, Ralph Clifton. "Frank French: Engraver on Wood." *Print Connoisseur* 8 (October 1928): 208–219.

French took up wood engraving in New Hampshire in 1870 and eventually found a position with the American Tract Society. His early work in cooperation with Southwick is difficult to identify; his first signed work appeared after 1875. He engraved several books, most importantly *Home Fairies and Heart Flowers*, and executed work for *Scribner's*, *Harper's* and *Century* magazines. He did many engravings after the drawings of the popular illustrators of the time. French's reputation is based in part upon his portrait painting; at the close of the century he abandoned engraving for that genre.

285. Koehler, Sylvester R. "Edmund H. Garrett." *American Art Review* 2, no. 2 (1881): 103.

Garrett worked as a wood engraver for eight years before taking up etching under the guidance of R. Swain Gifford. Koehler lists a selection of plates and characterizes Garrett's style as neat and delicate. He notes a lack of feeling for color which he attributes to the artist's training as an engraver, but it is more likely due to the fact that Garrett did not have experience as a painter.

286. Welsh, Caroline Mastin. "'A Passion for Fishing and Tramping': The Adirondacks Etched by Arpad G. Gerster, M.D." in *Adirondack Prints and Printmakers: The Call of the Wild*, 139–157. editor Caroline Mastin Welsh. Blue Mountain Lake and Syracuse, N.Y.: Adirondack Museum and Syracuse University Press, 1998.

A physician, man of letters, and amateur artist, Gerster (1848–1923) summered in the Adirondacks and was introduced to etching by one of his patients, James David Smillie, and Dr. Leroy Milton Yale, both founders of the New York Etching Club. Smillie presented Gerster with an etching press and a work table. Gerster produced twenty-three etchings of Raquette and Long Lakes, their inhabitants and environs. Welsh describes the prints using his diary (in the Adirondack Museum along with sketches and the plates) as primary documentation. Although not a great artist, Gerster produced a valuable pictorial and verbal record of the region between 1883 and 1906.

287. Hall, Elton W. *R. Swain Gifford, 1840–1905*. New Bedford: Old Dartmouth Historical Society, 1974. 113 pp.

This work, written for an exhibition of Gifford's painted and printed works in the summer of 1974, contains a short biography and a selection of paintings, watercolors, drawings, and etchings. Short descriptions are given for each plate. While only twenty-six etchings are illustrated, a complete catalog of the seventy-five or so etchings produced by Gifford, who was one of the moving forces in the etching revival of the late nineteenth century, remains to be compiled. The essential matter of this catalog, as well as some of the plates, appeared in the author's "R. Swain Gifford," *The American Art Review* 1:4 (1974): 51–67.

288. Koehler, Sylvester R. "R. Swain Gifford." *American Art Review* 1, no. 1 (1880): 5–6.

This short biography of Gifford includes comments on his methods of work. There is also a list of those etchings produced up to the date of this article, which is illustrated by an original etching.

289.———. "R. Swain Gifford, N.A." *American Art Review* 1, no. 2 (1880): 417–22.

This article is mainly concerned with Gifford as a landscape painter, but also provides a good background on the artist as etcher.

290. Darrach, Charles Gobrecht. "Christian Gobrecht, Artist and Inventor." *Pennsylvania Magazine of History and Biography* 30 (July 1906): 355–58.

Darrach, a descendant of Christian Gobrecht (1785–1844), briefly describes the artist's life and his major accomplishments, both in engraving and mechanics. The author claims that Gobrecht, an accomplished bank note engraver, invented a medal-ruling machine. Two of his drawing books, dated 1794 and 1802, are in the collection of the Historical Society of Pennsylvania.

291. O'Gorman, James F. "'Either in Books or in Architecture': Bertram Grosvenor Goodhue in the Nineties" in *A History of Book Illustration, 29 Points of View*, 548–566. editor Bill Katz. Metuchen, N.J., & London: The Scarecrow Press, Inc., 1994.

Goodhue (1869–1924) excelled in both architecture and book illustration. O'Gorman, an expert in the history of both fields, provides a biographical sketch of Goodhue, discussing his apprenticeship in New York in the 1880s, his association with the firm of Ralph Adams Cram in Boston, and his friendship with members of the Arts and Crafts Movement, under the influence of William Morris that led to designs for book illustrations in the 1890s. This essay was first published in the *Harvard Library Bulletin*, Spring 1987.

292. Koehler, Sylvester R. "Mrs. Eliza Greatorex." *American Art Review* 2, no. 2 (1881): 12.

An Irish immigrant, the artist (1820–1897) began to draw in 1869. In 1878 to 1879 she studied etching in Paris, and by the writing of this notice had completed etchings of Oberammergau, the environs of Paris, and northern Africa. Her work is characterized as having a delicate quality rather than a strong one.

293. Weitenkampf, Frank. "John Greenwood, an American-Born Artist in Eighteenth-Century Europe, with a List of Etchings and Mezzotints." *Bulletin of The New York Public Library* 31 (August 1927): 623–34.

Greenwood (1727–1792) never executed a print in his native land, although he painted portraits in the United States. Weitenkampf provides a biographical sketch of the artist, then lists the prints by Greenwood, also mentioning prints after his paintings found in The New York Public Library and in the lists found in various dictionaries of artists. The print descriptions are very detailed.

294. Marder, William, Estelle Marder, and Sally Pierce. "Philip Haas: Lithographer, Print Publisher, and Daguerreotypist." *The Daguerreian Annual* (1995): 20–39. Checklists of daguerreotypes and prints.

Philip Haas (1808–1863) was one of the few daguerreotypists who was able to publish his daguerreian portraits as lithographs. In turn the prints enable scholars and collectors to assess his work as a daguerreotypist. This article traces his multi-faceted career from his arrival in the United States in 1834 from Paris. He established himself as a lithographer in Washington in 1835 where he produced technical prints, portraits, and views of the capital city and of Mount Vernon. He also published a map and altas of the harbor of Bridgeport, Connecticut, and a book *Public Buildings and Statuary of the Government* issued in Washington in 1839 and 1840. He probably learned the daguerreotype process in Paris in 1839 and was producing them in Washington by 1843 when he published a lithograph from his portrait of John Quincy Adams. Other prints from his daguerreotypes are documented in this well annotated and researched article. Haas ended his career as a wet-plate photographer employed by the Union Army in the Civil War. Some of his photographs were reproduced in *Harper's Weekly Magazine*.

295. Lane, Gladys R. "Rhode Island's Earliest Engraver." *Antiques* 7 (March 1925): 133–37.

Born in Providence, William Hamlin (1772–1869) was apprenticed to Samuel Canfield, a metalsmith in Middletown, Conn. He spent his life in Providence as Rhode Island's first resident engraver. This biographical sketch is excellent, and a checklist of engravings is provided that was culled from various collections and from the Stauffer and Fielding lists; undoubtedly, it could be expanded today. Hamlin's style was naive but charming, and he engraved bank notes, views of several Providence churches, portraits used as book illustrations, and other miscellaneous items.

296. Harrison, William J. *William Harrison, Sr. and Sons, Engravers. A Checklist of Their Work*. South Yarmouth, Mass.: 1978. Unpag.

This mimeographed volume includes biographical material on members of the Harrison family who were engravers in the nineteenth century. Engravers in the family include William Harrison, Sr. (ca. 1750–1803), William Harrison, Jr. (b. 1774), Charles Peter Harrison (1783–1854), Richard Granville Harrison (1793–1870), and Samuel Harrison (1789–1818). There are checklists of the works by each of these men. Included are banknotes, book illustrations, separately published prints, and maps. Following the checklists is a genealogy of William Harrison's descendants.

297. Reading Public Museum and Art Gallery. "The Complete Work of Robert Havell, Jr." *Connoisseur* 126 (November 1950): 127.

Born in England, Havell (1793–1878) came to the United States after completing work on Audubon's *The Birds of America*, and painted landscapes of the Hudson River Valley. This brief note written by Helen Comstock records a Havell exhibition at the Reading [Pa.] Museum in 1950.

298. Williams, George Alfred. "An English Engraver of American Nature: Havell." *Antiquarian* 17 (July 1931): 26–30, 62, 64.

Robert Havell, Jr., is best known as the engraver of the plates for Audubon's *The Birds of America*, which he worked on from 1837 to 1839. The author, a direct descendant of Havell, had access to family papers which provide new insights into the relationship between Robert Havell, Jr., Robert Havell, Sr., and J.J. Audubon, and into the Havells' division of labor. A technical description of the aquatint process is included, with special emphasis laid on Havell's style. In 1839, Havell came to live in America, where he settled on the banks of the Hudson. He continued to engrave and produced several beautiful prints of the scenery and cities in the eastern United States. He later gave up engraving for oil painting. This is an excellent article containing valuable documentation.

299.———. "Robert Havell, Engraver of Audubon's 'The Birds of America'." *Print Collector's Quarterly* 6 (October 1916): 227–57.

This history of the Havell family includes an inventory of their publications. Searching for a publisher for his portfolio of paintings, Audubon discovered the Havells; their collaboration is recounted here in detail. Havell's later years in America are described, and several of his American drawings and plates are illustrated.

300. White, Luke Jr. *Henry William Herbert & The American Publishing Scene 1831–1858*. Newark, N.J.: The Carteret Book Club, 1943. 71 pp., biblio.

Herbert (1807–1858) wrote and illustrated his own books using the pseudonym of Frank Forester. Born and educated in England, Herbert arrived in America in 1831, ostensibly to travel and to hunt. He stayed for the rest of his life working as a teacher and a journalist. Although best known as an author, he did illustrate a number of his works; this book is illustrated with some charming wood engravings of birds. White firmly sets Herbert in the publishing world.

301. Drepperd, Carl W. "Rare American Prints Drawn from a Drawing Book." *Antiques* 16 (July 1929): 25–28.

The prints in this article are from the *Progressive Drawing Book* (Baltimore: Fielding Lucas, 1827–1828), containing "original views of American scenery" aquatinted by John Hill. Drepperd discusses the content of the volume, then lists the most important plates depicting American scenery. These charming prints had not been recorded by Stauffer or Fielding.

302. Koke, Richard J. *A Checklist of the American Engravings of John Hill (1770–1850), Master of Aquatint, Together with a List of Prints Colored by Him and a List of His Extant Original Drawings*. New York: New-York Historical Society, 1961. 87 pp.

This checklist of 161 engravings is based on the entries in Stauffer's and Fielding's volumes, as well as on collections in New York. Hill's account book for the years 1820 to 1834 (in The New-York Historical Society) provides new titles of prints and valuable documentation on the publication of portfolios containing Hill's aquatints. The checklist is chronologically arranged and the entries are very informative. It is followed by lists of the prints colored by Hill and of his drawings.

303.———. "John Hill (1770–1850), Master of Aquatint." *New-York Historical Society Quarterly* 43 (January 1959): 51–118.

John Hill, born in England, came to the United States in 1816 after attaining an excellent reputation in his native country for his skill with aquatint engraving. Koke discusses this process, Hill's English work, and his American career in Philadelphia and New York. His work in the two cities is carefully described, with reference made to each of the plates found in a variety of books and periodicals. This study is superbly doucumented, much of it based on John Hill's own account books, one of which (covering the years 1798 to 1816) can be found at The Metropolitan Museum of Art. The volume for 1820 to 1834 is a combination diary and account book, located at the New-York Historical Society together with original sketches, watercolors, and engraved proofs. Because of the existence of these books, Koke is able to provide many details on Hill and his family in this comprehensive article.

304.———. "Reflections: John Hill, Engraver in Aquatint." *Imprint* 4, no. 1 (April 1979): 13–19, 32.

Richard Koke summarizes the career of John Hill, the Anglo-American aquatint specialist, who created some of the most memorable prints of American scenery. Koke describes the process used by Hill and his major works (including some executed in London) pointing out Hill's contribution to the popularization of landscape as an American art form.

305. Shelley, Donald A. "William Guy Wall and His Water Colors for the Historic *Hudson River Portfolio*." *New-York Historical Society Quarterly* 31 (January 1947): 25–45.

Wall made the watercolors which John Hill engraved and aquatinted for the *Hudson River Portfolio*, one of the most significant books of American landscape published in the nineteenth century. His biography is meticulously reconstructed through newspaper notices and city directories, and his technique analyzed. The original watercolors are examined in detail and catalogued, including unpublished ones and those not owned by The New-York Historical Society. This is an important article for an understanding of John Hill's art because it allows a comparison to be made between the watercolors and the aquatints.

306. Sparling, Tobin Andrews. *American Scenery. The Art of John & John William Hill.* New York: New York Public Library, 1984. 23 pp.

John Hill and his son documented the changing and diverse topography of the United States for an expanding audience. The elder Hill focused on landscapes while his son focused on the urban scene. The checklist contains brief notes on the fifty-two prints exhibited.

307. Weitenkampf, Frank. "John Hill and American Landscapes." *American Collector* 17 (July 1948): 6–8.

Weitenkampf credits Hill with encouraging the interest in landscape in America through the use of the aquatint process, one particularly suited to the reproduction of watercolor and wash drawings. Before Hill's time the process was used only sporadically. This article, although not as thorough as Koke's *Checklist*, accords Hill a place among the artists of his time, and emphasizes the dominant techniques in American art in the second and third decades of the nineteenth century. It also indicates the part played by magazines in popularizing landscape prints and is the best general survey of American aquatints.

308. Koehler, Sylvester R. "J. Henry Hill." *American Art Review* 1, no. 2 (1880): 429–30.

A grandson of the aquatint specialist John Hill, John Henry Hill (1839–1922) was an American representative of the pre-Raphaelite movement in the 1860s. The first of his etchings appeared in his *Sketches from Nature* (1867). A number of his later plates were reproductions of his father's work and of Turner's paintings. He was influenced in part by the *Liber Studiorum*. Several of his finest etchings are listed here. Unlike many of his contemporaries, he worked with painstaking attention to detail and had an affinity for aquatint, which was rare in the last decades of the nineteenth century.

309. Finlay, Nancy. "The Hermit of Phantom Island: John Henry Hill's Etchings of Lake George" in *Adirondack Prints and Printmakers: The Call of the Wild*, 105–124. editor Caroline Mastin Welsh. Blue Mountain Lake and Syracuse, N.Y.: Adirondack Museum and Syracuse University Press, 1998. illus.

Finlay summarizes depictions of Lake George in the century prior to the residence of John Henry Hill in the 1870s. The son of a landscape artist who accompanied Ebenezer Emmons on a geological expedition in 1840, Hill first traveled to the region in 1867. From 1870 to 1876 or 1877, he lived in a cabin on Phantom Island. His illustrated diary (at the Adirondack Museum) from that period is filled with details of his daily life, his working methods, and his efforts to market his prints, eight of which describe Lake George. Finlay describes each of these prints relying on the diary to provide the context for each and concludes her essay by summarizing the rest of Hill's life.

310. Hitchings, Sinclair H. "Samuel Hill's Relief Engraving." *Printing and Graphic Arts* 8 (March 1960): 12–20.

Although best known for his copperplate engravings, it is evident in the correspondence between Isaiah Thomas and Ebenezer Andrews, and in other contemporary accounts, that Samuel Hill also produced relief cuts. One headpiece in Thomas's folio Bible was signed by Hill, and Hitchings speculates on his activities in this branch of engraving.

311. Shadwell, Wendy. "An Attribution for His Excellency and Lady Washington." *Antiques* 95 (February 1969): 240–41.

The author attributes two unsigned contemporary mezzotints of George and Martha Washington to Joseph Hiller, Sr. (1748–1814), earlier attributed by Charles Hart to Charles Willson Peale.

312.———. "Hancock by Hiller." *Imprint* 7, no. 1 (1982): 43–44.

This brief article notes the discovery of a second impression of Joseph Hiller's portrait of John Hancock at the New-York Historical Society, a print previously attributed to John B. Forrest (ca. 1814–1870). The impression of the portrait at the New-York Historical Society is the first state; the impression at the Peabody Essex Museum is the second state. Since another, privately owned, impression of the second state was on exhibition at the New York Public Library in 1928, Shadwell suggests that another impression is lurking in a collection somewhere.

313. Hart, Charles H. "An Etched Profile Portrait of Washington by Joseph Hiller, 1794." *Essex Institute Historical Collections* 43 (January 1907): 1–6.

Hart comments on a profile portrait of Washington by Joseph Hiller, Jr. (1777–1795), of Salem, Massachusetts. Dated 1794, the portrait appears on the backs of playing cards. The print was evidently made to be sent to England and copied as a seal. Hart discusses several impressions of the portrait, its style, and its derivation from an engraving by Joseph Wright; and briefly outlines the life of Jospeh Hiller, Jr.

314. Worman, Eugene C., Jr. "The Watercolors and Prints of Orra White Hitchcock." *Antiquarian Bookman* 83, no. 7 (13 February 1989):

Born in Amherst, Mass., Hitchcock (1796–1863) provided a number of sketches for works published by her husband Edward. In Deerfield she taught science and art. Some of her work remains at Deerfield Academy; some drawings survive in the Amherst College Archives. Most of her illustrations were done for her husband's publications on the geology of Massachusetts and other similar works.

315. Balge-Crozier, Marjorie P. "Through the Eyes of the Artist: Another Look at Winslow Homer's *Sharpshooter*." *Imprint* 21, no. 1 (1996): 2–10.

This essay takes a fresh look at one of Winslow Homer's (1836–1910) designs reproduced in the 15 November 1862 issue of *Harper's Weekly*. The author provides a synopsis of other visual works depicting sharpshooters and discusses the image in terms of its vision and different levels of meaning. The image is of particular importance because Homer used this subject for his first oil painting.

316. Beam, Philip C. *Winslow Homer's Magazine Engravings*. New York: Harper & Row, 1979. x, 274 p., index, biblio.

The volume includes a biographical sketch of the artist focusing on his activities as an illustrator before 1876. Other chapters discuss subjects and themes, compositions, processes and techniques, and the economics of Homer's work as an illustrator. The illustrations are listed chronologically and all (220) are reproduced. Beam relates many of Homer's illustrations to his paintings and watercolors.

317. Davis, Elliot Bostwick. "American Drawing Books and Their Impact on Winslow Homer." *Winterthur Portfolio* 31, no. 2/3 (1996): 141–163.

Using Homer's watercolor, *The Blackboard*, as a point of departure, Davis explores the influence of drawing manuals on Homer's early drawings and watercolors. One book used by students in the Cambridge (Mass.) High School was an American edition of Francoeur's *Introduction to Linear Drawing*. The geometric shapes in *The Blackboard* are possibly derived from the drawing book. Homer would have been exposed to other drawing manuals during his apprenticeship with John H. Bufford in Boston between 1855 and 1857. Davis also reveals the impact of drawing manuals on other artists in this well-argued and annotated essay.

318. Engel, Charlene. "'For Those in Peril on the Sea': The Intaglio Prints of Winslow Homer." *Print Review* 20 (1985): 23–40.

Engel relates the etchings of the 1880s to the illustrations of the 1860s and 1870s in terms of subject matter and contrasts them to the 'fine' prints of Whistler and others. Although related to paintings of the 1880s, these are not reproductive prints. The marine etchings relate to his work at Cullercoats on the North Sea and at Atlantic City. The etchings sold so poorly that he abandoned printmaking in 1889.

319. Fernandez, Rafael. "Winslow Homer, Printmaker" in *Winslow Homer in the Clark Collection*, 14–17. Alexandra R. Murphy. Williamstown: Sterling and Francine Clark Art Institute, 1986.

This overview of Homer's print oeuvre touches on the lithographs made for the Bufford firm and his work as an illustrator. Fernandez focuses on etchings by Homer and his work with George G. H. Ritchie, a New York printmaker who printed Homer's early prints. Christian Klackner, a New York dealer, served as a dealer for Homer's etchings and also published photogravures after his paintings. The etchings did not sell well and Homer abandoned the medium. He did, however, collaborate with Louis Prang in the production of two chromolithographs in the 1890s. A representative sample of the illustrations and prints are reproduced in the catalog.

320. Foster, Allen Everts. *Checklist of Illustrations by Winslow Homer in* Harper's Weekly *and Other Periodicals*. New York: New York Public Library, 1936. 13 pp.

This list, based in part on E.P. Richardson's list, adds illustrations which appeared in *Appleton's Journal*, *Ballou's Pictorial Drawing Room*, *Every Saturday*, *The Galaxy*, *Harper's Bazaar*, *Our Young Folks*, *Riverside Magazine*, and *Scribner's Monthly*. Reprinted from *The Bulletin of the New York Public Library* (Oct. 1936).

321. Gardner, Albert Ten Eyck. *Winslow Homer, American Artist: His World and His Work*. New York: Clarkson N. Potter, 1961. 263 pp., chronology, biblio., indexes.

As Homer's biography has been ably written by Lloyd Goodrich, Gardner prefers to approach the artist's work by examining it in its historical and artistic context rather than duplicating Goodrich's information. This interpretive approach is well suited to the discussion of Homer's style and provides illuminating information in the chapters on the art worlds of Boston and New York, on Homer's illustrations, and on his etchings.

322. Gelman, Barbara ed. *The Wood Engravings of Winslow Homer*. New York: Bounty Books, 1969. 204 pp.

The short introduction comments on the circumstances that took Homer to New York, where he worked for twenty years as a wood engraver. Technical aspects of wood engraving and Homer's stylistic development are among the topics analyzed. An excellent list of 284 of the artist's engravings, chronologically arranged, follows the introduction.

323. Grossman, Julia N. *Echo of a Distant Drum: Winslow Homer and the Civil War*. New York: Harry N. Abrams, Inc., 1974. 204 pp., biblio.

As a pictorial reporter for *Harper's Weekly* during the Civil War, Winslow Homer came of age artistically. Grossman surveys this very important aspect of Homer's oeuvre integrating sketches, drawings, and paintings with the wood engravings published during the first hal of the 1860s. The nearly two hundred reproductions, many in color, are superb.

324. Manning, Kathleen. "Winslow Homer's Wood Engravings." *Imprint* 2, no. 1 (1977): 11–12.

Homer's designs, as published in *Ballou's Pictorial* and *Harper's Weekly*, were wood engravings. Manning mentions the use of metal casts from the wood engraved blocks required by the large editions of these magazines. Some information is specifically directed at collectors of wood engravings.

325. Mather, Frank Jewett. "Winslow Homer as a Book Illustrator." *Princeton University Library Chronicle* 1 (November 1939): 15–32.

In addition to listing seventy-five illustrations found in twenty-four books, Mather discusses Homer's style and the possible influence English illustrators had upon it. Since sketches for most of Homer's illustrations do not exist, the author comes to the conclusion that he drew directly on the block of wood.

326. McCausland, Elizabeth. "Winslow Homer—Graphic Artist." *Prints* 7 (April 1937): 214–20.

This critic wishes more attention would be paid to the aesthetic value of Homer's illustrations and their place in the American tradition. She emphasizes his acute powers of observation and praises his innate sense of form and composition.

327. Museum of Graphic Art. *The Graphic Art of Winslow Homer*. New York: 1968. 136 pp.

This exhibition catalog with contributions by Lloyd Goodrich and Donald H. Karshan is a complete presentation of Homer's graphic art. Included are all of his etchings, the most important lithographs, many wood engravings, and related sketches and oils. The introduction traces Homer's career as a graphic artist, from his apprenticeship to the lithographer John H. Bufford, through his work for *Ballou's Pictorial Drawing-Room Companion*, and *Harper's Weekly*, for which he stopped working in 1874. The illustrations include all the material in the exhibition, and the catalog of prints is carefully prepared. A biographical chronology, a list of exhibitions featuring Homer's graphic works, and a bibliography complete this book.

328. Ormsbee, Thomas Hamilton. "Winslow Homer, Artist War Correspondent." *American Collector* 13 (September 1944): 6–7, 20.

Many illustrations of the Civil War, published in the pictorial weeklies of the nineteenth century, are of little historical or artistic interest. An exception to this lackluster body of work is the work of Winslow Homer, who created sympathetic sketches of the life of the soldiers. Ormsbee writes about Homer's experiences during the war years and mentions the titles and dates of wood engravings that appeared in *Harper's Weekly*.

329. Rash, Nancy. "A Note on Winslow Homer's *Veteran in a New Field* and Union Victory." *American Art* 9, no. 2 (June 1995): 88–93.

Rash relates Homer's painting depicting a veteran reaping wheat in a field to the imagery on patriotic envelopes issued during the Civil War, several of which associated wheat with the Union. The importance of wheat as an iconographical symbol adds additional meaning to the painting.

330. Richardson, Edgar P. "Winslow Homer's Drawings in *Harper's Weekly*." *Art in America* 19 (December 1930): 38–47.

From 1858 to 1875, Homer contributed about one hundred drawings, chronologically listed at the end of the article, to *Harper's Weekly*. Richardson emphasizes Homer's interest in his subjects, noting that his illustrations have a timeless quality that transcends their narrative content. This sensitive analysis of a large body of work goes beyond a simple biographical approach.

331. Rudd, Eric. "Winslow Homer and *Mr. Hardy Lee, His Yacht*." *Antiques* 106 (November 1974): 844–51.

Rudd proposes that the lithographs for *Mr. Hardy Lee, His Yacht* were made by Winslow Homer after drawings furnished to him by Stedman in 1857. His proof, however, is inconclusive.

332. Sherman, Frederic Fairchild. "Winslow Homer's Book Illustrations." *Art in America* 25 (October 1937): 173–74.

For fifteen years after the Civil War, Homer not only made drawings for *Harper's Weekly*, but simultaneously worked for James T. Fields, Roberts Bros. of Boston, D. Appleton Co. of New York, and other book publishers producing illustrations. The author has compiled a list of eleven books illustrated by Homer, but more recent research has added more.

333. Smith College Museum of Art. *Winslow Homer: Illustrator*. Northampton: 1951. 66 pp.

In the foreword, H. R. Hitchcock discusses the formation of the Smith College collection of Homer's illustrations, and the relationship between Homer and his European and American contemporaries. "Winslow Homer's America, 1860–1874," by Daniel Aaron, briefly touches on the rural life Homer attempted to capture in his illustrations. Mary Bartlett Cowdrey's short essay on the artist as an illustrator concentrates on his biography, activities as an artist, style, the relationship between some of the oils and wood engravings, and the engraver who cut the blocks. The major portion of the exhibition consisted of wood engravings from books and periodicals, but original sketches, watercolors, and paintings were included. The catalog is well arranged and illustrated, and the bibliography is very useful for the study of Homer's watercolors and drawings.

334. Tatham, David. *Winslow Homer and the Illustrated Book*. Syracuse: Syracuse University Press, 1992. 384 pp., biblio., index.

Tatham's research on Winslow Homer has spanned more than two decades. This definitive work focuses on Homer as a book illustrator. An introductory chapter on illustration in the industrial age is followed by chapters on illustrations for various genres: children's books, fiction, poetry, and history. The final section assesses the artist's final years in Maine as well as examines basic assumptions that can be made about Homer: his drawing was dynamic, definitive, and filled with commentary. He went beyond mere transcription of nature. Following the text are reproductions of most of his published illustrations and some drawings that relate to them.

335.———. *Winslow Homer in the 1880s. Watercolors, Drawings, and Etchings*. Syracuse: Everson Museum of Art, 1983. 32 pp.

In the 1880s, Winslow Homer produced a remarkable number of watercolors that sold well and experimented with etching. A section of this exhibition catalog is devoted to his etchings, some based on his oils, but thoroughly reworked. Although Homer hoped these prints would sell well, they did not and he abandoned the medium. Tatham relates these prints to Homer's other works of the decade, providing much background on them.

336.———. *Winslow Homer. Prints from Harper's Weekly*. Hamilton, N.Y.: Gallery Association of New York State, 1979. 14 pp.

The essay for this exhibition catalog summarizes all that is known about Homer's illustrations for *Harper's Weekly* created from 1857 to 1875. More than 130 illustrations by Homer were published in the pages of that popular weekly magazine that enjoyed a circulation of over 100,000 copies by 1860. Tatham's description of the technical processes that made these large runs possible includes useful information on electrotypes. Once the electrotypes were made, the wood engraved blocks were planed and reused.

337.———. "Some Apprentice Lithographs of Winslow Homer: Ten Pictorial Pages for Sheet Music." *Old-Time New England* 59 (1969): 87–104.

Among Homer's earliest lithographs were title pages for sheet music published in Boston by John H. Bufford. The author identifies the sheets drawn by Homer, the sequence of their production, and their inspiration. A checklist is appended.

338.———. "Some Newly Discovered Book Illustrations by Winslow Homer." *Antiques* 90, no. 6 (1976): 1262–1266.

In a further attempt to document Homers' formative years as an artist, Tatham discusses three books containing illustrations by Homer: *Hunter's Ottawa Scenery*; and two books for children, *The Hillside Farm* and *The Story* of *Our Darling Nellie*, all published in the 1850's. Homer's participation in these publications is well documented and a list of the illustrations is appended to the article.

339.———. "Winslow Homer's Adirondack Prints" in *Adirondack Prints and Printmakers: The Call of the Wild*, 125–137. editor Caroline Mastin Welsh. Blue Mountain Lake and Syracuse, N.Y.: Adirondack Museum and Syracuse University Press, 1998.

Homer visited the Adirondacks over twenty times from 1870 to 1910. In the 1870s five of his drawings were reproduced as wood engravings in popular magazines. Tatham analyzes these works thoroughly, setting them in the context of Homer's paintings and in the context of life in the Adirondacks. In 1889, Homer etched a plate, *Fly Fishing, Saranac Lake, 1889*, that is related to a watercolor, *Fly Fishing, Saranac Lake*. Tatham points out that the title is probably a misnomer, since Homer is not known to have been at Saranac Lake, but was probably done at Mink Pond, where he worked frequently.

340.———. "Winslow Homer's *Arguments of the Chivalry*." *American Art Journal* 5 (May 1973): 86–89.

Homer produced a lithograph, *Arguments of the Chivalry*, in response to the caning of Charles Sumner by Preston Brooks on May 22, 1856, in the United States Senate. Tatham provides the necessary historical background and speculates on the reasons behind the aborted publication of the lithograph.

341.———. "Winslow Homer in the Mountains." *Appalachia* (June 1966): 73–90.

Tatham describes Homer's trips to the White Mountains and the Adirondacks in the late 1860s and the 1870s, which provided him with visual material for several woodcuts and paintings, several of which are illustrated.

342.———. "Winslow Homer's Lithographic Portraits for Abner Morse's Genealogies." *Antiques* 106 (November 1974): 871–75.

This article adds seventeen signed lithographs and eight others attributable to Homer to the approximately two dozen the artist is known to have produced while at Bufford's shop. All twenty-five of the new plates appeared in genealogical studies written and published by Abner Morse in Boston between 1855 and 1857.

343.———. "Winslow Homer as a Book Illustrator: Further Notes." *Imprint* 22, no. 1 (March 1997): 25–26.

Tatham's *Winslow Homer and the Illustrated Book* was published in 1992. This brief note adds two additional books to Homer's oeuvre: *The White Rabbit and Other Stories from Robin-Wood* (Boston, 1857) and *Poetical Works of John Greenleaf Whitter* (Boston, 1871).

344. Weitenkampf, Frank. "The Intimate Homer." *Art Quarterly* 6 (1943): 306–321.

Weitenkampf points out that while much has been written on Homer's paintings and on his illustrations for *Harper's*, among other weeklies, little has appeared about his sketches, many of which are in the Cooper-Hewitt Museum in New York. The author analyzes many of the war and genre sketches that Homer drew both for *Harper's* and for his own paintings.

345.———. "Winslow Homer and the Wood Block." *Bulletin of the New York Public Library* 36 (November 1932): 731–36.

This is the earliest extended comment on Homer's illustrations for *Harper's Weekly* and other publications. Weitenkampf writes about the changes in Homer's style as a draughtsman, comparing Homer to his contemporaries who also furnished drawings for the illustrated magazines.

346. Weller, Allen. "Winslow Homer's Drawings in *Harper's Weekly*." *Art in America* 22 (March 1934): 76–78.

The author adds eight pictures that appeared in *Harper's Weekly* from 1860 to 1862 to the list of Homer's drawings compiled by E.P. Richardson. Weller attributes an additional eight or ten drawings on the basis of biographical information.

347.———. "Winslow Homer's Early Illustrations." *The American Magazine of Art* 28 (July 1935): 412–17, 448.

The author feels the study of Homer's illustrations for *Harper's Weekly* reveals a new aspect of his personality. His Civil War drawings and his seven-month stay in Paris in 1867 receive special mention. Weller maintains that the visit to Paris did not affect his style greatly, except for the subtle change caused by his exposure to Japanese prints. His drawings after 1870 reveal a more painterly approach to problems of reproducing tone, space, and atmosphere. Homer was not sentimental in his depiction of New England life, in contrast to some of his contemporaries.

348. Wilmerding, John. *Winslow Homer*. New York: Praeger, 1972. 224 pp., biblio., index.

In the first two chapters, Wilmerding concerns himself with Homer's apprenticeship as a lithographer and analyzes his engravings for *Harper's*. The author compares the objectivity of Homer's work to that of war photographs taken by men like Mathew Brady. Most of the volume, however, is devoted to Homer's paintings.

349. Wilson, Christopher Kent. "Winslow Homer's *Thanksgiving Day—Hanging Up the Musket*." *American Art Journal* 18, no. 4 (1986): 76–83.

The first national Thanksgiving Day was proclaimed by President Andrew Johnson on October 28, 1865. Winslow Homer designed a poignant illustration for *Frank Leslie's Illustrated Newspaper* that appeared in the issue of December 23, 1865, showing a man putting his musket above the parlor mantel in the presence of his wife and an older man. Wilson provides a thorough analysis of the meanings of this image relating it to the end of the Civil War and to images by other artists celebrating the end of the war. There are also religious overtones to the print because of the scenes on the Dutch tiles surrounding the fireplace opening.

350. Wood, Peter H., and Karen C.C. Dalton. *Winslow Homer's Images of Blacks. The Civil War and Reconstruction Years*. Austin: University of Texas, 1988. 144 pp.

This catalog was published to accompany a major exhibition mounted by the Menil Collection, Houston, in 1988–89. The text includes a foreword by Walter Hopps, an introduction by Richard J. Powell, "Winslow Homer, Afro-Americans, and the 'New Order of Things,'" and a major essay by Dalton and Wood on Homer's images of African Americans during the Civil War and Reconstruction. They explore the historical context of his work with respect to race relations and examine connections between his work and the popular press. The checklist of the exhibition is followed by a chronology of Homer, 1850–79, focusing on his works depicting African Americans. A list of works depicting African Americans in the same period by American and foreign artists follows.

351. Zalesch, Saul E. "Against the Current: Anti-Modern Images in the Work of Winslow Homer." *American Art Review* 5, no. 5 (September 1993): 120–125.

Zalesch focuses on Homer's iconography—the "mythic rugged Yankee individualist"—chosen because of his fear of industrialization and commercialization of American life after the Civil War. Among the images discussed are Homer's designs for wood engravings that appeared in *Harper's Weekly*. Homer could mix art and journalism in that medium, but not in paintings for individual patrons. This explanation for Homer's nostalgia is convincing and well documented.

352. Bolton, Theodore. "American Book Illustrators: A Checklist, Augustus Hoppin." *Publisher's Weekly* 140 (20 September 1941): 1, 162–63.

This checklist of Hoppin's (1828–1896) book illlustrations is arranged by title; included in each entry is information on the author, imprint, and number of illustrations.

353. Hogarth, Paul. *Arthur Boyd Houghton*. London: Gordon Fraser, 1981. 143 pp., biblio., index.

Houghton (1826–75) was a British painter, illustrator, and caricaturist who visited America in 1869 and 1870. His travels took him to New York City, the Shaker Village in Lebanon Springs, New York, Boston, and the West. The resulting sketches were published in the *Graphic* as the series "Graphic America." Hogarth's text provides an excellent overview of Houghton's life with four chapters devoted to the American work. A select list of works in public collections (including American institutions) and a partial list of works illustrated by him are very useful.

354. "Early American Artists and Mechanics: No.1–Nathaniel Hurd." *New England Magazine* (July 1832): 1–7.

This article on the Boston colonial engraver Nathaniel Hurd (1730–1777) begins with a survey of the history of engraving, then proceeds to a biography of the artist. Several of Hurd's engravings (the caricature of Seth Hudson, the bookplate for Harvard, and the small portrait of Joseph Sewell) are described, and an engraving of the Boston Massacre is misattributed to him. Curiously, the author of this sketch calls the portraits produced in England of Pitt, Wolfe, Amherst, and others "miserable productions.".

355. French, Hollis. *Jacob Hurd and His Sons Nathaniel & Benjamin: Silversmiths 1702–1781.* Cambridge, Mass.: Walpole Society, 1939. 148 pp.

Much of the silver of Jacob Hurd and his sons is still extant. Nathaniel also engraved bookplates and prints which are well described in this volume. French devotes an entire chapter to the approximately fifty-five bookplates.

356. Phillips, John Marshall. "An Unrecorded Engraving by Nathaniel Hurd." *Yale University Bulletin* 7 (June 1936): 26–27.

This brief note describes and illustrates an engraved compass dial by Hurd which contains a small vignette view of the lighthouse in Boston Harbor.

357. Carbonell, John. "Anthony Imbert, New York's Pioneer Lithographer" in *Prints and Printmakers of New York State, 1825–1940*, 11–41. ed. David F. Tatham. 277 pp. Syracuse: Syracuse University Press, 1986.

Born in 1794 or 1795 in France, Imbert arrived in New York probably around 1824. Carbonell provides an excellent summary of Imbert's earlier life in France and the beginnings of commercial lithography in New York in the early 1820s. Many of Imbert's early prints are documented in contemporary newspapers and Carbonell has made excellent use of those sources. Imbert tried to publish fine framing prints; these did not sell well so he issued sheet music, caricatures, and small prints suitable for "scrap books and tables." Carbonell discusses the sheet music and caricature production since they were such important parts of Imbert's print publishing business. He concludes by comparing the output of the Pendleton firm in Boston with Imbert's in New York. Imbert died in 1834.

358. Bolton, Theodore. "Henry Inman, an Account of His Life and Work." *Art Quarterly* 3 and Supp. 3 (1940): 353–57; 401–418.

Although this study concentrates on Inman's (1801–1846) oil paintings, mention is made of his activities in Philadelphia from 1831 to 1834 when he published lithographs in partnership with Cephas G. Childs. A supplement includes a list of portraits based on Bolton's own list, published in *Creative Art* (Feb. 1933). The list includes 168 oil portraits, as well as some figure compositions, landscapes, and miniatures.

359. Sherman, Frederic Fairchild. *Richard Jennys, New England Portrait Painter*. Springfield, Mass.: 1941. 96 pp.

The focus of this series of notes on Richard Jennys is his portrait painting. In the mid-1760s, however, he executed mezzotint portraits of the Reverend Jonathan Mayhew and of Nathaniel Hurd. Apart from these, Jennys worked entirely in oil, and this volume is devoted to that aspect of his work.

360. Rice, Foster Wild. "Nathaniel Jocelyn, Painter and Engraver: 1796–1881." *American Collector* 16 (December 1947): 6–9.

Jocelyn's work as an engraver is only briefly noted in this study, which concentrates on his portraits. Some of his early papers and diary notes are preserved at the Connecticut Historical Society.

361. Sherman, Frederic Fairchild. "Nathaniel Jocelyn, Engraver and Portrait Painter." *Art in America* 18 (August 1930): 251–58.

Jocelyn, along with Tisdale, Danforth, Doolittle, Buell and Reed, was a copperplate engraver in Connecticut during the first decades of the nineteenth century. In partnership with Danforth, he founded the National Bank Note Engraving Company. Sherman's study concentrates on Jocelyn's painted portraits, for he appears to have given up engraving about the age of twenty-seven.

362. Fales, Martha Gandy. "An Unrecognized Portland Engraver." *Old-Time New England* 57 (1967): 77–79.

This article concerns two engravings by David G. Johnson (1796–1881), previously known for his work in New York in the 1830s and 1840s, that he produced during his residence in Portland, Maine, from December of 1824 until 1830. Other of his Portland works have since come to light and are described by Earle G. Shettleworth in an article, "Portland, Maine, Engravers of the 1820s," *Old-Time New England* 61: 59–65, 105–110.

363. Kaskell, Joan Macy. "Eastman Johnson, Lithographer." *Imprint* 22, no. 1 (1997): 11–15.

The author, descended from Eastman Johnson, writes about a small group of portrait lithographs by Johnson (1824–1906), who was better known as a genre painter. Executed before he was thirty years old, the portrait prints depict members of the Folsom family and are now in the collection of the Metropolitan Museum of Art. Johnson did one later lithograph, *Marguerite*, issued about 1860.

364. Brigham, Clarence S. "David Claypoole Johnston, the American Cruikshank." *Proceedings of the American Antiquarian Society* 50 (April 1940): 98–110.

Among the collections of the American Antiquarian Society is a number of Johnston's letters, drawings, copperplates, watercolors, and prints. Johnston's arrival in Boston coincided with the opening of the Pendleton shop, and from that point on his output was prolific. Brigham mentions specific prints and summarizes the artist's work. Several letters to Johnston are quoted which provide a contemporary view of his career. The article finishes with mention of Johnston's children and their artistic achievements.

365. Johnson, Malcolm. *David Claypoole Johnston: American Graphic Humorist, 1798–1865*. Boston and Worcester, Mass.: American Antiquarian Society, Boston College, Boston Public Library, Worcester Art Museum, 1970. 47 pp.

The introduction contains a sketch of Johnston's life, with emphasis on a chonological discussion of his works. The catalog contains 235 items appearing in the exhibition including drawings, etchings, engravings, watercolors, oil paintings, lithographs, book illustrations, pictures collected by Johnston, and personal effects. Johnston is one of the best documented of American graphic artists. In the 1930s his descendents sold much material to Harvard and the American Antiquarian Society, although some items remained in the family.

366.———. *Great Locofoco Juggernaut, a New Console-a-tyory Sub-Treasury Rag-Monster: A Cartoon Bank Note by D.C. Johnston*. Barre, Mass.: Imprint Society, 1971. 36 pp., biblio.

A biographical sketch of D.C. Johnston, as well as a short history of the events leading to the bank crisis of the mid-1830s is provided. The imagery of the bank note is explained, and the volume contains a restrike from the original plate.

367.———. "David Claypoole Johnston: The American Cruikshank." *Antiques* 102 (July 1972): 101–107.

The author summarizes Johnston's career emphasizing his political and social caricatures.

368. Sullivan, John. "The Case of a 'Late Student:' Pictorial Satire in Jacksonian America." *Proceedings of the American Antiquarian Society* 83 (October 1973): 277–86.

The author draws upon contemporary newspaper accounts and letters to explain and date two lithographed caricatures of Duff Green, Russell Jarvis, and Daniel Webster by David Claypoole Johnston.

369.———. "Jackson Caricatured: Two Historical Errors." *Tennessee Historical Quarterly* 31 (March 1972): 39–44.

Sullivan writes about two of David Claypoole Johnston's political cartoons (*Symptoms of a Locked Jaw* and *Richard the III*) and correctly places them in their historical contexts. They were incorrectly dated by Frank Weitenkampf in his *Political Caricature in the United States in Separately Published Cartoons* (New York: New York Public Library, 1952), and Sullivan has corrected the errors through careful research in contemporary newspapers.

370. Tatham, David. *A Note About David Claypoole Johnston with a Checklist of His Book Illustrations*. Syracuse, N.Y.: Syracuse University Library Associates, 1970. 16 pp.

Tatham concentrates on the book illustrations designed and/or executed by Johnston, an artist, caricaturist, and illustrator, between 1819 and 1861. The introductory essay first appeared in *The Courier* (Spring 1970: 11–17). The checklist appeared in *The Courier* (Summer 1970: 26–31), and is the most complete compilation of his book illustrations, many of which were satirical.

371.———. "David Claypoole Johnston's *Militia Muster*." *American Art Journal* 19, no. 2 (1987): 4–15.

Tatham discusses the series of militia watercolors and prints by Johnston in terms of composition and cultural context. It was a theme that Johnston worked on from 1819 to 1862 and one of interest to other artists as well.

372.———. "David Claypoole Johnston's Theatrical Portraits" in *American Portrait Prints*, 162–193. ed. Wendy Wick Reaves. Washington: National Portrait Gallery, 1984.

Between 1821 and 1837, Johnston produced about thirty portrait prints of actors, the most important body of such prints produced in America at that time. Tatham summarizes Johnston's career in the theater and discusses the subjects of the prints. Because of Johnston's own interest in the theater, Tatham concludes that many of these prints are the artist's finest, aesthetically pleasing and powerful. A checklist of the prints follows the essay, including locations of prints in public collections.

373.———. "D.C. Johnston's Satiric views of Art in Boston, 1815–1850" in *Art and Commerce*, 9–24. Boston: Museum of Fine Arts, 1978.

After a brief overview of Johnston's career, Tatham focuses on this artist's social satire in general. Johnston's notions were anti-elitist and humor was an important tool for him. The place of the fine arts in a democracy was a theme that he explored and Tatham describes Johnston's prints and watercolors of the Muses and other subjects dealing with artists. Portrait artists, connoisseurs, panoramas, and satires on specific works of art are among the topics that Johnston satirized. One political print, the *Exhibition of Cabinet Pictures* is thoroughly analyzed.

374. Wood, Marcus. "The Influence of English Radical Satire on Nineteenth-Century American Print Satire: David Claypool Johnston's *The House That Jeff Built*." *Harvard Library Bulletin* 10, no. 1 (March 1999): 43–67.

Wood chooses *The House That Jeff Built* to demonstrate the impact that British satirical print production had on American practice. He examines the roots of this print that include a 1785 British print, *The House That Jack Built*, relating to the American Revolution; Thomas Rowlandson's *This is the House that Jack Built* of 1809; and Edward Williams Clay's *This is the House that Jack Built* of 1840. Wood describes pamphlet satires as well. He concludes that American printmakers adapted English print satire to local requirements.

375. Coburn, Frederick W. "The Johnstons of Boston." *Art in America* 21; 22 (December 1932 and October 1933): 27–36; 132–38.

Coburn attempts to unravel problematic attributions of art works to members of the artistically inclined Johnston family of Boston. For instance, a mezzotint likeness of Increase Mather was once attributed to Thomas Johnston of Boston. Relying on Murdock's monograph on the portraits of Increase Mather, Coburn proposes another Thomas Johnston, an Englishman, as the engraver, and then proceeds to a detailed and scholarly examination of the Boston engraver. Coburn concludes that Bayley and Goodspeed, in their edition of William Dunlap's *A History of the Rise and Progress of the Arts of Design in the United States*, have probably attributed far too much of the artistic production of the first half of the eighteenth century in Boston to members of the Johnston family.

376. Hitchings, Sinclair H. "Thomas Johnston" in *Boston Prints and Printmakers, 1670–1775*, 83–132. Boston: Colonial Society of Massachusetts, 1973.

In this outstanding work that traces Johnston's career through an examination of contemporary records, Hitchings includes an extensive bibliographical note on manuscripts of and about Johnston (ca. 1708–1767) and other members of his artistically talented family. The inventory of Johnston's estate is printed in full; all of the known engravings are described and illustrated, as well as several that are attributed to him, and those for which records exist but are no longer extant. Johnston's other pursuits—japanner, interior decorator, and organ builder—are also mentioned. Biographical information about his children is noted.

377. Wroth, Lawrence C. "The Thomas Johnston Maps of the Kennebec Purchase." in *In Tribute to Fred Anthoensen, Master Printer*, 77–107. Portland, Me.: 1952.

This study of the maps engraved by Johnston as a result of the controversy between the Town of Brunswick and the Proprietors of the Kennebec Purchase includes an excellent history of the controversy. The maps are examined in meticulous detail, and a checklist of titles of publications relative to the controversy, which took place from 1749 to 1755, is appended.

378. Koehler, Sylvester R. *Frederick Juengling*. n.p.: 1890. 12 pp.

Koehler wrote this laudatory essay on Juengling's (1846–1889) wood engravings for inclusion in an auction catalog of the artist's works. A biographical sketch is followed by a general description of his artistic endeavors, a character sketch, and a discussion of the wood engraving controversy. Koehler laments that few collectors regarded his work seriously, but mentions that an excellent collection of Juengling's prints is in the Museum of Fine Arts, Boston.

379.———. "Frederick Juengling Und Der Moderne Holzstich." *Zeitschrift Fur Bildende Kunst* (1891): 81–90; 112–22.

This article includes a detailed explanation of Juengling's working methods in white and black line. Koehler remarks on the tendency of the New School of wood engraving to move away from line toward form and color. The first part of this article, and much of the second, concentrates on modern wood engraving and new techniques of reproduction.

380. Connecticut Historical Society. *Kellogg Prints, an Exhibition of the Work of J.G., D.W., E.B., and E.C. Kellogg, Hartford Lithographers 1830–1866*. Hartford: 1952. 36 pp.

Biographical information is provided for the four Kellogg brothers: Jarvis Griggs (1805–1873), Daniel Wright (1807–1874), Edmund Burke (1809–1872), and Elijah Chapman (1811–1881). The catalog is divided into local views, the Mexican War, examples of Yankee ingenuity, Civil War battles and cartoons, animals, patriotic prints, lithographs illustrating the songs of Robert Burns, pin-up girls, memorial prints, religious subjects, book illustrations, and deathbed scenes. The one hundred lithographs and fifteen books mentioned illustrate the broad range of subjects treated by this most prolific firm. Very helpful is the list of addresses and respective dates for the firm. The successor to the firm was still in existence when this book was published in 1952.

381. Knittle, Rhea Mansfield. "The Kelloggs, Hartford Lithographers." *Antiques* 10 (July 1926): 42–46.

Beginning with a genealogy of the Kelloggs, the author provides biographical information on those in the family who were active in the lithography firm. A selection of various prints are discussed and illustrated. The author concludes by citing the prints she favors for their "personality, vigor, and character."

382. Morgan, S. St. J. "Collection of Kellogg Prints." *Connecticut Historical Society Bulletin* 13 (October 1948): 25–32.

This brief article begins with biographical sketches of the Kelloggs and others associated with their firm. A catalog of fifty lithographs published by E.C. Kellogg is reprinted, and several books containing lithographed illustrations by the Kelloggs are mentioned.

383. Phipps, Frances. "Connecticut's Printmakers: The Kelloggs of Hartford." *Connecticut Antiquarian* 21, no. 1 (June 1969): 19–26.

Of particular interest are details drawn from an 1849 article in the *Connecticut Courant* which suggests how widely circulated the Kellogg firm's prints were and provides additional information about job printing done by the firm, including banknotes, maps, and so on. The article also notes that in 1849 twenty-five or thirty women were employed coloring lithographs. Phipps also provides dates for the many different partnerships and shop locations of the firm over its long history. This is an useful article.

384. Ramsay, John. "Old Prints: The Kelloggs." *Hobbies* 45 (May 1940): 26–27.

About 1833, D.W. Kellogg opened a lithographic establishment in Hartford, Connecticut, where he produced the first of his cheap, popular prints. His brothers followed his lead closely, producing prints of sentimental and comic scenes and portraits. The prints rarely show date of publication or the artist's name. The author records the firm's expansion to other cities, and mentions that it was Currier & Ives's major competitor.

385. Steinway, Kate. "The Kelloggs of Hartford, Connecticut's Currier & Ives." *Imprint* 13, no. 1 (1988): 2–12.

The Kellogg firm was conducted by four brothers who were active from the 1830s to the 1870s. Their output was more than 1500 prints. Steinway discusses the impact of popular lithography on American culture, the history of the firm and the brothers, the style of the prints, sources, and the relationship between Currier & Ives and the Kelloggs. An appendix includes a useful chronology of the firm with its addresses.

386. Delaney, Edmund T. K. *The Kellys. Printmakers of New York and Philadelphia (1864–1881)*. Chester, Conn.: Connecticut River Publications, 1984. 27 pp.

Among the publishers of prints in the second half of the nineteenth century were Thomas Kelly and his brother, John. This modestly produced study contains biographical information on the family, a discussion of the genres of the prints they published (portraits, historical scenes, horses, views, sentimental and religious subjects, American life, Irish subjects). Thomas Kelly withdrew from print publishing in 1881, and turned to book publishing and the dry goods and furniture business. He died in 1914. A checklist of engravings and lithographs published by John and Thomas Kelly is very useful.

387. Martin, Francis Jr. "E. W. Kemble, 1861–1933, An American Illustrator." *Private Library* 7, no. 3 (1994): 130–144.

As a graduate student, Martin developed an interest in Edward W. Kemble and later avidly collected books and drawings by Kemble. While discussing the formation of his collection, Martin provides an overview of the illustrator's career which included providing illustrations to periodicals including *St. Nicholas*, *Century*, *Life*, *New York Daily Graphic*, and *Harper's Weekly*. Kemble, of course, illustrated works for Mark Twain and Joel Chandler Harris.

388. Williams, Hermann W., Jr. "A Rare Engraving by Kensett Identified." *Antiques* 41 (January 1942): 47.

The Metropolitan Museum of Art has an unfinished engraving titled "The Studious Boy," by John F. Kensett (1816–1872) after his own copy in oil of a painting by W.S. Mount. Correspondence from Samuel P. Avery to Mount identifies the subject and dates the work in the early 1840s.

389. Bunner, H. C. *A Selection of Cartoons from 'Puck' by Joseph Keppler*. New York: Keppler & Schwarzmann, 1893. 226 pp.

Joseph Keppler (1838–1894), born in Vienna, came to the United States in 1868. Bunner describes Keppler's experiences in this country, including his establishment of *Puck* in New York in 1876 in partnership with Adolph Schwarzmann. This volume contains reproductions of fifty six cartoons by Keppler.

390. Tatham, David. "Keppler versus Beecher: Prints of the Great Brooklyn Scandal." *Imprint* 23, no. 1 (1998): 2–8.

In 1872 the Brooklyn preacher, Henry Ward Beecher, became embroiled in a scandal over an affair with the wife of Theodore Tilton, a noted journalist. The scandal remained a target of cartoonists for three years. Among the artists who contributed to the pictorial documentation of the scandal was Joseph Keppler, whose lithographs appeared in his magazine *Puck*. Tatham provides the context for these prints and discusses seven of them in detail.

391. Weitenkampf, Frank. "Keppler and Political Cartooning." *Bulletin of the New York Public Library* 42 (December 1939): 906–908.

To celebrate the centenary of Keppler's birth, the Prints Division of The New York Public Library mounted an exhibition of his satirical works. Weitenkampf comments on Keppler's background and his influence on other satirists.

392. Weber, David J. *Richard H. Kern: Expeditionary Artist in the Far Southwest, 1848–1853*. Albuquerque: University of New Mexico Press for the Amon Carter Museum, 1985. 355 pp., biblio., index.

Kern (1821–1853) accompanied four major mapping and scientific expeditions in the Southwest. Weber provides an excellent commentary on this artist's career which was cut short by his death at the hands of Indians in Colorado. A newly discovered group of watercolors by Kern (located at the Amon Carter Museum) was the impetus for this study which concludes with an excellent essay assessing the documentary value of the prints published in government reports derived from Kern's original sketches. Weber was able to compare many of the original drawings with the lithographs and he tracked a number of illustrations derived from them without acknowledgement as well.

393. Koehler, Sylvester R. "C.F. Kimball." *American Art Review* 2, no. 2 (1881): 224.

Koehler praises Charles Frederick Kimball (1835–1907), a native Maine etcher, who, by the second of the three plates he had produced when the article was written, seemed an old hand at the art.

394. "Francis Scott King." *Scribner's Magazine* 17 (March 1895): 291–92.

This anonymous article recounts King's (1850–1913) life. His three masters in wood engraving were Linton, Marsh, and the Frenchman Pannemaker. King felt that the exclusive use of wood engraving for reproductive purposes precluded its use as an expressive form of art.

395. "Elbridge Kingsley." *Scribner's Magazine* 18 (July 1895): 32–34.

In his reproductions of paintings of the Barbizon School, as well as in his original blocks, Kingsley (1842–1918) is an interpreter of nature. This summary of his career documents his shift from magazine work to the production of wood engravings in limited editions on Japan paper.

396. Mount Holyoke College. *Catalog of the Works of Elbridge Kingsley*. South Hadley: 1901. 45 pp.

Elbridge Kingsley was noted for his wood engravings from nature. Born in 1842, he apprenticed in a printing office. After formal training in New York, he turned again to printing, then worked for several commercial wood engravers: Orr, Lossing & Barrett, and Edward Sears. Eventually Kingsley came under the influence of the New School of wood engraving. The excellent introduction to this catalog describes the rest of his career, including his contacts with contemporaries. The catalog records the substantially complete collection of Kingsley's work formed by Clara Leigh Dwight. Included in the 322 entries are proofs for book and magazine illustrations, Japan proofs for "Engravings Made for an Art Purpose," miscellaneous items, and experimental plates.

397. Mann, Maybelle. "Augustus Kollner." *Imprint* 6, no. 1 (1981): 19–22.

Among Kollner's works was a series of fifty-four views of American cities published between 1848 and 1851 by Goupil, Vibert & Co. of New York and Paris. Mann provides biographical background on Kollner (ca. 1812–1906) and mentions a variety of his productions including children's books, maps, and Civil War sketches reproduced photographically. The Historical Society of Pennsylvania has an important collection of his Pennsylvania views produced in the later years of his life. The Free Library of Philadelphia also has a large collection of his drawings and sketches.

398. Wainwright, Nicholas B. "Augustus Kollner, Artist." *Pennsylvania Magazine of History and Biography* 84 (July 1960): 325–51.

Drawing upon the substantial collection of Kollner's prints in Philadelphia institutions, Wainwright presents an excellent analysis and narrative of Kollner's career as a commercial lithographer and painter. Kollner, working in the 1840s, was also one of the first etchers in Philadephia. His partnerships with other lithographers, associations with various citizens of Philadelphia, Civil War experiences, and family life are among the topics which Wainwright has fully researched.

399. Naeve, Milo M. *John Lewis Krimmel: An Artist in Federal America*. Newark: University of Delaware Press, 1985. 204 pp., index., biblio.

Krimmel (1786–1821) died of drowning at the age of thirty-five, twelve years after arriving in America. Naeve provides background on Krimmel's life in Germany and his artistic training. Krimmel joined the Society of Artists of the United States in 1811 and participated in their exhibitions and other activities. He collaborated with printmakers to reproduce his sketches and watercolors listed in the catalogue raisonne of the artist's oil paintings, watercolors, and drawings, reproductive prints, and sketchbooks. In addition to the biographical sketch of Krimmel, Naeve's introduction includes chapters on Krimmel's "Approach to his Art" and "Krimmel and

American Taste." This volume is excellent—thorough, well documented, and handsomely produced as well.

400. "Gustav Kruell: A Sketch." *Scribner's Magazine* 17 (February 1895): 186–88.

Kruell (1843–1907), who was inspired by the works of Linton, engraved an outstanding series of portraits, a genre particularly suited to his style. Much of his best work appeared in *Scribner's Magazine*. Together with his friend Frederick Juengling, Kruell organized the Society of American Wood Engravers in 1881.

401. "Kruell's Portraits." *Nation* 50 (23 January 1890): 80.

Kruell's portraits of Darwin, William Lloyd Garrison, and Wendell Phillips excited much interest at a meeting of the Century Club. The editor of the *Nation* feels that while Kruell borrowed his technique from Linton, he was able to develop it further. The portraits were hand-printed on Japan paper.

402. Smith, Ralph Clifton. *Gustav Kruell, American Portrait Engraver on Wood.* Champlain, N.Y.: W.P. Truesdell, 1929. 98 pp., biblio., index.

This volume contains a biography and an analysis of Kruell's work for American magazines. The chronological checklist of 530 items indicates the locations of the works. This is the most complete of the existing volumes on Kruell, and contains indexes by artist and portrait, and a bibliography.

403.———. "Gustav Kruell: Wood Engraver." *Print Connoisseur* 6 (January 1926): 11–27.

During the heyday of American wood engraving, Kruell, whose technique differed from those of most other engravers, was particularly noted as an engraver of portraits. *The Portfolio of National Portraits* (1899) is his crowning achievement. There is a list, with dates, of American portraits cut by Kruell, and the author has identified over five hundred blocks engraved by Kruell.

404. Beckman, Thomas. "Louis Kurz: Early Years." *Imprint* 7, no. 1 (1982): 14–25.

This thoroughly researched article covers the career of Louis Kurz (1835–1917) before he joined with Alexander Allison in 1880. Beckman discusses a number of prints designed to serve a local audience, first in Milwaukee, then in Chicago, including city views, portraits, advertisements, and sheet music covers. Of particular importance are the 52 lithographs he produced for *Chicago Illustrated* published by Jevne & Almini beginning in 1866. After the Chicago fire, Kurz returned to Milwaukee, then went back to Chicago in 1878.

405. Holzer, Harold. "Art For The Parlors of America." *Civil War Times Illustrated* 24, no. 9 (January 1986): 26–35.

The Chicago lithographer Louis Kurz published lithographs of Civil War battles that were immensely popular but had little factual content. After Lincoln's assassination, Kurz even published a print showing the bearded Lincoln returning from campaigning in 1860 although Lincoln had not grown his beard until after the election and he did not campaign for the presidency. Holzer summarizes Kurz's career beginning in the 1850s and describes many representative prints, particularly the commemorative Civil War battle scenes published in the 1880s and 1890s, and depcitions of the American Revolution and the War of 1812.

406. Hitchings, Sinclair H. "A Boston Wood Engraver of the Eighties: G.J. LaCroix." *Printing and the Graphic Arts* 5 (December 1957): 71–79.

The Milton [Mass.] Historical Society has preserved twenty-eight of George James La Croix's wood blocks executed for a town history published in 1887. A brief biography of LaCroix (1854–1892) is given and his illustrations for a variety of publications, including *The Poetical Works of Henry Wadsworth Longfellow* (Boston, 1881), are discussed.

407. Weinberg, Helene Barbara. "John La Farge, the Relation of His Illustrations to His Ideal Art." *American Art Journal* 5 (May 1973): 54–73.

La Farge (1835–1910) created many wood engravings for book and magazine illustrations in the early part of his career. A study of these prints reveals his interest in idealistic themes.

408. Weitenkampf, Frank. "John La Farge, Illustrator." *Print Collector's Quarterly* 5 (December 1915): 473–94.

In the early days of his career, La Farge provided illustrations for *Enoch Arden* (1865), Browning's poems, and *Songs From the Old Dramatists* (1873). La Farge's attitude toward illustration was shared by his friend Horace Scudder, editor of *Riverside Magazine*, a juvenille publication. Weitenkampf emphasizes La Farge's individual approach to illustration, and includes a letter from La Farge's son that describes his father's method of working on wood.

409. Cape Ann Historical Association. *Paintings and Drawings by Fitz Hugh Lane.* Gloucester, Mass.: Cape Ann Historical Association, 1974. 14 pp., 65 leaves of plates, index.

The foreword by Edward Hyde Cox describes the formation of the Lane Collection at the Cape Ann Historical Association. John Wilmerding's essay focuses on Lane's art, the development of his oil painting and his subject matter. Also described are the drawings by Lane (about 110) in the last fifteen years of Lane's career. There are 135 reproductions of his work, most of which are drawings.

410. Crossman, Carl I. "Lithographs of Fitz Hugh Lane" in *American Maritime Prints*, 63–94. ed. Elton

W. Hall. New Bedford, Mass.: The Old Dartmouth Historical Society, 1985.

Through an examination of the lithographs executed on stone by Fitz Hugh Lane, Crossman documents the transformation of a draftsman to a full-fledged artist who became capable of transferring a painting composition to the medium of lithography. Lane worked in this medium from 1832 to 1855. He was a superb draftsman and his lithographed views of towns and harbors are unparalleled.

411. Davis, Elliot Bostwick. "Fitz Hugh Lane and John Gadsby Chapman's *American Drawing Book*." *Antiques* 144, no. 5 (November 1993):

This article focuses on the lessons learned by Lane and his contemporaries from Chapman's very influential drawing book published in 1847 and other drawing manuals. It was after 1847 that Lane's marine paintings showed an understanding of perspective.

412.———. *Training the Eye and the Hand: Fitz Hugh Lane and Nineteenth-Century American Drawing Books*. Gloucester, Mass.: Cape Ann Historical Society, 1994. 40 pp., biblio.

Drawn from the author's doctoral dissertation, the exhibition catalog discusses in detail Lane's use of drawing manuals to learn the art of surveying, also a goal of drawing instruction. Lane served an apprenticeship with the Pendleton and Moore lithography firms from 1833 to 1840 when he was also exposed to a variety of instruction materials being produced by the two firms, including Thomas Edwards's *Juvenile Drawing Book or Instructions in Landscape Drawing* and John R. Smith's *Compendium of Comparative Anatomy*. Davis has made excellent use of the Lane drawings at the Cape Ann Historical Society to understand Lane's perspective so important in his panoramic views and marine prints and paintings. The catalogue includes a list of works exhibited and a bibliography.

413.———. "American Drawing Books and Their Impact on Fitz Hugh Lane" in *The Cultivation of Artists in Nineteenth-Century America*, 55–80. ed. Georgia B. Barnhill, Diana Korzenik, and Caroline F. Sloat. Worcester: American Antiquarian Society, 1997.

Davis's careful analysis of Lane's sketches and paintings suggests that he assimilated information available in contemporary drawing manuals to develop his compositions. The lessons on perspective in John Gadsby Chapman's *The American Drawing Book* of 1847 may have been particularly useful to Lane in his marine paintings. Davis suggests other books that he might have known and learned from in this thoroughly researched and informative essay.

414. Wilmerding, John. *Fitz Hugh Lane*. New York: Praeger Publishers, 1971. 203 pp.

The author combines biographical information on Lane with an analysis of his prints and paintings. The first two chapters describe Lane's work for the lithographic workshops of the Pendletons and Thomas Moore. The rest of the volume is devoted to Lane's paintings. The appendix includes a list of the lithographs by the artist. Full titles, dates, dimensions, and imprints are provided. This list expands the one found in Wilmerding's earlier book, *Fitz Hugh Lane, 1804–1865: American Marine Painter*, (Salem, Mass.: Essex Institute, 1964).

415.———. "The Lithographs of Fitz Hugh Lane." *Old-Time New England* 54 (October 1963): 30–39.

Lane began his apprenticeship in lithography with the Pendleton firm in Boston in 1832. Wilmerding discusses Lane's style and his subsequent work for the lithographers Thomas Moore and J.W.S. Scott. A few of the prints are described in detail in this excellent introduction to Lane's lithographs. The discussion is continued in other publications by Wilmerding.

416. Christy, Bayard H. "Alexander Lawson's Bird Engravings." *The Auk* 43, no. 1 (1926): 47–61.

The Academy of Natural Sciences in Philadelphia houses two scrapbooks assembled by daughters of the engraver Alexander Lawson (1773–1846), known for his engravings for Alexander Wilson's *American Ornithology*. Christy describes the engravings and Wilson's drawings in the scrapbooks, discusses the friendship between the two men, and the role that Charles Bonaparte played in continuing Wilson's work. He concludes with an assessment of Lawson's engravings as a whole.

417. Ward, Townsend. "Alexander Lawson." *Pennsylvania Magazine of History and Biography* 28 (April 1904): 204–208.

Born in Scotland, Lawson arrived in Philadelphia in 1794, where he became associated with the engravers Thackara and Vallance. He made the acquaintance of Alexander Wilson, the ornithologist, and engraved most of the plates for Wilson's *American Ornithology*. The author particularly commends these plates in a discussion of Lawson's engravings.

418. Tatham, David. "Franklin Leavitt's Pictorial Maps of the White Mountains" in *Prints of New England*, 105–134. ed. Georgia Brady Barnhill. Worcester: American Antiquarian Society, 1991.

Franklin Leavitt (1824–98) was the producer of a remarkable series of tourist maps of the White Mountains of New Hampshire between 1852 and 1888. Tatham introduces the genre of the tourist map, outlines the history of tourism in the White Mountains, describes the Willey Slide disaster which plays a role in Leavitt's maps, and then focuses on Leavitt's life and productions. Most of the maps are illustrated with vignettes of White Mountain lore and history. The Lancaster (N.H.) Historical Society has a collection of Leavitt Family

Papers, some of which describe the publication of the maps. A list of the seven maps follows the essay.

419. Hendrick, Burton J. "William James Linton." *New England Magazine* New Series 18 (April 1898): 139–57.

This article, written in a casual manner, summarizes Linton's career as revealed in his *Recollections*. Linton's Appledore Press is mentioned, but little is written about the craft. Hendrick notes that in 1898 Linton presented the only complete collection of his work to the British Museum.

420. Hopson, W. F. "Side Lights on William James Linton, 1812–1897." *Papers of the Bibliographical Society of America* 27 (1933): 74–82.

This tribute to one of the most important wood engravers of the nineteenth century furnishes little information of substance on Linton's life or art.

421. Smith, Francis Barrymore. *Radical Artisan, William James Linton, 1812–97*. Manchester, England, and Totowa, N.J.: Manchester University Press and Rowman and Littlefield, 1973. 254 pp., biblio., index.

This impeccably researched biography focuses on Linton's political activism in England and provides important insights on his training and career as a wood engraver and illustrator. Linton became a leading wood engraver in New York after his arrival in 1866 and his life in the United States is well described. Linton left a voluminous amount of manuscripts, sketches, poetry, and other memorabililia so that his life could be fully reconstructed.

422. East, Charles. "Jules Lion's New Orleans." *Georgia Review* 40, no. 4 (1986): 913–936.

Jules Lion (d.1866) was a free man of color, born in France about 1810. His lithographed and painted portraits done in New Orleans provide an important view of the people of that city. He learned lithography in Paris and arrived in New Orleans in 1836. East summarizes what is known about Lion's life, the subjects of his portraits, his work as a daguerreotypist and teacher. The Historic New Orleans Collection acquired a portfolio containing 150 of his lithographic portraits in 1970 that might have been the basis for his proposed volume on eminent Louisianians. About fifteen of the portraits are reproduced.

423. Ver Nooy, Amy. "Benson J. Lossing, Nineteenth-Century Historian and Wood Engraver." *Antiques* 93 (April 1968): 524–29.

Lossing (1813–1891) wandered throughout the American countryside recording information on American history and sketching historical landmarks. The author concentrates on Lossing's *Pictorial Field-Book of the Revolution*, first published serially by *Harper's* and then issued in book format in 1855. Other publications by Lossing are mentioned and biographical information is supplied. The author concludes by stating that the *Pictorial Field-Boook of the Revolution* "still commands respect and the present-day antiquarian can still find in it information not to be located elsewhere.".

424. "William Mackwitz, Wood Engraver." *Missouri Historical Society Bulletin* 8 (January 1952): 176–79.

As little is known about Mackwitz (1831–1919), a wood engraver in St. Louis from 1857 to 1916, the anonymous author has searched and found some biographical information. Several wood engravings that were used for advertisements are reproduced, and each one is discussed in detail.

425. Malcom, James P. "Memoirs of James Peller Malcolm, F.S.A." *Gentlemen's Magazine* 85 (May 1813): 467–69.

Malcolm (1767–1815) wrote this memoir in 1806, nine years before his death. He was born in Philadelphia, but went to England after the revolution to study at the Royal Academy. He taught himself to engrave and many of his engravings appeared in English magazines and books, several of which are listed by the editors of the *Gentleman's Magazine*.

426. Hamilton, Sinclair. "Homer Martin as Illustrator." *New Colophon* 1 (July 1948): 256–63.

Martin (1836–1897), best known as a landscape painter, occasionally drew book illustrations. The author describes some of the illustrations and ties them to the paintings of the same period. Despite Martin's attitude that book illustrations were "derogatory to his dignity," he produced some charming prints.

427. Coffin, Annie Roulhac. "Audubon's Friend—Maria Martin." *The New-York Historical Society Quarterly* 49 (January 1965): 28–51.

Maria Martin (1796–1863) assisted Audubon in the preparation of watercolor sketches of plant backgrounds for his plates. This article considers her friendship with Audubon, her sketches of birds, and her copies of some of his water colors. The attributions here are helpful in distinguishing between Audubon's and Martin's work in *The Birds of America*.

428. Draper, Benjamin. "Alfred Edward Mathews, Soldier, Pioneer, and Delineator." *Antiques* 35 (March 1939): 127–29.

Mathews painted literal views of the West and the Civil War which were popular and widely sold. This informative article chronicles his multifaceted career, emphasizing his views of the West. Scant mention is given his more important Civil War drawings.

429. Martin, Elizabeth R. "The Civil War Lithographs of Alfred Edward Mathews." *Ohio History* 72, no. 3 (July 1963): 230–242.

After trying to compete with other soldier-artists during the Civil War for employment by the pictorial journals, Mathews (1831–1874) turned to Cincinnati lithography firms for reproductions of his Civil War sketches. There are forty known lithographs by Mathews, most of which are located at the Ohio Historical Society. Martin describes Mathews's Civil War experiences and the prints, ten of which are reproduced. After the War, Mathews exhibited a major panorama of battle scenes. A list of the lithographs at the Ohio Historical Society is appended to this essay.

430. Peters, Harry T. "Louis Maurer: The Last of the Currier & Ives Artists." *Print Connoisseur* 11 (January 1931): 39–47.

Maurer (1832–1932) worked for Thomas Strong and then for Nathaniel Currier. Later he transferred to the firm of Major & Knapp, gradually becoming involved with commercial work. At Currier & Ives he was an important member of the group of artists employed by the firm. His speciality was the drawing of horses, and his best-known work was the American Fireman series.

431. Stephens, Stephen DeWitt. *The Mavericks: American Engravers*. New Brunswick, N.J.: Rutgers University Press, 1950. 219 pp., biblio., indexes.

The long introduction to this checklist of prints by members of the Maverick family includes biographical sketches of Peter Rushton Maverick (1755–1811), and his descendants Peter (1780–1831); Peter, Jr., (1809–1845); Andrew (1782–1826); Samuel (1789–1845); Andrew Rushton (1809–1835); Aaron Howell (1809–1845), Catherine (1811–1887), Emily (1803–1850), Maria Ann (1805–1832), and Octavia (1814–1882). There is also a considerable amount of information on the craft of engraving and on other engravers. The volume consists primarily of a catalog of prints by the various Mavericks. Included are book illustrations, bookplates, trade cards, maps, and bank notes. Stephens checked many institutions for his catalog and the location of each print is noted. This excellent work is carefully researched, thoroughly documented, and well organized. A supplement, *Documentation, Corrections and Additions to The Mavericks*, was published by the author in 1964.

432. Ormsbee, Thomas Hamilton. "Christian Meadows, Engraver and Counterfeiter." *American Collector* 13 (January 1945): 6–9, 18.

Christian Meadows was a talented engraver in Vermont during the 1850s who was twice imprisoned for counterfeiting. Some of his finest engravings were made while he was in prison. Ormsbee discusses his life and work, and most the the engravings are illustrated. An informal list of Meadows's work was compiled by Harold G. Rugg, and Ormsbee includes the titles of the prints in his text.

433. Mendel, Claire. "Edward Mendel: Artist and Citizen." *Chicago History* 8, no. 2 (June 1979): 78–9.

A grandson of Edward Mandel, the author provides a succinct biographical sketch of the lithographer who was born in Berlin in 1827 and died in Chicago in 1884. Like so many others, he left Germany at the time of the political upheavals in that region.

434. Koehler, Sylvester R. "Anna Lea Merritt." *American Art Review* 1, no. 1 (1880): 299–300.

A Philadelphian, Merritt (1844–1930) travelled on the Continent for four years and spent most of her life in England. In 1879 she took up etching. During the next year she produced several plates, predominantly portraits, which are listed.

435. Weitenkampf, Frank. "An Etcher of New York: C.F.W. Mielatz." *Print Collector's Quarterly* 24 (October 1937): 236–52.

This is an excellent appraisal of the etchings by Charles Frederick William Mielatz (1864–1919) depicting New York. Weitenkampf feels they form the most salient part of the artist's work. Style and technique are closely analyzed and many prints are mentioned by title.

436. Drepperd, Carl W. "Found: A 'New' Early American Engraver." *Antiques* 42 (October 1942): 204–205.

Gabriel Miesse (b. 1807) was an untrained engraver whese known oeuvre includes three copperplates and one historical print. No original impressions of the first three plates, which were probably executed while he was in his teens, have been found. A list of works follows the article and each item is carefully described.

437. Cadbury, Warder H. "Alfred Jacob Miller's Chromolithographs" in *Alfred Jacob Miller: Artist on the Oregon Trail*, 447–450. ed. Ron Tyler. Fort Worth: Amon Carter Museum, 1982.

Alfred Jacob Miller contains several essays and a highly detailed catalog of the drawings, watercolors, and paintings of this artist of the west. A few of his works, listed on pages 445 and 446, were reproduced as lithographs and chromolithographs. Cadbury describes the relationship between Charles Wilkins Webber, a journalist and traveler, and Miller (1810–1874).

438. Tyler, Ron. "Alfred Jacob Miller's Western Prints" in *Prints of the American West*, 56–66. ed. Ron Tyler. Fort Worth: Amon Carter Museum, 1983.

In comparison to Bodmer and Catlin, Miller's western prints attracted little attention in the nineteenth century. Miller accompanied Captain William Drummond Stewart on an expedition of the American Fur Company to an annual rendezvous of fur trappers and traders in the Rocky Mountains. Tyler discusses the journey, Miller's work, and his subsequent exhibition of completed paintings in 1838 in Baltimore. Stewart returned to Scotland in 1838 and Miller followed to paint oils from his sketches. He refused Stewart's assistance in publishing a portfolio of prints because of severe rheumatism. Not until 1852 were any of Miller's works reproduced as chromolithographs in a book by Charles W. Webber, *The Hunter Naturalist: Romance of Sporting*. Additional subjects were reproduced in 1854 in Webber's *The Hunter Naturalist*. By the time he could have published a portfolio after his paintings, the market was flooded and he lacked the funds to undertake such a project.

439. Koehler, Sylvester R. "Charles H. Miller." *American Art Review* 2, no. 1 (1881): 102.

A native of New York City, Miller (1842–1922) studied medicine, but gave up his medical career after a trip to Europe in order to pursue an artistic one. He was a member of the Etching Club, and produced several plates after 1876 which are listed here. His poetical landscapes, often reminiscent of Jongkind, were not in accord with popular taste.

440. "William Miller." *Scribner's Magazine* 18 (October 1895): 525.

Miller (1850–1923), who did his first work for Frank Leslie, derived much of his style from the work of Juengling, Leslie's partner. Miller's best work is his reproduction of landscapes after Inness, Homer, and Swain Gifford.

441. McCue, Michael. *John Hill Millspaugh, 1822–1894, American Landscape Artist*. Ashville, N.C.: Michael McCue, 1999. 12 pp.

Although trained as a stereotyper as a young man, Millspaugh turned to a career in art after his brother's death in 1851. McCue summarizes what little is known about this artist's life and discusses his work as an etcher of landscapes in the 1880s.

442. Koehler, Sylvester R. "John Ames Mitchell." *American Art Review* 2, no. 2 (1881): 57–58.

Mitchell (1845–1918) first began etching in Boston. His preferred subject matter, architectural and figural themes, was an unusual choice for an American etcher of his time. A list of his etchings is provided. He is characterized as being a facile rather than meticulous draughtsman.

443. Everett, Morris T. "Etchings of Mrs. Moran." *Brush and Pencil* 8 (April 1901): 3–16.

At the 1887 exhibition of women etchers at the Museum of Fine Arts, Boston, Mary Nimmo Moran (1842–1899) exhibited fifty-four plates dating from 1879. Everett provides helpful biographical notes in this article, a discussion of Moran's method of working from nature, and a description of her style. There are several appreciations of her art from other critics. The illustrations provide a sampling of her work.

444. Koehler, Sylvester R. "Mrs. M. Nimmo Moran." *American Art Review* 2, no. 1 (1880): 183.

This brief note provides a list of twelve recent etchings by Moran. Koehler detects the influence in Moran's work of her husband, Thomas, especially in her disdain for detail.

445. F. Keppel & Co. *Catalogue of the Etched Work of Peter Moran*. New York: 1888. 28 pp.

Although lacking critical commentary on Moran (1841–1914), this printseller's catalog, compiled by Frederick W. Morton, includes five original etchings and provides a valuable listing of 105 additional etchings, twenty drawings, and eight monotypes.

446. Koehler, Sylvester R. "Peter Moran." *American Art Review* 1, no. 1 (1880): 149–51.

One of a large family of artists, Peter Moran (1841–1914) came to America as a child in 1842. He took up residence in Philadephia and began etching in 1874, making a careful study of French etchers. A complete list of his plates to 1879 is given. His forte was the correct and vigorous drawing of animals. In *American Art Review* 1 (Pt. 2): 164, Koehler adds eight additional plates to the list and comments on the changes in Moran's style and choice of subject matter. One of the plates, "A Burro Train, New Mexico," appears with the article.

447. White, Robert R. "The Southwestern Etchings of Peter Moran: A History and Catalog." *Imprint* 19, no. 1 (1994): 11–28.

Peter Moran, attracted to New Mexico by its scenery and people, made his first trip there by railroad in 1880. He returned during the next three years, producing an important body of work including fourteen etchings thoroughly described in this well researched essay. White adds another etching to the catalog in a brief note in the Spring 1995 *Imprint* (Vol. 20, no. 1, 34–35): *Santa Fe, 1883*, which is related to a photograph by William Henry Jackson.

448. "The Prang Commission" in *Thomas Moran*, 324–348. Nancy Anderson. Washington: National Gallery of Art, 1997.

Appendix 1 of this magnificent exhibition catalog contains a brief introduction to *The Yellowstone Park*, published in 1876 by Louis Prang and Company in Boston. Each of the fifteen chromolithographs is reproduced along with the text by F. V. Hayden.

449. Benson, Frances M. "The Moran Family." *Quarterly Illustrator* 1 (April 1893): 67–84.

The brothers Edward, John, Peter, and Thomas Moran, together with their wives and sons, formed an extended family of artists. This anecdotal account of the Morans' establishment in Philadelphia provides an informative record of the various family members.

450. Bruhn, Thomas. "Printmaker 'of the first rank'" in *Thomas Moran*, 282–299. Nancy Anderson. Washington: National Gallery of Art, 1997.

Bruhn's carefully crafted and thoroughly documented essay discusses Thomas Moran's (1837–1926) early exposure to the works of artists through books, his training as a wood engraver, his creation of several *cliche verre* prints, and a thorough discussion of his lithographs and etchings that span the years from 1860 to the 1890s. These are among the very finest and rarest of American artist's prints.

451.———. "Thomas Moran's Painter-Lithographs." *Imprint* 15, no. 1 (1990): 2–19.

Between 1859 and 1869 Moran drew at least thirty-nine lithographs on stone. They are rare and very beautiful images. Bruhn provides a synopsis of Moran's life and early artistic career, focusing on the prints which he suggests fall into three groups defined by subject, style, signature or date. Moran was one of the few American artists to use lithography as a medium of expression. Following the excellent analytical essay is a checklist of the lithographs including locations, notes, and comments on the images.

452. Kinsey, Joni. "Moran and the Art of Publishing" in *Thomas Moran*, 300–321. Nancy Anderson. Washington: National Gallery of Art, 1997.

Some two thousand of Moran's landscapes appeared as illustrations in books and magazines during the 1860s, 1870s, and 1880s. Kinsey explores Moran's "commercial career" that helped make him prominent, financially secure, and influential in shaping attitudes towards the American landscape. He worked as a literary illustrator, contributed illustrations to *Scribner's Monthly*, *The Aldine*, railroad guidebooks, government survey reports, *Picturesque America* and other illustrated books, and *The Yellowstone National Park* with the magnificent Prang chromolithographs. His paintings were also reproduced as calendars and posters.

453. Morand, Anne, and Nancy Friese. *The Prints of Thomas Moran in the Thomas Gilcrease Institute of American History and Art*. Tulsa, Okla.: Thomas Gilcrease Museum Association, 1986. 255 pp., biblio., index.

Three scholars, Victoria Hansen, Linda C. Hults, and Nancy Friese, have provided essays on Moran and contemporary printmaking, Moran and landscape prints, and his techniques, respectively. Each essay is an important contribution to the scholarship on American prints. Anne Morand provided the substantial checklist of his prints and illustrations (a separate list) beginning with an etched landscape issued in 1856. Each item is illustrated.

454. Morton, Frederick W. "Thomas Moran, Painter-Etcher." *Brush and Pencil* 7 (October 1900): 1–16.

The first part of this article concerns Moran's training as a painter and discusses several of his paintings. Although he took up etching as a diversion, he was noted for his experimentation, draughtsmanship, quantity, and quality of his plates. The author, who praises Moran's etchings, does not try to place them within the context of his paintings.

455. Pringle, Allan. "Thomas Moran: *Picturesque Canada* and the Quest for a Canadian National Landscape Theme." *Imprint* 14, no. 1 (1989): 12–21.

Between 1880 and 1882, Thomas Moran executed fifteen drawings of Canadian landscape for *Picturesque Canada* published between 1882 and 1884. In his well researched article, Pringle provides a detailed description of the creation of this publication and analyzes Moran's contributions to it, most of which described Niagara Falls, surely one of the most dramatic subjects of the book.

456. Cowdrey, Bartlett, and Hermann Warner Williams, Jr. *William Sidney Mount, 1807–1868: An American Painter*. New York: Metropolitan Museum of Art, 1944. 54 pp. plus plates.

Williams suggests in his introduction that Mount's interest in genre derives from popular "news prints" of the Revolutionary War era. The reproductions of his paintings made his paintings well known to his contemporaries. Appendix B to this catalog of his paintings is an excellent checklist of prints after his paintings. This list includes works reproduced in periodical literature and literary annuals as well as separately published engravings and lithographs. Collections owning these works are also noted.

457. Reilly, Bernard F., Jr. "Translation and Transformation: The Prints After William Sidney Mount" in *William Sidney Mount: Painter of American Life*, 132–147. Deborah Johnson. New York: American Federation of Arts, 1998.

Reilly argues convincingly that the prints reproduced from Mount's paintings allowed Mount such great exposure during the nineteenth century. In addition, sale of the prints generated revenue to supplement that which he earned from the sale of his paintings. Reilly discusses the production of these prints that ranged in format from bank notes to illustrations in gift books to separately published engravings and lithographs, some produced in Paris. Of particular interest is Mount's relationship with the publisher Wilhelm Schaus of New York.

Some of Mount's paintings were created with the print market in mind.

458. *Index to Signed Engravings by Thomas Nast As They Appeared in* Harper's Weekly *1863–1887*. Lansing, Mich.: Collectible Newspapers, 1985. 58 pp.

This useful pamphlet provides a chronological list of the engravings designed by Nast (1840–1902) for *Harper's Weekly*.

459. *Journal of the Thomas Nast Society*. Morristown, N. J.: Thomas Nast Society, 1987.

Since 1987, the Thomas Nast Society has published the *Journal*, one issue per year. In the tenth anniversary issue, a list of all the essays and authors was printed. Among the frequent contributors over the ten year period are Alice Caulkins, Draper Hill, Jeffrey Eger, Roger A. Fischer, and Lois R. Densky. Anyone interested in Nast should consult this journal.

460. Boime, Albert. "Thomas Nast and French Art." *American Art Journal* 2 (March 1972): 43–65.

Nast's work is usually studied for its political implications but Boime places it in an artistic perspective. Nast, who had no strong indigenous cartoon tradition to rely upon, turned regularly to French draughtsmen and painters for inspiration.

461. Caulkins, Alice A. *Th: Nast. Another Side of Thomas Nast*. Morristown, N.J.: Macculloch Hall Historical Museum, 1983. 8 pp., biblio.

This brief exhibition catalog explores Nast's images of daily life, a change from most publications that chronicle his political satire. Caulkins reprints comments made by Nast in 1894 about the changes made to an artist's work by engravers. He relished the introduction of process work permitting the exact reproduction of the artist's lines. There were 44 items in the exhibition—drawings, engravings from periodicals, and a cut and an uncut woodblock.

462. Goodrich, Lloyd. "Thomas Nast." *American-German Review* 2 (March 1935): 55.

The author insists that German printmakers influenced Nast's technique.

463. Hill, Draper. "Thomas Nast: Illustrator and Points Beyond." *Journal of The Thomas Nast Society* I, no. 1 (1987): 2–35.

Draper Hill, himself a noted political cartoonist, provides an excellent summary of Nast's career as an illustrator. Hill is able to provide some detail on the artist's early years in New York, his knowledge of contemporary European illustrations, and the influence of photography. Nast's first illustrations were published in 1859, the first of at least ninety book projects. Hill mentions some of the more important commissions, several of which are illustrated. His biographical sketch is followed by a checklist compiled by Lois R Densky, Alice Caulkins, and Jeffrey Eger covering the period 1860 to 1904.

464. Keller, Morton. *The Art and Politics of Thomas Nast*. New York: Oxford University Press, 1968. 353 pp., biblio.

This volume, concentrating on the historical and political context of Nast's cartoons, fails to discuss Nast's style, imagery, or technique in detail, although Keller does relate Nast to the European caricature tradition. The numerous reproductions of prints from *Harper's Weekly* are excellent, and the large format of the book permits them to be seen at two-thirds of their original size. The bibliography is good.

465. Knaufft, Ernest. "Thomas Nast." *Review of Reviews* 27 (January 1903): 31–35.

Written immediately after Nast's death in 1902, this article summarizes the artist's career, commending his ability as a draughtsman. Knaufft also mentions that his method of crosshatching allowed the printing block to be distributed among several engravers, which significantly speeded up the engraving process.

466. Kouwenhoven, John A. "Thomas Nast As We Don't Know Him." *Colophon* 1, no. 2 (1939): 37–48.

Kouwenhoven discusses about twelve of Nast's cartoons, none of which were among those that brought about the downfall of Tammany Hall. The author explains the meaning of each clearly, discussing the artist's understanding of and reactions to the problems of his era.

467. Maurice, A. B. "Thomas Nast and His Cartoons." *Bookman* 15 (March 1902): 19–25.

This short, illustrated article cites Nast's original contributions to American political caricature.

468. Paine, Albert Bigelow. *Thomas Nast: His Period and Pictures*. New York and London: Macmillan, 1904. 583 pp., index.

The six parts of this definitive study cover Nast's youth and association with Garibaldi up to 1860, his role in the Civil War, his attacks on the Tweed Ring (1870–1871), his relations with the Grant Administration, the cartoon campaigns from 1877 to 1886, and the last years of his life. It is profusely illustrated with his cartoons. This book was reprinted in Gloucester, Mass. in 1967.

469.———. "*Harper's Weekly* and Thomas Nast." *Harper's Weekly* 51 (5 January 1907): 14–20.

This article, which is illustrated with original cartoons of Nast, records a series of historical political victories against Tammany Hall. In this fiftieth anniversary issue of *Harper's*, Paine lauds the magazine for having fostered American cartooning. Before 1857 only three cartoon symbols had been invented: Brother Jonathan, Mistress Columbia, and the American eagle. Nast and *Harper's* enlarged the cartoonists' iconography.

470. Reaves, Wendy Wick. "Thomas Nast and the President." *American Art Journal* 19, no. 1 (1987): 60–71.

Reaves explores the relationship between Ulysses S. Grant and Thomas Nast. The article begins with a summary of Nast's career as an illustrator and cartoonist. She focuses on the 1872 portrait of Grant in the National Portrait Gallery collection reproduced in *Vanity Fair* (London, June 1, 1872). Also discussed is the portrait of Horace Greeley by Nast, also in the Portrait Gallery collection and issued during the 1872 election campaign. Reaves sets these satires in their appropriate context.

471. Vinson, J. Chal. *Thomas Nast, Political Cartoonist.* Athens, Ga.: University of Georgia Press, 1967. 46 pp., biblio., index.

The substantial introduction discusses Nast's career, the periodicals for which he worked, and the social and political events that shaped and inspired his work. Chapters are devoted to his early career, his work during the Civil War, his attacks on Boss Tweed, cartoons about presidential candidates, and his last years, when his work was largely unappreciated. The illustrations are a representative sampling, chronologically arranged, of the several thousand cartoons that he drew. The bibliography is excellent and includes several articles in contemporary periodicals.

472. Weiss, Harry B. "A Forgotten Version of Little Red Riding Hood, With Thomas Nast Illustrations." *Bulletin of the New York Public Library* 54 (January 1950): 61–73.

Several versions of Little Red Riding Hood are discussed as an introduction to Nast's illustrations for *Nast's Illustrated Almanac for 1872*. Although more famous for his political cartoons, Nast did illustrate some children's literature, titles of which are cited in this article. Eight pages of the almanac are reproduced which provide a good introduction to Nast's work in this vein.

473. Weitenkampf, Frank. "Thomas Nast, Artist in Caricature." *Bulletin of the New York Public Library* 37 (September 1933): 770–74.

Weitenkampf finds Nast's political prints successful because of the "telling juxtaposition of his figures, by firm insistence on facial and bodily characteristics, by directness, and, be it said again, by an intense expression of moral conviction." Several of his prints, his style, his use of symbols, and some of his contemporaries are briefly discussed in this description of the chronologically arranged collection that came as gifts from Nast's widow and their son Cyril.

474. Pyatt, Joseph O. *Memoir of Albert Newsam, Deaf-Mute Artist.* Philadelphia: Joseph O. Pyatt, 1868. 160 pp.

This informal biography of a renowned Philadelphia lithographer contains chapters on his early life, his education, his professional studies, his illness, his character, and the Galaudet monument. There is a general discussion of the artist's working methods.

475. Stauffer, David McNeely. "Lithographic Portraits of Albert Newsam." *Pennsylvania Magazine of History and Biography* 24 (October 1900 and January 1901): 267–89; 430–52.

Stauffer's introduction to this checklist of portraits drawn by Newsam (1809–1864) summarizes the lithographer's life, the development of his artistic talents, and his experiences as a lithographer. Newsam collected fine illustrated books and engravings, but these were lost in the fire that destroyed Duval's establishment. Since this checklist contains only the prints that Stauffer could examine, it is incomplete. Newsam was an excellent lithographer and it is hoped that his list will be revised.

476. Garvan, Beatrice B. "Matthew Clark's Charts. One Significant Example of Yankee Enterprise." in *Philadelphia Printmaking. American Prints Before 1860*, 42–69. ed. Robert F. Looney. West Chester, Penn.: Tinicum Press, 1976.

After surveying British coastal charts available for use in colonial America, Garvan describes in detail a set of charts published by Matthew Clark in Boston in 1790, engraved by John Norman (ca. 1748–1827) and Joseph Seymour.

477. Green, Samuel A. *Remarks on the* Boston Magazine, *the* Geographical Gazeteer of Massachusetts, *and John Norman, Engraver.* Cambridge, Mass.: J. Wilson & Son, 1904. 7 pp.

Reprinted from the *Proceedings of the Massachusetts Historical Society* (2d ser., May 1904: 326–30), this article concerns the "Society for Compiling a Magazine in the Town of Boston," whose manuscript records are in the Massachusetts Historical Society. The *Boston Magazine* began publication in the fall of 1783, with John Norman as one of the publishers. The *Geographical Gazeteer* was published serially. This Society was in a sense the forerunner of the Massachusetts Historical Society; their purposes were much the same, and several of the same men were involved in the founding of both. A few lines are devoted to Norman himself.

478. Hart, Charles H. "Some Notes Concerning John Norman, Engraver." *Proceedings of the Massachusetts Historical Society* 18 (October 1904): 394–96.

Hart expands on Green's remarks about John Norman. He provides further biographical information and cites additional engravings by Norman.

479. Weiss, Harry B. "John Norman: Engraver, Publisher, Bookseller; John Walters: Miniaturist, Publisher, Bookseller; and the *World Turned Upside-Down* Controversy." *Bulletin of the New York Public Library* 38 (January 1934): 3–14.

John Norman arrived in Philadelphia from London in 1774 and established himself as an engraver, architect, and drawing master. Using notices from Philadelphia newspapers, the author documents the artist's first years in Philadelphia. Weiss discusses his brief partnership with John Walters in 1779 and their joint publication of a children's book, *The World Turned Upside-Down*. A disagreement between the two men caused the partnership to break up in the midst of the preparation of the volume. Once it was settled, John Norman moved to Boston and Weiss cites some of his publications there. Various editions of *The World Turned Upside-Down*, which became a popular children's book, are described. A list of engravings by Norman in The New York Public Library is appended, but it is incomplete.

480. Jackson, Joseph. "Bass Otis, America's First [?] Lithographer." *Pennsylvania Magazine of History and Biography* 37 (October 1913): 385–94.

Jackson concentrates on his discovery of a portrait of Abner Kneeland executed by Otis (1784–1861) in 1818. Previous to this discovery, Otis's earliest lithograph was thought to have been an illustration to an article in the July 1819 issue of *Analectic Magazine*. Jackson discusses both prints and comments on a lithographic stone containing part of a design by Otis. Biographical data on Otis is presented.

481. Stow, Charles Messer. "America's First Lithographer, Bass Otis." *Antiquarian* 15 (July 1930): 55–66, 86.

Stow comments on Bass Otis's early experiments with lithography and quotes extensively from the article which appeared in the July 1819 issue of *Analectic Magazine*. Otis worked only briefly in lithography before devoting most of his long career to portrait painting.

482. Cowdrey, Mary Bartlett. "Fanny Palmer, an American Lithographer" in *Prints*, 217–34. ed. Carl Zigrosser. New York: Holt, Rinehart & Winston, 1962.

Between 1849 and 1868 Fanny Palmer (ca. 1812–1876) drew some two hundred landscape and genre prints on stone for Nathaniel Currier and Currier & Ives. She was undoubtedly the foremost woman lithographer of her time. Her career is carefully traced from the days of her own firm (1845 to 1849) through her years with Currier & Ives. Several lithographs are described in detail. In 1868 her career ended when James M. Ives insisted on the inclusion of figures in her landscapes, owing to changes in popular taste. Several other talented members of her family are discussed. Cowdrey, as a result of her scholarly research, is able to correct several errors made by Harry T. Peters in his work on Currier & Ives.

483. Daniels, Stephen. "Frances Palmer and the Incorporation of the Continent" in *Fields of Vision: Landscape Imagery & National Identity in England & The United States*, 174–199. ed. Stephen Daniels. Princeton: Princeton University Press, 1993.

Among Palmer's best known and latest works is *Across the Continent—'Westward the Course of Empire Takes its Way'*. After discussing Palmer's work in England, which included topographical views, Daniels discusses her work in New York for Nathaniel Currier and Currier & Ives. He sets *Across the Continent* in the context of Manifest Destiny and other pioneering pictures that she did. The role of the train in the composition, the new settlement on the left side of the tracks, and the power of the print as a view of land development are other topics that engage Daniels.

484. Rubinstein, Charlotte Streifer. "The Early Career of Frances Flora Bond Palmer." *American Art Journal* 17, no. 4 (1985): 71–88.

Fanny Palmer (1812–1876) was a professional lithographer in England before leaving in 1843 or 1844 to come to the United States with her husband. Her English period is well described as are the activities of the Palmers in their first years in New York. Their firm failed in 1851, but she had already been engaged by Nathaniel Currier to work for his firm. Her husband died in 1859.

485. Society for the Preservation of Long Island Antiquities. *Fanny Palmer. A Long Island Woman Who Portrayed America*. Cold Spring Harbor: Society for the Preservation of Long Island Antiquities, 1997. 16 pp.

The introduction by the SPLIA curator, Carolyn Oldenbusch, provides an introduction to lithography, the prints of Currier & Ives, and the impetus for collecting them in the early twentieth century. Charlotte Streifer Rubinstein's essay on Fanny Palmer summarizes her years in England, her work in the firm of F. & S. Palmer, and her work for Nathaniel Currier after he bought out the Palmer firm. She was one of the few regular, long-term staff members and was responsible for many of the most popular of the Currier & Ives prints. Rubinstein has analysed her contributions to the firm's output carefully. A checklist of all signed works by Palmer, published by Currier & Ives concludes the catalogue.

486. McPeck, Eleanor M. "George Isham Parkyns, Artist and Landscape Architect, 1749–1820." *Library of Congress Quarterly Journal* 30 (July 1973): 171–82.

The article consists of a biographical sketch of Parkyns and a discussion of his American landscape print series, with comments on his proposals for landscapes of the United States.

487. *A Catalogue of Etchings by Stephen Parrish, 1879–1883*. New York: 1883. unpag.

Eighty-six items appear in this catalog with notes on title, size, dates, description of etching, number of impressions or proofs if known, and location of each plate given. The ten etched plates are beautifully printed. The etchings are primarily landscapes or marine views.

488. Colby, Virginia Reed. "Stephen and Maxfield Parrish in New Hampshire." *Antiques* 115, no. 6 (June 1979): 1290–1298.

Stephen Parrish (1846–1938) moved to Cornish, N.H., in 1893 together with other artists, writers, and musicians. Charles A. Platt often visited him. Most of this article is devoted to "The Oakes," the house that Maxfield Parrish had built in Plainfield, N.H.

489. Hitchcock, Ripley. "Some Representative Etchings: Millet, Rajon, Parrish." *Art Review* 1 (December 1886): 1–5.

The etchings and style of Parrish, an American etcher, are discussed, and the author traces the influences of other artists on his work.

490. Koehler, S. R. "Stephen Parrish." *American Art Review* 2, no. Pt. 1 (1881): 5–6.

Koehler introduces Parrish, well known in Philadelphia, to a wider audience. Parrish's first etched plate is dated 1879. A selective list is given of the forty plates he had executed when this sketch was written.

491. Montclair Art Museum. *Charles Parsons and His Domain. An exhibition of Nineteenth Century American Illustration*. Montclair: Montclair Art Museum, 1958. 48 pp., biblio.

The introduction is by Kathryn E. Gamble. Born in England, Parsons (18221–1910) came to the United States in 1830 and in 1836 was apprenticed to the lithographer George Endicott. He became head of that firm's lithography department and also worked for Currier & Ives. In 1863 he became head of the art department of Harper's publication company. His work there is described at length and Gamble provides interesting accounts of Parsons's personality and appearance from artists who worked for Harper. In 1890 he retired and turned to painting in watercolor. He became an associate member of the National Academy of Design and a member of the American Watercolor Society. The catalog includes lithographs drawn by him, watercolors and oils, sketches and sketch books, photographs drawn by him, photographs of him and his family, and drawings for many of the books published while he was art editor at Harper's as well as several books and periodicals published by the firm.

492. Reaves, Wendy Wick. "His Excellency General Washington: Charles Willson Peale's Long-Lost Mezzotint Discovered." *American Art Journal* 24, no. 1/2 (1992): 44–59.

The National Portrait Gallery acquired a mezzotint portrait of Washington attributed to Peale (1741–1827) who mentioned such a portrait in his diary in 1778. Not only is the mezzotint an important print, it served as the source for other print makers including John Norman, the London engraver who arrived in Philadelphia in 1774. His engraving in turn was copied by many wood engravers. This richly illustrated article is well documented.

493. Richardson, Edgar P. "Charles Willson Peale's Engravings in the Year of National Crisis, 1787." *Winterthur Portfolio* 1 (1964): 166–81.

In the midst of a general economic collapse that affected his personal fortunes, Peale seized upon the idea of selling his prints, a successful business in England at the time. Difficulties with print production in Philadelphia dashed his hopes, although he did engrave several mezzotints, and he turned to a more successful career as a painter. His efforts at printmaking failed largely because he was ahead of his time.

494. Sellers, Horace Wells. "Engravings by Charles Willson Peale, Limner." *Pennsylvania Magazine of History and Biography* 57 (April and July 1933): 153–74; 284–85.

Sellers analyzes a pencil drawing of George Washington, made by Peale in 1777, which is now in the Historical Society of Pennsylvania. He discusses its provenance at length in order to substantiate its authenticity. The article also mentions engravings by Peale including portraits of George Washington, a series of mezzotint portraits, and a proposed series of Philadelphia street scenes. The study is well documented by contemporary manuscripts and newspaper notices. The July 1933 issue of the magazine contains a chronological list of eight engravings by Peale, dating from 1768 to 1787.

495. Shadwell, Wendy J. "The Portrait Engravings of Charles Willson Peale" in *Eighteenth-Century Prints in Colonial America. To Educate and Decorate*, 123–144. ed. Joan D. Dolmetsch. Williamsburg: Colonial Williamsburg Foundation, 1979.

Peale was a man of many talents and accomplishments. While in London studying with Benjamin West, he learned to engrave mezzotints and produced an ambitious portrait of William Pitt in 1769. He did another mezzotint in 1778 of George Washington. He executed a second portrait of Washington in 1780 followed by a series of four bust-length portraits in 1787. The production of these prints is thoroughly described and an appendix locates impressions of them in museum and library collections.

496. Mahey, John A. "Lithographs by Rembrandt Peale." *Antiques* 97 (February 1970): 236–42.

Among the first American artists to experiment with lithography, Peale (1778–1860) supplied designs to the Pendleton lithographic firm. All but three of the known Peale lithographs were produced between 1825 and 1833. A descriptive checklist of Peale's lithographs follows the article.

497. Gall, Dolores M. "Titian Ramsay Peale: An American Naturalist and Lithographer." *Yale University Art Gallery Bulletin* 38, no. 3 (December 1983): 6–13.

Peale (1799–1885) was the youngest son of Charles Willson Peale. Brought up in his father's museum, he acquired the talents and desire to become an artist-naturalist. The article focuses on his *Lepidoptera Americana*, a study of butterflies to be written and illustrated by Peale. Only one part was published in 1833. Due to lack of interest (only 39 subscribers), the subsequent plans for publication were abandoned. Gall discusses the lithographs by Peale for this publication as well as several others by this pioneer lithographer found in the Yale Art Gallery's collection.

498. Slade, Denison R. "Henry Pelham, the Half-Brother of John Singleton Copley." *Publications of the Colonial Society of Massachusetts* 5 (1902): 193–211.

Henry Pelham (1749–1806) was the son of Peter Pelham by his third wife, Mary Singleton Copley, which made John Singleton Copley and Henry Pelham half-brothers. Henry Pelham painted portraits in Boston, but left for England during the Revolution. There he turned to engraving and several of his works are described. Much of the information Slade has found comes from letters written by members of the Pelham family.

499. Allison, Anne. "Peter Pelham, Engraver in Mezzotinto." *Antiques* 52 (December 1947): 441–43.

The author wrote this article while preparing a biography of Pelham in hopes of obtaining further information on him. She discusses his life in Boston and Newport, the mezzotints which were published in Boston, and his occupations other than engraving.

500. Coburn, Frederick W. "More Notes on Peter Pelham." *Art in America* 20 (June 1932): 143–54.

This article supplements Whitmore's *Notes Concerning Peter Pelham*, correcting errors such as Pelham's birth date, and giving additional biographical data concerning the Pelham family. Part of the research is based on the Copley-Pelham correspondence in the Public Records Office in London, published by the Massachusetts Historical Society. Pelham's American mezzotints are listed and two oil portraits of Governor William Greene are reproduced. Pelham's pursuits outside art are also discussed.

501. Oliver, Andrew. "Peter Pelham (c. 1697–1751): Sometime Printmaker of Boston" in *Boston Prints and Printmakers, 1670–1775*, 133–74. Boston: Colonial Society of Massachusetts, 1973.

Using a variety of notes, articles, and references to Pelham and his prints from contemporary newspaper sources, Oliver has created an excellent study of this artist. The engraver's activities as dancing master, concert organizer, and teacher are also discussed. A catalog of the fifteen known mezzotints with locations in public collections is provided.

502. Whitmore, William H. *Notes Concerning Peter Pelham and His Successors Prior to the Revolution*. Cambridge, Mass.: John Wilson & Son, 1867. 31 pp.

This study was revised from a paper printed in the *Proceedings of the Massachusetts Historical Society* in May, 1866. Whitmore presents documentation from contemporary newspaper advertisements for Pelham's prints, and attempts to show his influence in the works of later engravers and artists, including Henry Pelham and Copley. Other artists mentioned are Nathaniel Smibert, John Greenwood, Richard Jennys, Nathaniel Hurd, Thomas Johnston, James Turner, Samuel Okey, Francis Dewing, and Paul Revere.

503. Palumbo, Anne Cannon. "Joseph Pennell: The Formative Years of an American Printmaker." *Imprint* 8, no. 2 (1983): 1 11.

In this well-researched exploration of the early years of Pennell's (1860–1926) career, Palumbo discusses some of Pennell's early contacts with prints on display at the Philadelphia Centennial Exposition, his art training, and the predominance of painter-etching over reproductive etching in the 1880's. The influence of Whistler and French etchers on the younger artist, his illustrations of the 1880s, his membership in etching clubs, exhibitions of his works, his marriage to Elizabeth Robbins, with whom he collaborated on many books, are all discussed. The Pennells lived in London for over thirty years, beginning in 1884. In the 1890s he became interested in lithography which resulted in a book on the subject as well as the creation of over 140 lithographs. Despite his residence abroad, his illustrations were published in the United States and he endeavored to make American art better known abroad through exhibitions, lectures, and publications.

504. Andrews, Carol Damon. "John Ritto Penniman (1782–1841), an Ingenious New England Artist." *Antiques* 120, no. 1 (July 1981): 147–170.

Well known for his ornamental painting and drawing in Boston in the first four decades of the nineteenth century,

Penniman was also active as a portrait painter and provided many drawings for engravers. He was also active briefly as a lithographer for the Pendleton shop in the late 1820s. This well-documented article treats all aspects of Penninman's artistic career.

505. Swan, Mabel M. "John Ritto Penniman." *Antiques* 39 (May 1941): 246–48.

Penniman, generally known as a painter in the first quarter of the nineteenth century in Boston, also executed lithographs on stone for the Pendleton firm, making him one of the first artists to draw directly on stone. Swan has summarized her findings about his life and has found references to paintings by him no longer in existance. His career as an artist ended in 1827 and he became a draftsman on board the *Independence* in the late 1830s. Nothing is known of him after that date.

506. "Memoir of Jacob Perkins." *Boston Monthly Magazine* 1 (February 1826): 475–84.

This anonymous memoir discusses a variety of Perkins's (1766–1849) inventions including his process for hardening steel and the technique he invented for bank note engraving to prevent counterfeiting.

507. Harris, Elizabeth. "Jacob Perkins, William Congreve, and Counterfeit Printing in 1820" in *Prints in and of America to 1850*, 193–214. ed. John D. Morse. Winterthur, Del.: Henry Francis du Pont Winterthur Museum, 1970.

In the early nineteenth century, the Bank of England appointed a committee to adopt new engraving methods in reaction to widespread forgery in the United States and England. Among the plans submitted were those of Jacob Perkins, an American, and Sir William Congreve, a member of the committee. Neither of their plans was selected, yet the technical innovations they suggested were widely used throughout the nineteenth century for bank notes, lottery tickets, stock certificates, paper seals, and even admission tickets. Harris explains the peculiar engraving technique and flaws of medal engraving. This technical article is clearly written and well researched.

508. O'Neill, Mora Dianne. *Robert Petley: Recollections of Nova Scotia*. Halifax: Art Gallery of Nova Scotia, 1999. 20 pp.

Robert Petley's fifteen lithographs of Nova Scotia were printed in London in 1837. O'Neill provides an excellent biographical sketch of Petley (1812–69), who received his early artistic training at the Royal Military College, Sandhurst. Stationed in the Maritime Provinces from 1831 to 1836, he later returned to Sandhurst where he taught military drawing and mathematics from 1845 until his death. O'Neill relates the lithographs to surviving watercolors and suggests the importance of the prints as documents of Mi'kmaq life in the region. An additional unpublished sheet of nine lithographed vignettes in the collection of the American Antiquarian Society was drawn in 1832, probably the first use of lithographic stone in Nova Scotia.

509. Alderfer, William K. "The Artist Gustav Pfau." *Journal of the Illinois State Historical Society* 60, no. 4 (1967): 383–390.

Gustav Pfau (d. 1884), an immigrant from Saxony, published at least two lithographs around 1850. Alderfer summarizes the known facts about Pfau's life and reproduces several watercolors by him from the collection of the Illinois State Library.

510. Fairbanks, Jonathan. "The Great Platte River Trail in 1853: The Drawings and Sketches of Frederick Piercy" in ed. Ron Tyler. *Prints of the American West* 67–86. Fort Worth: Amon Carter Museum, 1983.

Frederick Piercy, sponsored by Mormon missionaries in England, travelled from Liverpool to Salt Lake City in 1853. His journal and drawings formed the basis of a book, *Route from Liverpool to Great Salt Lake Valley* published in England in 1855. Fairbanks based his essay on two excellent collections of drawings at the Museum of Fine Arts and the Missouri Historical Society. He comments on the views Piercy took and the sights he saw, his skill as an artist, and the importance of these drawings as historical documentation of a precious part of the nation's heritage. A checklist of drawings in public and private collections follows the essay.

511. Lecheminant, Wilford Hill. "'Entitled to Be Called an Artist': Landscape and Portrait Painter Frederick Piercy." *Utah Historical Quarterly* 48, no. 1 (December 1980): 49–65.

Piercy (1830–1891), born in England, was a Mormon who traveled to Utah in 1853, producing sketches reproduced in his book *Route from Liverpool to Great Salt Lake Valley, Illustrated* published in 1855. The author discusses the background for this publication and Piercy's life. Some of his original sketches are located at the Museum of Fine Arts, Boston.

512. Anderson, Joan. "Charles A. Platt." *International Studio* 85 (1925): 180–85.

The author discusses Platt's (1861–1933) endeavors as an architect, painter, and etcher. His first plate was made when he was about twenty years of age, studying etching under Stephen Parrish.

513. F. Keppel & Co. *Catalogue of an Exhibition of Etchings and Dry-Points by C.A. Platt*. New York: 1907. 9 pp.

The introductory note written by M. G. Van Rensselaer in 1886 compares Platt with Stephen Parrish, noting the large strides the former had made since his first attempts at etching. The catalog lists 108 prints with their corresponding numbers in Rice's catalog. There are a few additional prints not included in Rice, and several of the prints are listed with multiple states included.

514. The Grolier Club. *Exhibition of the Etched Work of Charles A. Platt*. New York: 1925. 31 pp.

In 1889 a catalog of Platt's etchings was compiled by R.A. Rice. This catalog contains all of Rice's entries and adds twelve etchings done between 1889 and 1920. There are 120 etchings listed, and in many cases several states of a print are described.

515. Koehler, Sylvester R. "Charles Adams Platt." *American Art Review* 2, no. 2 (1881): 150.

Platt was one of the youngest artists to be associated with the etching revival. When he began to study painting in 1879, he confined himself to landscape and marine views. He started to etch in 1880 and had finished seventeen plates when this sketch was written. Koehler describes his technique and style. Another brief article, by Frank Weitenkampf, appears in *Print Connoisseur* 7 (Apr. 1927).

516. Rice, Richard A. *A Descriptive Catalogue of the Etched Work of Charles A. Platt*. New York: De Vinne Press, 1889. 60 pp.

This catalog describes 109 etchings and drypoints produced by Platt between 1880 and 1889. Prints are chronologically arranged, and notes on trial proofs are included in the entries. The title index is well arranged.

517. Weitenkampf, Frank. "Charles Adams Platt, Etcher." *Bulletin of the New York Public Library* 38 (January 1934): 17–19.

In early 1934, the Print Department of The New York Public Library held an exhibition of Platt's etchings. Weitenkampf summarizes Platt's work as an etcher and discusses his style and choice of subject matter.

518. Fern, Alan. "John Plumbe and the 'Plumbeotype'" in *Philadelphia Printmaking. American Prints Before 1860*, 149–164. ed. Robert F. Looney. West Chester, Penn.: Tinicum Press, 1976.

John Plumbe (1809–1857) was born in Wales, and came to the United States with his family in 1824. He followed a number of careers, and was active in the early 1840s as a daguerreotypist and owned several daguerrian galleries. He also reproduced thirty or so of his daguerreotype portraits as lithographs. The Prints and Photographs Division of the Library of Congress has several daguerreotypes of public buildings that can be attributed to him. Fern summarized his career as a photographer and as a promoter of a railroad route across the continent.

519. Fern, Alan, and Milton Kaplan. "John Plumbe, Jr., and the First Architectural Photographs of the Nation's Capitol." *Quarterly Journal of the Library of Congress* 31 (January 1974): 3–20.

Focusing on six daguerreotypes by John Plumbe acquired by the Prints and Photographs Division of the Library of Congress, the writers also discuss the lithographs published from the daguerreotypes, known as plumbeotypes. John Plumbe was a photographer, inventor, and entrepreneur. In 1846 he began to publish the *Daily National Plumbeotype Gallery*. A list of seventy-nine daguerreotypes and plumbeotypes photographed or published by Plumbe is appended to the article. Locations in public collections are noted.

520. Tolman, Ruel Pardee. "Plumbeotype." *Antiques* 8 (July 1925): 27–28.

Until this article was written, the word "plumbeotyped" was understood as a graphic arts process which used grained lead for the production of lithographs. By examining the inscriptions of several plumbeotypes, the author learned that the process refers instead to John Plumbe, a photographer and inventor who learned to copy daguerreotypes on stone in order that numerous copies could be produced.

521. Clapper, Michael. "Art, Industry, and Education in Prang's Chromolithographic Company" in *The Cultivation of Artists in Nineteenth-Century America*, 121–137. eds. Georgia B. Barnhill, Diana Korzenik, and Caroline F. Sloat. Worcester: American Antiquarian Society, 1997.

Clapper sets the production of Prang's famed chromolithographs in the context of his commercial job printing business, suggesting that machine production and capitalist marketing changed the way art was made and used. Prang's contributions to art education are also noted, particularly the books written by Walter Smith, a series of graduated lessons that emphasized the application of drawing skills to industry.

522. Freeman, Larry. *Louis Prang, Color Lithographer: Giant of a Man*. Watkins Glen, N.Y.: Century House, 1971. 192 pp.

Louis Prang (1824–1909) experimented with color printing and became the best known American chromolithographer. His company specialized in sentimental cards and advertisements, eventually producing reproductions of paintings. This narrative of Prang's career is often repetitive, but it includes a helpful list of Prang's early lithographs and facsimiles of sale catalogs. The illustrations display the full range of Prang's publications. The volume concludes with a summary of Prang's later career as a publisher of books for art education.

523. McClinton, Katharine Morrison. *The Chromolithographs of Louis Prang*. New York: Clarkson N. Potter, 1973. 246 pp., index.

This profusely illustrated volume, written for collectors, explains the technical aspects of chromolithography and gives the chronology of Prang's career. Many of the prints from the 1860s and 1870s are mentioned separately. Chapters are devoted to album cards, publications (books and games) for children, trade cards, greeting cards, flower prints, fine art books, educational publications, Civil War maps and views, landscape and sport series, and finally, notes on the artists whose paintings Prang reproduced. Appendices include lists of paintings owned and reproduced by Prang that were sold at auction.

524. Rushford, Edward A. "Lewis [sic] Prang, Engraver on Wood." *Antiques* 37 (April 1940): 187–89.

Although Louis Prang's chromolithographs are well known, relatively little has been written on his early years. Rushford discusses Prang's activities in Germany before his flight to the United States in 1850, and then analyzes his business career in Boston in the 1850s as a wood engraver and printer of labels. Some aspects of his later work are mentioned, but the emphasis is on Prang's early years in Boston.

525. Hitchings, Sinclair H. "The First American Printseller." *Print Collector's Newsletter* 2 (November 1971): 93–95.

William Price (1684–1771), who set up shop in Boston in 1720, sold a variety of imported objects, including prints. From time to time he also published maps and city views, and Hitchings discusses each of Price's publications in detail. His public life, musical, and church-related activities are also considered in this well-researched and documented article.

526. Waite, Emma Forbes. "William Price of Boston: Map Maker, Merchant, and Churchman." *Old-Time New England* 46 (September 1955): 52–56.

William Price was active in several areas of commercial and cultural life in colonial Boston. His publications of maps and views are discussed, but the article focuses on his church activities as musician, organ builder, designer of church spires, and philanthropist. This article offers several interesting insights into religious life in Boston in the eighteenth century.

527. Gregory, Jane Allen, and Elizabeth Hawkes. *Howard Pyle: Diversity and Depth*. Wilmington, Del.: Delaware Art Museum, 1973. 81 pp.

This exhibition catalog contains a biographical sketch by Jane Allen Gregory and bibliographical notes by Elizabeth Hawkes. Notes from Pyle's lectures of 1904 are also included. The subject categories in the catalog include colonial and Revolutionary War themes, works for children, and mystical, allegorical, medieval, and travel subjects. Both Pyle's oil paintings and illustrations published in books were exhibited.

528. Lykes, Richard Wayne. "Howard Pyle, Teacher of Illustration." *Pennsylvania Magazine of History and Biography* 80 (July 1956): 339–70.

Howard Pyle, whose career as a teacher spanned the years 1894 to 1910, began working as an illustrator in 1876. He wrote thirty-four books, most of which he illustrated, did the illustrations for another 160 volumes by other authors, and had about 2,200 drawings and paintings reproduced in periodicals. Lykes concentrates on Pyle's teaching and his students in this article. The descriptions of Pyle's classes and methods are superbly documented with statements from his students, some of whom the author contacted, and with the records of the Drexel Institute. In 1900 Pyle opened his own school in his Wilmington studio. He also taught a summer session at Chadd's Ford, Pa.

529. Morse, Willard S. and Brinchle, Gertrude. *Howard Pyle: A Record of His Illustrations and Writings*. Wilmington, Del.: Wilmington Society of the Fine Arts, 1921. 242 pp., index.

This volume contains a list of illustrations and writings by Pyle that were published in periodicals, another list of books containing illustrations by Pyle, as well as lists of programs, bookplates, etc., made by the artist. There is a subject index of illustrations and a general index.

530. Hawkes, Elizabeth H. "Drawn in Ink. Book Illustrations by Howard Pyle" in *The American Illustrated Book in the Nineteenth Century*, 201–231. ed. Gerald W. R. Ward. Winterthur: The Henry Francis du Pont Winterthur Museum, 1987.

Howard Pyle (1853–1911) became the leading illustrator of his generation as well as a writer, teacher, and mural painter. More than 3,000 of his illustrations were reproduced in over one hundred books. Hawkes traces the outlines of his career discussing the full range of his chosen subject matter and technique. She suggests that he was influenced by Durer and other artists of his generation for his work during the 1880s. By 1890 his style had changed in an effort to capture transitory effects of light and motion. His drawings could be reproduced by halftone process or by wood engraving. Near the end of his career, Pyle illustrated works on American history and a series of books on King Arthur.

531. Waite, Emma Forbes. "Pioneer Color Printer: F. Quarre." *American Collector* 15 (December 1946): 12–13, 20.

Quarre came to the United States from France about 1839, bringing with him a special printing process for engraving prints and embossing designs. His editorial projects are described and the characteristics of his peculiar process analyzed. His experiments were short-lived, however, for he stayed in the printing and publishing business only until 1845.

532. Cochran, Carl M. "James Queen, Philadelphia Lithographer." *Pennsylvania Magazine of History and Biography* 82 (April 1958): 139–75.

Few biographical facts are known about Queen (ca. 1821–1886). This article gives a careful analysis of his lithographs. Many of them are in a collection of more than three hundred items, including about one hundred and twenty sketches and paintings, owned (in 1958) by Mrs. Joseph Carson of Philadelphia. A wide variety of lithographs are discussed: chromolithographs, membership certificates, city views, landscapes, book and magazine illustrations, sheet music covers, and advertisements. Cochran's article is based on "James Fuller Queen—Artist and Lithographer," the dissertation that he submitted to the University of Pittsburgh in 1954. The author has constructed a useful biography through the study of Queen's artistic production.

533. Wilson, Christopher Kent. "Engraved Sources for Quidor's Early Work." *American Art Journal* 8, no. 2 (November 1976): 17–25.

John Quidor (1801–1881) was one of America's finest literary painters. Many of his paintings were derived from the stories and legends of Cooper and Irving. Wilson discusses some English and European prints which influenced Quidor's development.

534. Blanchard, Julian. "Cincinnati Branch of Rawdon, Wright & Hatch." *Essay Proof Journal* 35 (July 1952): 6 pp.

Although the headquarters of Rawdon, Wright & Hatch, engravers of bank notes, was in New York, Blanchard discovered a branch of the firm in Cincinnati, established about 1840, that was under the direction of William F. Harrison. Of great interest is the inclusion here of a brief notice from the *Cincinnati Miscellany* (Nov. 1844: 60), which details the process by which the engraving dies and plates were made.

535. O'Brien, Donald C. "Abner Reed: A Connecticut Engraver." *Connecticut Historical Society Bulletin* 44, no. 1 (January 1979): 1–16.

Drawing upon a variety of manuscript and printed sources, O'Brien has succeeded in describing Reed's (1771–1866) life and his work as an engraver over a long period of time. Footnotes to the article may be consulted at the Connecticut Historical Society.

536. ———. "The Promotion of Stafford Springs: Aquatints by Abner Reed." *Imprint* 17, no. 2 (1992): 27–34.

O'Brien discusses the handsome set of aquatints by Reed, *Six Views in Aquatinta* (1810), that depict the health spa at Stafford Springs, Connecticut. America's first recognized health spa was owned by Dr. Samuel Willard. O'Brien considers how Reed learned to make aquatints, the history of the spa, the purpose of the prints, and the views themselves.

537. Wister, Owen. *The Illustrations of Frederic Remington*. New York: Bounty Books, 1970. 192 pp.

The introduction and commentary are brief but provide the basic facts of Remington's (1861–1909) life. The artist's style and approach to his subject are discussed, but there is no detailed analysis of his drawings. Although the volume is profusely illustrated, the sources of the illustrations are not provided.

538. "Early Artists and Mechanics: Number 2--Paul Revere." *New England Magazine* 3 (October 1832): 305–314.

This sketch describes some of Revere's (1735–1818) engravings in a discussion of his life. It includes a long letter written to the corresponding secretary of the Massachusetts Historical Society in which Revere recounts his activities of April 18 and 19, 1775, and comments on the treacherous behavior of Church.

539. Agresto, John. "Art and Historical Truth: The Boston Massacre." *Journal of Communication* 29, no. 4 (1979): 170–4.

Agresto argues that Paul Revere's engraving of the Boston Massacre permanently altered the reality of the historical event. He compares the known facts with the engraving, concluding that it does portray the "correct understanding of the meaning and portent of the occurrence."

540. Andrews, William Loring. *Paul Revere and His Engraving*. New York: Charles Scribner's Sons, 1901. 171 pp., index.

Andrews's volume, which contains inaccuracies, has been superseded by Brigham's. It does, however, contain useful information on the Boston Massacre and on some of Revere's contemporaries, such as Bernard Romans. Moreover, it is a beautifully printed and illustrated book.

541. Brigham, Clarence S. *Paul Revere's Engravings*. Worcester, Mass.: American Antiquarian Society, 1954. 181 pp.

Brigham's volume reproduces all the known engravings by Revere. Documentation for most of the engravings comes from Revere's Day Books, located at the Massachusetts Historical Society. The author was remarkably successful in uncovering English sources as well as Revere's copperplate engravings and type metal cuts that are reproduced in full-size facsimile. This handsome work attests to what can be done in the field of American prints if time and sufficient funds are made available to a scholar. A revised edition was issued in New York in 1969.

542.———. "Boston Massacre, 1770." *Antiques* 68 (July 1955): 40–43.

This article is a condensation of a major chapter in Brigham's book *Paul Revere's Engravings*, which reveals that Henry Pelham created the original design for Paul Revere's print of the Boston Massacre. Several engravings of the massacre are reproduced, and the various versions, including several of the nineteenth-century prints, are compared and described.

543. Goss, Elbridge Henry. *The Life of Colonel Paul Revere*. Boston: J.G. Cupples, 1891. 2 vols.

Goss's extensive volume integrates biographical information with comments on Revere's work as an engraver. Several of the engravings are reproduced and original documents reprinted. Since this is a biography, it is not entirely superseded by Brigham's volume, which reproduces the engravings. Goss did an excellent job of documenting Revere's life and various political, artistic, and industrial activities.

544. Hart, Charles H. "Paul Revere's Portrait of Washington." *Pennsylvania Magazine of History and Biography* 18 (December 1903): 83–85.

This brief article concerns a portrait of George Washington attributed to Revere which was published in *Weatherwise's Town and Country Almanack* for 1781. It is known that Revere engraved a portrait of Washington at that time because his records show that he sent a copy of such a print to his cousin in France in 1781.

545. Sargent, George H. "Paul Revere's *Boston Massacre*." *Antiques* 11 (March 1927): 214–16.

This article, somewhat outdated, centers on the various versions of the "Boston Massacre" print. The version that was printed as a broadside, the impressions commonly handcolored and framed, the London reprints, the Jonathan Mullikan version, and nineteenth-century reprints are discussed.

546. Swan, Bradford F. *An Indian's an Indian; or The Several Sources of Paul Revere's Engraved Portrait of King Philip*. Providence, R.I.: Roger Williams Press, 1959. 7 pp.

The "Four Kings of Canada" engravings, and a Grignion plate that appears in Bouquet's *Expedition* (London, 1766), served as as sources for Revere's engraving of King Philip.

547. Welsh, Peter C. "Henry R. Robinson: Printmaker to the Whig Party." *New York History* 53 (January 1972): 25–53.

Little biographical information exists on Henry Robinson, the foremost lithographer of political cartoons in New York in the 1830s and 1840s. Welsh's excellent study uses Robinson's prints to establish his background and his political, economic, and social views.

548. Dalphin, George R., and Marcus A. McCorison. "Lewis Robinson—Entrepreneur." *Vermont History* 30 (October 1962): 297–313.

Lewis Robinson (1793–1871), of South Reading, Vt., was a publisher and distributor of prints. As background information, the authors describe other engravers active in Windsor and Orange Counties in the early nineteenth century. Biographical information on Robinson is provided and data from his account book of 1840 to 1855 (at the Vermont Historical Society) is reproduced in tabular form. Some of the prints were published by Robinson, others he distributed. His map publishing business was large, and between 1840 and 1855 he transacted business with 15 peddlars. Appended to the text is a list of the maps, books, and prints published by Robinson, with their locations in public collections. Carefully researched, this study makes excellent use of manuscript sources to document the business of this publisher.

549. Daniel, Forrest W. "The Artist Who Played 'Hooky'." *North Dakota History* 43, no. 3 (June 1976): 4–13.

While working for *Harper's Weekly* in 1878, William A. Rogers (1854–1931) covered the Minnesota State Fair in St. Paul. Daniel discusses Rogers's career in general and focuses on the works done by Rogers in the three months that he played "hooky" from his duties in New York. He drew Fort Garry in Manitoba and traveled to the Dakota Territory. Daniel traces his steps and discusses the illustrations that later resulted from this important trip.

550. Rogers, William A. *A World Worth While. A Record of"Auld Acquaintance"*. New York and London: Harper & Borthers, 1922. 305 pp.

This personal memoir spans the years from 1870 to 1900. Rogers writes of many men he encountered through his work as an illustrator for the Harper firm—Edwin A. Abbey, George William Curtis, Thomas Nast, and Mark Twain among others. There are many details to be gleaned about the lives of his contemporaries and the work of an illustrator, particularly in the descriptions of his relationships with publishers and other illustrators.

551. Decatur, Stephen. "William Rollinson, Engraver." *American Collector* 9 (December 1940): 8–9.

Little is known about Rollinson's (1762–1842) early years in England. He emigrated to New York in 1788, arriving just before Washington's inauguration. In New York, he began working as a chaser of fancy buttons, then turned to copperplate engraving in 1791. Some of his engravings are described and illustrated here, and Decatur notes two innovative engraving techniques invented by Rollinson.

552. Reid, Robert W. *William Rollinson, Engraver*. New York: Privately printed, 1931. 62 pp.

Rollinson's diary, located at the New York Public Library that documents his early attempts at engraving, was reproduced in facsimile in 1930. That and other records held by his descendants provide the documentation for this monograph. The author describes Rollinson's background, early engravings, invention of a bank note ruling machine, and other activities. The short biographical sketch is followed by illustrations of Rollinson's work.

553. Phillips, Philip Lee. *Notes on the Life and Works of Bernard Romans.* Deland, Fla.: Florida State Historical Society, 1924. 128 pp.

This analytical study of Bernard Romans (ca. 1720–1784) concentrates on his large map of Florida, published in 1774, a copy of which is in the Library of Congress. The publication of this map is discussed in great detail, with newspaper advertisements, extracts from account books, and letters published in newspapers providing documentation. Other topics considered in this volume are Abel Buell's collaboration with Romans, and Romans's book on Florida. A detailed list of Romans's map, books, letters, and articles is appended to the text.

554. Rosenthal, Albert. *List of Portraits: Lithographs, Etchings, Mezzotints by Max Rosenthal and Albert Rosenthal.* Philadelphia: By the author, 1923. 32 pp.

There was a strong interest among collectors of the late nineteenth century in prints copied from original works of art. The author and his father were well known in this area for their expertise in producing portrait prints. A group of collectors who specialized in autographed letters of famous colonial and Revolutionary Americans commissioned the Rosenthals to engrave the portraits contained in this list; Rosenthal gives the history of these prints. Further discussion of these collectors can be found in several works compiled by Stan V. Henkels: 1) Hampton L. Carson, *Collection of Engraved Portraits* (Philadelphia: William F. Fell Co., 1904. 4 pts); 2) *Rare Engraved Portraits of Gen. George Washington and Other Notable Americans* (Philadelphia: Davis & Harvey, 1906); 3) *The Collection of Engraved Portraits Belonging to Hon. James T. Mitchell* (Philadelphia, 1906–1908. 7 pts); 4) *The Collections of Engraved Portraits of Washington Belonging to Henry Whelen, Jr.*; and *The Extensive Collections of Engraved Portraits of Franklin* (Philadelphia, 1909).

555.———. "Albert Rosenthal, Painter, Etcher, Lithographer." *Print Connoisseur* 9 (April 1929): 96–130.

Rosenthal (1863–1939) briefly describes a few of the events and activities of his own career. His chief work was the copying of portraits by lithography or etching. A list of the plates executed by him, arranged by subject (members of Constitutional conventions, Supreme Court justices, and miscellaneous prints), is appended. Rosenthal reprinted this autobiographical article in Philadelphia in 1929 as an illustrated, unpaginated book.

556.———. "The Mezzotints of Max Rosenthal." *Print Connoisseur* 2 (September 1921): 2–25.

At an early age Max Rosenthal (1833–1918) was apprenticed to a lithographer in Paris. He returned to the United States in 1849 with the lithographer M. Thurwanger, who had signed a contract with P.S. Duval in Philadelphia. Rosenthal's career up to 1900 is described and a checklist of his mezzotint portraits, all executed after 1900 and primarily based on well-known paintings, follows. The author, son of the artist and a printmaker himself, offers no judgment on the artistic merit or historical importance of the prints.

557. Hall, Elton W. "Panoramic Views of Whaling by Benjamin Russell" in *Art & Commerce*, 25–49. Boston: Museum of Fine Arts, 1978.

Benjamin Russell (1803–1885) was born into a New Bedford merchant and whaling family. In the early 1830s the firm failed and Russell worked at a variety of jobs including a stint on a whaling ship. He produced designs for lithographed ship portraits as early as 1848 and painted the *Panorama of a Whaling Voyage Around the World* in 1848. It was 1300 feet long and eight and a half feet high. Hall focuses, however, on prints by Russell ranging in date from 1848 to 1871. The publications are thoroughly documented by contemporary newspaper advertisements and the original watercolors for some of the prints are extant. Hall concludes by noting the correct delineation by Russell of his subjects making these prints valuable documents.

558. *Montana: The Magazine of Western History.* 34, no. 3 (June 1984):

The entire issue is devoted to the work of Charles M. Russell (1864–1926) and includes a number of drawings on letters. Also included is an essay on his drawings of women.

559. Guignard, Philippe. *Notice Historique Sur la Vie et les Travaux de M. Févret de Saint-Mémin.* Dijon: Loireau-Feuchot, 1853. 22 pp.

This essay was originally read before the Academy in Dijon, Saint-Mémin's native city. Saint-Mémin (1770–1852) was exiled during the French Revolution, and took up the art of engraving in New York. He made two views of the city as well as etched views of projects for a new city, and then turned to the physiognotrace to make portraits. His travels in the United States and his life in France as director of the Dijon Museum after 1817 are described.

560. Miles, Ellen G. *Saint-Mémin and the Neoclassical Profile Portrait in America.* Washington: National Portrait Gallery and Smithsonian Institution Press, 1994. 461 pp., biblio., index.

In 1974 Mr. and Mrs. Paul Mellon presented the collection of 761 engravings by Charles Balthazar Julien Févret de Saint-Mémin that had belonged to Elias Dexter to the National

Portrait Gallery. This book presents the results of years of research by Miles on Saint-Mémin and contemporary profilists, the artist's life, and his career in America from 1796 to 1809. Concluding chapters present information about his years in France from 1809 to 1852 and his artistic legacy. There is a detailed catalogue of Saint Mémin's drawings, portrait prints, and other works by him. This latter group includes drawings of Niagara Falls, an engraved plan of Savannah, a trade card for Pierre Mourgeon, and a view of New York. The appendix lists Saint-Mémin's sitters by city. The book is thoroughly researched, beautifully designed and printed, and lavishly illustrated.

561. Morgan, John H. "The Work of M. Févret de Saint-Mémin." *Brooklyn Museum Quarterly* 5 (January 1918): 4–26.

Morgan discusses Saint-Mémin's lack of recognition in the United States and the provenance of several copies of his views of New York. He gives a detailed description of the history of portrait engraving in Europe and of Saint-Mémin's methods and style. Several of the artist's engravings are carefully analyzed, and Morgan concludes by noting the historical importance of Saint-Mémin's work.

562. Norfleet, Fillmore. *Saint-Mémin in Virginia; Portraits and Biographies.* Richmond, Va.: Dietz Press, 1942. 235 pp.

The starting point of this thoroughly researched biography of Saint-Mémin is his childhood in France. The artist's life and travels in the United States are well documented. The illustrations, Saint-Mémin's portraits of Virginians, are followed by exhaustive biographical notes on each subject. Sources for the notes are listed in the bibliography.

563. Rice, Howard C., Jr. "An Album of Saint-Mémin Portraits." *Princeton University Library Chronicle* 13 (1951): 23–31.

This article discusses some of the small albums of portraits that Saint-Mémin prepared as gifts for friends. The album in the Princeton University Library, done for Claude-Bernard-Marguerite-Henri Joliet, is thoroughly described. An extensive bibliographical note is included.

564.———. "Saint-Mémin's Portrait of Jefferson." *Princeton University Library Chronicle* 20, no. 4 (June 1959): 182–92.

Thomas Jefferson sat for Saint-Mémin in November 1804. The original drawing is in the collection of the Worcester Art Museum. Rice describes the process and reproduces a drawing of a physiognotrace machine. Saint-Mémin produced two different copperplates from this drawing, both of which are extant. Rice suggests that the second plate was made at the time of Jefferson's second inauguration.

565. Seaton-Schmidt, Anna. "St. Mémin and His Portraits." *American Magazine of Art* 11 (October 1920): 438–41.

Charles Balthazar Julien Févret de Saint-Mémin, a French nobleman, fled France for San Domingo in 1789. He stopped in New York during the voyage and decided to remain in that city. He made a successful living by producing small engraved portraits. The method of obtaining a full-size sihouette and the means of reducing it to a two-inch circular engraving is clearly explained. He saved copies of much of his work, and an extensive collection of his prints is at the Corcoran Gallery.

566. Weitenkampf, Frank. *Sketch of the Life of Charles Balthazar Julien Févret de Saint-Mémin.* New York: The Grolier Club, 1899.

The Grolier Club published this sketch to accompany their exhibition of Saint-Mémin's portraits. Weitenkampf's short but thorough biography emphasizes Saint-Mémin's inventiveness. The names of some of the eminent men who commissioned portraits from him are listed. In 1810 Saint-Mémin returned briefly to France, then spent several more years in the United States. His eyesight became impaired, however, and he returned to France in 1815, where he became the director of the musuem in Dijon in 1817. The recipient of many French honors, he died in 1852.

567. Brainard, Newton C. "Isaac Sanford." *Connecticut Historical Society Bulletin* 19 (October 1954): 122.

This brief note mentions two mechanical inventions by Isaac Sanford, otherwise known as an engraver and portrait painter. One was used in shearing and finishing wool, the other in the manufacture of hats. The patents for these are among Sanford's papers at the Connecticut Historical Society and the Wadsworth Atheneum.

568. Bellroche, Albert. "The Lithographs of Sargent." *Print Collector's Quarterly* 13 (February 1926): 30–45.

The author was closely associated with John Singer Sargent (1856–1925), who executed six lithographs between 1895 and 1905. These were drawn on transfer paper rather than on stone; all are reproduced in this study, and copies are in the British Museum. This article, a personal memoir, is valuable because Belleroche was the printer of Sargent's lithographs.

569. Jones, Karen F. "American Artist Prints." *Quarterly Journal of the Library of Congress* 23 (January 1966): 56–59.

This article concentrates on the history of Sargent's six lithographed prints, casting light on Sargent's involvement with lithography.

570. Bassham, Ben L. *The Theatrical Photographs of Napoleon Sarony*. Kent, Ohio: Kent State University Press, 1978. 122 pp., biblio.

After a successful career in commercial lithography Sarony (1821–1896) opened a photographic studio in New York in 1866 which continued for some thirty years. He allegedly photographed every actor and actress who appeared on the New York stage as well as people from all walks of life. Bassham provides an excellent overview of Sarony's lithographic business, his life, and the importance of his theatrical portraits, of which some forty-three are reproduced full size and discussed in detail.

571. Peet, Phyllis. "Emily Sartain: America's First Woman Mezzotint Engraver." *Imprint* 9, no. 2 (1984): 19–26.

John Sartain's daughter, Emily Sartain (1841–1927), was the only nineteenth-century female mezzotint engraver. Her desire to become an artist is well documented by letters written while in Europe with her father. She received training from him and produced her first print in 1865. Peet describes her training and analyzes a variety of her mezzotints, including genre scenes, religious prints, and portraits. As the demand for mezzotints waned, she became principal of the Philadelphia School of Design for Women, where a number of female wood engravers and etchers were trained.

572. "John Sartain and His Portraits." *Eclectic Magazine* 53 (May 1861): 138–39.

For many years Sartain did mezzotints for the *Eclectic Magazine*. This short eulogy emphasizes the portraits he engraved, and incorrectly credits him with introducing the mezzotint process to the United States.

573. Martinez, Ann Katharine. "The Life and Career of John Sartain (1808–1897): A Nineteenth-Century Philadelphia Printmaker." Ph.D. diss., George Washington University, 1986. 248 pp., biblio.

Martinez has based her excellent doctoral dissertation on archival collections of Sartain material at the Historical Society of Pennsylvania, Moore College of Art, and other Philadelphia institutions. Chapters are devoted to his training in England, illustrations for gift books, his involvement with social reform, the influence of transcendentalism and photography on his portrait prints, and the business of publishing his periodical illustrations and framing prints. This is a model for publications on other American engravers. Unfortunately the illustrations do not reproduce well in the photocopied version of the dissertation.

574. Martinez, Katharine. "John Sartain (1808–1897): His Contribution to American Printmaking." *Imprint* 8, no. 1 (1983): 1–12.

Sartain was a prolific mezzotint engraver with over one thousand prints to his credit, as well as an entrepreneur. Martinez has uncovered a substantial amount about his early training in Great Britain, his work in Philadelphia, and his style and technique. Until the panic of 1837, Sartain could rely on private commissions which were easliy available. After 1837, Sartain turned to book publishers, finding his niche in literary annuals and gift books. He also produced many "framing prints," several of which are reproduced and discussed.

575.———. "Portrait Prints by John Sartain." in *American Portrait Prints*, 135–161. ed. Wendy Wick Reaves. Washington: National Portrait Gallery, 1984.

John Sartain had a long career in Philadelphia as a mezzotint engraver, although he also turned to portrait painting, lithography, etching, bank-note engraving, and photography. In this well researched essay, Martinez discusses a sampling of his more than 1500 mezzotint portraits focusing on his portrait commissions of the 1830s and 1840s, the reintroduction of mezzotint plates for use in book and magazine illustration, and his involvement with photography.

576.———. "'Messengers of Love, Tokens of Friendship': Gift-Book Illustrations by John Sartain" in *The American Illustrated Book in the Nineteenth Century*, 89–112. ed. Gerald W. R. Ward. Winterthur: The Henry Francis du Pont Winterthur Museum, 1987.

Illustrated gift books flourished in the nineteenth century. Martinez explores the contributions of John Sartain, an Englishman who came to the United States in 1830 at the age of twenty-two. Already a specialist in the mezzotint technique, Sartain received many commissions, providing illustrations for more than sixty gift books between 1832 and 1855. Many were based on reproductive prints from European paintings in his own extensive collection, now owned by the Moore College of Art in Philadelphia. Sartain also copied the works of American artists and edited *The American Gallery of Art* (1848) for the publisher Lindsay and Blakiston. Martinez also considers Sartain's participation in various reform movements. The essay is followed by a list of gift books illustrated by Sartain.

577. Rash, Nancy. "New Light on George Caleb Bingham & John Sartain." *Print Collector's Newsletter* 25, no. 4 (September 1994): 135–137.

Rash has located correspondence in the Historical Society of Pennsylvania that sheds light on the publication of a mezzotint after Bingham's painting *Marshall Law* or *Order No. 11*, a Civil War episode that depopulated several Missouri counties to rid the area of Confederate sympathizers. The correspondence reveals the date and terms of the commission in 1869. Delays occurred and the print was not published until 1872 and the correspondence reveals that sales were disappointing.

578. Sartain, John. *Reminiscences of a Very Old Man, 1808–1897*. New York: D. Appleton & Co., 1899. 297 pp.

The reminiscences of John Sartain include anecdotes about his large circle of friends and acquaintances that included other engravers, artists, actors, publishers, and authors. The occasional details about his own prints should be of interest to those studying the graphic arts of the period. This book was reviewed by Richard H. Stoddard, *Book Buyer* 19 (Dec. 1899): 373–77; and by Minna Angier, *Dial* 27 (Nov. 16, 1899): 359–62.

579. Dickson, Harold E. "The Case Against Savage." *American Collector* 14 (January 1946): 6–7, 17.

Relying on Dunlap's history of the arts in the United States, Dickson proposes that many of the prints produced by Edward Savage (1761–1817) in Philadelphia reveal the hand of David Edwin. In particular the author writes about Savage's *The Washington Family* and *Congress Voting Independence*, also commenting on David Edwin and John Wesley Jarvis, both of whom worked for Savage. Dickson discusses Savage's prints further in *John Wesley Jarvis, American Painter, 1780–1840* (New York, 1949).

580. Fielding, Mantle. "Edward Savage's Portraits of Washington." *Pennsylvania Magazine of History and Biography* 48 (July 1924): 193–200.

Fielding discusses the Savage portrait of Washington painted in 1789, the history of the painting of *The Washington Family*, and the print of it completed in 1798. Statements by John Sartain and James R. Lambdin reinforce the theory that Edwin helped with the engraving of *The Washington Family.*

581. Hart, Charles H. "Edward Savage, Painter and Engraver." *Proceedings of the Massachusetts Historical Society* 19 (January 1905): 1–19.

In 1856 a large copperplate by an anonymous engraver, titled "The Congress Voting Independence," was presented to the Massachusetts Historical Society. In the 1890s, Hart purchased some of Trumbull's correspondence, including a letter from Edward Savage's son which proves that Savage engraved the plate. Hart discusses Savage's portrait of Washington for Harvard College, his work in England, his museum in Philadelphia, the mezzotint portraits, and other prints. He disputes the assertion that David Edwin engraved the plates for Savage. Appended to the article is a chronological catalog of Savage's engraved plates.

582. Jones, Louis C. "Liberty and Considerable License." *Antiques* 74 (July 1958): 40–43.

Edward Savage painted and engraved an image of Liberty that was evidently quite popular, for the author has found a substantial number of paintings on velvet, watercolors, and pieces of needlework based on it. He also lists five Chinese paintings on glass after the print. This is an interesting study of a print that acted as a source for other works of art.

583. Thorpe, Russell Walton. "Edward Savage." *Antiquarian* 5 (November 1925): 31–34.

That Savage's reputation as an engraver was disputed is evident by the disparaging contemporary criticism of him by David Edwin, John Wesley Jarvis, and William Dunlap. Thorpe, however, praises the mezzotint portraits by Savage, then discusses other aspects of the artist's career.

584. Rainey, Sue. "Recollections of a Leslie's Special Artist in the Civil War." *Imprint* 23, no. 1 (1998): 18–26.

Rainey has transcribed and provided an introduction to a memoir by Francis H. Schell (1834–1909) relating his experiences as an artist employed by the publisher of *Frank Leslie's Illustrated Newspaper* in the the early months of the Civil War. His account provides interesting details about pictorial journalism, the expectations of the publisher, and some of the pitfalls facing the many men who worked for the pictorial newspapers. The memoir, located in the Special Collections Department of the University of Virginia, has provided Rainey the ability to attribute some unsigned illustrations to Schell.

585. Harris, Elizabeth. *An Engraver's Potpourri. Life and Times of a Nineteenth Century Bank-Note Engraver*. Washington, D.C.: Smithsonian Institution, 1979. 8 leaves.

Harris provides a biographical sketch of Stephen Schoff (1818–1905), a professional engraver. The exhibition included examples of prints that he admired—other banknote engravings, portrait etchings, old master prints. He served his apprenticeship with Oliver Pelton and Joseph Andrews and then set off for Europe. He was influenced by J.M.W. Turner's school of engravers. Schoff later worked for John A. Lowell, a commercial publisher of greeting cards.

586. Fontana, Bernard L. "Drawing the line between Mexico and the United States." *American West* 20, no. 4 (July 1983): 50–56.

Arthur Carl Victor Schott (1814–1875) was a German-born survey artist who participated in the boundary survey in the early 1850s. His field sketches were published in the official report in 1859. Fontana provides excellent biographical information on this artist and notes the existence of a 1977 master's thesis on Schott by Gretchen Gause Fox (George Washington University).

587. Titterton, Robert J. *Julian Scott: Artist of the Civil War and Native America*. Jefferson, N.C. and London: McFarland & Company, Inc., 1997. 315 pp., index, biblio.

Julian Scott (1846–1901) was one of the youngest of the Civil War sketch artists. He served in the Third Regiment of Vermont Volunteers and recorded on paper some of what he saw. While recuperating from a wound, he was befriended by Henry E. Clark who arranged for his admission to the National Academy of Design. In May 1864 he traveled to the front lines to document Civil War battles. In later years he used these drawings in his paintings; others were reproduced in magazines, particularly *Harper's Weekly*. He also provided illustrations of the Revolutionary War for the popular press. In 1890 he joined the staff of the Eleventh Census and made sketches of Native American life that were reproduced in later reports. This book provides an excellent summary of Scott's life and work.

588. Holt, Mary E. "A Checklist of the Work of Francis Shallus, Philadelphia Engraver." *Winterthur Portfolio* 4 (1968): 143–158.

Many of Shallus's (1773–1821) works are book illustrations of a scientific or technical nature, such as those for Dobson's *Encyclopedia*. Several medals are among his extant engravings. Holt describes Shallus's life and work, then provides a carefully prepared checklist of his engravings.

589. Norton, Bettina A. "William Sharp: Accomplished Lithographer" in *Art & Commerce*, 50–75. Boston: Museum of Fine Arts, 1978.

William Sharp (1803–1875) was trained in England as a lithographic artist and emigrated to America in 1839, settling in Boston where he was responsible for introducing color lithography. Norton summarizes his years in England, provides information on his family and activities in Boston, distinguishing him from other lithographers working in Boston sharing the same surname, and then describes the prints for which he was responsible. The beginnings of color lithography in England and France are also described. Because of his experience in England, Sharp was able to start producing lithographs printed in colors soon after his arrival in Boston. Norton describes a number of book illustrations, sheet music covers, and separately published prints by Sharp. Some, particularly those for the *Victoria Regia* (1854), are among the finest lithographs produced in America in the nineteenth century.

590. Beckman, Thomas. "The Etchings of Robert Shaw (1859–1912)." *Delaware History* 24, no. 2 (1990): 75–108.

Robert Shaw was one of the three most significant artists active in Wilmington, Delaware, at the end of the nineteenth century. Between 1888 and 1910, Shaw created at least 120 etchings, all listed at the end of the article. Beckman discusses his childhood in Delaware, his art education, and his work in oil, watercolor, pen and ink, and etching. He etched a series of views that became *Picturesque Wilmington* (ca. 1890–1894). Beckman has determined that Shaw based some of his views on historical photographs. Beginning in 1903 Shaw worked for six years on *American Memorial Etchings*, containing sixty prints, the most complete set of which is in the New York Public Library. The Historical Society of Delaware has an extensive collection of Shaw's correspondence and related materials.

591. Shadwell, Wendy. "Louis Simond, Amateur Artist." *Antiques* 105 (January 1974): 174–77.

Simond (1767–1831), a French emigrant, provided the drawings for several engravings by William S. Leney in the beginning of the nineteenth century. This study provides information on Simond's artistic associations in New York from 1790 to 1814.

592. Walsh, Charles Harper. "The Earliest Engraving Executed in Copper in the American Colonies: A Map of Raritan River, Engraved on Copper by R. Simson in 1683." *Records of the Columbia Historical Society* 15 (1912): 54–72.

Walsh knew of two copies of a map of the Raritan River that was engraved on copper in 1683 by R. Simson. One is at the Library of Congress, the other at the New Jersey Historical Society. The compiler of the map, John Reid, came to New Jersey from Edinburgh in 1683; Walsh provides factual information about his life. Simson is more of an enigma; all that is known is that contemporary colonial records claim that the map was printed in the colonies. This article is well researched, although its information on the history of American engraving is somewhat dated. Wheat and Brun did not include this map in their bibliography of early American maps.

593. Hawkes, Elizabeth H. "John Sloan's Newspaper Career: An Alternative to Art School" in *The Cultivation of Artists in Nineteenth Century America*, 169–185. editors Georgia B. Barnhill, Diana Korzenik, and Caroline F. Sloat. Worcester: American Antiquarian Society, 1997.

Rather than obtaining formal art training, John Sloan (1871–1951) spent twelve years working as an artist for Philadelphia and New York newspapers beginning in 1892. Hawkes describes these years of Sloan's life and the importance of illustrations to the success of newspapers of that era. Some newspaper artists supplemented their on-the-job training with formal classes at academies and became painters; others turned to magazine illustration. Hawkes provides an excellent overview of Sloan and his contemporaries who worked for the press.

594. Sloan, Helen Farr. "John Sloan: His Early Years." *Imprint* 5, no. 1 (1980): 9–14.

The artist John Sloan (1871–1951) started his career as an etcher and illustrator. His second wife records his early life and training as an artist. He learned to etch, for example, by using Hamerton's *Handbook*. A number of his etchings, based on photographs, were made for A. Edward Newton, a Philadelphia merchant and collector. In 1892 he began to work for the Philadelphia *Inquirer*, which eclipsed his work as an etcher.

595. Allodi, Mary Macaulay, and Rosemarie L. Tovell. *An Engraver's Pilgrimmage. James Smillie in Quebec, 1821–1830.* Toronto: Royal Ontario Museum, 1989. 139 pp., biblio., index.

James Smillie (1807–1885) spent nine years in Quebec before settling permanently in New York where he became one of the best reproductive engravers of his era. Allodi and Tovell have transcribed his autobiography covering his years in Quebec. Smillie also compiled a scrapbook containing examples of his work. These have been very carefully described in a fully illustrated catalogue. The introduction describes his childhood in Scotland, his training, and his family. An appendix contains portions of letters received by Smillie between 1827 and 1839. This is an extremely informative publication.

596. Schweizer, Paul D. "'So exquisite a transcript': James Smillie's Engravings after Thomas Cole's *Voyage of Life*." *Imprint* 11 and 12, nos. 2; 1 (1986 and 1987): 2–13; 13–24.

Schweizer notes that four folio engravings by James Smillie (1807–1885) after Cole's allegorical paintings formed the most ambitious print publishing project of the 1850s and analyzes all aspects of this remarkable undertaking. Abundant documentation exists for these prints and Schweizer has used it all to excellent advantage. The article is continued in the following issue of *Imprint* (Spring 1987). The author includes a great deal of information on other works engraved by Smillie in the 1850s.

597. Weitenkampf, Frank. "The Evolution of Steel Engraving in America." *Book Buyer* New ser. 23 (September 1901): 93–95.

Weitenkampf concentrates on the work of James Smillie, artist, engraver, and etcher. This article was written when The New York Public Library received a large collection of his work, donated by a member of his family. Weitenkampf describes Smillie's prints and his technique for obtaining exact reproductions of the paintings he copied. Smillie was also a bank note engraver, and Weitenkampf comments briefly on his contributions in that field.

598. Witthoft, Brucia. "The History of James Smillie's Engraving After Albert Bierstadt's *The Rocky Mountains*." *American Art Journal* (1987): 40–49.

Bierstadt's painting was first exhibited in 1863 when it received favorable public notice. Witthoft's discussion of the creation of a print from the painting is based on the contract between the two men as well as on diaries of Smillie and his son.

599. Koehler, Sylvester R. "James D. Smillie." *American Art Review* 1, no. 2 (1880): 524–25.

Under the direction of his father, Smillie learned steel and bank note engraving. After a trip abroad, he began to paint. He was a founder of the American Water Color Society and, with Leroy Yale, organized the New York Etching Club. A list of his most important etchings is given.

600. Schantz, Michael W. "James D. Smillie's The Goldsmith's Daughter. The Making and Marketing of a Reproductive Master Print." *Imprint* 18, no. 1 (1993): 2–14.

Schantz opens his discussion with a summary history of reproductive engraving suggesting its importance as a genre and comparing the process to etching. Schantz bases his analysis of a reproductive engraving by Smillie (1833–1909) after Daniel Huntington's painting, *The Goldsmith's Daughter*, on materials and diaries in the Smillie Family Collection at the Archives of American Art. The creation of the print is described as well as its publication and marketing.

601. Schneider, Rona. "Career of James David Smillie (1833–1909) As Revealed in His Diaries." *American Art Journal* 16, no. 1 (December 1984): 4–33.

Smillie kept diaries now owned by the Archives of Amerian Art, from 1865 until his death. They contain a wealth of information on his artistic practices as well as comments on the New York art scene. Although trained as an engraver by his father, he turned to painting in oils and is best known for his landscapes. His etchings were in demand in the 1880's and his experiments with mezzotint and drypoint are also recorded in his diaries. This article is very well documented and illustrated.

602.———. "James David Smillie: The Etchings (1877–1909)." *Imprint* 6, no. 2 (1981): 2–13.

James David Smillie (1833–1909) was a versatile artist, working in oil, watercolor, and the various graphic media. Schneider provides an excellent, well-researched biographical sketch of the artist, focusing on his etchings done in conjunction with the New York Etching Club. His subject matter as an etcher was varied including western views, the New England landscape, portraits, and even an etching after Winslow Homer's *A Voice from the Cliff* of 1886. Large collections of his prints may be found at the New York Public Library, the Museum of Fine Arts in Boston, and the St. Louis Art Museum.

603. Witthoft, Brucia. *The Fine-Arts Etchings of James David Smillie.* Lewiston, N.Y.: The Edwin Mellen Press, 1992. 309 pp., biblio., index.

Witthoft's monograph is based on extensive surviving diaries owned by the Archives of American Art. The biographical sketch is excellent and is rich in documenting Smillie's relationships with other artists and etchers of the era, particularly those active in the New-York Etching Club. The catalogue raisonne is arranged chronologically. Witthoft provides excellent information about each one drawn from the diaries and other sources. Although this book is well documented, the illustrations are of poor quality and the book itself does not equal the merit of Smillie's prints.

604. Smith, Edward S. "John Reubens Smith, An Anglo-American Artist." *Connoisseur* 85 (May 1930): 300–307.

Born in England, John Reubens Smith (1775–1849) was the son of John Raphael Smith, an artist and engraver. The younger Smith was a successful artist in England when he left for the United States in 1806. His activities were three-fold: painting, engraving and teaching. This study, an excellent introduction to Smith's works, could be expanded.

605. Stauffer, Paul J. "Uriah Smith: Wood Engraver." *Adventist Heritage* 3, no. 1 (June 1976): 17–21.

Some of the engravings in the Adventist publications, the *Review and Herald* and the *Youth's Instructor*, in the 1850s and 1860s were made by Uriah Smith, who often signed with just his initials, U.S. Stauffer provides the little biographical information about Smith that is known. His engraving tools, located at Andrews University, are reproduced together with examples of his engravings.

606. Arthur, Helen. "Thomas Sparrow, an Early Maryland Engraver." *Antiques* 55 (January 1949): 44–45.

Primarily an Annapolis silversmith, Sparrow also engraved a few vignettes and title pages. Few examples of his work survive. Through diligent research the author has compiled the known facts of Sparrow's life. Three of his signed engravings are reproduced.

607. "Exploration and Survey of the Valley of the Great Salt Lake of Utah." *Nevada Historical Review* 3, no. 1 (1975): 32–40.

This article contains a brief biographical sketch of Howard Stansbury, a member of the Army Corps of Engineers who helped survey the territory between Fort Leavenworth and the Great Salt Lake in 1849–50. Sixteen plates from the report published in 1853 are reproduced.

608. Wright, Edith A. and Josephine A. McDevitt. "Henry Stone, Lithographer." *Antiques* 34 (July 1938): 16–19.

Henry Stone, English by birth, was advertising his lithographic press in Washington by 1822. Many details of his career are not known, but this article discusses the available facts, including information on the lithographed sheet music he produced in 1823, and the illustrations that appeared in books. A list of sheet music, illustrations from books and magazines, separately published items, engravings, and aquatints that he printed is appended. This list could be expanded, but it stands as a useful location guide for the items in public collections.

609. Dann, Peg. "The Strobridge Collection." *Cincinnati Historical Society Bulletin* 31 (December 1973): 253–260.

The Cincinnati Historical Society holds an important collection of materials relating to the Strobridge Company. Items include lithoraphs published by the company from 1867 to 1956, posters, photographs, bound volumes of lithographs, and business records. Few lithography firms can be as well documented.

610. Marzio, Peter C. "Chromolithography as a Popular Art and Advertising Medium: A Look at Strobridge and Company of Cincinnati" in *Prints of the American West,* 104–125. ed. Ron Tyler. Fort Worth: Amon Carter Museum, 1983.

The Cincinnati Historical Society has a superb collection of the business papers of Strobridge and Company, a very successful firm that filled orders for custom work, speculated on chromolithographic reproductions of oil paintings, and printed posters for circuses, theatrical productions, and miscellaneous road shows. Marzio discusses the business of producing chromolithographs based on the Strobridge Collection. The history of American lithography is marked by the bankruptcies of many firms; Marzio describes one of the successful firms that turned from fine art reproduction to poster production when the market for prints changed.

611. Merten, John W. "Stone by Stone Along a Hundred Years with the House of Strobridge." *Bulletin of the Historical and Philosophical Society of Ohio* 8 (January 1950): 3–48.

The Strobridge Company, still in existence when this article was written, began in 1847 when Elijah C. Middleton set up the firm in Cincinnati. The article traces its growth. Despite two fires, there are still many records in existence that Merten used in a judicious manner to compile this history. The author discusses both the artists who worked for the firm and commercial posters produced, including those for Barnum and Bailey's circus that were the firm's speciality.

612. Cuthbert, John A., and Jessie Poesch. *David Hunter Strother: 'One of the Best Draughtsmen the Country Possesses'.* Morgantown, W. Va.: West Virginia University Press, 1997. 168 pp., biblio., index.

Published at the time of an exhibition of Strother's (1816–1888) drawings in 1997, this volume contains Cuthbert's extensive biography of this talented draftsman, a welcome addition to the literature on American illustrators. Strother's work was reproduced in periodicals and books beginning in the 1840s. The forty-two catalog entries by Poesch are thorough and each of the drawings is reproduced in color.

613. Poesch, Jessie. "An Artists'Excursion, Illustrated by Porte Crayon (David Hunter Strother)." *Imprint* 21, no. 2 (1996): 23–35.

The Harper firm selected Strother to illustrate the excursion that a group of artists made on the Baltimore & Ohio Railroad in June 1858. Poesch provides excellent biographical information on Strother and details about the railroad and the trip. The original article, published in the June 1859 *Harper's New Monthly Magazine*, contains important information about the public's attitudes toward railroads and artists.

614. Poesch, Jessie F. "David Hunter Strother: Mountain People, Mountain Images" in *Graphic Arts & the South. Proceedings of the 1990 North American Print Conference*, 62–99. Judy L. Larson. Fayetteville: University of Arkansas Press, 1993.

A native of Virginia's Shenandoah Valley, Strother (1816–1888) wrote and illustrated articles for many publications, including *Harper's New Monthly Magazine*. Poesch provides biographical information on this writer-artist who often signed his articles "Porte Crayon." He received some formal academic training in Philadelphia and also studied with Samuel F.B. Morse before going to Europe for three years. In this essay, Poesch focuses on Strother's textual and visual depictions of Virginia scenery and its people, both before and after the Civil War. The essay is richly documented with original drawings and quotations from his diaries.

615. Cadbury, Warder H. "Arthur F. Tait." in *American Frontier Life*, 108–129. Fort Worth, Texas: Amon Carter Museum, 1987.

Cadbury, an expert on Tait's paintings, discusses his depictions of the Plains and prints published after his paintings by Nathaniel Currier and Currier & Ives. There were just 13 different compositions of this type, eight of which were published as lithographs. Tait (1819–1905) never traveled to the West, and Cadbury concludes that these compositions are fabrications, created to meet the market demands of Currier and Currier & Ives. The essay is filled with interesting information drawn from Tait's account books as well as contemporary reviews of the paintings.

616. Norton, Bettina A. "Tappan and Bradford: Boston Lithographers With Essex County Associations." *Essex Institute Historical Collections* 114, no. 3 (July 1978): 149–160.

This article discusses Eban Tappan (1815–1854), Lodowick H. Bradford (1820–1854), and their association as lithographic publishers in Boston in the 1840s and early 1850s. A number of their prints are discussed and reproduced.

617. Crompton, Robert D. "James Thackara, American Engraver." *Antiques* 74 (November 1958): 424–28.

This is a condensation of the author's article in the *Journal of the Lancaster County Historical Society*. In *Antiques*, Crompton focuses on Thackara's (1767–1848) engravings, a good number of which are mentioned and reproduced here. A note appears with the article indicating that Crompton was in the process of preparing a checklist of the engravings.

618.———. "James Thackara, Engraver of Philadelphia and Lancaster, Pennsylvania." *Journal of the Lancaster County Historical Society* 62 (April 1958): 65–95.

Although this study is poorly edited, it is well researched and does contain a great deal of information about Thackara's life, mentioning his family, engravings, political activities, and other pursuits. Much of the research is based on family papers, especially a diary kept by Thackara's son, William Wood Thackara. Many individual prints are mentioned and Crompion provides a good outline of the artist's career as an engraver.

619. Golovin, Anne Castrodale. "William Wood Thackara, Volunteer in the War of 1812." *Pennsylvania Magazine of History and Biography* 91 (July 1967): 299–325.

This introduction to Thackara's (1791–1839) own narrative of his activities in the War of 1812 concerns his family, his unsuccessful forays into commerce before joining his father in an engraving business, his experiences in the war, and the little information that is known about his life after the war. The diary, which begins in September 1814 and ends the following January, is a fascinating document but reveals nothing of Thackara's artistic pursuits. The diary itself is held by the Pennsylvania Historical Society.

620. Smith, Steven E. "Thure de Thulstrup: Harper's Workhorse." *Imprint* 21, no. 2 (1996): 2–11.

A prolific illustrator for *Harper's Weekly*, Thulstrup (1848–1930) worked for the Harper firm for almost thirty years. Smith provides an excellent biographical sketch of the artist and description of his work, which encompassed political and social events, portraiture, and military scenes.

621. O'Brien, Donald C. "Elkanah Tisdale. Designer, Engraver, and Miniature Painter." *Connecticut Historical Society Bulletin* 49, no. 2 (1984): 82–96.

O'Brien traces Tisdale's (1768–1835) development as a book illustrator, engraver, miniature and portrait artist in New York, Albany, Boston, and Hartford. In 1823, Tisdale returned to his native town, Lebanon, Connecticut, where he died in 1835.

622. Morris, Thomas F. "Charles Toppan of Bank Note Fame." *Essay-Proof Journal* 26 (December 1969): 3–13.

An important bank note engraver, Charles Toppan (1796–1874) became president of the American Bank Note Co. After growing up in Newburyport, Mass., he worked in Philadelphia with Jacob Perkins. The author outlines his various business relationships and illustrates and discusses a number of unusual proof sheets and miniature engravings.

623. Jackson, Russell Leigh. "Charles Cutler Torrey, 1799–1827." *Old-Time New England* 34 (July 1943): 1–5.

Raised in the Salem area, Torrey served his apprenticeship with George Murray in Philadelphia. A long letter from Torrey to his parents, quoted in the article, provides some insights into the firm of Kearney, Tanney, & Vallance in 1817. Returning to Boston about 1820, Torrey soon traveled to Nashville to seek work, where he died at an early age. Few of his engravings are recorded, although several are mentioned in the text of this article.

624. Crompton, Robert D. "James Trenchard of the 'Columbian' and 'Columbianum'." *Art Quarterly* 23 (December 1960): 378–97.

Trenchard (b. 1747), an engraver in Philadelphia during the late eighteenth century, was co-owner of the *Columbian Magazine* and a founder of a short-lived society of artists, the Columbianum. Crompton discusses the quality of Trenchard's engraving and sources for his work, such as drawings by C.W. Peale and earlier prints. This is a well-documented study of an engraver whose prints deserve recognition.

625. Hanson, David A. "A. A. Turner, American Photolithographer." *History of Photography* 10, no. 3 (July 1986): 193–211.

As a young man, Austin Augustus Turner (1831–66) worked as a photographer in Boston. Hanson provides details of his career and of his experiments in photography and later photolithography, a technique he may have learned while in Paris in 1856. Upon his return he was in business with James A. Cutting who later joined with Lodowick Bradford to produce photolithographs. In 1860 Turner moved to New York where he published *Villas on the Hudson* and several separately published photolithographs. In 1864 he moved to New Orleans while maintaining his New York office. This article is well annotated and illustrated.

626. Fales, Martha Gandy. "James Turner, Silversmith-Engraver" in *Prints of New England*, 1–20. ed. Georgia Brady Barnhill. Worcester: American Antiquarian Society, 1991.

James Turner (1722–1759) was born in Marblehead, Massachusetts, and spent his working life in Boston and Philadelphia. Fales has gathered his known engravings and relief cuts, and assembled the known facts of his life for this biographical study. Turner engraved maps, book and periodical illustrations, bookplates, trade cards, and portraits, and worked as a silversmith. His career as an engraver was more successful and only a few pieces of silver attributed to Turner are known.

627. Cincinnati Art Museum. *A Retrospective Exhibition: John Henry Twatchman. Introduction by Mary Welsh Baskett.* Cincinnati: Cincinnati Art Museum, 1966. 41 pp., biblio.

Much of this catalog is devoted to Twachtman's (1853–1902) paintings, but there is a small section on his etchings. The introduction provides information on Twachtman's contemporaries, working methods, and range of subject matter. The prints are arranged by subject and include over twenty etchings and one lithographed poster. This is the most complete record of Twachtman's etchings to date. A bibliography is supplied.

628. Ryerson, Margery A. "John H. Twachtman's Etchings." *Art in America* 8 (February 1920): 92–96.

Ryerson comments upon Twachtman's style and interest in nature, noting that some of the qualities of his oil paintings are found in his etchings. There is an appendix listing twenty-six of his prints, but no dates are provided for the works.

629. Koehler, Sylvester R. "Kruseman Van Elten." *American Art Review* 1, no. 2 (1880): 475–76.

Hendrick Dirk Kruseman Van Elten (1829–1904) reveals his Dutch birth and heritage in his choice of subjects, although he did not take up etching until he came to America in 1879. A list of his etchings of landscapes produced in the years 1879 to 1880 is included in this article. He was more interested in rendering color and tone than were most American landscape etchers. In *American Art Review* 2 (p. 198), Koehler lists seven additional plates. He notes that Van Elten's technique had improved, and adds that the artist had written to him that he had been working directly from nature and expected even better results.

630. "Vedder's Drawings for Omar Khayyam's "Rubaiyat"." *Atlantic Monthly* (January 1885): 113.

In this anonymous editorial, the writer commends Vedder's (1836–1923) designs for their intellectualism and symbolism.

631. Murray, Richard N. "Elihu Vedder's Drawings for the Rubaiyat." *American Art Review* 10, no. 2 (April 1998): 108–111.

Murray reproduces a selection of Elihu Vedder's original drawings owned by the National Museum of American Art for the *Rubaiyat of Omar Khayyam* published in Boston in 1884. The first edition sold out in days and its immediate popularity established Vedder's reputation.

632. Reich, Marjorie. "The Imagination of Elihu Vedder, as Revealed in His Book Illustrations." *American Art Journal* 6 (May 1974): 39–53.

Vedder, who sought haunting effects in his paintings, was inspired by Doré and Blake in his book illustrations. Particular emphasis is placed here on his illustrations for the *Rubaiyat*.

633. Tatham, David. "Elihu Vedder's *Lair of the Sea Serpent*." *American Art Journal* 17, no. 2 (March 1985): 33–47.

Tatham discusses the iconography of Vedder's painting, *Lair of the Sea Serpent* (1864) and relates it to other works by Vedder executed during the Civil War and to others done in Rhode Island. Of particular interest is the effort to reproduce the painting as an etching in the *American Art Review*. Correspondence between the editor, Sylvester Koehler, the artist, and the engraver, Stephen Alonzo Schoff (1818–1904), dated 1880 provides the basis for his discussion.

634. Chapin, Howard M. "An Unlisted Engraver and Printer of 1715." *American Collector* 2 (July 1926): 361–62.

Samuel Vernon (1683–1737), a silversmith in Newport, R.I., was employed to engrave and print Rhode Island currency from 1715 to 1737. His son, Samuel Jr., carried on the business after his father's death before ceding it to Claggett a year later.

635. Farquhar, Francis P. *Edward Vischer and His* Pictorial of California. San Francisco: Grabhorn Press, 1932. 9 pp.

This biographical sketch focuses on the compilation and publication of Vischer's (1809–1879) book in 1870. The information was obtained from Hubert Vischer in conversation with F.P. Farquhar.

636. Anderson, George McCullough. *The Work of Adalbert Johann Volck, 1828–1912*. Baltimore: By the author, 1970. 223 pp.

Anderson recounts the events in Volck's life which brought him to America about 1848 and that led to his participation in the Civil War. About fifty of Volck's satirical etchings are reproduced, accompanied by an explanatory text. Volck's later career in music, drama, and art are discussed. Thirty other works, including metalcrafts, are illustrated.

637. Voss, Frederick S. "Adalbert Volck, The South's Answer to Thomas Nast." *Smithsonian Studies in American Art* 2, no. 3 (September 1988): 66–87.

Adalbert Volck (1828–1912) did a series of anti-Lincoln prints during the Civil War signed V. Blada. Voss provides biographical information on this German-American dentist who emigrated to the United States in 1848 and discusses the lithographed and etched cartoons that Volck produced. Voss suggests that these cartoons, distributed in small numbers, had little impact. They do, however, epitomize Southern ideas and hatred of the north.

638. Force, Albert W. "H. Walton, Limner, Lithographer, and Map Maker." *Antiques* 82 (September 1962): 284–87.

Little biographical information about Henry Walton exists, but he was an active artist in Ithaca from the 1830s to the late 1840s, at which time he departed for California. The author examines a number of his signed works including several lithographed landscapes. Walton earlier worked for the Pendleton shop in Boston where he presumably learned lithography.

639. *Alfred R. Waud. Special Artist on Assignment. Profiles of American Towns and Cities 1850–1880.* New Orleans: The Historic New Orleans Collection, 1979. 21 pp.

In 1979 The Historic New Orleans Collection mounted an exhibition of 135 items from their strong collection of Waud (1828–1891) drawings and some related prints and illustrations. The introduction discusses Waud's work as a "special artist" for *Harper's Weekly* which hired him away from the *New York Illustrated News*. The artist also produced drawings for *Harper's New Monthly Magazine* and *Every Saturday*. The collection of about 2,000 items came from Waud's descendants and is an important archive. For a full biography, see Frederic E. Ray's *Alfred R. Waud, Civil War Artist* (New York: Viking Press,1974).

640. Katz, Harry L. "Love, Lies, and Wood Engraving: Alfred Waud in Boston, 1856–1860." *Imprint* 22, no. 2 (1997): 2–10.

Waud lived in Boston for several years, using a pseudonym (A. Hill) to conceal his illicit love affair with a married woman. Katz uncovered this aspect of Waud's career by comparing extant sketches in The Historic New Orleans Collection with published illustrations in *Ballou's Pictorial*. He discusses these years of Waud's life and work in detail. Eventually the woman was divorced, paving the way for Waud to marry her. The Civil War opened new opportunities for Waud in New York and his reputation as a "special artist" soared.

641. Ray, Frederic E. *Alfred R. Waud, Civil War Artist*. New York: Viking Press, 1974. 192 pp., index.

This well illustrated book is based on the collection of Waud's drawings at the Library of Congress. Waud was one of the best known sketch artists who worked for *The New York Illustrated News* and *Harper's Weekly*. Born in England in 1828, Waud came to the United States in 1850, originally looking for work as a scene painter. He soon went to Boston and began drawing on wood blocks and then returned to New York. Ray traces Waud's Civil War experiences and work of the sketch artists who worked for the illustrated magazines. Ray also provides extensive information on each of the drawings reproduced.

642. Cary, Elisabeth L. "Etched Work of J. Alden Weir." *Scribner's Magazine* 68 (October 1920): 507–512.

This article concentrates on Weir's style of etching, particularly the Isle of Man series and the plate entitled "The Blacksmith's Shop." The author notes that a common interest in contemporary American society is evident both in Weir's etchings and in the works of writers of his time, such as the books of Henry James.

643. Flint, Janet A. *J. Alden Weir, An American Printmaker, 1853–1919*. Provo, Utah: Brigham Young University Press, 1972. 96 pp., biblio., index.

Flint explores some of the relationships Weir had with other etchers and artists that stimulated his interest in etching. Individual prints are mentioned and his work as a whole is carefully characterized. The notes on other good collections of Weir's etchings are helpful. The catalog reproduces the sixty-five prints included in the exhibition and twenty-two others, mainly unfinished, that were included for their historical interest. The bibliography is good and includes references to general works on Weir.

644. Ryerson, Margery A. "J. Alden Weir's Etchings." *Art in America* 8 (August 1920): 243–48.

Weir etched during the 1880s and 1890s, specializing in figures and farm scenes. The most valuable part of this brief appreciation is its list of eighty-seven etchings, plus eighteen more from the Isle of Man series. Only measurements and titles are provided.

645. Spence, Robert, and John Nelson. *The Etchings of J. Alden Weir*. Lincoln: University of Nebraska Art Galleries, 1967. Unpag.

In his biographical sketch, Spence mentions influences on Weir's art, his training, and his painting, to provide background for his detailed discussion of Weir's etching. The introduction to the catalog by Nelson is concerned with Weir's technique, choice of subject matter, and method of work. Spence's catalog describes 128 prints and locates impressions of them in several different collections. The bibliography is excellent and includes exhibition and sales catalogs, standard articles, and articles in the *New York Times*.

646. Zimmermann, Agnes. "An Essay Towards a Catalogue Raisonne of the Etchings, Drypoints, and Lithographs of Julian Alden Weir." *Papers of the Metropolitan Museum of Art* 1, no. 2 (1923):

This catalog is comprised of one hundred and twenty-three entries arranged in four general groups: women and children, men, views and landscapes, and the Isle of Man series. Different states of each print are described and the content discussed.

647.———. "Julian Alden Weir, His Etchings." *Print Collector's Quarterly* 10 (October 1923): 289–308.

Weir etched over one hundred plates in only six years, some of which were accidentally destroyed. He looked upon etching as a form of relaxation from his painting. Zimmermann provides a thorough chronology of his printmaking career, describing some of his working methods. Weir generally printed his own plates, which he worked extensively, and was fond of old paper. Specific prints are mentioned and sensitively analyzed.

648. Bryant, William Cullen, II. "Robert Weir as Illustrator" in *Robert W. Weir of West Point. Illustrator, Teacher and Poet*, 7–29. compiler and editor Michael E. Moss. West Point, N.Y.: United States Military Academy, 1976.

Bryant discusses Weir's work as a book and magazine illustrator in the 1830's, 1840's, and 1850's. Detailed information on a variety of them is provided in the exhibition checklist. This pamphlet also discusses Weir as a teacher of art at West Point and his poetry.

649. Moss, Michael E. *Robert W. Weir of West Point. Illustrator, Teacher and Poet*. West Point, N.Y.: United States Military Academy, 1986. 68 pp.

This catalog documents an exhibition held at the West Point Museum from 1976 and 1977. Weir (1803–1889) was head of the Academy's department of drawing from 1834 to 1876. Included in the catalog are brief essays on Weir as an illustrator, Weir as a teacher, and Weir as a poet. The catalog of book illustrations after Weir's designs and drawings by his students numbers fifty-six items. This is a useful publication.

650. Wrightson, Pricilla. "Benjamin West, Thomas Rowlandson and William Combe." *Print Quarterly* 9, no. 4 (December 1992): 361–368.

Wrightson describes the circumstances around the creation of Benjamin West's (1738–1820) *Angel of the Resurrection* signed and dated 1801. There are four states, each of which is illustrated and described. Also described are verses reproduced lithographically by William Combe at Ackermann's press in London. Wrightson attributes *Two Women With a Fishwife* to Rowlandson, ca. 1817.

651. "Whistler in Painting and Etching." *Scribner's Monthly* 18 (August 1879): 418–95.

Whistler's ideals and work, are compared to those of his contemporaries. Those qualities attributed to Whistler (1834–1903) "explain his undisputed excellence as an etcher. An etcher is logically an impressionist."

652. Bacher, Otto H. "With Whistler in Venice, 1880–1886." *Century* 73 (December 1906): 207–218.

Bacher's anecdotal article touches on Whistler's association with Duveneck's "boys," his pastels, his method of printing, and his struggle to reproduce his master etching, "The Traghetto."

653. Cary, Elisabeth Luther. *The Works of James McNeill Whistler*. New York: Moffat, Yard & Co., 1913. 302 pp., index.

Cary discusses Whistler's artistic development and devotes separate chapters to topics such as his childhood drawings, his training in Paris, his life in England, Japanese influence, his etchings, and his theory of art. There are 426 items included in the checklist of etchings, and the titles are keyed to other catalogs. The lithographs are listed separately.

654. Caxton Club. *Catalogue of an Exhibition of the Etchings and Lithographs of James McNeill Whistler*. Chicago: 1900. Unpag.

This exhibition catalog contains a listing of 320 etchings and 120 lithographs. No dates are given for the prints, and there is no introduction.

655. Copley Society. *Loan Collection: Etchings, Dry-Points and Lithographs of James McNeill Whistler*. Boston: 1904. 33 pp.

In this checklist of 315 items, the etchings are numbered according to Wetmore's catalog and supplement and the lithographs according to Way's catalog. Both volumes supersede this work in importance.

656. Delaney, Paul. "Whistler, Shannon and the Revival of Lithography as Art." *Nineteenth Century* 4, no. 4 (December 1978): 75–80.

Whistler began to use lithography in 1878–79. Delaney discusses his work in the medium in 1887 and later years. The role of centenary exhibitions commemorating the invention of lithography is explained. Charles Shannon, a friend of Whistler's, also created lithographs, and Delaney discusses his work and the range of influences on it.

657. Dodgson, Campbell. "Two Unpublished Whistlers." *Print Collector's Quarterly* 7 (April 1917): 217–20.

Both of these unrecorded minor works—a rejected title to the *French Set* (1858), and a cancelled lithograph—are illustrated in this article. The former is possibly a unique impression. Both prints are in the British Museum.

658. Esko, Claudia T. "The Influence of Whistler on American Painter-Etchers." *Imprint* 10, no. 2 (1985): 12–20.

Esko chronicles Whistler's use of etching and his particular style. Among his American followers were Joseph Pennell, Frank Duveneck, Otto Bacher, Charles Abel Corwin, Henry Twachtman, Julian Alden Weir, and Childe Hassam. Their stylistic relationships are discussed.

659. Getscher, Robert H. *The Stamp of Whistler*. Oberlin, Ohio: Allen Memorial Art Museum, 1977. x, 285 pp., index, biblio.

The focus of this exhibition was the influence of Whistler on his contemopraries and on later generations of etchers. The introduction by Allen Staley discusses Whistler's printmaking career and concludes that he was "very much a part and product of his time." (p. 12) Half of the catalogue is devoted to extensive commentary by Getscher on Whistler's etchings and lithographs; the rest describes the work American, British, and French artists who fell under his influence. Americans include Frank Deveneck, Julian Alden Weir, John Henry Twatchman, George Edward Hopkins, Charles Abel Corwin, Joseph Pennell, and Frederick Childe Hassam.

660. The Grolier Club. *Catalogue of Etchings and Dry-Points by James McNeill Whistler*. New York: 1904. 88 pp., index.

A brief biography of Whistler is included in the introduction, which notes the different styles of etchings Whistler executed in England, France, and Italy. This exhibition catalog lists nearly four hundred plates, and in many cases several states of each print are described.

661.———. *Catalogue of Lithographs by James McNeill Whistler*. New York: 1907. 15 pp.

Whistler's lithographic style, his experimentation with the medium, and the reception accorded his lithographs by collectors and connoisseurs are discussed in the introduction. There was little interest in the lithographs when they were first issued, but later they became popular and scarce. The exhibition included all of Whistler's lithographs, and the checklist is keyed to Way's catalog, where fuller descriptions of the prints may be found.

662. Johnson, Una E. "The Wood Engravings of James McNeill Whistler." *Print Collector's Quarterly* 28 (October 1941): 275–87.

Whistler's early success abroad encouraged his production of prints. Among his efforts were four wood engraved illustrations for the magazine *Once a Week*, done in 1862. Drawn directly on the block by Whistler, the illustrations were engraved by the Dalziel brothers. Proof impressions can be found in the British Library, the Victoria and Albert Museum, and the Brooklyn Museum, among other collections. In addition, Whistler did two illustrations for a short story that appeared in the journal *Good Works*. All six illustrations are reproduced and a descriptive list is appended. Also mentioned are five uncut drawings on boxwood in the Library of Congress.

663. Knoedler & Co. "Fifty Lithographs by James McNeill Whistler." *Print Collector's Bulletin* 1 (1930): 1–71.

This special number of Knoedler's illustrated catalogs for museums and collectors includes an introductory note by Joseph Pennell and contributions by T. R. Way, E. L. Cary, and F. Weitenkampf. The introduction explains lithography and the plates are annotated with quotations from critical writings on Whistler.

664. Lane, James Warren. *Whistler*. New York: Crown Publishers, 1952. 112 pp., biblio.

The short text focuses on Whistler's personality as can be discerned in his painting and etching. The artistic training he received in Paris and the influence of Japanese prints on him are elaborated. There is a general discussion of his etchings and lithographs, several of which are illustrated.

665. Levy, Mervyn. *Whistler Lithographs*. London: Jupiter Books, 1975. Unpag., biblio.

Allen Staley summarizes Whistler's career, with particular emphasis on his lithographs and their subject matter. The introductions by Thomas R. Way published in 1896 and 1905 for Whistler's work are reprinted in full. Levy's introduction discusses Whistler's style and technique. Among the catalog entries are several preparatory sketches. The prints are well described and illustrated.

666. Lochnan, Katharine A. "The Gentle Art of Marketing Whistler Prints." *Print Quarterly* 14, no. 1 (March 1997): 3–14.

Whistler carefully laid plans for marketing his prints. Lochnan describes his efforts in the context of the etching revival of the 1860s in England, networks of family and friends, and patrons. He helped to create the market for unique proofs of etchings and contributed to the market. In exhibitions of his etchings, he controlled all aspects of the installation. He was able to apply some of these techniques to the sale of his lithographs.

667.———. *The Etchings of James McNeill Whistler*. New Haven: Yale University Press and the Art Gallery of Ontario, 1984. 308 pp., biblio., index.

Over the course of his long career, Whistler made 450 etchings. Lochnan's book provides an excellent overview of Whistler's life from his birth in Lowell, Massachusetts, in 1834 through his late etchings of the early twentieth century. Of particular interest is Lochnan's placement of the etchings in the context of the work of Rembrandt and other Old Masters. She also considers the influence of other artists on his work in this study arranged chronologically. The illustrations are excellent and the text is well documented. Because of Whistler's status as an expatriot (he even claimed to have been born in St. Petersburg), coverage of him in this bibliography is incomplete. Those interested in Whistler should certainly consult Lochnan's bibliography for additional works on this important artist.

668. Mansfield, Howard. *A Descriptive Catalogue of the Etchings and Dry-Points of James Abbott McNeill Whistler*. Chicago: The Caxton Club, 1909. lxvii, 267 pp., index.

This catalogue itemizes 440 etchings and drypoinots by Whistler. Careful attention is paid to the different states, and a short description is provided for each print. The introduction, which includes a biography of the artist, touches on his style, his methods, the publication of his etchings, locations in private collections, exhibitions of his work, and information about prior catalogues.

669.———. "Concerning a Whistler Portrait: 'Mr. Mann' or 'Mr. Davis'?" *Print Collector's Quarterly* 4 (December 1914): 383–91.

The etching alleged to be of Mr. Mann is in reality Mr. Henry Davis, while the drypoint alleged to be Mr. Davis is actually of Mr. Astruc.

670.———. "Whistler in Belgium and Holland." *Print Collector's Quarterly* 6 (December 1916): 375–95.

From the early 1860s Whistler was enthusiastic about Belgium and Holland. His first visit there was with Haden and Legros. Examples of the etchings and watercolors he produced during this and subsequent trips are cited.

671.———. "Whistler as a Critic of His Own Prints." *Print Collector's Quarterly* 3 (December 1913): 367–93.

Whistler's self-criticism is evident in the changes he made in his etched plates. It is known that plates existed from which no impressions were taken prior to their cancellation. Mansfield notes that the line of demarcation between trial proofs and various states is difficult to draw. He goes on to discuss a number of etchings in detail, pointing out changes and corrections made by Whistler. From time to time the artist noted on the backs of the impressions those prints which pleased him most. A list of those displayed at the Chicago World's Fair in 1893 is printed. A few corrections to his lithographs are also noted.

672. Mayor, A. Hyatt. "An Early Whistler Lithograph." *Print Collector's Quarterly* 24 (October 1937): 305–309.

Mayor writes about a Whistler lithograph dated 1855, proving that the artist was introduced to lithography well before his association with Thomas Way in 1878.

673. Morton, Frederick W. "Whistler the Etcher." *Brush and Pencil* 12 (August 1903): 305–319.

Whistler's death, just before this article was written, occasioned a number of attempts like this one to assess his career. Morton feels that the etchings are supreme accomplishments, and sets them in the context of Whistler's rebellious personality. Quotations from other critics, as well as Morton's own thoughts on the artist's viewpoint and style, are included.

674. Nash, Ray. "Rembrandt's Influence on Seymour Haden, Whistler, and the Revival of Original Etching." *Printing and Graphic Arts* 2 (December 1954): 61–73.

Seymour Haden, an English surgeon who was one of the first to study Rembrandt's etchings, was an amateur etcher. Whistler, the half-brother of Haden's American wife, visited London in 1848 and 1849, where he was introduced to Rembrandt's work by Haden. The etching revival in England in the 1850s began with the renewed interest in Rembrandt.

675. Palmer, Marlene A. "Whistler and the U.S. Coast and Geodetic Survey: An Influential Period in a Flamboyant Life." *Journal of the West* 8, no. 4 (October 1969): 559–77.

Whistler, who attended West Point for three years from 1851–54, learned etching and engraving while working for the Coast Survey after he was discharged from West Point. He left within a few months; he and the regimen were an unsuitable match. Palmer sets this episode of his early professional training within his larger success as an etcher and artist.

676. Pennell, Joseph. "Whistler as Etcher and Lithographer." *Burlington Magazine* 3 (October 1903): 160–69.

Beginning with the statement that "Whistler was the greatest etcher and most accomplished lithographer who ever lived," Pennell contrasts him with Rembrandt, concentrating on choice of subject matter, style, and technique. Pennell, who worked with Whistler, writes about Whistler's use of lithography as a form of multiplying sketches, rather than as the reproduction of finished works into black and white.

677. Stratis, Harriet K. and Martha Tedeschi. *The Lithographs of James McNeill Whistler*. Chicago and New York: Art Institute of Chicago and Hudson Hills Press, 1998. 2 vols., biblio, index.

The result of a decade's worth of preparation and scholarship, this definitive catalogue is a model of its type. The general editors gathered experts to prepare the catalogue which contains extended commentary on each state of each lithograph that Whistler produced. Each print is beautifully reproduced. Volume two includes the very valuable correspondence between Whistler and his printer, Thomas Way and Way's son. The letters span two decades and were edited by Nicholas Smale. Essays include one by Kevin Sharp on the chronology of exhibitions, publications and sales. Stratis contributed one on Whistler's papers, their selection and use. She and David Kiehl provided another essay on watermarks. The bibliography includes a list of lifetime exhibitions and reviews as well as books and articles on Whistler. It is exhaustive.

678. Tedeschi, Martha. "Whistler and the English Print Market." *Print Quarterly* 14, no. 1 (March 1997): 15–41.

Whistler's prints are considered within the context of the British print market in general, one in which mass-reproduced, reproductive engravings predominated during the late decades of the nineteenth century. Whistler was concerned about reproductions of his own paintings as well as the sale of his original prints. Some of the same conditions that existed in England in the second half of the nineteenth century were factors in the sale of prints in the United States.

679. Way, Thomas R. *Mr. Whistler's Lithographs*. London and New York: George Bell & Sons and H. Wunderlich & Co., 1905. 67 pp.

The introduction to the second edition goes into some detail about the fate of Whistler's lithographic stones after he executed the drawings. Some prints are discussed at length, and a very detailed catalog totaling 160 items, as well as a title index, complete the work.

680.———. "Whistler's Lithographs." *Print Collector's Quarterly* 3 (October 1913): 277–309.

The author's father introduced Whistler to lithography in 1878. By 1896 Whistler had produced about 163 prints. Way discusses some of the early and rare lithographs, then continues with an examination of Whistler's technique. The author examines several prints in detail to determine his methodology, and discusses a number of his themes: nudes, old buildings and shops, craftsmen at work, portraits, and a small group printed in up to six different colors. The author has produced a fine study on lithography and Whistler.

681. Wedmore, Frederick. *Whistler's Etchings: A Study and Catalogue*. London: P. & P. Colnaghi, 1899. 102 pp., index.

This catalog was first published in 1886. The second edition was enlarged to incorporate the etchings produced between 1886 and 1899. The introduction explains the genesis of the catalog, its arrangement, and the characteristics of Whistler's etching style. Each of the 268 entries includes a description of the print, date, dimensions, and location.

682. Wiehl, M. Lee. *A Cultivated Taste: Whistler and American Print Collectors*. Middletown, Conn.: Davison Art Center, 1983. 44 pp.

Wiehl examines the formation of Whistler's reputation in America and the mechanisms that brought his prints into private collections. Although Whistler made tentative plans to return to the United States, he never did. However, his brother-in-law Seymour Haden did, lecturing on etching in 1882. Among the major collectors were George Lucas and Samuel Avery who learned of modern etching in Paris in the 1850s and 1860s. Avery began selling Whistler's prints in the early 1870s. Howard Mansfield, another great collector, introduced Charles Freer to Whistler's work. These collectors collected for reasons of aesthetics and connoisseurship rather than to be encyclopedic.

683. Tovell, Rosemarie L. "Charles Henry White (1878–1918), Canada's Painter-Etcher of American Cities." *Imprint* 22, no. 1 (1997): 2–10.

In this well-documented article, Tovell establishes White as a founder of the etching revival of the early 1900s, a movement known for its realistic treatment of subject matter. She focuses on his etchings of American cities, particularly New York, executed beginning in 1901. At the same time he provided illustrations for popular magazines such as *Harper's Monthly*. Although he lived abroad beginning in 1909, he exhibited in Chicago, New York, and Philadelphia.

684. Taylor, Carl Jr. "George White—Vermont's "Unknown Artist"." *Vermont History* 42 (1974): 3–11.

White (1797–1873) was one of the few engravers in Vermont in the nineteenth century. He was briefly associated with the Eddys in Greenbush. The author of this article describes White's travels throughout Vermont and mentions his various prints. An appendix lists three maps of Vermont and New Hampshire and seven prints either signed by White, or attributed to him.

685. Angle, Paul M. "Whitefield's Views of Chicago." *Chicago History* 3, no. 1 (September 1951): 1–7.

The finest pre-fire prints of Chicago were executed by Edwin Whitefield (1816–1892). Angle presents biographical facts about the artist and provides a checklist of seven prints of Chicago done while Whitefield was there from 1860 to 1863.

686. Heilbron, Bertha L. "Edwin Whitefield's Minnesota Lakes." *Minnesota History* 33 (1953): 247–51.

The Minnesota Historical Society possesses a folio volume containing thirty-seven original watercolor sketches of Minnesota, Wisconsin, and the upper Mississippi, done in 1858 and 1859 by Edwin Whitefield. The artist had a particular interest in this area as he was one of the organizers of the Kandiyohi Town Site Co. He planned to use some of his pictures to promote this venture, perhaps by issuing them as lithographs. The sketches are well executed and form a valuable pictorial record of the northern regions of the United States.

687.———. "Edwin Whitefield: Settlers' Artist." *Minnesota History* 40, no. 2 (1966): 62–77.

This article focuses on Whitefield's work in Minnesota in the mid-1850s. Heilbron discusses in particular Whitefield's use of his artistic talents as he promoted settlement of the frontier. Whitefield lived in one of the frontier settlements, Kandotta, from 1858 to 1860. He made paintings of the region as well as lithographs, some issued in the *Series of Minnesota Scenery*. The article is well illustrated and documented with references to family papers in the Minnesota Historical Society.

688. Norton, Bettina A. *Edwin Whitefield. Nineteenth-Century North American Scenery*. Barre, Mass.: Barre Publishing, 1977. 158 pp., index, biblio.

Whitefield (1816–1892) is described in the foreword by Charles D. Childs as an artist-traveler. In her two essays, Norton uses these descriptors to good advantage. The essay, "The Traveler," describes Whitefield's attempts to paint and publish views of a large number of American towns and cities after his arrival from England in 1837. In "The Artist" Norton focuses on Whitefield's artistic training and efforts as a draftsmen, watercolorist, and artist in oils as well as the transformation of his works into commercially published lithographs. A large number of prints from many collections are reproduced. Norton provides a definitive catalog of his prints, book illustrations, and other printed materials generated by Whitefield. The text and catalog are based on diaries at the Boston Public Library and sketchbooks at the Society for the Preservation of New England Antiquities. The monograph is well researched and written and handsomely produced.

689.———. "Edwin Whitefield, 1816–1892." *Antiques* 102 (August 1972): 232–43.

The author traces the artist's peripatetic career beginning with his first published lithographed views in 1845. Appended is a chronological checklist of Whitefield's city views, ranging in date from 1845 to 1878. This study is well researched and illustrated. Some of the documentation comes from the artist's papers, now at the Boston Public Library.

690.———. "Sketching America. The New York Public Library's Sketchbook of the Nineteenth-Century Amerian Artist and Traveler Edwin Whitefield." *Bulletin of Research in the Humanities* 81, no. 2 (1978): 169–178.

This article concentrates on drawings Whitefield made as preparatory sketches for lithographed panoramas. The New York Public Library Prints Division has a sketchbook used by Whitefield from 1846–69, with a few later drawings added in 1864. Passages from the diary of Whitefield (Boston Public Librеary) document the sketches and Whitefield's travels.

691. Zukowsky, John. "Observations on Edwin Whitefield and *The Hudson River and Rail Road Illustrated*." *Winterthur Portfolio* 14, no. 3 (1979): 270–281.

Zukowsky attributes two sketchbooks at the Henry F. DuPont Winterthur Museum to Whitefield and relates them to books published by the artist. He compares some sketches to structures that are still standing.

692. Whitney, J. H. E. "My Experience as a Wood Engraver." *Lippincott* 40 (October 1887): 592–98.

The personal reminiscence of an engraver in New York City before and after the Civil War, this article contains little information of substance. John Henry Ellsworth Whitney (1840–1891) gives his opinions on Linton and the controversy over the New School of wood engraving. Linton once characterized Whitney's work as "the lowest things in art," and Whitney is correspondingly negative about Linton.

693. McDermott, John F. "J.C. Wild and Fort Snelling." *Minnesota History* 32 (March 1951): 12–14.

John Caspar Wild (ca.1804–1846) painted a view of Fort Snelling in late September 1844. Lithographs of the Mississippi and Ohio River Valleys are related to this painting. McDermott writes well about the few years Wild spent in the midwest before his untimely death at 42.

694.———. "J.C. Wild, Western Painter and Lithographer." *Ohio Archeological and Historical Quarterly* 60 (April 1951): 111–25.

McDermott, although mentioning some of Wild's activities in Philadelphia, concentrates on the paintings and lithographs he produced in St. Louis and Davenport. This excellent study is well documented with newspaper notices, manuscripts, and secondary sources, and is a valuable contribution to the existing body of information on lithography in the midwest.

695.———. "John Casper Wild: Some New Facts and a Query." *Pennsylvania Magazine of History and Biography* 83 (October 1959): 452–55.

In an article on Wild, Martin Snyder wrote that the artist had come to Philadelphia in 1837. A newspaper editorial shows that Wild had been in Philadelpia as early as 1831 or 1832. Other contemporary documents trace his path from Philadelphia in 1835 to Cincinnati, then back in 1837. The author, using this documentation on the artist's travels between Philadelphia and Cincinnati, attempts to date several paintings of Cincinnati done by Wild. The "query" of the title concerns a watercolor and gouache painting of Reading, Pa., in the Stokes Collection of The New York Public Library, thought to be by Zeno Schindler. McDermott attributes it to Wild instead of to Schindler.

696.———. "Some Rare Western Prints by J.C. Wild." *Antiques* 72 (November 1957): 452–53.

Wild did a series of eight views of St. Louis in 1840, as well as a large lithograph of the steamboat *Missouri*, adveritsed for sale in the St. Louis *Missouri Republican*. No copies of the lithograph are known, but McDermott believes that the "Steamer Alexander Scott" was done on the same stone as the "Missouri." Several other interesting prints are illustrated and described.

697. Snyder, Martin P. "J.C. Wild and His Philadelphia Views." *Pennsylvania Magazine of History and Biography* 77 (January 1953): 32–75.

Early in 1838 J.C. Wild began to publish a series of lithographed views of Philadelphia buildings. Snyder discusses their publication in great detail, using newspaper and broadside advertisements as documentation. He also describes other Philadelphia views by Wild, then provides new biographical information on the artist.

698. Cadbury, Warder. "The Adirondack Chromolithographs of Robert D. Wilkie" in *Adirondack Prints and Printmakers: The Call of the Wild*, 69–82. editor Caroline Mastin Welsh. Blue Mountain Lake and Syracuse, N.Y.: Adirondack Museum and Syracuse University Press, 1998.

After providing a brief discussion of the publication of chromolithographs by Louis Prang, Cadbury describes the sets of album cards issued by Prang in 1875 and 1876 after paintings by Robert D. Wilkie (1828–1903). These small cards are now very scarce, although they were published in large numbers for popular display in the home. In the auction of Prang's paintings in 1889, about fifty works by Wilkie of New England and New York were sold; most have disappeared from view.

699. Egerton, Frank N. "Notes Chiefly on the plates of Wilson's *American Ornithology*." *Journal of the Society for the Bibliogprahpy of Natural History* 4, no. 2 (1963): 125–37.

Egerton reprints several letters by Alexander Wilson (1766–1813) to William Bartram and lists the drawings for Wilson's book in the Academy of Natural Science, the Historical Society of Pennsylvania, and the Museum of Comparative Zoology at Harvard University. Several receipts noting payments for engraving and coloring plates are also reprinted.

700. Looney, Robert F. "Jacques Wissler, Painter and Printmaker." *Imprint* 7, no. 1 (March 1982): 37–42.

In 1971, the Free Library of Philadelphia received a box containing a memoir, sketches, and 28 prints by an artist born in Strasbourg. Looney presents an English translation of the memoir that covers Wissler's life through 1880. Wissler (1803–1887) came to Philadelphia in 1849 where he worked for the firm of Peter Duval. In 1860 he was sent to Richmond, Virginia, by a New York firm. There are few prints signed by him, but he clearly was technically proficient.

701. Osgood, Nancy. "Josiah Wolcott: Artist and Associationist." *Old-Time New England* 76, no. 264 (1998): 5–34.

Although best known as a portrait painter, Wolcott (1814–1885) worked at many trades—artist, ornamental painter, and illustrator in Boston. Osgood provides excellent documentation of all of these activities. Among his startling illustrations is "Invitation to the Spirit Land" for a book by John W. Edmonds and George T. Dexter, *Spiritualism* (1853).

702. "Henry Wolf." *Scribner's Magazine* 17 (January 1895): 20–22.

The anonymous author provides a short summary of Wolf's (1852–1916) early career in Paris and discusses his illustrations for magazines in the United States. This glowing appreciation focuses on the artist's skill in rendering the effect of the original work in his wood engraving. Another thumbnail sketch of his life appeared in *Print Collector's Quarterly* 1 (July 1911): 361–62.

703. Smith, Ralph Clifton. "Henry Wolf." *Print Connoisseur* 5 (July 1925): 209–221.

Among the dozen artists comprising the New School of wood engraving, Wolf was one of the most outstanding. A native of Alsace, he did work that first appeared in *Scribner's Magazine* in 1877. He engraved many blocks after American illustrators and painters, such as Sargent and Homer, because he preferred their work to that of European artists. Even when the halftone reproductive method replaced wood engraving, his work remained in demand; toward the end of his career he privately issued original proofs. Smith discusses the aesthetics of several of Wolf's blocks and includes a list of his engraved portraits.

704. Groce, George C., and J.T. Chase Willet. "Joseph Wood: A Brief Account of His Life and the First Catalogue of His Work." *Art Quarterly* 3 (1940): 148–161, 393–400.

Joseph Wood (ca. 1778–1830) worked mainly in oil and watercolor, painting portraits in New York, Philadelphia, and Washington. In addition to his paintings, the authors have found four prints signed by Wood. They also discuss drawings he made that were engraved by others. This study is well documented and includes a catalog listing eighty of the artst's paintings and engravings.

705. Worman, Paul. "The Etchings of Thomas Waterman Wood." *Imprint* 24, no. 1 (1999): 27–34.

Worman is engaged in the compilation of a catalog raisonne of Thomas Waterman Wood (1823–1903). In this essay, he presents Wood's biography and describes his use of the etching process beginning in 1877 at the first meeting of the New York Etching Club. He worked in this medium until 1894 when he refocused his attention on his painting career.

706. Rainey, Sue. "J.D. Woodward's Wood Engravings of Colorado and the Pacific Railways, 1876–1878." *Imprint* 18, no. 2 (1993): 2–12.

Popular journals met the need for more information about the West, particularly after the completion of the transcontinental railroad in 1869. John Douglas Woodward (1848–1924) was hired by D. Appleton's *Art Journal* to make drawings along the railroad's route in Colorado and Utah. Rainey provides information on Woodward's career relying on his extant drawings for much of her excellent discussion of this project published in *The Art Journal* in 1876 and 1877 and as a book titled *Scenery of the Pacific Railraods and Colorado* in 1878.

707. Rainey, Sue, and Roger B. Stein. *Shaping the Landscape Image, 1865–1910: John Douglas Woodward.* Charlottesville: Bayly Art Museum, University of Virginia, 1997. 123 pp., biblio.

Woodward produced a significant body of landscape drawings that were reproduced as illustrations in the latter part of the nineteenth century. This exhibition draws on the collection of Shrine Mont, a conference center of the Episcopal Diocese of Virgina. Stein's essay, "Shaping the Landscape Image," discusses the reasons for Woodward's obscurity after his death, the growing importance of landscape illustration in the second half of the nineteenth century, and Woodward's contributions to this genre. Rainey's essay discusses Woodward's entire career. Illustrations and the catalog of the exhibition follow the essays.

708. Merritt, Jesse. "Thomas Worth, Humorist to Currier & Ives." *American Collector* 10 (August 1941): 8–9.

Thomas Worth (1834–1917) conceived several series of humorous prints for Currier & Ives, including the Darktown Series and White Comics. He was also responsible for many of the excellent trotting-horse lithographs. Merritt also notes that Worth worked for *Harper's Weekly*, providing the periodical with drawings of high quality.

709. Weiss, Harry B. "Joseph Yeager, Early American Engraver, Publisher of Children's Books, and Railroad President." *Bulletin of The New York Public Library* 36 (September 1932): 611–16.

Weiss cites previously unrecorded examples of Yeager's (ca. 1792–1859) early work in Philadelphia and provides new insights on this engraver who, from 1848 until his death, was president of the Harrisburg and Lancaster Railroad. For several years after 1824, he published children's books in partnership with William H. Morgan. A list of books published by the two men is appended, as are lists of Yeager's prints and book illustrations housed in The New York Public Library.

Bibliographies

710. Boston Public Library. "List of Books and Magazine Articles on American Engraving, Etching, and Lithography." *Monthly Bulletin* 9 (December 1904): 481–87.

Published on the occasion of an exhibition of early American engravings at the Museum of Fine Arts, Boston, this valuable but little-known list includes many entries from nineteenth-century periodicals.

711. Bridson, Gavin, and Geoffrey Wakeman. *Printmaking and Picture Printing: A Bibliographic Guide to Artistic and Industrial Technique in Britain, 1750–1900*. Oxford and Williamsburg, Va.: The Plough Press and The Bookpress Ltd., 1984. 250 pp.

Although the works cited in this bibliography mostly are British, many are applicable to the history of the graphic arts in the United States since there was so much trans-Atlantic sharing of technology. The organization of the entries is as follows: printmaking and picture printing in general, intaglio plate processes, relief block processes, planographic processes, and photo-mechanical processes. Each in turn is logically subdivided. Entries are annotated when the contents deserve special attention. Among the literature searched were encyclopedias and periodicals; a list of the latter genre makes up the final section. There are indices by process and by authors. This is a superb resource which will serve to answer many questions.

712. Chase, Frank H. "A Bibliography of American Art and Artists Before 1835." in *History of Arts of Design in the United States*, 346–77. William Dunlap. ed. Frank W. Bayley and Charles E. Goodspeed. Boston: C.E. Goodspeed & Co., 1914.

Although dated, this bibliography is good, and includes references to architects, painters, and sculptors, as well as engravers. It is divided into several sections: bibliographies, general reference works, books containing reproductions, and periodical articles. Also issued as a separate pamphlet.

713. Garrett, Wendell D., and Jane N. Garrett. *The Arts in Early American History*. Chapel Hill: University of North Carolina Press, 1965. 170 pp.

This annotated bibliography is devoted to all the American arts. Sec. 7 pertains to the graphic arts, including engraving, caricature, printing, and bookbinding. The majority of entries under engraving relate to cartography and general works, with little emphasis on individual engravers or particular subjects. The introductory essay by Walter Muir Whitehill discusses the state of scholarship in American art and opportunities for further research.

714. Henry Francis du Pont Winterthur Museum. "A Tentative List of Books, Periodicals, and Catalogues Pertaining to Prints About America With Emphasis on the Period 1650–1850." *Walpole Society Note Book* (1962): 69–119.

This bibliography, reprinted in 1963, is arranged by subject. Its scope includes European prints of America. Many general works on American printing, as opposed to the graphic arts, have been included in this bibliography, which was prepared by a graduate seminar of fellows in the Winterthur Program of Early American Culture under the direction of Charles F. Montgomery.

715. Levis, Howard C. *A Bibliography of Amreican Books Relating to Prints and the Art and History of Engraving*. London: Chadwick Press, 1910. 79 pp., index.

The basis of this bibliography is Levis' own collection. Arranged by author, the listing contains many American publications relating to European prints. As the book excludes magazine articles, its usefulness is limited.

716.———. *A Descriptive Bibliography of the Most Important Books in the English Language Relating to the Art and History of Engraving and the Collecting of Prints*. London: Ellis, 1912. 571 pp.

This massive descriptive bibliography is arranged by subject matter and lists English-language books, including many American works. Readers interested in American prints would do better to consult Levis' earlier bibliography on the subject. Of particular interest is the section on collections and museum and library publications. Supplement and index: London, 1913.

717. Mason, Lauris. *Print Reference Sources: A Select Bibliography, 18th-20th Centuries*. Millwood, N.Y.: Kraus Thomson Organization Limited, 1975. 246 pp.

Organized alphabetically by printmaker, this work includes references to the artist in art historical literature (exhibition and dealers catalogs, monographs, articles) listed after the entries. The selection of printmakers seems rather random as do the bibliographical citations. This is not a definitive reference work for the scholar, but would be very useful to the collector and amateur.

718. Weitenkampf, Frank. *Prints and Their Production: A List of Works in the New York Public Library*. New York: New York Public Library, 1916. 162 pp., index.

Weitenkampf includes books dealing with print production around the world, categorized by individual nations. Usefulness of this work is limited by its early publication date and by its exclusion of periodical articles.

Book and Periodical Illustration

719. Best, James J. *American Popular Illustration: A Reference Guide*. Westport, Conn.: Greenwood Press, 1984. 171 pp., index.

Nineteenth-and twentieth-century book illustration is covered by this excellent guide. Best provides an historical overview covering the most important genres and artists, discusses major illustrated books and artists, delineates the social and artistic context of illustration, concludes with a chapter on techniques and publication media. Each chapter has its own bibliography. Appendices include a list of some of the periodicals that include articles on illustration, information on research collections that he has consulted in his own research and in the compilation of this reference work, a list of illustrated books arranged alphabetically by the illustrator.

720. *City Life Illustrated, 1890–1940*. Wilmington, Del.: Delaware Art Museum, 1980. 117 pp., biblio.

This exhibition catalog features the work of John Sloan, William Glackens, George Luks, and Everett Shinn, all of whom worked as illustrators in the 1890's and later. Also included in the exhibition are works by their friends and colleagues—Bellows, Henri, Kent, Frederic Gruger, Rollin Kirby among others—twenty-seven artists in all. Introductory essays examine aspects of book, magazine, newspaper illustration of the period. The essays and the exceptional biographical sketches were written by the museum's staff.

721. *The Golden Age of American Illustration, 1880–1914*. Wilmington, Del.: Wilmington Society of the Fine Arts, 1972. 68 pp.

The introduction to this catalog by Rowland Elzea touches on many aspects of American illustration including the social context which resulted in the explosion of illustrated material, changes in printing technology, the relationship of periodical and book publishing to illustration, distinctions between easel painters and illustrators, and factors that contributed to the decline of American illustration. A summary of the history of illustration to 1880 is given that relates the work of Americans to European trends. A final section treats American illustration from 1880 to 1914. Again, Elzea discusses the American contributions to this field in relation to the work of European illustrators. The themes of American artists—Art Nouveau, narrative subjects, and city life are discussed. The exhibition included both European drawings and watercolors and those of the major American illustrators of the period.

722. *The Cabinet of Natural History and American Rural Sports*. Barre, Mass.: Imprint Society, 1973. 150 pp.

The introduction to this edited reprint of a nineteenth-century periodical is by Wilson G. Duprey. In it, he summarizes the publication of this journal from 1830 to 1833. Containing a wealth of illustrations of unusual birds and animals of the United States, this journal is noted for the fine hand-colored lithographs, many drawn by Thomas Doughty of Philadelphia and printed there. Duprey notes, however, the interesting fact that some were drawn and printed in New York and Boston, suggesting a high degree of cooperation among early commercial lithographers. The text for the volume was drawn from many different accounts of explorers. Unfortunately a lack of subscribers led the publishers to cease publication. This is a handsome volume which reproduces all the illustrations of the original with the accompanying text.

723. Adelson, Fred B. "Art Under Cover: American Gift-book Illustrations." *Antiques* 125, no. 3 (March 1984): 646–653.

Adelson discusses the literary context and pictorial embellishments of the popular gift-book, common in nineteenth-century America. A number of different titles are discussed as are the role of publisher as patron, the popularity of work by American artists, and the difficult task of accurately reproducing an artist's design. A brief survey of the artists whose works were used and a comment on the pedagogical use of the gift-book concludes the essay which is particularly well illustrated and researched.

724. Andrews, William Loring. "The First Illustrated Magazine Published in New York." in *The Old Booksellers of New York, and Other Papers*, 53–67. New York: Privately printed, 1895.

New York Magazine, the first illustrated magazine in New York, was published from 1790 to 1797. Andrews discusses the history, facts of publication, content, and illustrations. Some of the engravings provide excellent documentation of the appearance of New York in the late eighteenth century, and the more interesting plates are described. Complete files of the periodical are scarce.

725. Barnhill, Georgia B. "Illustrations of the Adirondacks in the Popular Press" in *Adirondack Prints and Printmakers: The Call of the Wild*, 45–68, ed. Caroline Mastin Welsh. Blue Mountain Lake and Syracuse, N.Y.: Adirondack Museum and Syracuse University Press, 1998.

This survey of illustrations of the Adirondacks covers the late eighteenth and nineteenth centuries. Barnhill stresses the importance of considering these prints in the context of the publication in which they appeared. The role of illustrations in fostering tourism and hunting as well as conservation is described, with particular emphasis on the illustrations in *Frank Leslie's Illustrated Newspaper* and *Harper's Weekly* that reached an enormous audience.

726.———. "The Publication of Illustrated Natural Histories in Philadelphia, 1800–1850" in *The American Illustrated Book in the Nineteenth Century*, ed. Gerald W. R. Ward. 53–88 Winterthur, Del.: The Henry Francis du Pont Winterthur Museum, 1987.

Illustrated books on natural history by Benjamin Smith Barton, Alexander Wilson, William P. C. Barton, Thomas Say, John Godman, Samuel Stehman Haldeman, John Edwards Holbrook, and Thomas Nuttall are the focus of Barnhill's essay. These publications all faced problems due to the high cost of publishing illustrated works, often on a subscription basis. They also faced competition from European publications. These issues were only resolved by the subsidization of research and publication by federal and state governments.

727. Bennett, Whitman. *A Practical Guide to American Nineteenth-Century Color Plate Books.* New York: Bennett Book Studios, 1949. 132 pp.

This volume, written to introduce a new territory of book collecting to Americans, describes books published between 1800 and 1900 that contained colored plates. Each item is well annotated, with particular attention paid to the means of coloring the plates. The bibliography is arranged by author, and there is a chronological index at the end.

728. Blum, Ann Shelby. *Picturing Nature. American Nineteenth-Century Zoological Illustration.* Princeton: Princeton University Press, 1993. 403 pp., biblio., index.

This handsomely produced, impeccably researched and highly readable monograph treats in detail many aspects of illustration for zoological publications. Chapters are devoted to "The Naturalist-Illustrator" (the Peales and Alexander Wilson), "Divergence" (the impact of new natural history institutions on the work of scientists such as Lesueur, Say, Godman), "From Naturalist-Illustrator to Artist-Naturalist" (the work of Audubon), "Scientific Prestige, National Honor: Pictures for Federal Science" (the importance of state and federal natural history surveys and publications), "'A Better Style of Art'" The Consolidation of Convention in Midcentury Illustration" (the creation of a style for presenting scientific information), "Illustrations of Theory, Illustrations of Practice" (the works of Agassiz and Darwin), "The Lens and the Line: Photography and Microscopy," and "The Zoologist's Province" (illustrations in the last decade of the century).

729. Bogart, Michele H. "Artistic Ideals and Commercial Practices: The Problem of Status for American Illustrators." *Prospects* 15 (1990): 225–282.

The author provides an intensive analysis of the "Golden Age of Illustration" focusing on the "history of a new vocation structurally bound up on one side with fine art and on the other side with the development of national advertising and mass-market publishing." Bogart discusses illustrators such as Edwin A. Abbey, John LaFarge, and Howard Pyle who began their careers in the 1870's. Among the topics considered are the education of illustrators, the role of organizations, advertising art, the impact of World War I, and poster art. The author concludes that mass market art created restraints for illustrators and compromised the ideals of their own artistic identity. After World War I the tension ceased and illustrators realized that their patronage came from the commercial sector.

730. Bolton, Theodore. *American Book Illustrators: Bibliographic Check Lists of 123 Artists.* New York: R.R. Bowker Co., 1938. 290 pp., index.

This edition, planned as a companion volume to Merle Johnson's American First Editions (1936), represents the first attempt made to catalog the work of American book illustrators. While the book is oriented toward the twentieth century artists, it includes illustrators active in the nineteenth century: E.A. Abbey, W.A. Clark, F.O.C. Darley, A.B. Frost, C.D. Gibson, Winslow Homer, Thomas Nast, F.B. Opper, J. Pennell, H. Pyle, C.S. Reinhart, and F. Remington. Illustrators active before 1840 are not listed. Whenever possible, bibliographic references have been given.

731. Brandywine River Museum. *The Art of American Illustration.* Chadds Ford, Pa.: Brandywine River Museum, 1976. 62 pp.

This loan exhibition catalog presents the works of about ninety illustrators. Joan H. Gorman states in her introduction that an attempt was made to place Howard Pyle and his students in the context of American illustration. A discussion of technological changes in printing illustrations is followed by information on changing styles, the choice of subject matter, and the decline of illustration by the 1950's. The catalog of the exhibition includes biographical sketches of the illustrators as well as information on each drawing.

732. Braun, Robert. *American Natural History Illustrated.* Fairfield: Connecticut Audubon Birdcraft Museum, 1998. 7 pp.

This exhibition checklist describes 35 natural history subjects from books published between 1636 and the present, although most of the books were issued prior to 1900.

733. Brooklyn Museum. *A Century of American Illustration.* Brooklyn: 1972. 155 pp., biblio.

This exhibition catalog, which includes 120 illustrations dating from 1850 to 1972, emphasizes work done in the twentieth century. Linda S. Ferber, in her introduction to the section covering the years 1850 to 1920, writes about the distinction between painter and illustrator, the relationship of illustration to text, and processes for the reproduction of drawings. The American school of illustrators is discussed, with individuals such as Darley and Pyle singled out for special mention. The numerous reproductions are well photographed, and there are short biographical notes on each artist represented in the catalog.

734. Bumgardner, Georgia Brady. "American Almanac Illustration in the Eighteenth Century" in *Eighteenth-Century Prints in Colonial America. To Educate and Decorate,* 51–71. ed. Joan D. Dolmetsch. Williamsburg: Colonial Williamsburg Foundaion, 1979.

This essay traces the history of almanac publication and the audience for this genre, contrasting the contents of American and English almanacs. Various types of illustrations—portraits, astronomical diagrams, genre illustrations, and political images—are discussed with particular emphasis on the latter category.

735.———. "Aspects of American Book Illustration: Technology, Natural Science, and Literature." *Imprint* 5, no. 2 (1980): 2–11.

Bumgardner surveys three aspects of eighteeth-and nineteenth-century book illustration. The illustrations discussed document the growth of interest in American subject matter, the importance of illustrations as visual stimulation for children and their relation to the popularity of specific texts, and their significance as records of American thought, culture, and history.

736.———. "The Popularization of Gentility. Illustrations in American Literary Annuals" in *The Documented Image. Visions in Art History*, 13–26. eds. Gabriel P. Weisburg and Laurinda S. Dixon. Syracuse: Syracuse University Press, 1987.

This essay explores the illustrations found in literary annuals from the 1820s to the Civil War with particular attention paid to the critical response to the illustrations in the popular press and to the changes in subject matter from landscape to genre to romantic scenes. Annuals were particularly important in cultivating taste and making reproductions of the works of American and European artists widely available.

737. Burns, Sarah. "Yankee Romance: The Comic Courtship Scene in Nineteenth-Century American Art." *American Art Journal* 18, no. 4 (1986): 51–75.

William Sidney Mount painted two courtship scenes. Burns suggests that two slightly later paintings by Francis William Edmonds owe something to Mount's works. They are all related to prints and illustrations of the 1850s and later, particularly those for James Russell Lowell's poem "The Courtin" of 1857 by Augustus Hoppin and Winslow Homer. The male figures in Mount's paintings are descendants of "Brother Jonathan," the typical Yankee celebrated in song, literature, and image in the early decades of the nineteenth century. All of these sources and others are analyzed. Burns concludes that Lowell's poem and Homer's illustrations exploit the quaintness of a bygone era.

738. Drepperd, Carl. *Early American Advertising Art: Illustrations Used in American Newspaper, Almanac, and Magazine Advertising, 1750–1850*. New York: Youth Group of Magazines, 1943. 24 pp.

The short introduction comments on the growing interest in Americana, and provides a brief history of the subject. The chief value of this volume is in its reproductions.

739. Carlebach, Michael L. *The Origins of Photojournalism in America*. Washington: Smithsonian Institution Press, 1992. 194 pp., biblio., index.

Carlebach traces the history of American photography and its use in the production of wood engravings of events in popular magazines such as *Harper's Weekly* and *The Daily Graphic*. He argues that the combination of photographs and text changed the way information was gathered and disseminated to the public. Separate chapters are devoted to daguerreotypes, paper prints for the masses, photographs of war, the west, and dry plates and halftones.

740. Clarke, Karen B. "American Birds: Illustrated Books In The Watkinson Library, 1555–1869." *Imprint* 14, no. 1 (1989): 22–31.

Founded in 1858 in Hartford, Connecticut, The Watkinson Library became part of Trinity College in 1952. One of its special collections is the Ostrom Enders Ornithology Collection of 6,000 volumes. Clarke notes the importance of illustrated books to the science of ornithology. Her survey spans several centuries and includes examples from rare European imprints. Among American printed works are those by Alexander Wilson, Thomas Nuttall, John James Audubon, John Cassin, Spencer Fullerton Baird, and Daniel G. Elliot.

741. Coffin, William A. "American Illustration of Today." *Scribner's Magazine* 11 (January, February and March 1892): 106–17; 196–205; 33–49.

These articles study the many American artists who specialized in book illustrations. The author defends illustrations for instilling a love of art in their viewers and believes that woodcuts and photogravures provide better artistic nourishment than steel engravings and chromolithographs can. Part 1 concentrates on the work of Will Low, Kenyon Cox, and Elihu Vedder, discussing their respective illustrations of Keats's *Odes*, Rossetti's *Blessed Damozel*, and the *Rubaiyat*. Robert Blum, Irving Wiles, Twachtman, and William M. Chase are among the many painter-illustrators mentioned briefly in part 2, while Edwin A. Abbey, Pennel, Charles Reinhart, and H. Pyle are among those examined at length in part 3.

742. Comstock, Edward Jr. "Satire in the Sticks: Humorous Wood Engravings of the Adirondacks" in *Prints and Printmakers of New York State, 1825–1940*, 163–182. ed. David Tatham. Syracuse: Syracuse University Press, 1985.

Comstock writes about three generations of artists who produced a record of the lighter side of life in the Adirondacks after illustrated magazines proliferated. Comstock's survey begins with C.W. Webber's *The Hunter-Naturalist* (Philadelphia, 1852) which includes satirical illustrations on hunting and fishing. Among the artists discussed are Charles E. Whitehead, Thomas Bangs Thorpe, Harry Fenn, Will H. Low, W.L. Sheppard, Seneca Ray Stoddard, Augustus Hoppin, Daniel Carter Beard, Culver H. Lewis, C.W. Webber, William

Allen Rogers, and W.M. Cary. The survey ends with the end of illustrated magazines in the 1880's, although other artists, including Frederick Remington produced satires that were reproduced by halftones.

743. David, Beverly R. *Mark Twain and His Illustrators*. Troy, New York: The Whitston Publishing Company, 1986. 268 pp., index.

This volume describes the interaction between Samuel Clemens, his publisher, Elisha Bliss, and the illustrators who worked on his books, published on a subscription basis from 1869 through 1875. Among those who illustrated Twain were True Williams, Thomas Nast, and Augustus Hoppin. Much of the documentation comes from published volumes of the author's notebooks, letters, and journals. David's research effectively delineates the problems confronted by authors and publishers in issuing an illustrated text.

744. Davison, Nancy R. "Bickham's *Musical Entertainer* and Other Curiosities" in *Eighteenth-Century Prints in Colonial America. To Educate and Decorate*, 98–122. ed. Joan D. Dolmetsch. Williamsburg: Colonial Williamsburg Foundation, 1979.

Some of the handsomely engraved works by the two George Bickhams, Senior and Junior, found their way into the colonies. Davison discusses four major titles by them: *The Universal Penman*, *The British Monarchy*, *The Musical Entertainer*, and *An Easy Introduction to Dancing*. All were designed for the wealthy merchant class and were issued in the 1730s and 1740s. *The British Monarchy* has one Philadelphia subscriber. These publications provide insights into life in London in the 1730s and 1740s.

745. Dawson, Muir. *Prints of original wood blocks from the archives of McLoughlin Bros. Publishers, N.Y.* Los Angeles: Dawson's Book Shop, 1980. 2 vols. (472 sheets).

Some years ago, Dawson's Book Shop acquired a collection of blocks for illustrations published by the McLoughlin Brothers in New York in the last quarter of the nineteenth century. This firm specialized in children's books and the cuts are arranged according to the books in which they were published. Only thirty sets of this title were created; it is a valuable archive.

746. Dickenson, Victoria. *Drawn from Life: Science and Art in the Portrayal of the New World*. Toronto: University of Toronto Press, 1998. 320 pp., biblio, index.

Dickenson's meticiculously researched history of illustration of early natural history discoveries in the New World includes an important section, "Translating the Image: The Value of Repeated Pictorial Statement." The change from drawing to print can be done faithfully or not; Dickenson compares John White's drawings to the engravings in DeBry's *Voyages* as a case study. In addition to surveying a substantial literature, Dickenson offers a perceptive analysis of images on maps and the depiction of the landscape.

747. Dinnean, Lawrence. *Nineteenth Century Illustrators of California Sights and Scenes*. Berkeley: Friends of the Bancroft Library, 1986. 72 pp., index.

Dinnean summarizes work done by expeditionary artists in the early nineteenth century, then moves on to work done by artists of the gold rush era. Work in the 1870's and 1880's was generated by publicity for the Southern Pacific Railroad and luxury hotels. Biographical sketches for seventeen artists and examples of their work are very useful.

748. Dodd, Loring Holmes. *A Generation of Illustrators and Etchers*. Boston: Chapman & Grimes, 1960. 214 pp.

This collection of chatty newspaper articles on a variety of illustrators and etchers active in the late nineteenth and early twentieth centuries includes are Edwin Austin Abbey, Howard Chandler Christy, James Montgomery Flagg, A.B.Frost, Charles Dana Gibson, Maxfield Parrish, Howard Pyle, Remington, and N.C. Wyeth.

749. Dodge, Norman L. "Heavenly Days, A Glance at Some Old American Almanacs." *Antiques* 43 (January 1943): 12–15.

Dodge surveys the history and contents of almanacs, then discusses almanac compilers, including Benjamin Franklin, and several specific almanacs. Some of the engravers whose illustrations appeared in almanacs are mentioned, but the author provides little information on them. The reproductions are well chosen, and represent a variety of styles from the late seventeenth through the nineteenth centuries.

750. Drepperd, Carl W. "American Drawing Books." *Bulletin of the The New York Public Library* (November 1945): 795–812.

This chronological checklist of instruction manuals for drawing and painting covers the period of 1787 to 1860. Many of the instruction books are illustrated by well-known artists, such as John Hill, while some of the illustrators remain anonymous. This volume is still useful, but in need of revision to incorporate the quantity of new material discovered in recent years. This was printed as a separate text in 1946.

751.———. "Art Instruction Books for the People." *Antiques* 41 (June 1942): 356–59.

Art blossomed in the United States after the establishment of a peacetime economy in 1789, and instruction books began to be printed in the United States. Drepperd traces the growth of these books, and provides a brief checklist of those published before 1865.

752.———. "Drawing Cards, the Sunday Game That Gave Us Too Much Amateur American Art." *American Collector* 13 (November 1944): 6–7.

Drepperd's own collection contained several sets of drawing cards, measuring about three by five inches, that were issued in slip cases. Drepperd proposes that many primitive landscapes and portraits were copied from these cards, rather than from life. Titles of several of the sets are provided, and some of the lithographed cards are reproduced.

753.———. "Early Prints in Old Magazines." *Antiquarian* 9 (December 1927): 61–65.

The title of this article is misleading; Drepperd's sole concern is with Huddy & Duval's *The United States Military Magazine*, published in Philadelphia from 1839 to 1842. Of particular note is information on the price and type of plates in each issue. Individual artists employed by Huddy & Duval are mentioned, but no biographical material about them is proferred. Written specifically for collectors, the article also describes the subject matter of many of the prints.

754. Epstein, Stanley. "The Earliest American Color Plates." *Printing and Graphic Arts* 4 (May 1956): 42–45.

Until the advent of chromolithography, most colored plates were colored by hand, using watercolors applied to black and white impressions of a plate. Epstein discusses the earliest American deviation from this tedious process: Jacob Bigelow's *American Medical Botany*, published in Boston in three parts dated 1817, 1818, and 1820. After the first volume, the engraver used aquatint to convey the modeling of the plants, and then applied colors appropriate to the plants directly onto the plates before printing. Minute touches of color were added after printing. A long quotation by Bigelow about this process is included in this article.

755. Forman, Allan. "Newspaper Art and Artists." *Quarterly Illustrator* 1 (1893): 313–24.

Forman credits James G. Bennett of the *New York Herald* with publishing the first newspaper illustration in 1837. Illustrations were instrumental in the success of Pulitzer's rejuvenated *World* after 1884; one after another, other dailies were compelled to follow his example. John Baker, Leon Barritt, Henry Coultans, Walter Fox, Homer Davenport, C. deGrimm, and W.W. Denslow are among the numerous illustrators discussed.

756. Gambee, Budd L. "American Book and Magazine Illustration of the Later Nineteenth Century" in *Book Illustration: Papers Presented at the Third Rare Book Conference of the American Library Association in 1962*, 45–55. ed. Frances J. Brewer. Berlin: Gebr. Mann Verlag, 1963.

The author highlights the history of book illustration from the 1830s to the 1870s, discussing John Gadsby Chapman, Joseph Alexander Adams, Benson J. Lossing, F.O.C. Darley, Harry Fenn, and Timothy Cole. A short bibliography follows the article.

757. Gladstone, John. "Working-Class Imagery in *Harper's Weekly* 1865–1895." *Labor's Heritage* 5, no. 1 (1993): 42–61.

This interesting look at images in *Harper's Weekly* focuses on works by Winslow Homer, Paul Frenzeny, Jules Tavernier, Thomas Pollack Anshutz, Robert Koehler, and Thure de Thulstrup. These men created powerful images of working people, labor unrest, and disasters that reached a large audience. Gladstone suggests that these works affected the Ashcan painters of 1908 who in turn influenced social realists of the 1930s and 1940s.

758. Gottesman, Rita S. "Early Commercial Art." *Art in America* 43 (December 1955): 34–42, 55.

The author traces the growth of advertising art from small newspaper woodcuts and trade cards to large and colorful lithographed posters. She mentions advances in typographical design, packaging, premiums, and the use of comical characters. The illustrations, from the Landauer Collection at The New-York Historical Society, are well chosen.

759. Griffin, Gillett G. "The Development of Woodcut Printing in America." *Princeton University Library Chronicle* 20, no. 1 (1958): 7–17.

Gillett discusses the innovations in printing press technology that advanced the printing of woodcut illustrations in the early nineteenth century. This chronological survey of American book illustration is based on the Sinclair Hamilton Collection at Princeton University.

760. Gutjahr, Paul. *An American Bible: A History of the Good Book in the United States, 1777–1880.* Stanford: Stanford University Press, 1999. 256 pp., biblio., index.

Gutjahr provides an extended publishing history of Bibles in America. In Chapter Two, "Packaging," the author discusses illustrations and bindings commissioned by Bible publishers to enhance sales in a very competitive market. Among the publishers discussed are Isaiah Thomas, Mathew Carey, John Holbrook, and Harper and Brothers. Gutjahr discusses the marketing strategies of these publishers and the importance of illustrations within them.

761. Harris, Christopher H. "The Halftone and American Magazine Reproduction 1880–1900." *History of Photography* 17, no. 1 (1993): 77–80.

This discussion describes the innovative half-tone photographic process developed by Stephen H. Horgan in the late

1870's and its first use in the *New York Daily Graphic* in 1880. Harris compares it to wood engraving and describes the impact of the new technology on the older craft.

762. Harris, Neil. "Pictorial Perils: The Rise of American Illustration" in *The American Illustrated Book in the Nineteenth Century*, 3–20. ed. Gerald W. R. Ward. Winterthur, Del.: Henry Francis du Pont Winterthur Museum, 1987.

Harris's interest is the rise of pictorialism late in the nineteenth century. Illustrators such as Howard Pyle, Edwin Austin Abbey, Joseph Pennell, Frederic Remington, Arthur Frost, and Howard Chandler Christy flourished and produced works of artistic value, particularly when compared to works issued early in the century. However, there was criticism of works that were not faithful to reality or even to the texts illustrated. Harris explores the critical response to illustration, and the impact (sometimes negative) of photographic illustration and picture postcards, pictorial advertising, comic strips, and films on culture.

763. Haugh, Georgia C. "The Beginnings of American Book Illustration" in *Book Illustration: Papers Presented at the Third Rare Book Conference of the American Library Association in 1962*, 34–44. ed. Frances J. Brewer. Berlin: Gebr. Mann Verlag, 1963.

This succinct survey covers book illustration from the late seventeenth and early eighteenth centuries through Alexander Anderson. The useful bibliography is followed by a list of about fifty illustrated books from which the author drew her examples.

764. Hawkes, Elizabeth H. "Pursuing American Illustrations." *Private Library* 7, no. 3 (1994): 90–101.

Hawkes writes about six private collections of American illustrations, discussing their history and contents. Although the collections focus on the twentieth century, several of these collectors also possess works by nineteenth-century Americans.

765. Hoeber, Arthur. "A Century of American Illustration." *Bookman* 8 (November 1898; February 1899): 213–19 ; 317–24 ; 429–39 ; 540–48.

The author begins his survey with Alexander Anderson, and notes the dismal state of book illustration around 1800. Other topics considered include gift book illustrations, artists and growth of the illustrated magazines (particularly after the Civil War), subscription books, and the impact of American artists who were trained in Europe. He further discusses social satire, the poster movement, and the technique of process engraving. Although book illustration in the first half of the nineteenth century is slighted, this series of articles is quite detailed, and the author discusses the work of many illustrators.

766. Hoolihan, Christopher. "Wood Engraving and American Medical Publishing in the Early Nineteenth Century." *Imprint* 21, no. 1 (1996): 20–28.

Changes in publishing, the creation of an educated elite, and the professionalization of the medical profession increased the need for medical literature. Hoolihan discusses the alternative processes for the production of illustrations focusing on the most popular and economical—wood engraving. Between 1800 and 1810, the firm of Collins & Perkins pioneered the use of wood engravings in their medical texts and realized the great advantages to the publisher of publishing illustrations with the text, as opposed to printing the illustrations separately and binding them in. The observations of Hoolihan are applicable to other genres of literature.

767. Hopkins, Joseph G. E. "Plain Talk in Pictures." *New-York Historical Society Quarterly* 31 (April 1947): 97–105.

The tradition of American pictorial journalism began with *The Royal American Magazine*, published in the mid-1770s. These early illustrations were simple embellishments, however, and did not attempt to present news or tell a story. The arrival of skilled English and Scottish engravers in the early nineteenth century improved the quality of illustrations in magazines like the *Portfolio* and the *Analectic Magazine*, but did not change the concept of illustration as embellishment. True pictorial journalism would depend on newer and cheaper processes than engraving; lithography and electrotyped wood engravings provided the answers. Pictorial journalism did not begin until the 1850s, when it was employed in Harper's, Gleason's, and Frank Leslie's publications.

768. Hornung, Clarence P. *Handbook of Early American Advertising Art*. New York: Dover Publications, 1947. 176 pp.

In his introduction, Hornung discusses posters and broadsides that were used for advertising in the colonial era. He also mentions small advertisements found in newspapers and magazines, tracing the growth of this form of art through the nineteenth century. He comments on wood engraving in relation to advertising cuts, and singles out Alexander Anderson and four of his pupils for discussion. Then the author considers the type foundries which supplied "stock" cuts to printers, and discusses trade cards and typographic design. The period of 1840 to 1865 brought several innovations, including large newspaper cuts and color lithography. The plates in this book are reproduced from type specimen books of the nineteenth century, and a wide range of ornaments and type faces are displayed.

769. Hubbard, Geraldine H. "The Hopkins Flower Prints." *Antiques* 55 (April 1949): 286–87.

Bishop John Henry Hopkins of Vermont turned to lithography to supplement his meager income as Episcopal bishop of Vermont. He issued several drawing books, including *The Vermont Drawing Book of Flowers* (1847), *The Vermont Drawing Book of Landscapes* (1841), and *The Burlington Drawing Book of Figures* (1846?). The author, a great-grand-daughter of Hopkins, had access to family records and to copies of the publications, thereby enabling her to recreate the history of his publishing ventures. Copies of these drawing books are very scarce.

770. Hurd, Charles Edwin. "Art in Book Illustration." *New England Magazine and Bay State Monthly* 4 (January and December 1886): 37–47 ; 95–105.

These two articles present a survey of recently published books, mentioned because of the artistic merit of their illustrations. In the first installment, Hurd enthusiastically extols the wood engravings popular in the 1880s, which were capable of imitating any process of drawing or printing. He proceeds to cite several examples which demonstrate different styles and techniques. The second part concentrates on describing the different reproductive processes, and the effects which they produced. He says very little about the illustrators of these books, although they included artists of such renown as Pennell and Hassam.

771. Jones, Matt B. "The Early Massachusetts Bay Colony Seals, with Bibliographical Notes Based Upon Their Use in Printing." *Proceedings of the American Antiquarian Society* 44 (April 1934): 13–44.

Jones examines impressions of seals from 1629 to 1691 and their reproductions in printer's cuts. The article includes a chronological list of laws and proclamations carrying impressions of cuts of the Bay Colony seal. The printer, place of printing, and library locations of copies of these cuts are included.

772. Kiser, Joy. "America's Lady Audubon." *Biblio* 3, no. 9 (September 1998): 18–23.

One of the most exquisite natural history publications is *Illustrations of the Nests and Eggs of the Birds of Ohio* published in parts from 1879 through 1886. The original drawings, the drawings on lithographic stone, and the handcoloring were done by Genevieve Jones and her mother Virginia Jones; the text was by Howard Jones. This article discusses the roles of the various family members in the production of the book, which had little success at the time of publication.

773. Kramer, Sidney. "Pictorial Wood Blocks of the Amreican Nineteenth Century." *Quarterly Journal of Current Acquisitions* 1 (October 1943): 42–43.

In 1942 and 1943, the Library of Congress received some donations of wood blocks covering the period 1840 to 1890 from several American publishing firms. These and similar collections are described, particularly one cartoon by Thomas Nast. The Library of Congress also has the original drawings, lithographic stones, copperplates, and wood blocks for the reports of the United States Exploration Expedition (Wilkes Expedition) of 1838 to 1842.

774. Lacey, Barbara. "Visual Images of Blacks in Early American Imprints." *William and Mary Quarterly* 53, no. 1 (January 1996): 137–179.

Lacey has conducted a thorough survey of depictions of African Americans in eighteenth-century American imprints—pamphlets, books, periodicals, and broadsides. She finds that these images depict African Americans in a variety of roles and conditions—not all were slaves. She situates these images in the context of American social and intellectual history.

775. Larson, Judy L. "Dobson's *Encyclopaedia*: A Precedent in American Engraving" in *The American Illustrated Book in the Nineteenth Century*, 21–51. ed. Gerald W. R. Ward. Winterthur, Del.: The Henry Francis du Pont Winterthur Museum, 1987.

In 1789 Thomas Dobson, a successful Philadelphia publisher, advertised an American edition of the *Encyclopaedia Britannica*. It was published in ten volumes from 1789 to 1803 with 543 plates. Larson delves into the history of this massive project comparing the American and British editions and focusing on the engravers. Foremost among them were Robert Scot (ca. 1745–1823), John Vallance, James Thackara, Samuel Allardice, Alexander Lawson, and Francis Shallus. Larson also describes the encyclopaedias that followed Dobson's in the next twenty years. She concludes her essay by speculating on the usefulness of the illustrations for instruction. She concludes that Dobson's high standards contributed to the success of the genre and to raising standards for illustration in general.

776.———. "Stuff and Nonsense: Humor in American Childrens' Book Illustration." *Imprint* 10, no. 2 (1985): 2–11.

Nonsense literature for children was first published in England. Some Americans, Samuel Goodrich in particular, railed against nonsense books for children in the mid-nineteenth century. Mary Maples Dodge brought new vitality to American childrens' literature beginning in 1874. The works of Palmer Cox, A.B. Frost, Frank Burgess, and Peter Newell are discussed.

777. Lawall, David B. "American Painters as Book Illustrators, 1810–1870." *Princeton University Library Chronicle* 20, no. 1 (1958): 18–28.

Using the Sinclair Hamilton Collection at the Princeton University Library as his base, Lawall focuses on three major phases of the history of American painting reflected in book illustration. Factual and didactic painting predominating before 1840 resulted in illustrations for history books, children's literature, and Bibles. Artists of the Sentimental School included genre and landscape painters whose works were reproduced in books of poetry. In the post-Civil War era, artists such as Hennessy, Vedder, La Farge, and Homer combined an interest in style and subject matter. The author concludes by suggesting that the illustrations designed by artists add to the knowledge about their work.

778. Lewis, Benjamin Morgan. *A Guide to Engravings in American Magazines, 1741–1810.* New York: New York Public Library, 1959. 60 pp., biblio., index.

This guide lists engravings, arranged by date of issue, that appeared in magazines of the second half of the eighteenth and early nineteenth centuries. Indexes of the subject, title, and engravers of the prints, plus a list of signed plates, make this a very helpful reference book.

779.———. "Engravers in American Magazines, 1741–1810" in *Books in America's Past: Essays Honoring Rudolph H. Gjelsness*, 204–217. ed. David Kaser. Charlottesville: University Press of Virginia, 1966.

Lewis, who earlier had listed all engravings in periodicals issued through 1810, pulls interesting statistics out of his material. Forty-nine artists' names appear on engraved plates. Lewis briefly focuses on signed engravings and then turns to bibliographical problems. In a section of the essay, "Statistical Survey and Subject Content of Magazine Engravings," we learn sixty periodicals of some 2032 in this period, contained engravings, about 657. Among the most popular subjects were views, portraits, college buildings, and waterfalls.

780. Loomis, C. C., Jr. and M. A. Wilson. "The *Polaris* Expedition, 1871–73: A Newly Found Graphic Record." *Prologue* 2, no. 1 (1970): 1–9.

In 1871 an ill-fated expedition set off to the Arctic. This article discusses the graphic documents of the *Polaris* expedition including drawings, small oil paintings, and the book illustrations derived from them that were published in 1876. These documents are housed in the Center for Polar Archives in the National Archives.

781. Lovejoy, David S. "American Painting in Early Nineteenth-Century Gift Books." *American Quarterly* 7, no. 4 (1955): 345–61.

Lovejoy analyzes the 230 engravings published in the *Atlantic Souvenir* and *The Token* published between 1826 and 1850. More than half were reproductions of American paintings, all but one by contemporary American artists. Of particular interest in this essay are the citations of reviews of the illustrations from various literary magazines of the day. Lovejoy notes the absence of portraits from these two literary annuals.

782. Mahony, Bertha E. *Illustrators of Children's Books, 1774–1945.* Boston: The Horn Book, Inc., 1947. 527 pp.

This volume does not focus on American illustrators, but there are chapters on "Early American Illustrators" by Bertha E. Mahony and "Howard Pyle and His times" by Robert Lawson which deal with American topics. American publications are described in other essays as well. Also of importance is a section of biographies of living illustrators, a bibliography of illustrators and their works, and a bibliography of authors and titles of their work that contain illustrations. The focus of these sections is on American publications. This is an excellect reference work.

783. Marzio, Peter C. "American Drawing Books, 1820–1860" in *Philadelphia Printmaking. American Prints Before 1860*, 9–41. ed. Robert F. Looney. West Chester, Penn.: Tinicum Press, 1976.

Marzio focuses on the popular art instruction manuals by Rembrandt Peale, John Gadsby Chapman, and John Reubens Smith that served as models for other artist-authors. Over 145 drawing manuals were issued from 1820 to 1860. Marzio explores the range of these publications and describes the methodology of them as well, dealing with the basics of drawing figures and landscape, perspective, shading, and composition. Marzio points out their importance for public education, their indication of aesthetic thought, and their value as sources for the study of American printmaking.

784. Matthews, J. Brander. "The Comic Periodical Literature of the United States." *American Bibliopolist* 7 (August 1875): 199–201.

This is a list of forty-six comic newspapers and magazines published in the United States between 1807 and 1875. While not complete, it provides a starting point for the study of humorous literature and graphics in the nineteenth century.

785. McClinton, Katharine M. "American Flower Lithography." *Antiques* 49 (June 1946): 361–63.

The author mentions about twenty publications published in the first half of the nineteenth century containing lithographed plates of flowers. Her starting point is J.E. Smith's *Grammar of Botany*, containing plates lithographed by Barnet and Doolittle in 1822. Both books and periodicals are included in this survey.

786. McCorison, Marcus A. "The Idylls of the Triune Idol, or the Joys of Publishing in 1820" in *Prints of New England*, 69–81. ed. Georgia Brady Barnhill. Worcester: American Antiquarian Society, 1991.

This article describes the efforts of Caleb Atwater, Abner Reed, and Isaiah Thomas that resulted in the publication of an article on the antiquities of native Americans of the Ohio region in the first volume of *Archaeologia Americana* or the *Transactions and Collections* of the American Antiquarian Society. Original drawings for this article and correspondence survive in the Archives of the Society. McCorison provides information about Atwater, Reed, and Thomas, and uses the correspondence to suggest the difficulties encountered by Thomas, the founder of the Society, forced to become the mediator.

787. McGrath, Daniel F. *American Colorplate Books, 1800–1900.* 1988. 231 pp., biblio.

This survey focuses on both hand-colored book illustrations and those printed in color. The five chapters discuss copperplate and wood engravings, and colored lithographs, tinted lithographs, the origins of chromolithography, and the "gaudy" days of that technique and photomechanical color printing. McGrath discusses the artists and publishers of these books and includes a list of over seven hundred publications based on Whitman Bennett's *A Practical Guide to American Nineteenth Century Color Plate Books.* This is not a sophisticated study, but it does amplify Bennett's earlier work.

788. McKay, George L. "American Artists as Reporters." *American Collector* 16 (November 1947): 6–8, 24.

McKay examines the flowering of the news picture from 1851 to 1900. The role of photography in this development is discussed, for photographs could be used as original or source material for the wood engravings. Frank Leslie was the publisher who developed the illustrated news magazine, and his periodicals competed keenly with *Harper's Weekly.* Other illustrated periodicals are mentioned, and notes about the most important artists and cartoonists are provided. McKay's interest in the subject was encouraged by an exhibition at the New-York Historical Society that displayed over two hundred of these illustrations. The engravings in the exhibition were selected from the Harry T. Peters Collection at the Society.

789. Meigs, John. *The Cowboy in American Prints.* Chicago: The Swallow Press, Inc., 184 pp.

Meigs' introduction surveys the depiction of the cowboy in American illustrated books and periodicals. Such depictions were printed as early as the 1850's in *Harper's Weekly* and *Gleason's Pictorial.* Among the early artists of the west were William M. Carey, Paul Frenzeny and Jules Tavernier, W.J. Palmer, and William F. Sparks. The best known illustrator of this group was Remington.

790. Meyer, Susan E. *America's Great Illustrators.* New York: Harry N. Abrams, 1978. 310 pp., biblio.

The artists covered in this volume are Howard Pyle, N.C. Wyeth, Frederic Remington, Maxfield Parrish, J.C. Leyendecker, Norman Rockwell, Charles Dana Gibson, Howard Chandler Christy, James Montgomery Flagg, and John Held, Jr. Meyer provides a brief overview as well as a discussion of processes, publishers of magazines, and how American illustrators lived. The reproductions are lavish in size and color and are divided between original art work and final published versions.

791. Morgan, David. *Protestants and Pictures: Religion, Visual Culture, and the Age of American Mass Production.* New York: Oxford University Press, 1999. 417 pp., biblio, index.

Morgan sets the abundant number of religious prints and almanac, periodical, tract, and children's book illustrations in their larger historical context. The four parts of the book are: "The Mellennial Mission of the American Republic," "Adventism and Images of the End," "Visual Pedagogy," and "The Rise of the Devotional Image in American Protestantism." Morgan is adept at interpreting the larger cultural meaning of this wealth of material.

792. Moritz, Albert F. *America the Picturesque in Nineteenth Century Engraving.* Toronto: New Trend, 1983. 167 pp., biblio.

Moritz's text focuses on the history of printed depictions of scenery of the United States, William Henry Bartlett and *American Scenery,* contemporaries of Bartlett working in the picturesque tradition, the rise of American wood engraving, *Picturesque America,* and the final decades of wood engraving (1870–1890). Over 100 engravings are reproduced with extensive commentary in this volume that provides an excellent overview of book illustration in general.

793. Mosimann, Elizabeth. "The Useful and Beautiful: 19th-Century Botanical Illustration in Philadelphia." *Imprint* 12, no. 2 (1987): 12–20.

Mosimann examines the work of various commercial lithographers in the field of botanical illustration, beginning in the 1830s. She mentions a significant number of publications and makes useful judgments about the quality of individual plates.

794. Munch, Janet Butler. "*Villas on the Hudson*: An Architectural and Biographical Examination." *Hudson Valley Regional Review* 10, no. 2 (September 1993): 92–124.

Munch discusses the publishing history of an important architectural book and provides detailed information on the architects and owners of the buildings depicted in it. Contemporary advertisements note that the book orginally was to contain more plates, but Munch does not explain why the book was issued with views of thirty instead of forty villas.

795. Nickels, Cameron C. *New England Humor From the Revolutionary War to the Civil War.* Knoxville: University of Tennessee Press, 1993. 277 pp., biblio., index.

Nickels's book focuses on textual humor, but includes a chapter on the illustration of humor using broadsides, prints, sheet music covers, books and periodicals to document the emergence of Uncle Sam, a dominant figure in pictorial satire.

796. Nickerson, Cynthia D. "Artistic Interpretations of Henry Wadsworth Longellow's *The Song of Hiawatha*, 1855–1900." *American Art Journal* 16, no. 3 (June 1984): 49–77.

One of the most popular literary works of the nineteenth century, *The Song of Hiawatha* was illustrated by many artists. Currier & Ives, for example, published seven Hiawatha prints, several of which are illustrated. Nickerson examines oil paintings and sculpture as well.

797. Nipps, Karen. *Naturally Fond of Pictures. American Illustration of the 1840s and 1850s*. Philadelphia: Library Company of Philadelphia, 1989. 30 pp., biblio., index.

Nipps describes the 1840s and 1850s as an "especially creative and adventurous period in American book production" because of the technological advances of the period. Nipps organized the exhibition first by technique and then by special topics—F.O.C. Darley and other talented illustrators, genre scenes, natural history publications, ephemeral books and broadsides, illustrated magazines, sheet music covers, comic publications, and books about other places. The descriptions of each item are well written and incorporate much useful information.

798. O'Gorman, James F. "Billings, Cruikshank, and *Uncle Tom's Cabin*." *Imprint* 13, no. 1 (1988): 13–21.

The historical relationship and relative merits of two sets of illustrations to Harriet Beecher Stowe's abolitionist novel form the subject of O'Gorman's essay. Hammatt Billings produced 123 designs for the 1853 illustrated edition; George Cruikshank designed 27 illustrations for the 1852 English edition. O'Gorman concludes that Billings' designs are more sympathetic to the text.

799. Oakley, Thornton. "Remarks on Illustration and Pennsylvania's Contributors to its Golden Age." *Pennsylvania Magazine of History and Biography* 71 (January 1947): 3–18.

Oakley begins by philosophizing about illustration as art. He calls it "the expression of ideals," and "the revealer of man's noblest vision." The golden age of illustration, which came in the last half of the nineteenth century, is evident in the prints of magazines like *Harper's*, *Scribner's*, *Century*, and the early *Collier's*. Drawing on his own personal recollections, Oakley discusses illustrators for these magazines—E.A. Abbey, Arthur B. Frost, Joseph Pennell, Howard Pyle, Henry McCarter, F. Walter Taylor, Alice Barber Stephens, George Gibbs, Jessie Smith, and N.C. Wyeth.

800. Parker, Peter and Winkelbauer, Stefanie Munsing. "Embellishments for Practical Repositories: Eighteenth-Century American Magazine Illustration" in *Eighteenth-Century Prints in Colonial America. To Educate and Decorate*, 71–97. ed. Joan D. Dolmetsch. Williamsburg: Colonial Williamsburg Foundation, 1979.

This analysis of five American magazines—*The Royal American Magazine* and *Massachusetts Magazine* (Boston), the *New York Magazine*, the *Pennsylvania Magazine* and *Columbian Magazine* (Philadelphia)—discusses why illustrations were important, the range and proportion of subject matter, and the relationship of American magazines to English examples of the same period. The authors provide some detail about the principal engravers—Paul Revere, Robert Aitken, Samuel Hill, James Trenchard, and Cornelius Tiebout. The essay is followed by two tables: Comparative Biographical Data of 18th Century American Engravers and Illustrations in American Magazines Compared to those in the British *Gentleman's Magazine*.

801. Pearson, Andrea G. "*Frank Leslie's Illustrated Newspaper* and *Harper's Weekly*: Innovation and Imitation in Nineteenth-century American Pictorial Reporting." *Journal of Popular Culture* 23, no. 4 (1990): 81–112.

Instead of comparing the literary content and style of these two popular weekly magazines, Pearson focuses on the pictorial news content. Frank Leslie had worked for the *Illustrated London News* before coming to the United States in 1848. He learned the value of news pictures with that journal. Pearson compares the two magazines, using Civil War reporting as a focus. Thomas Nast first worked for Leslie, then for Harper's. His work was done in New York from others' sketches, not in the field, like that of Alfred Waud's. Although *Harper's* is the better known of the two, *Frank Leslie's Illustrated Newspaper* "established the significance and accuracy of the news image."

802. Pierce, Sally. "*Gleason's Pictorial*: Elevating and Celebrating American Life." *Ephemera Journal* 5 (1992): 12–24.

Modeled after the *Illustrated London News*, *Gleason's Pictorial* began publication in May 1851. From a beginning circulation of 50,000 copies, by 1856, 103,000 copies were printed of each issue. Pierce explains how Frederick Gleason and his editor Maturin Murray Ballou achieved such success, concentrating on its contributions to the art component of its pages. Illustrations were more than ornamentation. In 1856 after Ballou purchased the journal, there were seven designers of illustrations and thirty-four wood engravers employed by the company. Indeed, the cost of illustrations proved ruinous and the magazine ceased publication in 1859. At the close of the article, Pierce characterizes the illustrations that served to perpetuate the image of the American union.

803. Pitz, Henry C. *The Brandywine Tradition*. New York: Weathervane Books, 1968. 252 pp., biblio.

Preliminary chapters of this book discuss the history and people of the Brandywine Valley, including several literary figures. Succeeding chapters deal with F.O.C. Darley, Howard Pyle, N.C. Wyeth, Maxfield Parrish, Violet Oakley, Jessie Wilcox Smith, George Harding, Walter Everett, Sarah S. Stillwell, Thornton Oakley, William Aylward, Clifford Ashley, Frank E. Schoonover, Edward A. Wilson, Andrew Wyeth, Peter Hurd, and other members of this school of illustrators. Pyle and his students are the focus of this narrative written by a practicing illustrator trained by those familiar with Pyle.

804.———. *Two Hundred Years of American Illustration.* New York: Random House and Society of Illustrators, 1976. 436 pp.

This volume and accompanying exhibition were sponsored by the Society of Illustrators formed in 1901 to promote friendship among illustrators for philanthropic purposes. There were some 850 items in the exhibition dating from the late eighteenth century through the early 1970s. The text begins with the a chronological survey beginning in the late eighteenth century. Illustrated are numbers of published prints, as well as drawings for illustrations. Darley, Audubon, the Civil War, Wild West illustrations of the last quarter of the nineteenth century, Charles Dana Gibson, Howard Pyle and the Brandywine School, pen and ink drawings, pictures for children, historical subject matter, humor, magazine covers and posters, commercial designs for advertising are among the topics covered by Pitz. The illustrations are arranged in a rather haphazard order, but it is a delightful range of material.

805. Pollin, Burton R. "Edgar Allen Poe and His Illustrators." *American Book Collector* 2, no. 2 (March 1981): 2–17.

The first of this two part article begins with the illustrations by F.O.C. Darley and J.G. Chapman for works by Poe. Poe's own thoughts on the value of illustrations are also presented. Poe's works were more frequently published in illustrated editions abroad, so the focus of the article turns to English and European artists.

806. Price, Lois Olcott. "The Development of Photomechanical Book Illustration." in *The American Illustrated Book in the Nineteenth Century*, 233–256. ed. Gerald W. R. Ward. Winterthur: The Henry Francis du Pont Winterthur Museum, 1987.

The goal of publishers of illustrated books was to find ways in which to reproduce artist's drawings accurately at the lowest cost possible. Price's article describes a number of photomechanical processes used during the nineteenth century. Much of her discussion is based on patents and nineteenth-century technical manuals listed in the bibliography.

807. Princeton University Library. *Early American Book Illustrators and Wood Engravers, 1670–1870.* Princeton: Princeton University Press, 1958. 2 vols., biblio., index.

Sinclair Hamilton's introduction to this magnificent catalog of his collection traces the history of American book illustration, from works by John Foster, to those produced in the last quarter of the nineteenth century. It is a detailed history of the art, based on Hamilton's substantial collection of over two thousand volumes. The catalog is arranged chronologically for the eighteenth century, since most of the illustrations are anonymous wood and type metal cuts. For the nineteenth century, the entries are arranged by the name of the illustrator. The entries are detailed, and include bibliographical references and descriptions of each illustration. The separate indexes of illustrators, engravers, authors, and titles make this a very useful reference tool. In 1968 a supplement was published which follows the format of the first volume. The introduction to the catalog originally appeared in the *Princeton University Library Chronicle* 6 (Apr. 1945): 99–126, and was revised for publication in 1958. Both volumes have an index and bibliography.

808. Rainey, Sue. *Creating* Picturesque America*: Monument to the Natural and Cultural Landscape.* Nashville and London: Vanderbilt University Press, 1994. 383 pp., biblio., index.

William Cullen Bryant's *Picturesque America* published by D. Appleton and Company from 1872 to 1874 reached an enormous audience. Rainey's carefully researched monograph traces the origins of this publication and focuses on the people who made it possible—Oliver Bell Bunce and the many authors and artists who contributed to it. The text is followed by biographies of the artists, the two varying versions of the preface, a list of the proper placement of the steel engravings in the parts (important because so many of these engravings are found in the bins of print dealers), and the notices about the publication that appeared on the covers of the parts, as issued.

809. Rainey, Sue, and Mildred Abraham. *Embellished With Numerous Engravings: The Works of American Illustrators and Wood Engravers, 1670–1880.* Charlottesville: University of Virginia Library, 1986. 48 pp.

This pamphlet, issued to document an exhibition in the Department of Rare Books at the University of Virginia Library, contains two essays. The first, by Sue Rainey, discusses American wood engravers including Alexander Anderson and Abel Bowen, and designers such as Hammatt Billings, F.O.C. Darley, John Gadsby Chapman, David Claypoole Johnston, and Harry Fenn. The work of engravers and artists for the illustrated magazines is also discussed. Mildred Abraham's essay describes the exhibition which was divided into four chronological sections. It shows the increasing use of illustrations over two hundred years as well as the increasing skill of designers and engravers.

810. Reese, William S. *Stamped with a National Character: Nineteenth Century American Color*

Plate Books. New York: The Grolier Club, 1999. 120 pp., index.

The eminent rare book dealer, William S. Reese, has assembled a remarkable collection of books with illustrations in color. This exhibition catalog contains Reese's commentary on the artists and publishers of 114 books, including such treasures as William Birch's *The City of Philadelphia* and William G. Wall's *The Hudson River Portfolio*. The catalog is arranged topically and contains some surprises, such as books produced in Canada and Central and South America, unusual color printing techniques, and some trade catalogues. This book is illustrated in color and is a work of art in itself.

811. Reilly, Bernard F. "Comic Drawing in New York in the 1850s" in *Prints and Printmakers of New York, 1825–1940*, 147–162. ed. David Tatham. Syracuse: Syracuse University Press, 1985.

Reilly begins his thoughtful essay with definitions and applications of caricature (facial distortions of concrete things) and allegory (figurative forms given to abstract political principles). In the first half of the nineteenth century, Reilly suggests that the two kinds of imagery were combined. Thomas W. Strong is identified as the bridge between caricature of the 1830's and 40's and the very diffierent style of the 1870's typified by Thomas Nast. Strong published the first illustrated comic journal, *Yankee Notions* (1852–73). Artists who worked for him included John McLenan, Frank Bellow, Augustus Hoppin, J.H. Goater. Reilly discusses the works of these and other artists and suggests that Strong provided a vehicle for public exchange of visual humor and brought the works of a generation of artist humorists to the public.

812. Reilly, Elizabeth Carroll. *A Dictionary of Colonial American Printers' Ornaments and Illustrations*. Worcester, Mass.: American Antiquarian Society, 1975. 515 pp., index.

This superb referece work reproduces over two thousand ornaments and illustrations that appeared in American pamphlets, books, and broadsides before 1776. Copper engravings are excluded. The reproductions are arranged by subject, and the date, place of publication, printer, and entry number corresponding to Charles Evans's *American Bibliography* is given. The well-written introduction considers the significance of ornaments and illustrations, the history of English ornament, and the reliance of American printers on European and English models. The biographical information included and the sketch drawn of commercial and artistic relations among printers make this a valuable work for serious scholarly research.

813. Reveal, James L. *America's Botanical Beauty: Illustrations from the Library of Congress*. Golden, Col.: Fulcrum Publishing, 1996. 162 pp., biblio., index.

First published by Starwood Publishing, Inc., under the title, *Gentle Conquest*, this beautifully illustrated book describes European and American illustrated books on botany from the 1500s through the 1800s. Reveal's knowledge of the history of botany is substantial as is his interest in the history of exploration that led to botanical description.

814. Ricciotti, Dominic. "Popular Art in *Godey's Lady's Book*: An Image of the American Woman, 1830–1860." *New Hampshire History* 27, no. 1 (March 1972): 3–26.

The role of art in society sets the stage for a discussion of *Godey's Lady's Book*. Sarah Josepha Hale was the editor of this successful magazine that promoted domestic culture. The illustrations to the magazine are discussed in terms of sonological content—the image they present of women and their place and function.

815. Rice, Howard C., Jr. *Sampler from the Class of 1926 Memorial Collection of Illustrated Books Published in New England, 1769–1869*. Hanover, N.H.: Dartmouth College Library, 1970. Unp.

Held to celebrate the college's bicentennial, this exhibition focuses on the books published during the college's first century, including such works as the *New England Primer* (1822), *The Spiritual Mirror* (1844), *The Female American* (1800) and *Thomas Starr King's The White Hills* (1860). The *Sampler* is not a checklist of the exhibition, rather it presents some of the highlights with explanatory text.

816. Rowland, Benjamin. "Popular Romanticism: Art and the Gift Books." *Art Quarterly* 20, no. 4 (December 1957): 364–81.

Rowland surveys the art of literary annuals and uses the engraved and lithographed reproductions of works of American art as an index to taste in the era, reflecting public enthusiasm for romantic and gothic subject matter. Native Americans, the struggle for Greek independence, the Orient, landscape, and genre scenes all appeared in the period from the 1820s into the 1850s.

817. Ruge, Valice F. *Life Along the Hudson. Wood Engravings of Hudson River Subjects from* Harper's Weekly, *1859–1903*. Woodstock, N.Y.: The Overlook Press, 1994. 180 pp.

Long a resident of the Hudson River region, Ruge collected the Hudson River images and their related texts for this volume. The modest introduction provides some basic information about the importance of the illustrations in *Harper's Weekly* and discusses some of the most important sites depicted. This volume achieves its goal—the linking of the images with their descriptive texts, permitting the reader and viewer to fully understand the meaning of these wood engravings, many designed by the foremost illustrators of the century including

Winslow Homer, Thomas Nast, William Allen Rogers, and Howard Chandler Christy.

818. Schmidt, Martin F. "*The Kentucky Stock Book*. A Search for the Elusive." *Filson club History Quarterly* 48, no. 3 (July 1974): 217–227.

Kentucky cattle and horse breeders attempted to publish the *Kentucky Stock Book* from 1837 to 1841 with illustrations after sketches and paintings by Edward Troye. This essay provides the history of this subscription publication, which was never brought to completion. However, a group of rare lithographs issued for the book do exist in the Louisville Free Public Library; Schmidt provides a checklist of them.

819. Scholnick, Robert J. "*Scribner's Monthly* and the 'Pictorial Representation of Life and Truth' in Post-Civil War America." *American Periodicals* 1, no. 1 (September 1991): 46–69.

Scholnick writes about innovations in illustrative technology practiced by *Scribner's Monthly*. Alexander W. Drake was the head of the art department; he worked closely with Theodore Low Devinne to obtain fine results, applying photographic technology and encouraging the employment of the best engravers. Scholnick also summarizes the content of *Scribner's* in broad terms and discusses the ways in which it recruited a new class of readers.

820. Scott, Kenneth. "Advertising Woodcuts in Colonial Newspapers." *Antiques* 67 (February 1955): 152–53.

The earliest pictorial advertisements appeared in newspapers during the colonial era. This article surveys the various types of advertisements, but does not identify the artists, or explain production techniques of the prints.

821. Seavey, Charles A. "Government Graphics: The Development of Illustration in U. S. Federal Publications, 1817–1861" in *A History of Book Illustration, 29 Points of View*, 514–547. ed. Bill Katz. Metuchen, N.J., & London: The Scarecrow Press, Inc., 1994.

Seavey investigates several aspects of the illustration of government documents: when did the practice originate, which volumes are illustrated, and which agencies took the lead. This chronological survey is well organized and researched and concludes with a checklist of the publications noted in the text, a very useful guide. This essay was earlier printed in *Government Publications Review* vol. 17 (1990).

822. Simon, Janice. "Consuming Pictures: *The Aldine, The Art Journal of America* and the Art of Self-Promotion." *The American Transcendental Quarterly* New Series 12, no. 3 (September 1998): 221–245.

The New York printer James Sutton began *The Aldine* as an advertising supplement in 1868 and transformed it into a successful art journal that lasted a decade and contained quality reproductions of American and European fine art. Simon provides an overview of the history of the journal focusing on its illustrations which were rather conservative.

823.———. "Imaging a New Heaven on a New Earth. *The Crayon* and Nineteenth Century American Periodical Covers." *American Periodicals* 1, no. 1 (September 1991): 11–24.

Simon examines several illustrated journals that "visually proclaimed ... the role of the arts in assuring a free and prosperous republic." Although many periodicals were profusely illustrated, few discussed the fine arts. The establishment of *The Crayon* in 1855 by editors William J. Stillman and John Durand filled the void. Simon analyses the iconography of the *The Crayon's* cover and those of *Sartain's Magazine*, *Graham's Magazine*, the *Western Art Journal*, the *Cosmopolitan Art Journal*, and *Gleason's Pictorial Drawing-Room Companion*.

824.———. "'Nature's Forest Volume'": *The Aldine*, the Adirondacks, and the Sylvan Landscape" in *Adirondack Prints and Printmakers: The Call of the Wild*, 83–103. ed. Caroline Mastin Welsh. Blue Mountain Lake and Syracuse, N.Y.: Adirondack Museum and Syracuse University Press, 1998.

The Aldine presented original wood engravings of extraordinary quality featuring American scenery, particularly sylvan views. Simon describes the role of the magazine's editor from 1872 through 1876, Richard Henry Stoddard, in the publication of these images and their expression of post-Civil War concerns such as national and regional character, and conceptions of masculinity, femininity, and Darwinism. Many of the forest views were drawn in the Adirondacks by artists such as John A. Hows, F. T. Vance, Thomas Moran, and John S. Davis. Stoddard declared the region "the noblest of the forest parks.".

825. Slee, Jacquelynn. *A Summary of the English Editions of Illustrated Bibles Published in America Between 1790 and 1825, with Indices of Subjects Illustrated and Engravers*. Ann Arbor, Mich.: Master's Thesis, 1973. 89 pp., biblio.

In her introduction, Slee provides the history of illustrated Bibles in America, a publishing feat that began just before peace was declared with Great Britain in 1782. She traces some of the European sources for the American engravings and notes the importance placed upon the engravings by the American publishers. Small reproductions of 26 engravings follow the introduction. The catalog contains Slee's extensive commentary on each publication including information on the sources and engravers. These descriptions are followed by a list of the illustrations in each Bible and the useful indices.

826. Smith, David E. "Illustrations of American Editions of *The Pilgrim's Progress* to 1870." *Princeton University Library Chronicle* 26, no. 1 (1964): 16–25.

Pilgrim's Progress was a frequently illustrated book in England and later in America. Smith traces American illustrations to their English sources and briefly describes the works of various American engravers including Alexander Anderson, Garret Lansing, William Mason, and George Gilbert. He concludes with descriptions of enormous painted panoramas that became popular entertainments in the 1850s. One was painted by artists including Frederick E. Church, Jasper F. Cropsey, F. O. C. Darley, and Daniel Huntington. A selection of book illustrations accompanies this study.

827. Smith, F. Hopkinson. *American Illustrators*. New York: Charles Scribner's Sons, 1892. 68 pp.

F. H. Smith, who wished to recreate the milieu of artists in the late nineteenth century, wrote this book as a series of imagined discussions at the Century Association, the Tile Club, and other places where artists of the time congregated. Whether or not he succeeded in this aim is debatable, but the results are interesting. Reproductions abound, and include works by Abbey, Pyle, Frost, Homer, and Kingsley.

828. Smith, Steven E., Catherine A. Hastedt, and Donald H. Dyal eds. *American Book and Magazine Illustrators to 1920*. Detroit: Gale Research Company, 1997. 450 pp.

This volume contains 42 biographical and bibliographical sketches on American illustrators. Among those active in the nineteenth century are E. A. Abbey, Alexander Anderson, Hammatt Billings, F.O.C. Darley, W. W. Denslow, Harry Fenn, Mary Hallock Foote, A. B. Frost, Winslow Homer, Augustus Hoppin, D. C. Johnston, D. W. Kemble, W. R. Leigh, Thomas Nast, Edward Penfield, Joseph Pennell, Howard Pyle, Frederic Remington, J. Allen St. John, John Sloan, Jessie Willcox Smith, Alice Barber Stephens, Thure de Thurstrup, and A. R. Waud. The volume concludes with an 80 page cumulative index to the various volumes in the series, *Dictionary of Literary Biography*, in which this is volume 188.

829. Smithsonian Institution. *Western Views and Eastern Visions*. Washington, D.C.: Smithsonian Institution Traveling Exhibition Service, 1981. 118 pp., biblio.

Although this exhibition catalog focuses on photographic views of the West, the examples include drawings by Thomas A. Ayres and William Henry Holmes, paintings, and lithographs after photographs. The particular interest of the exhibition is the relation of art and photography to the scientific surveys of the West during the nineteenth century. The text is by Eugene Ostroff.

830. Smyth, Albert Henry. *The Philadelphia Magazines and Their Contributors, 1741–1850*. Philadelphia: R.M. Lindsay, 1892. 264 pp., index.

The emphasis in this volume is on the history of, and contributors to, Philadelphia magazines. From time to time, illustrations are mentioned and briefly described.

831. Steinway, Kate. "Early Nineteenth-Century American Children's Books and Their Relationship to Currier and Ives Lithographs." *Imprint* 18, no. 1 (1993): 17–26.

Considering illustrations in children's books as the earliest genre images, Steinway suggests that their audience in the 1820s and 1830s formed the audience for popular prints published by Nathaniel Currier and Currier & Ives in the 1840s and later. She describes several types of imagery as a visual language that formed sterotypes and conventions that appear in both sets of images. Steinway concludes that the motifs became so accepted that the images could be read without the texts.

832. Stern, Madeleine B. "Mathew B. Brady and the *Rationale of Crime*: A Discovery in Daguerreotypes." *Quarterly Journal of the Library of Congress* 31, no. 3 (July 1974): 127–35.

The American edition of a book by Marmaduke B. Sampson, *Rationale of Crime* (1846), contains nineteen wood engravings after daguerreotypes by Mathew Brady. Stern discusses the background of this publishing effort which combines popular phrenology with penology.

833. Thompson, Neville. "Tools of Persuasion. The American Architectural Book of the Nineteenth Century" in *The American Illustrated Book in the Nineteenth Century*, 137–169. ed. Gerald W. R. Ward. Winterthur: The Henry Francis du Pont Winterthur Museum, 1987.

After surveying the collection of architectural design books at Winterthur, Thompson concludes that they were designed to be "tools of persuasion." Their inexpensive means of production and wide distribution meant that the books were designed to be used. The books reveal a great deal about the goals of the architects and builders of the period. Thompson discusses the illustrations, generally designed by the architects and reproduced by other hands as engravings, lithographs, or wood engravings, and then provides a chronological survey of the books beginning with Asher Benjamin's *The Country Builder's Assistant* (Boston, 1798) and concluding with Frank L. Smith's *A Cosy Home* (Boston, 1887).

834. Thompson, Susan Otis. "The Arts and Crafts Book in America" in *The American Illustrated Book in the Nineteenth Century*, 171–200. ed. Gerald W. R. Ward. Winterthur: The Henry Francis du Pont Winterthur Museum, 1987.

The arts and crafts movement started in England as a reaction to the industrial revolution. William Morris's Kelmscott Press was instrumental in the revival of fine printing. Thompson discusses the influence of this revival on American book designers and printers, particularly Daniel Berkeley Updike, Copeland and Day of Boston, Bruce Rogers, Will H. Bradley, Clarke Conwell's Elston Press, Frederic W. Goudy, W. A. Dwiggins, and Dard Hunter. All were active between 1890 and 1905.

835. Twyman, Michael. "The Emergence of the Graphic Book in the 19th Century" in *A Millenium of the Book: Production, Design & Illustration in Manuscript and print 900–1900*, 135–180. eds. Robin Myers and Michael Harris. Winchester, England, and New Castle, Delaware: St. Paul's Bibliographies and Oak Knoll Press, 1994.

This well-annotated study focuses on the British booktrade, but Twyman's observations apply as well to the development of the "graphic" book in the United States. Twyman considers books that have charts and diagrams as well as books that have illustrations, but no text.

836. Waite, Emma Forbes. "Beginnings of American Color Printing." *American Collector* 15 (July 1946): 12–13, 18.

Waite discusses the evolution of processes to print illustrations in color, commenting on the demand for color printing in book and periodical illustration. She touches upon the techniques of lithotinting and chromolithography, the printing of steel plate engravings in color, and the printing of wood blocks in oil colors. Unfortunately, the illustrations of each process are in black and white.

837.———. "Early Artists of Godey's *Lady's Book*." *Antiques* 59 (April 1951): 300–301.

The fashion plates of the *Lady's Book* are very elegant. Shunning the lithographic process, Godey insisted on hand-colored steel engravings. Edward W. Clay, Francis Humphreys, Joseph Ives Pease, and the firm of Capewell & Kimmel were among those who provided plates for the magazine. Many of the plates, however, were anonymously produced.

838. Wakeman, Geoffrey. *Victorian Book Illustration: The Technical Revolution*. Detroit: Gale Research Co., 1973. 182 pp., index.

Although the examples used are from English publications, this volume is equally applicable to American book publishing. Techniques discussed include wood engraving, etching, engraving, mezzotint, aquatint, lithography, color relief printing, chromolithography, electrotyping, photomechanical processes. The bibliography is excellent, and should be consulted by anyone interested in the technical aspects of book illustration.

839. Ward, Gerald W. R. *The American Illustrated Book in the Nineteenth Century*. Winterthur: The Henry Francis du Pont Winterthur Museum, 1987. 273 pp., index.

Edited by Ward, this volume is based on a conference held at the Winterthur Museum in 1982. The nine essays include the following: "Pictorial Perils: The Rise of American Illustration" by Neil Harris, "Dobson's *Encyclopaedia*: A Precedent in American Engraving" by Judy L. Larson, "The Publication of Illustrated Natural Histories in Philadelphia, 1800–1850" by Georgia B. Barnhill, "'Messengers of Love, Tokens of Friendship': Gift-Book Illustrations by John Sartain" by Katharine Martinez, "F. O. C. Darley's Outline Illustrations" by Sue W. Reed, "Tools of Persuasion: The American Architectural Book of the Nineteenth Century" by Neville Thompson, "The Arts and Crafts Book in America" by Susan Otis Thompson, "Drawn in Ink: Book Illustrations by Howard Pyle" by Elizabeth H. Hawkes, and "The Development of Photomechanical Book Illustration" by Lois Olcott Price. The foreword is by E. McSherry Fowble and Ian M. G. Quimby of the Winterthur Museum. Each essay is described individually. The volume is copiously illustrated.

840. Weitenkampf, Frank. "American Illustrators of Shakespeare." *Bulletin of the New York Public Library* 40 (February 1956): 70–72.

Weitenkampf describes editions of Shakespeare's plays, beginning with publications in 1852, that were illustrated by Americans. T.H. Matteson, W.J. Hennessey, and E.A. Abbey are artists mentioned in this note.

841.———. "American Bible Illustration." *Boston Public Library Quarterly* 10 (July 1958): 154–57

Bible illustrations of the eighteenth and early nineteenth centuries were often copied after European engravings of paintings. Weitenkampf, however, concentrates his discussion on wood engravings, beginning with the 1600 engravings for the *Illuminated Bible*, published by Harper's in 1846, 1400 of which were designed by J.G. Chapman. Also cited are W. Croome and J.B. Brightly's Illustrations for the New Testament, published in Philadelphia in 1849, and Hitchcock's *New and Complete Analysis of the Holy Bible*, with illustrations by Thomas Nast and F.B. Carpenter (New York, 1872). Weitenkampf ends his survey with a discussion of some illustrated Bibles of the twentieth century.

842.———. "American Illustrators of Dickens." *Boston Public Library Quarterly* 5 (October 1953): 189–94.

American publishers reprinted vast numbers of Dickens' novels. The etchings of the original editions were frequently copied, without much success. By the 1860s, American artists began to create their own images. F.O.C. Darley made a number of illustrations that Weitenkampf discusses, together with examples by Sol Eytinge, Jr., John McLenan, Thomas Nast, and Thomas Worth. Several twentieth-century illustrators are also mentioned.

843.———. "American Illustrations Abroad." *Art in America* 47 (1959): 58–61.

Weitenkampf surveys the illustration of foreign books by American artists. He begins by discussing an edition of Shakespeare, illustrated by T.H. Matteson, that was published in 1852. Illustrators of Shakespeare, Dickens, Tennyson, and other Brisish authors are mentioned, but Weitenkampf devotes most of this brief survey to twentieth century work.

844.———. "The Emergence of the American Illustrator." *Art Quarterly* 18 (1955): 394–402.

The various processes of book illustration (copper and steel engraving, woodcut, and wood engraving) are described in Weitenkampf's discussion of the mid-nineteenth-century flowering of wood engraving. Among the many artists he mentions are F.O.C. Darley, William Croome, and Winslow Homer. The author identifies a variety of social and historical factors which he feels were responsible for this creative outburst continuing through the 1870s.

845.———. "The Keepsake in Nineteenth-Century Art." *Boston Public Library Quarterly* 4 (July 1952): 139–48.

Keepsakes are elegantly bound volumes containing engravings and short literary pieces. Many publishers issued one per year, and they were popular gift items in the Victorian era. Weitenkampf examines the European influence on these volumes, and then discusses the illustrations, generally steel engravings. Among the illustrations in early volumes were reproductions of English paintings. But, as time went on, engravers such as Durand, Smillie, and J. Cheney reproduced the paintings of Asher B. Durand, Thomas Cole, Thomas Doughty, J.G. Chapman, and W.S. Mount. Weitenkampf points out that keepsakes were important in helping to bring American art and literature to the attention of the public.

846.———. "Nineteenth-Century History in Illustrated Weeklies." *Art in America* 45 (1957): 28–31.

The author contrasts photography with wood engravings of the second half of the nineteenth century. He emphasizes the wide range of subject matter of wood engravings, which he finds useful as documents of social history. Among the artists he briefly mentions are Homer, E.A. Abbey, W.A. Rogers, and F. Remington.

847. Welch, Margaret. *The Book of Nature: Natural History in the United States, 1825–1875*. Boston: Northeastern University Press, 1998. 289 pp., biblio., index.

This well written and thoroughly docmented study focuses on the importance of published natural histories to their audience. Welch discusses the books in three chronologically arranged chapters. The first is a survey of natural histories to 1825. Two chapters are on books published between 1825 and 1850 and the natural history surveys published by local, state, and national governments. Additional chapters focus on print culture, visual imagery, and the figure in the landscape.

848. Whalley, Joyce Irene. *Cobwebs to Catch Flies. Illustrated Books for the Nursery and Schoolroom, 1700–1900*. London: Elek, 1974. 163 pp., biblio.

Illustrated educational books for young children flourished in the nineteenth century. Although most of the examples reproduced are English, Whalley uses many American examples as well. Among the topics are alphabet books, counting and reading books, religious instruction books, moral improvement, history, street cries, natural history and science, grammar, music and languages. The text is well researched and informative.

849. White, Frank Linston. "Fifty Years of Book Illustrating in the United States." *Independent* 44 (January 21 and 28 1892): 80; 119.

The first part of this article emphasizes wood engraving, mentioning the works of Darley, William Croome, Alfred R. Waud, Nast, and many others. The second part concentrates on illustrators whose drawings were reproduced by mechanical means, and on artists including Vedder, Pyle, and Thomas Moran.

850. Winearls, Joan. *Art on the Wing: British, American, and Canadian Illustrated Bird Books from the Eighteenth to the Twentieth Century*. Toronto: University of Toronto, 1999. 80 pp., biblio.

Ornithological illustration has been important to the development of scientific knowledge of bird species since the sixteenth century. Focusing on more recent publications in the Anglo-American world, Winearls provides an excellent survey touching upon the great artists and their works and describing clearly the technical problems of reproducing their drawings and sketches. Most of the reproductions are printed in color.

851. Wolfe, Richard J. *Jacob Bigelow's American Medical Botany, 1817–1821*. North Hills, Pa.: Bird & Bull Press and Boston Medical Society Library, 1979. 121 pp.

Based on Bigelow's papers preserved in the Francis A. Countway Library at Harvard University, Wolfe's research reconstructs the planning, printing, binding, and distribution of Bigelow's *American Medical Botany*, the first book published in America with color-printed illustrations. A further aspect of this work is that the illustrations were printed from stones—the first use of lithography in the United States. This conlusion, however, has been recently refuted by Philip Weimerskirch in "The Beginning of Color Printing in America" (*Printing History* volume 22, number 5).

852. Wood, Charles B. III. "American Scientific Illustration, 1675–1775" in *Boston Prints and Printmakers, 1670–1775*, 221–39. Boston: Colonial Society of Massachusetts, 1973.

The few scientific illustrations published in Boston were printed before 1718. After considering prints of astronomy found in almanacs, and then several book illustrations, Wood turns to English illustrations depicting North American natural history. He discusses some of the fundamental problems and concerns of the scientific illustrator, such as the accuracy of the engravings when compared to the original drawings.

853.———. "Prints and Scientific Illustration in America" in *Prints in and of America to 1850*, 161–92. ed. John D. Morse. Winterthur, Del.: Henry Francis du Pont Winterthur Museum, 1970.

Wood presents a well-documented survey of scientific illustrations found in books and periodicals from about 1750 to 1850. Numerous books are cited, and processes (line engraving, aquatint, lithography, and chromolithography) are discussed in terms of their suitability for scientific illustration. The emphasis is on American natural history, since illustrations for most other scientific books were copied from European works. This is an excellent survey of a largely unexplored topic.

854. Yarnell, James L. "Tennyson Illustration in Boston, 1864–1872." *Imprint* 7, no. 2 (1982): 10–16.

Yarnell describes the illustrations that resulted when two rival publishing houses "engaged in what can be considered a Tennysonian publishing war." In 1864 the firms of Ticknor and Fields and J.E. Tilton and Company each published editions of *Enoch Arden*. The Tilton edition contained six full page anonymous wood engravings; Ticknor and Fields commissioned nineteen illustrations from Felix O.C. Darley, William John Hennessey, Elihu Vedder, and John LaFarge. It is to the works of the latter two artists that Yarnell directs his attention. Ironically, Ticknor and Fields did not continue to publish such distinctive illustrations in subsequent editions of Tennyson's works. J.E. Tilton's publications were more successful.

City Views

855. "Artists Draw South Dakota: Panoramic Views of Pioneer Towns." *South Dakota History* 8, no. 3 (1978): 221–249.

This article is largely based on John R. Hebert's *Panoramic Maps of Anglo-American Cities*. The South Dakota Historical Society's collection includes about twenty-four views, all reproduced in this photographic essay. A useful table compares populations in the towns depicted in the 1880s, 1900, and 1970.

856. "Images of Historical Cincinnati." *Cincinnati Historical Society Bulletin* 38, no. 4 (1980): 233–64.

Depictions of Cincinnati in many media—paintings, prints, photographs—provide an excellent overview of the collections of the Cincinnati Historical Society. The article celebrates the 150th anniversary of the Society.

857. Andrews, William Loring. *Iconography of the Battery and Castle Garden*. New York: Charles Scribner's Sons, 1901. 44 pp.

Castle Garden was situated on the southwest tip of Manhattan, known as the Battery. Andrews describes the history of this section of New York and the views and maps made of it. The Garden was constructed upon Fort Clinton, built around 1810. In 1824 it was roofed and converted into a popular place of entertainment and amusement. In 1855 it became an emigration depot, then in 1896 it became a public aquarium. The list of illustrations provides titles and publication data.

858.———. *New Amsterdam, New Orange, New York: A Chronologically Arranged Account of Engraved Views of the City from the First Picture Published in 1651 Until the Year 1800*. New York: Dodd, Mead & Co., 1897. 142 pp.

Andrews begins by giving information on Henry Hudson and the Dutch West Indies Co., both important to New York's history. He proceeds to describe each engraving of the city to 1800. His commentaries are descriptive and contain valuable bits of information. Reprinted in the appendix are extracts from George M. Asher's bibliography of early Dutch books and pamphlets on New Netherland, and publications by Hugh Gaine, William Smith, and others concerned with the history of the city. This volume is outdated, although handsome in appearance.

859.———. *A Prospect of the Colleges in Cambridge in New England: Engraved by Wm. Burgis in 1726*. New York: Dodd, Mead & Co., 1897. 38 pp.

Andrews begins his account of the Burgis view of Harvard engraved in 1726 with a long quotation from *First Foundation of the Colleges at Cambridge in New England* (London, 1642). Two states of the engraving were described in the *Proceedings of the Massachusetts Historical Society* for 1881. Writing in his unique discursive style, Andrews discusses other copies of the plate and other engravings, the Hollis family and their association with Harvard, the early buildings of the college, and various other topics. He concludes with descriptions of other views of Harvard. Letters from Thomas Hollis and Edward Holyoke, president of Harvard, about Hollis Hall and Hollis's collection of books, are reprinted in full.

860.———. *An Index to the Illustrations in the Manuals of the Corporation of the City of New York, 1841–1870*. New York: Society of Iconphiles, 1906. 107 pp., index.

David T. Valentine compiled the *Manuals of the Corporation of the City of New York* from 1842 to 1866. Beginning in 1844, these volumes contained historical data on the city and many illustrations copied from old prints, paintings, and sketches that were reproduced as lithographs and wood engravings. The last of these manuals was published in 1870. The primary list of illustrations is arranged by date of publication and includes all the plates; there is an additional list of maps and plans arranged by date of original issue, and another for facsimiles of letters, broadsides, certificates, etc. The general index to all the illustrations is of great value, and is an excellent and useful guide to views of New York.

861. Angle, Paul M. "American City Prints." *Chicago History* 7, no. 2 (1963): 51–61.

Angle discusses the collection of city views at the Chicago Historical Society, many of which were on display at the time the article was written, and sets them within the history of the growth of American cities. Drawing on original correspondence at the Historical Society from two viewmakers (Smith Brothers and Edwin Whitefield), the author asserts that the prints were used to promote towns. The Whitefield document also points out the problems of obtaining subscribers.

862.———. "Views of Chicago, 1866–1867." *Antiques* 63 (January 1953): 60–61.

In 1866, two interior decorators, Otto Jevne and Peter M. Almini, began publishing *Chicago Illustrated*, with lithographs by Louis Kurz of the Chicago Lithographing Co. Four plates appeared each month, together with descriptive text. The venture lasted only thirteen months, but the lithographs produced form the best and most complete pictoral record of Chicago before the Great Fire of 1871. Further details about the publication and its creation appear in this article.

863. Ashton, Jean. "Tall Tales and Whales: Wonders of Barnum's Museum." *Imprint* 16, no. 2 (1991): 15–25.

This article focuses on prints and posters describing Barnum's Museum in New York. Ashton's well-researched essay provides detailed information on Barnum, his activities, and his efforts to enhance his own reputation through self-promotion.

864. Bail, Hamilton Vaughan. *Views of Harvard: A Pictoral Record to 1860.* Cambridge, Mass.: Harvard University Press, 1949. 264 pp., index.

Almost half of the views of Harvard reproduced in this volume are prints ranging in date from the Burgis view of 1726, to the birds-eye lithograph published in 1858 by Prang & Meyer. Detailed descriptions of the prints include contemporary accounts from newspapers, subscription forms, identifications of the buildings depicted, and information about the artists and publishers. A bibliography for each print is also included. There are several opportunities in this volume to study the preparatory drawings and watercolors in comparison with the finished engravings or lithographs.

865. Baine, Rodney M. and Louis De Vorsey, Jr. "The Provenance and Historical Accuracy of *A View of Savannah as it Stood the 29th of March, 1734.*" *Georgia Historical Quarterly* 73, no. 4 (December 1989): 784–813.

One of the rarest city views is the 1734 engraving of Savannah. This essay discusses the recently found sketch of the city that served as the source for P. Fourdrinier's engraving. The authors discuss the creation of the engraving and assign responsibility for the original sketch to George Jones. This careful analysis of an important city view is thoroughly documented.

866. Baird, Joseph A., Jr. *Historical Lithographs of San Francisco.* San Francisco: Burger & Evans, 1972. [93 ll.], biblio.

In 1972, an elephant folio book containing about fifty reproductions of lithographs of San Francisco was compiled by Baird and Edwin Clyve Evans. A reduced photocopy of the text alone was made available in 1980. The introduction provides an excellent and thoroughly annotated survey of lithography in San Francisco. The catalog includes detailed entries on 231 prints and variant states. Locations in public institutions are provided.

867. Beckman, Thomas. *Milwaukee Illustrated: Panoramic and Bird's-Eye Views of a Midwestern Metropolis, 1844–1908.* Milwaukee: Milwaukee Art Center, 1978. Unp.

Beckman distinguishes between panoramic and bird's-eye views, discusses the various commercial printmaking media, prices and sales techniques, and some of the important publishers and artists. The catalog of the exhibition includes almost fifty views of Milwaukee. The entries are very informative providing excellent background on the artists and the prints.

868. Boorse, Henry A. "Bush Hill: An Historic Philadelphia House." *Imprint* 9, no. 2 (1984): 12–18.

Bush Hill was built in 1740 by Alexander Hamilton, the Philadelphia lawyer who had defended the newspaper printer Peter Zenger against a charge of seditious libel. Boorse examines several eighteeth-century engravings of the house, describes its role in the nation's history (it housed Vice President John Adams and his wife in 1790), and its eventual demise in 1875.

869. Boutros, David. "The West Illustrated: Meyer's Views of Missouri River Towns." *Imprint* 9, no. 2 (1984): 2–11.

Two little known publishers of American views were Joseph Meyer (1796–1856) and his son, Herrmann Julius Meyer (1826–1909). Boutros provides biographical sketches of both men and describes their various publications, *Meyer's Universum* and *The United States Illustrated*. In these publications eight views of Missouri River towns, including St. Louis, Jefferson City, and Van Buren appeared. Sources for these views include lithographs and daguerreotypes. Boutros concludes his well researched article by suggesting that Meyer's views may not be entirely accurate.

870. Breitenbach, Edgar. "Little Loretto, Kentucky" in *American Printmaking Before 1876, Fact, Fiction, and Fantasy*, 47–52. Washington, D.C.: Library of Congress, 1975.

An odd print of the religious settlement at Little Loretto, Kentucky, is the subject of this article. Published to recruit priests and funds in Europe in 1806 or 1807, it is a blend of truth and fiction. Breitenbach discusses the origin of the print, the reasons for its publication, and the history of the settlement it depicts.

871. Brigham, Clarence S. "Timothy Dexter Mansion Prints." *Essex Institute Historical Collections* 91 (July 1955): 193–94.

Brigham carefully describes four variations of a print depicting Timothy Dexter's mansion in Newburyport. The first is an aquatint by John Rubens Smith executed in Boston between 1810 and 1812. Three lithographs were published in the 1850s, all copied from the aquatint.

872. Brodherson, David. "Souvenir Books in Stone: Lithographic Miniatures for the Masses." *Imprint* 12, no. 2 (1987): 21–28.

Brodherson provides a survey of city views in different media following the 1876 Centennial, concentrating on the small view books issued by publishers to serve as souvenirs in the 1880s. There were four major publishers of this genre, one of which was the Wittemann Brothers of New York, the focus of this excellent study which includes information on the illustrations as well as on the bindings and text. He notes their usefulness to researchers interested in urbanization and social values, as well as graphic arts.

873. Buisseret, David. "Printed Maps of the Chicago Portage." *Imprint* 12, no. 1 (1987): 25–7.

The author provides an interesting survey of maps describing the portage around the Chicago River from 1733 to 1853. He notes the enjoyment that can be obtained from collecting narrowly on one geographic area or feature.

874. Burr, Nelson R. "The Federal City Depicted, 1612–1801." *Quarterly Journal of the Library of Congress* (November 1950): 64–77.

Burr describes early plans for the city, beginning his discussion with seventeenth century maps of the Washington, D.C., region. There is substantial documentation on both the planning of the capital and its early buildings.

875. Chace, Laura L. "Otto Onken: His Cincinnati Scenes." *Queen City Heritage* 49, no. 3 (1991): 21–29.

Onken published a series of eight lithographs of Cincinnati in the early 1850s. Each is reproduced in color in this brief article that provides essential biographical information on the lithographer and a brief overview of the printing and publishing industry of Cincinnati which ranked fourth in the nation by 1856.

876. Cilella, Salvatore G. "Eighteenth Century Views of Bethlehem." *Pennsylvania Heritage* 6, no. 2 (1980): 10–14.

Founded in 1741 by German Protestants, Bethlehem, Pennsylvania, flourished. Cicella discusses the important views of Bethlehem beginning with Nicholas Garrison's view issued in London in 1757. Garrison was a resident of the community, although he lived for many years in Philadelphia. A later view by him was published in 1784; this was copied for Isaac Weld's *Travels Through the States of North America* in 1798. Another important view by Thomas Pownall appeared in the *Scenographia Americana* in 1768.

877. Clark, Donald F. "Six Remarkable Views, 1761: The Collaboration of Governor Pownall and Paul Sandby." *Imprint* 4, no. 1 (1979): 23–28.

Thomas Pownall (1722–1805) was the British topographical draftsman and political figure responsible for a series of drawings engraved and published in London in 1761. Clark provides the historical context for this important series of prints engraved by Paul Sandby (1725–1809). These views were reprinted in 1768 in the *Scenographia Americana* with views of other cities in the American colonies and West Indies. The appendices include lists of the prints published in 1761, other views by Pownall and Sandby, and the contents of the 1768 publication.

878. Cogswell, Ledyard Jr. "Some Albany Views." *Antiques* 60 (July 1951): 39–41.

The ten views of Albany discussed are from the collection of Ledyard Cogswell. For some of the prints, the author was fortunate in finding the original drawings, which lends greater interest to this article. Cogswell is more concerned with the subject matter of the prints than with the artists who created them.

879. Comstock, Helen. "The Hoff Views of New York." *Antiques* 51 (April 1947): 250–52.

This series of twenty lithographed views is found in *The Empire City of New York*, a book published in New York by Henry Hoff in 1850. Most of the text of this article concerns the histories of the buildings portrayed; the author was not able to reveal much about the artists and lithographers who collaborated in this venture. The set of views is very rare; The New York Public Library and The New-York Historical Society possess sets that are almost complete.

880. Cresswell, Donald H. "Late Eighteenth-Century American Harbor Views Derived From Joseph Vernet and Richard Paton" in *American Maritime Prints*, 41–62. ed. Elton W. Hall. New Bedford, Mass.: The Old Dartmouth Historical Society, 1985.

Cresswell provides a brief overview of views of the American colonies and then focuses on a group of French prints of American cities actually derived from prints after Vernet's paintings of European cities. Another group of prints, known as "vues d'optiques" are also fictitious and some are based on a print derived from a painting by Richard Paton. Cresswell suggests that these derivations not be considered "frauds," but that we look to see what kind of aesthetic theory produced them and what elements of truth are contained within them.

881. Cresswell, Donald H., and Christopher W. Lane. *Prints of Philadelphia at the Philadelphia Print Shop, Featuring the Wohl Collection*. Philadelphia: 1990. 128 pp., biblio., index.

This handsome catalogue of a private collection being sold is scholarly and informative, providing information on subject matter and printmakers. Milton and Joan Wohl formed the collection over a forty year period.

882. Cummings, Abbott Lowell. "A Recently Discovered Engraving of the Old State House in Boston" in *Boston Prints and Printmakers, 1670–1775*, 175–84. Boston: Colonial Society of Massachusetts, 1973.

Nathaniel Hurd engraved the "South Prospect of the Court House in Boston" in 1751, which was, in 1973, only recently discovered. Cummings uses the engraving to discuss the architecture of the Old State House, the significance of Thomas Dawes, and Nathaniel Hurd.

883. Dann, John C. "Views of New Orleans in 1840." *The American Magazine and Historical Chronicle* 4, no. 2 (1988): 32–8.

Thirty-five views of New Orleans buildings were printed in the *Historical Epitome of the State of Louisiana* (New Orleans, 1840). These images are reproduced with a brief prefatory note.

884. Deak, Gloria-Gilda. *American Views Prospects and Vistas*. New York: Viking Press and New York Public Library, 1976. 134 pp., index.

The introduction to this volume is by James T. Flexner. He discusses the growth of settlements, the movement of the frontier, and the importance of the city in American life. About fifty prints are reproduced and each plate is accompanied by a page of text providing background on the subject of each print.

885.———. *Picturing America, 1492–1899*. Princeton: Princeton University Press, 1988. 2 vols., biblio., index.

This magnificent and scholarly reference work describes the collection of American city views at the New York Public Library. Volume one contains 657 pages of text; volume two has 880 illustrations. The introduction touches on a variety of subjects—public interest in the early views in the sixteenth and seventeenth centuries, the history of the New York Public Library's print collection, and a brief overview of the history of printmaking in the United States. The catalog has 880 entries and each is described in great detail with special emphasis on the subject matter of each print and on those who were responsible for the design and execution of them. There are two indices—one for subject and one for artist, printmaker, publisher. The bibliography is extensive. Any serious collector of American prints should find shelf space for this reference work. It is not likely to be surpassed.

886.———. "Picturing America, 1492–1899." *Imprint* 13, no. no. 2 (1988): 1–76.

This issue of *Imprint* serves as the catalog for an exhibition of prints, maps, and drawings at the New York Public Library. The introduction discusses early cartographers; the print room of the Library; I.N. Philps Stokes, the creator of the collection; and the history of printmaking in the United States. The catalog lists and reproduces eighty-two items. The subject matter of each is well described. A selective bibliography is included.

887. Dooley, William German. "Early Boston Seen in Prints." *Antiques* 44 (December 1943): 278–80.

In 1943 the Museum of Fine Arts sponsored an exhibition entitled, "Boston, Its Life and Its People, from the Founding to the Great Fire and the New Metropolis, 1630–1872." Nine of the prints from the exhibition are reproduced here with an excellent text about the subjects depicted. The display actually included almost a thousand items of many types: prints, paintings, silver, glass, pottery, furniture. The variety of prints represented is described in general terms in the introduction to the article.

888. Dorrill, Lisa K. "Illustrating the Ideal City: Nineteenth-Century American Bird's Eye Views." *Imprint* 18, no. 2 (1993): 21–31.

The use of bird's-eye city views as promotional pieces, especially views of Mid-western and Western cities, is the subject of this article. Dorrill uses prints of Lawrence, Kansas, 1858–1880, to trace shifting attitudes towards that city as it changed from an abolitionist stronghold to a metropolitan center. Her analysis of these prints is thorough and her methodology can be used on other bird's-eye views.

889. Drury, John. "'The City in a Garden,' Chicago Before the Fire of 1871." *Antiques* 43 (February 1943): 66–69.

The title of this article comes from a letter written by an immigrant in 1864. Because of the 1871 fire, books, pamphlets, prints, and all printed materials about Chicago are scarce. The prints illustrating this article are from the Joseph T. Ryerson Collection, which was on display at the Lakeside Press Galleries in 1943. Drury describes the growth of the city until the fire, then concentrates on some of the rarer prints. The captions for the illustrations provide helpful documentation on the buildings and areas depicted.

890. Dykshorn, Jan. "Artists Draw South Dakota: Panoramic Views of Pioneer Towns." *South Dakota History* 8, no. 3 (June 1978): 221–249.

Basic information about the production of city views and their makers is provided. Twenty-one views are reproduced with a table providing comparative populations statistics for the 1880s, 1900, and 1970.

891. Edmonds, John H. "The Burgis Views of New York and Boston." *Proceedings of the Bostonian Society* (19 January 1915): 29–50.

In 1913, rumors circulated about the sale of a perfect copy of the first state of the Burgis view of New York. Many incorrect statements were made about the print and Burgis which inspired Edmonds to set the record straight. He begins by discussing the date of the view of New York, later states of it, and then turns to the Burgis view of Boston. Much of this discussion is taken from an earlier essay that he wrote, published by the Colonial Society of Massachusetts in 1907, but Edmonds has incorporated new findings and interpretations in this article.

892.———. "The Burgis-Price View of Boston." *Publications of the Colonial Society of Massachusetts* 11 (February 1907): 245–62.

Many references to the Burgis-Price view of Boston, first published in 1723, are found in contemporary newspapers. Using these references as documentation, Edmonds is able to provide a history of the publication of the engraving. The plate was reissued in 1736 with "pasters" over the parts of the skyline that had changed; Edmonds recommends soaking these off the British Museum copy to restore it to its original condition. He locates five copies of the 1743 edition. Facts about William Price and his other views are provided, and information on John Harris is also supplied. This excellent account of the engraving, artist, engraver, and publishers is extensively documented.

893. Emlen, Robert P. "The Great Gale of 1815: Artifactual Evidence of Rhode Island's First Hurricane." *Rhode Island History* 48, no. 2 (May 1990): 50–61.

A powerful hurricane struck the Rhode Island Coast on September 23, 1815. The artist James Kidder (1776–1852) produced an aquatint in 1816 which incorporates a great deal of information on the storm and the damage it caused. Emlen closely reads the print closely to tell the story of the storm.

894. Freeman, Larry. *Historical Prints of American Cities*. Watkins Glen, N.Y.: Century House, 1952. 100 pp., index.

Freeman provides "a representative sampling of the cradle places of United States industry and commerce," through the compilation of views of American cities, generally printed around 1850. The book is well illustrated, but the descriptions of the prints lack substantive information on the artists and publishers and contain errors on processes. The index is by city.

895. The Grolier Club. *A Catalogue of Plans and Views of New York City From 1651 to 1860*. New York: 1897. 38 pp.

The introduction discusses important views made in the eighteenth century: views made in Holland, the Burgis views of 1717, and the Popple view of 1733. There is also a brief note on the profusion of views printed after the Civil War. The catalog is arranged according to the print's date of execution rather than date of publication, and contains descriptions of almost 150 items.

896. Gross, Sally Lorensen. *Toward an Urban View: The Nineteenth-Century American City in Prints*. New Haven: Yale University Art Gallery, 1989. 48 pp.

In her extensive and thoughtful essay accompanying this exhibition catalog, Gross perceives that printed views reveal changing perceptions of the urban environment and the changing markets for the prints. Gross also examines the changing modes of looking at cities and towns. Interior views of cities are also described, a genre surveyed through the 1890s. The catalog consists of fifty-four prints arranged chronologically.

897. Guarino, Charles E. "A Dozen Eggs on the Street. The Panics of Wall Street Recorded in Print." *Imprint* 3, no. 2 (November 1978): 17–20.

Guarino provides an interesting array of depictions of Wall Street and the stock market found in nineteenth-century illustrated journals including *Ballou's Pictorial*, *Harper's Weekly*, and *Frank Leslie's Illustrated Newspaper*. He provides the historical background of the most prominent financial panics and related events that were depicted in the pictorial press.

898. Hall, Elton W. "Domestic Life in a Whaling Port" in *American Maritime Prints*, 130–188. ed. Elton W. Hall. New Bedford, Mass.: The Old Dartmouth Historical Society, 1985.

As an important whaling port, New Bedford is the subject of a large array of prints. Hall surveys views of the town, prints of homes and civic buildings, and factory views. Trade cards, membership certificates, prints of steamships, atlas illustrations, yachting prints, and portraits are also part of this survey. Finally, Hall reproduces two prints lithographed in New Bedford by the firm of Mack, Dixon and Co. in 1834. Hall suggests that all these prints provide a valuable record of life in nineteenth-century New Bedford.

899. Hallam, John. "The Eighteenth-Century American Townscape and the Face of Colonialism." *Smithsonian Studies in American Art* 4, no. 3–4 (September 1990): 145–163.

This is a perspective analysis of the Burgis views of New York (ca. 1719) and Boston (ca. 1725) and the John Smibert oil painting of Boston, 1738. Hallam focuses on the accuracy of these images and the relationship of factual accuracy to the colonial policies of Great Britain. They are also discussed in terms of their usefulness as promotional images. The Smibert painting introduces people in the foreground—a colonial couple and a native American couple. Hallam suggests that this reflects "a kind of ecclesiastical and moral imperialism." Hallam provides excellent historical background for the production of these views.

900. Harley, Robert L. "George Washington Lived Here: Some Early Prints of Mount Vernon." *Antiques* 47 (February 1945): 103–105; 166–167.

Harley begins with a history of Mount Vernon's owners and architecture and discusses views made of the residence, with special emphasis on "The Washington Family at Mount Vernon," by Edward Savage; an aquatint by George Isham Parkyns; and Samuel Seymour's engraving after the painting by William Birch. The second part of the article concerns the popularity of the subject in the 1850s and 1860s, when Mount Vernon was being restored. The author discusses which prints he thinks are copies of earlier ones, basing his arguments on fictive depictions portrayed in some of the views. Harley does not mention the many engraved book and magazine illustrations of the subject, but the prints reproduced for this article are well chosen.

901.———. "Learning in the Wilderness, Some Notes on Early American Colleges." *American Collector* 14 (February 1945): 6–7, 18.

The histories of Harvard University, the College of William and Mary, King William's School (University of Maryland), and several other colleges support Harley's comments on early views of the institutions.

902.———. "Old American College Views." *Antiques* 26 (November 1934): 185–87.

An exhibition of views of colleges at the Old Print Shop in New York in 1934 was the impetus for this article. The author was able to find only ten pre-1800 views. As lithography was more common in the nineteenth century, Harley notes more important examples executed using that process.

903. Hebert, John R. *Panoramic Maps of Anglo-American Cities*. Washington, D.C.: Library of Congress, 1974. 118 pp.

Hebert's informative introduction discusses how the city views were made, promoted, and sold. Several of the publishers who specialized in this genre are discussed. The giants were Albert Ruger, Thaddeus Mortimer Fowler, Lucien R. Burleigh, Henry Wellge, and Oakley H. Bailey. These views remain significant for thieir ability to capture the vitality of American urban centers. The checklist numbers over one thousand items. Arranged by state, each entry includes the name of the city and date, artist (if recorded), publisher, lithographer, or printer, and dimensions. This is an excellent record of the Library of Congress collection.

904.———. *Panoramic Maps of Cities in the United States and Canada*. Washington, D.C.: Library of Congress, 1984. 181 pp., index.

This checklist records 1,726 panoramic maps or views of North American cities and towns held by the Geography and Map Division of the Library of Congress. An essay by John Hebert on the creation, publication, and distribution of these views precedes the checklist. Information is included on several of the most prolific publishers including Albert Ruger, Thaddeus Mortimer Fowler, Lucien R. Burleigh, Henry Wellge, and Oakley H. Bailey. The checklist is arranged by state and city with an index by location and artist/publisher. Each entry includes the name of the town depicted, LC call number, and artist.

905. Hitchings, Sinclair H. "A New England Album." *Archives of American Art* 9 (October 1971): 17–26.

Hitchings relies on portraits, maps, and illustrations that appear in books, almanacs, and broadsides for this discussion of Boston prints. He feels that visual matter can reveal much about life in colonial New England, if considered thoughtfully.

906. Horton, Loren H. "Through the Eyes of Artists: Iowa Towns in the 19th Century." *Palimpsest* 59, no. 5 (September 1978): 133–147.

Horton discusses panoramic views and viewmakers of Iowa towns, focusing on common elements found in these views, the artists who drew them, particularly Henry Lewis, John Caspar Wild, and the publisher of illustrated atlases, Alfred T. Andreas, who employed over 100 people as artists, cartographers, writers, and canvassers. Another native of Iowa active in this business of producing views was Alexander Simplot. The article is well illustrated.

907. Howitson, Brenda, Claire Goodwin, and Mary Micarelli. "An Index to Illustrations of Massachusetts People and Places in *Ballou's* and *Gleason's Pictorials.*" *Imprint* 19, no. no. 2 (1994): 30–41.

The introduction to this useful checklist provides background on the two periodicals published consecutively from 1851 to 1859. The index is very useful for those who must respond to the question, "Do you have a picture of ________?".

908. Jackson, Joseph. *Prints, Documents, and Maps Illustrative of Philadelphia Real Estate in the Office of Mastbaum Bros. & Fleisher*. Philadelphia: 1926. 85 pp.

Albert Rosenthal, a Philadelphia artist, formed the collection of prints owned by Mastbaum Bros. & Fleisher. The introduction describes the growth of Philadelphia from colonial times to the 1920s, concentrating on the history of real estate and realtors. This interesting catalog of prints and documents has been carefully compiled.

909.———. "Iconography of Philadelphia." *Pennsylvania Magazine of History and Biography* 59 (January 1935): 57–73.

Jackson's discussion of views of Philadelphia begins with the painting by Peter Cooper, ca. 1720—now in the Library Company of Philadelphia—and ends with Frank H. Taylor's twentieth-century views of buildings. This article forms a good general guide to views of Philadelphia. Artists such as Krimmel, John Hill, Birch, Cephas Childs, William L. Breton, J.C. Wild, and Joseph Pennell are discussed, as are the photographic views of John C. Browne, stereoscopic photographs, and illustrations in the city directories and nineteenth-century guidebooks. This article was also printed privately with illustrations in 1934.

910. Kies, Emily Bardack. *The City and the Machine: Urban and Industrial Illustration in Aemrica, 1880–1900*. Ph.D. Dissertation: Columbia University, 1971. 284 pp., index by artist, biblio.

Kies relies on periodical illustrations that reflect the moods and thoughts of an era and examined them as works of art apart from the visual information they provide. She provides the historical context for the illustrations, discusses the genre, magazines, the art of illustratin, humanistic views of cities that focus on people, industrial still life, and the inconography of the city and machines. Among the artists in her study are Edwin A. Abbey, Otto H. Bacher, Arthur B. Frost, Charles Parsons, Thure de Thulstrup, and Rufus Zogbaum.

911. Lane, Mills B., IV. "Glimpses of New Orleans." *Walpole Society Note Book* (1975): 23–32.

This survey of prints and drawings of New Orleans concentrates on the period from settlement in 1726, to 1852. This article was written in conjunction with the Society's visit to New Orleans in 1975.

912. Lyttle, Rebecca. "People and Places: Images of Nineteenth Century San Diego In Lithographs and Paintings." *Journal of San Diego History* 24, no. 2 (March 1978): 152–171.

Lyttle surveys images of San Diego with some attention paid to the criticism levied against A. E. Mathews' 1873 view of the growing city, published as a promotional piece. The author contrasts these topographical views with paintings done in the final quarter of the nineteenth century and concludes the survey with an examination of portrait paintings.

913. Magill, John T. "Pelican's Eyes: Views of New Orleans." *Imprint* 15, no. 2 (1990): 20–31.

Magill surveys bird's-eye views of New Orleans from 1803 through the 1880s. He attempts, in particular, to assess the accuracy of these images. Distortion of New Orleans is caused by the topography of the city, sprawled along the curves of the Mississippi River.

914. Marks, Matthew S. "The Brooklyn Bridge: Symbol of American Progress." *Imprint* 8, no. 1 (1983): 26–30.

Completed in 1883, the Brooklyn Bridge became both a potent symbol of American industrial power and a favored subject of artists and printmakers. Lithographs, steel engravings, wood engravings, and etchings were made of the Bridge. Marks provides an interesting survey of images as well as historical background on the building of the Bridge and its importance as a symbol to the American people.

915. Mason, Charles E., Jr., and Bettina A. Norton. "Hotels for Business or Pleasure in Lithographs." *Antiques* 104 (July 1973): 100–107.

This carefully researched article focuses on lithographed advertisements for hotels in and near Boston and for vacation spots favored by Bostonians. All were produced in Boston by the Pendletons, John Bufford, and other mid-nineteenth-century firms. Much factual information is included on the buildings themselves, and the article is handsomely illustrated.

916. Mason, Glenn. "Early Images of Spokane." *The Pacific Northwesterner* 29, no. 1 (December 1984): 1–13.

Spokane, on the banks of the Palouse River, was depicted by many artists beginning with Henry James Warre in 1846. Mason mentions the early artists who depicted the Spokane Falls and focuses his attention on views made during the city's boom period of the 1880s and 1890s. The Northern Pacific Railroad published promotional views and other depictions appeared in a variety of books and magazines, including *West Shore*.

917. Mayer, Grace M. "Views of Manhattan Island." *Antiques* 62 (December 1952): 498–501.

Mayer's article reproduces views, mainly watercolors, from the Blair Collection in the Museum of the City of New York. These views are an important complement to the Stokes Collection at The New York Public Library.

918. Mayor, A. Hyatt. "Aquatint Views of Our Infant Cities." *Antiques* 88 (September 1965): 314–18.

The author begins by describing the process of making aquatints, and emphasizing its degree of difficulty. Two of the best aquatint artists were John Hill and William J. Bennett, and Mayor focuses on the works of these two men. Their aquatints were done after paintings by Joshua Shaw, William Guy Wall, George Cook, and Antoine Mondelli. The superb illustrations to this article were owned by Harry W. Havemeyer and were exhibited at The Metropolitan Museum of Art from Dec. 1965 to Feb. 1966.

919.———. "Prints." *American Art Journal* 7 (May 1975): 43–51.

The theme of the May 1975 issue of the *American Art Journal* is "1776: How America Really Looked." In his article, Mayor surveys the history of prints in America to 1800. Some choice views are reproduced: a 1625–1628 etching of New Amsterdam, the Burgis view of New York (ca. 1720), the Scull and Heap view of Philadelphia (1756), and two Revere engravings, all with excellent commentary.

920. Munsterberg, Margaret. "Early Views of Beacon Hill." *Boston Public Library Quarterly* 8 (October 1956): 171–80.

The Boston Public Library possesses five watercolors by John Rubens Smith, which he made in 1811 or 1812. In 1857 and 1858, chromolithographs of the watercolors were published by George G. Smith. Information given in this article includes biographical material on the artist and lithographer, and on the subject of each print.

921. Muscalus, John A. *The Views of Towns, Cities, Falls and Buildings on 1800–1866 Bank Paper Money*. Bridgeport, Pa.: John A. Muscalus, 1939. 10 pp.

This index to vignettes on bank notes, which gives the name and denomination of the bank note carrying the vignette, is divided into appropriate sections, and then arranged geographically by state and town. Muscalus has compiled at least thirty-eight other pamphlets on bank notes; since these are of peripheral interest, an exhaustive listing of them has not been made. Copies of the pamphlets are available at the Library of Congress.

922. Museum of Art, Pennsylvania State University. *Pennsylvania Prints from the Collection of John C. O'Connor and Ralph M. Yaeger*. University Park: Museum of Art, Pennsylvania State University, 1980. [180] pp., biblio.

O'Connor and Yaeger were college classmates who established a restaurant in State College in 1948 and adorned the walls with views of Pennsylvania. Their collection numbered over three hundred items in 1980, all carefully researched. This exhibition catalog reproduces eighty-one of them. The entries written by Judith W. Hansen are succinct and informative. Harold Dickson and Walton Lord wrote the introduction and selected prints for the exhibition. The owners of the collection provide an overview of the style of city views and formation of the collection. Nancy Miller wrote a brief essay on the collectors. A checklist of the portion of the collection not on exhibition is appended to the catalog.

923. Nash, Chauncey C. "A Prophetic Engraving." *Walpole Society Note Book* (1936): 45–48.

In 1825 Abel Bowen published *A History of Boston*, written by Caleb H. Snow, with line and wood engravings by Bowen himself. "View of the Proposed Building West of the Common, Boston," engraved by Bowen, is inserted in some copies of the book. Nash comments on the history of this section of Boston, and notes that when developed in 1856, the building did indeed resemble the proposed building in the engraving.

924. The New York Public Library. "Check List of Engraved Views of the City of New York in the New York Public Library." *Bulletin of the New York Public Library* 5 (June 1901): 222–26.

Chronologically arranged, this selective checklist includes views of the city through 1852, and mentions many rare items in the collection.

925.———. "Loan Exhibition of Historical Prints, Early Views of American Cities, Etc." *Bulletin of the New York Public Library* 21 (May 1917): 317–24.

This was the first major print exhibition in New York to bring together a collection of historical prints and early views of American cities. With a few early exceptions, the prints range in date from the mid-eighteenth century to 1850. The exhibition included maps, city views, landscapes, military prints, and views of colleges. Some drawings and watercolors are included in this important exhibition.

926. Phillips, Philip Lee. *A Descriptive List of Maps and Views of Philadelphia in the Library of Congress, 1683–1865*. Philadelphia: Philadelphia Geographical Society, 1926. 91 pp., index.

Arranged by subject, this list of 490 items describes separately published views, book and magazine illustrations, and drawings of Philadelphia. Most of the prints date from the first half of the nineteenth century, although the list includes a large body of Revolutionary War material.

927. Pierce, Sally. "The Railroad in the Pasture: Industrial Development and the New England Landscape." in *Aspects of American Printmaking*, 53–80. ed. James O'Gorman. Syracuse, N.Y.: Syracuse University Press, 1988.

Pierce examines the interaction of the pastoral ideal landscape with the increasing industrialization of New England. A theme developed by Leo Marx in *The Machine in the Garden*, Pierce looks at the expression of it in a variety of town and factory views published in Boston from the mid-1820's through the 1850's. In the 1860's the pastoral foreground of town and city views is eliminated and the full text of urban development is portrayed.

928. Podmaniczky, Christine Bauer. *Through a Bird's Eye: Nineteenth-Century Views of Maine*. Rockland, Me.: William A. Farnsworth Museum, 1981. 44 pp., biblio.

This exhibition catalog reproduces an excellent variety of printed and painted bird's eye views of towns in Maine. The introduction focuses on the publication of printed views; the interest in topographical accuracy; artists such as Edwin Whitefield, Fitz Hugh Lane, and John William Hill; views issued by J. J. Stoner of Madison, Wisconsin; works by George E. Norris; and the problems of publishing such prints by subscription. Earle G. Shuttleworth provides a brief afterword on the usefulness of these prints as historical documents. Finally, a checklist of views of Maine, 1835–1905, completes the publication.

929. Reeves, Sally K. "The Plan Book Drawings of the New Orleans Notarial Archives: Legal Background and Artistic Development" in *The Cultivation of Artists in Nineteenth-Century America*, 81–101. eds. Georgia Brady Barnhill, Diana Korzenik, and Caroline F. Sloat. Worcester: American Antiquarian Society, 1997.

Founded in 1867, the New Orleans Notarial Archives has among its collections a superb collection of architectural and topographical drawings dating from 1803 to 1918. Reeves provides the history of the Archives and then focuses on the drawings made at the time that properties were sold. Many of the renderings have true artistic value as well as historical signficance and much about the appearance of New Orleans can be learned from this collection.

930. Reps, John. *Bird's Eye Views: Historical Lithographs of North American Cities*. New York: Princeton Architectural Press, 1998. 116 pp.

In the introduction to the more than 100 color reproductions of bird's eye views, Reps discusses in general terms the more than 5,000 prints of this type published in the nineteenth century, touching upon some of the artists who worked in this genre. Reps also discusses the urbanization of America during the second half of the century and the ways in which the prints document this transformation. Each reproduction is accompanied by a caption providing information on the city depicted.

931. Reps, John W. *Cities on Stone: Nineteenth Century Lithographic Images of the Urban West*. Fort Worth: Amon Carter Museum, 1976. 99 pp.

Reps discusses city views from a historical perspective, the graphic media used by artists and publishers, the work of several artists who specialized in this genre, and the cities depicted in the prints. A checklist of the exhibition follows the section devoted to reproductions of about fifty of the city views.

932.———. *Panoramas of Promise: Pacific Northwest Cities and Towns on Nineteenth-Century Lithographs*. Pullman: Washington University Press, 1984. 93 pp.

This handsomely illustrated volume includes information on 130 lithographed views dating from 1880 to 1910, of British Columbia, Idaho, Montana, Oregon, and Washington. The entries for each print are very informative including date, title, dimensions, lithographer, printer, publisher, presence of vignettes and key, locations in public collections and entry number in Reps' *Views and Viewmakers of Urban America*. The introductory text provides information on the usefulness of these prints for the study of urban history, the promotional aspects of them, the history of printed city views, means of production, the lithographers and publishers responsible for them, and the prints themselves. Almost half of the prints are illustrated, increasing the usefulness of this volume.

933.———. *Views and Viewmakers of Urban America. Lithographs of Towns and Cities in the United States and Canada, Notes on the Artists and Publishers, and A Union Catalogue of Their Work, 1825–1925*. Columbia: University of Missouri Press, 1984. 570 pp., biblio., index.

This is an essential reference work for any collection or collector of historical American prints. Reps has provided well-documented information on the drawing, printing, technology, and selling of city views. Other portions of the extensive introduction are devoted to the public response to these images and the usefulness of city views in documenting urban America. Biographical sketches are provided for the makers of views from John B. Bachelder to John C. Wild. Each is informative and definitive. The union catalogue is arranged by state, city, and date and includes locations in many public collections. Titles, dimensions, dates, artists, lithographers, printers are all part of this extensive record.

934.———. *Saint Louis Illustrated. Nineteenth-Century Engravings and Lithographs of a Mississippi River Metropolis*. Columbia: University of Missouri Press, 1989. 198 pp., biblio., index.

This thorough study examines the pictorial record of St. Louis improving our understanding of the city's history and the ways in which the views can reveal urban change and growth. Contemporary descriptions enhance the reproductions of the prints. In the introduction, Reps provides a history of European city views and reproduces some eighteenth-century views of other American cities. Other chapters discuss the earliest printed views, the work of John Caspar Wild, viewmakers on the eve of the Civil War, bird's eye views, views of the 1860s and 1870s, *Pictorial St.Louis* by Camille N. Dry published in 1875, and later prints of the 1880s and 90s. A detailed checklist of illustrations follows the text. A chronological list of views not illustrated in the volume follows.

935.———. *Washington on View. The Nation's Capital since 1790*. Chapel Hill: The University of North Carolina Press, 1991. 297 pp., biblio., index.

This sumptuous volume is a combination of many elements. Reps provides information on the planning and construction of the nation's capital, the artists and printmakers who depicted it, and the publication of views of the city. Accompanying the rich visual documentation are observations of travelers to the city.

936.———. "Boston by Bostonians: The Printed Plans and Views of the Colonial City by Its Artists, Cartographers, Engravers, and Publishers" in *Boston Prints and Printmakers, 1670–1775*, 3–56. Boston: Colonial Society of Massachusetts, 1973.

An extraordinary series of maps and views of colonial Boston exists today. This well-researched article examines and reproduces all of these prints. Much of the documentation is from contemporary sources, and Reps carefully uses information provided by the maps and views themselves.

937.———. "Upstate Cities on Paper and Stone: Urban Lithographs of Nineteenth-Century New York" in *Prints and Printmakers of New York State, 1825–1940*, 111–132. ed. David Tatham. Syracuse: Syracuse University Press, 1985.

Reps has worked for many years to create his definitive checklist of city views. This essay looks at a subset of the whole: views of upstate New York. The earliest of these were three views of Rochester by John Young done in 1836. Other prints listed by Reps were done in the same year. Edwin Whitefield, a prolific view maker also worked in New York producing prints of Buffalo, Albany, and Troy. Reps talks about the marketing of these prints—an important aspect of this particular genre. Other artists who worked in this genre were John W. Hill, Lewis Bradley of Utica, Melville Martin of Syracuse, Leopold and Julius Laass, Howard H. Bailey, Oakley H. Bailey, Augustus Koch, Herman Brosius, Albert Ruger, H.H. Rowley, L.R. Burleigh, and John Lyth. Prints by all these men are discussed chronologically with an emphasis on changes in style and content.

938. Roylance, Dale, and Nancy Finlay. *Pride of Place. Early American Views from the Collection of Leonard L. Milberg '53*. Princeton: Princeton University Library, 1983. 66 pp., biblio.

This exhibition draws on the collection of Leonard Milberg, who contributed a preface to the catalog in which he discusses his own interests in collecting American prints. The introduction by Dale Roylance provides a chronological overview of American landscape and topographical prints. The works of Joshua Shaw and John Hill, William Guy Wall, William Birch, George Harvey, William Henry Bartlett, and William James Bennett are mentioned as artists and engravers. Lithographers of note in this genre include Edwin Whitefield, Henry Walton, Fitz Hugh Lane, and Augustus Kollner. The exhibition entries by Nancy Finlay cover the period from the 1740s to the 1870s. The entries provide interesting information about the artists and printmakers as well as the subjects. There were one hundred and thirty prints, watercolors, and drawings on display.

939. Rub, Timothy F. "American Architectural Prints." *Print Review* 18 (1984): 7–19.

Rub finds prints of American architecture in abundant numbers, but architecture often plays a subordinate role. Included in this survey are engraved and lithographed examples from the nineteenth century. The prints are related to changes in the architectural profession as well as in style. The growth of photomechanical reproductive techniques rendered printmakers obsolete, but the artist-etcher continued to focus on buildings. These picturesque etchings were by artists such as Whistler, and Joseph Pennell. Much of this article pertains to twentieth-century prints.

940. Ruell, David. "The Bird's Eye Views of New Hampshire: 1875–1899." *Historical New Hampshire* 38, no. 1 (March 1983): 1–88.

This issue of *Historical New Hampshire* was devoted to this excellent study of bird's eye views of the state. During 1983 and 1984, an exhibition of twenty-two views traveled to nearly a dozen locations. Ruell discusses the popularity of bird's eye views, their history in the United States, techniques of the view makers and salesmen. These topics are very thoroughly documented. The general observations are followed by a chronological account of the views arranged by the publishers and based on research in contemporary newspapers. Finally, there is a checklist of the sixty-six views.

941. Scharff, Maurice R. "Collecting Views of Natchez." *Antiques* 65 (March 1958): 217–19.

The author has a collection of twenty engravings and lithographs of Natchez, all printed before 1880. Scharff outlines the history of exploration in the area, then describes items in his collection and elsewhere. Audubon, Lesueur, Frederick Piercy, and Henry Lewis are among the artists who produced views of Natchez.

942. Schuyler, David. "Green-Wood Cemetery As Image and Cultural Artifact." *Imprint* 14, no. 1 (1989): 2–11.

Green-Wood Cemetery in Brooklyn, along with Mount Auburn in Cambridge, Massachusetts, and Laurel Hill in Philadelphia, are the three great rural cemeteries of the nineteenth century. Schuyler's article discusses the history of the rural cemetery movement in general and the history of Green-Wood in particular. The well-researched article is illustrated with reproductions of elegant engravings by James Smillie (1807–1885) issued in *Green-Wood Illustrated* published in 1846.

943. Shadwell, Wendy. "The Statue of Liberty: A Century in the Graphic Arts." *Imprint* 10, no. 1 (1985): 20–27.

After presenting a brief history of the Statue of Liberty, finally erected in New York Harbor in 1886, Shadwell surveys the depictions of it from 1883 through 1941.

944. Smith, Jerome Irving. "The Fire Engine in Prints." *Antiques* 48 (July 1945): 32–34.

A substantial body of American prints depicts fire engines. These include engravings executed for patents, advertisements, book illustrations, genre prints, and lithographs of specific engines. The prints are sufficiently detailed to provide documentation on the history of fire fighting machines, and Smith provides a good deal of information on individual engines. The artists and lithographers who created the prints, however, are not discussed at all.

945.———. "Fire Laddies—Past and Present." *American Collector* 11 (May 1942): 8–9, 17.

The history of fire fighting is the focus of this article. It is illustrated with a variety of engravings and lithographs depicting fires and fire fighting equipment.

946.———. "New York's Fire of 1845 in Lithographs." *Antiques* 38 (September 1940): 119–20.

The author proposes that "fire offered sensational subjects for the most spectacular delineation." There are five existing lithographs of the July 19, 1845, conflagration in New York City that destroyed three hundred buildings. Three were by Nathaniel Currier, one was published by Henry R. Robinson, and one by G. and W. Endicott. Although Smith discusses the fire itself, he also emphasizes the role of the sensational lithograph in commerical sales of prints.

947. Sniffen, Harold S. "Southern Views in Prints." *Antiques* 60 (October 1951): 300–302.

Numerous views of southern subjects exist, despite the lack of printmakers working south of Baltimore. Sniffen mentions some early European views from the sixteenth and seventeenth centuries, but concentrates on eighteenth- and nineteenth-century examples. Views of the south are less frequent than those of the northeast, but Sniffen has found many important and beautiful prints.

948. Sniffen, Harold W. "Views of Port Cities as Depicted by Vernet and Other Eighteenth-Century Artists" in *Eighteenth-Century Prints in Colonial America. To Educate and Decorate*, 32–50. ed. Joan D. Dolmetsch. Williamsburg: Colonial Williamsburg Foundation, 1979.

Sniffen begins by surveying books containing city views that would have been intriguing to colonists and then focuses on Claude Joseph Vernet (1714–89), who painted a series of views of European ports that were engraved by French engravers Jacques Philippe LeBas and Charles Nicolas Cochin. These were among the prints available for export to the colonies.

949. Snyder, Martin P. *City of Independence. Views of Philadelphia before 1800*. New York: Praeger Publishers, 1975. 304 pp., index.

Snyder traces the development of Philadelphia through engravings, paintings, drawings, maps, made in this country and Europe from 1680 to 1800. Almost 200 items are reproduced with detailed information about each, including title, artist, size, medium, source (if book illustration) and owner. The text includes excellent background information on Philadelphia and the prints.

950.———. "Views of Philadelphia, 1750–1770." *Antiques* 88 (November 1965): 674–80.

The author feels that Philadelphia, of all the American cities, was the subject of the most colonial views. Martin Snyder, relying on his own collection and the one at the Historical Society of Pennsylvania, reproduces nine of these views, discussing each in detail.

951. Stokes, Anson Phelps Jr. *Historical Prints of New Haven, Connecticut*. New Haven: Tuttle, Morehouse & Taylor Co., 1910. 33 pp., index.

This chronological list of seventy-four prints begins with a reproduction of a map of Hew Haven in 1641, and ends with a view of Yale College, dated 1909. Maps, books and periodical illustrations, and separately published views are included. The annotation for each item is excellent. Appendixes include reproductions of original drawings, a chronology of New Haven, and an index of engravers, artists, and publishers. Biographical information on the engravers is not included.

952. Stokes, I. N. Phelps. *The Iconography of Manhattan Island, 1498–1909*. New York: Robert H. Dodd, 1915. 6 vols.

Stokes states in his preface that his purpose was "to collect, to condense, and to arrange systematically ... the facts and incidents which are of the greatest consequence and interest in the history of New York City ... and to illustrate this material by the best reproductions obtainable of ... contemporary maps, plans, views, and documents." Stokes succeeds admirably in his task, and his reference work bears testimony to his skill and determination. The first volume is concerned with the history of New York from its founding until 1811, and includes plates with detailed annotations. The second volume discusses the specific topics of cartography, the Dutch grants, early newspapers in New York (1725 to 1811), and the plan of Manhattan in 1909. Volume three completes the historical survey, and volumes four and five provide a detailed historical chronology of New York City, illustrated with relevant documents. Material in volume six includes an extensive bibliography, an index, and additional views of the city. The Arno Press reprinted this important reference work.

953. Stout, Leon J. "Pennsylvania Town Views, 1850–1922: A Union Catalogue." *Western Pennsylvania Historical Magazine* 58 (July and October 1915): 409–28; 546–71.

Over three hundred panoramic and birds-eye views are cited in this checklist. In his introduction, Stout distinguishes between the two types of prints, and discusses the various artists, production techniques and sales methods of the prints. The description of each print is excellent, and the indexes by artist, publisher, lithographer, and date make the contents of the checklist readily accessible. The inventory begun in the *Historical Magazine* was continued in subsequent issues.

954. Tolles, Bryant F. Jr. "College Architecture in New England Before 1860 in Printed and Sketched Views." *Antiques* 103 (March 1973): 502–509.

In a fresh approach to a time-worn subject, the author discusses the planning and shifting design concepts of college architecture.

955. Ugast, Ann. "American Pictorial Lettersheets." *Imprint* 4, no. 2 (1979): 2–10.

Lettersheets were issued to comply with postal regulations promulgated about 1845. Some publishers, particularly Charles Magnus of New York and many California stationers, included illustrations on the lettersheets to increase their commercial appeal. Most were produced lithographically in black and white, but occasionally colors were added. Of particular interest are the lettersheets issued in California depicting the Gold Rush. Ugast provides sketches of the firms that issued the most of these fascinating pictorial vignettes.

956. Vail, R. W. G. "Unknown Views of Old New York." *The New-York Historical Society Quarterly* 33; 34; 39; 43 (Apr. 1949; July 1949; Jan. 1950; Oct. 1955; Apr. 1959): 96–101; 149–59; 12–17; 124–33; 380–84; 221–35.

Several parts of this series contain previously unpublished views of New York found in John W. Francis' *Old New York* (New York, 1865) in the collections of The New-York Historical Society. Other views include a Dutch watercolor of 1673, a copy of a 1794 view by Saint-Mémin, the William Burgis view of Fort George of 1730–1731, fifteen wash drawings by Joel H. Barlow, a cartoon by Will Crawford from Punch (1909), the Burgis engraving of the New Dutch Church of 1731, and a painting by John W. Hall of the Van Nest Homestead (1832). Each article is well documented and illustrated.

957. Van Devanter, Willis. *American Places Represented in Prints and Watercolors, 1588–1875: From the Collection of Mr. and Mrs. Paul Mellon.* Upperville, Va.: 1970. 12 pp.

This catalog was printed in honor of the Walpole Society's 1970 visit to the Mellon's collection, which is best known for its examples of English art. The selection of city views emphasizes those with architectural detail.

958. Wainwright, Nicholas B. "Scull and Heap's East Prospect of Philadephia." *Pennsylvania Magazine of History and Biography* 73 (January 1949): 16–25.

One of the great views of American cities is the Scull and Heap view of Philadelphia. Wainwright discusses the history of all editions published of the print, and lists the collections which are known to contain impressions. Relevant correspondence and references in contemporary newspapers provided the sources for this well-documented study.

959. Weddell, Alexander Wilbourne, and Douglas S. Freeman. *Richmond, Virginia in Old Prints, 1737–1887.* Richmond, Va.: Johnson Publishing Co., 1932. 254 pp., index.

This volume contains reproductions of ninety-one views of Richmond, Virginia. The commentary on each print is extensive including substantial information on the buildings and scenes depicted. Items discussed include prints, watercolors, paintings, maps, woodcuts, engravings, and lithographs. The foreword provides a brief social and architectural history of the city. Little information is given on individual artists.

960. Weiner, Mina Rieur. "New York Built Ships, 1818–1865: Prints Document an Industry." *Imprint* 16, no. 1 (1991): 20–30.

This well documented article shows how prints can be used to document commercial activity, in this case, ship building in New York. She found that illustrations from *Harper's Weekly* and *Harper's New Monthly Magazine* were particularly useful.

961. Weitenkampf, Frank. "American City Views in American Prints." *Print Connoisseur* 5 (January 1925): 25–47.

Weitenkampf presents a survey of views of cities published in America. Representative prints are mentioned from each period; eighteenth-century copper engravings, early aquatints, lithographs, and wood engravings are all discussed. Although brief, this article provides a good introduction to the subject.

962.———. "City Types in American Prints." *Print Connoisseur* 6 (April 1926): 9–40.

Urban sterotypes appeared in nineteenth-century American prints, city views, book and magazine illustrations, and caricatures. Auctioneers, children, coal men, dogcatchers, draymen, salesmen, messengers, and emigrants were among popular urban subjects. Weitenkampf enumerates a wealth of specific examples in this study.

963.———. "The Eno Collection of New York City Views." *Bulletin of the New York Public Library* 29 (May and June 1925): 327–54; 385–414.

The Amos F. Eno collection of views of New York City, containing about 450 American and European prints ranging from the seventeenth to the early twentieth century, is in The New York Public Library. Weitenkampf uses this collection as an example of art that illustrates the social and cultural history of a place and era. He concludes by saying that art is an "expression of the spirit of its time and land." The views are arranged by date and individually described. The introduction was reprinted in the *Print Connoissuer* 5 (Oct. 1925): 305–323. The entire list was reprinted by The New-York Public Library in Sept. 1925, as a separate publication.

964.———. "New York in the Illustrated Weeklies." *The New-York Historical Society Quarterly* 42 (July 1958): 300–308.

Selecting examples from *Ballou's Pictorial*, *Harper's Weekly*, *Frank Leslie's Illustrated Newspaper*, and *Gleason's Pictorial Drawing-Room Companion*, Weintenkampf discusses life in New York City from 1850 to 1900. His sampling reveals a rich and varied panorama, in accordance with his view that an illustration can provide more information than a photograph.

965.———. "Peep Show Prints." *New York Public Library Bulletin* 25 (June 1921): 359–66.

A number of the views of American cities published during the eighteenth century in Europe are gaudy and inaccurate. They were designed for use in peep shows or raree (portable box) shows. This eighteenth- and nineteenth-century form of amusement is explained in detail by Weitenkampf, who illustrates his article with numerous contemportary pictures of the mechanism.

966. Whalen, Catherine L. "From the Collection: The Pickman Family *Vues d'optique*." *Winterthur Journal* 33, no. 1 (1998): 75–88.

Whalen discusses the history and use of the eighteenth-century print known as a "vue d'optique," as well as the devices used to view them. Following the essay is a checklist of a collection formed by the Pickman family in Salem in the eighteenth century. From this collection found in a secretary, Whalen speculates about how the family acquired them and used them within their domestic circle.

967. Wilson, Raymond L. "Prints of Early California." *Art of California* 2, no. 4 (August 1989): 20–26.

Wilson begins his survey with a primer on techniques and then mentions and illustrates works by Currier and Ives, Gene Kloss, Herman Volz, and Roc Partirdge.

968. Wright, Helena. "New City on the Merrimack: Prints of Lawrence 1845–1876." *Occasional Reports* 2 (1974): 32 pp.

The Merrimack Valley Textile Museum has several hundred drawings, watercolors, wood engravings, lithographs, and maps relating to Lawrence, Massachusetts. In 1973, the Museum held an exhibition containing twenty-five of these items. The catalog entries for these prints are reprinted in this report.

969. Younger, Rina C. "A Tale of Two Cities." *Pittsburgh History* 76, no. 2 (1993): 92–95.

Derived from the author's dissertation at the university of Pittsburgh, *Paintings and Graphic Images of Industry in Nineteenth Century Pittsburgh* (1991), this article focuses on the competition between one-time partners Edwin Whitefield and George Warren Smith to produce the first printed view of Pittsburgh in 1848 and 1849. Smith's view was published first and was reprinted in an 1854 issue of *The Ladies' Repository*, a widely circulated magazine with a circulation of 18,000 that year. Younger draws on newspaper accounts for her documentation in this excellent study.

Collecting and Collectors

970. Baragwanath, Albert K. "Harry T. Peters: A Collector's Collector." *Imprint* 2, no. 2 (November 1977): 4–5, 11.

Peters (1881–1948), the donor of the Currier & Ives collection at the Museum of the City of New York, was one of the great collectors of American lithographs in the twentieth century. This biographical sketch, written by the print curator at the Museum, describes Peters' various interests that brought him to collecting prints. Peters, of course, was also the author of many books on American prints, including the indispensible *America on Stone*.

971. Brown, Lloyd A. *Notes on the Care and Cataloguing of Old Maps*. Windham, Conn.: Hawthorn House, 1941. 110 pp.

Drawing on his experience as curator of maps at the William L. Clements Library at the University of Michigan at Ann Arbor, Brown incorporates in his text many fine suggestions for the care and cataloging of maps. With regard to cataloging, many aspects of production and nomenclature are clarified, making this a useful work for curators and scholars, even if the ideal system that Brown suggests cannot be easily implemented. The bibliography includes general references, historical sketches, bibliographies, regional studies, and collection catalogs.

972. Comstock, Helen. "Print Processes." *Antiques* 84 (September 1963): 294–301.

This is a good introduction to prints for the newcomer. Comstock discusses various print processes: wood engraving, line engraving, etching, dry point, soft-ground etching, mezzotint, crayon manner, stipple, aquatint, and lithography. Many of the examples chosen to illustrate the processes are American.

973. Cunha, George M. "Print Care." *Imprint* 5, no. 1 and 2 (1980): 24–6; 31–33.

Cunha briefly describes important aspects of print care, including storage in a stable environment in which appropriate temperature and humidity levels are maintained, low levels of light, and storage in acid-free materials. The second installment discusses simple cleaning procedures.

974.———. "Print Care." *Imprint* 6, no. 1 and 2 (1981): 28–31; 29–33.

In the first installment, Cunha discusses the controversial and rather complicated techniques of deacidifying paper, and, in the second, solubility of inks and colors, and characteristics of machine-made versus hand-made paper.

975. Dolmetsch, Joan D. "Colonial America's Elegantly Framed Prints." *Antiques* 99, no. 5 (May 1981): 1106–1112.

Dolmetsch draws upon wills, inventories, and newspaper advertisements to discuss the framing practices common in colonial America. These records show that gilt frames were very popular. Many of these frames were painted black as the gilt wore off or the styles changed. Colonial Williamsburg has found evidence of gilt under black paint and started the arduous task of restoring the frames to their original appearances.

976. Doloff, Francis W., and Roy L. Perkinson. *How to Care for Works of Art on Paper*. Boston: Museum of Fine Arts, 1971. 46 pp.

This handbook contains chapters on the history of papermaking, matting and framing, causes of the deterioration of paper, and restoration. There is a helpful list of sources for materials used in matting and restoration. The bibliography cites many excellent references for further reading, particularly emphasizing books on paper conservation.

977. Gascoigne, Bamber. *How to Identify Prints*. New York: Thames and Hudson, 1986. 208 pp., glossary, index.

In addition to relief, intaglio, and planographic techniques, Gascoigne describes process prints, screenprints, monotypes, and cliches verres. This book is extremely well organized with excellent photographic reproductions, including many in color. This volume is an indispensible guide for the collector and curator.

978. Grace, Trudie. "Methods of American Printmaking 1830 to 1930." *Antiques* 155, no. 2 (February 1999): 310–17.

Grace's essay is a discussion of four printmaking processes—etching, engraving on metal, wood engraving, and lithography—using American prints as examples. Written with the assistance of active printmakers, the explanations are very concise and clear. Among the nineteenth-century printmakers mentioned are Alfred Jones, Asher B. Durand, Henry Farrer, Mary Nimmo Moran, Otto Henry Bacher, James D. Smillie, and John Taylor Arms.

979. Griffiths, Antony. *Prints and Printmaking: An Introduction to the History and Techniques*. New York: Alferd A. Knopf, 1980. 150 pp., glossary, index.

This volume is an expanded version of a *Guide to the Processes and Schools of Engraving* by A.M. Hind, first published by the British Museum in 1914. Chapters are devoted to relief printing processes, intaglio printing processes, lithography, screenprinting, color printing, and photomechanical processes. The illustrations are excellent teaching devices, for they are reproduced as full-size facsimilies of the originals. Each chapter includes a technical description of the media as well as a summary of the historical development of each. It was reprinted by the University of California Press in 1996.

980. Hathaway, Richard O. "Finders Keepers." *Imprint* 17, no. 2 (1992): 35–37.

Hathaway provides a series of anecdotes about his own collection and comments on the collecting of figures such as the Collyer brothers and William Randolph Hearst. He concludes with reasons why we collect—to make order out of chaos, to uncover objects that are transcendent, to create a buffer against mortality.

981. Ivins, William M. *How Prints Look*. New York: Metropolitan Museum of Art, 1943. 164 pp.

Since the first edition was published in 1943, Ivin's excellent handbook has been reprinted several times. The book is arranged according to the three major groups of print processes: planographic, relief, and intaglio. The characteristics of each process are clearly explained; photographic enlargements of details from prints provide the necessary visual aids. There are also discussions on color, copies and facsimiles, and "notes on a few points of interest.".

982. Klackner, C. *Proofs and Prints, Engravings and Etchings: How They are Made and How to Select Them.* New York: 1884. 16 pp.

This pamphlet was written in response to the "growing taste for fine proof engravings and etchings in this country." Its remarks on artist's proofs, states, and techniques are still valid today.

983. Lane, Christopher, Donald H. Cresswell, and Carolyn Cades. *A Guide to Collecting Antique Historical Prints.* Philadelphia: Philadelphia Print Shop, Ltd., 1995. 48 pp.

This well-illustrated and useful guide discusses a variety of topics including the definition of historical prints, reproductions, restrikes, illustrations and separately issued prints, sets, preservation issues, terminology, and the importance of historical prints.

984. Maberly, Joseph. *The Print Collector.* New York: Dodd, Mead & Co., 1880. 336 pp., biblio.

Many topics are discussed in this massive handbook: classification of prints, subject matter, the selection of specimens, states and prices of prints, etc. Maberly includes catalogs of the works of individual engravers. Except for Robert Hoe's chapter on contemporary etching, which contains a brief note on Whistler, the amount of material on American prints is negligible.

985. Metropolitan Museum of Art. *American Paintings & Historical Prints from the Middendorf Collection.* New York: 1967. 111 pp.

Works in the Middendorf Collection range in date from the early eighteenth to the early twentieth century. In the introduction to this exhibition catalog, Middendorf explains his collection and its genesis. About twenty American prints, dating from 1728 to 1815, are described in detail. They range in subject from portraits and views to battle scenes and political prints.

986. Middendorf, J. William II. "Notes on Collecting American Historical Prints." *Walpole Society Note Book* (1958): 17–34.

Rather than presenting advice on acquisition of prints, Middendorf writes about a number of prints from his own collection. The article includes interesting enlargements of details from the unique copy of the first state of Revere's engraving of the Boston Massacre and also from the more common second state.

987. Rawls, Walton. "Audubon, Bodmer, and Catlin: Facsimile Editions from the Editorial Side." *Imprint* 16, no. 1 (1991): 2–10.

Rawls writes knowledgeably about the recent publications in facsimile of three of the great illustrated works of the nineteenth century. He justifies these extravagant projects by their making otherwise rare works accessible to a larger public. He recognizes the problems of close facsimiles on the market and cautions collectors.

988. Rotskoff, Lori E. "Decorating the Dining-Room: Still-Life Chromolithographs and Domestic Ideology in Nineteenth-Century America." *Journal of American Studies* 31, no. 1 (April 1997): 19–42.

The popularity of chromolithographs in home decoration began with the advice of Harriet Beecher Stowe and Catherine Beecher, focusing particularly on prints for the dining room published by Louis Prang in Boston. Rotskoff sets her study of these prints in the context of consumerism and domestic idealogy. The marketing of these prints and the relation of the prints to the vogue for still-life paintings are other subjects of interest to the author.

989. Shaffer, Linda. "Restoration of Works of Art on Paper." *American Art Review* 1 (May 1974): 74–82.

Shaffer discusses the problems encountered and techniques involved in the restoration of prnts, drawings, and watercolors. The illustrations are particularly useful.

990. Spooner, Shearjashub. *An Appeal to the People of the United States, in Behalf of Art, Artists, and the Public Weal.* New York: 1854. 27 pp.

Spooner pleads for public support in publishing a collection of engravings of works of art in the Louvre from the restored copper plates. Beyond that, he calls eloquently for support of American artists who usually were forced to live and work in Europe where their work was more appreciated than in this country. The situation for artists deteriorated after the demise of the American Art Union. Spooner's little pamphlet provides a good assessment of the state of the arts in the mid-nineteenth century.

991. Weitenkampf, Frank. *The Quest of the Print.* New York: Charles Scribner's Sons, 1932. 286 pp.

In this general treatment of various aspects of print collecting, Weitenkampf considers how, why, and what to collect, states of a print, copies and frauds, notable collectors in the past, print collecting in the United States, public print collections, and the care of prints. The text includes specific references to American prints, and is well written, as is typical of Weitenkampf's writing.

992.———. *How to Appreciate Prints.* New York: Charles Scribner's Sons, 1929. 330 pp., biblio.

This volume contains descriptions and histories of various printmaking processes: etching, line engraving, mezzotint, aquatint, stipple engraving, wood engraving, lithography, and photomechanical processes. Other chapters discuss color prints, collecting, the making of prints, the care of prints, and the collecting of prints according to subject matter. The first edition was printed in New York by Moffat, Yard, & Co. in 1908.

993. Zigrosser, Carl, and Christa M. Gaehde. *A Guide to the Collecting and Care of Original Prints.* New York: Crown Publishers, 1965. 120 pp., biblio.

This is an excellent handbook for serious print collectors. Printmaking processes, definitions of originals, and the relationships between artists, dealers, and the print market are among the topics treated. Much of the text is devoted to twentieth-century prints, but the principles of connoisseurship outlined by the authors are applicable to all periods.

Collections

994. Chapin, Willis O. *Illustrated Catalogue: Collection of Prints.* Buffalo, N.Y.: Albright-Knox Art Gallery, The Buffalo Fine Arts Academy, 1905. 122 pp.

This small collection, which numbers scarcely one thousand prints, includes a series of wood engraving proofs by Wolf and Cole, as well as some etchings by American artists. The collection was also the subject of a short article by Chapin in the *Print Collector's Quarterly* 2 (Feb. 1912): 51–55.

995. Barnhill, Georgia B. "Political Cartoons at the American Antiquarian Society." *Inks. Cartoon and Comic Art Studies* 2, no. 1 (February 1995): 33–36.

Barnhill describes the collections of political prints at the American Antiquarian Society. Among the holdings are prints by Paul Revere, British prints describing America, about 600 single sheet cartoons published as lithographs, and a large collection of images clipped from illustrated nineteenth-century magazines.

996. Bumgardner, Georgia B. "Print Collection Resources of the American Antiquarian Society." *Imprint* 3, no. 1 (April 1978): 3–4.

This article introduces the collections housed in the graphic arts department of the American Antiquarian Society, a research library located in Worcester, Massachusetts. Among the important holdings are engravings by Paul Revere and his contemporaries, political prints, commercially published lithographs, maps, and broadsides.

997. Paine, Nathaniel. "Remarks on Early American Engravings and the Cambridge Press Imprints (1640–1692)." *Proceedings of the American Antiquarian Society* 17 (April 1906): 280–98.

Paine calls attention to some of the 200 prints then on permanent display at the American Antiquarian Society, including Simon's Indian portraits, Pelham's mezzotints, various topographical views, and engraved portraits of presidents. Most of the article is devoted to books published in Cambridge in the seventeenth century.

998. Winkelbauer, Stefanie Munsing. "William Bentley: Connoisseur and Print Collector" in *Prints of New England*, 21–38. ed. Georgia Brady Barnhill. Worcester: American Antiquarian Society, 1991.

Born in Boston in 1759, Bentley was educated at Harvard College. After a brief stint as a teacher, he worked from 1780 to 1783 as assistant librarian in the Harvard College Library. In July of 1783 he became an assistant to the preacher of the East Church in Salem where he remained until his death in 1819. Bentley kept a diary during those years in which he recorded his impressions about the places he went and the people he met. Among his hobbies was collecting portraits in all media—paintings, drawings, and prints. His collection went to the American Antiquarian Society after his death. Winkelbauer has used the *Diary* to provide information about his collection—its formation and use in his home and public places.

999. Pratt, Dallas. "Historical Maps at the American Museum in Britain." *Imprint* 15, no. 1 (1990): 20–26.

One of the founders of the American Museum in Bath, England, Dallas Pratt presented to it his collection of two hundred maps of the world and the Americas issued prior to 1610. In this article, Pratt presents an overview of the exhibitions from his collection at the Museum and reproduces a selection of the maps.

1000. Hughston, Milan R. "The Print Collection of the Amon Carter Museum." *Imprint* 7, no. 2 (1982): 17–27.

Hughston begins his survey by describing works by "historian/ artists" who documented the American West. Included in this group are James Otto Lewis, James Hall, Thomas L. McKenney, Karl Bodmer, George Catlin, and Alfred Jacob Miller. The holdings of Mexican War prints and views of California are also described. Landscapes and city views are also an important category for the museum. Other areas of interest are prints after Bingham's paintings, Currier & Ives, chromolithography, and illustrated books of the West.

1001. Reese, William S. "The Bonaparte Audubons at the Amon Carter Museum and the Friendship of John James Audubon and Charles Lucien Bonaparte" in *Prints of the American West*, 13–24. ed. Ron Tyler. Fort Worth: Amon Carter Museum, 1983.

In 1965 the Amon Carter Museum acquired the first fifteen plates of Audubon's *Birds of America*. These plates had been presented to Charles Lucien Bonaparte by Audubon in 1827. Although Bonaparte never saw the plates, the story of Audubon and Bonaparte's friendship is an interesting one as is the rupture of that friendship and the ensuing bitterness. This essay, well researched from correspondence between Audubon, Bonaparte, and William Cooper, is an excellent excursion into the provenace of this most important set of prints.

1002. Arthur J. Breton, Nancy H. Zembala, and Anne P. Nicastro. *A Checklist of the Collection*. Washington, D.C.: Archives of American Art, 1975.

More complete than *Archives of American Art: A Directory of Resources*, compiled by Garnett McCoy and published by R.R. Bowker in 1972, this concise checklist presents the holdings of the Archives in tabular form. It contains information on nearly two thousand artists and institutions and is an extremely valuable finding list for original source materials.

1003. Wallace, Robert K. "Melville's Prints and Engravings at the Berkshire Athenaeum." *Essays in Arts and Sciences* 15 (June 1986): 59–89.

Herman Melville's grand-daughter donated a collection of artifacts belonging to the author to the Berkshire Athenaeum in 1952. Included in the gift were some framed prints and three portfolios of prints containing about 300 items. Wallace relates these prints to Melville's interest in art dating from his years in New York in the 1840s when he visited the galleries of the American Art Union. Later he visited the most important museums in Europe. Wallace provides a brief catalog of the prints, all of which are European in origin.

1004. Villa, Nicole. "Iconography of the United States in the Bibliotheque Nationale." *Quarterly Journal of the Library of Congress* (October 1973): 262–67.

Part of the October 1973 issue of the *Quarterly Journal* was devoted to resources in France for the American historian. The section by Nicole Villa concerns prints about America in the print department of the Bibliotheque Nationale in Paris, and the different approaches a scholar might use in researching a particular subject. This would be a very helpful article for anyone venturing to France to do research on prints of America.

1005. Mason, Charles E., Jr. *New England Historical Prints*. Boston: Boston Athenaeum, 1980. 20 pp.

This exhibition catalog describes about sixty prints from the collection largely formed by Charles E. Mason at the Boston Athenaeum. The introduction consists of reminiscences of print collecting by Mason, a hobby beginning in the late 1930s that led to the formation of a very important collection.

1006. Pierce, Sally. "The Print Collection of the Boston Athenaeum Library." *Imprint* 9, no. 1 (1984): 18–25.

The history of the print collection and its focal points—lithographs showing the commercial development of lithography in Boston, historical prints of New England, productions of Boston lithographic firms—are well described by the collection's curator. Another portion of the collection includes some 21,000 views, mainly of Boston, but of other American cities as well. The portrait file contains some 30,000 images.

1007. Hoover, Catherine, and Robert Sawchuck. "'From the place we hear about ...' A descriptive checklist of pictorial lithographs and letter sheets in the CHS Collection." *California Historical Quarterly* 56, no. 4 (1977): 346–367.

A brief overview of lithography in California precedes a checklist of prints in the collection of the California Historical Society arranged topically. Among the genres included are letter sheets, urban views, sites of interest, portraits, the gold rush and mining, events such as parades and celebrations, architecture, and scenery. Specific titles as well as an overview is provided for each section. The article is well illustrated.

1008. Will, Maureen O'Brien. "The Graphics Collection of the Chicago Historical Society." *Imprint* 8, no. 1 (1983): 31–36.

This article sumarizes the high points and general topics covered by prints in the graphics collection. Not necessarily focused on Chicago scenes, the collection pertains to American history in a broad way. The collection of city views is noteworthy as is that of portaits. There are some one thousand Currier & Ives lithographs and a substantial collection of broadsides, as well as fine art posters.

1009. Dolmetsch, Joan D. *Rebellion and Reconciliation: Satirical Prints on the Revolution at Williamsburg*. Charlottesville, Va.: Distributed by the University Press of Virginia, 1976. 230 pp.

This selection of political satires—English, Dutch, French, and American—is important for the iconographical and historical background it provides on American political prints. Many American political prints were influenced by English models (see Herbert M. Atherton, *Political Prints in the Age of Hogarth*, Oxford: Oxford University Press, 1974, for background on the English tradition), which were, in turn, influenced by Continental prints. A fully descriptive text is provided for each of the prints in the Williamsburg collection.

1010.———. "The Maps and Pictures." *Antiques* 95, no. 1 (January 1969): 138–144.

The article reproduces a variety of maps and prints on display in the exhibition buildings at Colonial Williamsburg. Among the types of prints are portraits, sporting prints, maritime scenes, genre scenes, and views, all of European origin.

1011. Hood, Graham. "The Role of the British Eighteenth-Century Print at Williamsburg" in

Eighteenth-Century Prints in Colonial America. To Educate and Decorate, 1–10. ed. Joan D. Dolmetsch. Williamsburg: Colonial Williamsburg Foundation, 1979.

This introductory essay explains why Colonial Williamsburg displays original prints in its exhibition buildings. Several of them are thoughtfully analyzed to demonstrate what decorative arts curators, in particular, can learn from the display of eighteenth-century prints. They help create settings in which eighteenth-century people would have felt comfortable, an important part of Colonial Williamsburg's mission.

1012. Wroth, Lawrence C. "Account of Things Seen at Hartford: Maps and Charts." *Walpole Society Note Book* (1950): 29–35.

On the occasion of the Society's excursion to the Connecticut Historical Society in 1950, an exhibition of various rare maps and prints was held. Items described are Thomas Johnston's *Plan of Kennebeck and Sagadahock Rivers*, Abel Buell's chart of Saybrook Harbor and map of the United States, Bernard Roman's map of Connecticut, and the Doolittle engravings of Lexington and Concord. This discussion is thorough and detailed.

1013. Corcoran Gallery of Art. "American Prints in the Corcoran Gallery of Art." *Bulletin* 2 (May 1949): 16 pp.

The preface is by Hermann W. Williams, Jr., and the introduction is by John Palmer Luper. The catalog describes some of the highlights of the American print collection in the Corcoran, singling out a series of portraits by Saint-Memin as the collection's strongest point.

1014. Shackelford, George T. M. *Nineteenth-Century American Prints from the Dartmouth College Collection*. Hanover, N.H.: Carpenter Galleries, 1977. 96 pp., biblio.

Started as a senior project, the description of the collection of American prints at Dartmouth resulted in an exhibition of fifty-three of the prints as well as a checklist of all the prints in the collection. The introduction provides a broad overview of American printmaking during the nineteenth century. The prints in the catalog range from one of the plates from Alexander Wilson's *American Ornithology* (1808) to Edward Penfield's poster for the November 1896 issue of *Harper's*.

1015. Kanes, Michael. "American Historical Print Resources in the Burton Historical Collection." *Imprint* 4, no. 1 (April 1979): 11, 36.

Clarence Monroe Burton formed The Burton Historical Collection of the Detroit Public Library in the late nineteenth century. It focuses on the social, cultural and commercial history of the Old Northwest and French Canada, and includes broadsides, lithographs, maps, and city plans.

1016. Gartland, Joan W. "The Print Collection of the Robert H. Tannahill Research Library." *Imprint* 5, no. 2 (1980): 24–27.

Gartland, the librarian at Greenfield Village and the Henry Ford Museum in Dearborn, Michigan, notes a number of interesting broadsides, prints, trade catalogues, almanacs, maps, and prints in the collection.

1017. Wojack, David E. "American Historical Print Resources at the Henry Ford Museum & Greenfield Village, Dearborn, Michigan." *Imprint* 3, no. 2 (November 1978): 7.

Among the vast collections of the Henry Ford Museum are examples of prints, maps, music, broadsides, and frakturs, housed in the Tannahill Research Library. Wojack provides a very brief introduction to these collections.

1018. Penrose, Boies. "Prints and Drawings in the Collections of the Historical Society of Pennsylvania." *Pennsylvania Magazine of History and Biography* 66 (January and July 1942): 140–60; 379–84.

This checklist of the most important views of Philadelphia and elsewhere is a very helpful guide to the collections of the Historical Society of Pennsylvania. The introduction provides a discussion of watercolors and drawings in the collection and an explanation of the catalog's arrangement. Information on each print includes subject, artist, publisher or engraver, medium, date, coloring or tinting, and references in standard works. Following the Philadelphia views are views of the Delaware River, commercial prints, diplomas, Pennsylvania views, miscellaneous prints. The second part of the article supplements the list of Philadelphia and miscellaneous views.

1019. Telian, Diane M. "The Print Collection of the Historical Society of Pennsylvania." *Imprint* 4, no. 2 (1979): 21–25.

Some of the highlights of the print collection of the Historical Society are presented in this overview. Mentioned are William Birch's Philadelphia views, William S. Baker's Washingtoniana Collection, ink and wash drawings by Benjamin West, lithographs, and twentieth-century prints by Joseph Pennell and Henry Pullinger. The Society also has rich holdings of maps, photographs, and architectural plans.

1020. Cherbosque, Cathy. "American Historical Prints at the Huntington—The Prints and Ephemera Collections." *Imprint* 23, no. 2 (1998): 27–34.

The Henry E. Huntington Library in San Marino, California, has broad collections relating to both American and British history and culture. Cherbosque provides an overview of the history of the collections and the current policy for adding to the print collection. Several representative highlights are reproduced drawing from collections of posters, broadsides, genre prints, portraits, and social and political caricature.

1021. Brewington, M. V., and Dorothy Brewington. *Kendall Whaling Museum Prints.* Sharon, Mass.: Kendall Whaling Museum, 1969. 209 pp., indexes.

The Kendall Whaling Museum formed one of the largest collection of whaling prints in North America. This handsomely printed and profusely illustrated catalog is divided into several broad subject areas: whaling ships and scenes, sealing, views of whaling ports, sea life, Japanese prints, stranded whales, and miscellaneous. There are about six hundred entries, each carefully described and illustrated. Even the small reproductions are helpful. Indexes for titles and books, and for artists, engravers, and publishers complete a very useful volume.

1022. Benoit, Jean M. "Iconographic Treasures at the Library Company of Phliadelphia." *Pennsylvania Heritage* 9, no. 4 (September 1983): 9–13.

Founded in 1731 by Benjamin Franklin, the Library Company of Philadelphia is an independent research library with rich holdings of prints and photographs relating to Philadelphia and colonial America. This article describes seven major prints and photographs including John Smither's engraved trade card commissioned by Benjamin Randolph, a colonial cabinet maker; Benjamin Franklin's etching, *Magna Britannia: her Colonies Reduc'd*, and an illustrated advertisement for the Atlantic Petroleum Storage Company of 1866.

1023. *The John Rubens Smith Collection. A Life Portrait of the Young Republic.* Washington: Library of Congress, 1993. 8 pp.

Issued to commemorate the one hundred millionth acquisition of the Library of Congress, this pamphlet provides a tantalizing overview of the John Rubens Smith Collection of drawings and prints. Smith was versatile, talented, and prolific as this pamphlet suggests. He excelled as a teacher, topographic artist, and creator of allegorical designs for currency and membership certificates.

1024. Beall, Karen F. *American Prints in the Library of Congress.* Baltimore: Johns Hopkins Press, 1970. 568 pp., biblio., index.

Prefaced by a foreword by Carl Zigrosser and an introduction by Alan Fern, this catalog lists some 12,000 prints, dating before 1966, by 1,250 artists. Only "fine" prints appear, to the exclusion of Currier & Ives and other such commercial publishers. Also not included are book and magazine illustrations. The collection is strongest in twentieth-century prints. Accompanying the entry for each artist are small reproductions representative of his work.

1025. Cresswell, Donald H. *The American Revolution in Drawings and Prints: 1765–1790. A Checklist of Graphics in the Library of Congress.* Washington, D.C.: 1975. 455 pp., biblio., indexes.

Sinclair Hitchings's foreword sketches the historical and cultural significance of prints of the Revolution. Cresswell's preface explains the arrangement and terminology of the checklist. There are five major sections: portraits, events, views, cartoons and allegories, and weapons and implements. The list was compiled from material in three divisions of the Library of Congress: Prints and Photographs, Rare Books, Geography and Maps. Over 920 prints are described with helpful background information, and nearly all are illustrated. Appendix A includes books and atlases containing prints and drawings; Appendix B lists secondary sources cited in the text. There are separate indexes of titles, subjects, artists, and publishers. An excellent reference work, this checklist is a fine accompaniment to the catalog of fine prints in the Library of Congress compiled by Karen Beall.

1026. Fern, Alan, and Milton Kaplan. *Viewpoints: A Selection from the Pictorial Collections of the Library of Congress.* Washington, D.C.: 1975. 223 pp., index.

This volume covers a wide variety of subject matter, with the sections on transportation, United States history, the American scene, and architecture in the United States containing a number of American prints. Drawings, watercolors, and photographs are also included in these sections. Finally, a few nineteenth-century American prints appear in the section called "Artists' Prints." The excellent captions provide helpful background on the subjects depicted, although little material is provided on the artists or the publishers. *Viewpoints* contains a variety of popular prints excluded from *American Prints in the Library of Congress.*

1027. Katz, Harry. "Prints and Drawings" in *Gathering History: The Marian S. Carson Collection of Americana*, 73–96. Washington: Library of Congress, 1999.

The Library of Congress acquired The Marian S. Carson Collection in 1996. This vast collection contains unique manuscripts as well as rare books, photographs, prints and drawings. Katz's chapter describes some of the choice drawings and prints including works by John Rubens Smith, Thomas and William Birch, and James Queen. Other treasures include drawings of historical subjects by Mather Brown and eighteen watercolors of Civil War scenes by William McIlvaine. The collection also includes ephemera such as bank notes, tickets, pictorial labels, and the like.

1028. Library of Congress. *Prints and Photographs. An Illustrated Guide.* Washington: Library of Congress, 1995. 80 pp.

This guide provides an overview of the pictorial collections of the Library of Congress. The collections encompass a range of media, covering not just the United States, but Europe and Asia as well. There are six sections to this guide: "An American Gallery," "Pictorial Journalism," "Politics and Propaganda," "The World at Large," "Architecture, Design, and Engineering," and "The American Landscape and Cityscape." The text is informative about the history of this great collection, the works reproduced, and the artists and photographers who created them.

1029. Parker, Alice Lee. "Pictorial Americana, 1590–1801." *Quarterly Journal of Current Acquisitions* 8 (November 1950): 541–63.

Parker considers a variety of prints relating to America drawn from several divisions of the Library of Congress: Prints and Photographs, Manuscripts, Music, Rare Books, and Maps. She mentions foreign views, American views, caricatures and cartoons, portraits, other historical prints, architectural drawings, and photographs.

1030. Parsons, Arthur J. *Catalog of the Gardiner Greene Hubbard Collection of Engravings, Presented to the Library of Congress*. Washington, D.C.: Government Printing Office, 1905. 516 pp., biblio.

The catalog of the Hubbard Collection contains a chronological index of engravers of the American school, but the largest portion of the collection is devoted to foreign prints. It is superseded by Beall's catalog.

1031.———. "The Division of Prints of the Library of Congress." *Print Collector's Quarterly* 3 (October 1913): 310–35.

Written by the chief of the Prints Division, this article describes the collection under Parson's care. Of greatest interest to those concerned with American prints is the discussion of the copyright law of 1846, which required the deposit of a copy of each print in the Copyright Office (although the copy was not necessarily transferred to the Library of Congress). There were some 350,000 items, including prints, photographs, and posters on deposit by 1913, and the collection was growing at the rate of 15,000 items a year. Most of Parson's article is devoted to the collection of European prints, the care of the collection, and the growth of the reference library.

1032. Shaw, Renata V. *Graphic Sampler*. Washington, D.C.: Library of Congress, 1979. 368 pp.

Arranged chronologically, this volume presents essays by members of the prints and photographs division, past and present, on specific aspects of the collection of Library of Congress. Of American interest are essays on Latrobe's architectual designs, tobacco label art, sketchbooks of Emamuel Leutze, lithographed letterheads, pictorial essays on women, John Singer Sargent, and architectural collections. The volume is well-illustrated and of general interest.

1033. Vanderbilt, Paul. *Guide to the Special Collections of Prints and Photographs in the Library of Congress*. Washington, D.C.: 1955. 200 pp., index.

This guide describes the 802 collections within the Prints and Photographs Division of the Library of Congress, noting the provenance, nature, and scope of each. Some contain only a dozen items, while others contain thousands. Many of them are not American in subject matter, yet the guide provides excellent information on one of the greatest pictorial archives in the world.

1034. Hewes, Lauren B. "Ponderous Folios and Curious Engravings: The Print Collection of the Henry Wadsworth Longfellow Family." *Imprint* 22, no. 2 (1997):

The Longfellow National Historic Site in Cambridge, Massachusetts, houses nearly 1,200 prints acquired by the Longfellow family. Hewes provides a synopsis of Longfellow's life and identifies several themes evident in the family's collections: portraits of acquaintances and views of places they visited, prints acquired for their usefulness as reference tools, prints by local artists, and reproductions of important works of art. Both European and American prints are discussed and reproduced.

1035. Nadzeika, Bonnie-Lynn and Alice A. Caulkins. "Macculloch Hall Historical Museum." *Inks* 4, no. 2 (May 1997): 32–5.

The Macculloch Hall Historical Museum in Morristown, New Jersey, houses an important collection of the work of Thomas Nast, including over 300 original drawings, illustrated books, wood engravings from *Harper's Weekly*, and assorted memorabilia. This article includes biographical information on George Macculloch whose estate was eventually purchased by W. Parsons Todd for his collection of American and European decorative arts and works by Nast.

1036. Mariners Museum. *Catalog of Marine Prints and Paintings*. Boston: G.K. Hall & Co., 1964. 3 vols.

The Mariners Museum in Newport News, Virginia, has a collection of approximately ten thousand marine prints and paintings. Volume one contains main entries; the other two volumes contain secondary entries with information on each vessel, its builder and owner, and the artist and lithographer. The main entries are listed by the name of the ship, or the subject of a portrait or place.

1037. Velthuys, Paula. "The Print Collection of the Maryland Historical Society." *Imprint* 8, no. 2 (1983): 20–26.

Founded in 1844, the Maryland Historical Society focuses on material relating to the state and the region. Of primary interest are views of Baltimore beginning with a 1752 wash drawing. The Society also has many prints by two Baltimore lithographic firms—E. Sachse & Co. and A. Hoen & Co. The later firm was in business from 1835 to 1981. Also mentioned are three individuals—Fielding Lucas, Jr., publisher of illustrated books; Alfred Jacobs Miller, landscape and portrait painter; and Adalbert Johann Volck, political cartoonist of the Civil War. In addition collections of Frakturs, currency, and sheet music are described.

1038. Riley, Stephen T. *Prints, Maps and Drawings, 1677–1822: A Massachusetts Historical Society Picture Book*. Boston: 1957. 32 pp.

In his foreword, Walter Muir Whitehill briefly describes the highlights of this selection of graphic arts from the Massachusetts Historical Society collections. Stephen T. Riley, librarian of the society, supplied detailed notes on the twenty-nine reproductions. Works include several early maps, rare historical prints, watercolors, and drawings.

1039. Urquhart, Ross. "The Print Collection of the Massachusetts Historical Society." *Imprint* 5, no. 2 (1980): 20–23.

Founded in 1791, the Massachusetts Historical Society has collected prints from its earliest days. Urquhart mentions a number of rare and interesting eighteenth-century British and American prints. The Society also has nineteenth-century lithographs and an interesting collection of the work of Will Bradley, given in 1957 by the artist's daughter.

1040. Watson, Arthur C. *The Forbes Collection of Whaling Prints at the Francis Russell Hart Nautical Museum*. Cambridge, Mass.: Massachusetts Institute of Technology, 1941. 14 pp.

The Forbes collection of whaling prints numbered over 1, 000 items and it joined other marine collections at the Nautical Museum of the Massachuestts Institute of Technology. Watson describes the wide variety of prints present, technology, odd depictions of the whale in various journals, and humourous prints. Of some interest are the watercolors by Benjamin Russell (1804–1885) of New Bedford, Mass. Several Prang lithographs were derived from his watercolors. There is a list of the Russell pictures and the corresponding lithographs.

1041. Byrne, Janet S. *American Ephemera*. New York: Metropolitan Museum of Art, 1976. Unpag.

This pamphlet consists of examples of advertising ephemera drawn from the collection of the Metropolitan Museum of Art. Examples of labels, packaging, valentines, ball tickets, rewards of merit, billheads, sheet music, trade cards, calling cards, copybooks, a paper doll, cigar bands, fashion plates, mechanical cards, and posters are reproduced. Explanatory notes provide the barest explanations for these colorful items.

1042. Shadwell, Wendy J. "Some Rare American Prints in the Middendorf Collection." *Antiques* 92 (1967): 558–62.

Nine rare eighteenth-century historical prints are reproduced in this article. A brief preface to the reproductions emphasizes the importance of these prints and the development of printmaking processes. The captions contain information on the subject and on the engraver. Although some of the prints are familiar, this article concentrates on rare states or new discoveries, such as the first state of Revere's "Boston Massacre.".

1043. Lehr, Marie C. "The Print Department of the Minneapolis Institute of Arts." *Print Collector's Quarterly* 7 (October 1917): 289–97.

Opened to the public in 1915, the Print Department had a stong collection of Whistler's work in 1917. This article gives no indication of other American prints held by the Institute.

1044. Lucas, Ann M. "Jefferson's Print Collection." *Antiques* 144, no. 1 (January 1993): 86–91.

The year 1993 was the 250th anniversary of Thomas Jefferson's birth. Monticello, Jefferson's home in Charlottesville, celebrated by reassembling as many objects owned by Jefferson as possible. He recorded his art collection in a catalog and this essay is based on that document. Additional documentation came from family correspondence and his memorandum books. He collected maps, city plans, architectural views, landscapes, and portraits. Several are reproduced in this well documented article.

1045. Reaves, Wendy Wick. "The Prints." *Antiques* 135, no. 2 (February 1989): 502–11.

A detailed inventory of the contents of Mount Vernon at the time of George Washington's death has enabled Reaves to identify a number of prints in Washington's collection, from a portrait of Louis Seize to Cornelius Tiebout's *Sacred to Patriotism* of 1798. Many prints, particularly portraits of Washington, came to him as gifts. In 1797 he apparently purchased a number of prints in Philadelphia published in London by Boydell. Reaves concludes that these prints are evidence of Washington's interest in the development of the arts in America.

1046. Baragwanath, A. K. "The Print Collection of the Museum of the City of New York." *Imprint* 4, no. 2 (1979): 18–20.

Founded in 1929, the print collection of the Museum of the City of New York focuses on the iconography of the City, attempting to collect every view published. At the time this article was written, the collection included about 6,800 prints including Harry T. Peters' collection of lithographs by Currier & Ives donated in the 1950s. There are also about 200,000 photographs and negatives and thousands of reproductions and uncatalogued images.

1047. Reaves, Wendy Wick. "A Decade of Print Collecting at the National Portrait Gallery." *Imprint* 10, no. 2 (1985): 21–28.

The Print Department at the National Portrait Gallery was established in 1974 with a mission to collect, research, and exhibit portrait prints of Americans. Reaves describes some of the most significant acquisitions of the preceding decade which include 761 engravings by St. Memin, 53 lithographs by Charles Fenderich, and many individual prints of the eighteenth and nineteenth centuries. The collection also includes portrait prints of the twentieth century, such as fine etchings by Anders Zorn and Childe Hassam. Caricature portraits have also been eagerly sought by the Portrait Gallery and Reaves is seeking contemporary images as well.

1048. The New York Public Library. *A Handbook of the S.P. Avery Collection of Prints and Art Books in the New York Public Library*. New York: 1901. 84 pp.

Samuel P. Avery was a wood engraver who became an art dealer, with the intention of collecting one or more examples of the work of every well known comtemporary artist. The resulting collection numbered 17,757 etchings, photographs, and lithographs by 978 artists. Although the collection is heavily French, the German, Belgian, Dutch, and English schools are also represented. Since Avery knew many of the artists himself, the collection contains an unusual number of proofs and dedicated prints. The collection, almost exclusively European with the exception of Whistler, Cassatt, and a few others, is arranged by etcher and lithographer. The number of prints by each artist is noted. There is a separate section of illustrated books arranged by the name of the artist.

1049.———. "The Burt Engravings." *Bookman* 13 (April 1901): 108–11.

Charles Burt, a bank note engraver, collected etchings and portraits of his contemporaries. Also part of the collection are some of his own designs for engravings and some of his original drawings. Thanks to the generosity of Samuel P. Avery and others, these were added to The New York Public Library's print collection.

1050. Roth, Elizabeth E. "American Historical Print Resources in the Prints Division of the New York Public Library." *Imprint* 3, no. 2 (November 1978): 8.

This brief overview of the Print Division of the New York Public Library focuses on its American prints, particularly the I. N. Phelps Stokes Collection so fully described by Gloria Deak. The Amos F. Eno Collection of New York City views is another important facet of the division as is the David McNeely Stauffer Collection of early American engravings. There are strong collections of portraits of George Washington, American social and political caricatures, and banknote engravings.

1051. Stokes, I. N. Phelps, and Daniel C. Haskell. *American Historical Prints, Early Views of American Cities, Etc., from the Phelps Stokes and Other Collections*. New York: New York Public Library, 1932. 327 pp., indexes.

In 1930, I.N. Phelps Stokes presented his collection of American historical prints to the New York Public Library. This magnificent catalog was printed serially in the *Bulletin of the New York Public Library* 1931–1932, then issued as a separate volume. The introduction is a survey of the most important items in the collections, and discusses the general field and its importance to the study of American culture and history. Other points raised include references to prints in the furnishing of eighteenth-century homes. A general description and history of the Stokes Collection is presented, together with summaries of other important collections such as those formed by DuPont, Garvan, Peters, and Taylor. There are also descriptions of public collections. The catalog itself includes references to other collections of prints of the New York Public Library. Chronologically arranged from 1497 to 1909, the catalog contains maps, paintings, watercolors, engravings, and lithographs. Each entry is thoroughly described and includes information on the subject and bibliographical references. Following the catalog of prints is a section of historical notes on the cities represented in the collection. These include information on the founding of each city and important events that occurred there.

1052. Weitenkampf, Frank. "The Print Collection of the New York Public Library." *Print Collector's Quarterly* 1 (October 1911): 457–63.

Established in 1899, the Department of Prints in the library was endowed with the remarkable gift of Samuel P. Avery, a collection of about 19,000 prints. Other substantial gifts followed. American prints are well represented in the collection, which places particular emphasis on the work of etchers and line engravers.

1053. New York State Library. *Catalogue of New York State Library, 1856: Maps, Manuscripts, Engravings, Coins, Etc.* Albany, N.Y.: Charles Van Benthuysen, 1857. 274 pp.

The collections of the New York State Library include a great deal of material that is not pertinent to the state. The catalog of atlases and maps lists many European specimens; the same is true of the list of prints, although it does contain a substantial amount of material of American interest. A separate listing itemizes the paper currency in the collection.

1054. Black, Mary. *American Advertising Posters of the Nineteenth Century*. New York: Dover Publications, Inc., 1976. 119 pp., index.

The brief introduction discusses Bella C. Landauer collection of advertising materials gathered and housed at the New-York Historical Society. The 101 posters reproduced in this volume were the focal point of an exhibition at the Society. They reflect New York's commerical life from 1840 through the 1890's. Following the reproductions are notes on each poster including title, artist or lithographer, printers, place of publication, date, and size. The subject matter of each poster is well documented. Indices by advertiser and by artist, lithographer, and printer follow.

1055. Shadwell, Wendy. "Pictorial Ephemera in the New-York Historical Society." *Picturescope* 31, no. 2 (1983): 44–49.

Shadwell describes the collections of ephemera at the New-York Historical Society, most of which was collected by Bella C. Landauer from 1923–1960. Various themes and genres of the collection, such as tobacco and patent medicines, billheads and admission tickets are described. Shadwell suggests ways in which ephemera can be used in a scholarly fashion. This is an excellent introduction to an enormous and wide ranging collection.

1056.———. "Prized Prints: Rare American Prints Before 1860 in the Collection of The New-York Historical Society." *Imprint* 11, no. 1 (1986): 1–27.

This is the catalog for an exhibition mounted at the New-York Historical Society in conjuncion with the 1986 North American Print Conference. Shadwell's criterion for inclusion in this exhibition is rarity—prints known by fewer than three or four impressions. Thirty-eight prints are described in superb detail and almost all are reproduced. Among the rarest of the prints are several early lithographs printed in New York in 1821 and 1822.

1057. Sullivan, Larry. "The Print Collection of the New-York Historical Society." *Imprint* 6, no. 2 (1981): 20–24.

Chronologically the print collection of the New-York Historical Society begins in the seventeenth century and concludes in the twentieth. Although the primary focus is on New York City and State, the subject matter covers all parts of the United States. Special collections include clipper ship cards, naval prints (The Irving S. Olds Collection), circus posters, portraits of prominent Americans, political cartoons, architectural drawings, and the enormous Bella C. Landauer Collection of Business and Advertising Art.

1058. Zinkham, Helena. *A Guide to Print, Photograph, Architecture & Ephemera Collections at the New-York Historical Society*. New York: New-York Historical Society, 1998. 175 pp., biblio., index.

This guide assembles for the first time information on the vast pictorial collections of the New-York Historical Society. The introduction provides suggestions for pursuing pictorial research at the Society and the history and scope of the collections. Zinkham describes 75 different collections with details on arrangement, access, restrictions on use, and provenance. This publication is very well illustrated with excellent explanatory captions.

1059. Norton, Bettina A. *Prints at the Essex Institute*. Salem, Mass.: Essex Institute, 1978. 50 pp.

Norton provides an overview of the Essex Institute collection founded in 1821. Included are European prints collected by Salem residents and a broad array of American prints of the eighteenth and nineteenth century. The text is well illustrated and arranged by type: town views and landscapes, commercial buildings, buildings, portraits, certificates, political prints, historical prints, sheet music and genre illustration, and prints for Salem's houses. A final section includes information on Essex County and Salem printmakers including Samuel Blyth, James Akin, Henry Dean, Mary Jane Derby, and J. Warren Thyng. Harriet Frances Osborne and later Frank Benson were noted etchers. An appendix explains various printmaking processes.

1060.———. "The Print Collection of the Essex Institute." *Imprint* 6, no. 1 (1981): 23–26.

Among the print holdings at the Peabody Essex Museum, formerly the Essex Institute, Salem, Massachusetts, are topographical prints, portraits, certificates of membership, historical and political prints, and genre scenes. Also present are portfolios of European prints collected by Salem residents while abroad, and prints by Salem artists including Samuel Blyth, Mary Jane Derby, and Frank Benson. Many of the prints are displayed in historic houses owned by the Museum.

1061. Finlay, Nancy. "American Graphic Arts in the Princeton University Library: A Cumulative subject Index to the Princeton University Library Chronicle, 1930–1980." *Princeton University Library Chronicle* 42, no. 2 (1981): 127–138.

The Graphic Arts Department of the Princeton University Library was founded in 1940 by Elmer Adler, the first curator. From that time to the present, the *Princeton University Library Chronicle* has included many references to American prints within its pages. This article is a valuable reference tool for scholars of American historical prints. Skimming it reveals interesting collections of prints and drawings, as well as specific references to individual artists and books.

1062. Roylance, Dale. *American Graphic Arts. A Chronology to 1900 in Book Prints and Drawings*. Princeton, N.J.: Princeton University Library, 1990. 213 pp.

This handsomely produced and thoroughly illustrated exhibition catalog is arranged chronologically and contains the highlights of the collections of illustrated books and American prints in the Princeton University Library. Roylance aimed to select items that "give the most authentic graphic and visual embodiment to North America's past" and he succeeded. The bibliography is useful.

1063.———. "Graphic Arts in America, 1670–1900." *The Princeton University Library Chronicle* 42, no. 2 (1981): 83–103.

This essay documents an exhibition mounted in the Graphic Arts Exhibition Room in the fall of 1980. It demonstrated the strength of Princeton's holdings in the arts of the book in America from 1670 to the present. Roylance relates the graphic arts in America to the technical developments of lithography and photography in Europe and traces the history of Princeton's collection of graphic arts. The exhibition included sections on the inconography of America, early American graphic arts, wood engraved book illustration, lithography, and the printmaking revival of the late nineteenth-century. This is a good overview of a massive subject expanded in Roylance's 1990 catalog. A checklist of the exhibition appears on pages 113–126. That list includes twentieth-century material as well.

1064. Burant, Jim. "The Print Collection of the Public Archives of Canada: An Unknown Treasure." *Imprint* 11, no. 2 (1986): 20–27.

The Print Collection of the Public Archives relates to events, places, and personalities in Canadian history, from its earliest settlement into the present. The collection of this visual documentation began seriously in 1904; Arthur Doughty, the second Dominion Archivist, started the Picture Division in 1905. Purchases were made in England, Canada, and the United States, although the number of purchases slowed during the Depression. Burant describes the important acquisitions of the past three decades during which interest in the pictorial record of Canada has emerged. The collection also includes fine art prints by artists such as Walter J. Phillips (1884–1963) and David Milne (1882–1953). The article concludes with an excellent bibliography of the major publicatons on Canadian printmaking to 1950.

1065. Jeffreys, Charles W. *A Catalogue of the Sigmund Samuel Collection: Canadiana and Americana.* Toronto: Ryerson Press, 1948. 180 pp., index.

The Sigmund Samuel Collection is housed in the Royal Ontario Museum and the Canadiana Gallery. It contains many American views, military prints, and maps dating from the seventeenth, eighteenth, and nineteenth centuries. Indexes are by subjects and artists.

1066. Santa Barbara Museum of Art. *The Gloria and Donald B. Marron Collection of American Prints.* Santa Barbara, Calif.: Santa Barbara Museum of Art, 1981. 159 pp., biblio., glossary.

A graduate student seminar at the University of California at Santa Barbara prepared this catalog describing the collection covering the period from the mid-nineteenth century to about 1940. Included in the exhibition are works by Homer, Whistler, John Taylor Arms, Joseph Pennell, Mary Cassett, and the twentieth century masters through Milton Avery. The 105 catalog entries are descriptive, thorough, informative, and well annotated.

1067. Stephens, Sloane. "Electra Havemeyer Webb's Print Collection at the Shelburne Museum." *Imprint* 24, no. 2 (1999): 16–24.

Long before the Shelburne Museum was opened, its founder, Electra Havemeyer Webb (1888–1960), collected American prints and related Americana for her homes in Vermont and Westbury, Long Island, beginning in 1919. Stephens, Managing Curator of the Museum, documents the collection and its installation at Shelburne, founded in 1947. Collections include important Currier & Ives prints, circus posters, textiles related to prints, as well as railroad, naval, whaling and maritime prints that reflect other major parts of the Museum's interests.

1068. Claassen, Lynda Corey. *Finders' Guide to Prints and Drawings in the Smithsonian Institution.* Washington: Smithsonian Institution Press, 1981. 210 pp., indexes.

The Smithsonian Institution is large and complex. This very useful guide was issued to assist researchers in locating works of art on paper. Organized by museum and collection, brief descriptions of the collections are provided. Furthermore, information on finding aids, selected descriptive publications, photoduplication service, exhibition programs, loan policies, and public access is provided. There is an index by graphic artist as well as a general index.

1069. Harris, Elizabeth. *G.A. 100. The Centenary of the Division of Graphic Arts.* Washington: National Museum of American History, 1986. 51 pp.

Harris's introduction presents the history of the division developed by Sylvester Koehler and established in 1886. The original aim was to collect scientifically, not considering the subject matter, but the processes by which prints were made. The division numbered some 45,000 accessions by 1986 including prints, photographs, printing presses and type, and related materials. The catalog of the exhibition contains descriptions of some of the major collections and most interesting items. Helena Wright contributed the narrative of the division focusing on the contributions of the curators over the years. The catalog concludes with lists of special exhibitions and select bibliographies of past division staff. It's an impressive list.

1070. Wright, Helena E. *Prints at the Smithsonian. The Origins of a National Collection.* Washington: The National Museum of American History, 1996. 71 pp.

In the introduction, Alan Fern sets the creation of the print collection at the Smithsonian Institution within the framework of other great collections in the United States and Europe. The Smithsonian purchased the George Perkins

Marsh collection in 1849, an unusual step. Wright's essay and exhibition catalog, celebrating the 150th anniversary of the Smithsonian, focuses on collecting and print publishing in the nineteenth century, the acquisition of the Marsh collection, the creation of the Division of Graphic Arts in 1886, the role of Sylvester R. Koehler as curator in the 1880s and 1890s, and other collections acquired in more recent decades. The essay is followed by summaries of the important collections and a checklist of the exhibition arranged to show the chronological development of the collection.

1071. Lawrence, Richard Hoe. *Catalogue of the Engravings Issued by the Society of Iconophiles of the City of New York, 1894–1908*. New York: 1908. 878 pp., index.

The introduction by William Loring Andrews reviews the history of the society, its publication of prints, its members, and its aims. There is a formal description and discussion of subject matter for each of the seventy or so prints. Among the etcher-engravers working for the Society were E.D. French, Mielatz, F.S. King, and S.L. Smith. Some of the prints issued were original works, while others were copies of historical prints and decorations on Staffordshire ware (often itself copied from historical prints). The catalog closes with an autobiographical sketch by E.D. French.

1072. State Street Trust Company. *A Collection of Interesting and Historic Prints*. Boston: State Street Trust Company, 1909. 48 pp.

The State Street Trust Company owns a significant collection of Americana. The captions in this publication are minimal, but it is interesting to know the genesis of the Company's collection.

1073. University Club. *Catalogue of the Collection of Engravings in the University Club*. New York: 1926. 78 pp.

This catalog contains reproductions of both English and American prints, with a particular emphasis on the American examples. The aim of the collection was to assemble views of colleges and universities and portraits of professors, presidents, and distinguished graduates of various colleges. The catalog is arranged in these categories, and the entries have been carefully compiled. Most of the prints date from the nineteenth century, but there are some twentieth century restrikes and facsimiles of eighteenth century American views, particularly of the colleges.

1074. McKissick Museum. University of South Carolina. *From Artist to Patron. The Fraser Collection of Engravings Presented to Dr. Robert Gibbes*. Columbia: McKissick Museum, 1985. 50 pp.

Prior to 1857, Charleston artist Charles Fraser gave to his patron Robert Gibbes a collection of 143 engravings. Gibbes' collection was recorded in an exhibition catalogue dated 1857 and was destroyed in 1865 by fire. There are three essays in this catalogue. The first, by Walter Edgar, focuses on Gibbes and his collecting interests. The second, by Paula Locklair, focuses on Fraser's taste in art and how this affected the collection he created for Gibbes. The third essay, by Georgia Brady Bumgardner, discusses print collecting in antebellum America. The catalog of Gibbes' art collection is reproduced and there is a checklist of the eighteen prints borrowed for the exhibition. This is an interesting excursion into taste and collection building of nineteenth-century America.

1075. Moss, Michael E. "Early Prints of the Military Academy in the West Point Museum." *Imprint* 5, no. 1 (1980): 20–23.

Opened in 1854, the Museum at West Point contains some 20,000 artifacts including some 3,000 prints depicting American battle scenes, military uniforms, and West Point itself. Moss surveys this portion of the collection which appeals to those interested in the Hudson River Valley as well as military history. Included are prints by John Hill after George Catlin, the designs by William Henry Bartlett, and works published in the pictorial press.

1076. Patterson, Margaret Sloane. *Views of Old New York: Catalogue of the William Sloane Collection*. New York: Privately printed, 1968. 80 pp., biblio., index.

The sixty-one items in the collection are all illustrated in this chronologically arranged catalog. Detailed notes indicate the artist, engraver (or lithographer), subject of the prints, and bibliographical references. This is a beautifully produced catalog; the descriptions of each print are so detailed and complete that one wishes the collection were far larger.

1077. Fowble, E. McSherry. *Two Centuries of Prints in America, 1680–1880: A Selective Catalogue of the Winterthur Museum Collection*. Charlottesville: University Press of Virginia for The Henry Francis du Pont Winterthur Museum, 1987. 543 pp., biblio., index.

The Winterthur Museum has a fine collection of European and American prints published between 1680 and 1880. Most were originally designed to be used as household decoration. This catalogue, divided into two sections, discusses and illustrates nearly 400 prints. The first section, "To Please Every Taste: Prints for the American Market" includes maps, views, portraits, political and social satire, historical subjects, genre, allegorical prints, prints for the instruction and amusement of children, and certificates. "Executed with Neatness and Dispatch: Prints Produced in America" includes portraits, genre, views, architecture, maps, historical and current events, allegorical prints, satire, scientific and technological illustration, job printing, prints to instruct and amuse children, and artists' prints. For each print, Fowble provides an extensive commentary about the artists and engravers as well as the subject matter. Essays that introduce each of the two major sections provide brief histories of printmaking, the roles of publishers, and details on technology. This collection catalogue is an exceptionally useful reference work.

1078.———. *To Please Every Taste. Eighteenth-Century Prints from the Winterthur Museum.* Alexandria, Virginia: Art Services International, 1991. 215 pp. biblio.

This exhibition marked the fortieth anniversary of the opening of the Winterthur Museum to the public. The introduction discusses the British print trade, techniques, publishers, engravers, and artists in England and America. The exhibition consisted of 92 prints and related objects, each of which is thoroughly described and illustrated.

1079. Richards, Nancy E. "The Print Collection at Winterthur." *Antiques* 100 (October and November 1971): 586–90; 734–39.

This two-part article highlights Winterthur's print collection, which numbers over one thousand prints, dating from the mid-seventeenth to mid-nineteenth centuries. In addition, the musuem's library holds many English mezzotint portraits from the Belknap Collection, nineteenth-century maps and city views, and illustrations from printed sources. The well-annotated examples that illustrate the article were chosen to show the variety of imprints and the comprehensiveness of the museum's collection.

1080. Dresser, Louisa. "Notes on the Goodspeed Collection of American Prints." *Prints* 6 (April 1936): 208–215.

Charles Goodspeed's fine collection of American prints was acquired by the Worcester Art Museum in 1910. The Goodspeed Collection includes over four thousand prints, dating from the seventeenth through the mid- to late nineteenth centuries, and includes portraits, city views, caricatures, maps and plans, and book illustrations.

1081. Gross, Sally Lorensen. "American Historical Prints at Yale University Art Gallery." *Imprint* 14, no. 2 (1989): 18–30.

This survey of the print collection at the Yale University Art Gallery includes the history of the collection, its arrangement, finding aids, and history of exhibitions from the collection. Some uncommon prints are reproduced and discussed in detail, including several extraordinary eighteenth- and nineteenth-century prints.

1082. Jandorf, Lisa C. "American Prints at the Yale University Art Gallrey." *Antiques* 117, no. 6 (June 1980): 1296–1299.

Among the collections at Yale are the Garvan Collection and the Whitney Collections of Sporting Art. Holdings of twentieth century prints are very strong and growing. Eight prints representative of the various periods—eighteenth to twentieth centuries—in which Yale has holdings are reproduced.

Dictionaries of Printmakers

1083. Baker, William Spohn. *American Engravers and Their Works.* Philadelphia: Gebbie & Barbie Publishers, 1875. 184 pp.

Baker's biographical dictionary contains brief sketches of eighteenth- and nineteenth-century engravers, noting several works by each artist. The volume is far from complete in its listing of engravers and their works, but it was a pioneering effort by a collector who compiled the notes largely for his own use. In spite of occasional inaccuracies, Baker's comments on specific prints are also of interest.

1084. Barnhill, Georgia Brady. "The Catalogue of American Engravings: A Manual for Users." *Proceedings of the American Antiquarian Society* 108, no. 1 (1999): 113–247.

This guide assists researchers to access the Catalogue of American Engravings, a definitive listing of some 16,800 engraved prints, book and periodical illustrations issued prior to 1821. After a history of the project and suggestions for its use are lists of artists, sculptors, architects, and inventors whose works are reproduced; engravers; genre and subject headings.

1085. Belknap, Henry Wyckoff. *Artists and Craftsmen of Essex County, Massachusetts.* Salem, Mass.: Essex Institute, 1927. 127 pp.

The sources for this compilation, which covers the period from 1600 to 1860, include probate and vital records for the towns of Essex County, files of Salem newspapers, town directories, and town and family histories. Brief biographies of about forty engravers are also included. Many of these engravers are obscure, and little other information exists on them, beyond the entries in the above sources.

1086. Brown, H. Glenn, and Maude O. Brown. *A Directory of the Book-Arts and Book Trade in Philadelphia to 1820, Including Painters and Engravers.* New York: New York Public Library, 1950. 129 pp.

The introduction to the directory explains its scope and clarifies potential problems. Arranged by name, this easy-to-use directory includes trades, addresses, and dates. The bibliography includes other directories and newspapers.

1087. Dow, George Francis. *The Arts and Crafts in New England, 1704–1775: Gleanings From Boston Newspapers.* Topsfield, Mass.: Wayside Press, 1927. 326 pp., index.

The introduction to this volume includes a brief history of engraving in Boston together with information on other arts and crafts. The section on painting and engraving includes subdivisions on engravers, engravings, maps and charts, mezzotints, and a list of relief cuts which appeared in the early newspapers examined. As with other compilations of this sort, this is an excellent source of information for the documentation of American prints.

1088. Fielding, Mantle. *American Engravers Upon Copper and Steel: Biographical Sketches and Check-Lists of Engravings. A Supplement to David McNeely Stauffer's American Engravers.* Philadelphia: Privately printed, 1917. 365 pp.

Fielding's supplement to Stauffer's checklist includes additional biographical sketches of engravers and another two thousand entries. Many of these additional entries are book illustrations, and there is a large number of entries by anonymous engravers. There is a subject index at the end.

1089.———. *Dictionary of American Painters, Sculptors, and Engravers.* Philadelphia: Printed for the subscribers, 1926. 433 pp.

This dictionary contains biographical entries on artists of the eighteenth, nineteenth, and early twentieth centuries. The descriptions are good, but the sources of information for each entry are not cited, although there is a general bibliography at the end. This volume is particularly useful for the second half of the nineteenth century and early twentieth century since *The New-York Historical Society's Dictionary of Artists in America, 1564–1860* does not cover this later period. The revised edition by James F. Carr (New York, 1965) contains additional material, but no additional artists.

1090. Gottesman, Rita S. *The Arts and Crafts in New York, 1726–1776.* New York: New-York Historical Society, 1938. 450 pp.

1091.———. *The Arts and Crafts in New York, 1777–1799.* New York: New-York Historical Society, 1954. 484 pp.

1092.———. *The Arts and Crafts in New York, 1800–1804.* New York: New-York Historical Society, 1954. 537 pp.

The only comprehensive gathering of this material, these three volumes contain thousands of transcripts of advertisements and news items from all the extant files of the New York City newspapers of the period. These admirable source books, useful for studies of individual artists, are divided into categories by crafts. The sections on painting and engraving are especially valuable for the study of graphic arts. In the first volume there is a list of woodcuts illustrating New York newspapers, and in the second volume, there is a list of woodcuts and engravings depicting different trades. All three indexed volumes are part of the series, *Collections of the New-York Historical Society*, although they were issued separately.

1093. Groce, George Cuthbert, Jr., and David H. Wallace. *The New-York Historical Society's Dictionary of Artists in America, 1564–1860.* New Haven: Yale University Press, 1957. 757 pp.

This may be the single most useful volume yet published for the study of American art. It contains information on all types of artists, including both well-known and obscure engravers and lithographers. The introduction discusses the proper use of primary and secondary sources and makes suggestions for the use of the volume. The sources include census records, city directories, books, pamphlets, periodicals, newspapers, and unpublished manuscripts. The entry for each artist provides biographical information culled from these sources, titles for several of their works, and a short title for each source utilized to compile the entry. Complete citations are found in the massive bibliography at the end of the volume. In the *American Collector* 16 (Jan. 1948): 6–9, Groce discusses the history of the *Dictionary* and some of their more interesting discoveries.

1094. Harper, J. Russell. *Early Painters and Engravers in Canada.* Toronto: University of Toronto Press, 1970. 376 pp., biblio.

This dictionary of over four thousand Canadian artists, all born before 1867, includes vital dates, place of birth and death, and details of the artist's life, and public and semipublic collections that contain examples of the artist's work.

1095. Hessler, Gene. *The Engraver's Line. An Encyclopedia of Paper Money & Postage Stamp Art.* Port Clinton, Ohio: BNR Press, 1993. 437 pp., index.

This reference work features biographical sketches of hundreds of artists and engravers active from colonial times into the twentieth century. The illustrations include reproductions of their work and portraits of them. Hessler includes a great of valuable and elusive information about engravers who created other kinds of commercial engravings.

1096. Kane, Patricia E. *Colonial Massachusetts Silversmiths and Jewelers.* New Haven: Yale University Art Gallery, 1998. 1241 pp., biblio., index.

This masterful biographical dictionary contains a great deal of information about colonial Massachusetts engravers including Nathaniel Hurd, Nathaniel Morse, Paul Revere, and James Turner. Their works on paper are mentioned along with more extensive information about their silver and other decorative work. Introductory essays by Barbara McLean Ward on tools and the goldsmithing trade, Patricia Kane on artistry in Boston silver, and Gerald W. R. Ward on rural silversmiths add a great deal to the importance of this volume. The biographical dictionary is followed by several appendices including a very useful glossary, biographies of allied craftsmen including engravers, and a chronology of colonial Massachusetts silversmiths and jewelers.

1097. Mallett, Daniel Trowbridge. *Mallett's Index of Artists: International-Biographical, Including Painters, Sculptors, Illustrators, Engravers, and Etchers of the Past and Present.* New York: R.R. Bowker Co., 1935. 493 pp., biblio.

This international index contains basic data on 27,000 artists and provides a key to sources for further information. It is doubtful that it contains entries on Americans working before 1860 that cannot be found in the *New-York Historical Society's Dictionary*. The supplement adds several thousand more names and a necrology is provided for artists who died between the publication of the first volume and the supplement. A separate list of American silversmiths, who frequently made engravings on copper, is also included. Extensive list of biographical sources. A supplement was issued in 1940 (319 pp.).

1098. McKay, George L. *A Register of Artists, Engravers, Booksellers, Bookbinders, Printers and Publishers in New York City, 1633–1820.* New York: New York Public Library, 1942. 78 pp.

The introduction to this useful volume lists the principal works consulted for its compilation: directories, newspapers, and books. The register lists individuals by name, and the entries include their trade, address, and dates. Also included are the titles and dates of activity of newspapers and periodicals. The register was published serially in the *Bulletin of the New York Public Library* from 1939 to 1941.

1099. Prime, Alfred Coxe. *The Arts and Crafts in Philadelphia, Maryland, and South Carolina, 1786–1800: Gleanings from Newspapers.* Walpole Society, 1929 and 1932. 2 vols., index.

The two volumes of Prime's compilation were gleaned from forty-six newspapers and include sections on engravers and engravings. The two volumes presumably include all the entries from his *Colonial Craftsmen of Pennsylvania: Reproductions of Early Newspaper Advertisements from the Private Collection of Alfred Coxe Prime* (Philadelphia: Pennsylvania Museum and School of Industrial Art, 1925).

1100. Prime, Phoebe Phillips. *The Alfred Coxe Prime Directory of Craftsmen.* 1960. 4 vols.

Culled from Philadelphia directories from 1785 to 1800, vols. 1 and 2 contain entries arranged by trade. Within each section, the entries are arranged alphabetically by name and contain the trade, address, and dates of the directory entries. Vol. 3 is an alphabetical listing of all the directory entries, regardless of trade. Vol. 4 contains entries taken from the advertisement file which Alfred Coxe Prime compiled for his *Arts and Crafts in Philadelphia, Maryland and South Carolina*. Copies of this directory may be found at the library of the Henry Francis du Pont Winterthur Museum and at the American Antiquarian Society in Worcester, Mass. Reproduced by xerography, 1960.

1101. Sherman, Frederic Fairchild. *Early Connecticut Artists and Craftsmen.* New York: Privately printed, 1925. 78 pp., biblio.

This volume, which includes a listing of engravers and lithographers, is divided into sections by crafts. Little data is supplied beyond the names, dates, and locations of the artists which limits the usefulness of the book.

1102. Silver, Rollo G. *The Boston Book Trade, 1800–1825.* New York: New York Public Library, 1949. 48 pp.

This directory of persons involved in the book trades in Boston was compiled from city directories and contemporary newspapers. A few engravers are included with their addresses and dates. The introduction provides an excellent synopsis of book publishing in Boston, and discusses topics such as apprenticeships, journeyman's work, wages, book trade organizations, and output. Most of this introduction does not relate specifically to engravers, but some of the information is analogous. It is reprinted from the *Bulletin of the New York Public Library* (Oct.-Dec. 1948).

1103.———. "The Baltimore Book Trade, 1800–1825." *New York Public Library Bulletin* 57 (1953): (Mar. 1953) 114–25; (Apr. 1953): 182–201; 57 (May 1953): 248–51; (June 1953): 297–305; (July 1953): 349–57.

The introduction to this series of articles traces the history of publishing in Baltimore, and discusses those men who were particularly active in literary pursuits. The directory of those involved in the Baltimore book trades, based on city directories and files of newspapers, is arranged alphabetically. There are a few names associated specifically with the graphic arts. The list was also published separately by the New York Public Library.

1104.———. "The Boston Book Trade, 1790–1799." in *Essays Honoring Lawrence C. Wroth*, 279–303. Portland, Me.: 1951.

Compiled from newspapers and city directories, this list contains the names of those associated with the book trades in Boston. The arrangement is alphabetical, and the entries include addresses, dates, and sources for information.

1105. Smith, Frank Bulkeley. "An Artist Index to Stauffer's *American Engravers*." *Proceedings of the American Antiquarian Society* 30 (October 1920): 295–341.

In his introduction, Thomas Hovey Gage emphasizes the usefulness of this index, for engraved copies are often all that remain of many American paintings. The index is in two parts, one for Stauffer's volume, and one for Fielding's. It is a very helpful list and relatively unknown.

1106. Smith, Ralph Clifton. *A Biographical Index of American Artists*. Baltimore: William & Wilkins Co., 1930. 102 pp.

This index of 4,700 names lists birth and death dates for each artist, mentions his working medium, and indicates sources where further information may be found. Artists through the early twentieth century are included. Forty-two reference works, on which the compiler relied for his information, are listed. This index is less thorough than *The New-York Historical Society's Dictionary of Artists in America, 1564–1860*, but it is useful for its information on artists active in the late nineteenth and early twentieth centuries.

1107. Stauffer, David McNeely. *American Engravers Upon Copper and Steel*. New York: Grolier Club, 1907. 2 vols.

Volume one of Stauffer's work consists of biographical sketches of about seven hundred American engravers through the nineteenth century, excluding the artists associated with the etching revival. The prints themselves, with their dates, signatures, and publishers, form the basis of his compilation. The introduction provides a survey of the history of American engraving. The second volume is a list of over 3,400 engravings made by printmakers working before 1825. The second volume, therefore, is more restrictive than the first. For the most part, book illustrations are excluded from the list, which is arranged by engraver. There are detailed descriptions for each print which include the complete inscription taken from the original work. A subject index for the second volume is found at the end of the biographical sketches.

1108. Young, William. *A Dictionary of American Artists, Sculptors and Engravers*. Cambridge: William Young & Co., 1968. 515 pp.

Young's compilation includes individuals from the colonial era to the turn of the twentieth century. The brief entries provide basic biographical data but no bibliographical references.

Engraving

1109. "Medal Ruling." *Miss Leslie's Magazine* (August 1843): 33–34.

This brief notice recalls that in 1816 or 1817, Asa Spencer of Philadelphia invented a type of pantograph which made it possible to reproduce medals and medallions in engravings. The plate accompanying this notice was so engraved by Spencer.

1110. Allen, Charles Dexter. *American Book-Plates*. New York: Macmillan Co., 1905. 437 pp.

First published in London in 1894, Allen's pioneer work on early American bookplates still stands as the best on the subject. The book's topics include: name labels, armorial plates; bookplates of colleges, libraries, societies and associations; signature of the engraver; date; and special pictorial matter. In a chapter devoted to the bookplates of early American engravers, Allen calls special attention to the work of Nathaniel Hurd, Alexander Anderson, Joseph Callender, Henry Dawkins, Amos Doolittle, John M. Furnass, Thomas Johnston, Peter R. Maverick, Paul Revere, William Rollinson, and James Turner. Allen's catalog of early American bookplates is dated, of course, but the almost one thousand examples cited in this work, alphabetically arranged, form an excellent basis for studies in the field. A chronological list of plates up to 1800, and an alphabetical list of signed plates are included. Allen writes further on mottoes with translations, American collectors, collections, and Ex Libris Societies. Eben Newell Hewins complied the bibliography on American bookplates, which joins a similar list for English plates. The index includes a breakdown of engravers by state, and references to them in the text are indexed.

1111. Blanchard, Julian. "Signed Vignettes on Obsolete Banknotes." *Essay Proof Journal* 6, 7 (April 1946):

In his examination of 1,350 bank note vignettes of the firsf half of the nineteenth century, Blanchard found work signed by Asher B. Durrand, Freeman Rawdon, George W. Hatch, James Smillie, A.B. Ellis, C.C. Wright, G. Murray, Peter Maverick, and Childs. However, only fifty-two vignettes out of the total studied were signed.

1112. Mann, Maybelle. "The Arts in Banknote Engraving, 1836–1864." *Imprint* 4, no. 1 (1979): 29–30, 35–6.

Mann provides a brief overview of banknote engraving, explaining why the lack of a uniform currency resulted in such a proliferation of engraving companies. She explains the contributions of Jacob Perkins, James Barton Longacre, Asher B. Durand, Francis William Edmonds, among other artists and engravers.

1113. Means, Mary Elizabeth. "Early American Trade Cards." Ph.D. diss., M.A. thesis, Winterthur Program, 1958. 205 pp.

It is unfortunate that this excellent study has not been published and made available to large numbers of scholars. As part of her research, the author visited all the major collections which contain trade cards. Among the topics discussed are the British heritage of the cards, the growth of American printing and engraving to 1800, techniques and materials for engraving, and trends and characteristics of style and subject matter. A major portion of the study is devoted to the discussion of specific trade cards by engravers such as T. Johnston, N. Hurd, J. Turner, Revere, John Hutt, H. Dawkins, Dunlap Adams, J. Smither, J. Norman, David Tew, Joseph Seymour, J. Callender, S. Hill, S. Harris, C. Tiebout, Abraham Godwin, A. Doolittle, Rollinson, Saint-Mémin, Boudier, J. Akin, Thackara & Vallance, Barber, A. Reed, W. Hooker, W. Hamlin, A. Bowen, E. Tisdale, G. Fairman, and the Mavericks. The study is well documented with a variety of sources, and contains an excellent bibliography. The thesis is illustrated with photographic reproductions and may be found in the libraries of the American Antiquarian Society, Worcester, Mass.; the Henry Francis du Pont Winterthur Museum, Winterthur, Del.; and the University of Delaware, Newark, Del.

1114. O'Brien, Donald C. "Training in the Workshop of Abner Reed" in *The Cultivation of Artists in Nineteenth-Century America*, 19–44. eds. Georgia Brady Barnhill, Diana Korzenik, and Caroline Sloat. Worcester, Mass.: American Antiquarian Society, 1997.

This essay is a careful distillation of diaries kept by John Warner Barber (1798–1866) during his apprenticeship with Abner Reed in East Windsor, Connecticut. O'Brien talks about the lives of apprentices—their work, reading, and leisure activities. Reed trained a good number of engravers and O'Brien presents a chart at the end of his essay with the names, dates, companies they later worked for, and the locations of those businesses. Since so little is known about the apprenticeship system, this a particularly useful essay.

1115. Scott, Kenneth. *Counterfeiting in Colonial America*. New York: Oxford University Press, 1957. 283 pp., index.

This book, which discusses bank note engraving as practiced by criminals, is well documented with eighteenth-century manuscripts, newspapers, and other contemporary sources. The bibliography on counterfeiting is very good, and incorporates many of Scott's other detailed studies on the subject.

1116.———. "Colonial Silversmiths as Counterfeiters." *Antiques* 67 (January 1955): 54–55.

Almost as much is known about the counterfeiters of colonial currency as about its legitimate engravers. Scott considers a few specific cases of counterfeiting, then reprints the story of Owen Sullivan, who was eventually hanged for his counterfeiting activities, found in the *Connecticut Gazette* of April 3, 1756.

1117.———. "Counterfeiting in New York During the Revolution." *New-York Historical Society Quarterly* 42 (July 1958): 220–59.

Most of this article is devoted to the court cases against those who passed counterfeit bills during the Revolution in conjunction with the British government. Conterfeiting was an official policy of the British at that time, and New York was the center of an activity which succeeded in depreciating colonial currency. Scott discusses in detail the cases of counterfeiters Henry Dawkins, the Philadelphia engraver; Benjamin Church, Director General of Hospitals of the Continental Army; and Church's brother-in-law, printer John Fleming.

1118. Wax, Carol. *The Mezzotint: History and Technique*. New York: Harry Abrams, Inc., 1990. 296 pp., biblio.

The book serves two purposes—the history of the use of the technique and the creation of mezzotints. In the historical section are chapters devoted to Dutch and English mezzotints, printselling and publishing, the market for mezzotints, steel mezzotints, the demise of the mezzotint in the nineteenth century and the revival of the technique in twentieth. Little attention is paid to American examples, but prints by Peter Pelham, Edward Savage, John Sartain, and Thomas Doney are reproduced. This is a very beautifully produced volume—a work of art in itself. The technical section certainly aids in the appreciation of the medium.

1119. Weitenkampf, Frank. "The Steel Plate in American Art." *American Collector* 16 (September 1947): 18–20.

Weitenkampf's article concerns the role that steel plate engraving played in the dissemination of fine art. Steel replaced copper for most engraving because of its durability: larger editions could be pulled from one plate. Steel engravers tended to reproduce portraits, landscapes, city views, historical scenes, and genre pictures by the finest American painters. These reproductions reached the public at a time when no large museums were open to them. Weitenkampf mentions the best of the engravers and cites their finest productions.

Etching and Other Processes

1120. *American Etchers*. New York: F. Keppel, 1886. 31 pp.

This pamphlet contains text from Mariana Griswold van Rensselaer's article in the February 1883 issue of *Century*, text from the *New York Star*, and an account of Meryon by Frederick Keppel.

1121. *Famous Etchers: A Series of Twenty Original Etchings by Famous Foreign and American Artists, among whom are Otto Bacher, Unger, Farrer, Gaugengigl, and Gifford. With Descriptive Text*. Boston: Estes & Lauriat, 1889. unpag.

Each plate in this collection is accompanied by a brief note on its etcher, with a textual description in a poetic vein. Most of the illustrations are reproductions of paintings; the descriptions try to relate the etchings to the paintings in terms of style and ability to reproduce painterly values. The importance of this volume lies in the quality of the plates, which are excellent examples of late nineteenth-century etching.

1122. "Professor Herkomer's New Art." *Scientific American* 74 (22 February 1896): 122.

Although Sir Hubert von Herkomer was English, his experiments with graphics were noticed in America and may have, in some measure, encouraged similar experimentation by American artists. This technical article considers the methods Herkomer used to print his "New Black and White Art" in a demonstration given before the Fine Art Society in London. This "art," unlike the usual monotype, does not reverse the image in printing; rather, it relies on the reproduction, by rather complicated means, of a thin metallic mold of the inked surface of the original plate. A further description of this process, also called a "spongotype," is fouud in W.A. Coffin's article.

1123. Ackley, Clifford S. "Sylvester Rosa Koehler and the American Etching Revival" in *Art and Commerce*, 143–150. Boston: Museum of Fine Arts, 1978.

Koehler, the curator of prints at the Museum of Fine Arts from 1887 until his death in 1900, was a critic and scholar of the graphic arts and a key figure in the American etching revival of the late nineteenth century. Ackley provides an excellent biographical sketch, including information on Koehler's ten year stint as technical manager for the Louis Prang firm. As editor of the *American Art Review* (1880–1), he promoted the etchings of American artists. Ackley, a connoisseur of prints himself, is an excellent interpreter of Koehler's taste in the printing of etchings.

1124. Art Institute of Chicago. *Catalogue of an Exhibition of Works by American Etchers*. Chicago: 1913. unpag.

Useful only as a finding list, this publication mentions 225 items by over sixty artists.

1125. Austin, George Lowell. "With Acid and Needle." *Galaxy* 18 (November and December 1874): 639–46; 768–77.

Most of this article is devoted to a discussion of the technique of etching and an explanation of how certain effects can be achieved. The author furnishes little historical background, although he does mention contemporary French and English etchers. The article is significant for being one of the first published in America on etching, a branch of the graphic arts that became very popular in the following decade.

1126. Brinton, Christian. "Monotypes." *Scribner's Magazine* 47 (April 1910): 509–12.

This article discusses the differences between monotype printing and other graphic processes, using the monotypes of Albert Sterner as examples of the art. (Sterner was a member of the Monotype Club in New York City, a group composed of men who had studied at Julien's in Paris.) Given the date of the article, one is surprised that the author is seemingly unaware of Davies's and Prendergast's work.

1127. Bruhn, Thomas. *American Etching: The 1880s*. Storrs, Ct.: The William Benton Museum of Art, 1985. 134 pp.

Bruhn provides an overview of American etching of the late nineteenth century and then discusses the marketing of etchings, the use of special papers, sizes of editions, and collectors. An interesting feature of the catalog is an annotated checklist of contemporary publications that contained etchings. They were deluxe publications issued in relatively limited numbers. The exhibition featured five etchers: Thomas Moran, Mary Nimmo Moran, Robert Swain Gifford, Samuel Colman, and Stephen Parrish. The catalogue is extremely well-researched. In all, ninety-four prints were exhibited and many are reproduced.

1128. Carey, E. L. "Collecting American Etchings." *The American Magazine of Art* 11 (May 1920): 235–41.

The author, recommending that the novice collector begin by assembling a small group of works by Whistler, Duveneck, Twachtman, and Alden Weir, cites examples of their finest labors. Of contemporary etchers, Carey recommends Mary Cassatt and Childe Hassam. The remainder of the article concentrates on noteworthy twentieth-century copper engravings.

1129. Coffin, W. A. "Monotypes with Examples of an Old and New Art." *Century Magazine* (February 1897): 517–24.

The term "monotype" was first used by Charles A. Walker of Boston, who rediscovered the process in 1877 without knowledge of its earlier use by Castiglione and others. Along with Walker, other American artists who exhibited examples of monotypes after 1877 included William Chase, Whistler, Robert Blum, Otto Bacher, Duveneck, Henry Sandham, Joseph Lauber, and A.H. Bicknell. This article, one of the first published in America on the monotype, is noteworthy for the historical perspective that it provides.

1130. Everett, Morris T. "Revival of Interest in Etching." *Brush and Pencil* 8 (August 1901): 233–46.

Frederick Keppel predicted that commercialism coupled with new reproductive techniques could bring about the downfall of the etching revival of the 1880s. By 1901 only James D. Smillie continued to work in the "old" tradition. The classes he taught at the National Academy of Design are described in this article, and some of the work of his students is reproduced. Smillie led the second "revival" of the early 1900s.

1131. Hall, Elton W. "R. Swain Gifford and the New York Etching Club" in *Prints and Printmakers of New York State, 1825–1940*, 185–121. ed. David Tatham. Syracuse: Syracuse University Press, 1985.

This essay focuses on R. Swain Gifford, one of the founders of the New York Etching Club in 1877 and one of the foremost etchers in the etching revival of the 1860s and 1870s. Hall explores the history of etching in the United States, the problems of printing, publishing, and exhibiting them. Among the other artists discussed are Leroy M. Yale, James D. Smillie, Henry Farrer, John M. Falconer, James Craig Nicoll, Thomas Moran, Mary Moran, Charles A. Platt, and Charles A. Vanderhoof. This overview of the New York Etching Club closes with the observation that these prints contain much merit and afford great pleasure.

1132. Hamerton, Philip G. *The Etchers Handbook*. London: Roberson & Co., 1871. 88 pp.

An examination of this book on old and new etching techniques would aid in understanding the controversy between the various schools of etching. Hamerton developed some novel techniques himself, which he describes here. He also discusses etchings worthy of study, etchers from nature, and the training of etchers. Several plates illustrate the various techniques.

1133.———. *Etching and Etchers*. Boston: Roberts Bros., 1876. 459 pp.

The publication of the first British edition of this work in 1868 proved to be a tremendous factor in the international revival of etching. This was about twelve years after the beginning of the revival in France, at a time when it was just beginning in England. The work is in five sections: "Powers and Qualities in Art," "The Dutch and Other Schools," "The French School," "The English School" (from Turner on), and "Reproductive Etching," followed by an appendix of practical notes on etching processes. No attention is paid to American etchers, but the work as a whole provides the international context for American practices.

1134. Hewes, Lauren B. *Forgotten Etchers: Nineteenth-Century Prints*. New York: 1998. 42 pp.

This exhibition catalog documents an exhibition at the New-York Historical Society of works from the collection of Dave and Reba Williams. The introduction sets the etchings in the context of the period of great productivity and change in New York from 1880 to 1900. The exhibition features landscapes, urban views, portraits, and genre prints by a range of artist-etchers. The introduction is followed by artists' biographies and a checklist of the exhibition.

1135. Hind, Arthur M. *The Processes and Schools of Engraving*. London: British Museum, 1952. 63 pp.

Historically well informed, this succinct and readable exposition of the processes of print production stands as a good introduction of Hind's larger work, *A History of Engraving and Etching from the Fifteenth Century to the Year 1914* (London: Constable & Co., 1923). Although the larger work is considered the standard reference for engraving, etching, and the allied processes, it devotes little attention to Americans and Canadians in its classified list of artists, and there is no discussion of them in the text.

1136. Hitchcock, James Ripley Wellman. *Etching in America*. New York: White, Stokes & Allen, 1886. 97 pp.

Hitchcock differentiates between the engraver's etching, used as an auxillary to engraving, and the artistic nature of painter's etching, a freehand drawing upon a grounded plate. The earliest group of artistic etchers was formed in New York in 1877. Hitchcock makes a few comments on etchers of the late eighteenth century and nineteenth centuries. This first book devoted to etching includes a list of American etchers and another of private and public American print collections.

1137.———. *Notable Etchings by American Artists*. New York: White, Stokes & Allen, 1886. 54 pp.

Hitchcock believes that the most striking fact to emerge from this survey is that little original etching has been done directly from nature. Even though he finds that original etching is in decline both here and abroad, Hitchcock states that there is much good reproductive etching being produced. He describes the characteristics of English, French, and American etching, and includes thumbnail biographies of artists such as G. Ferris, F. Frear, Van Etten, Calahan, Gregory, Yale, and Volkman who are responsible for the plates in the volume.

1138.———. *Recent American Etchings*. New York: White, Stokes & Allen, 1885. Unpag.

The original plates in this volume by J.S. King, W.H. Shelton, Henry Farrer, Hamilton Hamilton, J.C. Nicoll, Charles Volkmar, Katherine Levin, J.A.S. Monks, K. Van Elten, and J.J. Calahan are each accompanied by brief remarks on the artist. A prefatory essay on etching in America traces the history of the art in some detail through 1883. This succinct survey is worth reading, although the author repeats some of the material found in his *Etching in America*. He casts doubt on the existence of a distinctive American school of etching, and expresses the belief that American etching represents a composite of influences, particularly French and English. Hitchcock also attributes the great demand for etching to "fickle fashion.".

1139.———. *Representative Etching By Artists of Today in America*. New York: Frederick A. Stokes, 1887. 54 pp.

Ten original etchings by artists including Church, Blum, King Parish, Ferris, and Mielatz, form the basis of this volume. Each etching has an accompanying text by Hitchcock commenting on the plates, and providing information on the artists. The prefatory essay focuses on the present and future state of etching.

1140.———. *Selective Etchings: Important Plates By Stephen J. Ferris, Stephen Parrish, and Others.* New York: Frederick A. Stokes, 1889. 24 pp.

Each of the ten etchings in this volume is accompanied by biographical information on the artist and notes on the subject matter and technique.

1141.———. *Some Modern Etchings: Original Plates By S.G. McCutcheon, Frank Walker, and Others.* New York: White, Stokes & Allen, 1884. 25 pp.

Hitchcock's introduction to this collection considers the growth, characteristics, and various styles of painter-etching in the United States. Each plate is accompanied by an interpretative text.

1142. Holland, Leicester B. "American Painter-Etchers." *Quarterly Journal of Aquisitions* (July 1943): 37–39.

This brief note describes several painter-etchers whose works are in the Prints Division of the Library of Congress. Artists mentioned include Duveneck, Weir, and Charles Woodbury, all of whom made etchings in the late nineteenth century.

1143. Jenkins, Will. "America" in *Modern Etching and Engraving, European and American*, ed. Charles Holme. New York: International Studio, 1902. 6 pp.

Focusing on Whistler, Stephen Parrish, Duveneck, and Mary Moran, this is a listing of American etchers that includes a few critical words for each. Sections separately paginated.

1144. Kellner, Sydney. "Early Aquatints in America." *Prints* 6 (February 1936): 143–50.

Kellner discusses a variety of aquatints in this article. He begins by examining English topographical prints, including illustrations found in the *Atlantic Neptune*, published in London from 1763 to 1784. Parkyn's proposed portfolio of American views is mentioned, as are prints that were made after Alexander Robertson's drawings. John Hill and William Bennett came to the United States in 1816, and they both produced beautiful aquatints. Finally, Robert Havell's reproductions of Audubon's work are briefly noted. Many early American aquatints that appeared in periodicals and book prior to 1820 are ignored.

1145. Keppel, Frederick. *The Golden Age of Engraving.* New York: Baker & Taylor Co., 1910. 314 pp.

Most of the material in this book concerns British and French engravers and Old Masters. There are, however, two chapters on Whistler, one of which is Keppel's personal reminiscence of a day spent with the artist. There is also a long chapter on Pennell, and another entitled "What Etchings Are." Several of the author's previously published periodical articles are reprinted herein.

1146. Kiehl, David. "American Monotypes" in *Art & Commerce*, 151–165. Boston: Museum of Fine Arts, 1978.

Monotypes are the synthesis of drawing and printmaking, a technique popular in France among the Impressionists and Post-Impressionists. The earliest American examples were created in 1879 and 1880; more were created at the turn of the century. Kiehl's study is the first comprehensive examination of American monotypes and in it he discusses the work of Frank Duveneck, Charles A. Corwin, William Merritt Chase, Charles A. Walker, Maurice Pendergast, John Sloan, Robert Henri, Arthur B. Davies, Albert Sterner, and William Hopson. This is a distinctive body of work that deserves a great deal of attention.

1147. Koehler, Sylvester R. *Etching, an Outline of Its Technical Processes and Its History, with Some Remarks on Collections and Collecting.* New York: Cassell & Co., 1885. 238 pp.

Koehler presents a chapter by chapter survey of etching, spanning the period from its invention through the eighteenth century. Several technical chapters are also included. American etching is traced from its eighteenth century origins with West, to the work of George Loring Brown in the 1850s. Koehler places the renaissance of etching in the United States to 1866, with Cadart in New York City. He states that etching did not take lasting root in this country until American art, with the encouragement of Whistler, came under the pervasive influence of the French school. In an important chapter providing an overview of nineteenth-century etchers, plates by the following artists are discussed: R. Swain Gifford, Henry Farrer, Stephen Parrish, James Smillie, Charles Platt, Thomas Moran, Mary Moran, Peter Moran, Charles Vanderhoof, Whistler, Duveneck, Charles Corwin, and I. Gaugengigl. The chapter on collections includes the following: the Phillips at the Pennsylvania Academy, the Gary at the Museum of Fine Arts, Boston, the Tosti at the Boston Public Library, the George P. Marsh at the Smithsonian, the Charles B. King at the Redwood Library, and others in New York and Baltimore.

1148.———. *Twenty American Etchings, Original and Reproductive.* Troy, N.Y.: Nims & Knight, 1887. unpag.

Each plate in this book is accompanied by an excellent text. There is a sensitive analysis of subject matter, and often of the etcher's style. The plates in this volume are beautiful and provide a good survey of American etching in the 1880s.

1149. Laver, James. *A History of British and American Etching*. New York: Dodd, Mead & Co., 1929. 195 pp., biblio., index.

This work contains chapters on satirical etching and sporting prints in Britain; eighteenth-, nineteenth-, and early twentieth-century British etchers; and a comprehensive chapter on American etching from 1870 through the 1920s. Also included are important sections on Whistler and his influence. Although this book is a well-written and comprehensive survey on the subject, it is not as detailed as Weitenkampf's chapters on the same topic.

1150. Lawrence, Alfred E. "American Etchings at the St. Louis Exposition." *Brush and Pencil* 12 (July 1903): 269–80.

The etcher James D. Smillie arranged an exhibition of American etchings for the St. Louis Exposition. By 1903 the etching revival had already passed, and the popularity of the medium had begun to wane. This article discusses some of the exhibition plans, then comments on changes in the appreciation of the art. A history of the etching revival is provided.

1151. Mandel, Patricia C. F. "A Look at the New York Etching Club 1877–1894." *Imprint* 4, no. 1 (1979): 31–4.

Mandel describes the founding of the New York Etching Club in 1877 and discusses the major participants in the group including James D. Smillie, R. Swain Gifford, and Leroy M. Yale. The group held annual exhibitions at the National Academy of Design and published catalogues of them beginning in 1882. Among those who exhibited that year was James Whistler.

1152. Monks, J. A. S. *How Etchings Are Made*. Boston: Casino Art Co., n.d. 3 pp.

Monks, an etcher, briefly describes the etching process of preparing a plate, drawing, then biting it. The plates are charming examples of Monk's expertise, and have dates of 1886 and 1888.

1153. Montclair Art Museum. *The New York Etching Club: American Etchings from the collection of William Frost Mobley*. Montclair: Montclair Art Museum, 1979. unpag.

The introduction by Maureen C. O'Brien describes the revival of interest in etching in the United States in the late nineteenth century and the role of the New York Etching Club. Forty-eight prints were included in this exhibition including examples by Otto Bacher, Frederick S. Church, R. Swain Gifford, Peter Moran, and James D. Smillie.

1154. Morrow, B. F. *The Art of the Aquatint*. New York: G.P. Putnam's Sons, 1935. 140 pp.

This helpful and instructive book on the aquatint process includes examples taken from work of the early twentieth century.

1155. New York Etching Club. *Catalogue of the Exhibition Illustrated with Etchings, 1882–1889*. New York: 1882.

Each number contains original etchings by members of the Club, the roster of officers and members, and a list arranged by artist of prints exhibited. These catalogs are important records of the activity of etchers in the 1880s.

1156. O'Brien, Maureen, and Patricia C. F. Mandel. *The American Painter-Etcher Movement*. Southampton, N.Y.: The Parrish Art Museum, 1984. 62 pp., biblio.

This exhibition catalog contains essays by O'Brien and Mandel. The former discusses the superb collection at the Parrish Art Museum, formed by Henry E. F. Voigt, a master printer in New York in the 1880s, who produced the plates for the *American Art Review* edited by Sylvester Koehler. Much of this essay addresses technical issues of printing plates for the magazine. Mandel's essay, "Death, Despair, and Copyrights" focuses on problems of the market for prints and commercialization. The catalog is arranged by artist and each print is carefully described. The bibliography should be consulted by specialists in the painter-etcher movement.

1157. O'Keeffe, Ida T. E. "Monotypes." *Prints* 7 (June 1937): 258–67.

This layman's explanation of monotype printing draws its examples mainly from the twentieth century. The author does mention that after Chase's experiments, Peter Moran, as well as Duveneck's "boys," employed the medium in the 1890's. The members of the Tile Club in New York, under the leadership of Hopkinson Smith, experimented with monotypes at their meetings; passing references such as this in the article hint at the larger and yet unstudied role played by the Tile Club, and others such as the Art Club of New York, in introducing and reviving unusual graphic processes in America.

1158. Patterson, William C. "The Philadelphia Society of Etchers." *Imprint* 19, no. 2 (1994): 17–29.

Patterson sets the Philadelphia Society of Etchers in the context of the etching revial of the late nineteenth century. The founding members included Peter Moran, Stephen Parrish, Stephen James Ferris, Joseph Pennell, and Henry Rankin Poore. Moran was president for the twenty-four years the Philadelphia Society of Etchers was active. Works of each of the major artists are discussed and examples reproducted. The organization's records exist in the Bucks Country Historical Society.

1159. Peet, Phyllis. *American Women of the Etching Revival.* Altanta: High Museum of Art, 1988. 72 pp., biblio.

In 1887 Koehler mounted an unjuried exhibition of female etchers at the Boston Museum of Fine Arts. The next year, the Union League Club of New York recreated and expanded it. The exhibition at the High Museum marks the centennial of those exhibitions. Peet's excellent essay discusses the earlier exhibitions, women as professional artists, training for women etchers, their work abroad, subject matter, and a separate sphere for women. The catalog contains 117 entries and is followed by biographical sketches of the artists who participated in the 1887–1888 exhibitions. The bibliography is exhaustive.

1160. Pennell, Joseph. *Etchers and Etching.* New York: Macmillan Co., 1936. 343 pp., index.

These are somewhat idiosyncratic views of a practicing etcher on the history of his medium. Pennell combines his chronicle with valuable technical explanations of modern artistic methods. He also offers interesting insights into Whistler's graphic art, although his main emphasis is on European etchers.

1161. Rowlands, Walter. *American Painter-Etchings: Ten Original Etchings by the Best American Artists.* Boston: Estes & Lauriat, 1888. unpag.

Each of the ten etchings is accompanied by text describing the subject matter and the artist. Among the artists included in this elegant publication are R. Swain Gifford, F.S. Church, and Thomas Moran.

1162. Sartain, John. *A Brief Sketch of the History and Practice of Engraving.* Philadelphia: Franklin Institute, 1880. 23 pp.

Sartain, a leading American engraver of the time, delivered this lecture before the Franklin Institute of Philadelphia. He discusses engraving, etching, and mezzotint in some detail; aquatint and engraving on stone are considered briefly.

1163. Schneider, Rona. *American Painter Etchings 1853–1908.* New York: Grolier Club, 1989. 48 pp., biblio.

This exhibition stresses the importance of place to American etchers—in the United States, Canada, and Europe. Schneider's entries are very informative in terms of information about each print, the artists, and subject matter. The bibliography should be consulted by those with a serious interest in the subject.

1164.———. *The Quiet Interlude: American Etchings of the Late Nineteenth Century.* Amherst: Mead Art Museum, 1984. 5 pp.

This exhibition brochure contains information on forty-six etchings from the author's collection. She notes that the etchers focused their talents on landscape, domestic scenes, and nostalgia for rural America. Schneider has tried to identify the sources for many of the published prints, a difficult task.

1165.———. "The American Etching Revival: Its French Sources and Early Years." *American Art Journal* 14, no. 4 (1982): 40–65.

Derived from Schneider's master's thesis, "The Birth of American Painter-Etching, 1860–1882," this essay traces the French influence on American painter-etchers. Alfred Cadart exhibited French etchings in New York beginning in 1866; within a year Samuel Putnam Avery was buying examples in Paris, and American artists became familiar with these works. More French works were available at the Centennial Exhibition in Philadelphia. Schneider has found compositional and stylistic similarities in the works of American and French etchers, well documented by her text and illustrations.

1166.———. "The Canadian Etchings of Stephen Parrish and Charles Adams Platt." *Imprint* 23, no. 2 (1998): 2–19.

Parrish and Platt traveled together to the Canadian maritime provinces in August and September of 1881, lured by the scenery and stories of other artists. Parrish made fourteen etchings and Platt eight as a result of this trip. In this thoroughly documented essay, Schneider provides biographical information on each artist, background on the etching revival, and information about the creation, publication, and exhibition of the etchings of the two men.

1167. Smillie, James D. "Etching and Painter-Etching." *Quarterly Illustrator* 2 (July 1894): 260–63.

Smillie extols the virtues of modern etching in this article. He discusses the medium in terms of style in an attempt to broaden public interest in the medium. No specific artists are discussed in this impressionistic article.

1168. Taylor, E. A. "Etching." in *Modern Etchings, Mezzotints and Drypoints*, 107–111. ed. Charles Holme. London: Studio, 1913.

The author states that the primary strengths of American etchers have been their supreme technical ability and their adherence to English tradition. As to the influence of Whistler, Taylor notes a welcome change in American etching in the direction of greater originality. Hornby, Pennell, Armington, Koopman, and Gleeson are among the many artists whose etchings are summarily mentioned in this chapter.

1169. Trumble, Alfred. "Etching in America, the False Gospel and the True." *Art Review* 2 (September 1887): 26–31.

The author begins this article by calling the United States the "country of crazes." He goes on to apply this term to etching, citing a plate by C.Y. Turner that measures two by four feet. Trumble comments that etching originally served as a diversion for painters, and was a good medium in which to express a thought. He is highly critical of the "charlatanry of criticism" which fed the etching craze, although he notes that the public did gain a valuable appreciation and familiarity with art from the craze. Trumble goes on to discuss the difference between original and reproductive etching, citing specific examples. This is an excellent article, very different from most of the literature on etching. It is refreshingly objective.

1170. Tyler, Francine. *American Etchers of the Nineteenth Century*. New York: Dover Publications, 1984. xxviii, 115 plates, biblio.

The excellent introduction touches on the market for etchings, the French and English etching revivals, Hamerton's book on etching, Seymour Haden's tour to America, Whistler, American etching clubs, women etchers, Sylvester Koehler, favored subject matter, the search for picturesque subjects by artists, reproductive etching, the "business and the etching craze" and subsequent overproduction, and the end of the etching revival. Biographical sketches precede the reproductions.

1171. Van Rensselaer, M. G. "American Etchers." *Century Magazine* 25 (February 1883): 483–99.

This article, of major importance to the subject, reproduces plates by Whistler, Duveneck, Bacher, Farrer, Gifford, Parrish, Pennell, Moran, and others. The process and limitations of etching are explained, its history is briefly sketched, and the Centennial Exhibition is established as the starting point for the etching renaissance in America. Van Rensselaer then considers Whistler's influence on the art. Like other critics, she is convinced that American artists are at their best with American themes, and analyzes the work of several artists in detail. This is a good contemporary introduction to the subject.

1172. Weitenkampf, Frank. "American Painter-Etchings: A Revival." *Scribner's Magazine* 52 (September 1912): 381–84.

Weitenkampf is gratified to see a revival of etching, and to note the frequent occurence of American subjects in the art. Among the younger etchers, he mentions C.H. White, H. Winslow, Washburn, Pennell, Mielatz, and John Sloan. This article adds little information, however, to that found in the corresponding chapter of the author's history of American graphic arts.

1173.———. "Some Women Etchers." *Scribner's Magazine* 46 (December 1909): 731–39.

Weitenkampf mentions several European etchers of the nineteenth century, and then discusses the work of several American women: Mary Nimmo Moran, Eliza Greatorex, Anna Lea Merritt, and Mary Cassatt, whom he contrasts in style and subject matter to Kathe Kollwitz. Several other European women are mentioned in passing.

1174. Wray, Henry Russell. *Review of Etching in the United States*. Philadelphia: R.C. Penfield, 1893. 91 pp.

Three aspects of American etching are examined: etching as an art form, the history of etching in America, and the formation of etching clubs and societies, which encouraged the widespread acceptance of the art. The first chapter is largely an attempt to raise the reputation of modern etching to the artistic heights of masterworks of the seventeenth century, while other chapters focus on various groups in the late nineteenth century who helped to popularize etching. The copy consulted at the Museum of Fine Arts, Boston, was annotated by Sylvester R. Koehler, whose remarks and comments often chide and contradict Wray.

1175. Wright, Charles Lennox, II. "The Pioneer of Zinc Etching: Introduction to the Charles Lennox Wright I Collection." *New-York Historical Society Quarterly* 36 (April 1952): 194–209.

In 1884 and 1885, Charles L. Wright made the first relief-etched metal plate of a photographically transferred subject. The plate was capable of being printed in an edition of up to 100,000 copies on high-speed presses. Wright had a diverse career that included experiments with photographing drawings on wood blocks, making collotypes and photolithographs, etching halftone plates, and experimenting with three color halftone plates and photography. According to the author of this article, modern reproductive printing techniques are variations on Wright's zinc etchings. The New-York Historical Society's holdings include examples of Wright's works and other memorabilia. Unfortunately this article does not give as clear an explanation of the various terms and methods of printing as it might.

Exhibitions

1176. "A Checklist of Prints Pertaining to America in the Collection of the Henry Francis du Pont Winterthur Museum." *Walpole Society Note Book* (1962): 36–68.

This checklist is arranged by subject and contains 119 items. The description of each print is excellent. The exhibition was prepared for a visit made to Winterthur by the Walpole Society, and was arranged by a graduate seminar of Fellows in the Winterthur Program of Early American Culture. The checklist is an excellent guide to the holdings of the museum in early American prints and European works about the United States.

1177. American Federation of Arts. *America D'Altri Tempi: Mostra Di 138 Incisoni Americane dal 1722 al 1875*. Rome: 1954. 95 pp.

This exhibition was organized for the United States Information Agency in Italy. Its purpose was to provide the Italian public with a glimpse of American life in the eighteenth and nineteenth centuries. In his introduction, Marshall Davidson points out that the artists were more concerned with recording the world around them than with creating masterworks. The majority of the prints exhibited are lithographs and aquatints from the nineteenth century. Davidson deposited a typescript of the catalog in English at the American Antiquarian Society in Worcester, Mass.

1178. Anthony, A. V. S. *Exhibition of American Engravings on Wood*. Boston: Alfred Mudge & Son, 1881. 58 pp.

The introduction to the catalog surveys the history of wood engraving in England, France, and America, as well as an examination of the process itself. The first four hundred prints in the exhibition were made by living artists, including Timothy Cole, S.S. Kilburn, and Elbridge Kingsley. Another section was devoted to a historical survey of American woodcuts, beginning in 1747. There was also a selection of European wood engravings, and a few examples of color printing.

1179. Bruhn, Thomas P. *The American Print: Originality and Experimentation 1790–1890*. Storrs: William Benton Museum of Art, University of Connecticut, 1993. 120 pp., index, biblio.

This splendid exhibition catalog contains an introductory essay by Bruhn suggesting that American prints of this period are original statements by their creators, not just reproductions of works in other media. A second essay by Kate Steinway examines the early prints in the exhibition looking at unconventional aspects of them. The catalogue is arranged chronologically and each of the 71 prints is reproduced and thoroughly described.

1180. Club of Odd Volumes. *Catalog of an Exhibition of Mezzotinto Portraits*. Boston: 1892. 20 pp.

Almost half of this exhibition was comprised of portraits of American military officers during the Revolution. The rest was a miscellany of European and American portraiture of the seventeenth and eighteenth centuries.

1181.———. *An Exhibition of Prints, Maps, Broadsides, Newspapers, Autographs, Appertaining to Boston Revolutionary Times*. Boston: 1911. unpag.

Sixty-six items are listed in this exhibition handbook. Subjects of the prints include portraits, views, cartoons, maps, and plans.

1182.———. *Notes on an Exhibition of Early American Lithographs, 1819–1859, Selected Mainly from the Collections of Members of the Club of Odd Volumes*. Boston: 1924. 22 pp.

The beginnings of American lithography are discussed in the introduction to this catalog, together with an analysis of some of the prints on display. A list of the lithographers whose work was exhibited is given at the end.

1183. Detroit Institute of Arts. *Early American Prints, A Check List of an Exhibition Held at the Detroit Institute of Arts*. Detroit: Detroit Institute of Arts, 1957. unpag.

This exhibition contained 156 prints, covering the years from 1670 to 1875. Wide in scope and of good quality, the exhibition also included prints originally published in books.

1184. Dresser, Louisa. *Early New England Printmakers*. Worcester: Worcester Art Museum, 1940. 77 pp.

This exhibition catalog describes eighty-five prints, by artists from John Foster to Winslow Homer, from the collections of the Worcester Art Museum and the American Antiquarian Society. It is arranged chronologically and the notes on each print are detailed and informative; it is especially strong on eighteenth-century prints. The introduction discusses the work and versatility of engravers, the historical value of the prints, and the different processes represented in the exhibition. The text has also been printed in *Art in New England: The Arts and Crafts of New England and a Survey of the Taste of its People* (Cambridge, Mass. : Harvard University Press, 1940).

1185. Fitchburg Art Museum. *Homer and Whistler. The American Artist at Home and Abroad*. Fitchburg, Mass.: Fitchburg Art Musem, 1983. Unpag.

Etchings by Whistler and wood engravings after Homer are the focus of this exhibition which sought to show the interests of the two artists. In his essay, Eric Rosenberg seeks to differentiate the two artists in their lives and art. Miriam Stewart prepared the checklist for the exhibition.

1186. Flint, Janet A. *The Print in the United States from the Eighteenth Century to the Present*. Washington: National Museum of American Art, 1981. 22 pp.

Roughly half of the prints in this exhibition date from the eighteenth and nineteenth centuries. All are from various collections within the Smithsonian Institution. The introduction provides a brief overview of the history of printmaking in the United States, stressing the rich heritage of twentieth century printmakers.

1187. Flint, Janet A. and Joseph Goddu. *Creation & Craft. Three Centuries of American Prints*. New York: Hirschl & Adler Galleries, 1990. 135 pp., biblio., index.

This exhibition catalog marked the tenth anniversary of the establishment of the print department at Hirschl & Adler, a prominent New York gallery. The descriptions of the seventy eighteenth- and nineteenth-century prints are detailed and scholarly. Included are many rare items and works by fine artists of the 1880s and 1890s.

1188. Goldman, Judith. *American Prints: Process & Proofs*. New York: Whitney Museum of Art and Harper & Row, 1981. 187 pp., biblio., glossary.

Although the focus of this exhibition is on twentieth-century American artists, there is an introductory chapter on American prints from 1670 to 1900 focusing on a few colonial prints and later works by engravers, illustrators, and lithographers such as Asher B. Durand, Winslow Homer, and Currier & Ives. The work of several painter-etchers is noted. A checklist of the prints in the exhibition appears at the end of the volume.

1189. Greenleaf, E. H. *Catalogue of Etchings Exhibited at the Museum of Fine Arts (Gray Room), January 1879*. Boston: Alfred Mudge & Son, 1879. 20 pp.

Containing the work of few American etchers other than Whistler, Gifford, and Smillie, this catalog does mark one of the first times that American etchings were exhibited alongside those of Rembrandt, Turner, Daubigny, Millet, and other European and English etchers. The 441 etchings were borrowed from many collections, including those of S.P. Avery, C.E. Norton, and H. Wunderlich, as well as from the artists themselves. Still others came from the Gray Collection at Harvard.

1190. The Grolier Club. *Modern Wood Engraving: Works of the Society of American Wood Engravers*. New York: 1890. 16 pp.

This exhibition catalog records the titles of 157 wood engravings by about twenty engravers. The American engravings exhibited at the Paris Universal Exhibition of 1889, with the names of those artists who won awards, are also listed.

1191.———. *Catalogue of an Exhibition Illustrative of a Centenary of Artistic Lithography*. New York: 1896. 83 pp., biblio., index.

Although oriented toward European lithographers, this exhibition of 224 prints did include the works of Whistler, Rembrandt Peale, John Cheney, Albert Newsam, Thomas Cole, and Joseph Cole. In his introduction, the lithographer Louis Prang discusses the discovery of lithography and its subsequent introduction throughout Europe and America.

1192.———. *Catalogue of an Exhibition of Early American Engraving Upon Copper, 1727–1850*. New York: The Grolier Club, 1908. 100 pp.

This catalog contains 296 examples of engraving by 147 artists. The biographical notes and textual information have been summarized from Stauffer's *American Engravers*. There is also a section of portraits of engravers. The introduction contains a discussion of the growth of interest in American engravings, and provides a very brief history of the art to 1900. There are a few errors and simplifications.

1193. Halsey, R. T. Haines. *Exhibition of Prints Relating to American History: Being a Part of the Prints Contained in the Mabel Brady Garvan Collection of American Arts and Crafts at Yale University*. Washington, D.C.: 1931. 28 pp.

Included in the Mabel Brady Garvan Collection at Yale University are about five thousand prints. This selection of 322 of those prints concentrates on historical scenes, portraits, and city views of American and European origin. The introduction describes the exhibition and then emphasizes the rarest of the prints.

1194. Helfand, William H. *Potions, Pills, & Purges: The Art of Pharmacy*. Madison, Wisc.: American Institute of the History of Pharmacy for the Philadelphia Museum of Art, 1995. 60 pp.

This exhibition was drawn from The Ars Medica Collection of the Philadelphia Museum of Art and the collection of the author. Eighty-three prints from the collection, each focusing on some aspect of pharmacies or drugs, are thoroughly described. About one quarter of the prints are American, and it is interesting and instructive to see them set among their European counterparts of the eighteenth and nineteenth centuries. Each item is illustrated, making this a valuable record of the exhibition held in 1995.

1195. Henry Francis du Pont Winterthur Museum. *Philadelphia Reviewed: The Printmaker's Record, 1750–1850*. Winterthur, Del.: 1960. 43 pp.

Charles Montgomery's foreword sets the prints in their proper context by providing historical background on Philadelphia. Almost fifty prints are described in the exhibition catalog, depicting views of Philadelphia, leading citizens, buildings, and social life. The entries are excellent, and include information about the subject matter and artist.

1196. John Carter Brown Library. *American Woodcuts and Engravings, 1670–1800*. Providence: 1946. 44 pp.

This exhibition was held in honor of the Walpole Society's visit to the John Carter Brown Library in 1945. The catalog, compiled by Lawrence C. Wroth and Marion W. Admas, was also printed in the *Walpole Society Note Book* for that year. Clarence Brigham's introduction is a discussion of the history of illustration in New England. The sixty-five entries, arranged topically, contain thorough descriptions of and bibliographical references for each item. The appendix includes a discussion of several woodcuts signed "J.F." which were at one time attributed to John Foster, but here are convincingly assigned to James Franklin.

1197. Kennedy Galleries. *Notable American Prints: The Collection of Henry Graves, Jr.* New York: 1959. 63 pp.

American and New York City views, American historical and naval prints, and American historical portraits were featured in this exhibition. Nearly all the prints were published before the 1830s, and many date from the late eighteenth century.

1198. Koehler, Sylvester R. *Exhibition of American Etchings.* Boston: Alfred Mudge & Son, 1881. 51 pp.

In his introduction to this catalog, Koehler desribes and contrasts the processes of etching, engraving, and lithography, emphasizing the particular qualities of etching. The catalog includes the work of about one hundred artists, a number of them amateurs, and gives prices for the prints, most of which were for sale. A contrast to the American examples was provided by the inclusion of a number of European etchings in the exhibition.

1199.———. *Exhibition of the Works of Women Etchers of America.* Boston: Alfred Mudge & Son, 1887. 26 pp.

Koehler provides a historical survey of women etchers, beginning in the early seventeenth century. The catalog itself includes a nearly complete listing to 1887 of the prints of about fifteen American female etchers.

1200.———. *Exhibition Illustrating the Technical Methods of the Reproductive Arts From the Fifteenth Century to the Present Time, with Special Reference to the Photomechanical Processes.* Boston: Alfred Mudge & Son, 1892. 98 pp.

This excellent catalog describes printmaking processes, utilizing European and American prints as examples. Large sections of text provide information on each of the processes, and analyze specific prints in terms of their deviations from standard techniques. There is also a clear explanation of photomechanical processes.

1201.———. "Catalogue of the Contributions of the Section of Graphic Arts to the Ohio Valley Centennial Exposition." *United States National Museum, Smithsonian Institution Proceedings* 10 (1888): 701–731.

Included in this catalog, which appears in the appendix to the *Proceedings*, are the following sections: twenty-four engraving processes used for pictorial purposes, from the sixteenth century to the present; wood engraving in the United States; etching in the United States, with mention of the leading women etchers in America; and modern photomechanical processes, including photolithography, halftone, and collographic methods. The last three sections in particular provide a valuable survey of items illustrating the history of graphic arts.

1202. The Library Company of Philadelphia. *Made in America: Printmaking 1760–1860. An Exhibition of Original Prints From the Collections of the Library Company of Philadelphia and the Historical Society of Pennsylvania.* Philadelphia: 1973. 63 pp., biblio.

Stefanie Munsing's preface briefly surveys both print collections in Philadelphia and characteristic features of prints in the colonial era and the nineteenth century. The catalog is chronologically arranged and includes a description of subject and printmaker. Eighty-five items are annotated. The bibliography is excellent.

1203. Museum of Fine Arts, Boston. *Exhibition of the Society of American Wood-Engravers, Supplemented by an Exhibition of Old and Modern Woodcuts.* Boston: 1890. 28 pp.

This three-part exhibition included proofs from members of the Society of American Wood Engravers, proofs from exhibitors not members of the Society, and old and modern black-line facsimile work, along with modern European white-line work. This last group was shown for purposes of comparison with the work of the contemporary American school. The works of thirty-one American artists were included in the exhibition.

1204.———. *Exhibition of American Engravings and Etchings.* Boston: 1893. 6 pp.

Nearly six hundred prints by American engravers and etchers were displayed at the 1893 World's Columbian Exposition in Chicago. A few early nineteenth century examples were included, but the emphasis fell on later prints of a more artistic nature.

1205.———. *Summer Exhibition 1897: Wood Engravings, Dry-Points, Aquatints, Mezzotints, Stipples, and Line-Engravings by American Artists.* Boston: 1897. 15 pp., index.

Over 640 prints dating from the eighteenth and nineteenth centuries appeared in this notable exhibition. Unfortunately only the engravers' names are listed in the catalog, with the artists' names excluded, and the checklist is arranged according to the layout of the exhibition. There is an index by engraver.

1206. Museum of Graphic Art. *American Printmaking: The First 150 Years.* Washington, D.C.: Smithsonian Institution Press for Museum of Graphic Art, 1969. 180 pp., biblio., index.

From 1969 to 1971, the Museum of Graphic Art circulated an exhibition of American historical prints, drawn largely from the collection of J. William Middendorf II, to thirteen institutions. In the introduction, Middendorf comments on the significance of the prints and on his collection. The catalog by Wendy Shadwell is excellent and impressions in public collections are noted. Of particular significance is the identification of various states of some of the prints, a detail of print connoisseurship rarely noted on American prints. Also noteworthy are the resumes of holdings of major collections, the bibliography, and an index by engraver.

1207. National Collection of Fine Arts. *A Measure of Beauty: The Diffusion of Style in Early Nineteenth-Century America.* Washington, D.C.: Smithsonian Institution, 1973. 6 pp.

This exhibition examined the development of the neoclassical style in prints and drawings. The catalog is divided into four sections: "Style As an Institution," "A Likeness Beyond Time," "The Feminine Muse," and "Living a Style" (dress and fashion).

1208. National Museum of History and Technology. *The Victorian American.* Washington, D.C.: Smithsonian Institution, 1961. 30 pp.

The preface includes a memoir of Harry T. Peters, whose America on Stone Collection is at the Smithsonian Institution, and background on the Victorian era. The introduction focuses on the history of lithogrpahy in the United States. Sections in the exhibition catalog by curators Anthony N. B. Garvan and Peter C. Welsh are: technical process, sports, fashion, the West, the sea, patriotism, associations, politics, warfare, and humor. One hundred lithographs were exhibited.

1209. The New York Public Library. *One Hundred Notable American Engravers, 1683–1850.* New York: 1928. 38 pp.

I. N. Phelps Stokes discusses the focus of this exhibtion: the development of the art of engraving in the United States until 1850. Almost four hundred examples were exhibited, representing the work of 125 engravers. Included is a detailed checklist, chronologically arranged, which was originally printed in the *New York Public Library Bulletin* 32 (Mar. 1928): 139–74.

1210.———. *Currier & Ives, Printmakers to the American People: A Catalogue of an Exhibition Held at the New York Public Library.* New York: 1931. 19 pp.

In the introduction Harry T. Peters discusses the history of Currier & Ives and subjects favored by the firm in their prints. The catalog compiled by Charles F. McCombs lists 194 prints, gathered together to provide a pictorial record of a fascinating period in American life. There are occasional notes on the prints and the artists who created them. The catalog also appeared in the *New York Public Library Bulletin* 35 (Jan. 1931): 3–18.

1211. Philadelphia Society of Etchers. *Catalogue of the First Annual Exhibition.* Philadelphia: 1882. 26 pp.

In his introduction, Sylvester R. Koehler describes the characteristics and techniques of painter-etchings and compares etching to other graphic processes. The catalog lists almost eleven hundred etchings, arranged by artist. The illustrations include etchings by Church, P. Moran, and Ferris.

1212. Richter, Emil H. *Descriptive Catalogue of an Exhibition of Early Engraving in America.* Boston: Boston Public Library, 1904. 151 pp.

The catalog lists 665 items by 157 artists. It represents the first noteworthy exhibition of the works of early American engravers. The catalog contains sections on coins, paper money, and seals of governments, colleges, and universities, with an index of subjects arranged by artist. In December 1904, on the occasion of this exhibition, the Boston Public Library published a complementary list of books and articles on American prints.

1213. Union League Club. *Exhibition Catalogue of the Work of the Women Etchers of America.* New York: 1888. 23 pp.

Mrs. Schuyler Van Rensselaer's introduction describes the international role of women in the arts, noting that the exhibition was open to all women etchers in America, regardless of training or level of expertise. The catalog lists over five hundred plates by thirty-five women. The best-known artists in the exhibition were M. Nimmo Moran and Eliza Greatorex.

1214. Watson, Arthur C. *Special Exhibition of the Henry P. Kendall Whaling Collection.* Cambridge, Mass.: Massachusetts Institute of Technology, 1937. 16 pp.

Watson briefly desribes the history of whaling. The exhibition includes materials from as early as the sixteenth century. They include attempts at the accurate scientific depiction of whales, Dutch prints showing the northern whale fishery, cartoons, lithographs by Benjamin Russell other works by VanBeest, R. Swain Gifford, Clifford W. Ashley, Currier & Ives, and prints of various aspects of the whaling industry. The Kendall Collection included European and Far Eastern works as well.

1215. Webster, Donald B. Jr. *American Historical Prints: Engraving of a Golden Age.* Binghamton, N.Y.: Roberson Memorial Center, 1965. 30 pp.

The prints in this exhibition, covering the period 1760 to 1850, are each fully described in a short commentary.

Historical Prints

1216. Abrams, Ann Uhry. "Visions of Columbus: The 'Discovery' Legend in Antebellum American

Paintings and Prints." *American Art Journal* 25, no. 1 and 2 (1993): 74–101.

Abrams examines the use of Washington Irving's scene of Columbus discovering America (*A History of the Life and Voyages of Christopher Columbus*, 1828) as the source for the imagery appearing in numerous paintings and prints in the nineteenth century. Her analysis of the prints is excellent. The essay again demonstrates how some prints must be viewed and used with caution; artists could be very creative.

1217. Andrews, William Loring. *Fragments of American History, Illustrated Solely by the Works of Those of Our Own Engravers Who Flourished in the Eighteenth Century*. New York: Privately Printed, 1898. 69 pp.

In this small volume the author discusses various historical prints by Amos Doolittle, Samuel Hill, Robert Aitken, John Norman, Samuel Harris, James Turner, and James Trenchard. Andrews concentrates on the historical and cultural significance of the prints, acknowledging their lack of artistic merit. It is an interesting essay by a renowned collector, although not useful for its factual information on the engravers.

1218. Cobb, Josephine. "Prints, the Camera, and Historical Accuracy" in *American Printmaking Before 1876, Fact, Fiction, and Fantasy*, 1–10. Washington, D.C.: Library of Congress, 1975.

Many mechanical aids were used in the production of paintings and prints. Cobb discusses the camera obscura, the camera lucida, the physiognotrace, photography, and other less common devices. The devices are well described, and there is discussion of American prints produced with the help of these aids during the late eighteenth and nineteenth centuries.

1219. Comstock, Helen. "Spot News in American Historical Prints, 1755–1800"; "Spot News in American Historical Prints, 1805–1821." *Antiques* 80 and 81 (November 1961 and January 1962): 446–49; 97–100.

Each article contains reproductions of seven prints with detailed commentary on the prints and their publication. The second article concentrates on naval actions during the Tripoli War and the War of 1812. Both articles are carefully prepared and informative.

1220. Davidson, Marshall. *The Drawing of America: Eyewitness to History*. New York: Harry N. Abrams, 1983. 256 pp., biblio., index.

This book uses drawings and watercolors to elucidate the history of the United States from the colonial era to the present. Works by both academic artists and naive observers of the American scene are included. The narrative text places the drawings in their historical context. Few comments relate to the works of art themselves. This is a lavishly illustrated, handsome volume. The works are selected from the collections of many museums and libraries.

1221. Deak, Gloria-Gilda. *Other Voices, Other Times: American Historical Prints of the 18th and 19th Centuries*. New York: Kennedy Galleries, 1985. 65 pp., biblio., index.

This exhibition catalog features reproductions of fifty-four prints with extensive, thoroughly researched descriptions. The prints range from a nineteenth-century engraving of the landing of Columbus to a lithograph of the Crane Paper Company's plant in Dalton, Massachusetts, issued in 1899. Deak's commentary concentrates on the subject matter of each print, but the captions also provide relevant information on the publisher and artist.

1222.———. "Christopher Columbus and the Flowering of American Iconography." *Imprint* 17, no. 1 (1992): 2–37.

This issue of *Imprint* honors the Quincentenary of the "discovery" of America. Deak poses twenty-five questions about the Columbus story, illustrating each response with an appropriate print, focusing on early images of America.

1223. Franco, Barbara. "Masonic Imagery" in *Aspects of American Printmaking, 1800–1950*, 1–29. ed. James F. O'Gorman. Syracuse, N.Y.: Syracuse University Press, 1988.

Masonic imagery permeated American culture. Franco discusses this phenomenon with a brief introduction to the history of freemasonry in the United States, provides the symbolic meaning of masonic tools and the apron, connects freemasonry to architecture, presents the widespread use of masonic imagery on objects and in prints, relates freemasonry to the federal style, and provides information about several engravers who were responsible for most of the membership certificates issued between 1775 and 1825. Engravers of particular importance include Paul Revere, Amos Doolittle, Val de Nuit, Abner Reed, Samuel Maverick, and Oliver Eddy.

1224. Greenberg, Jonathan. *America as Emblem*. New York: Kennedy Galleries, 1992. 25 pp., biblio.

Greenberg surveys emblems representing America from the late sixteenth century to the Centennial Exposition of 1876. This thematic exhibition and accompanying essay provide a useful listing of fifty-six rare prints and reproductions of some of the most interesting.

1225. Halsey, R. T. H. *Exhibition of Prints Relating to Early American History*. Washington, D.C.: Library of Congress, 1931. 28 pp.

This exhibition was drawn from the Mabel Brady Garvan Collection at Yale University. Halsey's introduction of the checklist of 332 prints highlights some of the major maps, political caricatures, city and town views, portraits, and depictions of events on display.

1226. Halsey, R. T. Haines. "Prints Relating to Early American History." *Metropolitan Museum of Art Bulletin* 26 (1931): 164–68.

This article was published on the occasion of an exhibition of prints from the Mabel Brady Garvan Collection. Halsey, in an earlier article, pointed out that engravings were lavishly displayed in northern houses during the colonial period. On the basis of both this exhibition and newspaper advertisements, he concludes that while the southern colonies had few outstanding engravers, they valued engravings as much as the northern colonies did.

1227. Hicks, Frederick S. "Amiable Frauds" in *American Printmaking Before 1876, Fact, Fiction, and Fantasy*, 72–79. Washington, D.C.: Library of Congress, 1975.

As a collector of American naval prints, Hicks has found several examples of "duplicity" on the part of printmakers. He discusses several battle scenes, portraits, and landscape prints published during the first half of the ninteenth century.

1228. Keazor, Henry. "Theodore De Bry's Images for *America*." *Print Quarterly* 15, no. 2 (June 1998): 131–49.

This superbly documented essay discusses the pictorial sources for De Bry's *America* published in fourteen volumes between 1590 and 1634. The importance of John White's drawings has long been recognized; Keazor looks at other works produced in Europe.

1229. Marks, Arthur S. "The Statue of King George III in New York and Iconology of Regicide." *American Art Journal* 13, no. 3 (1981): 61–82.

On April 26, 1770, a monumental statue of King George III was dedicated in New York. On July 9, 1776, it was torn down shortly after the Declaration of Independence was read; only a few scraps survive. Marks tells this story in detail and reproduces prints and paintings that relate to this statue and its demise including a variety of book illustrations and fictitious prints by Franz Joseph Habermann. In 1848 the German refugee Johannes Adam Oertel painted *Pulling Down the Statue of George III* which was reproduced as a large folio engraving in 1859. Marks connects these images with contemporary political movements in Europe and the United States.

1230. Marzio, Peter C. "Illustrated News in Early American Prints" in *American Printmaking Before 1876, Fact, Fiction, and Fantasy*, 53–60. Washington, D.C.: Library of Congress, 1975.

Marzio considers illustrations of events that appeared in newspapers, almanacs, and prints of the colonial era. The items discussed and illustrated include newspaper cuts (unusual at the time), almanac illustrations of recent events, and historical prints such as Thomas Johnston's engraving of the Lake George battle fought during the French and Indian Wars.

1231. Marzio, Peter C., and Milton Kaplan. "Lithographs as Historical Documents." *Antiques* 102 (October 1972): 669–74.

Nineteenth-century lithographs have often wrongly been assumed to be an objective account of our everyday past. In this important article, the authors put forth arguments in support of a "curious and biased style" in these prints. The authors make a plea for the judicious use of lithographs as historical evidence.

1232. Masur, Louis P. "'Pictures Have Now Become a Necessity:' The Use of Images in American History Textbooks." *Journal of American History* 84, no. 4 (March 1998): 1409–1424.

Masur argues that textbook publishers and authors of textbooks fail to provide the historical or artistic context for the illustrations that appear in their volumes. Illustrations are used as ornamentation, not documentation. Masur suggests that new approaches are needed and makes appropriate suggestions.

1233. Mills, Laura K. *American Allegorical Prints: Constructing an Identity*. New Haven: Yale University Art Gallery, 1996. 31 pp.

Mills demonstrates that American allegorical prints issued from 1780 through 1865 provided national symbols and popular heroes and were, therefore, important in molding American identity. After the nation was firmly established, allegorical prints also served individual needs. This exhibition catalog discusses such prints. Among the themes addressed are the development of national symbols, the cult of George Washington and other American heroes, moralizing America, temperance, material progress, and democracy and individualism. The essay is thoroughly researched and is followed by the detailed checklist of the fifty-two prints in the exhibition.

1234. Nelson, Christina H. "Transfer-printed Creamware and Pearlware for the American Market." *Winterthur Portfolio* 15, no. 2 (1980): 93–116.

Among the topics discussed in this article are the print sources for the images that decorated this pottery produced between 1790 and 1825. Many American engravings—portraits, views of ships and battles—have been identified as sources.

1235. Nesheim, Kenneth M. "Images of America, 1494–1788." *Yale University Library Gazette* 51, no. 2 (October 1976): 9–73.

Nesheim describes 118 items exhibited at the Beinecke Library in two separate exhibitions during 1976. The first one illustrated the discovery, exploration, and settlement of the Western Hemisphere. The second concerned the Revolution. Both include verbal as well as pictoral images of America, including European and American prints and drawings.

1236. Reid, Robert W. "Some Early Masonic Engravers in America." *Transactions of The American Lodge of Research, Free and Accepted Masons* 3 (1938): 97–125.

Reid presents biographies of several American engravers and printers who were masons, including N. Hurd, P. Pelham, M.G. de Bruhl, H. Dawkins, J. Thomas, B. Franklin, P. Revere, A. Doolittle, Andrew Billings, R. Scot, T. Aberbethie, P.R. Maverick, S. Maverick, W. Rollinson, C. Rollinson, and Jervis Cutler. The sketches are brief but include both newspaper advertisements and individual works, particularly Masonic certificates.

1237. Shadwell, Wendy. "Some Pre-Revolutionary Prints and Broadsides." *Antiques* 99 (February 1971): 262–267.

The author demonstrates how the text of a broadside often provides information germane to incidents illustrated by prints. She further illustrates her point with a selection of six pairs of prints and broadsides from the Middendorf Collection.

1238. Sommer, Frank H., III. "Prints as Documents of Early American History" in *American Printmaking Before 1876, Fact, Fiction, and Fantasy*, 25–33. Washington, D.C.: Library of Congress, 1975.

Basing his material on the print and rare book collections at the Henry Francis du Pont Winterthur Museum, Sommer has found illustrations that depict life in the United States during the eighteenth and early nineteenth centuries. Among the subjects treated are architecture, travel and transportation, agriculture, heat and light, clothing, etiquette, advertising, and the world of the child, the ill, the insane, and the criminal. Many of the prints described and illustrated are English, but are also suitable as depictions of American life.

1239. Weitenkampf, Frank. "Early American Historical Prints." *Print Connoisseur* 2 (March 1922): 196–217.

Weitenkampf begins with a discussion of reasons for print collecting, touching on general considerations such as technique and the aesthetic, historical, personal, and local qualities of prints. He then concentrates on American historical prints, commenting on their artistic qualities and historical accuracy. In a survey of the subject, he mentions most of the eighteenth-century engravers, then goes on to describe examples of prints published throughout the 1800s.

Landscape Prints

1240. Albright-Knox Art Gallery, Buffalo Fine Arts Academy. *Three Centuries of Niagara Falls*. Buffalo, N.Y.: Albright-Knox Art Gallery, 1964. 63 pp.

This exhibition included depictions of Niagara Falls in all media—oil, watercolors, pen and pencil, and the various graphic media. Most of the entries are brief in format, but they provide an excellent guide to available depictions of the Falls. The compilers included advertisements, posters, cartoons, and sheet music covers.

1241. Dahl, Harold J., and George Connor. "The Falls of the Passaic." *Antiques* 74 (October 1958): 326–28.

The authors have found over forty-five depictions of the Passaic Falls, ranging in time from the colonial era to the age of stereograph views. Several of the most interesting views are discussed.

1242. Diebold, William. *Rockland County in Old Prints 1750–1900*. Nyack, N.Y.: Edward Hopper Landmark Preservation Foundation, 1986. Unpag.

This exhibition catalog contains a nice variety of prints depicting a part of New York State along the Hudson River. Diebold's text discusses the artists responsible for the views (William Guy Wall, Jacques Gérard Milbert, William Henry Bartlett, Benson Lossing, John Henry Hill, and Jules Tavernier), some of the remarkable features of the landscape, and the importance of Major John Andre to the region. A mimeographed list of the 138 prints in the exhibition accompanies the pamphlet.

1243.———. "Four Great Sequences of Hudson River Prints." *Imprint* 20, no. 2 (1995): 2–18.

After summarizing notable eighteenth- and early nineteenth-century views of the Hudson River, Diebold describes the production and contents of four signficant sequences of Hudson River views: the aquatints of the *Hudson River Portfolio* by John Hill after William Guy Wall; the lithographs of Jacques Gérard Milbert's *Itinéraire pittoresque du Fleuve Hudson*; the steel engravings in Willis's *American Scenery* after William Henry Bartlett; and Benson J. Lossing's *The Hudson, from the Wilderness to the Sea*. The essay is well-researched and documented.

1244. Frankenstein, Alfred. "The Great Trans-Mississippi Railroad Survey." *Art in America* 64, no. 1 (1976): 55–58.

This brief article summarizes the topographical views in *Reports of Explorations and Surveys to Ascertain the Most Practical and Economical Means for a Railroad from the Mississippi to the Pacific Ocean*, published in Washington in 1859–1860. Many of the landscapes depict mountain passes and riverbeds because those features were important to the planning of the eventual route. Among the artists on the survey were Richard H. Kern, F. W. von Egloffstein, Heinrich Baduin Mohlhausen, John Mix Stanley, and Charles Koppel.

1245. Hachey, Paul A. *The New Brunswick Landscape Print, 1760–1880.* Fredericton, Canada: Beaverbrook Art Gallery, 1980. 111 pp., biblio.

This catalog was prepared for an exhibition which toured several Canadian provinces during 1980 and 1981. One hunderd and seventeen prints are described—all depicting out-of-door subjects of identifiable and specific places, including waterfalls, rivers, harbours, mountains, public and private buildings, panoramas, sporting subjects, and topographical views. Technically, only lithographs, aquatints, and engravings are included; chromolithographs and relief prints have been excluded from consideration. Of the prints only four were printed in Canada, the others being of English or American origin. All entries are illustrated.

1246. Hatch, John Davis. "John Vanderlyn's Prints of Niagara Falls." *Antiques* 138, no. no. 6 (December 1990): 598–601.

In the early years of the nineteenth century, John Vanderlyn painted several views of Niagara Falls and decided to publish two views as prints in London. Hatch provides the publication details of these uncommon and beautiful prints engraved by J. Merigot in 1804 and by Frederick Christian Lewis in 1804. The sale of the prints was disappointing, even though they received critical acclaim.

1247. Johnson, Una E. "Life on the Mississippi." *Antiques* 50 (August 1946): 108–109.

Johnson discusses early commentators on the Mississippi River, such as Audubon, Dickens, Mrs. Trollope, and the French naturalist Charles Lesueur. Various prints depicting life on the Mississippi before the Civil War are used as illustrations.

1248. Kendall, Douglas. *Rural Visions. American County Atlas Illustrations as Historical Sources.* M.A. Thesis, University of Delaware, 1987. 85 pp., biblio.

Kendall suggests that atlas illustrations produced in the latter part of the nineteenth century are in fact based on fact and are useful as visual documentation of the nineteenth-century town and landscape. He studied the atlases of New Jersey's Salem and Gloucester counties, Pennsylvnaia's Lancaster County, and New York's Genessee County. Farmsteads were most frequently depicted in these atlases which contained over 300 views.

1249. Lane, Christopher W. *Impressions of Niagara. The Charles Rand Penney Collection of Prints of Niagara Falls and the Niagara River from the Sixteenth to the Early Twentieth Century.* Philadelphia: Philadelphia Print Shop, Ltd., 1993. 194 pp., biblio., index, glossary.

A native of Buffalo, New York, Penney started collecting prints of Niagara Falls as a young man. Over 700 prints, European and American, are described and reproduced in this exhibition catalog. An introductory essay, "The Niagara and Its Wondrous Falls" was written by Gloria Deak. She discusses explorers and early visitors to the Falls including Louis Hennepin and Charles Dickens. Lane provides a chronological survey of the prints of the Falls providing a great deal of local history and lore in addition to information on the prints and their creators. This is a valuable, well-produced reference work.

1250. Lawson, Karol Ann Peard. "An Inexhaustible Abundance: The National Landscape Depicted in American Magazines, 1780–1820." *Journal of the Early Republic* 12, no. 3 (September 1992): 303–330.

A signficant number of landscape prints appeared in magazines prior to the emergence of the Hudson River School. Publishers of periodicals solicited such views from amateur artists to promote American culture and American independence. In her well-researched essay, Lawson effectively and intelligently analyzes this important body of landscape imagery.

1251. Mann, Maybelle. "American Landscape Prints." *Art & Antiques* 4, no. 3 (May 1981): 90–99.

Mann discusses landscape prints by engravers and artists such as John Hill, Jacques Milbert, William J. Bennett, Asher B. Durand, E. Wade, William Henry Bartlett, and Edwin Whitefield. Most of these prints mentioned are found in books, as opposed to landscape views issued separately.

1252. Norton, Bettina A. "This Bridge of the Yankees: Engineers and Indians at the Niagara Frontier." in *Prints and Printmakers of New York State, 1825–1940*, 133–146. ed. David Tatham. Syracuse: Syracuse University Press, 1985.

A print in the collection at the Essex Institute, *Queenston and Lewiston Suspension Bridge* (New York, 1850), is the focus of this essay. Drawn by Frederick L. Knight, this print bears an inscription noting that the print was "presented by Maungwudaus." Norton discusses the creation of the bridge, the Native Americans of the region, and their relations with the English and French settlers. The bridge, designed for foot traffic across the Niagara River, one and three-quarter miles from the Falls, survived for only thirteen years. One of the first to cross it was Maungwudaus, one of the Native Americans who traveled with George Catlin in Europe in 1844. Norton describes the activities of the group in Europe and suggests Maungwudaus was with P.T. Barnum in Salem when he gave the print to the Peabody Museum, who in turn gave it to the present owner. This is an interesting introduction into the subject matter of a topographical print and its provenance.

1253. Ramsay, John. "The American Scene in Lithograph: The Album." *Antiques* 60 (September 1951): 180–83.

In the early nineteenth century, portfolios of landscape prints were popular in Europe; interest in them quickly spread to the United States. Ramsay considers a number of volumes depicting American scenery and cities, including the work of Whitefield, Kollner, J.C. Wild, and Alfred E. Mathews. This article is a good survey of American landscape views.

1254. Reese, William S. *The Illustrating Traveler: Adventure & Illustration in North America & the Caribbean 1760–1895*. [New Haven]: The Beinecke Library, 1996. 34 pp.

This checklist of an exhibition mounted at the time of the North American Print Conference held in New Haven in the spring of 1996 describes some of the finest illustrated travel narratives describing the Americas.

1255. Spendlove, F. St. George. "Niagara Falls Pictured." *Antiques* 69 (April 1956): 334–37.

Niagara Falls was a popular subject with American and foreign artists. Spendlove discusses depictions which he selected from the collection of the Royal Ontario Museum. Although paintings and water colors are included in the article, a number of fine prints are described: a set of four prints by W.J. Bennett; eight prints by August Kollner published in Paris; and other works by Currier & Ives, Charles Magnus & Co., and Sarony & Major.

1256. Weimerskirch, Philip J. "Two Great Illustrated Books about the Hudson River: William Guy Wall's *Hudson River Port Folio* and Jacques Gérard Milbert's *Itineraire pittoresque du fleuve Hudson*" in *Adirondack Prints and Printmakers: The Call of the Wild*, 25–44. ed. Caroline Mastin Welsh. Blue Mountain Lake and Syracuse, N.Y.: Adirondack Museum and Syracuse University Press, 1998.

Two of the most beautiful portfolios of views of America published in the 1820s and 1830s focused on the Hudson River. Weimerskirch provides background on the artists involved in their creation. Of particular importance is the discussion of the roles of John Rubens Smith and John Hill in the production of Wall's *Port Folio*. One of Milbert's original sketches is reproduced demonstrating the extent that the lithographers embellished the original drawings when making lithographed copies. The article includes a list of the plates from each series relating to the Adirondack region.

1257. Weitenkampf, Frank. "Early American Landscape Prints." *Art Quarterly* 8 (December 1945): 40–67.

This excellent survey traces the development of landscape prints from the mid-eighteenth century to about 1845. The earlier prints are primarily English in origin, but the late eighteenth century saw the publication of landscape prints in American periodicals. Weitenkampf discusses the growing appreciation for landscape art in America as evidenced by the rapid appearance of landscape imagery in separately published prints, portfolios, periodicals, and illustrated books.

1258. Wiesendanger, M. W. "The American Scene and the Graphic Arts." *Avocations* 1 (February 1938): 406–412.

The writer presents a survey of landscape and city views, concentrating on the works of John Hill, William G. Wall, and W.J. Bennett. He barely mentions lithographs, and disregards most woodcuts and line and steel engravings because their lines are so stiff.

1259. Wunderlich, Rudolf G. "Early Railroad Prints." in *The Concise Encyclopedia of American Antiques*, 376–80. ed. Helen Comstock. New York: Hawthorn Books, 1958. biblio.

Wunderlich begins by recording a few basic facts on the history of the railroad in the United States. He then discusses prints of historical significance, Western prints, Currier & Ives prints, music sheet covers, bank notes, stock certificates, and prints of trains, viaducts, and bridges. There are abundant references to specific prints and to their lithographers and publishers. A list of well-known designers of railroad prints is included, as is a bibliography.

Lithography

1260. *Lithography in Cincinnati. Part I. To the Advent of the Steam Press*. Cincinnati: Young and Klein, Inc., 1958. 33 pp.

Cincinnati was one of the major centers for the production of lithographs. This well illustrated study covers the history of lithography in Cincinnati from 1836 to 1868. The text, excerpted from Peter G. Duval's article on lithography from J. Luther Ringwalt's *Enclyclopedia of Printing* published in 1871, discusses the process involved in producing lithographs. Other commentary describes the individual firms who were active in the city and specific prints. Among the illustrations are several depicting the creation of lithographs.

1261. "Lithography." *Boston Monthly Magazine* (December 1825): 378–384.

This article on lithography closely followed the establishment of the first American commercially successful lithography firm, Pendleton's in Boston. The article is illustrated by three plates, a bouquet of flowers and two landscapes. The text is based on Senefelder's lengthy description of the process and on Raucourt's work on lithography. The anonymous author praises John Pendleton for bringing to Boston the materials necessary for establishing a lithography firm.

1262. "Lithography." *United States Literary Gazette* (15 June 1826): 224–27.

This article provides a description and history of the lithographic process. Its general diffusion is held to be beneficial "to the progress of the useful and ornamental arts." The Pendletons are praised for having established a press in Boston. Such articles, contemporary with the beginnings of lithography in the United States, provide little in the way of new information, but are interesting as chronicles of its acceptance.

1263. "The New Art of Lithotint." *Miss Leslie's Magazine* 7 (April 1843): 113–14.

This explanation of the process of lithotinting includes the plate, "Grandpapa's Pet," that was drawn and lithotinted by John H. Richards for P.S. Duval. It is credited as the "first specimen of this art ever produced in the United States." The invention of lithotinting is attributed to Charles Joseph Hullmandel in London. In 1841, after seeing examples of Hullmandel's work, Richards and Duval experimented to see if they could duplicate his method.

1264. Comstock, Helen. *American Lithographs of the Nineteenth Century*. New York: M. Barrows & Co., 1950. 170 pp., glossary, index.

Comstock discusses the applications of lithography, its technique, various subject areas of interest to collectors, early lithographic firms, and Currier & Ives. Each plate in this profusely illustrated volume bears a caption providing information on the artist, lithographer, and subject of the print.

1265. Cooper, Thomas. "Lithography." *Analectic Magazine* (July 1819): 67–73.

This article explains the new technique of lithography and the efforts to find a satisfactory lithographic stone in Kentucky. It is accompanied by a Bass Otis lithograph, one of the earliest specimens of the process. The editors of *Analectic Magazine* were obvously interested in the lithographic process; in 1817 and 1818 they republished short articles from British and French magazines on the new art.

1266. Crosby, Everett V. *Chromos*. Nantucket, Mass.: Tetankimmo Press, 1954. 13 pp.

Crosby began collecting chromolithographs as a hobby after finding some in old attics. He describes the process, the development of chromolithography in the United States, and the work of Louis Prang. He quotes extensively from Parton's article in the *Atlantic Monthly* of March 1869, and from one of Prang's catalogs, both of which give very full descriptions of the process.

1267. Drepperd, Carl W. "Why Only Currier & Ives?" *Antiques* (February 1927): 108–112.

Currier & Ives prints have always been a favorite of collectors. This article, written by an authority on prints, presents the work of other lithographers he considers equal to, or superior to, Currier & Ives. Among those mentioned are Napoleon Sarony, the firm of Childs & Inman, M.E.D. Brown, William E. Hitchcock, and the firm of Huddy & Duval. It is a spirited article and a pleasant change from the mass of literature on Currier & Ives.

1268. Eckhardt, George H. "Early Lithography in Philadelphia." *Antiques* 28 (December 1935): 249–252.

Eckhardt discusses early Philadelphia publications that were interested in lithography. He incorrectly cites the June 1822 issue of the *Journal of the Academy of Natural Sciences* as containing the first "true" lithograph. *The Children's Friend*, a small children's book published in New York in 1821, with each page printed by lithography, was the first. Further discussion centers on the Franklin Institute, which devoted much attention in its *Journal* to lithography, and also awarded prizes for various lithographs during the first half of the nineteenth century. The article contains a wealth of contemporary comments, and the sources are well identified to facilitate further research.

1269. Flint, Janet. "The American Painter-Lithographer." in *Art & Commerce*, 126–150. Boston: Museum of Fine Arts, 1978.

Flint focuses on a small group of painters who chose to engage in lithography out of interest rather than employment. Included in this group are Thomas Cole, William Rimmer, William Morris Hunt, and Thomas Moran. Representative prints by each artist are described. All are very scarce because, for the most part, they were not published commerically.

1270. Fuchs & Lang Manufacturing Co. *Catalogue of Lithographic Prints in the Gallery of the Fuchs & Lang Mf'g Co.* New York: 1913. 63 pp., biblio., index.

This catalog contains a bibliography, chronologically arranged, of technical books on lithography that were primarily published in Germany. Another feature is a list of books illustrated by lithographs, including several American publications. The catalog of Fuchs & Lang lithographs is arranged by date, and includes some of the finest American examples of the art.

1271. Gandy, Lewis Cass. "The Story of Lithography." *Lithographers' Journal* Supp. 24 (February 1940): 16 pp.

The author commences with Senefelder's discovery of lithography, and concentrates on the growth of American lithography through the era of commercial posters. The last section is devoted to a discussion of commercial printing processes based on lithography. The article is well illustrated.

1272. Gascoigne, Bamber. *Milestones in colour printing 1457–1859*. Cambridge: Cambridge University Press, 1997. 123 pp., index.

Most of this book is devoted to the highlights of European color printing beginning with German relief printing in 1457. Of particular interest is the chapter on the beginnings of chromolithography and the final chapter on the inexpensive topographical books published by Thomas Nelson. Established in Edinburgh, the firm had branches in London and New York. The firm published many booklets of American views including *The Falls of Niagara and the Vicinity*, *Nelson's Guide to the City of New York*, and *Nelson's Guide to Lake George and Lake Champlain*, issued in 1858. These and other titles are listed in a descriptive bibliography with a separate index of titles of individual prints in the 117 books listed.

1273. Golden, Jack. "Posters Past and Present." *Imprint* 2, no. 2 (November 1977): 6–8.

Citing the popularity of posters of the 1890s, Golden looks at some of the precursors—lithographed advertisements for consumer products as diverse as beer and insurance. He provides a brief synopsis of the development of chromolithography and its application to this most commercial of uses. The illustrations, all drawn from his private collection, provide an excellent survey of styles and techniques.

1274. Hitchings, Sinclair H. "Fine Art Lithography in Boston: Craftsmen in color, 1840–1900" in *Art & Commerce*, 103–125. Boston: Museum of Fine Arts, 1978.

Begining with a brief survey of commericial color printing in Boston, Hitchings focuses on the work of William Sharp, John H. Bufford, Louis Prang, and Charles Armstrong. The firm of Charles Armstrong developed a speciality in interpreting and reproducing watercolors. Louis Prang printed art nouveau designs in the 1890's that are a striking departure from the earlier reproductions of oil paintings. Winslow Homer approved of Prang's reproductions of two of his watercolors issued in 1893. Hitchings suggests that the four leading color lithography firms made intense and sustained contributions to the progress of color lithography, locally and internationally.

1275. Jackson, Joseph. "Some Notes Towards a History of Lithography in Philadelphia." in *Official Reference Book of the Lithographers International Protective and Beneficial Association*, 9–21. Philadelphia: Published by the association, 1899.

Beginning with Senefelder and Bass Otis, Jackson follows the development of lithography in Philadelphia through a study of the reports of the Franklin Institute exhibitions. The Institute's first exhibition was in 1824. By mid-century, interest in photography was superseding that in lithography at the exhibitions, and the 1874 exhibition was the last in which a prize was awarded for lithography. The author includes brief sketches of the lithographers who were awarded prizes, including Newsam, Frederick Bourquin, Thomas Sinclair, and P.S. Duval. The ten illustrations are portraits of various lithographers.

1276. Last, Jay T. "Trade Card Lithographers." *Advertising Trade Card Quarterly* 1, no. 1 (1994): 18–19.

Last, a collector of trade cards and historian of commercial American chromolithography, contributed frequently to this journal. His articles describe lithographic firms including the Donaldson Brothers of New York, lithographers of Buffalo, the Calvert Lithographic Company of Detroit, Hoen and Company of Baltimore, Shober & Carqueville of Chicago, and Major & Knapp of New York. These brief illustrated articles appeared in this journal from 1994 through 1996. This material and much more appears in expanded form in his book, *The Color Explosion: Nineteenth-Century American Lithography* published in 2005.

1277. Levinson, Luna Lambert. "Images That Sell: Color Advertising and Boston Printmakers, 1850–1900." in *Aspects of American Printmaking, 1800–1950*, ed. James F. O'Gorman. 81–103 Syracuse, N.Y.: Syracuse University Press, 1988.

Several Boston lithography firms issued color advertising prints. Lambert discusses the imagery of the prints and the history of the firms that produced them. Show cards were used by manufacturers and retail traveling salesmen to procure orders. Some were mounted on conposition board or were stretched and framed. Several printing innovations are described by Lambert. Among the firms whose works are described are John H. Bufford, Charles H. Crosby, William H. Forbes, Hatch Lithographic Co., and Louis Prang & Co. Some of the corporate histories are unravelled using the R.G. Dun & Co. collection in the library of the Harvard School of Business Administration.

1278. Marzio, Peter C. *The Democratic Art*. Fort Worth: Amon Carter Musuem of Western Art, 1979. 112 pp.

This exhibition catalog discusses various aspects of American chromolithography including the process, its origins in Europe, its genesis in America, histories of American firms and individuals employing the process, and the impact of the Dusseldorf Academy on American chromolithography. A separate chapter is devoted to Louis Prang and the prints that issued forth from his firm. The focus of the exhibition was on chromolithography as a medium for the reproduction of fine art and this fact is discussed in some detail. At the end of the text is the checklist of the exhibition.

1279.———. *Chromolithography 1840–1900: The Democratic Art. Pictures for a 19th-Century America.* Boston: David R. Godine and the Amon Carter Museum of Art, 1979. 357 pp., biblio, index.

In the second half of the nineteenth century, many firms published chromolithographs as advertisements, separately published prints for framing, and illustrations. Marzio explores the aesthetic issues prompted by these prints, the technology of this pictorial explosion, as well as the firms and artists that produced them. There are close to 100 illustrations in color and an additional seventy-five in black and white. Marzio's documentation for this study is impressive. The bibliography should be consulted by any scholar rsearching the visual culture of the second half of the nineteenth century.

1280.———. "American Lithographic Technology Before the Civil War" in *Prints in and of America to 1850*, 215–56. ed. John D. Morse. Winterthur, Del.: Henry Francis du Pont Winterthur Museum, 1970.

In this clearly written article, Marzio discusses many technical aspects of lithography: choice and preparation of the stones, drawing on the stones, application of the ink, and printing. The greater part of the article deals with lithographic presses themselves, and several drawings illustrate the principles of the special presses needed for lithography. The rapid growth of lithography after 1850 was made possible by mechanized presses. Marzio asserts that the technology was European in origin and spread slowly to the United States. The study is well documented, its information culled from contemporary magazines and newspapers and from more recent studies.

1281.———. "The Democratic Art of Chromolithography in America: An Overview." in *Art in Commerce*, 76–102. Boston: Museum of Line Arts, 1978.

The commercial process of multicolor lithography provided inexpensive reproductions of oil paintings, watercolors, and chalk drawings for a broad public. Marzio explains the process, the significance of chromolithographs, and the history and use of the process in America. In the 1880's, critical opinion turned against chromolithography and only in recent years have they received the recognition they deserve as purveyors of culture to Americans. This article is enriched with much contemporary commentary.

1282. McCauley, Lois B. *A. Hoen on Stone: Lithographs of E. Weber & Co. and A. Hoen & Co.* Baltimore: Maryland Historical Society, 1969. 52 pp.

The sixty-five lithographs and ten illustrated books that were included in this exhibition provide a survey of the lithographs published by E. Weber & Co., the second lithographic firm established in Baltimore, and its successor, A. Hoen & Co.

1283. Ormsbee, Thomas Hamilton. "Advertising Prints, A Phase of American Lithography." *American Collector* 3 (July 1938): 8–9, 20.

Since newspapers and other publications offered limited space for advertisements, broadsides in the eighteenth century and lithographs in the nineteenth century were often used as advertisements. The author discusses several of the earliest lithographed posters and provides a broad range of illustrations from the 1840s to the 1880s. This is a good survey of the subject, and it reveals many details of nineteenth-century social life and customs.

1284. Parton, James. "Popularizing Art." *Atlantic Monthly* 23 (March 1869): 348–57.

After describing Senefelder's discovery of lithography, Parton discusses chromolithography. Parton reveals valuable details about the process. Up to twenty-six stones, which require three months of preparation, are used to reproduce one painting. Another five months are required to print one thousand copies, each of which sold for five dollars. Using Eastman Johnson's *Barefoot Boy* as an example, Parton describes how each stone is colored. The lithographer Louis Prang, who specialized in this branch of lithography, is also discussed. Parton argues that prints produced by chromolithography are valuable aids for art education. He prefers that public taste in the fine arts be shaped by high-quality lithographs rather than by cheap, inept copies of well-known paintings produced by the hundreds in New York.

1285. Pennell, Joseph. "Lithography." *Print Collector's Quarterly* (December 1912): 459–482.

Pennell, a noted lithographer and artist, remarks on the practical aspects and aesthetics of lithography. He predicts that lithographs will someday be accorded the same respect enjoyed by etchings.

1286. Pennell, Joseph, and Elizabeth Pennell. *Lithography and Lithographers: Some Chapters in the History of the Art.* New York and London: Century Co. and T. Fisher Unwin, 1898. 279 pp., index.

This excellent and beautifully illustrated volume on the history of lithography devotes only a few pages to its practice in America. Pennell felt that very few lithographs of artistic importance were published in the United States, so this volume is rather useless to those interested in that subject. On the other hand, it is invaluable for the comparison afforded of American lithographs and those published abroad, particularly in England and France. The illustrations include original lithographs, and the volume is indexed.

1287. Peters, Harry T. *America on Stone: The Other Printmakers of the American People. A Chronicle of American Lithography Other Than That of Currier*

& Ives, From Its Beginning, Shortly Before 1820, to the Years When the Commercial Single-Stone Colored Lithograph Disappeared From the American Scene. New York: Doubleday, Doran & Co., 1931. 415 pp., biblio.

Peters's introduction to this monumental volume provides an excellent survey of American lithography, discussing business methods, aesthetics, and subject matter. The alphabetical list of lithographers is tremendously helpful in documenting prints. Each entry provides dates and addresses taken from city directories and mentions several prints. For the more important lithographers, entries run to four or more pages. There are some omissions and errors that could be corrected with a full revision of this valuable reference book. The collection formed by Peters, known as the America on Stone Collection, is at the National Museum of American History, a part of the Smithsonian Institution, Washington, D.C.

1288.———. *California on Stone.* Garden City, N.Y.: Doubleday, Doran & Co., 1935. 227 pp., index.

In *America on Stone*, Peters mentions that lithography in California is an area of special interest. He calls it the "fourth geographical school," following Boston, New York, and Philadelphia. Peters estimates that there are about 750 important California prints, although more have undoubtedly come to light since 1935. The introduction discusses different types of lithographs: letter sheets, song and music sheets, pictures of the missions, views of vigilantes, and genre scenes. The major lithographers are discussed briefly, and an alphabetical list of artists, lithographers, publishers, and craftsmen, together with their dates, addresses, and notes on their most important prints are included. The list includes non-Californians who produced views of California. The illustrations are delightful in their evocation of a marvelous period in American history.

1289.———. "The Little-Known American Lithograph." *Prints* 3 (March 1933): 1–13.

Peters presents two reasons for the growing interest in American historical lithographs in the 1930s: America had finally grown old enough to appreciate her past, and prints were among the last reasonably priced "antiques" on the market. Peters mentions some of the fine American lithographs by Homer, Darley, Rembrant Peale, and Whistler available, and then cites a few more popular items in this defense of nineteenth-century American lithography.

1290. Pierce, Sally, Catharina Slautterback, and Georgia Brady Barnhill. *Early American Lithography. Images to 1830.* Boston: The Boston Athenaeum, 1997. 87 pp.

Published on the occasion of an exhibition at the Boston Athenaeum, this catalog contains detailed information on the 77 prints, sheet music covers, and books displayed. The introductory essay by Pierce discusses the introduction of lithography into America, early practitioners including doctors and scientists, the formation of commercial presses in New York, Boston, Philadelphia, and Washington, the transition from engraving to lithography, amateurs, and the style and content of examples from this important first decade. Classical themes are of particular interest to Pierce in this fine essay.

1291. Pierce, Sally, and Catharina Slautterback. *Boston Lithography, 1825–1880.* Boston: Boston Athemaeum, 1991. 191 pp., biblio., index.

The text for this excellent book on lithography is based on the collection of prints at the Boston Athenaeum and is the result of twenty years of exhibitions and research. The introduction by Sally Pierce records the transformation of lithography from a shopcraft to an international major industry. There are 125 illustrations, many in color. The captions include information about the subject when appropriate. Catharina Slautterback compiled the directory of lithographic artists. This directory contains valuble information, making this volume not just a handsome one, but an excellent reference work for collectors, dealers, and curators.

1292. Reed, Cleota. "On the Trail of the Arkansas Traveller." *Imprint* 20, no. 2 (1995): 19–28.

Henry Chapman Mercer's decorative fireplace surrounds (1916) titled "The Arkansas Traveller" were based on a nineteenth-century print. Reed, an historian of ceramics, traces the history of this image both in folklore and fine art. Edward Payson Washborne painted the subject about 1856 and the painting was reproduced lithographically by Leopold Grozelier in 1859. An invoice from the lithographer, John H. Bufford, documents the size of the edition and the agents engaged to sell it. This lithograph in turn served as the source for other lithographs published by J. H. Bufford's Sons and Currier & Ives in the 1870s. Reed provides substantial information on Mercer as well.

1293. Schmidt, Martin F. "The Artist and the Artisan: Two Men of Early Louisville." *Filson Club History Quarterly* 66, no. 1 (January 1988): 32–51.

The collaboration of an artist, Thomas Campbell (ca. 1810–1847), and a lithographer and job printer, Colin R. Milne (1813–1897), is the subject of this article. Anthony Imbert trained Milne in New York in 1833. Campbell and Milne were born in Scotland and met in Baltimore in 1834. They decided to work together, first in Baltimore, then in Louisville. The essay is based on letters owned by a descendant of Milne and on an autobiographical statement writtenby Milne shortly before his death. Included in the essay are titles of prints issued by the firm in the 1830s and 1840s. After Campbell's death, Milne formed a partnership with Charles Bruder. Milne left the business in 1852.

1294. Shadwell, Wendy. "The Perkins' Sun Lithographic Establishment: A New York Mystery." *Imprint* 18, no. 2 (1993): 32–34 and 22, no. 2 (1997): 22–23.

The first article reprints a lengthy advertisement from the August 1850 New York *Sun* for a lithographic firm whose output is scanty. Joseph Perkins' firm advertised only briefly and only one print bearing its imprint had been found by 1993. In 1997 Shadwell added another print to Perkins' known output, *American Superiority at the World's Great Fair* (1851).

1295. Silliman, Benjamin. "Notice of the Lithographic Art, of the Art of Multiplying Designs, by Substituting Stone for Copper Plate, With Introductory Remarks by the Editor." *American Journal of Science and Arts* 4 (1822): 169–71.

Benjamin Silliman recommends printing by the new method of lithography because of its comparative cheapness and rapidity of execution. Silliman considers lithography an auxiliary art to copperplate engraving rather than a rival one. The plates in this volume of the *American Journal* were printed by Barnet & Doolittle in New York.

1296. Tatham, David. "The Lithographic Workshop, 1825–50" in *The Cultivation of Artists in Nineteenth-Century America*, 45–54. eds. Georgia Brady Barnhill, Diana Korzenik, and and Caroline Sloat. Worcester, Mass.: American Antiquarian Society, 1997.

Using a variety of sources, Tatham pulls together a number of first person accounts of work in the lithography firms of the 1820s, 1830s, and 1840s. He observes that the lithographic shop provided a new form of education for artists. Among those who emerged from this background were Fitz Hugh Lane, Winslow Homer, William Rimmer, Alfred Jacob Miller, and Thomas Cole. The decline of the workshops occurred with the influx of European trained lithographers in the late 1840s. At the same time, art academies developed to provide professional training for artists. Two charts showing names of artists active in the Boston firms from 1825–50 and the various firms in Boston follow the essay.

1297.———. "The Pendleton-Moore Shop: Lithographic Artists in Boston, 1825–1840." *Old-Time New England* 62 (1971): 29–46.

Tatham emphasizes the lithographic firm of John and William Pendleton in Boston. The Pendletons were succeeded by Thomas Moore and other artists who had worked for the firm, either as apprentices, or on a free-lance basis. A history of the two firms is followed by a discussion of eleven artists associated with the companies, including Rembrant Peale, John H. Bufford, and Nathaniel Currier. The shop's prestige was strong enough to attract men of talent who later became artists in their own right. Carefully researched and documented, this article is very helpful as a chronicle of an important era in lithography.

1298. Taylor, Charles Henry. "Some Notes on Early American Lithography." *Proceedings of the American Antiquarian Society* 32 (April 1922): 68–80.

Charles Henry Taylor, whose collection of early American lithographs is at the American Antiquarian Society, presents notes on the earliest lithographers. The work of Bass Otis, the New York firm of Barnet & Doolittle, Henry Stone, J.B. Martin (Richmond, Va.), John Pendleton, Abel Bowen, the firm of Pendleton, Kearney & Childs, the Senefelder Lithography Company, Stodart & Currier, and Anthony Imbert are described. There are some factual errors (it was Isaac Doolittle, not Amos the engraver, who worked in New York), but most of the information is factual, and several articles published in the 1820s on lithography are quoted. Taylor's notes are also at the American Antiquarian Society.

1299. Twyman, Michael. *Lithography 1800–1850*. London: Oxford University Press, 1970. 302 pp.

This volume is a "study of the various techniques used by artists in England and France for making drawings on stone" with particular reference to topographical prints. The text includes discussions on the invention and spread of lithography in Germany, England, and France; the literature and technique of lithography; and topographical lithography in England and France.

1300. Von Groschwitz, Gustave. *One Hundred and Fifty Years of Lithography*. Cincinnati: Cincinnati Museum Association, 1948. 35 pp.

The introduction to this exhibition catalog provides a brief outline of the history of lithography. The distinctive qualities of lithography are discussed and a few individual prints are analyzed. Several nineteenth-century American examples are included in the exhibition, many printed in Cincinnati, to show the development of art in that city.

1301. Wainwright, Nicholas B. *Philadelphia in the Romantic Age of Lithography: An Illustrated History of Early Lithography in Philadelphia with a Descriptive List of Philadelphia Scenes Made By Philadelphia Lithographers Before 1866*. Philadelphia: Historical Society of Pennsylvania, 1958. 261 pp., index.

Lithography was established in Philadelphia in 1827, after a few tentative attempts at the process by Bass Otis in 1818 and 1819. This superb book provides a complete history from the time of its beginning in Philadelphia through the Civil War. Wainwright has written comprehensively on the major lithographers Cephas Childs, Child's partners, P.S. Duval, and J.T. Bowen. The careers of a host of lesser lithographers who have been less well documented in the past are also discussed. Wainwright has made good use of the manuscripts of some of the lithographers that are in the Historical Society of

Pennsylvania. The major part of the volume is devoted to an exhaustive list of 480 prints depicting Philadelphia. The prints, listed by title, are accompanied by a complete transcription of the text and an interpretive paragraph. The list provides an excellent catalog of the prints in the Historical Society of Pennsylvania, the Library Company of Philadelphia, and other public collections in that city. The illustrations are handsomely reproduced. This is a monumental work.

1302. Weimerskirch, Philip J. "The Beginnings of Lithography in America." *Journal of the Printing Historical Society* , no. 27 (1998): 49–67.

This carefully researched essay documents the earliest knowledge and uses of lithography in the United States, beginning in 1808. As early as 1814, etchings on stone were made in Philadelphia, but no impressions of these prints have been located. Works by Bass Otis, Charles Alexandre Lesueur, Arthur J. Stansbury, among others are documented using contemporary periodical references and correspondence.

1303.———. "Lithographic Stone in America." *Printing History* 11, no. 1 (1989): 2–16.

Weimerskirch discusses the properties of stone used for lithography with particular attention paid to the attempts by Americans to find a substitute for imported stone from Solnhofen in Bavaria. Weimerskirch also describes some of the earliest American experimental lithographs. Businesses were formed to import stone and to sell presses, ink, and paper to support the lithography industry in the second half of the nineteenth century. The essay concludes with transcriptions of three letters from Dr. Samuel Brown to John Brown about the properties of Kentucky limestone and the possibility of using it to make lithographs.

1304.———. "Naturalists and the Beginnings of Lithography in America" in *From Linnaeus to Darwin: Commentaries on the History of Biology and Geology*, 167–177. London: Society for the History of Natural History, 1985.

Although an 1819 lithograph by Bass Otis is frequently cited as the first lithograph made in America, Weimerskirch has found evidence in periodicals and correspondence that the first lithographic stone arrived in America in 1807. From this beginning, Weimerskirch docments other early attempts at lithography. Among the naturalists interested in the subject were Samuel L. Mitchill, Charles A. Lesueur, Samuel Brown, James Blythe, William Maclure, Jacques Gerard Milbert, and Stephen Elliott.

1305. Weitenkampf, Frank. "Lithographs" in *The Concise Encyclopedia of American Antiques*, 371–75. ed. Helen Comstock. New York: Hawthorn Books, 1958.

This brief survey prints out that lithographs are important not only for their artistic value, but have additional significance as historical documents. The best-known lithographers are discussed in terms of their preferred subject matter: portraits, views, transportation, sports, political caricatures, and theater posters. The glossary contains sketches on the lithographers included in the survey, and mentions their most typical works.

1306.———. "Painter-Lithography in the United States." *Scribner's Magazine* 30 (May 1903): 537–50.

Lithographers who were also painters are the subject of this essay: Rembrant Peale, Henry Inman, Thomas Sully, Thomas Doughty, M.E.D. Brown, Albert Newsam, F. D'Avignon, and Napoleon Sarony. Later in the century Thomas Moran and J. Foxcroft Cole worked in landscape, whereas Winslow Homer and William Morris created genre scenes of American life. In 1895 a renewed interest in lithography among artists led to the production of some good drawings on stone.

1307.———. "Vereinigte Staaten Von Nordamerika" in *Die Lithographie*, ed. Richard Graul, and Friedrich Dornhoffer. Vienna: Gesellschaft fur Vervielfaltigende Kunst der Gegenwart, 1903.

Weitenkampf studies the use lithography in America from its beginnings with Bass Otis, through the period of commercial lithography with Inman, Pendleton, and others, to the rise of such painter-lithographers as Sargent, Cassatt, and Whistler. As was his habit, Weitnekampf exhaustively enumerates artists and publications.

1308. Welsh, Peter C. "The Lithograph: A Mirror of Victorian Taste." *Antiques* 80 (September 1980): 240–43.

This well-illustrated article is based on the exhibition, *The Victorian American*, shown at the National Museum of History and Technology of the Smithsonian Institution. Welsh discusses several aspects of lithography: its questionable veracity, its historical value, and its importance as social documentation. The eleven illustrations have excellent captions.

1309. White, John H., Jr. "Locomotives on Stone." *Smithsonian Journal of History* 1, no. 1 (1966): 49–60.

White focuses on the accuracy of lithographs issued as advertisements by manufacturers of locomotives. Contemporary notices and advertisements suggest the importance of this market to lithographers. This body of prints, usually drawn on stone by the engineers themselves, also preserves technical information otherwise lost to the historian of technology. White notes works by Zerah Colburn, Matthias N. Forney, Charles T. Parry, James Hinkley, and Franklin D. Childs, among others.

Marine and Naval Prints

1310. *American Naval and Other Historical Prints and Paintings, Including Portraits of American Naval Commanders and Some Early Views of New York*. New York: United States Steel Corp., 1951. unpag.

This list of 818 items from the collection of Irving S. Olds includes descriptions for each print. The arrangement of the catalog is by subject: views of New York City, the French and Indian War, the Revolutionary War, the Quasi-War with France, the war with Tripoli, the Little Belt Incident, the War of 1812, the war with Algiers, privateer action, miscellaneous naval prints, caricatures of the War of 1812, portraits of naval commanders, and miscellaneous historical prints. Five hundred of the prints and paintings from the collection were exhibited at the offices of the United States Steel Corporation in New York City in November 1951.

1311. Brown, Alexander Crosby. "The 'Grand Saloons' of Nineteenth-Century American Steamboats." *Antiques* 58 (August 1950): 100–102.

Many paintings and prints depict the exterior appearance of American ships, but interior views are relatively scarce. In this article, Brown discusses several mid-nineteenth-century prints from the Mariners Museum in Newport News, Virginia, which record the elegant and spacious interiors of the ships. Coupled with written descriptions by travelers on the steamboats, the prints provide a valuable source of documentation.

1312.———. "The Reign of the Clipper: A Romantic Chapter in the American Merchant Marine." *Print Collector's Quarterly* 7 (October 1917): 257–69.

This article discusses the history and growth of the American merchant marine in the nineteenth century. At the time of writing, the author felt that the collections of Grenville Kane and Arthur H. Clark were the best sources of prints pertaining to the United States Navy.

1313.———. "Steamship Disasters in Nineteenth-Century American Lithographs." *Antiques* 53 (March 1948): 208–210.

There are a large number of lithographed prints which depict disasters at sea. Several lithographers and publishers, such as Nathaniel Currier, made such shipwrecks an important part of their trade. Brown discusses many of these prints, pointing out the lack of veracity and sophistication in many of them.

1314. Brust, James, and Wendy Shadwell. "The Many Versions and States of the *The Awful Conflagration of the Steam Boat Lexington*." *Imprint* 15, no. 2 (1990): 2–13.

The authors examine the publication history of one of the most important and popular images issued by Nathaniel Currier and other lithographers in 1840. Many thousands of impressions of three versions poured forth. The article includes a list of versions and states with locations in collections and a bibliography on the disaster.

1315.———. "The Many Versions and States of *The Awful Conflagration of the Steam Boat Lexington*: An Update." *Imprint* 18, no. 1 (1993): 27–31.

This article adds a new state of the first version and a location for another item. They also describe another European depiction and provide some biographical data on a couple of the passengers as well as the full list of passengers and crew.

1316. Donnell, Edna. "Early American Fighting Frigates." *American Collector* 11 (January 1943): 6–7.

This article documents changes in the style of naval prints. During the Revolution, naval prints depicted scenes at the height of a battle, such as the one between the *Bon Homme Richard* and the *Serapis*. Prints of vessels shown in profile rather than in battle, such as those by Edward Savage, were common during the Quasi-War with France. Those of the War of 1812 tended to emphasize the victory, or to show an entire fleet fighting together against the enemy. This article was derived from the exhibition at The Grolier Club, *The United States Navy, 1776 to 1815*.

1317. Frank, Stuart M. "*Moby-Dick*: The Two 'Missing' Prints by 'H. Durand'." *American Neptune* 46, no. 4 (September 1986): 252–7

In *Moby-Dick*, Herman Melville mentions two whaling prints after paintings by Ambroise Louis Garneray. Frank identifies these prints, describes various editions of them (including one by Currier & Ives). Melville attributed two other prints to "H. Durand." Frank identifies this French artist as Jean-Baptiste Henri Durand-Brager (1814–1879) and reproduces these two formerly elusive prints.

1318. The Grolier Club. *Exhibition of Naval and Other Prints, Portraits and Books Relating to the War of 1812*. New York: 1912. 14 pp.

This catalog lists seventy-two engravings, mostly American in origin, depicting naval actions in the War of 1812. There are also thirty-six portraits, including examples by Edwin, Maverick, and Strickland, and thirteen caricatures by William Charles. No commentary is given.

1319.———. *The United States Navy 1776 to 1815*. New York: 1942. 158 pp., index.

This exhibition catalog forms a pictorial document of the United States Navy in its early years. This compehensive exhibition includes prints from abroad, and provides copious information for each of the 295 entries. A review of the exhibition was written by Harry Shaw Newman in *Antiques* 43 (Jan. 1943): 16–19.

1320. Hall, Elton W. *American Maritime Prints.* New Bedford, Mass.: The Old Dartmouth Historical Society, 1985. 293 pp.

In 1977 the North American Print Conference convened in New Bedford to learn about prints relating to whaling and to the sea. The papers presented were revised for publication and include the following: "The Atlantic Neptune" by Augustus P. Loring; "Late Eighteenth-Century American Harbor Views Derived from Joseph Vernet and Richard Patron" by Donald H. Cresswell; "Lithographs of Fitz Hugh Lane" by Carl Crossman; "Commercial and Job Printing Serving the Maritime Industries" by Wendy Shadwell; "Domestic Life in a Whaling Port," by Elton W. Hall; "John Paul Jones and the Heroic Naval Print" by Bernard F. Reilly, Jr.; "American Ship Portraits: The Romantic Fallacy" by John O. Sands; and "American Whaling Prints copied From European Sources" by Elizabeth Ingalls. Each essay is described individually. The volume, which is copiously illustrated, concludes with the checklist of an exhibition of whaling prints organized by Hall.

1321. Ingalls, Elizabeth. *Whaling Prints in the Francis B. Lothrop Collection.* Salem, Mass.: Peabody Museum, 1987. 341 pp., biblio.

This monumental catalog describes and illustrates just over 600 prints. Introductory text provides information on Lothrop as a collector, an overview of the importance of whaling prints as documents, the publication of them, the derivitive nature of some of the iconography as scenes were copied and recopied, and the history of whaling. The catalog itself is divided by topic and by nationality. American prints form an important proportion of the whole. The bibliography includes books containing whaling prints and images as well as books and articles useful to scholars.

1322.———. "Amerian Whaling Prints: Copied From European Sources" in *American Maritime Prints*, 207–225. ed. Elton W. Hall. New Bedford, Mass.: The Old Dartmouth Historical Society, 1985.

Despite the importance of the whaling industry, there are few prints relating to it; whalemen were not artists and American artists did not go whaling. Three American firms—Currier & Ives, Baillie, and the Kelloggs—produced prints that focused on the romance and perils of whaling, not on accurate depictions. Also, they reproduced imported prints to satisfy the demand for images. Ingalls has identified many sources for American prints and traces them as one firm copied work of another.

1323. Loring, Augustus P. "The Atlantic Neptune" in *American Maritime Prints*, 1–40. ed. Elton W. Hall. New Bedford, Mass.: The Old Dartmouth Historical Society, 1985.

Since the *Atlantic Neptune*, a collection of 110 charts, forty sheets of views, and twenty pages of text, was published over a thirty year period from 1774 to 1803, the charts and views come in many different states. Loring, a collector, describes the publishing history of the collection and follows several of the charts and views through various states from simple outline plans without much detail to the final states which often became too fussy. A number of the views are compared with photographs by the author to show the extent of distortion of certain natural landforms. The charts, on the other land, are excellent, particularly when compared to what else was available at the end of the eighteenth century.

1324. McCann, E. Armitage. "Ship Prints." *Antiquarian* 4 (July 1925): 17–19, 34, 37.

This article, addressed to collectors, contains several errors in its discussion of processes and artists. Watercolors, drawings, lithographs, engravings, and woodcuts of naval art are all included in the article.

1325. Olds, Irving S. *Bits and Pieces of American History: As Told by a Collection of American Naval and Other Historical Prints and Paintings, Including Portraits of American Naval Commanders and Some Early Views of New York.* New York: 1951. 463 pp., index.

This lavishly produced and illustrated catalog focuses on the early days of the United States Navy, The prints are chronologically arranged according to subject, and each print is carefully described, with information supplied on the event depicted. Five hundred prints, American and European, are included in this catalog of the Olds Collection.

1326.———. *Catalog of a Special Exhibition of the Irving S. Olds Collection of American Prints and Paintings at the Peabody Museum of Salem.* Salem: Peabody Museum, 1959. 61 pp.

The descriptions of the prints and paintings provide special emphasis on the historical context of each of the 203 items in the exhibition.

1327.———. "Early American Naval Prints." *Art in America* 43 (December 1955): 22–29, 54–55.

Olds comments on the genesis of his collection of naval prints, some of the naval battles depicted in the prints, and discusses some of the prints in detail. Most of these are rare, and a few may be unique. This article emphasizes the historical context of these prints, which illustrate early naval battles.

1328. Pool, Eugene H. *'Don't Give Up the Ship:' A Catalog of the Eugene H. Pool Collection of Captain*

James Lawrence. Salem: Peabody Museum, 1942. 82 pp., biblio., index.

This volume opens with a biographical sketch of Captain James Lawrence. The collection includes Lawrence's letters and manuscripts, reprinted in full, personal memorabilia, and relevant prints, paintings, and ship models. The section on prints and paintings is arranged by subject, with portraits and memorial prints listed separately. There is a good description of each print.

1329. Sands, John O. "Amerian Maritime Prints: The Romantic Fallacy" in *American Maritime Prints*, 207–225. ed. Elton W. Hall. New Bedford, Mass.: The Old Dartmouth Historical Society, 1985.

The custom of making ship portraits dates from the eighteenth century and began in the Mediterranean area. The China trade also spawned portraits of American ships. Sands traces the transition from sail to steam as it is mirrored in the prints. Two major firms, Currier & Ives and Endicott and Company, produced the best of the prints. Endicott, however, issued three "different" portraits from one stone. Sands suggests that prints of steamboats are as "romantic" as those of sailing vessels.

1330. Shadwell, Wendy. "Commercial and Job Printing Serving the Maritime Industries" in *American Maritime Prints*, 95–129. ed. Elton W. Hall. New Bedford, Mass.: The Old Dartmouth Historical Society, 1985.

Shadwell's survey of various printed materials for the maritime industries focuses on trade cards, membership certificates, shipping papers, billheads, tickets and passes, and clipper ship cards. A valuable contribution of this essay is the information gathered relating to George F. Nesbitt, the printer of many of these cards and other material as well. Shadwell finds that this commercial printing provides accurate pictorial information about the maritime industries and that this material mirrors the history and development of the United States.

1331. Smith, Edgar Newbold. *American Naval Broadsides: A Collection of Early Naval Prints (1745–1815)*. New York: Clarkson N. Potter for the Philadelphia Maritime Museum, 1974. 225 pp., biblio.

Although the description of each print includes biographical information on the artist, the emphasis is on the events depicted in each print. The catalog is chronologically arranged, with separate chapters devoted to the colonial period, the Revolution, the Quasi-War with France, the Tripoli War, and the War of 1812. Portraits and political cartoons are included, as well as views of naval battles.

1332. Sniffen, Harold S. "Marine Paintings and Prints." in *The Concise Encyclopedia of American Antiques*, 456–70. ed. Helen Comstock. New York: Hawthorn Books, 1958.

The first part of this survey pertains to the United States Navy from 1776 to 1865. Sniffen mentions artists, engravers, and lithographers of many battle scenes and ship portraits. A few English prints, and book and magazine illustrations are included. The second part discusses merchant ships, both sailing and steam vessels, depicted in paintings. Lithographs by Currier & Ives, Henry Robinson, the Endicotts, the Pendletons, Bufford, and others are briefly mentioned.

1333. United States Naval Academy Museum. *American Naval Prints from the Beverley R. Robinson Collection*. Washington: International Exhibitions Foundation, 1976. 121 pp.

Roger B. Stein's introduction discusses the documentary value of these prints, their value as works of art, imagery, their ability to interpret American history. The catalog contains information on 65 prints, all of which were illustrated. European prints were included in this exhibition as were ninteenth-century prints of eighteenth-century battles.

1334. Weitenkampf, Frank. "American Naval Prints." *Print Connoisseur* 2 (June 1922): 284–303.

This chronological survey of naval prints depicting battles begins with an engraving by Henry Dawkins dated 1746. Many specific prints are mentioned, including separately published engravings and lithographs, as well as book and magazine illustrations. Weitenkampf concludes by mentioning a few Civil War lithographs, and then explains that the illustrated magazine, rather than lithographs, became the major source for illustrations of newsworthy events after 1860.

1335. Wilson, Claggett. "Jack Afloat and Susan Ashore." *Antiques* 42 (July 1942): 22–23.

This article records the response to the enthusiastic demand for prints of the United States Navy in the first half of the nineteenth century. Most of the prints illustrated reflect the sentimentality of the Victorian era, showing tender adieus and joyous reunions. A number of these lithographs are mentioned; Nathaniel Currier, Kellogg and Comstock, and James Baillie are among those who published them. Currier also produced prints showing sailors at sea; these can be helpful for the documentation of naval uniforms of the 1840s and 1850s.

1336. Wisendanger, Martin W. "The Story Back of Naval Prints." *Prints* 8 (December 1937): 81–89.

The author recounts the history behind several prints produced during the Quasi-War with France, the Tripolitan campaign in 1804, the War of 1812, and the Civil War. Naval prints depicting battle scenes ceased after the Spanish-American War.

Military Prints

1337. *The Civil War: A Centennial Exhibition.* Washington: National Gallery of Art, 1961. 150 pp., biblio.

This catalog of 281 items by 35 artists contains useful information on pictorial journalism of the Civil War and the role of the special artist. Many of the drawings in the catalog were designed for publication and they are often accompanied by extensive quotes from the appropriate issue. The catalog includes useful biographical information on the artists who include Theodore R. Davis, Winslow Homer, Francis Schell, Alfred and William Waud, among others.

1338. Bishop, Alison. "Civil War Sketches." *Boston Public Library Quarterly* 4 (January 1952): 27–33.

Winslow Homer's *Campaign Sketches* and A.J. Volck's *Sketches from the Civil War in North America* are the subject of this study. The author discusses the subject matter of both sets of prints. Adalbert John Volck was a Baltimore dentist who tried to do for the South what Homer and cartoonists had done for the North. Volck printed thirty etchings. The Boston Public Library has a complete set of both publications.

1339. Carbonell, John. "Prints of the Battle of New Orleans" in *Prints of the American West*, 1–12. ed. Ron Tyler. Fort Worth: Amon Carter Musuem of Western Art, 1983.

Carbonell introduces his subject by providing background on the War of 1812 and the Battle of New Orleans. He then goes on to discuss prints of the battle itself. The most accurate one is by the French engraver Philibert-Louis Débucourt after Hyacinthe Laclotte; other depictions are more superficial. Multiple states of prints by Joseph Yeager and Francisco Scacki are discussed after which Carbonell focuses on a print of the battle by John Landis dated 1840 which he derived from a panorama he painted and exhibited.

1340. Cook, William C. "The Early Iconography of the Battle of New Orleans, 1815–1819." *Tennessee Historical Quarterly* 48, no. 4 (1989): 218–237.

Cook focuses on the years immediately following the Battle of New Orleans because in this short period the most important prints appeared. He examines book illustrations, prints, battle plans, textiles, and other media and describes the images in each category. A checklist describing the various states of each print presents the bibliographical information after the essay. Cook has provided locations for each item in public collections.

1341. Drepperd, Carl W. "Selling Jackson's Great Victory." *Antiques* 38 (November 1940): 220–21.

Several different engravings exist of the Battle of New Orleans. Drepperd cites documentation for the one engraved by J. Yaeger of Philadelphia. A copy of the print, once owned by the publisher, is reproduced along with the manuscript prospectus, the list of subscribers, and the prices. All three states of the engraving are carefully described, and Drepperd notes that a large group of the third-state proofs had been stored in an attic until 1897, later sold *en bloc* in 1925. Such documentation on a historical print is rare.

1342.———. "Three Battles of New Orleans." *Antiques* 14 (August 1928): 129–31.

Drepperd describes three contemporary folio prints depicting the Battle of New Orleans. Although he errs in his notes on the print engraved by J. Yaeger [*see Antiques* (Nov. 1940)], the other prints are well described. Since it is rare to find the three prints juxtaposed, the illustrations in this article are a helpful reference tool.

1343. Garrett, Rev. Edwin Atlee, III. "William Massey Huddy, 1807–1846: Artist, Soldier, Publisher, and Lithographer." *Military Collector & Historian* 25, no. 1 (1973): 5–17.

A descendent of Huddy's brother, Garrett provides accurate and interesting information about Huddy, the publisher of the *United States Military Magazine* together with Peter S. Duval from 1839 to 1842. Garrett suggests that the magazine ceased publication because of a fire in the building housing the magazine, difficulties with Albert Newsam, and incompatibility between Huddy and Duval. In his last years, Huddy drew a few lithographs.

1344. Hamilton, Edward P. *The War of 1812.* Boston: Massachusetts Historical Society, 1962. 16 pp.

This collection of twenty prints, illustrated broadsides, and book illustrations depicts various events of the War of 1812. This pamphlet suggests the range of visual material available on the war.

1345. Harwell, Richard. *The War 1861–1865, as Depicted in Prints by Currier & Ives.* Columbus, Ohio: Nationwide Mutual Insurance Co., 1960. 34 pp.

This small booklet traces the progress of the Civil War year by year, using selected prints by Currier & Ives to illustrate outstanding battles and events.

1346. Holzer, Harold, Gabor S. Boritt, and Mark E. Neely Jr. "Every Picture Tells A Different Story: Showing Lee's Surrender—Images of Peace." *Civil War Times Illustrated* 26, no. 3 (May 1987): 22–29.

Although Lee surrendered to Grant inside the McLean House in Appomattox Court House, Virginia, the legend quickly arose that the surrender took place in an apple orchard. The authors provide information on the origins of the story and the lithographs published by firms such as James Queen and

Kurz and Allison that perpetuated the myth. These are contrasted to more realistic portrayals of the event.

1347. John Carter Brown Library. *The French and Indian War: An Album*. Providence, R.I.: Associates of the John Carter Brown Library, 1960. 33 pp.

This pamphlet reproduces a variety of materials relating to the French and Indian War: title pages of pamphlets and books, maps, prints, and portraits. Detailed notes on each item follow the reproductions. Much of the material is rare, providing a unique pictorial guide to the French and Indian War.

1348. Library of Congress. *An Album of American Battle Art, 1775–1918*. Washington, D.C.: Government Printing Office, 1947. 319 pp., index.

The prints in this exhibition catalog are thoroughly documented; excellent historical data on each of the prints is included. Prints from abroad have also been included. There is an index by artist and a detailed table of contents.

1349. National Gallery of Art. *The Civil War. A Centennial Exhibition of Eyewitness Drawings*. Washington, D.C.: National Gallery of Art, 1961. 153 pp.

This loan exhibition of 281 drawings was held to commemerate the Civil War. The exhibition was assembled by William P. Campbell. His essay describes the role of the "special artist" during the Civil War, many of whom worked for the illustrated newspapers such as *Frank Leslie's Illustrated Newspaper*, *Harper's Weekly*, and the *New York Illustrated News*. The essay is well researched and informative. Among the artists included in the catalogue are: Conrad Wise Chapman (1842–1910), Edwin Forbes (1839–1895), Winslow Homer (1836–1910), Arthur Lumley (1837–1912), Frank Vizetelly (English, 1830–1993), Alfred R. Waud (1828–1891).

1350. Parker, Tom. *The Huddy & Duval Prints*. New York: Rampart House, 1955. Unpag.

This volume reproduces some of the text and all of the plates published in the *United States Military Magazine* (Philadelphia: Huddy & Duval, 1839–1842). The preface by Tom Parker provides information on the publication of the lithographs, and the introduction by Anne S. K. Brown gives a brief historical survey of military prints. The original copies of the magazine are scarce, and the plates are very popular.

1351. Pierce, Sally and Temple D. Smith. *Citizens in Conflict. Prints and Photographs of the American Civil War*. Boston: Boston Athenaeum, 1981. 50 pp.

This exhibition catalog contains an essay, "Soldier-Artists of the Civil War," and detailed entries on prints of the Civil War by Sally Pierce. The essay provides an overview of the experiences and works of soldier-artists who generally focused their attentions on views of camps. Few did satirical subjects and some continued to depict the Civil War for many years. The catalog provides biographical information on almost twenty-five printmakers and publishers. It is interesting to be able to compare the contributions of photographers to the documentation of the Civil War.

1352. Sandweiss, Martha A., Rick Stewart, and Ben W. Huseman. *Eyewitness to War. Prints and Daguerreotypes of the Mexican War, 1846–1848*. Fort Worth and Washington: Amon Carter Museum and Smithsonian Institution Press, 1989. 368 pp., index.

The Amon Carter Museum has long collected prints and photographs depicting Mexico and the Mexican War. This handsomely produced and informative volume presents essays by Stewart on artists and printmakers of the War and by Sandweiss on daguerreotypes produced during the War. The catalog of prints and photographs by Huseman presents views of Northern Mexico and the West, daguerreotypes taken during the Mexican War, and prints of the War in central and southern Mexico. This volume provides a thoroughly researched and detailed analysis of the War and its pictorial record.

1353. Thompson, W. Fletcher. *The Image of War: The Pictorial Reporting of the American Civil War*. New York and London: Thomas Yoseloff, 1960. 248 pp., index.

The aims of this volume are twofold: to study the images of the Civil War as created by photographers, illustrators, lithographers, and cartoonists, and to explore how historians can use these images as historical documents. This is a well-considered examination of the subject. Thompson begins, for example, with an analysis of the romantic image of war, a concept perpetuated by printmakers from the Revolution through the Mexican War. The growth of pictorial newspapers, the activities of various illustrators at the outset of the war, and the subsequent role of photographers, illustrators, cartoonists, and lithographers for the duration of the war are carefully analyzed. The final chapter discusses various representations of Lincoln. The documentation for this study is excellent, and the index is very helpful.

1354. Todd, Frederick P. "An Adventure in Military Lithography." *Antiques* (November 1940): 212–14.

William H. Huddy and Peter S. Duval successfully began to publish an illustrated journal in 1839 named the *Military Magazine*. It was handsomely illustrated with lithographs drawn by the best of the Philadelphia lithographers. Todd discusses the establishment and finances of the journal, its lithographs, and its demise in June 1842.

1355.———. "The Huddy & Duval Prints, An Adventure in Military Lithography." *American Military Institute Journal* 3 (1939): 166–76.

Todd discusses William H. Huddy and Peter S. Duval, publishers of the *United States Military Magazine*, which appeared from March 1839 to June 1842. The contents of the magazine are briefly described; the subjects and lithographers of the plates are discussed in greater detail. The article concludes with a list of the plates in each issue and includes a transcription of the legend on each print. This is a useful compilation because, for the most part, the plates are in scattered collections, complete files of the periodical being scarce.

1356. Truesdell, Winfred Porter. "The Mexican War and Its Prints." *Print Connoisseur* 10 and 11 (October 1930; January, April and July 1931): 329–42; 55–78; 97–115; 186–96.

The first article in this series focuses on events leading up to the Mexican War. The second part discusses prints of the different battles, but makes no attempt to assess these prints in terms of their faithfulness to the actual event. The selection of portraits in the third part are limited to those executed during the war. The final section lists books containing illustrations of the war. Most of the prints discussed are lithographs by N. Currier, the Kelloggs, James Baillie, J. Magee, and Sarony & Major.

1357. Tyler, Ronnie C. "The Mexican War: A Lithographic Record." *Southwestern Historical Quarterly* July 1973 (1977): 1–84.

This article, which was also published as a book by the Texas State Historical Association (1973), with an introduction by Stanley R. Ross, examines the historical accuracy of lithographs depicting the Mexican War (1846 to 1848). Fifty prints are reproduced, making this a valuable contribution to the study of military prints of the era.

1358.———. "Prints of the Mexican War as Historical Sources" in *American Printmaking Before 1876, Fact, Fiction, and Fantasy*, 61–71. Washington, D.C.: Library of Congress, 1975.

Tyler assesses the accuracy of the hundreds of prints of the Mexican War published in the United States. Lithographs published by Nathaniel Currier, for example, were frequently drawn without the benefit of sketches from life. Tyler discusses the use of Mexican war prints by various historians, then identifies those illustrations that could be used as documentary evidence by historians. He notes that others, although inaccurate, are useful as sociological documents.

1359. Weitenkampf, Frank. "American Military Prints." *Print Connoisseur* 6 (March 1921): 254–77.

Weitenkampf discusses more than a hundred military prints depicting uniforms, military groups, and battles that originally appeared as separately published prints, and as book, magazine, and sheet music illustrations. Weitenkampf is less analytical and more descriptive in this article than usual; the large number of descriptions of eighteenth- and nineteenth-century prints are of interest to the collector.

1360. Williams, Hermann Warner. *The Civil War: The Artists' Record*. Washington: The Corcoran Gallery or Art and Museum of Fine Arts, Boston, 1961. 251 pp., index.

The focus of this major publication was the non-professional soldier embroiled in war. Although few of the items are prints, many of the drawings were designed for the pictorial press. The exhibition was arranged by subject—camp scenes, preparing and eating rations, camp discipline, tedium of waiting for battle, recruiting soldiers, the calvary, combat, naval life, illness and death, hearth and home. The volume ends with a descriptive catalog of the items in the exhibition.

1361.———. *Civil War Drawings*. Washington: International Exhibitions Foundation, 1975. unpag.

This modest exhibition catalog discusses a group of drawings owned by the American Heritage Publishing Company. The drawings had been made for a publication of the Century Company, *Battles and Leaders of the Civil War* (1888). Fortunately many of the drawings survived and eventually became the property of American Heritage. Twenty-three artists are represented in the catalog of 100 items. Among the artists singled out for recognition are Edwin Forbes, Theodore Russell Davis, Francis H. Schell, James E. Taylor, William and Alfred R. Waud. Two Confederate artists mentioned are Allen Carter Redwood and William L. Sheppard.

1362. Wunderlich, Rudolf. "The Civil War in Prints." *Kennedy Quarterly* 2 (May 1961): 89–147.

This catalog of over four hundred prints about the Civil War offered for sale by the Kennedy Galleries is a handy reference list on the topic. Arranged by subject—battles, portraits, cartoons, camps, ships—the prints are nearly all separately published lithographs. Illustrations such as wood engravings from magazines are not included.

Political Prints

1363. "America in a Mirror: Caricature as History." *The Quarto* 1, no. 3 (April 1995): 1–13.

This brief history of caricature in the United States from colonial times through the 1930s also notes the usefulness of political prints in historical research. The article reproduces rare and interesting examples from the important collection at the Clements Library of the University of Michigan. The collection includes illustrations from books and periodicals as well as separately published prints.

1364. "The Limits of Caricature." *The Nation* 3 (19 July 1866): 55.

This interesting essay criticizes caricature for its malicious nature. In reference to political satire of the Civil War, the writer believed that "the Federal generals and Statesmen were, as a rule, rendered quite as ridiculous as the Confederate magnates.".

1365. Altschuler, Glenn C. and Stuart M. Blumin. "'Where is the Real America?' Politics and Popular Consciousness in the Antebellum Era." *American Quarterly* 49, no. 2 (June 1997): 225–267.

This essay presents an interesting examination of popular prints and periodical illustrations in a discussion of political engagement in antebellum America. Of particular interest are the political prints of Currier & Ives that present a form of "visual fiction" similar to novels. The authors also examined *Gleason's Drawing Room Companion*, *Frank Leslie's Illustrated Newspaper*, and *Harper's Weekly* in their attempt to discover the level of popular participation in American politics.

1366. American Antiquarian Society, and Worcester Art Musuem. *An Exhibition of American Political Caricature, 1765–1865*. Worcester: 1937. 22 pp.

This leaflet lists the seventy-seven prints in the exhibition jointly sponsored by the American Antiquarian Society and the Worcester Art Museum. The American Antiquarian Society holds a typescript which contains the explanatory material used on the exhibition labels.

1367. Appel, John, and Selma Appel. "Pat-Riots to Patriots: St. Patrick's Day in American Cartoons and Caricature." *The Critic* (1989): 36–52.

The Appels provide a survey of caricature relating to Irish immigrants from the mid-nineteenth century through the 1920s and 1930s. The annual St. Patrick's Day celebration in New York was often marred by violence and the Appels inquire into the origins of the riots and other disputes between the Irish and Protestants.

1368. Barnhill, Georgia B. "Political Cartoons of New England, 1812–61" in *Prints of New England*, 83–104. ed. Georgia Brady Barnhill. Worcester: American Antiquarian Society, 1991.

From 1812 to 1861, about eight hundred political caricatures were published as separate prints in the United States. Fewer than fifty were published in New England in those years, although another ten published in other cities referred to events in New England. This essay focuses on the local affairs that spawned these prints and suggests that political caricature did not flourish because of the absorption of New England in local, not national, affairs. Among the artists who produced these prints are William Charles, Thomas Kensett, and David Claypoole Johnston, certainly the most prolific graphic artist in this genre in the region.

1369. Becker, Stephen. *Comic Art in America*. New York: Simon & Schuster, 1959. 387 pp., index.

The emphasis of this volume is on work of the late nineteenth and twentieth centuries, although the chapters on magazines and on political satire include some information on political caricatures of the late eighteenth and nineteenth centuries. Illustrated periodicals including *Puck*, *Judge*, and *Harper's Weekly*, are described in detail. There is an index for the numerous illustrations, but not for the text.

1370. Bishop, Joseph B. "Early Political Caricature in America." *Century Magazine* 44 (June 1892): 219–31.

Bishop begins with a comparison of American and English caricatures. The author ignores almost all of the American cartoons published before 1852 because of the crudeness in their execution. The emphasis is on the cartoons published by Currier & Ives, a number of which are explained by the author. Thomas Nast and Joseph Keppler are also discussed in detail.

1371. Bivins, Thomas H. "The Body Politic: The Changing Shape of Uncle Sam." *Journalism Quarterly* 64, no. 1 (1987): 13–20.

Bivins looks at the changing physical appearance of Uncle Sam from tall and thin to short and plump over a 150–year period and suggests that cartoonists present their messages partly through body type. In the late twentieth century, the endomorphic Uncle Sam predominates, although Bivins finds that Uncle Sam's image is passing out of use.

1372. Blaisdell, Thomas C. Jr., and Peter Selz. *The American Presidency in Political Cartoons: 1776–1976*. Berkeley: University Art Museum, 1976. 277 pp., biblio.

A general historical background, emphasizing the events depicted in the cartoons, is provided in the introduction to this catalog. Over one hundred prints and drawings are described in detail; the information accompanying each plate includes biographical data on the artist and an analysis of subject matter. The cartoons all relate to American presidents, and almost half date from before 1900. The catalog is arranged by artist and follows a brief bibliography.

1373. British Museum. *Catalogue of Political and Personal Satires*. London: British Museum, 1883. 10 vols.

Compiled by Frederic George Stephens and M. Dorothy George, this scholarly reference work is essential to the study of English and European political caricature of America. The historical context for each print is given in the detailed annotations. A few prints of American origin are included in the volumes dealing with the period of the American Revolution; the work as a whole covers the entire collection in the British Museum up to 1827. This reference work is indispensable for the study of the iconography of political prints of the Revolutionary War era, and most books on English political prints of the late eighteenth century depend on the work of M. Dorothy George. Volumes one to four were compiled by Stephens, and volumes five to ten were compiled by George.

1374. Brown, Bruce. "Two Versions of the *Arkansas Traveler*." *American Collector* 6 (May 1937): 6.

Prints of the *Arkansas Traveler* and *The Turn of the Tune* were published in 1870. Political in nature, they recall Col. Sandford Faulkner's electioneering jaunt through Arkansas in 1840. From 1858 to 1860, E.P. Washburn produced genre paintings on this subject, which were much later published as lithographs by Currier & Ives and John Bufford. The article includes anecdotes on Faulkner's visit to a rural cabin and factual information about the prints themselves.

1375. Bunker, Gary. "Illustrated Periodical Images of Mormons, 1850–1860." *Dialogue* 10, no. 3 (1977): 82–94.

Several events in Mormon country in the 1850s stimulated negative caricatures of Mormons in the popular press. The authors present a variety of illustrations from journals such as *The Lantern*, *Yankee Notions*, *Frank Leslie's Illustrated Newspaper*, *Harper's Weekly*, and *The Old Soldier*. Some of these magazines had circulations of 100,000 copies or more at that time. The authors provide a detailed analysis of the historical context of these caricatures of Mormons in the 1850s.

1376. Bunker, Gary L. "*The Comic News*, Lincoln and the Civil War." *Journal of the Abraham Lincoln Association* 17, no. 1 (1966): 53–87.

London's illustrated weekly, the *Comic News*, contained harsh satires on Lincoln during its short existence, July 1863 to March 1865. During the final six months, the British illustrator Matt Morgan provided a series of important cartoons. Bunker analyzes the images from this magazine and its successor, *The Bubble*, and takes note of work by other British illustrators in these magazines.

1377. Bunker, Gary L., and Davis Bitton. "The Death of Brigham Young: Occasion for Satire." *Utah Historical Quarterly* 54, no. 4 (1986): 358–370.

Bunker and Bitton have complied an excellent array of caricatures on Brigham Young's death and have explored the historical context for this unusual burst of satire in the United States and even in Great Britain over a twenty year period.

1378.———. "Political Caricature and Mormonism" in *Prints of the American West*, 87–103. ed. Ron Tyler. Fort Worth: Amon Carter Museum, 1983.

Part of a larger project which seeks to document all pictorial images dealing with Mormonism between 1830 and 1914, this essay focuses on prints that relate Mormonism and the political scene. Among the issues Bunker and Bitton discuss are the Utah War, anti-polygamy legislation, Supreme Court decisions, the refusal by Congress to seat two Congressmen from Utah, and the grudging acceptance of a Mormon senator after a four-year battle. Among the prints are separately published cartoons by Currier & Ives and many periodical illustrations from journals such as *The Daily Graphic*, *Frank Leslie's Illustrated Newspaper*, *Puck*, and *Judge*.

1379. Burns, Sarah. "Party Animals: Thomas Nast, William Holbrook Beard, and the Bears of Wall Street." *American Art Journal* 30, no. 1 and 2 (1999): 8–35.

Wall Street was the site of occasional pandemonium from the 1850s through the 1870s. Burns addresses both paintings and periodical illustrations that resulted from the lack of order, focusing on Thomas Nast among others, providing information on Wall Street's financial market and analyzing works of contemporaries of Beard and Nast such as A.B. Frost, Matthew Morgan, and E. C. Steele. After the Stock Exchange imposed new regulations at the end of the 1870s, Nast and others had to turn to other subjects.

1380. Bushman, Richard L. "Caricature and Satire in Old and New England Before the American Revolution." *Proceedings of the Massachusetts Historical Society* 88 (1976): 19–34.

Bushman compares political caricature in New England with the art that flourished abundantly on the eve of the American Revolution in England. In an attempt to explain the paucity of the caricature in New England, Bushman discusses English satire and the essay form which, when transplanted to the colonies, became the medium of expression. The greater part of this article concentrates on literary satire, particularly as found in newspapers.

1381. College Art Association. *Catalogue of the Salon of American Humorists: A Political and Social Pageant From the Revolution to the Present Day.* New York: College Art Association, 1933. 95 pp.

This exhibition included four hundred cartoons ranging in time from 1754--when Benjamin Franklin's "Unite or Die" print was published—to 1933. The exhibition was assembled to show the development of political prints as an art form. William Murrell's brief foreword provides an outline of the history of political satire. There are notes on both individual artists and on the historical background of the prints.

1382. Cook, Karen Severud. "Benjamin Franklin and the Snake that would not Die" in *Images & Icons of the New World*, 88–111. Cambridge, England: The British Library, 1996.

Cook reads Benjamin Franklin's famous segmented snake cartoon that appeared in the *Pennsylvania Gazette* in 1754 as a map and relates it to other political prints and designs of a similar nature through the Civil War. Although this may seem far-fetched, the segments of the snake are given geographical designations and these run in order from north to south. The essay is extensively documented.

1383. Craven, Thomas. *Cartoon Cavalcade*. New York: Simon & Schuster, 1943. 456 pp., index.

Although a survey of American social and political cartoons of the twentieth century, this anthology has an opening chapter devoted to the late nineteenth-century precursors of modern cartoons.

1384. Davison, Nancy R. "Andrew Jackson in Cartoon and Caricature" in *American Printmaking Before 1876, Fact, Fiction, and Fantasy*, 20–24. Washington, D.C.: Library of Congress, 1975.

Jackson was one of the most colorful and controversial political figures of his day. Davison traces his political career from the War of 1812 through the 1844 election. Themes and symbols which frequently recurred in depictions of Jackson are described. No illustrations accompany this article, but most of the cartoons mentioned can be found in large print collections, or in other books on political cartoons.

1385. Dolmetsch, Joan D. "Political Satires at Colonial Williamsburg" in *Eighteenth-Century Prints in Colonial America. To Educate and Decorate*, 175–196. ed. Joan D. Dolmetsch. Williamsburg: Colonial Williamsburg Foundation, 1979.

After discussing collectors of political prints in the eighteenth century, Dolmetsch describes the collection formed by H. Dunscombe Colt in the twentieth century that was acquired by Colonial Williamsburg in 1960. A sampling of those prints whose style was influential and those whose delineation was particularly well done are discussed in chronological order from 1740 to the conclusion of the American Revolution.

1386. Dupuy, Pascal. "The French Revolution in American Satirical Prints." *Print Quarterly* 15, no. 4 (1998): 371–384.

A French scholar, Dupuy explores in a well illustrated article the reaction of American graphic artists to the French Revolution. He was able to locate sixteen prints which he carefully analyzes. He finds that English influences give way to an autonomous expression on the part of American artists such as James Akin, and others who anonymously produced their satires.

1387. Field, Ruth K. "Early Political Cartoons." *Bulletin of the Missouri Historical Society* 25 (October 1968): 31–34.

Eight cartoons from the Missouri Historical Society's picture collection are reproduced in this article, spanning the years from 1828 to 1856. Although the text accompanying the reproductions contains some minor inaccuracies, the article is helpful for its information on the scope of the collection.

1388. Fischer, Roger A. *Them Damned Pictures: Explorations in American Political Cartoon Art*. North Haven, Conn.: Archon Books, 1996. 253 pp., biblio., index.

Pictorial political satire of the period 1870 to 1900 is the subject of this book. Among the artists whose works are analyzed are Thomas Nast, Joseph Keppler, Bernhard Gillam, and Grant Hamilton. Their work appeared in popular magazines such as *Harper's Weekly*, *Puck*, and *Judge*. After a general survey of the genre, Fischer examines caricatures of aliens (foreignors and African Americans), native Americans, and iconography derived from the Statue of Liberty, Abraham Lincoln, and Lucifer. In these chapters, contemporary American caricatures are juxtaposed with those of the late nineteenth century. The book is generously illustrated and is a valuable reference work.

1389.———. "The 'Monumental' Lincoln as an American Cartoon Convention." *Inks. Cartoon and Comic Art Studies* 2, no. 1 (February 1995): 12–25.

This well researched and thoughtful analysis of images of Abraham Lincoln in a variety of cartoons of the nineteenth and twentieth centuries includes Lincoln as portrayed by Currier & Ives, John Tenniel, and others after the assassination as he became an American icon in the last quarter of the ninteenth century.

1390.———. "Rustic Rasputin: William A. Peffer in Color Cartoon Art, 1891–1899." *Kansas History* 11, no. 4 (1988): 222–39.

Kansas Populist William Alfred Peffer served in the U.S. Senate from 1891 to 1897. During that period, he appeared in over sixty cartoons in *Puck* and *Judge*, a selection of which are carefully analyzed by Fischer who points out that seldom was a single figure so consistently misrepresented.

1391.———. "William Windom. Cartoon Centerfold, 1881–1891." *Minnesota History* 51, no. 3 (1988): 99–109.

William Windom was a Republican congressman, senator, and secretary of the treasury. Fischer takes a close look at cartoons that appeared in *Judge* and *Puck* concerning this Minnesota politician, one of the few from the mid-west to receive so much attention by political satirists.

1392. Fleming, E. McClung. "The American Image As Indian Princess, 1765–1783." *Winterthur Portfolio* 2 (1965): 65–81.

Fleming identifies five stages in the evolution of the allegorical figure used to represent "America," with emphasis on the prints in which the Indian figure appeared. Examples of both European and American origin are considered.

1393.———. "From Indian Princess to Greek Goddess: The American Image, 1783–1815." *Winterthur Portfolio* 3 (1967): 37–66.

The author continues his study of the symbolic representation of "America," drawing heavily from the graphic arts. This iconographic discussion is of great interest, touching on several allegorical prints published in the United States during the period considered, and on the importance of personifications to the young nation.

1394.———. "Symbols of the United States: From Indian Queen to Uncle Sam" in *Frontiers of American Culture*, 1–24. ed Ray B. Browne. Lafayette, Ind.: Purdue University Studies, 1968.

In this essay, Fleming studies six major images of the United States: The Indian Princess, the Neoclassic Plumed Goddess, American Liberty, Columbia, Brother Jonathan, and Uncle Sam. These symbolic figures were used primarily in the graphic arts, but also in decorative objects and paintings. Fleming treats these iconographic themes chronologically beginning with 1765 and ending in 1877.

1395. Halsey, R. T. Haines. "Impolitical Prints: The American Revolution as Pictured by Contemporary English Caricaturists—An Exhibition." *Bulletin of the New York Public Library* 43 (November 1939): 759–829.

This exhibition included one hundred and fifty British cartoons relating to the American Revolution and the preceding events. Each cartoon is described and given its historical background. The introduction provides a general discussion of the prints and of the history of the era.

1396.———. *The Boston Port Bill as Pictured by a Contemporary London Cartoonist.* New York: Grolier Club, 1904. 322 pp., index.

Halsey discusses in great detail five humorous mezzotints drawn in response to the Boston Port Bill and published by Robert Sayer and J. Bennett in London in 1774. This well-researched volume is more a history of a complex period than a discussion of prints.

1397.———. "English Sympathy With Boston During the American Revolution." *Old-Time New England* 46 (1956): 85–95.

Political prints depicting the sympathy of the British press toward the American colonies during the American Revolution form the focus of this article. Halsey's "Impolitical Prints" is a more detailed discussion of the subject.

1398. Hancock, LaTouche. "American Caricature and Comic Art." *The Bookman* 16 (October 1902): 263–74.

Statements by the following late nineteenth- and early twentieth-century cartoonists highlight this article: C.G. Bush, Homer Davenport, Frederick Burr, Opper, Charles Nelan, Walt McDougall, T.E. Powers, R.F. Outcault, James Swinnerton, C. Marriner, Leon Barritt, C.S. Rigby, E.M. Howarth, T.S. Allen, Frank M. Kelly, Dan Smith, George Herriman, Gene Carr, Max de Lipman, C. Haydon Jones, Kate Carew, Frank Crane, Archie Gunn, Louis Dalrymple, Dan McCarthy, and Carl Schultze. The comments of these artists provide insights into their working habits.

1399. Hatcher, James Brush. "The Patriotic Envelope in Civil War Days." *American Collector* 12 (May 1943): 12–13.

Just before and during the Civil War, envelopes with patriotic illustrations and mottoes flourished in both the north and south. Hatcher describes a variety of the envelopes, which featured portraits. flags, battle scenes, memorials, and cartoons of the war.

1400. Helfand, William H. *Medicine & Pharmacy in American Political Prints (1765–1870).* Madison, Wis.: American Institute of the History of Pharmacy, 1978. 84 pp., biblio.

The prints in this interesting iconographic study are arranged by topic: diagnosis, examination, types of illness, medical procedures, systems of medicine, drugs and pharmacy, and administration of drugs. Foreign influences and the social role of the medical professions are also discussed briefly. Each print is accompanied by explanatory notes. The author compiled a chronological list of illustrations which is useful as well as a list of Civil War envelopes decorated with medical motifs.

1401.———. "The Medical Theme in American Political Prints." *Imprint* 5, no. 1 (1980): 2–8.

Through the analysis of medical imagery in political cartoons, Helfand explores the intensity of popular political sentiment and the practice of medicine, dentistry, and pharmacology in the eighteenth and nineteenth centuries. Helfand's survey covers the period from Paul Revere through Thomas Nast.

1402.———. "The Physician in Political Caricature." *Transactions and Studies of the College of Physicians of Philadelphia* 12, no. 4 (1990): 445–474.

The iconography of the physician and patient in British and American political caricature is the subject Helfand's interesting study. Appended to the text is a list of sixty-three prints that form the basis of the article.

1403. Hess, Stephen, and Milton Kaplan. *The Ungentlemanly Art: A History of American Political Cartoons*. New York: Macmillan Co., 1968. 252 pp., biblio., index.

Hess and Kaplan concentrate on cartoons of the nineteenth century. A large number of caricatures, including lithographs, magazine and newspaper illustrations, are reproduced. The section of notes and plates is unnecessarily complicated in its arrangement limiting its usefulness.

1404. Hess, Stephen and Sandy Northrup. *Drawn & Quartered: The History of American Political Cartoons*. Montgomery, Alabama: Elliott & Clark Publishng, 1996. 164 pp., biblio., index.

The authors devote the first half of this book to eighteenth- and nineteenth-century political prints, beginning with Benjamin Franklin's "Join, or Die" device that appeared in 1754. The authors include a range of separately published prints and illustrations from topical magazines. There are interesting juxtapositions of twentieth-century caricatures with earlier images demonstrating a continuity in the use of symbols, such as Uncle Sam and Liberty.

1405. Jeansonne, Glen. "Goldbugs, Silverites, and Satirists: Caricature and Humor in the Presidential Election of 1896." *Journal of American Culture* 11, no. 2 (1988): 1–8.

The 1896 presidential campaign between William Jennings Bryan and William McKinley was accompanied by millions of pieces of propaganda distributed by McKinley's strategists. The Populists struck back. Jeansonne provides excellent commentary on the campaign and the use of pictorial satire.

1406. Jones, Michael Wynn. *The Cartoon History of the American Revolution*. New York: G.P. Putnam's Sons, 1975. 191 pp., biblio.

This profusely illustrated book provides a history of the American Revolution. The text gives factual information on the period, and the lengthy captions relate the cartoons to specific episodes of the war. Unfortunately the quality of the reproductions is uneven. Many of the cartoons are book and periodical illustrations, but the titles of the publications they appeared in are not given. Although Jones acknowledges the institutions that aided him in his research, he does not credit the illustrations individually to the institutions housing them. This substantially reduces the usefulness of this work to scholars and curators. Jones is to be thanked, however, for including brief notes on each of the engravers represented.

1407. Kelly, James C. and Lovell, B. S. "Thomas Jefferson. His Friends and Foes." *Virginia Magazine of History and Biography* 101, no. 1 (January 1993): 133–157.

In 1993, the year that marked the 250th anniversary of Jefferson's birth, the Virginia Historical Society mounted an exhibition for which this article serves as the catalog. In it are reproduced portraits of Jefferson and several of his friends as well as rare political caricatures of Jefferson. The historical backgrounds of these prints are thoroughly described. Having these prints well reproduced in a single publication is a great service.

1408. Keyes, Willard E. "The Cow and the Sleeping Lion." *Antiques* 39 (January 1941): 25–27.

Keyes discusses the imagery of a well known political print, "A Picturesque View of the State of the Nation for February 1778," published in the *Westminister Magazine*, Feb. 1778. The cow, representing British commerce, is slyly milked by a Dutchman, with representatives of other nations aiding and abetting him. The lion, symbol of British authority, dozes quietly. Keyes discusses other versions of the print, and discloses that the imagery stems from a print published in 1670. During the embargo of the early nineteenth century, the print re-emerges on Liverpool pottery, presumably based on a design of James Akin. This is an excellent analysis of one of the most popular prints of the Revolutionary era.

1409. Kirkland, Frederick R. "An Unknown Franklin Cartoon." *Pennsylvania Magazine of History and Biography* 73 (January 1949): 76–79.

Benjamin Franklin designed at least three political prints. The earliest appeared in the pamphlet "Plain Truth," published in 1747, in which Franklin urges citizens of Pennsylvania to prepare for their own defense. "The Join or Die" cut appeared in the *Pennsylvania Gazette* of May 1754, and was reproduced elsewhere in several variations. Among the Franklin papers, acquired by the Historical Society of Pennsylvania in the late 1940s, is an engraving, *Magna Britannia her Colonies Reduced*. A similar print appeared in the December 1768, issue of the *The Political Register*. Franklin used the cartoon as a calling card in England, and was known to have given copies of it to each member of Parliament.

1410. Korshak, Yvonne. "The Liberty Cap as a Revolutionary Symbol in America and France." *Smithsonian Studies in American Art* 1, no. 2 (1987): 52–70.

The author traces the use and meaning of the Liberty Cap in a variety of media, focussing on prints of the revolutionary era. The use of the cap declined in the post-revolutionary era, although it remained as an element in coins throughout the nineteenth century.

1411. Le Corbeiller, Clare. "Miss America and Her Sisters: Personifications of the Four Parts of the

World." *Metropolitan Museum of Art Bulletin* 19 (April 1961): 209–223.

The collection of James Hazen Hyde, left to the Metropolitan Museum as a bequest in 1959, is featured in this article. Hyde collected personifications of the four continests as found in European decorative arts. "America" is one of the four figures, and its iconography is traced in European prints, porcelain, plates, medals, and textiles. "America" was also widely used in American prints, which gives particular value to this interesting study.

1412. Lorant, Stefan. *The Presidency: A Pictorial History of Presidential Elections from Washington to Truman*. New York: Macmillan Co., 1951. 775 pp., biblio., index.

This volume, a pictorial history, contains no information on the artists. It is a gold mine of illustrations, however, including many nineteenth-century political prints taken from magazines and newspapers. The sources for those illustrations are identified whenever possible.

1413. Mastin, Caroline L. *'Am I Not a Man and a Brother?'*. Wellesley, Mass.: Wellesley College Museum, 1970. 18 pp., biblio.

This exhibition featured over sixty prints providing varying attitudes towards African Americans in the nineteenth century. The introduction explores various meanings of the word "black" and the creation of stereotypes. The exhibition illustrates the prejudices of the nineteenth century and suggests that printed imagery promoted racial prejudice.

1414. Matthews, Albert. "The Snake Devices, 1754–1776, and the *Constitutional Courant*, 1765." *Transactions of the Colonial Society of Massachusetts* 11 (December 1907): 409–453.

Snake devices became prominent symbols three times during the colonial era: before the Albany Congress of 1754, during the Stamp Act Crisis, and just before the outbreak of the Revolution. Matthews points out the many inaccurate statements made about the image and provides a detailed chronicle of its use, setting it in its historical context. The *Constitutional Courant*, a broadside published in 1765 in response to the Stamp Act, employed the snake device. Matthews discusses its publisher and place of publication, verification of which had led to debate throughout the nineteenth century. The article concludes with descriptions of snake devices used on various newspaper mastheads in 1774 and 1775. This study is exceedingly well documented and researched.

1415. Maurice, Arthur Bartlett, and Frederic Taber Cooper. *The History of the Nineteenth Century in Caricature*. New York: Dodd, Mead & Co., 1904. 363 pp.

The treatment of German, French, and English caricature in this book furnishes important background for the chapters on American caricature. Examples of American caricature, inspired by the Mexican War, the Civil War, the political campaigns of 1880 and 1884, and American parties and platforms, are included in this well-illustrated volume, as are many cartoons by Thomas Nast.

1416. McDonald, Robert M. S. "Race, Sex, and Reputation: Thomas Jefferson and the Sally Hemings Story." *Southern Cultures* 4, no. 2 (1998): 46–63.

One of the most vitriolic cartoons of Thomas Jefferson was *A Philosophic Cock*, an aquatint by James Akin. This essay discusses the role of politics and fears of miscegenation that circulated around Jefferson's alleged liason with his slave Sally Hemings, particularly the role played by James Thomson Callender.

1417. McVay, Georgianne. "Yankee Fanatics Unmasked: Cartoons on the Burning of a Convent." *Records of the American Catholic Historical Society of Pennsylvania* 83 (September 1972): 159–68.

The burning of the Ursuline Convent in Charlestown, Mass., was part of a wave of anti-Catholicism. The author discusses the event and a series of eleven cartoons by D.C. Johnston, published in his *Scraps* for 1835, criticizing the incident. These interesting cartoons reveal religious attitudes of the nineteenth century. The study has been well-researched, and is documented from contemporary accounts.

1418. Mitchell, John Ames. "Contemporary American Caricature." *Scribner's Magazine* 6 (December 1889): 728–45.

This well-illustrated article surveys American caricature published in periodicals from the Civil War through the 1880s. Mitchell focuses his attention on Joseph Keppler and other artists associated with *Puck*, the sympathetic drawings of blacks by W.L. Sheppard and E.W. Kemble, and *Life's* cartoonist, W.A. Rogers. Many observations about America and its society are made, such as the desire for an intellectual art, or art with an idea. F.G. Attwood, M.A. Woolf, Oliver Herford, Frank and F.P.W. Bellew, and Charles Dana Gibson are among those whose work is illustrated and discussed.

1419. Murrell, William. *A History of American Graphic Humor*. New York: Whitney Museum of American Art, 1933. 2 vols., index.

Murrell's profusely illustrated work is still the standard exposition of American political satire, caricature, and humor in the graphic arts. A revision that includes a more thorough bibliography and more analytic discussions of individual artists would be welcome.

1420.———. "The Rise and Fall of Cartoon Symbols." *The American Scholar* 4 (1935): 306–315.

Murrell discusses cartoon symbols of political parties current before the advent of the Republican elephant, the Democratic donkey, and the Tammany Tiger. The "Join or Die" design by Benjamin Franklin, the devil, Columbia, the American eagle, the Gerrymander, and Uncle Sam are among the popular symbols whose histories are traced.

1421. Neely, Mark E., Jr., Harold Holzer, and Gabor S. Borritt. *The Confederate Image: Prints of the Lost Cause*. Chapel Hill and London: University of North Carolina Press, 1987. 257 pp., index.

The authors have collected the images that "served to revive and sustain Southern identity after the collapse of the Confederacy" (p. xiii). Prior to the Civil War, there were few print makers or print publishers in the south. Baltimore was part of the Union during the war and New Orleans fell to the union Navy in April 1862. The Confederate government had to import lithographic material and lithographers from Great Britain to make currency. There were, therefore, few Confederate prints until after the war when northern publishers celebrated southern heros and commemorated battles and places.

1422.———. "The Confederate Image: Prints of the Lost Cause." *Imprint* 12, no. 1 (1987): 2–12.

This article discusses images published in the Confederate States of America during the Civil War. The authors point out that Adalbert Volck's prints were actually issued from Union territory and discuss some fallacies inherent in those prints. Several of the Appomattox prints are analyzed as are portraits of Robert E. Lee, Jefferson Davis, and other military figures.

1423. Nevins, Allan, and Frank Weitenkampf. *A Century of Political Cartoons: Caricature in the United States From 1800 to 1900*. New York: Charles Scribner's Sons, 1944, 190 pp.

The introductory essay, providing a survey of American political cartoons, is followed by reproductions of one hundred prints. Extensive commentary on the historical context of each cartoon is included. The selection is excellent, and the commentaries help illuminate the meanings of the cartoons.

1424. Olson, Lester C. *Emblems of American Community in the Revolutinary Era*. Washington: Smithsonian Institution Press, 1991. 306 pp., index.

In a well researched and illustrated book, Olson examines the use of emblems to depict the American colonies. Chapters discuss the depiction of the colonies as a snake, as Indian, as children, and assesses the use of other imagery. His sources include book and periodical illustrations, newspapers, currency, medals, and separately published prints. A chapter of this book was published in the Autumn 1992 issue of *Imprint* (vol. 17, no. 2).

1425. Oveson, Catharine S. "Civil War Envelopes." *Antiques* (June 1928): 490–92.

At the beginning of the Civil War, envelopes with political and satirical illustrations were printed. Although a few envelopes may have been published in the South, most of them were printed in 1861 in northern cities. The author supposes that after 1861 the war became too serious an issue to be used for pictorial puns. The various types of illustrations which appeared are discussed, and the author quotes some of the verses and jokes used.

1426. Palumbo, Anne Cannon. "Averting 'Present Commotions' History as Politics in *Penn's Treaty*." *American Art* 9, no. 3 (September 1995): 29–56.

Benjamin West's *William Penn's Treaty with the Indians* was reproduced endlessly from the time it was painted in 1771–2. Palumbo discusses the painting in the context of Anglo-American relations in the early 1770s and relates it to a number of prints, maps, and medals. She convincingly argues the strong relation of the painting to the political passions of the times.

1427. Parsons, Arthur H., Jr. *American Political Cartoons: A Bibliography*. New York: Prints Division, The New York Public Library, 1938.

This typewritten annotated bibliography is divided into two sections. The first lists materials on political caricature, while the second lists books containing collections of cartoons.

1428. Parton, James. *Caricature and Other Comic Arts in All Times and in Many Lands*. New York: Harper Bros., 1877. 340 pp., index.

This is a general survey of caricature from the time of the ancient Egyptians to the third quarter of the nineteenth century. The last two chapters are a general discussion of American caricature. A large portion of this profusely illustrated book appeared in *Harper's Monthly Magazine* during 1875.

1429. Payne, Harold. "Our Caricaturists and Cartoonists." *Munsey's Magazine* 10 (February 1894): 530–535.

Payne provides brief sketches on Joseph Keppler, Bernhard Gillam, Frederick B. Opper, Grant E. Hamilton, Thomas Worth, Thomas Nast, J.A. Woolf, P. Beard, W.A. Rodgers, Charles J. Taylor, Charles Dana Gibson, Frank B.W. Bellew, and some younger cartoonists. Representative cartoons by each of the artists are reproduced.

1430. Penn, Arthur. "The Growth of Caricature." *The Critic* 2 (25 February 1882): 49–50.

This is a brief survey of caricature from ancient times through the nineteenth century, with special emphasis on Thomas Nast.

1431. Peterson, William J. "Cartoons in Presidential Elections." *Palimpsest* (November 1968): 449–540.

This collection of political cartoons emphasizes presidential campaigns of the twentieth century, although Peterson includes illustrations from *Harper's Weekly* and *Frank Leslie's Illustrated Newspaper* from the campaign of 1864. The illustrations are well reproduced, but detailed commentary is not provided.

1432. Preston, Paula Sampson. "The Severed Head of Charles I of England: Its Use as a Political Stimulus." *Winterthur Portfolio* 6 (1970): 1–13.

The tradition of exhibiting the heads of executed political prisoners in England dates to the death of Sir Thomas More. Preston traces the use of the image of the severed head in British political prints relating to colonial America. Patrick Henry made explicit the similarlities in political behavior between Charles I and George III.

1433. Reilly, Bernard F. *American Political Prints, 1766–1876: A Catalog of the Collections in the Library of Congress*. Boston: G.K. Hall & Co., 1991. 638 pp., index, biblio.

Reilly's catalog of political prints is a masterful compilation. The introduction provides an excellent overview of the history of the collection of the Library of Congress, the prints and some of the artists who created them, the importance of prints as documents, the concentration of this form of graphic expression in New York City, and other sources of political imagery. Each of the 758 prints is illustrated and Reilly provides a thorough discussion of the significance of each one. The catalog is arranged chronologically by date of copyright deposit, when known. All text from the prints is transcribed. Included are some sheet music covers, ballots, and campaign banners. There are indices for subject, artists, and titles. This is a superb reference work.

1434. Richardson, Edgar P. "The Birth of Political Caricature" in *Philadelphia Printmaking. American Prints Before 1860*, 70–89. ed. Robert F. Looney. West Chester, Penn.: Tinicum Press, 1976.

Richardson suggests the scarcity of political caricature in the American colonies was due to economics of producing and selling them in a limited market. In this article he provides the historical and political background for a series of prints issued in Philadelphia during the 1750s and 1760s when the frontier was besieged by Indians and the frontier looked to the government in Philadelphia for assistance. Two aspects of these cartoons were of particular importance for the future: the introduction of well-observed portraits and the "device of placing the characters in real, but ridiculous, situations." These joined the use of allegory and symbol in the vocabulary of political caricaturists.

1435.———. "Four American Political Prints." *American Art Journal* 6 (November 1974): 36–44.

This is a reassessment of the interpretation of three caricatures relating to the American Revolution, previously thought to be English. A fourth cartoon from a New York newspaper is published here for the first time. Richardson's treatment is scholarly, and his attributions are well substantiated.

1436.———. "Stamp Act Cartoons in the Colonies." *Pennsylvania Magazine of History and Biography* 96 (July 1972): 275–97.

This detailed analysis of seven English and American cartoons published in the wake of the Stamp Act describes one cartoon by John Singleton Copley and another by Benjamin Franklin. A third cartoon was first published in England, then copied by Wilkinson, a Philadelphia engraver. The cartoons discussed are exceedingly rare and infrequently reproduced.

1437. Rogers, W. A. "Recollections of A Harper's Weekly Cartoonist." *Harper's Weekly* 51 (5 January 1907): 21–23.

Rogers began as a "special artist" for *Harper's* during the heyday of wood engraving. Using this medium to report news events was a specialty of the late 1870s. The value of the article lies mainly in the anecdotes it contains.

1438. Serio, Anne Marie. *Political Cartoons in the 1848 Election Campaign*. Washington: Smithsonian Institution Press, 1972. 21 pp., biblio.

Nine political cartoons issued during the 1848 presidential campaign are in the Harry T. Peters America on Stone Collection in the National Museum of American History. This study provides excellent historical background on the election and on each of the cartoons. The author emphasizes the history of the period, but gives some information on the lithographers as well.

1439. Shadwell, Wendy. "Britannia in Distress." *American Book Collector* 7, no. 3 (March 1986): 11–22.

This article surveys British caricature relating to America from 1778 to the conclusion of peace in 1783.

1440. Shaw, Albert. *Abraham Lincoln, His Path to the Presidency*. New York: Review of Reviews, 1929. 236 pp., index.

Included in this volume, a history of Lincoln's political career up to his bid for the presidency in 1860, is a wide selection of political cartoons published between 1824 and 1860. There is some information provided on each cartoon, although the work does not deal primarily with prints.

1441.———. *Abraham Lincoln: The Year of His Election*. New York: Review of Reviews, 1929. 277 pp., index.

Like Shaw's history of Lincoln's path to the presidency, this volume does not focus primarily on prints. However, the profuse illustrations, many of them cartoons and caricatures, are clearly explained, making the work useful for the historian of political cartoons.

1442. Sheppard, Alice. *Cartooning for Suffrage*. Albuquerque: University of New Mexico Press, 1994. 276 pp., biblio., index.

Sheppard provides a coherent and well-researched analysis of cartoons about the suffrage movement in the second half of the nineteenth century and the first part of the twentieth. Beginning with images antagonistic to woman's suffrage, she turns to suffrage cartoonists, a group of women who used their art to shape public opinion. This book provides excellent information on the history of caricature, its imagery, language, and meaning, as well as background on the suffrage movement.

1443. Sink, Brenna Maloney. "Abraham Lincoln & the Political Cartoon." *Lincoln Herald* 97 (December 1995): 154–164.

Sink surveys political cartoons of Abraham Lincoln from 1860 to 1865, introducing her subject with a persuasive discussion of the importance of political cartoons in historical research and analysis. Sink accumulated 182 cartoons from a variety of sources for her study, including images from popular magazines as well as separately published prints. She notes that in England Matthew Somerville Morgan and Sir John Tenniel were particularly vicious in their attacks on the American president. The essay is arranged thematically.

1444. Smith, Kristen M. *The Lines are Drawn. Political Cartoons of the Civil War*. Athens, Georgia: Hill Street Press, 1999. 155 pp.

The foreword by Emory M. Thomas provides a brief introduction to the history of editorial cartoons in newspapers comparing the work of sketch artists to photographers of the era. Smith (a cartoonist herself) introduces some of the publishers and artists and discusses the use of stereotypes in her introduction. Sources for the cartoons include publications such as *Harper's Weekly*, *Southern Illustrated News*, *New York Illustrated News*, *Punch*, and *Frank Leslie's Illustrated Newspaper*. Several seprately published prints are also reproduced. The captions to each of the cartoons interprets the meaning of the images and notes the artist.

1445. Smylie, James H. "Presbyterians and the Cartoonists: A Pictorial Lampoon, 1884–1898." *Journal of Presbyterian History* 50, no. 3 (September 1972): 171–86.

A very brief note introduces cartooning in the post-Civil War era focusing on the publications *Puck* and *Judge*. Eighteen cartoons, all focusing on Presbyterians, are reproduced with extensive commentary.

1446. Sommer, Frank H., III. "Emblem and Device: The Origin of the Great Seal of the United States." *Art Quarterly* (1961): 57–76.

Sommer provides a scholarly investigation into the sources of the Great Seal of the United States in the emblem books of Francis Quarles and Jacob Cats, as well as in gravestones. Benjamin Franklin, printer of the first book of devices to be published in America, depended on such a work for his famous "Join or Die" cartoon. This article is important for the light it sheds on emblematic sources of American cartoons, as well as on the representation of symbols in the colonies. It also examines in detail the history of the Great Seal design.

1447.———. "Thomas Hollis and the Arts of Dissent" in *Prints in and of American to 1850*, 111–60. ed. John D. Morse. Winterthur, Del.: Henry Francis du Pont Winterthur Museum, 1970.

In the generation preceeding the Revolution, there was an interesting interplay between Thomas Hollis III and Thomas Hollis V in England and dissenters in Massachusetts. Sommer discusses the resulting expression of this interplay in paintings, prints, and coins. The article deals with the political and artistic climate of Boston in pre-Revolutionary days.

1448. Swasey, Charles A. G. *American Caricatures Pertaining to the Civil War: Reproduced From the Original Lithographs Published From 1856 to 1872*. New York: Brentano's, 1918. 6 pp., 80 plates.

This book presents a collection of eighty lithographed political cartoons issued by Currier & Ives between 1856 and 1872, documenting one of the major productions of this prolific firm. The first edition of this volume, published in 1892 by Wright and Swasey in New York, lacks the brief introduction found in the 1918 volume, which contains a history of the period.

1449. Sweeney, Erin Michaela. "The Patriotic Ladies of Edenton, North Carolina: The Layers of Gray in a Black-and-White Print." *Imprint* 23, no. 2 (1998): 20–24.

One British mezzotint that has long fascinated scholars is *A Society of Patriotic Ladies at Edenton in North Carolina* published by Robert Sayer and John Bennett in 1775. Sweeney analyses the economic, political, and social motives behind the publication of this print that shows women of Edenton signing a petition against the importation of British goods and the consumption of tea. In spite of its ostensibly pro-American sentiment, Sweeney points out aspects of the image that make its meaning ambiguous.

1450. Tatham, David. "The Half Horse-Half Alligator and Other Southern Members of the Jacksonian Bestiary: A Study in American Iconography" in *Graphic Arts & the South. Proceedings of the 1990 North American Print Conference*, 2–29. ed. Judy L. Larson. Fayetteville: University of Arkansas Press, 1993.

The beginning point of this study is a political print attributed to William Charles, *John Bull Making What He Calls a Demonstration on N. Orleans and a Kentucky Volunteer Meeting Him*. A curious figure, half-horse and half-alligator, has bitten off John Bull's lower left leg. Tatham examines this and other similar images that relate to the life and history of the southeastern frontier during the Jacksonian era. Among the images reproduced are several from the series of Crockett Almanacs of the 1830s and 1840s. Tatham suggests that the riotous imagery derives from the people who settled the region, generally from the north of England, Scotland, and Ireland as well as from the contrasts between the deep south and Kentucky and Tennessee.

1451.———. "Jack Downing: A Jacksonian Hero Personalized." *Imprint* 6, no. 2 (1981): 14–19.

Seba Smith created the mythical hero Jack Downing in 1830. Tatham explains the importance of Downing and other mythical heroes within the study of American culture. Although most disappeared after a brief moment, Jack Downing remained vital for over thirty years. Tatham surveys the images derived from Smith's creation including works by David Claypoole Johnston, Edward Williams Clay, and Anthony Imbert. Tatham suggests that a full study of Major Jack Downing would be useful.

1452.———. "Pictorial Responses to the Caning of Senator Sumner" in *America Printmaking Before 1876, Fact, Fiction, and Fantasy*, 11–19. Washington, D.C.: Library of Congress, 1975.

Tatham has located prints depicting the caning of Sumner by Preston Brooks. Included in his article are an illustration for *Frank Leslie's Illustrated Newspaper*, lithographs by John L. Magee and Winslow Homer, and caricatures by David Claypoole Johnston. Tatham draws some interesting conclusions about the value of studying images as popular responses to an event and their merit as works of art.

1453. Thomas, Samuel J. "The Tattooed Man Caricatures and the Presidential Campaign of 1884." *Journal of American Culture* 10, no. 4 (1987): 1–20.

British-born artist Bernhard Gillam (1856–1896) created a series of cartoons for *Puck* between April and November 1884 portraying James G. Blaine as covered with tattoos of his alleged political sins. Thomas provides excellent background on the 1884 presidential election campaign and explains the complex caricatures very clearly. Thomas asserts that this series of cartoons was a factor in Grover Cleveland's defeat of Blaine.

1454. Thompson, W. Fletcher. "Pictorial Propaganda and the Civil War." *Wisconsin Magazine of History* 46 (1962): 21–31.

Thompson studies the role of illustrated journalism in America, a method of news reporting that began about the time of the Civil War. This article, which documents the social conditions that brought the cartoons popular acceptance, emphasizes the role of Fletcher Harper and his publications.

1455. Tyler, Francine. "The Impact of Daumier's Graphics on American Artists: c.1863–c.1923." *Print Review* 11 (1980): 108–126.

Thomas Nast was among the Americans influenced by Daumier's political cartoons. Tyler draws convincing parallels in the two artists' work and also discusses how Daumier's work was known in New York. Likewise, Joseph Keppler was affected by Daumier. Daumier's influence continued in the work of Art Young (1866–1943), Boardman Robinson (1876–1952), Robert Minor (1844–1953), and John Sloan (1871–1951).

1456. Tyler, Ronnie C. *The Image of America in Caricature and Cartoon*. Fort Worth, Tex.: Amon Carter Museum of Western Art, 1975. 192 pp.

The introduction provides the historical context to the cartoons, which cover the period from 1754 to 1974. Each of the prints in the exhibition is illustrated, and the explanatory captions are helpful. The exhibition assembled cartoons from many different collections. The catalog is a good permanent record of these cartoons since many are unfamiliar and seldom reproduced.

1457. Vail, Robert W. G. "Our Friendly Enemies, the Pro-American Caricatures of a London Woman Printseller of 1776–1778." *New-York Historical Society Quarterly* 42 (January 1958): 39–46.

Vail begins by emphasizing the sympathy in England for the Americans in the Revolution, which forced King George to hire Hessians to fight in America. Hundreds of pro-American political prints were published after 1765. Vail focuses on one series published by Mrs. Mary Darley, based on the outlandish headdresses popular in London and Paris. All but one of the series can be found in the collections of the New-York Historical Society.

1458. Watt, Andrew. "Mr. Golightly and His Friends." *Ephemera Journal* 7 (1994): 5–24.

Watt uses caricatures to show the reaction of nineteenth-century Americans and Europeans to technological progress in transportation. Among the questions that Watt raises is how conservative were caricatures and whether there were differences between European and American views of progress. Most of the visual documentation comes from comic magazines and separately published prints. The subjects of the caricatures ranges from railroads to automobiles.

1459. Weitenkampf, Frank. *Uncle Sam Through the Years: A Cartoon Record.* New York: 1949. 24 leaves, typewritten.

Weitenkampf's article, "The Cartoonist's Uncle Sam," traces the evolution of Uncle Sam in pictorial terms. In this typescript in the Prints Division of The New York Public Library, a brief discussion of the literary origins of Uncle Sam is followed by an analysis of the pictorial evolution. The important contribution of this typescript is the list of cartoons with which the evolution can be documented. They range in date from 1813 to 1899.

1460.———. *Political Caricature in the United States in Separately Published Cartoons: An Annotated List.* New York: New York Public Library, 1953. 184 pp.

This list of cartoons is chronologically arranged from 1787 to 1898, excluding those cartoons issued in colonial days, as well as those published in books and periodicals. The annotations identify the characters in the cartoons. The locations given for cartoons in public collections are helpful, because so many of them are very rare. The subject index is useful. The checklist was originally published in serial form in the *Bulletin of the New York Public Library* and has been reprinted by the Arno Press.

1461.———. "The Cartoonist's Uncle Sam." *Antiques* 46, no. 1 (July 1944): 16–17.

The figure of Uncle Sam evolved from Brother Jonathan, an image popular in the early nineteenth century. Although the term Uncle Sam may have developed during the War of 1812, he did not begin to assume his current form until 1834, when he appeared in a political caricature in the swallowtail coat and striped trousers that were to become part of his image. Weitenkampf discusses other changes in his appearance in the second half of the nineteenth century by referring to well-chosen illustrations from periodicals.

1462.———. "Notes on Women in American Caricature." *American Collector* 15 (July and August 1946): 6–7, 18; 8–9, 24.

In the years before and during the Civil War, the involvement of women in the suffrage and abolition movements often resulted in caricatures of them. Weitenkampf describes many cartoons satirizing women's involvement in politics and temperance, their new modes of dress, and their social behavior. The second part of the article is concerned with social caricatures of women, on subjects such as marriage, manners, fashionable life, and servants. Most of these caricatures date from after the Civil War.

1463.———. "Political Cartoons as Historical Documents." *Bulltetin of The New York Public Library* 50 (March 1946): 171–76.

In this essay, Weitenkampf combines a historical survey of cartoons with a discussion of their value as documents. He discusses the various biases that shaped their content, and speculates about the "corrective nature" of cartoons. He concludes by recommending the study of cartoons to historians if they scrutinize the prints carefully.

1464. Wilson, Rufus Rockwell. *Lincoln in Caricature.* New York: Horizon Press, 1953. 327 pp.

This volume reproduces some 163 cartoons by caricaturists such as Louis Maurer, Sir John Tenniel, Henry Louis Stephens, Frank Bellew, Matt Morgan, and Thomas Nast. Wilson drew upon caricatures published in American and British periodicals as well as separately published prints, particullarly those issued by Currier & Ives. Each cartoon is throughly explained in terms of iconography. Biographical sketches of the most important artists are presented. Earlier editions of his work were published in 1903 and 1945.

1465.———. *Lincoln in Caricature.* Elmira, N.Y.: Primavera Press, 1945. 331 pp.

In the first edition of *Lincoln in Caricature*, the illustrations are reproduced from *Harper's Weekly*, *Vanity Fair*, *Punch*, and *Frank Leslie's Illustrated Newspaper*. Among the cartoonists represented are Frank Bellew, Henry Louis Stephens, and Sir John Tenniel. The commentary on each cartoon is adequate, and the source of each illustration is noted. In 1945, Wilson expanded the number of illustrations and enlarged the introduction to accommodate biographical sketches on a larger number of cartoonists. In addition to cartoons from magazines, single sheet lithographed cartoons by Currier & Ives and other publishers are included.

1466. Wolf, Edwin 2nd. "Benjamin Franklin's Stamp Act Cartoon." *Proceedings of the American Philosopical Society* 99, no. 6 (December 1955): 388–396.

A political cartoon designed by Franklin, *Magna Britannia her Colonies Reduc'd* is the subject of this detailed analysis. After summarizing all that had been written on it, Wolf describes its background, significance, and the dating of various versions of the device.

Portrait Prints

1467. "Early American Engraved Portraits: An Exhibition at The New York Public Library." *The American Magazine of Art* 7 (September 1916): 452–57.

A review of the first public exhibition of early American portraits in New York, this article mentions some of the most important and rare prints included in the exhibition. A few interesting details about the prints are noted, such as the fact that Paul Revere's engraving of Benjamin Church is copied after a portrait of Churchill, the English poet. Some of the portraits produced in Europe are of interest when compared to American portraits of the same sitter.

1468. Amyx, Clifford. "The Authentic Image of Daniel Boone." *Missouri Historical Review* 82, no. 2 (January 1988): 153–164.

Amyx discusses portraits of Daniel Boone, including the portrait of the frontier hero painted by Chester Harding and engraved by James Otto Lewis in 1820. The publication of this subscription print is discussed in some detail as is the fate of Harding's original painting which is contrasted to other images of Boone during his lifetime and afterwards.

1469. Andrews, William Loring. *An Essay on the Portraiture of the American Revolutionary War, Being an Account of a Number of the Engraved Portraits Connected Therein.* New York: Printed by Gillis Brothers for the author, 1896. 100 pp., index.

The brief preface explains the author's interest in the subject and his choice of illustrations. In the essay he discusses many American and European portraits of individuals involved in the Revolution. Sources for some of the prints are noted, and Andrews points out that a number of the portraits are fictitious. Although there are a few errors in the publication, Andrews's knowledge of the subject is thorough. Also included are biographical notes on some of the American engravers, and a list of portraits in American and British books and periodicals of the eighteenth and early nineteenth centuries.

1470. Baker, William S. *The Engraved Portraits of Washington, With Notices of the Originals and Brief Biographical Sketches of the Painters.* Philadelphia: Lindsay & Baker, 1880. 221 pp., index.

Baker devised a sensible system for arranging the many engraved portraits of Washington. The prints are classified according to the painters of the original portraits on which the prints are based and the paintings are arranged by date of execution. In the catalog, brief biographical sketches are provided for the artists, followed by a list of prints arranged by engraver, since many are not dated. There are 434 engravings described in this excellent reference volume.

1471. Berkhofer, Robert F., Jr. *The White Man's Indian: Images of the American Indian from Columbus to the Present.* New York: Alfred A. Knopf, 1978. 261 pp.

This book works with literary and artistic imagery of the Indian, including a chapter called the "The Indian and the Rise of an American Art and Literature.".

1472. Boritt, Gabor S., Mark E. Neely, Jr. and Harold Holzer. "The European Image of Abraham Lincoln." *Winterthur Portfolio* 21, no. 2/3 (1986): 153–184.

Lincoln's image in Europe was based upon a photograph made by Alexander Gardner in Washington shortly before his inauguratation. The authors survey European prints and illustrations of Lincoln, including political prints. Ironically, the authors find that Lincoln's image flourished in countries with repressive governments; Lincoln was used as a symbol of freedom.

1473. Boston Public Library. "Franklin Portraits." *Bulletin of the Boston Public Library* 11 (July 1892): 139–50.

Almost 250 prints are described in this list which is arranged by artist or "type." The list includes book illustrations and separately published prints.

1474. Bumgardner, Georgia B. "Political Portraiture: Two Prints of Andrew Jackson." *American Art Journal* 18, no. 4 (1986): 84–95.

This article discusses two portrait prints of Andrew Jackson after paintings by Ralph E. W. Earl. Existing documentation at the American Antiquarian Society suggests the important role these prints and others played in the presidential elections of 1828 and 1832 as Jackson's supporters sought to counter the devastating rumors circulating about Jackson and his wife and the political caricatures and broadsides issued by his opponents.

1475. Casper, Scott E. "First First Family: Seventy Years with Edward Savage's *The Washington Family.*" *Imprint* 24, no. 2 (1999): 2–15.

Edward Savage's painting *The Washington Family* was reproduced by Savage himself as a print in 1798 and by a host of printmakers and publishers over the next seventy years. Casper analyzes Savage's painting and print and their copies finding changing cultural and political ideas expressed in the varying adaptations through the nineteenth century.

1476. Chace, Laura L. "Indian Portraits." *Queen City Heritage* 48, no. 2 (1990): 42–48.

Chace provides biographical information on Charles Bird King, Thomas McKenney, and Joseph C. Hall, the creators of the *History of The Indian Tribes of North America*, containing portraits of 120 Native Americans and biographical sketches. Information about the publication of the volume, which spanned almost twenty years from inception to completion, is provided as well.

1477. Cunningham, Noble. *The Image of Thomas Jefferson in the Public Eye: Portraits for the People,*

1800–1809. Charlottesville, Va.: University Press of Virginia, 1981. 185 pp.

Cunningham has selected a small chronology from within which to set the portrait prints of a public person. The painted, sculpted, and drawn sources for these prints have been well researched as have the thirty-nine prints and the fifteen other objects—transfers on pottery, medals, and other objects. A rich context for these prints has been created.

1478.———. *Popular Images of the Presidency from Washington to Lincoln*. Columbia: University of Missouri Press, 1991. 312 pp., index.

Cunningham has assembled a wide array of images relating to American Presidents and has organized them into topics that provide added meaning to the images. The text is documented by contemporary newspaper advertisements and by correspondence. The chapters include: The First President Enshrined, The Presidency Celebrated and Enshrined, The Presidency and the Declaration of Independence, The Presidency and the Union, The Presidential Stance, Heads of State, Presidents Caricatured, The Drama of the Presidency, The Presidency Popularized and Exploited, and Presidential Images in American Culture. The text is very well written and informative, providing the kind of context that these images deserve.

1479. Doherty, Amy S. "Grace Woodworth's Portrait of Susan B. Anthony 'Outside the Common Lines'" in *Prints and Printmakers of New York State, 1825–1940*, 243–251. ed. David Tatham. Syracuse: Syracuse University Press, 1986.

A portrait of Susan B. Anthony by the photographer Grace Woodworth is the subject of this essay. It was reproduced in the *The Life and Work of Susan B. Anthony* (1904–8), volume three. Doherty provides biographical data on Woodworth (1872–1967), her artistic efforts, her ownership of photographic studios in Union Springs, N.Y. and Rochester where she photographed Anthony and her subsequent life in Seneca Falls.

1480. Ewers, John C. "An Anthropologist Looks at Early Pictures of North American Indians." *The New-York Historical Society Quarterly* 33 (October 1949): 222–34.

This article follows up a survey by Weitenkampf on early printed depictions of American Indians. Ewers discusses the same prints as Weitenkampf, but is concerned with their accuracy in portraying racial differences between Caucasians and Indians. The engravings of De Bry, made after the drawings of Le Moyne and John White, and the drawing of A. De Batz, "The Four Kings of Canada," are among the early works examined. Later images are analyzed as well.

1481. Feest, Christian. "The Virginian Indian in Pictures, 1612–1624." *Smithsonian Journal of History* 2, no. 1 (1967): 1–30.

Feest discusses the engravings by Theodore de Bry after John White and their influence on other prints, including those in John Smith's *Generall Historie of Virginia* (1612) and Robert Beverley's *History and Present State of Virginia* (1705). Also important in Feest's essay are Georg Keller (1568–1634) of Frankfurt and Robert Vaughan (fl. 1622–78) of London. The image of the "noble savage" comes from a variety of sources.

1482. Fern, Alan. "Introspection and Imagination: Portraiture in Twentieth-Century Prints" in *American Portrait Prints*, 256–269. ed. Wendy Wick Reaves. Washington: National Portrait Gallery, 1984.

Although focusing on prints of the twentieth century, Fern's essay documents the changes in the production of portrait prints caused by photography. Fern also contrasts artists' attempts to portray the subject's personality with the nineteenth-century emphasis on likeness. Twentieth-century artists have also used graphic media to create self-portraits. Continuing in the twentieth century is the joining together of photography and printmaking.

1483. Fielding, Mantle. "American Naval Portraits Engraved by David Edwin After Gilbert Stuart and Others." *Print Connoisseur* 2 (December 1921): 122–37.

Fielding briefly describes the career, techniques, and style of Gilbert Stuart. He then lists portraits engraved by David Edwin of the naval commanders in the War of 1812. The biographical sketch of Edwin emphasizes his friendship with Stuart. None of the engravings is discussed in detail.

1484. Finlay, Nancy and Julia Van Haaften. "Four Hundred Years of Native-American Portraits: Prints and Photographs from the Collections of The New York Public Library." *Biblion* 2, no. 1 (1993): 100–139.

A brief introduction precedes the checklist of an exhibition held at the New York Public Library in 1992–1993. It is useful introduction to the subject of images of Native Americans.

1485. Flint, Janet. *Prints and Personalities: The American Theater's First Hundred Years*. Washington: The National Collection of Fine Arts, 1979. 15 pp.

Assembled for the 1979 American Print Conference hosted by the National Portrait Gallery, this exhibition included sixty-one prints ranging in date from 1790 through the Civil War. Each entry includes artist, title, medium, size, and biographical information on the subject. The introduction provides a brief sketch of the theater in the United States.

1486. Franco, Barbara. "Museum of Our National Heritage Exhibition. George Washington: American Superhero." *Imprint* 7, no. 1 (1982): 33–36.

In this review of a major museum exhibition at the Museum of Our National Heritage, Lexington, Massachusetts, Franco mentions a number of historical prints in the exhibition and their importance in documenting Washington's image as superhero. Six prints are reproduced, all from the collection of the Museum.

1487. Frazier, Patrick. *Portrait Index of North American Indians in Published Collections.* Washington: Library of Congress, 1996. 200 pp., index.

This valuable reference work is an index to portraits of Native Americans in 115 publications housed at the Library of Congress, spanning the colonial period to the 1990s. It is arranged by tribe and then name of the sitter and is keyed to the reference work and location in it. There is an index arranged by name of the sitter. This reference work will be useful to historians, curators, collectors, genealogists, and others.

1488. Gilreath, James. "George Catlin and Karl Bodmer: Artists Among the American Indians." *Folklife Annual* (1988): 34–45.

Catlin and Bodmer covered almost the same territory in their travels in 1832 in search of frontier Indians. Catlin thought them "a superior but vanishing race." Bodmer was a scientific illustrator which explains a difference in their watercolors, many of which were later reproduced. A selection of their works are reproduced and a selective bibliography is appended to the article.

1489. Green, Samuel A. "Remarks on a Portrait of Increase Mather." *Proceedings of the Massachusetts Historical Society* 8 (March 1893): 143–51.

Green discusses John Van der Spriett's oil portrait of Increase Mather, painted in London in 1688, and copies of it engraved by Robert White, John Stuart, and Thomas Emmes in London and Boston in the seventeenth and early eighteenth centuries. He also mentions several nineteenth-century prints.

1490. The Grolier Club. *Exhibtion of the Engraved Portraits of Washington Commemorative of the Centenary of His Death.* New York: 1900. 51 pp.

The purpose of the exhibition was to draw comparisons between the rare, early prints of Washington, and a number of later, more common portraits. Over 270 prints were exhibited, as well as a few of the oil paintings and drawings from which many of the prints were copied.

1491. Grote, Suzy Wetzel. "Engravings of George Washginton in the Stanley DeForest Scott Collection." *Antiques* 112, no. 1 (July 1977): 128–133.

About twenty eighteenth- and early nineteenth-century American and European prints of George Washington are illustrated and discussed. The author was particularly eager to identify paintings that served as sources for the prints and in the faithfulness to life to the prints. No information on the Scott collection itself is presented.

1492. Hart, Charles H. *A Catalogue of a Collection of Engraved and Other Portraits of Lincoln.* New York: The Grolier Club, 1899. 66 pp.

This is the first attempt at assembling a record of the engraved portraits of Lincoln. Hart includes a description of Lincoln's physical characteristics and mentions several life portraits made of him. The catalog includes lithographs, etchings, and wood engravings of Lincoln, but concludes by noting that photographs form the truest record. The entries are arranged by medium.

1493.———. *Catalogue of the Engraved Portraits of Washington.* New York: Grolier Club, 1904. 406 pp., indexes.

Hart's magnificent compendium describes 880 plates and 634 variant states of those prints, for a total listing of 1,514 prints of American and European origin. Baker's system of classifying the portraits by the original oil portrait is followed, and there is a checklist of Baker numbers with the corresponding Hart numbers. The introduction describes Hart's methodology and a few of the most unusual prints. The twenty-one plates, for which there are detailed entries, handsomely reproduce the rarest of the prints. The indexes of engravers, publishers, place of publication, owners of the paintings, and titles of publications make this a superb reference work.

1494. Holzer, Harold. *Washington and Lincoln Portrayed. National Icons in Popular Prints.* Jefferson, N.C.: McFarland & Company, Inc., 1993. 252 pp., index.

This well-documented and illustrated study demonstrates how revered Washington and Lincoln were in the nineteenth century, particularly at the time of the Civil War and Lincoln's assassination. Separate chapters on portrait prints of Washington and Lincoln are followed by one in which the two figures appear in the same images.

1495.———. "How America Met Mr. Lincoln." *Nineteenth Century* 6, no. 1 (1980): 52–57.

There was a sudden demand for images of Lincoln after his nomination by the Republican Party in 1860. Since Lincoln did not personally campaign, his success depended on the proliferation of printed copies of speeches, photographs, and printed portraits. Holzer discusses original portraits and their engraved and lithographed copies.

1496.———. "How the Printmakers Saw Lincoln: Not So Honest Portraits of 'Honest Abe'." *Winterthur Portfolio* 14, no. 2 (1979): 143–170.

Lincoln was apparently aware that flattering portraits could help him politically. Print publishers generally issued idealized portraits. Holzer discusses a number of these prints chronologically, concentrating on "why" they were issued. Pirated editions are discussed as well.

1497.———. "The Image Makers: Portraits of Lincoln in the 1860 Campaign." *Chicago History* 7, no. 4 (December 1978): 198–207.

Holzer writes about the need for accurate and flattering portraits of Abraham Lincoln at the beginning of the 1860 presidential campaign. The article is very well illustrated and documented by contemporary advertisements. A brief note in the Summer 1979 issue of *Chicago History* reproduces a letter from Abraham Lincoln to Edward Mendel praising Mendel's portrait of him.

1498.———. "Lincoln and the Ohio Printmakers." *Ohio History* 89, no. 4 (1980): 400–419.

Prints issued in Ohio during Lincoln's administration include several striking images among which was a lithograph by Ehrgott, Forbriger & Co. after David Gilmore Blythe's painting of Lincoln drafting the Emancipation Proclamation. Several important prints showing the funeral cortege that went through Ohio on the way to Illinois after Lincoln's assassination were also published in Ohio. Finally, Holzer reproduces several portrait prints issued as memorials to the martyred president.

1499.———. "Memorial Prints of Washington and Lincoln." *Antiques* 115, no. 2 (February 1979): 352–356.

Holzer illustrated and described thirteen prints which honor both Lincoln and Washington. The brief text provides some historical background to these prints, some of which served as campaign propaganda.

1500.———. "Prints of Abraham Lincoln." *Antiques* 105, no. 2 (February 1974): 329–35.

This interesting account explains how printmakers devised ingenious ways of supplying the demand for pictures of Lincoln. The artists often invented poses and created "friendships that must have suprised even the president." This approach to portraiture underlines the importance of the caution with which one must approach prints as historical documents.

1501. Holzer, Harold, Gabor S. Boritt, and Mark E. Neely, Jr. "Francis Bicknell Carpenter (1830–1900): Painter of Abraham Lincoln and His Circle." *American Art Journal* 16, no. 2 (1984): 66–89.

This thoroughly documented article focuses on paintings of Lincoln and his cabinet that served as sources for paintings by Carpenter, *The First Reading of the Emancipation Proclamation*, *The Lincoln Family*, and portrait prints of Lincoln. The circulation of his paintings through the reproductive prints is an important part of the legacy of Lincoln.

1502. Holzer, Harold, Gabor S. Boritt, and Mark E. Neely, Jr. "The Lincoln Image: Abraham Lincoln and the Popular Print." *Imprint* 9, no. 1 (1984): 7–17.

The authors describe and analyze the variety of prints depicting Abraham Lincoln between 1860 and 1865. Included are portrait prints and their photographic sources, political prints, group portraits featuring Lincoln, the assassination, and Wiest's lithograph derived from John James Barralet's 1802 engraving showing the apotheosis of George Washington. This essay is adapted from the authors' full-length monograph, *The Lincoln Image: Abraham Lincoln and the Popular Print*, published in 1984.

1503. Holzer, Harold, Gabor S. Boritt, and Mark E. Neely. *The Lincoln Image: Abraham Lincoln and the Popular Print*. New York: Charles Scribner's Sons, 1984. 234 pp., index.

To celebrate the 175th anniversary of Lincoln's birth, Gettysburg College held an exhibition of some one hundred engravings and lithographs of Abraham Lincoln. This book is based on the exhibition and discusses the inconographic sources and uses of these prints—cartoons, illustrated sheet music, separately published portrait prints. The text is well researched with excellent commentary on the portraits and their role in the political events of the era.

1504. Jones, Karen M. "Collector's Notes: A Long-lost Portrait of Benjamin Lay." *Antiques* 115, no. 1 (January 1979): 194, 196.

The portrait of Benjamin Lay engraved by Dawkins was copied from an oil owned by Benjamin Franklin. Information on the newly discovered painting is presented here with reproductions of it and the engraved print.

1505. Kaplan, Milton. "Heads of States." *Winterthur Portfolio* 6 (1970): 135–50.

Portraits of heads of state are commonly regarded as realistic likenesses, yet in fact many are visual cliches varied only by facial features. For instance, Kaplan notes the similarity of some portraits of Andrew Jackson and Abraham Lincoln.

1506. Lipton, Leah. "Chester Harding and the Life Portrait of Daniel Boone." *American Art Journal* 16, no. 3 (June 1984): 4–19.

One of the rarest portrait prints is the stipple engraving by James Otto Lewis after Chester Harding's portrait of Daniel Boone, published in 1820. In her well documented essay, Lipton discusses the various versions of the painting.

1507.———. "The Portrait Painter and the Engraver: Cooperation and Conflict" in *Painting and Portrait Making in the American Northeast*, 167–180. ed. Peter Benes. Boston: Boston University Press, 1995.

In 1820 Chester Harding made a portrait of the legendary Daniel Boone in Missouri, which served as the source of an engraving by James Otto Lewis published in 1820. Based on existing correspondence between Harding and the engraver James Barton Longacre, Lipton discusses the relationship between artist and engraver including financial disputes, means of obtaining subscriptions, and the distribution of prints.

1508. Marshall, Gordon M. "The Golden Age of Illustrated Biographies, Three Case Studies" in *American Portrait Prints*, 29–82. ed. Wendy Wick Reaves. Charlottesville: University Press of Virginia, 1984.

Marshall presents a detailed analysis of three monumental collections of portraits: Joseph Delaplaine's *Repository of the Lives and Portraits of Distinguished Americans* (1816); John and Joseph M. Sanderson's *Biography of the Signers to the Declaration of Independence* (1819–27); and James B. Longacre and James Herring's *National Portrait Gallery of Distinguished Americans* (1833–39). Appended to the essay are lists of the engravings and engravers in each volume and the names of the authors of articles in the volumes (when appropriate).

1509. Marzio, Peter C. *Perfect Likenesses: Portraits for History of the Indian Tribes of North America (1836–1844)*. Washington: Smithsonian Institution, 1977. 27 pp.

In the introduction to this exhibition catalog, Marzio discusses the production of the lithographed Indian portraits for the three volume *Indian Tribes of North America* by Thomas L. McKenney and James Hall. The lithographs were produced from copies by Henry Inman from oil paintings by Charles Bird King. Marzio focuses on the accuracy of the lithographs and the problems of translating oil painting into the lithographic medium. The exhibition consisted of the lithographs, some of King's paintings, and actual artifacts depicted in the portraits.

1510. McDermott, John F. "Indian Portraits: The First Published Collection." *Antiques* 51 (May 1947): 320–22.

In 1835 *The Aboriginal Port Folio* was published, containing lithographs of portraits of Native Americans made after paintings by James Otto Lewis. McDermott describes the genesis of this project and details of publication. Unfortunately the original paintings by Lewis are no longer extant, but *The Aboriginal Port Folio*, a remarkable achievement, remains as a good record.

1511. Miles, Ellen G. "Portraits of the Heroes of Louisbourg, 1745–1751." *American Art Journal* 15, no. 1 (1983): 48–66.

In 1745, British and American soldiers captured Louisbourg, the French outpost in Nova Scotia. Miles examines the eight portraits of the military heroes, focusing on the direct pictorial references to the battle. Miles discusses the tradition of portrait paintings of this type, the battle itself, the paintings and their histories, and the mezzotint copies of them, including two by Peter Pelham of Boston.

1512.———. "Saint-Mémin, Valdenuit, Lemet, Federal Profiles" in *American Portrait Prints*, 1–28. ed. Wendy Wick Reaves. Charlottesville: University Press of Virginia, 1984.

In 1974 the National Portrait Gallery acquired a collection of engraved profiles by Saint-Mémin, numbering 761 items. This essay focuses on the physiognotrace method of portraiture practiced by three French emigre artists: Saint-Mémin, Thomas Bluget de Valdenuit, and Louis Lemet. The first two worked together in New York in 1797. Miles succeeds in differentiating their works by a careful analysis of their styles. In 1797 Valdnuit returned to France; Saint-Mémin moved to Burlington, N.J., which he used as a base until his return to France in 1814. Lemet appeared in Philadelphia in 1803 and worked in a similar style. Miles explains the process clearly and provides biographical sketches of the three artists. Saint-Mémin was far more prolific than the other two and left a lasting legacy in his portraits of federal society.

1513. Murdock, Kenneth B. *The Portraits of Increase Mather, With Some Notes on Thomas Johnson, An English Mezzotinter*. Cleveland: For private distribution by William Gwinn Mather, 1924. 70 pp.

The author traces the history of all known portraits of Mather. He disposes of the theory that the 1683 mezzotint portrait of Increase Mather is by Thomas Johnston of Boston. Murdock considers the Thomas Emmes plate of Mather to be the first copperplate portrait done in America.

1514. Murray, Patricia. *A Catalogue of Eighty Indian Portrait Lithographs from the History of the Indian Tribes of North America*. Providence, R.I.: Patricia Murray, 1990. 83 pp., biblio.

Murray's introduction provides a brief sketch of Thomas L. McKenney and the Indian gallery that he sponsored in Washington which featured 147 portraits by Charles Bird King, most of which were later destroyed by fire. McKenney and James Hall published a portfolio of 120 portraits. The catalogue describes eighty of them with information on extant oil paintings and biographical information on the subjects.

1515. Nolan, J. Bennett. "When Benedict Arnold Was A Hero." *Antiques* 27, no. 2 (February 1935): 56–57.

Benedict Arnold was a popular hero until he became a traitor during the Revolution. In the brief span of time between the victory at Saratoga and his treason, several portraits of him were published in France, Germany, and even England. They were imported to the United States through the West

Indies and became popular with Americans. Several of the portraits are illustrated in the article, which brings together some scarce prints.

1516. Ormsbee, Thomas Hamilton. "18th-Century Anglo-American Relations Mirrored in Prints." *American Collector* 13 (February 1944): 6–7, 15.

Noting that wars stimulate interest in a nation's leaders, Ormsbee examines a variety of printed portraits of American and British heroes during the French and Indian War and the Amerian Revolution. Most of the prints mentioned were executed in Europe. Some of the images were pirated, while others were fictitious.

1517. Poulter, Gillian. "Representation as Colonial Rhetoric. The image of 'The Native' and 'The Inhabitant' in the Formation of Colonial Identities in Early Nineteenth-Century Lower Canada." *The Journal of Canadian Art History* 16, no. 1 (1994): pp. 10–25.

Poulter argues that there are differences in representations of Native Americans and French Canadians by British and Canadian artists. Illustrations for this thesis include prints as well as watercolors and paintings. Artists whose works are discussed include Robert A. Sproule, James Duncan, James Gray, William H. Bartlett, Mary Millicent Chaplin, and Joseph Legare.

1518. Reaves, Wendy Wick. "'Effigies Curiously Engraven': Eighteenth-Century American Portrait Prints" in *Prints of New England*, 39–67. ed. Georgia Brady Barnhill. Worcester: American Antiquarian Society, 1991.

Reaves sets American portrait prints into the long tradition of engraved portraiture, beginning in the sixteenth century, and discusses the purposes that they served. She then surveys American prints from the portrait of Richard Mather by John Foster through the elegant portraits by Edward Savage, David Edwin, Charles Willson Peale, and Robert Field. She discusses the use of portraits in almanacs, periodicals, and in other publications. Sources for some of these prints are revealed in this useful survey.

1519.———. "Portraits for Every Parlor: Albert Newsam and American Portrait Lithography" in *American Portrait Prints*, 83–134. ed. Wendy Wick Reaves. Charlottesville: University Press of Virginia, 1984.

The popularity of lithographed portrait prints is well documented by Reaves who focuses her attention on the lithographic draftsman Albert Newsam, a deaf-mute who received some training from George Catlin and Hugh Bridport. He was placed with Cephas C. Childs, the noted lithographer and engraver, and quickly started producing prints. Reaves describes a number of Newsam's commissions of important public figures and the influence of French lithography on him. Documentation includes newspaper and magazine advertisements and correspondence.

1520. Reaves, Wendy Wick, ed. *American Portrait Prints*. Washington: National Portrait Gallery, 1984. 285 pp., index.

This volume presents essays based on lectures presented at the North American Print Conference held at the National Portrait Gallery in May 1979. The authors and titles of the essays are: Ellen Miles, "Saint Mémin, Valdenuit, Lemet, Federal Profiles;" Gordon M. Marshall, "The Golden Age of Illustrated Biographies, Three Case Studies;" Wendy Wick Reaves, "Portraits for Every Parlor, Albert Newsam and American Portrait Lithography;" Katharine Martinez, "Portrait Prints by John Sartain;" David Tatham, "David Claypoole Johnston's Theatrical Portraits;" William F. Stapp, "Daguerreotypes onto Stone, The Life and Work of Francis D'Avignon;" Daryl Rubenstein, "American Portrait Etching of the Late Nineteenth Century;" and Alan Fern, "Introspection and Imagination. Portraiture in Twentieth-Century Prints." The book is handsomely produced and lavishly illustrated. The preface by the editor discusses several themes that relate the essays—the commercial spirit that motivated the creation of these popular prints, the reproductive nature of them, and their validity as historic documents and works of art.

1521. Reilly, Bernard. "John Paul Jones and the Heroic Naval Print" in *American Maritime Prints*, 189–206. ed. Elton W. Hall. New Bedford, Mass.: The Old Dartmouth Historical Society, 1985.

John Paul Jones became a legend in Europe during the American Revolution as he made many raids on British shipping. The defeat of the *Serapis* by Jones's *Bonhomme Richard* brought forth a number of portrait prints. Reilly discusses a group of English and French prints produced during the years 1779–1781 and suggests some of the terms of the contemporary language of portraiture. Some of these prints are more ideal than actual representations and reflect contemporary interest in the study of physiognomy.

1522. Rubenstein, Daryl R. "American Portrait Etching of the Late Nineteenth Century" in *American Portrait Prints*, 232–255. ed. Wendy Wick Reaves. Washington: National Portrait Gallery, 1984.

Rubenstein surveys the two traditions of etched portaits—closely worked reproductions of portraits in other media and freely drawn original etchings, concentrating on the latter issued during the etching revival. Works by Anna Lea Merritt, Stephen Ferris, Walter Shirlaw, William Bicknell, Whistler, Robert Blum, J. Alden Weir, and Ignatz Gaugengigl are discussed and reproduced.

1523. Samuel, Bunford. "Index to American Portraits." *Pennsylvania Magazine of History and*

Biography 25 (April, July and October 1901): 47–70; 228–47; 384–99.

Samuel complied his index from twenty-two eighteenth- and nineteenth-century English and American periodicals and from a variety of books. The titles of the magazines which he searched are listed, although the titles of the books are not. The list is arranged by name, and the portraits of each man are arranged by date of publication. Artists of the original portraits the engravings copied are given, as well as the title of the magazine or book which contains the print described.

1524. Sellers, Charles Coleman. *Benjamin Franklin in Portraiture*. New Haven: Yale University Press, 1962. 452 pp., index.

In the first half of his book, Sellers surveys portraits of Franklin in chronological order. In the second half he makes a detailed catalog of the paintings, miniatures, prints, and sculptures of his subject. Arranged by artist, the catalog contains valuable notes, including information on copies, artists, and contemporary references to the works. Although the emphasis of the volume is on portraits painted from life, portrait prints and caricatures are also included. About one hundred of the portraits are reproduced. The documentation of this monumental compilation is superb.

1525. Simmons, William S. "The Earliest Prints and Paintings of New England Indians." *Rhode Island History* 41, no. 3 (August 1982): 73–85.

Simmons discusses the reasons for the poor visual record of the early natives of New England. His research has revealed a few important engravings which are reproduced along with eighteenth-century portrait paintings.

1526. Smith, John Chaloner. *British Mezzotinto Portraits: Being a Descriptive Catalogue of These Engravings from the Introduction of the Art to the Early Part of the Present Century*. London: Henry Sotheran & Co., 1884. 4 vols.

The compiler used the collections of the British Museum, the Bodleian Library, Windsor Castle, and the Bibliothèque Nationale, among others, to compile this list of portraits executed in mezzotint by British engravers. Mentioned are Peter Pelham and Samuel Okey, two of the best known English mezzotinters who worked in America. Abundant biographical information is provided for each engraver.

1527. Stoddard, Roger E. "Notes on American Play Publishing, 1765–1865." *Proceedings of the American Antiquarian Society* 81, no. 1 (April 1971): 161–187.

This survey of the American theater and American book trade concludes with a list of American dramatic illustrations from 1776 to 1800. Arranged chronologically, each entry includes the inscription on the plate with the title, author, and imprint of its publication, and the entry number in Stauffer.

1528.———. "Poet and Printer in Colonial and Federal America: Some Bibliographical Perspectives." *Proceedings of the American Antiquarian Society* 92, no. 2 (October 1982): 265–36.

This essay contains a great deal of information on the publication of poetry in America. Pages 353 to 359 contain citations to editions with illustrations and some of the finest portraits of poets are reproduced. This is a useful guide to both portraits and book illustrations.

1529. Swan, Bradford F. "Prints of the American Indian, 1670–1775" in *Boston Prints and Printmakers, 1670–1775*, 240–82. Boston: Colonial Society of Massachusetts, 1973.

Swan comments on late seventeenth and eighteenth century prints and oil portraits of American Indians, concentrating on three specific sets of prints: the DeBry engravings of 1590, the mezzotints by John Simon after Verelst's paintings, and the prints of Cherokees and Creeks who visited London in 1730, 1734, and 1762. The illustrations for this article are excellent and most of the prints mentioned are reproduced.

1530. Swan, Mabel M. "American 'Kings'." *Antiques* 19, no. 4 (April 1931): 278–81.

A newspaper notice appeared in Boston in 1825 heralding the arrival from France of lithographic portraits of the first five American presidents. The lithographs were prepared for John Doggett, a Boston importer. Swan had studied the Doggett records for other purposes, and chanced to find the complete account of these prints in the diary of Jonathan Cobb, one of Doggett's sons-in-law. She discovered that Monsieur Maurin, a French artist, drew the portraits on stone, not John Pendleton as had been previously assumed. Swan's article, well researched and clearly written, sheds light on some of the earliest productions of the Pendleton shop in Boston. In the "Editor's Attic" of *Antiques* 20 (July 1931): 11–13, further information is given on the original portraits painted by Gilbert Stuart for the series. Three portraits were burned in 1851, one was in a private collection in 1931, and the fifth, of James Monroe, is in The Metropolitan Museum of Art.

1531. Thorpe, Russell Walton. "Alexander Hamilton: Rare Portraits of This American General and Statesman." *Antiquarian* 4 (July 1925): 20–23, 37.

Thorpe describes the five known life portraits of Hamilton by Peale, Trumbull, James Sharples, Archibald Robertson, and Ezra Ames, and the engravings derived from them. Most of the six engravings described in detail are rare, and four are reproduced.

1532.———. "Portraits of John Hancock." *Antiquarian* 5 (October 1925): 27–29, 40.

About fifteen engraved portraits of John Hancock, most of which derive from the portrait painted by Copley in 1765, are the subject of this article. Several English and continental mezzotints are also described. All of the prints illustrated are rare. The author has not attempted to compile a complete checklist of portraits of Hancock.

1533. Truesdell, Winfred Porter. "A Checklist of the Portraits of General Winfield Scott." *Print Connoisseur* 11 and 12 (July and October 1931; January 1932): 202–236; 260–92; 56–66.

No text accompanies this list of 190 portraits of Scott, which is arranged by publisher and artist. Included are engravings, wood engravings, and lithographs. Unfortunately, no locations for the prints appear, nor is the rarity of individual prints indicated.

1534.———. "The Engraved and Lithographic Portraits of Abraham Lincoln." *Print Connoisseur* 5 (January, April, and July 1925): 67–83; 128–53; 246–60.

Beginning in the mid-nineteenth century, portrait prints were commonly based on photographs rather than oil paintings. This list of portraits is based on the arrangement of Frederick Hill Meserve's *The Photographs of Abraham Lincoln* (New York, 1911). Meserve found 110 photographs of Lincoln, and the prints in this list follow the photographic sequence. The description of each print is excellent.

1535.———. "Washington and Lincoln Portraits." *Print Connoisseur* 1 (March 1921): 278–99.

Truesdell discusses the importance of Washington and Lincoln in American history, and then describes some prints of them. Truesdell mentions some of the rare—and in some cases fictitious—portraits of Washington and Lincoln, noting that photographs had largely replaced oil portraits by Lincoln's time. The article was written to show collectors the range of prints available and to encourage the collecting of these and similar historical documents.

1536. Vail, Robert W. G. "Portraits of 'The Four Kings of Canada,' a Bibliographical Footnote." in *To Dr. R.*, 218–26. Philadelphia: 1946.

Vail describes in detail prints of the four Indian chiefs who were taken to England in 1710. He includes the four mezzotint prints by John Simon after the paintings by John Verelst, and describes three states for each print. Vail also comments on a series of four miniatures by Bernard Lens, Jr., which were reproduced as mezzotints by his father, Bernard Lens, Sr., two series by John Faber and Peter Schenck, and portraits of King Hendrick, who visited England in 1710 and again in 1740.

1537. Van Ravenswaay, Charles. "A Rare Midwestern Print." *Antiques* 43, no. 2 (February 1943): 77, 93.

The year 1820 found Chester Harding, a prolific portrait painter, in Saint Louis. Among the portraits he painted that year was one of Daniel Boone. In partnership with James Otto Lewis, Harding agreed to produce prints copied from this painting. The author, in his well-written history of this scarce print, asserts that it was the first produced west of the Mississippi River. Only one copy, now at the Missouri Historical Society in Saint Louis, was known at the time the article was written.

1538. Viola, Herman J. *The Indian Legacy of Charles Bird King*. Washington: Smithsonian Institution Press//Doubleday & Company, 1976. 152 pp., biblio., index.

The introduction by John C. Ewers discusses earlier Indian portraiture and the involvement of the Bureau of Indian Affairs in collecting portraits of Indians. Chapters discuss Charles Bird King, his portraits, and his travels. Of particular interest is the chapter on the publication of Bird's portraits in McKenney and Hall's *History of the Indian Tribes of North America*, which was completed in 1844 after years of problems. A final chapter discusses the locations of the remaining few portraits left after the fire at the Smithsonian in 1865.

1539. Waite, Emma Forbes. "Heyday of the Lithographic Portrait." *American Collector* 17 (December 1948): 12–14, 21.

Waite describes publishers who issued lithographed portraits, such as the Pendletons, Childs & Inman, P.S. Duval, Nathaniel Currier, Henry R. Robinson, and William Sharp, and the artists who worked for them.

1540. Weitenkampf, Frank. "Early Pictures of North American Indians: A Question of Ethnology." *Bulletin of The New York Public Library* 53 (December 1949): 591–614.

Weitenkampf surveys illustrations of American Indians with emphasis on the accuracy of the portrayals. He begins with the earliest German woodcuts, often fictitous representations, and concludes with more realistic depictions by artists such as Catlin and Bodmer.

1541.———. "How Indians Were Pictured in Earlier Days." *The New-York Historical Society Quarterly* 33 (October 1949): 212–21.

Weitenkampf notes that the earliest depictions of Native Americans were imaginary. Later, artists drew upon literary descriptions, and finally drew from life. Beginning with a survey of European prints dating back to the 1500s, the author concentrates on prints of the first half of the nineteenth century, both American and European.

1542.———. "Portraits." *Bulletin of The New York Public Library* 10 (January 1906): 29–81 in *List of*

Works in the New York Public Library by or Relating to Benjamin Franklin.

The January 1906 issue of the *Bulletin*, devoted to Benjamin Franklin, includes detailed descriptions of each of the 307 prints of Franklin in the collection at The New York Public Library.

1543. Wick, Wendy. "American Icon: The Eighteenth Century Image of George Washington." *Imprint* 7, no. 2 (1982): 1–9.

This article is based on Wick's book, *George Washington, An American Icon: The Eighteenth Century Graphic Portraits*, published in 1982 by the Smithsonian in conjunction with a traveling exhibition. The exhibition included prints of Washington issued from 1775 through 1800, the year after his death. Artists who produced the portraits had two challenges: the need to create a likeness and finding the symbolic context for it. A range of portraits has survived—from naive woodcuts to elegant mezzotints by Peale and Savage.

1544. Wick, Wendy C. *George Washington, An American Icon: The Eighteenth-Century Graphic Portraits*. Washington: National Portrait Gallery, 1982. 186 pp., biblio., index.

Wick's goal was to provide a detailed analysis of the portrait prints of George Washington published between 1775 and 1800 including separately published prints, book and periodical illustrations, and relief cuts that appeared on broadsides. The fully illustrated catalog records in great detail 101 of these portraits with descriptive text placing each print in its historical, publishing, and aesthetic context. Lillian Miller's introduction discusses the transformation of Washington into a national icon. Wick's essay places and discusses portraits of Washington in various categories: commander-in-chief, presidential image, and national symbol. This volume is an extremely useful reference work.

1545. Wiet, John Phillip. "McKenney-Hall Prints from the *History of the Indian Tribes of North America*." *Imprint* 5, no. 2 (1980): 12–19.

After a brief survey of relations between native Americans and settlers, Wiet discusses McKenney's idea that resulted in the series of portraits painted by Charles Bird King and the published lithographs issued in Philadelphia between 1836 and 1844 with text by Thomas Loraine McKenney and James Hall. Wiet also describes the publication history of this complex project that involved several publishers and lithographers.

1546. Wilker, Jenny Squires. *The Hall Park McCullough Collection: Portraits of George Washington*. Middlebury, Vt.: Middlebury College Museum of Art, 1995. 38 pp.

This exhibition catalog focuses on a portion of the print collection formed by a Vermont lawyer, Hall Park McCullough (1872–1966). The collection was split among several institutions; this exhibition reassembles the portraits of Washington from those institutions. J. Robert Maguire's introduction discusses the collector and his collection. Wilker's introduction discusses Washington's military career briefly and provides a history of the interest in portraits of Washington as well as a chronology of the prints of him. The catalog of the exhibition is arranged by artist. Each entry provides information such as title, medium, date, dimensions, publisher, and bibliographical references. The illustrations are particularly good.

1547. Wright, Helena E. "A 'Transatlantic Stranger': Portrait Prints of John James Audubon." *Imprint* 23, no. 1 (1998): 9–17.

In this well-researched article, Wright asserts that Audubon's style of self-promotion influenced his reception and reputation, using portrait prints and verbal descriptions of him as the basis for her thesis. He even admitted in a letter to his wife that his long hair was as important to his success as his talent. The portrait prints discussed by Wright were derived from life portraits.

Prints

1548. *Art and Commerce: American Prints of the Nineteenth Century*. Boston: Museum of Fine Arts, 1978. 179 pp., index.

American prints, printmakers, and painter-printmakers of the nineteenth century were the focus of the North American Print Conference held in Boston in 1975. The eight presentations published in this volume are as follows: "D.C. Johnston's Satiric Views of Art in Boston, 1825–1850" by David Tatham; "Panoramic Views of Whaling by Benjamin Russell" by Elton W. Hall; "William Sharp: Accomplished Lithographer" by Bettina A. Norton; "The Democratic Art of Chromolithography in America: An Overview" by Peter Marzio; "'Fine Art Lithography' in Boston: Craftsmanship in Color, 1840–1900" by Sinclair H. Hitchings; "The American Painter-Lithographer" by Janet Flint; "Sylvester Rosa Koehler and the American Etching Revival" by Clifford S. Ackley; and "American Monotypes" by David Kiehl.

1549. *Gesellschaft Fur Vervielfaltigende Kunst. Vervielfaltigende Kunst Der Gegenwart*. Vienna: 1887.

This massive four-volume undertaking, profusely illustrated, comprehensively surveys contemporary graphic arts throughout the world, each volume being devoted to a particular process. While volume two *Der Kupferstich* contains no section on America, the sections in the other three volumes constitute one of the most valuable surveys published on American graphics in the nineteenth century.

1550. Ahlborn, Richard E. "American Beginnings: Prints in Sixteenth-Century Mexico." in *Prints in and of America to 1850*, 1–22. ed. John D. Morse. Winterthur, Del.: Henry Francis du Pont Winterthur Museum, 1970.

The earliest printing in the Americas commenced in Mexico in 1539 under the leadership of Juan Pablos. This article discusses the earliest Mexican prints, generally book illustrations, the changes in personal publishing in Mexico, and the growth of the Mexican press. Stylistic and thematic changes are also described. Although the focus of the article is on Mexican prints, not American, it is included here because it was part of the 1970 Winterthur Conference.

1551. Blakely, Judith. "The American Art-Union Contribution to American Prints." *Imprint* 1, no. 2 (1976): [6–11].

Blakely points out the importance of the American Art Union as a publisher of reproductive prints from 1839 to 1852. It issued thirty-six folio prints, a list of which is appended to the article. This useful list includes year of publication, title, artist, and number of subscribers.

1552. Bloch, E. Maurice. "The American Art-Union's Downfall." *The New-York Historical Society Quarterly* 37 (October 1953): 331–59.

Bloch discusses the management of the Art Union and its relationship to its artists, based on an examination of the organization's manuscripts, correspondence with Thomas W. Whitley, whose volcanic temperament and byzantine schemes to persuade the Art Union to purchase his paintings eventually made him one of the institution's most bitter critics.

1553. Breitenbach, Edgar. "American Graphics in the Late Nineteenth Century." *Archives of American Art Journal* 9 (July 1969): 1–11.

This article was one of the papers presented at a conference on "Needs and Opportunities for the Re-evaluation in the Arts in America, 1860–1910," sponsored by the Archives of American Art in April 1962. Starting with the transmittal of etching from Europe to New York, Breitenbach discusses the early etchers, etching clubs, women etchers, and critics of etching (Ripley Hitchcock and Sylvester Koehler). The discussion on wood engraving centers on the stylistic medium, and the article closes with a re-evaluation of the poster movement and lithography. This is an excellent study of American wood engraving, poster art, and lithography.

1554. Bunner, H. C. "American Posters, Past and Present." *Scribner's Magazine* 18 (October 1895): 429–43.

Although written in a rambling style, this article is valuable for its reproductions of early commercial, theatrical, and circus posters. The author points out that while puritanical attitudes kept pictorial material out of many American homes, the utilitarian character of posters gave them a place on barn walls. The old system of printing posters from roughly engraved wood blocks was current until the 1870s. Bunner also comments on the new work of Bradley and Penfield.

1555. Cantor, Jay. "Prints and the American Art-Union" in *Prints in and of America to 1850*, 297–326. ed. John D. Morse. Winterthur, Del.: Henry Francis du Pont Winterthur Museum, 1970.

Using the annual reports of the Art Union and manuscripts of several artists as documentation, Cantor makes a detailed examination of the prints the organization published for its members. Also analyzed is the philosophy of the American Art Union, the reasons for its popularity, and its influence upon mid-nineteenth-century culture.

1556. Cowdrey, Mary Bartlett. *American Academy of Fine Arts and American Art-Union*. New York: New-York Historical Society, 1953. 2 vols., index.

Volume one contains detailed chronicles of the American Academy of Fine Arts, written by Theodore Sizer, and of the American Art Union, by Charles E. Baker. The bibliography of publications of the Art Union was compiled by Cowdrey, and includes titles of prints that were included in the annual reports, or published separately as premiums. Several of the prints are illustrated. Volume two contains an exhibition list for the American Academy and the Art Union covering the years 1816 to 1852. It is arranged by artist, with a chronological listing of each painting exhibited. Among the graphic artists represented are D.C. Johnston, Fitz Hugh Lane, and Robert Cooke.

1557. Dolmetsch, Joan D. *Eighteenth-Century Prints in Colonial America. To Educate and Decorate*. Williamsburg: Colonial Williamsburg Foundation, 1979. 206 pp., index.

This volume edited by Dolmetsch presents nine essays presented at a symposium of print curators at Colonial Williamsburg in 1973. The essays are as follows: "The Role of the British Eighteenth-Century Print at Williamsburg" by Graham Hood, "London's Images of Colonial America" by Sinclair Hitchings, "Views of Port Cities as Depicted by Vernet and Other Eighteenth-Century Artists" by Harold Sniffen, "American Almanac Illustration in the Eighteenth Century" by Georgia B. Bumgardner, "Embellishments for Practical Repositories" by Peter Parker and Stefanie Munsing Winkelbauer, "Bickham's *Musical Entertainer* and Other Curiosities" by Nancy R. Davison, "The Portrait Engravings of Charles Willson Peale" by Wendy Shadwell, "*The Prodigal Son* in England and America" by Edwin Wolf 2nd, and "Political Satires at Colonial Williamsburg" by Joan D. Dolmetsch. Each essay is well researched and annotated and each is described separately in this bibliography.

1558.———. "European Prints in Eighteenth-Century America." *Antiques* 101, no. 5 (May 1972): 858–63.

Newspaper advertisements, early inventories, and diaries disclose that by 1770 large quantities of engravings were being imported from England. Portraits, sporting prints, and reproductive engravings of old masters were favored subjects.

1559.———. "Prints in Colonial America: Supply and Demand in the Mid-Eighteenth Century" in *Prints in and of America to 1850*, 53–74. ed. John D. Morse. Winterthur, Del.: Henry Francis du Pont Winterthur Museum, 1970.

Dolmetsch's examination of early colonial newspapers, letters, and inventories has yielded much information about the importation of prints from England and the Continent to the colonies. In this study, Dolmetsch discusses many prints for which she has found references in mid-eighteenth-century documents. Battle scenes, landscapes, satirical prints, and portraits were particularly popular.

1560. Drepperd, Carl W. *Early American Prints*. New York: Century Co., 1930. 232 pp., biblio., index.

Intended for the collector, this book surveys American prints through Currier & Ives. Lists of printmakers and significant examples of their work constitute the major portion of the book. Also included are chapters on magazine illustrators, caricature, and print processes.

1561.———. "Some Other Prints." *Antiques* 9 (February 1926): 81–84.

Drepperd discusses a variety of prints in this article as part of his apparent campaign for the recognition of American prints. He mentions book illustrations, lithographs, naval prints, and political cartoons.

1562. Ebert, John, and Katherine Ebert. *Old American Prints for Collectors*. New York: Charles Scribner's Sons, 1974. 277 pp., biblio., index.

Presented to the general reader as a history of American graphics as well as a primer on their production and preservation, the book is unfortunately full of minor errors. Lacking in perspective, the text is mainly devoted to lithography, while other media and periods are poorly represented. The glossary of terms, a list of selected names in American printmaking until 1880, and the list of nineteenth-century colorplate books that is included are helpful.

1563. Gabriel, Ralph Henry, ed. *The Pageant of America*. New Haven: Yale University Press, 1925. 15 vols.

The Pageant of America is a copiously illustrated fifteen volume series devoted to various aspects of American history. Vol. 12 is titled "The American Spirit in Art" and several of the chapters, written by Frank Jewett Mather, Jr., are concerned with graphic arts. The chapter on reproductive engraving discusses technique, individual engravers like John Foster, Paul Revere, and James B. Longacre, landscape portfolios, the American Art Union prints, and wood engraving. A separate chapter covers painter-engraving, which deals with the etching revival. The chapter on book illustration discusses individual illustrators of the nineteenth and early twentieth centuries, while the last of the graphic arts chapters focuses on social and political caricature in the late nineteenth and early twentieth centuries. In each of these chapters Mather quickly dispenses with the eighteenth century, but the volume is useful for its reproduction of nineteenth-century prints.

1564. Glaser, Lynn. *Engraved America: Iconography of America Through 1800*. Philadelphia: Ancient Orb Press, 1970. 314 pp., index.

The introduction describes European literature that published illustrations of North and South America. The arrangement of the volume is chronological but somewhat confusing. For example, views of a city are grouped together, but not in alphabetical or chronological order. The notes on the plates are curiously uneven, some fairly good, others poor. Glaser continually refers the reader to other publications. Moreover, there are no acknowledgments for the illustrations, so it would be difficult for the serious researcher to find the original prints. Some of the book illustrations are not credited to their books, but are presented completely out of context. All in all, the work is not very helpful, though picture researchers may find it useful.

1565. Halsey, R. T. Haines. "Early Engravings in Colonial Houses." *Bulletin of the Metropolitan Museum of Art* 19 (August 1924): 196–202.

Enough importance was accorded to prints in the colonial period that they were frequently hung on the walls of homes and collected in portfolios. Several early views, portraits, and maps, as well as advertisements for them are cited here as examples. This is an important article for an understanding of the print trade in the colonies.

1566. Harris, Neil. *The Artist in American Society*. New York: George Braziller, 1966. 432 pp., biblio., index.

Although there is little direct reference to the graphic arts in this work, it is indispensable for the background it provides on the interactions of the artist and American society in the eighteenth and nineteenth centuries. The book is particularly valuable for its scholarly discussions of artistic communities both here and abroad.

1567. Hartmann, Sadakichi. "The Graphic Arts." in *A History of American Art*, Boston: L.C. Page & Co., 1901.

First printed in 1901, the chapter on graphic arts in the second volume concentrates on the last half of the nineteenth century. Prints created before the Civil War are dismissed entirely. Various book illustrators, comic artists, etchers, and wood engravers receive some mention, but there is no extensive commentary on any individual. A revised edition was issued in New York by Tudor in 1934.

1568. Hitchings, Sinclair. "London's Images of Colonial America" in *Eighteenth-Century Prints in Colonial America. To Educate and Decorate*, 11–31. ed. Joan D. Dolmetsch. Williamsburg: Colonial Williamsburg Foundation, 1979.

The maps and prints depicting the North American colonies produced in London in the age of Hogarth and later are the subject of this survey. Among the prints mentioned are vues d'optique, the Lewis Evans map of the middle colonies; the great views of Boston, New York, and Philadelphia; Mark Catesby's *Natural History*; Thomas Pownall's drawings for the *Scenographia Americana*; portrait prints; and caricatures.

1569. Holman, Richard B. "Seventeenth-Century American Prints" in *Prints in and of America to 1850*, 23–52. ed. John D. Morse. Winterthur, Del.: Henry Francis du Pont Winterthur Museum, 1970.

This study begins by considering most of John Foster's prints, book illustrations, and printer's ornaments. Holman mentions citations from contemporary sources about works of Foster that are no longer extant. A crude but powerful woodcut of King David, tentatively attributed to Richard Pierce, a Boston printer of the 1680s, is also considered. Holman concludes by briefly mentioning the Massachusetts Colony Bills of 1690, engraved on copper by John Coney. The section on Foster is well documented and includes references to recently published studies on the portrait of Richard Mather and the map of New England.

1570. Karshan, Donald H. "American Printmaking." *Art in America* 56 (1968): 22–55.

This overly ambitious survey discusses the context, honesty, and realism of early American prints. Lithography is covered briefly; Homer and later artists are treated more thoroughly. The article is lavishly illustrated, primarily with prints of the twentieth century.

1571. Klumpp, H. Parks. "Whence and Whither America? A Note on the Importance of Prints." *Antiques* 34, no. 9 (1938): 126–29.

At the time this article was written, few public collections considered American prints to have artistic or historic value. This article is a plea to the Library of Congress to organize its vast collection of such prints by taking them from storage and housing them in a central location.

1572. Koehler, Sylvester R. "Nordamerika." in *Der Holzscnitt*, ed. Carl Von Lutzow. Vienna: Gesellschaft fur Vervielfaltigende Kunst, 1887.

This article concentrates on woodcuts and wood engravings after the Civil War. Most of the important artists, as well as the influence of illustrated periodicals, are noted.

1573.———. "Vereinigte Staaten Von Nordamerika." in *Die Radierung*, ed. Richard Graul. Vienna: Gesellschaft fur Vervielfaltigende Kunst, 1892.

In this volume, Koehler traces the history of etching in the United States from Cadart's arrival in New York in 1866 through the 1880s. Detailed attention is given to the period 1866 to 1877, when the etching clubs were founded, and the impact of the French influence was felt. Especially worthwhile are Koehler's opinions on the later developments in etching. Etchers are enumerated by groups: portraitists, landscapists, followers of Whistler, Duveneck's circle, reproductive etchers, women etchers, and monotypists. Since no American copperplate engravers were included in the preceding volume, Koehler closes with a mention of the most outstanding exponents of this art.

1574. Larson, Judy L. "Separately Published Engravings in the Early Republic: An Introduction to Copperplate Engraving and Printing in America Through 1820." *Printing History* 6, no. 1 (1984): 3–24.

This article is in two parts. The first provides an overview of the engraving and printing trades which produced separately published prints. Interactions of artists, engravers, and publishers are discussed as are subscription methods, advertising, sizes of editions, etc. The second part discusses eleven categories of prints—portraits, political cartoons and caricatures, genre prints, landscape and city scenes, allegorical prints, religion, broadside illustrations, certificates, educational aids, contemporary events, and historical events.

1575. Little, Nina Fletcher. "Engraved Sources for American Overmantel Panels." *Antiques* 88, no. 9 (October 1965): 494–501.

Numerous overmantel paintings were derived from printed sources. The sources were generally European, but the author has found several American sources through her extensive research into American folk art.

1576. Mann, Maybelle. *The American Art Union*. Otisville, N.Y.: ALM Associates, Inc., 1977. 90 pp.

The author discusses various aspects of the American Art Union and its predecessor the Apollo Association. Touched upon are the paintings reproduced as engravings, relations with the artists, the National Academy of Design, medals issued by the Art Union, the lotteries, exhibitions, American genre painting, and the demise of the Art Union. The prints that were widely circulated are reproduced as are examples of the medals. Biographical sketches of the artists involved in the American Art Union publications are included in this catalog.

1577.———. "The American Art-Union: Missionaries of the Art World." *American Art & Antiques* 1, no. 1 (July 1978): 58–67.

The author traces the existence of the American Art-Union from its founding in 1839 to its demise in 1851. The article focuses on the distribution of the prints, and each one is reproduced on a small, but useful scale. Following the article is an afterword "Hints for American Art-Union Print Collectors." Discussed are the values and prices on the current market, margins, water damage, and sources for the purchase of the prints.

1578. Mayor, A. Hyatt. *Popular Prints of the Americas*. New York: Crown Publishers, 1973. 183 pp.

This book is an uneven treatment of the history of prints in the western hemisphere until 1900. There is some discussion of the purpose of prints and their role in society. The book is notable for drawing attention to prints produced in Spanish-American countries, a matter too frequently ignored in such general discussions. The book is a compilation of brief essays, designed for a general audience.

1579. McClinton, Katherine M. "American Engravings on Papier-Mache Snuffboxes." *Antiques* 48 (November 1945): 284–85.

Engraved portraits, city views, depictions of historical events, and satirical comments often furnished the subject matter for the decoration of snuffbox lids. Some of the covers appear to be copied after well-known prints by American engravers, and a few are signed. The author discusses these prints and their sources, and provides information on the engravers.

1580. Miller, Jo. "America's Forgotten Printmakers." *The Print Collector's Newsletter* 1 (March 1973): 1–4.

Miller argues for a reassessment of several late nineteenth-century printmakers, such as Peixotto, Greatorex, Alden Weir, and Washburn.

1581. Morse, John D., ed. *Prints in and of America to 1850*. Winterthur, Del.: Henry Francis du Pont Winterthur Museum, 1970. 355 pp.

Chaired by Jonathan L. Fairbanks, the Winterthur Conference for 1970 was devoted to American prints before 1850. The following ten papers were published in the report: "American Beginnings: Prints in Sixteenth-Century Mexico" by Richard E. Ahlborn; "Seventeenth-Century American Prints" by Richard B. Holman; "Prints in Colonial America; Supply and Demand" by Joan Dolmetsch; "The Graphic Arts in Colonial New England" by Sinclair Hitchings; "Thomas Hollis and the Arts of Dissent" by Frank H. Sommer III; "Prints and Scientific Illustration in America" by Charles B. Wood; "Jacob Perkins, William Congreve, and Counterfeit Printing in 1820" by Elizabeth Harris; "American Lithographic Technology before the Civil War" by Peter Marzio; "The Grand Triumphal Quick-Step, or, Sheet Music Covers in America" by Nancy Davison; and "Prints and the American Art-Union" by Jay Cantor. Also included is a list supplied by Wendy J. Shadwell entitled "Early American Print Research Resources in the United States.".

1582. O'Gorman, James F., ed. *Aspects of American Printmaking, 1800–1950*. Syracuse, N.Y.: Syracuse University Press, 1988. 245 pp., index.

This volume of nine essays is based on the talks presented at the seventeenth North American Print Conference sponsored by the Museum of Our National Heritage and the Grace Slack McNeil Program in American Art at Wellesley College. Other institutions in Boston cooperated by mounting exhibitions and hosting sessions. The essays in this volume are as follows: "Masonic Imagery" by Barbara Franco; "The Poet and the Illustrator," James F. O'Gorman; "The Railroad in the Pasture," Sally Pierce; "Images That Sell," Luna L. Levinson; "Photo-lithography of L.H. Bradford, " David Tatham; "American Master Prints, 1900–1950," Sinclair Hitchings; "The Imperious Mr. Pennell and the Implacable Mr. Brown," Clinton Adams; "The Etchings of Ernest Roth and Andre Smith," Elton W. Hall; and "Yankee Printmakers in Mexico, 1900–1950," Richard Cox. Separate entries on the essays appropriate to this bibliography are located in their respective sections. All the essays are well researched and illustrated. They illuminate the emergence of a tradition of fine art printmaking.

1583. Palumbo, Anne Cannon. "Prints into Paint: The Influence of Prints on Eighteenth-Century American Painting." *Imprint* 18, no. 2 (1993): 13–20.

Using the Winterthur Museum exhibition of 1992–93 *To Please Every Taste*, Palumbo focuses on artists who relied on prints as learning devices and as sources for historical paintings. Artists mentioned include Benjamin West, J.S. Copley, and William Williams. The latter artist used prints as sources for settings and poses in portrait painting. John Greenwood was indebted to a print by Hogarth for his painting of *Sea Captains Carousing at Surinam*. Palumbo also suggests that West derived part of his painting *William Penn's Treaty With the Indians* from the cartouche of Henry Popple's 1733 map of the British Empire in America. This essay points to an important fact about prints relating to North America—the appropriation of them by artists to create additional works of art.

1584. Pittman, Linda Lee. *Prints for America: T. B. Freeman and Company, 1795–1797*. M.A. Thesis, University of Delaware, 1982. 51 pp., biblio.

This excellent study of a Philadelphia print dealer is based on correspondence and an account book located in the Division of History and Archives, Pennsylvania Historical and Museum Commission, Harrisburg. Tristram Bampfylde Freeman emigrated from England where he had been a print seller. At first Freeman imported prints, but he also fostered American production. Existing records document all aspects of this business including management of the store. Among the engravers he employed were George Isham Parkyns, George Graham, and H. H. Houston. Several women were also in his employ.

1585. Roth, Elizabeth E. "Engravings" in *The Concise Encyclopedia of American Antiques*, ed. Helen Comstock. New York: Hawthorn Books, 1958. biblio., illus.

This survey begins with a description of European views of America. It mentions both those engraved by Theodore de Bry after paintings by Jacques Le Moyne and John White, and other views that appeared in English and Dutch publications. The author notes that Americans imported many European prints with which to adorn their homes, although after the Revolution, engravers came to the United States from England and Scotland. Roth discusses landscape views, woodcuts and wood engravings, historical subjects, college views, and portraits. A glossary provides brief notes on the most important engravers and gives definitions of technical terms.

1586. Weitenkampf, Frank. *American Graphic Art.* New York: Macmillan Co., 1912. 328 pp., biblio.

No work has yet appeared to rival Weitenkampf's history of American graphics from its beginnings to World War I. Longtime keeper of prints in The New York Public Library, Weitenkampf demonstrates a knowledge of American prints and print bibliography that is staggering. The only shortcomings of the work are a lack of annotations and footnotes, owing no doubt to the exigencies of packing so much information into one volume. In case of doubt about a reference, one can consult the mammoth clipping file the author kept in the New York Public Library until his retirement. In his work Weitenkampf approaches the history of prints through the treatment of various media, not chronologically. There are chapters on etching, line and stipple engraving, mezzotint, aquatint, wood engraving, and lithography. Weitenkampf also considers the applications of graphic art in chapters on illustration, caricature, the daily press, bookplates, and sundry arts such as business cards and posters, much as he did in his bibliography of prints. It goes almost without saying that each chapter of this book is the necessary first introduction to any given problem. The excellent bibliography, given its chronological limitations, is thoughtfully arranged. The index is unusually thorough. A revision or a new version of *American Graphic Arts* is sorely needed, for the last fifty years have seen new advances in the state of the art, many described by Weitenkampf himself. In any case, until such a work appears, one should consult the drastically Revised Second Edition, published in 1924. It is readily available in a Reprint Edition, edited by Maurice Bloch (New York: Johnson, 1970), with a bibliography of books and articles by Weitenkampf.

Regional Studies

1587. *Boston Prints and Printmakers, 1670–1775.* Boston: Colonial Society of Massachusetts, 1973. 294 pp., index.

This volume on colonial engraving in Boston contains eight scholarly articles based on lectures presented at a conference held in 1971. The authors and titles are as follows: John W. Reps, "Boston by Bostonians: The Printed Plans and Views of the Colonial City by its Artists, Cartographers, Engravers, and Publishers;" Richard B. Holman, "William Burgis;" Sinclair H. Hitchings, "Thomas Johnston;" Andrew Oliver, "Peter Pelham (c. 1697–1751), Sometime Printmaker of Boston;" Abbott Lowell Cummings, "A Recently Discovered Engraving of The Old State Housein Boston;" Martha Gandy Fales, "Heraldic and Emblematic Engravers of Colonial Boston;" Charles B. Wood, "American Scientific Illustration, 1675–1775;" and Bradford F. Swan, "Prints of the American Indian, 1670–1775." The introduction by Walter Muir Whitehill and Sinclair H. Hitchings provides the background on the conference.

1588. "Panoramic Views of Connecticut." *Connecticut Historical Society Bulletin* 20 (April 1955): 52–61.

This anonymous article discusses the artists and lithographers who produced panoramic views of Connecticut. A list of fifty-one views of Connecticut contained in the collections of the Connecticut Historical Society follows the introduction.

1589. Adams, Katherine J. "Texas Impressions: Graphic Arts and the Republic of Texas, 1836–1845" in *Prints and Printmakers of Texas*, 1–19. ed. Ron Tyler. Austin: Texas State Historical Society, 1997.

Katherine Adams reviews the images produced during the period that the Republic of Texas flourished. Presses were active in Houston, Brazoria, Galveston, San Augustine, Washington, Clarksville, and Austin. Printers issued over 500 imprints, some of which were ornamented with advertising cuts, mastheads, and typographic ornamentation. Banknotes were also printed decoratively. Adams also surveys images of Texas during this period printed elsewhere, looking at books with views, idealized battle scenes from the Texas Revolution, comic almanacs and prints, and sheet music covers.

1590. Allodi, Mary. *Printmaking in Canada. The Earliest Views and Portraits.* Toronto: Royal Ontario Museum, 1980. 244 pp., biblio., index.

Most early views of Canada were printed in Europe, not Canada. For this exhibition catalog, Allodi sought, with great success, to locate views and portrait prints separately issued in Canada before 1850. Her essay chronicles the history of printmaking by city, medium, and genre discussing works by professional printmakers and amateurs. Detailed entries on the 104 entries in the checklist set each work in its historic and artistic context.

1591. Avery, B. P. "Art Beginnings on the Pacific." *Overland Monthly* 1 (July and August 1868): 28–34; 113–19.

This summary of the artistic life of San Francisco, from its beginnings through the mid-nineteenth century, discusses the work of painters, wood engravers, and lithographers. Avery concentrates on Charles Nahl, who was an illustrator, engraver, and lithographer, as well as painter.

1592. Baird, Joseph Armstrong, Jr., *California's Pictorial Letter Sheets: 1849–1869*. San Francisco: David Magee, 1967. 171 pp., biblio.

The illustrations of letter sheets in this book are well reproduced in their original size. The information provided in each entry includes title, artist, publisher, seller, copyright date, description, process, size, variations of issue, and current location. Following the 343 entries is an excellent selective bibliography.

1593. Baird, Joseph Armstrong, Jr., and Edwin Clyve Evans. *Reduced Xerox of the Original Text of Historic Lithographs of San Francisco*. San Francisco: 1980.

In 1972, Baird and Evans produced a very handsome volume on views of San Francisco containing fifty fine reproductions. A few years later, Baird produced a reduced facsimile to make the fine text and thorough checklist of views available to a wider audience. Baird's introduction discusses the production of the views, using Kuchel & Dresel as a case study. His notes are extensive, relating his text on the views to related prints. The annotated catalog is arranged chronologically. Baird includes prints distributed abroad and "partial" views of the city—events, buildings, and the like.

1594. Baird, Joseph Armstrong, Jr., "California's Pictorial Letter Sheets." *Antiques* 96 (September 1969): 412–17.

This article emphasizes the importance of letter sheets as contemporary visual accounts of California between 1849 and 1869. The sheets were wood engraved or lithographed. Editions of ten thousand or more were printed, indicating the immense popularity of these sheets.

1595. Barnhill, Georgia B. *Wild Impressions. Prints in the Collection of the Adirondack Museum*. Blue Mountain Lake, N.Y. and Boston: The Adirondack Museum and David R. Godine, 1995. 99 pp., biblio., index.

For much of its history, the Adirondack Museum has collected prints describing the Adirondack region in New York State. The catalog essay discusses these prints in terms of their use to describe, promote, and celebrate the region. The checklist of the collection, arranged by process, is particularly useful because it lists the titles of the books and periodicals in which these images first appeared. Many appeared in *Harper's Weekly* and other illustrated journals. Currier & Ives published many of the separately published lithographs including a number after the paintings of Arthur Fitzwilliam Tait (1819–1915), the foremost sporting artist of his era.

1596. Barnhill, Georgia Brady, ed. *Prints of New England*. Worcester: American Antiquarian Society, 1991. 164 pp., index.

This volume presents seven essays presented at a conference sponsored by the Worcester Art Museum and the American Antiquarian Society in 1976. The authors and titles are as follows: Martha Gandy Fales, "James Turner, Silversmith-Engraver;" Stefanie Munsing Winkelbauer, "William Bentley: Connoisseur and Print Collector;" Wendy Wick Reaves, "Effigies Curiously Engraven: Eighteenth-Century American Portrait Prints;" Marcus A. McCorison, "The Idylls of the Triune Idol, or the Joys of Publishing in 1820;" Georgia Brady Barnhill, "Political Cartoons of New England, 1812–61;" David Tatham, "Franklin Leavitt's Pictorial Maps of the White Mountains;" and Jane D. Kaufmann, "Calico Printing." Checklists of exhibitions held in conjunction with the conference at the American Antiquarian Society and the Worcester Art Museum and a list of the North American Print Conferences and Publications follow the essays, each of which is described separately in this bibliography.

1597. Barnhill, Georgia Brady. "Depictions of the White Mountains in the Popular Press." *Historical New Hampshire* 54, no. 3 & 4 (1999): 107–124.

Barnhill discusses the range of nineteenth-century images of the White Mountains published in books and periodicals or issued by print publishers such as Currier & Ives and Louis Prang. Barnhill argues that the intentions of the publishers and the audience determined the appearance of these illustrations and prints. Other essays in this special issue of *Historical New Hampshire* concern paintings and photographs of the White Mountains.

1598. Burant, Jim. "The Growth and Protection of a Cultural Industry: The Graphic Arts in Canada, 1850–1914." *Imprint* 24, no. 2 (1999): 25–37.

Based on his presentation at the North American Print Conference held in Ottawa in 1984, Burant's essay documents the imposition of protective tariffs, the growth of a distinctively Canadian graphic arts industry, its commercialization, and the development of a tradition of fine-art printmaking. Prior to the establishment of a protective tariff in 1858, many Canadian artists turned to the centers of print production in Europe and the United States for lithographs after their works. Burant provides ample examples of each of his major themes in this seminal article.

1599. Clark, Edna Maria. *Ohio Art and Artists*. Richmond: Garrett & Massie, 1932. 509 pp., index.

Two chapters in this volume pertain to prints. The first chapter on graphic arts discusses Ohio etchers, including Otto Bacher, Frank Duveneck, and Ellis F. Miller. Robert Blum, who was both a lithographer and etcher in the late nineteenth century, is also mentioned. In the chapter on newspaper artists, the works of Frederick B. Opper, Grant E. Hamilton, and William A. Rogers, who were late nineteenth-century caricaturists, are described. The emphasis in this volume, however, is on the twentieth century, although no mention is made of this century's commercial lithographers.

1600. Connell, Neville. "Colonial Life in the West Indies as Depicted in Prints." *Antiques* 99 (May 1971): 732–37.

This article examines Edward's *History of the British Colonies in the West Indies* and supplies information on early artists who illustrated the volume. Mention is made of a number of other prints on the same subject.

1601.———. "Cuddy's Aquatints of the West Indies." *Antiques* 101 (March 1972): 524–27.

John H. Cuddy's set of twelve colored aquatints of the West Indies was published in London in 1838. Connell describes the aquatints in detail, and gives a brief summary of the artist's career, noting that Cuddy later turned his attention to Canadian scenes.

1602.———. "Some Early Printed Views of the West Indies." *Antiques* 99 (January 1971): 127–31.

From the late seventeenth until the mid-nineteenth century, views of the West Indies were printed from wood cuts, copperplates, and lithographic stone. Most of them were published in England and France. The article contains a good selection of illustrations.

1603. Currier, John James. "Authors, Artists, and Engravers" in *History of Newburyport, Mass., 1764–1909*, 311–79. Newburyport, Mass.: Privately printed, 1909. index.

This chapter provides information on several engravers who worked in Newburyport in the late eighteenth and nineteenth centuries, including Jacob Perkins, Abraham Perkins, James Akin, William Hooker, and Gideon Fairman. A number of engravings are reproduced in the chapter and elsewhere in the volume. The biographies of the men are quite good, and pertinent facts have been extracted from newspapers, contemporary documents, and local tradition.

1604. Dexter, Arthur. "The Fine Arts in Boston" in *Memorial History of Boston*, 383–414. ed. Justin Winsor. Boston: J.R. Osgood & Co., 1880.

The greater part of this chapter is devoted to painters. Among the engravers and lithographers given brief mention are Peter Pelham, Paul Revere, Nathaniel Hurd, John and Seth Cheney, and John Andrews. Dexter only touches the surface of a vast subject worthy of more thorough treatment.

1605. Elwert, Philip. *Windsor County Engravers, 1809–1860*. Montpelier: Vermont Historical Society, 1982. 16 pp.

This brief publication discusses the work of Isaac Eddy (1777–1847), Oliver Tarbell Eddy (1799–1868), James Wilson (1763–1855), John G. Darby, Ebenezer Hutchinson, Moody Morse Peabody (1787–1866), Lewis Robinson (1793–1871), George White (1797–1873), Christian Meadows (b. 1814), and Sarah Wood. Biographical information and a checklist of the works of each engraver is provided.

1606. Fales, Martha Gandy. "Heraldic and Emblematic Engravers of Colonial Boston" in *Boston Prints and Printmakers, 1670–1775*, 185–220. Boston: Colonial Society of Massachusetts, 1973.

The author points out that work such as seal cutting and arms engraving constitutes the bulk of most engravers' work. Other work includes currency and coins, early seals and stamps for embossing legal documents, college seals, armorial engravings on silver or for bookplates, trade cards, and membership certificates. The study is well documented and profusely illustrated.

1607. Giffen, Daniel H. "Summer in the White Mountains." *Antiques* 88 (August 1965): 195–99.

Giffen begins with a few words on the development of the White Mountains as a summer retreat. He then describes several wood engravings, engravings, broadsides, and lithographs that depict the region.

1608. Gillingham, Harold E. "Old Business Cards of Philadelphia." *Pennsylvania Magazine of History and Biography* 53 (July 1929): 203–229.

Gillingham's introduction to the subject emphasizes American independence in the design of trade cards. He discusses in detail about fifteen trade cards in the collection of the Historical Society of Pennsylvania designed by engravers such as James Smither, Thackara & Vallance, Henry Dawkins, James Akin, Gideon Fairman, and William E. Tucker. Other trade cards mentioned were either printed or engraved anonymously. City directories, newspapers, and other sources were used in the research for this article, so much valuable information on the tradesmen and engravers involved in the production of these cards is presented.

1609. Glanz, Dawn. *How the West was Drawn: American Art and the Settling of the Frontier*. Ann Arbor: UMI Research Press, 1982. 205 pp., biblio., index.

This volume discusses four themes recurrent in art of the American West: Daniel Boone, fur trappers and traders, American pioneers and homesteaders, and wild animals. The visual matter under discussion includes sculpture and paintings as well as drawings, prints and book illustrations. As Glanz explains, this study of iconography of the West is part of a larger context which includes the conflict between wilderness and civilization, white man and the Indian, the sense of Amerian mission and the nature of progress.

1610. Harlow, Thompson R. "Connecticut Engravers, 1774–1820." *Connecticut Historical Society Bulletin* 36 (October 1971): 97–136.

This exhibtion catalog lists eighty-two engravings by Connecticut artists, arranged by the engraver's name. Each engraver's prints are listed chronologically. The biographical sketches are excellent; several are based on manuscript materials held by the Connecticut Historical Society. Almost half of the prints described are reproduced, making this a very useful checklist for a fine collection.

1611. Hitchings, Sinclair H. "The First Philadelphia Printsellers" in *Philadelphia Printmaking. American Prints Before 1860*, 3–8. ed. Robert F. Looney. West Chester, Penn.: Tinicum Press, 1976.

Hitchings writes about the various men, who in addition to other activities, sold prints in Philadephia during the colonial era. Documentation is drawn from contemporary newspapers and other sources.

1612.———. "The Graphic Arts in Colonial New England" in *Prints in and of America to 1850*, 75–110. ed. John D. Morse. Winterthur, Del.: Henry Francis du Pont Winterthur Museum, 1970.

This discursive survey briefly touches on many aspects of the graphic arts in New England: city views, book illustrations, portraits, maps, and paper currency. All of the artists involved in these various branches of the graphic arts are also discussed, although none of the engravers is closely analyzed. This survey also suggests topics to pursue that would help eliminate the large gaps in our knowledge about prints of this era.

1613.———. "New York's Pioneer Printsellers." *The Print Collector's Newsletter* 4 (March 1973): 4–6.

This is the second in a series of articles which discuss the business of selling prints. In the first half of the eighteenth century, Hitchings notes that William Bradford and Gerardus Duyckinck in New York City were pioneers of print commerce. The article is well researched, with references to contemporary notices in newspapers and inventories of works for sale.

1614. Hogarth, Paul. *Artists on Horseback: The Old West in Illustrated Journalism, 1857–1900*. New York: Watson-Guptill, 1972. 288 pp., index, biographical notes.

Hogarth deals with British sketch artists of the American west and the reproduction of their works in British publications.

1615. Howell, Warren R. "Pictorial California." *Antiques* 65 (January 1954): 62–65.

In this article, Howell considers a collection of prints and drawings formed by Robert B. Honeyman that were displayed at the Los Cerritos Museum in 1954. He has selected several lithographs for analysis, and comments on Francis S. Marryat, Thomas A. Ayers, Alexander Edouart, and Albertis del Orient Browere, among others.

1616. Hulse, Elizabeth. *Engravers & Lithographers in 19th Century Canada*. Toronto: Thomas Fisher Rare Book Library, 1980. 14 pp., mimeo.

This exhibition checklist was prepared for the meeting of the North American Print Conference in Toronto in 1980. Particular attention is paid to the engravers and lithographers whose work appeared in books and periodicals published between 1824 and 1885.

1617. Huseman, Ben. "The Beginnings of Lithography in Texas" in *Prints and Printmakers of Texas*, 20–47. ed. Ron Tyler. Austin: Texas State Historical Society, 1997.

Huseman has identified two German immigrants, Dr. Karl Adolf Daniel Douai and J. Martin Riedner, as the first lithographers in Texas. Working in San Antonio, they advertised in 1854 that they could produce maps, ephemera, views, architectural plans, caricatures and charts. Few prints are extant, but one caricature, *Sam Recruiting*, drawn by Wilhelm C. A. Thielepape, does survive and Huseman explains its meaning. Thielepape became the sole proprietor of the firm in 1855, but gave up the business soon after. Other lithographers included Iwonski and Lungkwitz, William DeRyee, and Joseph Paul Henri, a French immigrant. After the Civil War, additional lithographic firms became active in the state. Until that time, inadequate transportation and a small population hindered the development of commercial lithography.

1618. Kent, Alan E. "Early Commercial Lithography in Wisconsin." *Wisconsin Magazine of History* 36, no. 4 (1953): 247–251.

This brief article summarizes the practice of commercial lithography in Milwaukee. Kent discusses each of the important lithographers who began to work in that city in 1852. Excellent biographical information is presented on them. Also mentioned are lithographers working elsewhere who did lithographs of Milwaukee.

1619. Kimball, Gregg D. "'The South as it Was': Social Order, Slavery, and Illustrators in Virginia, 1830–1877." in *Graphic Arts & the South. Proceedings of the 1990 North American Print Conference*,

128–157. ed. Judy L. Larson. Fayetteville: University of Arkansas Press, 1993.

Using illustrations by David Hunter Strother, Eyre Crowe, William Ludwell Sheppard, and James E. Taylor, Kimball examines their vision of slavery and contrasts that vision to the reality in antebellum Virginia. Later illustrations deal with race relations in the era of Reconstruction. The author also analyzes the illustrations to show cultural biases in the stories and their pictures.

1620. Larson, Judy L., ed. *Graphic Arts & the South. Proceedings of the 1990 North American Print Conference.* Fayetteville: University of Arkansas Press, 1993. 277 pp.

This volume of nine essays derives from the presentations made at the 1990 North American Print Conference hosted by the High Museum in Atlanta, Georgia, in 1990. The essays are as follows: "The Half Horse-Half Alligator and Other Southern Members of the Jacksonian Bestiary: A Study in American Iconography" by David Tatham; "F. O. C. Darley's Illustrations for Southern Humor" by Georgia B. Barnhill; "David Hunter Strother: Mountain People, Mountain Images" by Jessie J. Poesch; "Two Perspectives on the Cotton Kingdom: 'Yeoman' and 'Porte Crayon'" by Dana F. White; "'The South as it was': Social Order, Slavery,and Illustrators in Virginia, 1830–1877" by Gregg D. Kimball; "Victims, Stoics, and Refugees: Women in Lost-Cause Prints" by Mark E. Neely, Jr., and Harold Holzer; "Images of the South in *Picturesque America* and *The Great South*" by Sue Rainey; "Alfred Hutty and the Charleston Renaissance" by Boyd Saunders; and "Graphic Images and Agrarian Traditions: Bayard Wootten, Clare Leighton, and Southern Appalachia" by Caroline Mesrobian Hickman. Separate entries on the individual essays are located in their respective sections. All are well researched and illustrated and contribute to an understanding of southern culture.

1621. Looney, Robert F. "Philadelphia Views, 1800–1830; A Preliminary Investigation." *Imprint* 3, no. 1 (April 1978): 12–15, 19.

This article focuses on prints of Philadelphia that appeared in books and periodicals beginning with the important works by William Birch. This survey reveals considerable diversity of style and some works of fine quality.

1622. Looney, Robert F., ed. *Philadelphia Printmaking. American Prints Before 1860.* West Chester, Penn.: Tinicum Press, 1976. 175 pp.

This volume contains eight essays based on presentations at a conference sponsored in 1973 by the Free Library of Philadelphia, the Historical Society of Pennsylvania, the Library Company of Philadelphia, and the Philadelphia Museum of Art. The essays are as follows: "The First Philadelphia Printsellers" by Sinclair H. Hitchings, "American Drawing Books" by Peter C. Marzio, "Matthew Clark's Charts" by Beatrice B. Garvan, "The Birth of Political Caricature" by E.P. Richardson, "William Charles and His War of 1812 Caricatures" by Lorraine Dwelling Lanmon, "Liveliness: A Quality in Prints of Philadelphia" by Martin P. Snyder, "Thomas Doughty, Printmaker" by Robert F. Looney, and "John Plumb and The 'Plumbeotype'" by Alan Fern. Each essay is well researched and written. The volume also includes checklists of exhibitions at the host institutions.

1623. Los Angeles County Museum of Art. *Los Angeles Prints, 1883–1980.* Los Angeles: Los Angeles County Museum of Art, 1980. 112 pp.

This exhibition catalog is divided into two chronological sections—1883–1959, organized by Ebria Feinblatt, and 1960–1980, by Bruce Davis. The introduction provides a narrative history of printmaking in Los Angeles, including organizations of printmakers, exhibitions, teachers and schools, and dealers. The discussion of printmakers is organized by medium. The catalog includes 136 entries and is arranged chronologically. This catalog is an excellent record of the printmaking activity of the region.

1624.———. *Early Prints and Drawings from the Robert B. Honneyman, Jr., Collection.* Los Angeles: 1955. 44 pp.

Compiled by Ebria Feinblatt and Ruth Mahood, this exhibition catalog provides a brief history of the artists and publishers who produced California views, as well as a history of the Gold Rush. The lithographs and drawings (some of which are preparatory sketches for the prints) have an important pictorial record of the major mining sites, scenery, ships, and cities in California at that time. There were 145 items in the exhibition, and the collection is now at the Bancroft Library, University of California.

1625. Lyttle, Rebecca. "People and Places: Images of Nineteenth Century San Diego in Lithographs and Paintings." *Journal of San Diego History* 24, no. 2 (1978): 152–171.

The earliest views of San Diego were made by artists employed by government surveys and makers of city views including Alfred E. Mathews. H. C. Ford, a landscape painter, made a series of watercolors and etchings of missions, including one of the Mission San Diego. Much of Lytle's article is devoted to landscape and portrait paintings.

1626. McCauley, Lois B. *Maryland Historical Prints, 1752 to 1889.* Baltimore: Maryland Historical Society, 1975. 259 pp., index.

Almost 350 prints of views, landmarks, and events relating to Maryland are reproduced and annotated in this volume. Many private and public collections in Maryland were culled to obtain this fine selection, drawn from maps, cartoons, sheet music, advertising, book illustrations, and separately published views. The descriptions are particularly well done, with attention paid to contemporary documentation and various print states. Added features are a glossary, biographical sketches of Maryland printmakers, a bibliography of books containing prints, and a list of secondary references.

1627. McClintock, Gilbert Stuart. *Valley Views of Northeastern Pennsylvania*. Wilkes-Barre, Pa.: Wyoming Historical and Geological Society, 1948. 45 pp., index.

This volume, concerned with the settlement and growth of northeastern Pennsylvania, discusses both the history and pictorial views of the area. There are detailed descriptions of the excellent illustrations.

1628. McCracken, Harold. *Portrait of the Old West*. New York: McGraw-Hill Book Co., 1952. 232 pp., index.

Over thirty artists born before 1875 are discussed in this documentary history of the West. Although McCracken writes primarily on oil paintings, the works of several illustrators, ranging from Darley to Remington, are included in this profusely illustrated volume. There is a biographical checklist of individuals other than those discussed in the text. The foreword was written by R.W.G. Vail.

1629. McGuire, James Patrick and David Haynes. "William DeRyee, Carl G. von Iwonski, and Homeography, A Printing Process, 1858–1872" in *Prints and Printmakers of Texas*, 48–79. ed. Ron Tyler. Austin: Texas State Historical Society, 1997.

The authors describe homeography, a photographic printing process that enabled the reproduction of pencil drawings, and the lives and activities of DeRyee (1825–1903) and Iwonski (1830–1912). The pair produced a small number of views and caricatures while they were active in San Antonio.

1630. Neely, Mark E., Jr., and Harold Holzer. "Victims, Stoics, and Refugees: Women in Lost-Cause Prints" in *Graphic Arts & the South. Proceedings of the 1990 North American Print Conference*, 158–183. ed. Judy L. Larson. Fayetteville: University of Arkansas Press, 1993.

The authors wonder why women figure so rarely in prints depicting the Confederacy. Few wives of Confederate generals appear with their husbands in portraits, rather women appear as victims and refugees, individuals who sacrificed much for the war effort. Works by Adalbert Johann Volck, comic valentines issued in Richmond in 1864–65, James Massalon, William D. Washington, and Joseph E. Baker are used as examples. The authors conclude their survey with a Currier & Ives caricature showing Jefferson Davis, dressed as a woman, escaping from Union soldiers. They suggest that this image so humiliated the south that southerners could not bear to have their cause feminized.

1631. Neuwirth, Steven D. "The Images of Place: Puritans, Indians, and the Religious Significance of the New England Frontier." *American Art Journal* 18, no. 2 (1986): 42–53.

Neuwirth sets early images of American natives and wilderness in their historical and religious context, using the definitions of wilderness established by Thomas Shepard in his Election-Day Sermon of 1672.

1632. The New-York Historical Society. "Gold Fever: A Catalogue of the California Gold Rush Centennial Exhibition." *New-York Historical Society Quarterly* 33 (October 1949): 235–71.

This extensive catalog by R. W. G. Vail, also issued separately, contains both historical background on the Gold Rush and a detailed checklist. Prints, maps, and cartoons are included. This is a good guide for anyone interested in this frequently illustrated event.

1633. O'Dea, Shane. "Strangers and Livyers: Perspectives on Newfoundland Seen through Prints and Engravings from the Seventeenth, Eighteenth and Nineteenth Centuries." *Newfoundland Studies* 1, no. 1 (1985): 1–16.

O'Dea differentiates between views of a place made by visitors and residents. This chronological description of prints of Newfoundland is an important contribution to the study of Canadian views issued in Canada, Europe, and the United States.

1634. Pennsylvania Academy of the Fine Arts. *Philadelphia Painting and Printing to 1776*. Philadelphia: 1971. 50 pp.

Although the seventeenth annual Winterthur Conference concentrated on furniture making, this exhibition, which was organized in conjunction with the conference, included paintings and engravings. City views, bookplates, book and periodical illustrations, and trade cards were among the types of engravings displayed. While the paintings are fully annotated, little information is given on the prints.

1635. Pepper, Jerold. "When Men and Mountains Meet: Mapping the Adirondacks" in *Adirondack Prints and Printmakers: The Call of the Wild*, 1–24. ed. Caroline Mastin Welsh. Blue Mountain Lake and Syracuse, N.Y.: Adirondack Museum and Syracuse University Press, 1998.

Pepper describes the discovery of the region by Samuel de Champlain, military maps, early surveyors, cartographic efforts of the New York State Legislature beginning in 1836, and maps produced by promoters of railroads and tourism including articles by William Watson Ely in *Moore's Rural New-Yorker* in 1860 and Alfred Billings Street's *Woods and*

Water of 1860. Particularly important to tourism were Seneca Ray Stoddard's guidebooks published annually from 1873 to 1915. Maps appeared in editions from 1874 forward. Finally, the efforts of Verplanck Colvin to survey the region are described. Later maps were produced to assist the State in its efforts to protect the forest and water resources within the park.

1636. Perry, Claire. "Art and exploration in California, 1791–1827." *Antiques* 155, no. 4 (April 1999): 576–585.

Perry discusses the important role that expeditionary artists played during the period of exploration in providing visual intelligence to monarchs and merchants. Among those discussed are Jose Cardero (b. 1768), Louis Choris (1795–1828), and William Smyth (1813–1878). Their subjects included natural history studies, views of towns and landscapes, and depictions of Natives and Spaniards.

1637. Peters, Harry T. "The Lithographs of California." *Prints* 5 (March 1935): 1–9.

Peters wrote this article partly to elicit additional information on lithography in California for use in his forthcoming volume entitled *California on Stone*. The introduction to that book expands upon the information given here. Peters obviously loved the subject.

1638. Philbrook, Douglas A. "Louis Prang and the White Mountain School of Art." *Imprint* 2, no. 1 (1977): 9–10.

One of the foremost collectors of White Mountain material was Douglas Philbrook. He lists here about two dozen reproductions of paintings of White Mountain scenery by Louis Prang's firm in Boston and several sets of album cards.

1639. Rainey, Sue. "Images of the South in *Picturesque America* and *The Great South*" in *Graphic Arts & the South. Proceedings of the 1990 North American Print Conference*, 184–215. ed. Judy L. Larson. Fayetteville: University of Arkansas Press, 1993.

Two important popular publications providing Northerners with images of the South were *Picturesque America* edited by William Cullen Bryant and published by D. Appleton and Company between 1872 and 1874 and Edward King's *The Great South* issued by the American Publishing Company of Hartford in 1875. Rainey provides the history of both publications exploring the demand for images of the South and focusing on Harry Fenn's illustrations for the Appleton volume and James Wells Champney's (1843–1903) for King's. The former publication featured views of scenery and cities while the latter incorporated views of agriculture, mineral resources, and manufacturing with attention to people. Both books promoted national unity.

1640. Reilly, Bernard F. "The Prints of Life in the West, 1840–60." in *American Frontier Life: Early Western Painting and Prints*, 166–196. New York: Abbeville Press, 1987.

This essay is the last chapter of an exhibition catalog that explores different aspects of art of the West. Reilly provides a chronological survey of a generation focusing on works by or after F.O.C. Darley, Seth Eastmen, George Catlin, Charles Edward Wagstaff, Nathaniel Currier, Arthur Fitzwilliam Tait, George Caleb Bingham, Richard Caton Woodville, and William Sidney Mount, among others. Reilly touches on the appearance of genre painting in the unusual formats of banknote engravings as well as examples published by the American Art Union. Following the essay is a checklist of prints in the exhibition.

1641. Samuels, Peggy and Harold. *Samuels' Encyclopedia of Artists of the American West.* n.p.: Castle, 1985. 549 pp.

This book contains basic biographical information on over 1700 painters, illustrators, and sculptors who depicted the American West from the days of exploration to those active by 1950. Each entry provides places and dates of birth and death, references in other reference works, education, and a synopsis of work relating to the West. European artists are, of course, included.

1642. Scharf, John Thomas, and Thompson Wescott. "Arts and Artists" in *History of Philadelphia, 1609–1884*, 1029–1075. Philadelphia: L.H. Everts & Co., 1884.

This chapter discusses artists in Philadelphia, particularly portrait painters. The discussion of engravers centers on the prints of John Sartain, and touches on the work of other engravers, such as Dawkins, Smithers, Aitken, Poupard, Scot, Trenchard, Thackara, and Vallance. There are some brief comments on lithography, with detailed attention paid to Albert Newsam's career.

1643. Schmidt, Martin F. "Early Prints and Maps of Kentucky, 1784–1850." *Antiques* 105 (March 1974): 556–60.

The author traces the history of views of Kentucky, from the first known map of the state, dating from 1784, and the first view of a local scene, made about 1795, to the mid-nineteenth century.

1644. Sheldon, Francis E. "Pioneer Illustration in California." *Overland Monthly* 11 (April 1888): 337–55.

The first generation of illustrators of California life and landscape are discussed in this early article; illustrators mentioned include Thomas Armstrong, and Charles and

Arthur Nahl. The thorough descriptions of illustrated books, letter sheets, and magazines make them readily accessible to scholars today.

1645. Shettleworth, Earle G. "Portland, Maine, Engravers of the 1820's." *Old Time New England* 61 (January-March and April-June 1971): 59–65; 105–110.

Shettleworth's excellent documentation on the first engravers who worked in Portland during the 1820's comes from a careful examination of contemporary newspapers. The artists discussed are Danforth Newcomb, Abel and Sidney Bowne, Orramel Hinckley and Daniel Scrope Troop, David G. Johnson, and George Washington Appleton. Individual engravings are carefully described.

1646. Snyder, Martin P. *Mirror of America. The Developing Life of Philadelphia Seen in Engravings, 1801–1876*. Gladwyn, Penn.: Martin P. Snyder, 1996. 256 pp.

This volume, inexpensively mimeographed, is divided into two sections. The first focuses on engraved views of Philadelphia, Cephas G. Childs's *Views in Philadelphia*, aquatint and mezzotint views, and wood engravings. The second section is a detailed list of 800 engravings, arranged by subject, followed by appendices listing the prints in a selected number of books and periodicals. Snyder's essay draws upon his profound knowledge of the city and the artists and engravers who depicted it. It is only unfortunate that the illustrations are derived from photocopies and that the production of the volume was not more professional.

1647.———. "Liveliness: A Quality in Prints of Philadelphia" in *Philadelphia Printmaking. American Prints Before 1860*, ed. Robert F. Looney. West Chester, Penn.: Tinicum Press, 1976.

Snyder suggests that American city views, even those that emphasize buildings, are of universal interest because they also show people and their customs, costumes, celebrations, and occupations. To demonstrate this thesis, Snyder describes a variety of prints from the mid-1760s through the 1850s.

1648. Spalding, Philip L. "Two Early Boston Engraved Advertisements." *Walpole Society Note Book* (1935): 33–36.

Two early trade cards are reproduced and described in this brief note. One, engraved by Thomas Johnston about 1732, advertises his own japanning business. The other was engraved by James Turner, about 1743, for Joseph and Daniel Waldo. Information is included on both engravers.

1649. Speed Art Museum. *Early Views of Kentucky*. Louisville, Ky.: 1949. unpag.

Fifty-two views are represented in this exhibition checklist; subjects include cities in Kentucky such as Louisville and Frankfurt, the Ohio River, and the Mammoth Cave. The exhibition included prints, paintings, and maps.

1650. Taft, Robert. *Artists and Illustrators of the Old West, 1850–1900*. New York: Charles Scribner's Sons, 1953. 400 pp., index.

In this excellent study Taft discusses over thirty painters and printmakers of the West. Included are such artists as John Mix Stanley, Alfred E. Mathews, Frederic Remington, Frenzeny-Tavernier, W.M. Cary, and H.B. Mollhausen; their work appeared as illustrations in books and periodicals. The text is well documented by letters, quotes from diaries, and other sources, all of which are noted in a separate section. Much of the material in this volume originaly appeared in a series of articles in the *Kansas Historical Quarterly* from 1946 to 1952.

1651. Tatham, David ed. *Prints and Printmakers of New York State, 1825–1940*. Syracuse: Syracuse University Press, 1986. 277 pp., index.

The twelfth North Amrican Print Conference was held in Syracuse in 1981 and the lectures are presented in this volume. The essays and authors are as follows: "Anthony Imbert" by John Carbonell; "George and William Endicott" by Georgia Brady Bumgardner; "St. Lawrence Country, 1838, as Seen Through the Eyes of Salathiel Ellis" by Wendy Shadwell; "E.W. Clay and the American Political Caricature Business," by Nancy R. Davison; "Upstate Cities on Paper and Stone," by John W. Reps; "This Bridge of the Yankees," by Bettina A. Norton; "Comic Drawing in New York in the 1850's," by Bernard Reilly; Satire in the Sticks, " by Edward Comstock, Jr.; "R. Swain Gifford and the New York Etching Club," by Elton W. Hall; "Bolton Brown, Artist Lithographer," by Clinton Adams; "Grace Woodworth's Portrait of Susan B. Anthony," by Amy S. Doherty; Woodstock in the 1930s," by Grant Arnold. The essays are well researched and illustrated, and are described individually.

1652. Tovell, Rosemarie L. *A New Class of Art. The Artist's Print in Canadian Art, 1877–1920*. Ottawa: National Gallery of Canada, 1996. 192 pp., biblio., index.

This beautifully produced and carefully researched exhibition catalog focuses on the etching revival in Canada. Tovell's essay sets Canadian artists within the European and American context, discusses the early exhibitions of artist's prints, the Association of Canadian Etchers, professional education for printmakers, the Society of Canadian Painter-Etchers, and the works of individual artists. A checklist of the 132 prints in the exhibition follows the essay and the endnotes.

1653. Tyler, Ron ed. *Prints of the American West*. Fort Worth: Amon Carter Museum, 1983. 144 pp., index.

The ninth North American Print Conference was convened by the Amon Carter Museum in 1978. Eight essays are published in this volume: "Prints of the Battle of New Orleans" by John Carbonell; "The Bonaparte Audubons at the Amon Carter Museum," by William S. Reese; "For European Audiences: George Catlin's *North American Indian Portfolio*," by William H. Truettner; "The Western Prints of Karl Bodmer," by George P. Tomko; "Alfred Jacob Miller's Western prints" by Ron Tyler; "The Great Platte River Trail in 1853: The Drawing and Sketches of Frederick Piercy," by Jonathan Fairbanks; "Political Caricature and Mormonism," by Gary L. Bunker and Davis Bitton; and "Chromolithography as a Popular Art and Advertising Medium," by Peter C. Marzio. The essays are followed by the checklist of an exhibition at the Amon Carter Museum assembled by the conference.

1654.———. *Prints and Printmakers of Texas*. Austin: Texas State Historical Association, 1997. 274 pp., index.

This volumes contains essays based on lectures presented at the 1988 North American Print Conference held in Austin, Texas. The three essays describing nineteenth-century prints are "Texas Impressions: Graphic Arts and the Republic of Texas, 1836–1845" by Katherine J. Adams; "The Beginnings of Lithography in Texas" by Ben Huseman; and "William DeRyee, Carl G. von Iwonski, and Homeography, a printing Process, 1858–1872" by James Patrick McGuire and David Haynes. The other ten essays are on subjects such as prints, photographs, posters, and T-shirts of the twentieth century.

1655. Watson, Douglas S. *California in the Fifties*. San Francisco: John Howell, 1936. unpag.

This publication contains reproductions of fifty lithographs executed by San Francisco artists depicting cities and mining towns in California during the 1850s. Although the caption for each view contains some background information, little attention is given to the individual craftsmen.

1656. Weber, David J. "The Artist, the Lithographer, and the Desert Southwest." *Gateway Heritage* 5, no. 3 (1984): 32–41.

The historian David Weber assesses the accuracy of nineteenth-century lithographs of the southwest and stresses their importance as the earliest depictions of the region. In comparisons of drawings to published images in government reports, Weber points out embellishments, changes, and errors yet asserts that the published lithographs are generally accurate copies of work by topographical artists. This striving for fidelity is not necessarily present in commercial publicaions of the same era.

1657. Weiss, Harry B. "The Growth of the Graphic Arts in Philadelphia, 1663–1820." *Bulletin of the New York Public Library* 56 (February and March 1952): 76–83; 56; 139–45.

This statistical analysis on the graphic arts in Philadelphia is based on information in H. Glenn Brown and Maude Brown's *A Directory of Book-Arts and Book Trade in Philadelphia to 1820, Including Painters and Engravers*. The book contains graphs which illustrate the growth of the various book trade professions, and also gives information on allied trades.

1658.———. "The Number of Persons and Firms Connected with the Graphic Arts in New York City, 1633–1820." *Bulletin of The New York Public Library* 50 (October 1946): 775–86.

This statistical analysis is based on George McKay's *Register of Artists, Engravers, Booksellers, Bookbinders, Printers and Publishers in New York City, 1633–1820*. Weiss has rearranged McKay's list to show the growth, year by year, of the graphic arts. Separate charts have been prepared on artists, engravers, bookbinders, booksellers, and printers. Other occupations associated with printing have also been analyzed. The text explains Weiss's methods and provides information on the various trades and craftsmen.

1659. Weitenkampf, Frank. "The Fine Arts in New York City" in *Memorial History of the City of New York*, 334–70. New York: New York History Company, 1892.

As Weintenkampf surveys all the fine arts in New York City in this chapter, his comments on graphic arts are necessarily brief. Among the topics touched upon are late eighteenth-century and nineteenth-century engravers, bank note engraving, etching, lithography, wood engraving, and book illustration.

1660.———. "The West in American Prints." *Scribner's Magazine* 69 (April 1921): 507–512.

This survey touches upon book illustrations and separately published prints of Western life. Subjects of these nineteenth-century prints include Indians, the Gold Rush, and pioneer life. Lithographs by Currier & Ives, and prints executed after Bierstadt's and Moran's paintings, are discussed.

1661. Welsh, Caroline Mastin, ed. *Adirondack Prints and Printmakers: The Call of the Wild*. Blue Mountain Lake and Syracuse, N.Y.: Adirondack Museum and Syracuse University Press, 1998. 212 pp., index.

This volume contains nine essays presented at the North American Print Conference held at the Adirondack Museum in 1995. The titles and authors of the essays are as follows: "When Men and Mountains Meet: Mapping the Adirondacks" by Jerold Pepper; "Two Great Illustrated Books about the Hudson River: William Guy Wall's *Hudson River Port Folio* amd Jacques Gérard Milbert's *Itinéraire pittoresque du fleuve Hudson*" by Philip J. Weimerskirch; "Illustrations of the Adirondacks in the Popular Press" by Georgia B. Barnhill; "The Adirondack Chromolithographs of Robert D. Wilkie" by Warder H. Cadbury; "'Natures's Forest Volume': *The Aldine*, the Adirondacks and the Sylvan Landscape" by Janice Simon; "The Hermit of Phantom Island: John Henry Hill's Etchings of Lake George" by Nancy Finlay; "Winslow Homer's Adirondack Prints" by David Tatham; "'A Passion for Fishing and Tramping': The Adirondacks Etched by Arpad G. Gerster, M.D." by Caroline Mastin Welsh; and "Responding to Nature: David Milne's Adirondack Prints" by Rosemarie L. Tovell. The introduction by Welsh provides an overview of the challenges that faced artists in the region, the works of early travelers and geographers, and relates the essays to each other.

1662. White, Dana F. "Two Perspectives on the Cotton Kingdom: 'Yeoman' and 'Porte Crayon'" in *Graphic Arts & the South. Proceedings of the 1990 North American Print Conference*, 100–127. ed. Judy L. Larson. Fayetteville: University of Arkansas Press, 1993.

Dana White compares and contrasts the two views of antebellum Virginia life presented by Frederick Law Olmstead and David Hunter Strother. Although better known for his work as a landscape architect, Olmstead also was an influential authority on the south. Strother was raised in Virginia and illustrated his own travel narratives. One place that both visited and described was the Dismal Swamp, and White uses their descriptions to compare the two and to suggest why Olmstead's reputation has been revived while Strother's has languished.

1663. Whitmore, William H. "The Early Painters and Engravers of New England." *Proceedings of the Massachusetts Historical Society* 9 (May 1866): 197–216.

Among the engravers discussed in this pioneering study are Peter Pelham, Nathaniel Hurd, Thomas Johnston, James Turner, and Paul Revere. Sources contemporary with the engravers were used for this well-documented study, although far more is now known about these men.

1664. Wolff, W. Martin. "Five Printmakers of Connecticut." *American Collector* 3 (7 March 1935): 3, 9.

The five printmakers of the title are: Amos Doolittle, John Finch, Nathaniel Jocelyn, George H. Durrie, and John W. Barber. The life and work of each artist is summarized.

1665. Wright, Helena. *New City on the Merrimack.* North Andover, Mass.: Merrimack Valley Textile Museum, 1974. Unpaged.

Wright provides information on the history of Lawrence, Massachusetts, established in 1845, a center for the production of textiles in New England. Twenty-six maps, drawings, and prints are reproduced and described.

Religious Prints

1666. Andrews, Faith, and Edward Deming. *Visions of the Heavenly Sphere.* Charlottesville: University Press of Virginia for the Henry Francis duPont Winterthur Museum, 1969. 138 pp., index., biblio.

This book deals with the art of the Shakers commonly executed on paper. The introduction provides much information on the Shakers, their communal life, and religious beliefs. The illustrations are handsomely produced and the text on the objects are reprinted for easy reference. One of the appendices lists all extant Shaker inspirational drawings in public and many private collections. The library of Edward Deming Andrews is at the Winterthur Museum.

1667. D'Oench, Ellen G. *Prodigal Son Narratives 1480–1980.* New Haven: Yale University Art Gallery, 1995. 40 pp., biblio.

The story of the prodigal son was the most frequently illustrated parable in Western art. This exhibition catalog focuses on European prints, but includes several American prints including those by Amos Doolittle and Nathaniel Currier. D'Oench's excellent essay addresses the changes in the treatment of the theme over a five hundred year period. The illustrations are excellent and are useful for comparative purposes. Since the American series were dependent on British prints, D'Oench sets the American prints within the context of changes in society. A checklist of the exhibition follows the endnotes.

1668. Emlen, Robert P. "The Shaker Dance Prints." *Imprint* 17, no. 2 (1992): 14–26.

Part of a study of the depiction of Shaker life in the popular press, Emlen focuses on prints showing Shakers dancing. At least eighteen prints derive from one engraving issued about 1830 depicting a scene inside the meeting house at New Lebanon, New York. Emlen traces the lines of descent in a careful analysis that includes the architecture of the original meeting house. He suggests that this image "became the one image most people held of Shakerism in the nineteenth century.".

1669. Field, Richard S. "Further Notes on *The Rescue of John Wesley*, Philadelphia Style." *Yale University Art Gallery Bulletin* (March 1989): 62–67.

This issue of the *Yale University Art Gallery Bulletin* contains an essay by Amy Green on a painting by H.P. Parker, *The Rescue of John Wesley*. Field's essay is about a lithograph published in Philadelphia about 1865–70 derived from a copy of that painting. Field compares the painting and print, carefully noting the changes that turned "a historical epic into a popular illustration." Field also provides what information can be gleaned on the lithographer, D. Wiest, and the publisher William Smith. Smith published at least three Wesley prints, but Field could not identify any special relationship between him and the Methodists. This is an interesting excursion into the history of a single print.

1670. Flint, Janet. *The Way of Good and Evil: Popular Religious Lithographs of Nineteenth-Century America. An Exhibition at the National Collection of Fine Arts.* Washington, D.C.: National Collection of Fine Arts, 1972. 9 pp.

The introduction to this catalog discusses the religious life of America, providing historical background for the prints. Subjects in the exhibition include illustrations of Bible stories, allegories, portraits of ministers, and temperance prints.

1671. Gifford, Don. *An Early View of the Shakers. Benson John Lossing and the* Harper's *Article of July 1857.* Hanover: University Press of New England for Hancock Shaker Village, Inc., 1989. 77 pp.

Lossing wrote an article on the Shaker community in New Lebanon, N.Y., published in 1857. Gifford extensively annotated Lossing's text. Many of Lossing's sketches and watercolors are found in the Huntington Library in San Marino, California. Several pertaining to the Shaker community are reproduced with the finished illustrations as seen in *Harper's New Monthly Magazine*. This publication furnishes a contemporary view of the Shaker community.

1672. Holt, Elizabeth Gilmore. "Revivalist Themes in American Prints and Folksongs, 1830–50" in *American Printmaking Before 1876, Fact, Fiction, and Fantasy*, 34–46. Washington, D.C.: Library of Congress, 1975.

Holt discusses a variety of religious prints in this article, relating them to their European origins, American society, and the religious ideals of the nineteenth century. The texts of folksongs that relate to the prints are also reprinted. This article is based on materials gathered for a volume on religious prints of the Jacksonian era.

1673. Neuerburg, Norman. "The Function of Prints in the California Missions." *Southern California Quarterly* 67, no. 3 (September 1985): 263–80.

Neuerburg suggests the importance of prints for practical and didactic purposes in the New World, particularly since religious paintings were scarce. He cites instances of engravings serving as sources for colonial Mexican paintings and in use in churches. Archival records from the California missions are a rich source of documentation for the importation of European prints.

1674. Promey, Sally M. *Spiritual Spectacles. Vision and Image in Mid-Nineteenth-Century Shakerism.* Bloomington and Indianapolis: Indiana University Press, 1993. 292 pp., biblio., index.

From 1839 to 1859, elaborate drawings and watercolors were made by Skakers expressive of their spiritual experiences. Promey explores the context and meanings of these drawings, most of which were generated in Hancock, Massachusetts, and New Lebanon, New York.

1675.———. "Celestial Visions: Shaker Images and Art Historical Method." *American Art* 7, no. 2 (1993): 78–99.

Promey uses two art historical approaches—contextual analysis and careful visual scrutiny—to consider a significant body of American art. She finds that these tools of analysis enables us to understand these images as impressions of "the deepest spiritual concerns of one of the largest and most long-standing utopian religious communities in the United States.".

1676. Wolf, Edwin 2nd. "*The Prodigal Son* in England and America" in *Eighteenth-Century Prints in Colonial America. To Educate and Decorate*, 145–174. ed. Joan D. Dolmetsch. Williamsburg: Colonial Williamsburg Foundation, 1979.

In the 1940s Wolf found copperplates with episodes of the Prodigal Son story. This essay begins with these images which he attributed to William Priest who also was a musician and music engraver. Wolf looked for English prototypes and uncovered many versions produced during the eighteenth and nineteenth centuries. Interestingly the figures are presented in contemporary dress, not in Biblical costume. Among the American prints are sets by Amos Doolittle (1814) copied by D. W. Kellogg & Company as lithographs in the late 1830s. Nathaniel Currier also published a set as did Henry R. Robinson. These prints are rare and seldom do full sets exist.

Serials and Periodicals

1677. *American Art*

During its brief career from October 1886 through December 1887, this monthly magazine published articles on the arts—fine, graphic, and applied. The communications are brief, not scholarly, and intended for a general audience of collectors. Pages are filled with current news of exhibitions, descriptions of collections, and discussions of art instructional methods.

1678. *American Art Journal*

Published in New York from April 1864 through October 1905, this journal attempts to extend the knowledge of its female audience on the arts and fashion. It contains small anecodotes, gossip, and notices on various graphic artists. Published as *Walton's Weekly Arts Journal* (vols. 1–4); *American Art Journal* (vol. 5–7:8); *Watson's Art Journal* (vols. 7:9–87).

1679. *American Art Journal*

Published twice annually by Kennedy Galleries in New York from 1969 through 2004, this journal was dedicated to the presentation of new scholarship on American art. Areas covered include painting, sculpture, architecture, decorative arts, and graphics. The occasional articles on prints are scholarly, well written, and of great interest.

1680. *American Art Review: A Journal Devoted to the Practice, Theory, History, and Archaeology of Art*

Under the editorial direction of Sylvester R. Koehler, this periodical was published in Boston from 1879 through 1881. It corresponds in format and importance to Philip G. Hamerton's English *Portfolio*. Containing many illustrations, including a large number of original etchings, it is especially important for its many notices on contemporary graphic artists. Notices on archaeology, collections, sculpture, and architecture are also included. The book and exhibition reviews, and the notices on art society activities, constitute a potentially fertile source of information and documentation for detailed studies. There is also a four-volume edition published of the Columbian Exhibition.

1681. *American Art Printer*

This bimonthly magazine, issued in New York from 1887 through 1893, is basically a trade journal of the typographic arts and related industries. It is useful for the technical background it provides on the high-speed printing of illustration.

1682. *Imprint*

Initiated in February 1976, *Imprint*, the journal of the American Historical Print Collectors Society, is the only journal exclusively devoted to the study of American prints. A bibliography of the articles that appeared in volumes one to twenty-five was published in the Autumn 2000 issue.

1683. *On Paper: The Journal of Prints, Drawings and Photography*

Published bimonthly in New York from September 1996 through July 1998, *On Paper* continued the *Print Collectors Newsletter*. In turn, *Art on Paper* continues *On Paper* with an emphasis on contemporary American and European prints, photography, and drawings.

1684. *Print: A Quarterly Journal of the Graphic Arts*

Issued in New Haven and then Woodstock, Vermont, from 1940 to 1950, *Print* published well-written articles on all aspects of graphic arts, old and new, from wallpaper to Durer. With volume six (winter 1950–1951), it combined with the *Print Collector's Quarterly* and became bimonthly. After the merger, *Print* became more and more of a trade organ; articles of interest to art historians were no longer published after 1950.

1685. *Print Collector's Newsletter*

Published six times a year in New York by Paul Cummings from 1970 tp 1996, the *Newsletter* placed equal emphasis on old masters and contemporary printmaking. Little was written in the *Newsletter* on American prints before 1900. Lists of museum and dealer's catalogs, reviews of print auctions and books, and notices of prints and portfolios recently published provide information on current activities in the print world. It was continued by *On Paper*, a magazine also devoted to contemporary graphics.

1686. *Print Collector's Quarterly* New York; Boston; London; Kansas City, Mo.; Woodstock, Vt.

This periodical, which was chiefly concerned with the works of the recognized masters of engravings and etching, old and modern, began its useful career in February 1911, published by F. Keppel & Co. in New York. Publication was suspended from 1918–1920. It was revived with volume 8 in 1921 by J.M. Dent, Ltd., and continued by them in London through 1936. In 1937, the magazine was purchased by J.H. Bener of Kansas City, Missouri. Publication was again suspended in April 1942. William E. Rudge of Woodstock, Vermont, resumed publication of the quarterly and merged it with his *Print: A Quarterly Journal of the Graphic Arts.*

1687. *Print Connoisseur*

Published quarterly in New York by W.P. Truesdell from 1920 through 1932, the *Print Connoisseur* evenly balanced its articles between modern and old masters, American and foreign prints. In addition to carrying many fine articles on American prints, the journal published printmaker's oeuvre catalogs.

1688. *Print Quartorly*

Published in London, England, beginning in 1984, *Print Quarterly* emphasizes European and modern prints. Some of the articles do set American print production in a global context.

1689. *Printing and Graphic Arts*

Published by the Stinehour Press in Lunenburg, Vermont, from 1953 to 1965, *Printing and Graphic Arts* presented articles on various aspects of printing from ancient times to the present. This periodical contains several contributions on eighteenth- and nineteenth-century prints in America which have not been superceded.

1690. *Prints*

Published in New York five times a year from 1930 to 1938, *Prints* was devoted mostly to contemporary American prints. Pieces of interest, if not of great scholarship, occasionally appeared on old masters and American prints before 1900. Book reviews and exhibition notes were frequently included in each issue.

1691. *Quarterly Illustrator*

Containing occasional articles on graphic artists, this journal published in New York reproduced from 1893 to 1897, in popular form, illustrations copied from original sources such as paintings and drawings. Reproduced as well were illustrations from *Scribner's* and *Harper's*. Essentially a *Reader's Digest* of illustration and art, the *Quarterly Illustrator* is of value today as an example of the nineteenth-century interest in "popularizing art." It was published as: *Quarterly Illustrator* 1–3 (1893–1895); *Monthly Illustrator* and *Home and Country* (1895–1897).

1692. *Scribner's Magazine*

Appearing monthly in New York from 1887 to 1939, *Scribner's* frequently printed articles on American artists and their graphic works. Unlike *Scribner's Monthly* and its successor, *Century Illustrated*, the journal was not noted for the quality of its illustrations, since it relied heavily on photo engraving and halftone work.

1693. *Winterthur Portfolio*

Published annually by the Henry Francis du Pont Winterthur Museum beginning in 1964, the *Portfolio* presents scholarly articles on all aspects of American material culture, including prints. These carefully researched essays, profusely illustrated, have made valuable contributions to the field of graphic arts. Since 1990, the magazine has been published quarterly.

Sheet Music Illustration

1694. Beaumont, Cyril W. "Some Prints of the Romantic Ballet." *Print Collector's Quarterly* 18 (July 1931): 220–43.

This article concentrates on European prints of ballet scenes, several of which served as models for American sheet music illustrations.

1695. Davis, Aaron. "Music Covers." *Antiques* 12 (November 1927): 394–96.

Writing for the novice collector, the author discusses the proliferation of lithographed sheet music covers in the mid-nineteenth century, and points out some of the possible areas in which a collector could specialize. The basic information and advice is still useful, even for non-collectors.

1696. Davison, Nancy R. *American Music Illustration: Reflections of the Nineteenth Century*. Ann Arbor, Mich: William L. Clements Library, 1973. 24 pp.

In the fall of 1973, the William L. Clements Library at the University of Michigan sponsored on exhibition of American music to celebrate a gift of 30,000 musical scores donated to the library by Mr. and Mrs. Bly Corning. This catalog discusses the illustrators of the sheet music on display, and places the music in its historical context. The technical problems of printing in color, and the use of wood engravings and photography are briefly discussed. The subjects mentioned in the article include portraits, yachts, inventions, the Civil War, and even the discovery of oil.

1697.———. "The Grand Triumphal Quick-Step; or, Sheet Music Covers in America" in *Prints in and of America to 1850*, 257–96. ed. John D. Morse. Winterthur, Del.: Henry Francis du Pont Winterthur Museum, 1970.

Much nineteenth-century sheet music was published with illustrated covers, most of which were lithographed. This survey of the subject discusses over thirty covers and the artists who created them: D.C. Johnston, FitzHugh Lane, Winslow Homer, Benjamin Champney, and Robert Cooke. Some information is given on the business of music publishing. The sheet music mentioned in the article is listed with information on dates, publishers, artists, and lithographers. The bibliography is excellent, and much of it is devoted to American music.

1698. Delarue, Allison. "Ballet Music Titles." *Antiques* 37 (May 1940): 230–32.

This article, aimed toward collectors, presents background information on ballet and notable ballerinas in New York from the 1820s to the 1850s. The author notes that most of the illustrated sheet music covers concerned with ballet were copied from English and French ballet prints. The names of several lithographers are mentioned.

1699.———. "Some American Lithographs of the Romantic Ballet." *American Collector* 11 (November 1942): 8–9, 12–13, 19.

The history of the ballet in America is the focus of this study. The text discusses illustrations of ballerinas, and provides information about the lithographers and publishers responsible for the prints. Although this is not emphasized in the article, many of the lithographs were probably used for sheet music covers.

1700. Dichter, Harry, and Elliott Shapiro. *Early American Sheet Music: Its Lure and Its Lore, 1768–1889, Including a Directory of Early American Music Publishers*. New York: R.R. Bowker Co., 1941. 287 pp., index.

This volume does not pertain specifically to sheet music illustration, but it does list important illustrated sheet music covers. The book discusses various types of music, such as music of the American Revolution, early Negro songs, political songs, dance music, songs about Abraham Lincoln, and baseball songs. The appendix of lithographers and artists working on American sheet music covers before 1870 was compiled by Edith Wright and Josephine McDevitt. This list expands their previous one published in *Antiques* (May 1933). The bibliography emphasizes the history of music.

1701. Jones, Matt B. "Bibliographical Notes on Thomas Walter's 'Grounds of Musick Explained'." *Proceedings of the American Antiquarian Society* 42 (October 1932): 235–46.

There are six editions of Thomas Walter's *Grounds of Musick Explained*. First published in 1721, it contained the first engraved music printed in the colonies. Presumably Thomas Johnston engraved the plates for the fifth edition, but the engraver responsible for the earlier editions is not known. The sixth edition appeared after Johnston's death, and another publisher had additional music engraved which he had bound with unsold copies of the 1764 edition.

1702. Jumonville, Florence M. "Set to Music: The Engravers, Artists, and Lithographers of New Orleans Sheet Music" in *The Cultivation of Artists in Nineteenth-Century America*, 103–120. eds. Georgia Brady Barnhill, Diana Korzenik, and Caroline F. Sloat. Worcester: American Antiquarian Society, 1997.

Music played an important role in New Orleans from its founding in 1718. Jumonville's essay describes the contributions made to the publishing of sheet music in New Orleans by Henri and Clementine Wehrmann, French immigrants who arrived in 1849. Their firm produced some 8,000 pieces of sheet music by the end of the century. This essay provides a brief history of lithography and music in the city, concentrating on the contribution of the Wehrmanns who printed music for several different publishers and then on their account. It should be noted that Clementine was an engraver.

1703. Landauer, Bella C. *My Country 'Tis of Thee: New York City on Sheet Music Covers*. New York: New-York Historical Society, 1951. unpag.

The introduction discusses music composed for various occasions in New York's history. Among subjects covered are politics, the water celebration of 1842, districts and streets of New York, transportation, the Brooklyn Bridge, hotels, churches and cemeteries, the Crystal Palace, concert halls, parks and squares, estates on Manhattan, the Hudson River, beaches, and the bay of New York. A fascinating array of music covers is presented, and the checklist notes the most important aspects of the eighty plates.

1704. Leininger-Miller, Theresa A. *Picture Cincinnati in Song: Illustrated Sheet Music, 1840–1920*. Cincinnati: University of Cincinnati, 1996. 12 pp., biblio.

This exhibition catalog contains detailed descriptions of a variety of illustrated sheet music covers published in Cincinnati. The introduction includes a history of music publishing in that city and a synopsis of the each of the major lithography firms. The catalog is arranged topically—architecture, Ohio River, *Uncle Tom's Cabin*, Civil War Marches, patriotic hymns, exposition marches, train tunes, campaign songs, songs about newspapers, racial stereotypes, racial uplift, local musicians, infant mortality, children, beautiful women, Kentucky girls and schools, novelty pieces, and baseball. The bibliography is a useful one.

1705. Levy, Lester S. *Picture the Songs: Lithographs from the Sheet Music of Nineteenth-Century America*. Baltimore: Johns Hopkins University Press, 1976. 213 pp., biblio., index.

The author of several compilations of popular American music, Levy incorporates information on the lithographers and artists responsible for this array of over ninety lithographed covers arranged chronologically. The collection is now at the John Hopkins University and available over the University's website with excellent subject and name access.

1706. Porter, Howard F. "Early Sheet Music Mirrored American Life." *American Collector* 2 (20 September 1934): 3, 11.

The author mentions a number of interesting pieces of music in this article, written as a brief introduction to the field for collectors.

1707. Tatham, David. *The Lure of the Striped Pig: The Illustration of Popular Music in America, 1820–1870*. Barre, Mass.: Imprint Society, 1973. 157 pp., biblio.

The scholarly introduction to this handsome volume is in two parts. The first part discusses various types of musical illustration and its roots in George Bickham's *Musical Entertainer* (London, 1736–1739), the growth of musical publishing and lithography, which gave a strong impetus to the rapid development of music illustration, and the various subjects depicted on sheet music covers. The second surveys the history of music illustration, concentrating on specific artists (David C. Johnston, Robert Cooke and others), different stylistic trends, the use of chromolithography, and the influence of photography. Sixty music covers are reproduced in full size, and notes on each piece of music include information on the composer, the subject of illustration, and the artist. There are lists of the illustrators represented in the volume, and of their work. The bibliographical essay provides titles of influential books on English and European sheet music, as well as of books on American music.

1708. Waite, Emma Forbes. "Light on the Blackface Minstrel." *Antiques* 42 (October 1942): 197–200.

Waite provides background information on the blackface minstrel tradition and discusses some of the illustrated music covers made for this type of music. The history of the minstrel show, and the individuals made famous by their participation in such shows are described. The well-chosen illustrations, identified by artist when possible, are representative of covers used in the nineteenth century.

1709. Weitenkampf, Frank. "Social History in American Music Covers." *American Collector* 17 (March 1948): 9–11, 22.

Sheet music covers often act as mirrors of daily life. They can reveal the costumes, tastes, customs, amusements, fads, and many other facets of a society. Weitenkampf deals with specific subjects, citing pieces of music pertinent to each topic. The illustrations to the article are well chosen.

1710. Wright, Edith A. and Josephine A. McDevitt. "Collecting Early American Sheet Music." *Antiques* 29 (May 1936): 202–205.

The authors discuss various subject categories in which a collector might specialize, such as Civil War, individual composers, and literary topics. Although a pleasant survey and well illustrated, the content of the article is not very substantial.

1711.———. "Fire Fighters and American Sheet Music." *Antiques* 41 (May 1957): 448–50.

The authors collected sheet music illustrations depicting fires, fire fighters, and related subjects. They have listed more than one hundred titles on the subject, the earliest of which was published in Philadelphia in 1819. The illustrations to the article provide a good representative sampling of the collection, now at the Free Library of Philadelphia.

1712.———. "Music Sheets for Stamp Collectors." *Antiques* 41 (March 1942): 183–85.

The authors suggests an unusual speciality for print collectors: sheet music covers depicting conveyances that carry mail, such as railroads, boats, balloons, and carriages. Far more attention is paid to the subject matter of the prints than to the artists who created them. The article is well illustrated, and some of the covers shown are rare.

1713. Wright, Edith A., and Josephine A. McDevitt. "Early American Sheet Music Lithographs." *Antiques* 23 (February and March 1933): 51–53; 99–102.

The authors provide an introduction to the subject, mentioning some of the more interesting pieces from the 1820s to the 1870s. At the end of the second part of the article is a list of lithographers and the artists who worked for them, arranged by city. Although the authors admit it is incomplete, the list is still a useful tool.

Social History in Prints

1714. *Winter's Tale*. Glens Falls, N.Y.: The Hyde Collection, 1994. 24 pp.

The celebration of Christmas and related winter activities, as seen in wood engravings from periodicals such as *Harper's Weekly*, the *Illustrated London News*, and *Punch*, is the subject of this exhibition catalog. The text provides background information on the sources for customs such as feasting and gathering greens and aspects of Christmas such as Santa Claus. The checklist provides information on the illustrations. Artists represented include Winslow Homer, Granville Perkins, Jules Tavernier, and Thure de Thulstrup.

1715. Baird, Elizabeth. "American Printed Valentines." *Imprint* 3, no. 2 (November 1978): 13–16.

Baird discusses valentines printed in America from the 1830s to the late 1860s—as woodcuts, engravings, or lithographs. These productions of such firms as Turner and Fisher often followed the lead of English Valentines and often their images resembled the children's book illustrations of the publishers. Some "fancy" ones with lace and embossing were produced by such well-known stationers as Howland and Whitney. Interesting special types included bank note valentines and Civil War valentines.

1716. Breeskin, Adelyn D. *Labor in Art*. Baltimore: Baltimore Musuem of Art, 1938.

This exhibtion catalog focuses on depictions of workers in fine art. Drawing upon European and American art of the 18th and 19th centuries (as well as the earlier prints of the 15th, 16th, and 17th centuries), work by Americans such as Winslow Homer and James Smillie are included.

1717. Bunker, Gary. "Antebellum Caricature and Women's Sphere." *Journal of Women's History* 3, no. 3 (1992): 6–43.

The 1840s and 1850s were a period of social change for women. Bunker's well researched and documented survey of the subject describes caricatures from periodicals and almanacs, as well as separately published prints.

1718. Bunker, Gary L. and Bitton, Davis. "Double Jeopardy: Visual Images of Mormon Women to 1914." *Utah Historical Quarterly* 46, no. 2 (1978): 184–202.

The authors have surveyed pictorial images of Mormon women and grouped them in various categories. The Mormon system was portrayed as victimizing women because of the effects of polygamy. Mormon women were portrayed as impoverished and subjugated, uncultured, unsightly, fickle, even domineering. Many of these stereotypes occurred because of the negative view of Mormons. Further information on this subject was published in the authors' *The Mormon Graphic Image, 1834–1914* published in 1983.

1719. Bunker, Gary L., and John Appel. "'Shoddy,' Anti-Semitism, and the Civil War." *American Jewish History* 82, no. 1–4 (1994): 43–71.

At the outbreak of the Civil War, anti-Semitism was on the rise as a result of the wave of immigration during the 1850s and strong nativist sentiments among the Protestant majority. Bunker and Appel examine the graphic record as found in the popular illustrated press, examining economic stereotypes that were charged with overtones of political subversion. "Shoddy," although technically referring to wool that can be made into a sturdy fabric, became tied to poorly made goods sold to the Army and by extension to those who made them, expecially Jews.

1720. Bunker, Gary L., and Carol B. Bunker. "Woman Suffrage, Popular Art, and Utah." *Utah Historical Quarterly* 59, no. 1 (1991): 31–51.

Women's rights became a popular issue for caricaturists in the latter half of the nineteenth century. The Bunkers trace the history of suffrage for women in Utah relating the movement to criticism of polygamy and analyze prints that appeared in journals such as *Frank Leslie's Illustrated Newspaper*, *Puck*, and *Judge*.

1721. Bunker, Gary L., and Davis Bitton. *The Mormon Graphic Image, 1834–1914. Cartoons, Caricatures, and Illustrations.* Salt Lake City: University of Utah Press, 1983. 154 pp., biblio.

This study of the Mormon image is well-researched and fully illustrated. The authors have set the pictorial response to Mormons within the context of the history of this religious organization. The text is divided into two broad sections: The Development of the Visual Image and Image Themes. The first section uses a chronological approach. The second treats the imagery thematically focusing on Mormons and other minorities, Henry Ward Beecher and the Mormons, political caricature amd Mormonism, visual images of Mormon women, mischievous Puck and the Mormons.

1722. Davis, Aaron. "Cigar Smoking Prints." *Antiques* 8 (December 1925): 345–47.

The author, who has a collection of prints relating to the smoking of cigars, presents in this article a brief history of smoking and discusses a sampling of his own prints. Most are American lithographs of the mid-nineteenth century, humorous in nature. The article is addressed to collectors and suggests other subjects appropriate for print collectors.

1723. Goodrich, Lloyd. *American Genre; the Social Scene in Paintings and Prints.* New York: Whitney Museum of American Art, 1955. 30 pp.

Goodrich focuses on the history of American genre painting and its most important practitioners from the early nineteenth century throughout the Ashcan School. In the exhibition itself there were numerous prints and watercolors that supplement paintings by artists such as George Caleb Bingham, Alvan Fisher, Winslow Homer, and William Sidney Mount.

1724. Gordon, Jean. "Early American Women Artists and the Social Context in Which They Worked." *American Quarterly* 30, no. 1 (1978): 62–67.

Quantitative in nature, this study basically relies on the New-York Historical Society's *Dictionary of Artists in America: 1564–1860*. The discussion of the artistic careers of several women provides the "social context."

1725. Hoglund, Kenneth G. "'The Least of These': Visions of the Mid-Nineteenth Century City Missions Movement in New York." *Imprint* 7, no. 1 (1982): 26–32.

The poor in New York City faced increasing problems as the nineteenth century progressed. Religious and other voluntary organzations founded city missions to combat the problems of homelessness. Hoglund discusses the background for the establishment of the missions and reproduces an array of depictions of the missions from a variety of illustrated journals. This article proves the importance of illustrated journals in understanding the nineteenth century.

1726. Landauer, Bella C. "Literary Allusions in American Advertising as Sources of Social History." *The New-York Historical Society Quarterly* 31 (July 1947): 148–59.

The author furnishes many examples of nineteenth-century advertisements that exploited the use of literary allusions to promote products. Her discussion includes trade cards, books, pamphlets, miniature books, and broadsides, and she suggests ways in which these advertisements might be used by a social historian.

1727. Magriel, Paul. "American Prize Fight Prints." *Antiques* 56 (November 1949): 352–53.

Although boxing was outlawed in the United States until late in the nineteenth century and prints depicting the sport are rare, there is a small body of works showing prize fighters and fights. This article discusses several prints, emphasizing subject matter.

1728. Montclair Art Museum. *Piscatorial Pictorials of America.* Montclair, N.J.: Montclair Art Museum, 1973. 30 pp.

This exhibition catalog deals with the sport of fishing as portrayed in prints, paintings, and watercolors. The prints include such diverse types as lithographs of fishing scenes, trade cards, political cartoons, sheet music covers, and modern reproductive prints. The collector of these angling works describes the formation of his collection in the catalog's introduction.

1729. Newman, Ewell L. "Graceful Vines, Common Scolds, and Shameless Devils: The Image of Woman in Nineteenth-Century American Historical Prints." *Imprint* 6, no. 1 (1981): 2–18. biblio.

In a well-researched and thoughtful essay, Newman uses lithographs published by Currier & Ives and other firms to examine the way in which graphic artists portrayed women. His survey includes sentimentalized images of women with and without family members and several of the forty portraits of women published by the firm. He turns to other publishers, including Kurz & Allison of Chicago, and the pages of popular magazines to find images of strong women. Winslow Homer was among the artists who depicted the useful lives of women in his Civil War illustrations.

1730. Ormsbee, Thomas Hamilton. "Sports of Our Grandfathers." *American Collector* 6 (October 1937): 6–8, 14–17.

Prints of American sporting events in the first half of the nineteenth century are scarce. Ormsbee concentrates on depictions of competitive sports, often found in lithographs by Currier & Ives. Among those mentioned are horse racing, yacht racing, baseball, football, prize fighting, skating, and ice boating. The occurrence of these themes in humorous political prints is briefly noted.

1731. Pennoyer, A. Sheldon. "The Scope of Railroad Prints." *Antiques* 28 (August 1935): 58–61.

This article includes a survey of collections specializing in railroad prints. Pennoyer mentions Currier & Ives lithographs, wood engravings from the magazines of the nineteenth century, and a few water colors and paintings.

1732. Peters, Harry T. "The Greatest Show on Earth." *Antiques* 38 (July 1940): 15–17.

Peters owned a collection of circus posters, dating from early nineteenth-century printed broadsides to late nineteenth-century chromolithographs. In this article he examines the origin of circus posters and the development of the circus in America. He emphasizes subject matter and does not mention the artists.

1733. Reilly, Bernard F., Jr., "The Art of the Antislavery Movement" in *Courage and Conscience: Black & White Abolitionists in Boston*, 47–73. ed. David M. Jacobs. Boston: Boston Athenaeum and Indiana University Press, 1993.

Reilly chronicles the contributions of graphic artists to the antislavery movement through their designs for political and portrait prints, newspaper banners, and book and periodical illustrations. This essay is well illustrated and provides many examples of pictorial propaganda used by the abolitionist movement.

1734. Rock, Howard B. "'All Her Sons Join as One Social Band': New York City's Artisanal Societies in the Early Republic" in *American Artisans: Crafting Social Identity, 1750–1850*, 155–175. Baltimore: The Johns Hopkins University Press, 1995.

Among the most handsome of eighteenth- and nineteenth-century engravings are the membership certificates issued by various voluntary associations. This essay examines the English background of artisanal societies in general and then focuses on such institutions in New York. Of particular interest to the author are the certificates, bookplates, and banners used by these organizations. Rock explains their iconography and the meanings of these documents to their contemporaries. He concludes that, as the century progressed, the harmony they depicted occurred less and less.

1735. Rubinstein, Charlotte Streifer. *American Women Artists: From Early Indian Times to the Present.* Boston: G.K. Hall, 1982. 560 pp., biblio., index.

This work incorporates biographical sketches of American women artists into a narrative text which places these women in a social and cultural context. The work is well-researched, annotated, and profusely illustrated.

1736. Ruge, Valice F. "Life along the Hudson and a Checklist of *Harper's Weekly* Hudson River Subjects." *Imprint* 15, no. 1 (1990): 27–45.

Harper's Weekly carried pictorial material of all types. Ruge has examined a complete run of the magazine (1857–1903) and cited the 104 pictures of Hudson River scenes. Fifteen are reproduced with accompanying text from the magazine. The checklist is arranged chronogically and provides text page, title, page number of illustrations and names of artist, photographer, and engraver when cited.

1737. Shadwell, Wendy. "The Mad Hatter." *Seaport* 34, no. 1 (1999): 22–27.

Presented as a lecture at the 1997 annual meeting of the American Historical Print Collectors Society, this article describes the use of prints to promote a man and his trade. John N. Genin (1819–1878) was a manufacturer and importer of hats who used printed and pictorial materials lavishly to promote himself and his wares. Shadwell delineates his career and reproduces several of the important prints, pamphlets, and illustrations that propelled his business and fame.

1738. Stambaugh, James D. "Evangel in the Wilderness: The Nineteenth Century Camp-Meeting." *Imprint* 7, no. 1 (1982): 7–13. biblio.

The year 1800 witnessed two major religious revivals in New England and in Kentucky and Tennessee. Stambaugh provides the historical background for understanding the prints depicting camp-meetings that occurred as a result of renewed interest in religion. His survey ranges from 1819 through 1872. The illustrations for the article came from the collection of the Billy Graham Center Museum in Wheaton, Illinois.

1739. Tyler, Francine. "The Angel in the Factory: Images of Women Workers Engraved on Ante-bellum Bank Notes." *Imprint* 19, no. 1 (1994): 2–10.

Tyler has assembled images of women at work, including some depicting women in the textile industry. Many bank notes were issued by banks in communities noted for their textile factories. Tyler provides a brief history of textile manufacturing in New England and the makers of the images and their sources. A vignette of a female slave and child is also reproduced in this article.

1740. Weitenkampf, Frank. "American Sporting Prints." *Scribner's Magazine* 67 (June 1920): 763–68.

Drawing mainly on Currier & Ives, the author presents prints of hunting, fishing, horse racing, and various athletic events. This article, written for collectors, provides little critical information on this largely unstudied subject.

1741.———. "Country Life in American Prints." *Print Connoisseur* 11, 12 (October 1932): 296–315; 51–57.

The subject matter of the prints under consideration in this article are country houses, country scenes, country life, sports, the farmer, the farmer's work, the farmer's diversions, the blacksmith, and winter in the country. Nearly all the examples cited are lithographs of 1840 to 1860, although some steel engravings after William Sidney Mount are included. The second part completes a list of prints started in the first article, for each category of country life. In addition to the use of separately published prints, Weitenkampf suggests that reseach on banknotes by Burt and Darley, and wood engravings by Alexander Anderson and Winslow Homer could yield further information on the subject.

1742. Welsh, Peter C. *The Trotter in America*. Washington, D.C.: Smithsonian Institution, n.d. 22 pp.

The introduction to this exhibition catalog of thirty prints from the Harry T. Peters America on Stone Collecion gives a short history of horse racing in the United States.

1743.———. *Track and Road: The American Trotting Horse*. Washington, D.C.: Smithsonian Institution Press, 1967. 174 pp., index.

This selection of prints of trotting horses comes from the Harry T. Peters America on Stone Collection at the Smithsonian Institution. The text covers the general history of lithography in the United States and presents information on the history of horse racing. A list of the trotting prints in the Peters Collection (eighty-three items) and the names of the printmakers is included. The index is very helpful.

1744. Wright, Helena E. "The Image Makers: The Role of the Graphic Arts in Industrialization." *Journal of the Society for Industrial Archeology* 12, no. 2 (1986): 5–18.

Wright pursues the relationship between commercial lithography and industrialization through the proliferation of views of cities planned for industry, particularly Lowell and Lawrence, and through the publication of advertisements for industries such as railroads and iron works.

Wood Engraving

1745. *The Century Gallery: Selected Proofs From the* Century Magazine *and* St. Nicholas. New York: Century Co., 1893. 8 pp., 64 plates

A variety of wood engravings are presented in these sixty-four plates, reproduced from two magazines. Publication dates for the engravings, as well as artists and titles of the original works, provide a potentially useful index to the taste of wood engravers and magazine publishers in the late nineteenth century.

1746. "American Wood-Engraving." *Engraver and Printer* 5 and 6 (May and July 1894): 67–72; 1–7.

This anonymous article replies to the severe criticism of the work of American engravers that appeared in 1893 in the *English Magazine of Art*. A defense of Timothy Cole and the American New School is presented to counter charges of decadence in the art in the 1890s. The second part of the article attempts to demonstrate that freehand drawing with a graver on the block (as often recommended by Linton as being the essence of the art) is nearly impossible. In a curious appeal for aesthetic appreciation of New School work, the author proposes that the cheapness of halftone engraving and the rapid replacement of reproductive engraving by photographic processes gives artistic value to such work.

1747. "Art of Wood-Engraving." *Harper's Monthly* 60 (May 1880): 939–40.

This editorial, which defends wood engraving as an art, points out that despite the mechanical means used for the production of wood engravings, the pleasure viewers can derive from them is not diminished.

1748. "The Century Gallery: Selected Proofs From the *Century* and *St. Nicholas*." *Nation* (7 December 1893): 434–35.

Following the tradition of illustrated gift books, *Century* and its children's magazine *Saint Nicholas* published collections of their best woodcut illustration. This review examines outstanding plates by artists such as Cole, Juengling, Kingsley, and H. Wolf, and mentions the controversy between Linton and the exponents of the New School of wood engraving.

1749. "Decline of Wood Engraving." *Brush and Pencil* 13 (March 1904): 461–65.

This anonymous article speculates on the causes of the decline of wood engraving in America. By 1904, original wood engravings were rarely published, and only two artists were still producing them. The author attributes the decline to inexpensive new reproductive techniques.

1750. "Designers on Wood: Note on the Engraver's Art." *Scribner's Magazine* 20 (July 1896): 125–27.

The author notes that reproduction of drawings on wood blocks by hand is a fading profession owing to advances in photographic transfer processes. Especially interesting is the account of the wood engraver's profession; the author provides valuable and detailed sidelights on the practice of an art that had passed from its former glory by the mid-1890s.

1751. "Desultory Thoughts on Wood-Engraving and Wood-Cut Printing." *Knickerbocker Magazine* 41 (January 1853): 51–57.

This early article on woodcuts and wood engravings lists many artists and firms, especially in New York, who were practitioners of the art. From this article along with Linton's history, much information can be gleaned about the art before its so-called renaissance after the Civil War.

1752. "Development of Wood-Engraving as Shown in *Harper's Magazine*." *Harper's New Monthly Magazine* 63 and 64 (October 1881 and April 1882): 789–90; 788–89.

The first part of this article mentions a forthcoming exhibition of wood engravings at the Museum of Fine Arts, Boston, and remarks that these two issues of Harper's constitute a repository of the art. The second part contains an editorial comment on the first installment of Woodberry's *History of Wood Engraving*, which appeared in this same issue of the magazine. The belief is expressed that the "actual instruction conveyed by the illustrations of this magazine ... is incalculable." Woodberry feels that wood engraving has quickened the demand for reading, and the demand has in turn stimulated the development of wood engraving. Without mentioning names, the editor is clearly on the side of Cole and not Linton in the controversy over fidelity of reproduction in wood engraving.

1753. "Engraving on Wood." *Scribner's Magazine* 18 (July 1879): 456–57.

In this anonymous reply to Linton's article in the June 1879 issue of the *Atlantic*, *Scribner's* takes exception to Linton's accusations against Cole. Cole was one of *Scribner's* most eminent engravers, and they understandably were upset with Linton's inference that the great improvement in American wood engravings had occurred in spite of the work done in *Scribner's*. Linton, in turn, is branded a conservative in his approach to engraving; *Scribner's* criticizes him for not acknowledging that desirable effects may be produced from their technique of photographing on the block.

1754. "How Our Pictures Are Made." *The Child at Home* 1 (May 1860): 19.

Published by the American Tract Society, this magazine printed many wood engravings. This step-by-step description of the process is excellent. Much work still remains to be done by print historians in this neglected antebellum era of American wood engraving.

1755. "Modern Wood Engraving." *Nation* 50 (27 February 1890): 189.

This is a favorable review of the Grolier Club's 1890 exhibition of wood engravings, many of which originally appeared in *Century*, *Harper's* and *Scribner's*. Despite the small scale of such prints, the reviewer is struck by their distinctness and clarity. He gives special mention to Timothy Cole's wood engravings after Italian paintings. The reviewer closes by wishing that the Society of American Wood Engravers had a permanent exhibition hall in New York, so that the public could be exposed to the beauty of their art.

1756. "Outlook for Wood Engraving." *Century Magazine* 40 (June 1890): 312–13.

This anonymous editorial, inspired by the successful auction of Juengling's proofs and the exhibition of proofs by wood engravers at the Grolier Club, exhorts museums to collect such proofs. It is predicted that mechanical processes will not supersede wood engravings in importance, the mechanical processes being unable to reproduce the fine tonalities of paintings.

1757. "Wood Engraving in America." *American Historical Record* 1 (April 1872): 152–53.

The fourteenth edition of Noah Webster's spelling book (1791) contained a portrait of Washington engraved in relief on type metal. This article considers both this cut and other early American work.

1758. "Wood-Engraving." *Nation* 29 (3 July 1879): 14–15.

In this review of Linton's article in the June 1879 *Atlantic*, the writer clearly explains both sides of the wood engraving as art issue, providing a better statement of the basic premises of the polemic than does Linton, who is vague at times. In the *Nation* 29 (July 17, 1879), Linton replies. He disagrees with the explanation given here, but does not clarify the statements he made in the *Atlantic* article.

1759. "Wood-engravings as works of art." *Nation* 26 (28 March 1878): 218.

In 1878, in a letter to the New York *World*, John La Farge expressed his desire to see some of the best specimens of American wood engraving and painting sent to Paris for exhibition purposes. A rebuttal by George Inness appeared in the *Evening Post*, denying the value of wood engravings as art. This article recapitulates the arguments that ensued between La Farge in the *World* and Inness in the *Evening Post*.

1760. "Wood-engraving and the Scribner Prizes." *Scribner's Monthly* 21 (April 1881): 937–45.

This article announces the award of the Scribner prizes to young engravers not yet commercially employed. It goes on to discuss the success of the New School of wood engraving, the merit of American work as compared to European, and revives the controversy over whether the engraver's personality or fidelity in reproducing the original is more important.

1761. "Wood-Engraving: Reply to a Letter Concerning the *Century* Woodcuts." *Century Magazine* 57 (January 1899): 474–5.

In this response, the editor explains various technical methods employed by the magazine: the electrotyping of woodblocks to keep them from wearing, and the engraver's use of process plates of line drawings, halftone process plates, and halftone plates.

1762. Bale, Edwin I. "Timothy Cole and American Wood-Engraving." *Magazine of Art* 16 (1893): 138–39.

Bale discusses wood engraving as a "triumph of science." His arguments are technical, and he refers specifically to Timothy Cole's engravings in *Old Italian Masters*.

1763. Bradley, William Aspenwall. "The Advantages of Wood-Engraving for Magazine Illustration." *Print Collectors Quarterly* 1 (1911): 381–84.

The author, perhaps in a nostalgic mood, predicts that a revival of wood block magazine illustration may not be far off. He presents an interesting technical argument in favor of wood block illustration: halftone plates have many limitations, and require careful handling on the press, while wood block electrotypes, which are used on high speed presses, have an advantage in terms of clarity and longevity.

1764. Caffin, Charles H. "American Wood-Engraving." *International Studio* Supp. 18 (November 1902): 99–102.

This short article reviews the 1902 exhibition of wood engraving held at the Lenox Library in New York. Included in the exhibition were imprints spanning the period from Alexander Anderson and Abel Bowen through the late nineteenth century. Caffin provides a coherent discussion of the chronological and technical changes in the medium and analyzes several works exhibited. This excellent article provides a carefully reasoned and objective treatment of the subject, free from the taint of controversy which raged over wood engraving in the last quarter of the century.

1765. Carr, J. Comyns. "Gravure Sur Bois en Amérique." *L'Art* 2 (January 1881): 3–11.

Carr discusses early techniques for printing wood cuts and examines the methods of modern wood engraving. He concludes that the use of photography with wood blocks has given the engraver greater flexibility in his technique. The illustrations are drawn from *Scribner's Monthly* and the *Saint Nicholas Magazine*, two leading publishers of wood engravings.

1766. Carrington, James B. "American Wood-Engravers." *The American Magazine of Art* 18 (August 1927): 415–23.

These few pages by a practicing wood engraver clearly explain white-line engraving on wood. There follows a succinct history of the progress of wood engraving in America. Much of this history relies on quotations from the symposium of artists published by G.W. Sheldon in *Harper's Monthly* (Feb. 1880).

1767. Cary, Elisabeth L. "Two Masters of Modern Wood-Engraving." *Print Collectors Quarterly* 1 (1911): 319–33.

The author explains the meaning of the New School and discusses its ability to translate the tone as well as the line of the original work of art into engraving. By the time this article was written, halftone and other photographic processes had caused the school of modern wood engraving to shrink to two practitioners, Timothy Cole and Henry Wolf. Cole was interested in making as exact a copy of the original as possible, while Wolf believed in freedom of interpretation for the wood engraver.

1768. Chandler, Bruce. "The Imp of the Reverse" in *The Cultivation of Artists in Nineteenth-Century America*, 141–142. eds. Georgia B. Barnhill, Diana Korzenik, and Caroline F. Sloat. Worcester: American Antiquarian Society, 1997.

Bruce Chandler, a wood engraver working in Boston, describes the creation of a wood engraving from the original sketch to the final proof.

1769. Closson, W. B. "Painter-Engraving." *Century Magazine* 38 (August 1889): 583–87.

This is the third article in this issue written by a member of the Original Workers on Wood. Closson discusses the importance of individual expression in engraving, commending techniques which allow the artist a great amount of stylistic freedom. He finds reproductive engraving of use only in the rare circumstance when the artist and engraver have a good working relationship. Like the other members of his group, he is especially attracted to the production of high-quality proofs handprinted on Japanese paper from a wood block.

1770. Cole, Timothy. *Considerations on Engraving*. New York: William E. Rudge, 1921. 15 pp.

In his lecture delivered in 1921, Cole discusses the different fashions in woodcuts and engravings that were prevalent during his career.

1771.———. "Some Difficulties of Wood Engraving." *Print Collector's Quarterly* 1 (July 1911): 335–43.

In his discussion of wood engraving, Cole argues for softness, tone, and reproduction of the "air" as well as the line of the original. Cole is particularly concerned with the engraving of heads, which he believes was never done properly by the old school.

1772. Davis, John P. "The New School of Engraving." *Century Magazine* 38 (August 1889): 587–89.

Davis, a member of the Original Workers on Wood group, was a staunch supporter of William Linton's claims for the engraver's freedom in interpretation of subject matter. Davis's use of the term New School is in contradistinction to its prevailing use as a description of reproductive engravers such as T. Cole, who worked for the illustrated monthlies.

1773. DeVinne, Theodore. "Growth of Wood-Cut Printing." *Scribner's Magazine* 20 (May 1880): 34–35.

The author attributes the renaissance of wood engraving after the Civil War to mechanical printing. DeVinne provides a good discussion of the various types of presses and of the steps involved in producing a print from a wood block. He naturally emphasizes the work which appeared in *Scribner's*. This is the second of two articles by DeVinne. The first part concentrates on woodcuts, generally of European origin, that were printed on hand presses.

1774. DeVinne, Theodore L. "The Printing of Wood-Engravings." *Print Collector's Quarterly* 1 (July 1911): 365–78.

A great printer himself, DeVinne differentiates between the problems of early woodcut printing from pear wood blocks, and the later nineteenth-century wood engravings which were electrotyped and then printed. This knowledgeable essay sheds much light on the decline of wood engraving.

1775. Duyckinck, Evert Augustus. *Early American Wood Engravings by Dr. Alexander Anderson and Others*. New York: Burr & Boyd, 1877. unpag.

This little volume contains impressions from a series of wood blocks. Engraved for tracts and juvenile books, they were published in the nineteenth century by Samuel Wood, the New York Quaker bookseller and employer of Anderson. There is neither commentary nor artist attribution accompanying the impressions.

1776. Emerson, William A. *Practical Instruction in the Art of Wood Engraving*. East Douglas, Mass.: Charles J. Batcheller, 1876. 52 pp.

This volume contains a brief history of wood engravings with detailed and well-illustrated instructions for their execution. A revised edition was published as William A. Emerson, *Handbook of Wood Engraving* (Boston: Lee & Shepard, 1881).

1777. Farmer, Jane M. *American Prints from Wood*. Washington, D.C.: Smithsonian Institution Press, 1975. 64 pp., biblio.

This exhibition catalog surveys American relief prints from the late eighteenth century to the present era, looking especially at the contributions of Alexander Anderson, Winslow Homer, and Elbridge Kingsley. A special attribute of this catalog is the section at the end that focuses on techniques used in engraving on wood.

1778. Fraser, W. Lewis. "A Word About the *Century's* Pictures: New Developments in Wood Engraving and Other Methods." *Century Magazine* 49 (January 1895): 478–79.

Fraser writes briefly about the changes in reproductive processes. Twenty years before the writing of the article, artists saw their designs mutilated by the hand of the engraver. The New School of engravers, headed by Cole and Juengling, was far more precise in reproducing works of art on wood, although at times they were too intent on attempting to reproduce tones and textures of the original. The introduction of the halftone process proved more successful; an engraver, by reworking the halftone plate, could compensate for its weakness in rendering the extreme tonalities of the original.

1779. French, Frank. "Wood Engravers in Camp." *Century Magazine* 38 (August 1889): 569–75.

This is the first of four articles, written by members of the Original Workers on Wood, which appeared together in this issue of the *Century*. French recounts a camping excrusion to central Massachusetts taken by Kingsley, Closson, J.P. David and himself. As a result of this trip, a guild was loosely formed to encourage wood engraving from nature. Although chatty and anecdotal, this account is important for two things: its chronicle of the new movement's evolution, and its discussion of engraving directly from nature.

1780. Gokey, Edward A. "The New School of Wood Engraving." *Syracuse University Library Associates Courier* 25, no. 1 (1990): 53–83.

Gokey's well researched essay summarizes the debate over wood engraving in the late nineteenth century. Beginning with an appeal by John LaFarge to the committee on American art at the Paris Exposition in 1878, Gokey contrasts that letter with one by George Inness who believed that wood engravers were merely imitators. The essay provides an excellent summary of the state of wood engraving at the end of the nineteenth century.

1781. The Grolier Club. *Wood Engraving: Three essays by A.V.S. Anthony, Timothy Cole, and Elbridge Kingsley, With a List of American Books Illustrated With Woodcuts*. New York: The Grolier Club, 1916. 84 pp., index.

Anthony's essay, a posthumous publication, yields little information of substance, while Cole's seeks to establish an analogy between the techniques of wood engraving and those of painting. Kingsley reminisces about the growth of original work in wood engraving. Most valuable in this small book, of which 260 copies were printed, is its list of American books that are illustrated with woodcuts and engravings. Exhibited at the Grolier Club in 1915, these books and magazines are chronologically grouped by the publisher. About forty publishers are listed, including the American Tract Society, Harper's, Putnam's, and Scribner's. There is also a list of proof engravings, mostly of a reproductive nature, by Anthony, Cole, Dana, French, Kingsley, and others, constituting a veritable Who's Who of wood engravers.

1782. Hamerton, Philip G. *The Art of the American Wood Engraver*. New York: Charles Scribner's Sons, 1894. 2 vols., biblio.

The first volume contains a discussion of the status of wood engraving in America and compares wood engraving in America to photography. The second volume contains the forty wood engravings described in the first volume. James B. Carrington compiled the bibliography.

1783. Harvey, Clifford A. "Before Rosebud was a Sled: Documentation and Reprinting of Early 19th Century Commercial Wood Engravings from the GramLee Collection." *Printing History* 10, no. 2 (1988): 4–18.

Samuel George (1827–1903) printed flour sacks during the last quarter of the nineteenth century. This article discusses that business and the acquisition of the wood and metal engraving plates, over nine tons of them, by Bob Graham and Pat Lee. Harvey helped document the cuts, reprinted some of the best, and has produced a brief history of wood engraving.

1784. Hitchings, Sinclair H. "Some American Wood Engravers, 1820–1840." *Printing and Graphic Arts* 9 (1961): 121–38.

Hitchings discusses several collections of proof engravings, assembled in the nineteenth century, which provide valuable insights into the formative years of the white-line style of wood engraving. Religious societies, such as the American Tract Society, exerted a powerful influence on the evolution of book illustration during the mid-nineteenth century, as is evident from these collections. A detailed account, this article includes engravers who were outside the circle of Alexander Anderson, and is thus a valuable supplement to Linton's history of wood engraving.

1785. Johnson, Una E. *American Woodcuts, 1670–1950*. Brooklyn: Brooklyn Museum, 1950. 55 pp., biblio.

Johnson's introduction to this profusely illustrated exhibition catalog provides a broad survey of the topic. The catalog is well written, and pulls together much diverse material. The exhibition contained almost two hundred items including books, pamphlets, broadsides, and prints, drawn from the finest collections specializing in Americana.

1786. Kaufmann, Jane D. "Calico Printing." in *Prints of New England*, 135–150. ed. Georgia Brady Barnhill. Worcester: American Antiquarian Society, 1991.

Many examples of broadside texts, maps, and pictures printed on various textiles exist in libraries and museums. Kaufmann describes the production of printed cottons in general focusing on calico in an effort to understand why and how the specialty items were produced. The process of cylinder printing, patented in England in 1783, was used in the United States to produce fabrics for furnishings and clothing. Kaufmann suggests that letterpress printers possibly used special inks to produce commemorative broadsides and speeches on fabrics, but any special techniques remain unknown.

1787. Keppel, Frederick. "Golden Age of Engraving." *Harper's Monthly* 57 (August 1878): 321–36.

Keppel wrote this article, discussing the relative merits of wood engraving, in the wake of the LaFarge-Inness dispute over the medium. Keppel comes to its defense by evoking its long and illustrious past. The illustrated magazines, whose fortunes were in great part based on woodcut illustration, were primarily defenders of the art in the dispute.

1788. Kingsley, Elbridge. "Originality in Wood-Engraving." *Century Magazine* 38 (August 1889): 576–83.

An outdoorsman and nature lover, Kingsley was greatly interested in the potentials of engraving on wood directly from nature. Along with J.P. Davis, Frank French, and W.B. Clossen, he organized the Original Workers on Wood (OWW). This is the second of a collection of articles the group published in this issue of the *Century*. The OWW was interested in showing that wood engraving could be more than photographic reproduction; the group defended the rights of the engraver to put the medium to imaginative use. The new concern with originality in wood engraving was largely due to the example and influence of painter-etchers in America.

1789.———. "Wood-Engraving Direct From Nature." *Century Magazine* 25 (November 1882): 48.

At the request of the editor of the magazine, Kingsley prepared a wood engraving *en plein air* (in the open air), and wrote an account of his procedures. Kingsley firmly believed that wood engravers—as well as etchers and painters—could work directly from nature, as opposed to working indoors. This article marked a major shift in wood engraving away from the New School of reproductive engravers.

1790. Koehler, Sylvester R. "New School of Wood-Engraving." *Art Review* 2 (December 1887): 76–81.

Koehler reviews the two types of wood engraving: black-line work, current from the fifteenth to the nineteenth centuries, and white-line work, which developed in the nineteenth century. The discussion is general without specific reference to individual prints, yet the quality of the article is much higher than other contemporary discussions of wood engraving.

1791.———. "Wood-Engraving." *American Art Review* 1, no. 1 (1880): 123–25.

The author of this review, Sylvester Koehler, is the founder of the *American Art Review* and the first keeper of prints at the Museum of Fine Arts, Boston. In this article, Koehler examines William J. Linton's *Some Practical Hints on Wood-engraving* (Boston, 1879), and the *Portfolio of Proof Impressions Selected from Scribner's Monthly and St. Nicholas* (1879), one of the first compendia of fine art wood engravings addressed to the public at large. Koehler defends Linton's theories on the purpose and practice of the craft and rather forcefully criticizes much of the work presented in the *Portfolio*.

1792. Laffan, William M. *Engravings on Wood, by Members of the Society of American Wood-Engravers*. New York: Harper & Bros., 1887. unpag.

Laffan's introduction ascribes the remarkable development of wood engraving in the United States to two factors: the growth of the publishing trades, and the increasing appetite for luxury and culture of a burgeoning population. He briefly contrasts the American and European schools, characterizing the American as one faithful to the work it reproduces. A descriptive text accompanies each plate, with a comparison of the style of the original work of art to the style of the wood-engraved reproduction.

1793. Lankes, J. J. "The Techniques of Wood-Cutting and Wood-Engraving." *Print* 1 (September 1940): 66–76.

This is a precise and clear exposition of these two arts by a practicing engraver. Tools, supplies, drawing, cutting, and printing are all discussed in straightforward terms. Lankes's article is not well known, but is still one of the best introductions to these processes.

1794. Linton, William James. *The History of Wood-Engraving in America*. Boston: Estes & Lauriat, 1882. 71 pp.

Subjects included in the book are Alexander Anderson and his followers, type-metal cuts. illustrated newspapers and magazines, gift and large format books, *Scribner's* and *Harper's* magazines, the New School of engraving, and a final chapter in which Linton emphasizes the importance of artistry in successful wood engravings. A valuable source of information for little known wood engravers, the text is somewhat spoiled by too much attention to detail and too little emphasis on the development of the art. The author criticizes the recent tendency of wood engravers toward excessive fineness in execution. All of the chapters, except for the last, were written for the *American Art Review*, appearing consecutively in numbers 5 to 12 in 1880. As with any volume by Linton, this one was extensively reviewed in the following magazines: *Academy* (July 21, 1883); *Atlantic* (February 1883); *Critic* (January 13, 1883); *Century* (February 1883); *Saturday Review* (December 23, 1882); and *Athenaeum* (February 1883). Nancy Carlson Schrock prepared a new edition with an excellent historical introduction and valuable bibliography that was published in 1976 by The American Life Foundation in Watkins Glen, New York.

1795.———. *The Masters of Wood-Engraving*. New Haven, Conn.: Chiswick Press, 1889. 229 pp.

A product of the Chiswick Press, the elephant folio, of which one hundred copies were printed for American distribution, is certainly the most handsome volume printed on the subject. There is historical coverage of knife work from the fifteenth century onwards, although the only coverage of American work is the repetition of Linton's criticisms of the New School. There were several reviews: *Nation* (June 30, 1892); *Art Journal* (October 1893); and *Library* (February 1889).

1796.———. *Some Practical Hints on Wood-Engraving*. Boston: Lee & Shepard, 1879. 92 pp.

A masterpiece of vituperation, this is Linton's riposte to the attacks made by various reviewers on his article which appeared in the June 1879 issue of *Atlantic*. Linton is particularly hard on the *Scribner's* reviewer, who in turn reviewed this book in *Scribner's* for March 1880. This small book marks an important stage in the development of the wood engraving controversy.

1797.———. *Threescore and Ten Years: 1820 to 1890.* New York: Charles Scribner' Sons, 1894. 229 pp., index.

This work primarily consists of Linton's recollections of his career as a wood engraver and artist in England and America. In spite of Linton's involvement in the late nineteenth-century controversy over the New School of wood engravings, these memories yield very little information on Linton's practice of, and attitude toward, his art.

1798.———. "Art in Engraving on Wood." *Atlantic* 43 (June 1879): 705–15.

A professional engraver and historian of his art, Linton opened a major controversy with his views on the aesthetics of wood engraving. He distinguishes two schools: that of Bewick, which he considers the more artistic because of its originality, and the school of Branston, which he found imitative of copperplate technique. Careful notice is given various contemporaries of both schools, although Timothy Cole is a particular object of Linton's ire. Influenced perhaps by the painter-etchers, Linton makes his cause for "bringing back a taste for the original and peculiar worth of wood-engraving.".

1799.———. "The Engraver: His Function and Status." *Scribner's Monthly* 16 (June 1887): 237–42.

The New York newspapers, during the LaFarge-Inness dispute, published Inness's pronouncement that "wood engravers, properly speaking, are not artists." In reaction to this view, Linton wrote this article to defend the status of the engraver. This proved to be the first in a series of articles and books by Linton which opened a controversy over the nature of the engraver's art.

1800. Martin, Morris. "George Baxter and His Oil Color Prints." *Princeton University Library Chronicle* 40, no. 2 (1979): 155–170.

George Baxter (1804–1867) experimented and perfected a method of producing color prints by combining engraving and block printing with oil colors in England in the late 1820's. Martin explains the process very lucidly, describes various examples of the process, and summarizes what is known about Baxter's life. He also discusses the use of the Baxter process in the United States. The Princeton University Library held an exhibit, "George Baxter: Painting by Printing," in March-April 1978.

1801. Merrill, Hiram C. *Wood Engraving and Wood Engravers.* Boston: Society of Printers, 1937. 16 pp.

Five hundred copies were printed of this short essay, originally delivered as an address to the Society of Printers by a practicing engraver. In the address, Merrill recounts his career and his association with the wood engravers of the last decades of the nineteenth century. Glimpses into the artist's methods, as well as thumbnail sketches of prominent engravers, make this a worthwhile backward glance at the golden age of American wood engraving.

1802. Michie, Thomas S. "American Wallpapers of the Nineteenth Century at the Museum of Art, Rhode Island School of Design." *Imprint* 16, no. 2 (1991): 4–14.

Among the collections at the Rhode Island School of Design is one of wallpapers from the seventeenth century to the present. Michie's article describes American papers, the most commercial form of printmaking. Many of the samples are found on boxes and in trunks; other examples came to RISD with larger collections of ephemera and decorative arts.

1803. Pennell, Elizabeth Robins. "An English Estimate of American Illustration: A Criticism of Mr. Linton's Lecture Before the Society of Arts at London, 1889." *Nation* 48 (11 April 1889): 189.

Pennell criticizes Linton's opinion that American wood engravers are responsible for everything wrong with modern illustration. To the contrary, she finds that Linton's arguments, when carried to their logical conclusion, prove the truth of the assertions made by the New School of wood engraving. She also feels that Linton is unfair in laying blame on America; he seems blissfully unaware of the fact that the techniques used by the Americans have European precedents.

1804. Pomeroy, Jane R. "On the Changes Made in Wood Engravings in the Stereotyping Process." *Printing History* 17, no. 2 (1995): 35–40.

Pomeroy has been studying the wood engravings of Alexander Anderson for some time. In this article, she explains how stereotyped blocks are made and altered. Five pairs of blocks illustrate her careful and well-documented analysis. A related essay by Michael Winship in *Printing History* (vol. 5, no. 2, 1983), "Printing with Plates in the Nineteenth Century United States," provides important information on the steoreotyping of text.

1805. Pyle, Howard. "American Wood-Engraving of the Present." *Book Buyer* 4 (December 1887): 394–96.

Pyle, a talented illustrator in his own right, briefly reviews the wood engravings in *Engravings on Wood, by Members of the Society of American Wood Engravers.* The works by Elbridge Kingsley are cited for their particular merit.

1806. Sheldon, George William. "A Symposium of Wood-Engravers." *Harper's Monthly* 60 (February 1880): 442–53.

This article, which solicits testimony from seven engravers as to American superiority in wood engraving, is one of the most important statements published on wood engraving during its nineteenth-century revival. A.V.S. Anthony sides with William Linton in the white-line controversy; he believes in drawing directly on the block versus using photography, which was a popular practice of magazines of the time. Timothy Cole, on the other hand, is at odds with Linton, and defends the use of wood engraving for the reproduction of paintings. J.P. Davis expresses the belief that the nature of the art precludes the engraver from reproducing and interpreting works from other media. Frederick Juengling finds Linton's criticisms irrelevant to the necessities of modern printing in large editions. Richard A. Muller is also on the side of engravers who use the medium for photographically faithful reproduction of art. John Tinkey believes in the importance of the engraver's artistic expression, while Henry Wolf criticizes Linton's idea of originality in wood engraving as being too personal.

1807. Silver, Rollo. "Trans-Atlantic Crossing: The Beginning of Electrotyping in America." *Journal of the Printing Historical Society* 10 (May 1974): 84–103.

Mass-produced periodicals and books in the latter half of the nineteenth century were often printed from electrotyped plates. Silver docments the beginnings of this technology in Britain and its adaptation by American experimenters and printers. It was particularly useful for the reproduction of fine wood engravings, because the original blocks were preserved.

1808. Sturgis, Russell. "The Public Library Exhibition of American Wood-Engravings." *Scribner's Magazine* 33 (January 1903): 125–28.

In this critical review of an exhibition of wood engravings at the New York Public Library, Sturgis differentiates between the work of the New School, and the work of earlier nineteenth-century engravers. In his opinion, the new tendency toward precise reproduction reformed earlier excesses. Examples chosen from the art of Cole, King, Closson, Wolf, and others are discussed for their artistic merits; the omission of works by Linton and Marsh from a representative exhibition is decried.

1809. Sugden, Thomas D. *A History of Wood Engraving in the United States*. New York: By the author, 1903. 3 pp.

This brief and unimportant historical sketch mentions Alexander Anderson, Abel Bowen, Juengling, and other late nineteenth-century engravers.

1810. Van Rensselaer, M. G. "Wood-Engraving and the Century Prizes." *Century Magazine* 23 (June 1882): 230–39.

This is the announcement of the winners of the second contest for wood engravers in the Scribner's-Century series. The development of wood engraving in America is sketched, and the phenomenal growth of the art after the Civil War is attributed to three factors: the influence of magazines like the *Century*, which needed illustrative material; the introduction of the profusely illustrated gift book; and the introduction of photography, which encouraged the reproduction of the tone of the original drawing or painting in the engraving.

1811. Wagner, Ann Prentice. "The Graver, the Brush, and the Ruling Machine: The Training of Late-Nineteenth-Century Wood Engravers" in *The Cultivation of Artists in Nineteenth-Century America*, 143–167. eds. Georgia Brady Barnhill, Diana Korzenik, and Caroline F. Sloat. Worcester: American Antiquarian Society, 1997.

Wagner briefly summarizes wood engraving during the final quarter of the nineteenth century and discusses the training of wood engravers drawing on the experiences of Hiram Merrill (1866–1958) whose life is well documented by the Hiram Campbell Merrill Collection at the Boston Public Library. Other engravers whose work is described include Elbridge Kingsley (1841–1918), William B. Closson (1848–1926), Henry Herrick, Carolina Amelia Powell, Sarah E. Fuller, and Ann Maverick (c. 1810–1863), the daughter of Alexander Anderson (1775–1870). Wagner also discusses the importance of art clubs and the impact of changing technology on the employment of these artisans.

1812. Warner, Charles Dudley. "Reaction in Wood Engraving." *Art Interchange* 5 (22 December 1880): 133.

Without taking sides, Warner briefly examines the wood engraving controversy. He then analyzes the engraving, drawn by E.A. Abbey and engraved by H. Wolf, that appears in the December 22, 1880, issue of *Art Interchange*.

1813. Whittle, George Howes. "Wood Engravings in America." *The American Magazine of Art* 10 (November 1918): 3–10.

This study of the New School engravers, who began to command recognition about 1877, was written by George Whittle, long associated with the art department of *Century Magazine*. He interprets the chief function of wood engravings to be the reproduction of the design of the illustrator. Whittle summarizes the dispute between Linton and the other engravers of the New School, providing a clear introduction to the problems raised by the growth of a distinctly national school of wood engraving.

1814. Wolf, Henry. "Concerning Wood-Engraving." *Print Collector's Quarterly* 1 (July 1911): 349–58.

The artist recounts his own life in terms of his wood engraving. In discussing the New School, he attributes its development to the perfected method of photographing drawings on the block, and its demise caused by the halftone process. He predicts that the art of wood engraving in America will die from lack of encouragement.

1815. Woodberry, George E. *A History of Wood-Engraving*. New York: Harper & Bros., 1883. 221 pp.

Although the main concern of Woodberry's book is with European wood engravers, it does contain an informative chapter on modern American engravers such as Linton, F.S. King, H. Marsh, T. Cole, and Hoskin. This chapter essentially repeats the information in two articles by Woodberry that appeared in *Harper's New Monthly Magazine* (April 1882 and July 1882).).

Index of Authors

C

D

E

F

G

H

I

J

K

L

M

N

O

P

Q

R

S

T

U

V

W

Y

Z